MEDIEVAL SAINTS

READINGS IN MEDIEVAL CIVILIZATIONS AND CULTURES: IV
series editor: Paul Edward Dutton

MEDIEVAL SAINTS

A READER

edited by

MARY-ANN STOUCK

LIBRARY AND ARCHIVES CANADA CATALOGUING IN PUBLICATION

Medieval Saints: a reader
Readings in medieval civilizations and cultures ; 4
ISBN 978-1-4426-0101-7

1. Christian saints – Biography – Early works to 1800. 2. Europe – Church history – Middle
Ages, 600–1500. 3. Church history – Middle Ages, 600–1500 – Sources. I. Stouck, Mary-Ann,
1941– . II. Series

BX4654.M42   1998   282'.92'2   C98-932233-5

We welcome comments and suggestions regarding any aspect of our publications—please
feel free to contact us at news@utphighereducation.com or visit our Internet site at
www.utppublishing.com.

North America	*UK, Ireland, and continental Europe*
5201 Dufferin Street	NBN International
North York, Ontario, Canada, M3H 5T8	Estover Road, Plymouth, PL6 7PY, UK
	TEL: 44 (0) 1752 202301
2250 Military Road	FAX ORDER LINE: 44 (0) 1752 202333
Tonawanda, New York, USA, 14150	enquiries@nbninternational.com

ORDERS PHONE: 1-800-565-9523
ORDERS FAX: 1-800-221-9985
ORDERS E-MAIL: utpbooks@utpress.utoronto.ca

Every effort has been made to contact copyright holders; in the event of an error or omission,
please notify the publisher.

The University of Toronto Press acknowledges the financial support for its publishing activities
of the Government of Canada through the Canada Book Fund.

CONTENTS

List of Illustrations • viii
Chronological Guide • x
Introduction • xv
Suggestions for Further Reading • xxi

CHAPTER ONE: MARTYRS OF THE EARLY CHURCH • 1

1. The Martyrdom of St. Polycarp, Bishop of Smyrna • 3
2. The Martyrs of Lyons and Vienne • 10
3. The Passion of SS. Perpetua and Felicitas • 21
4. *Tertullian's Address to the Martyrs* • 33
5. Augustine Preaches on the Feast of SS. Perpetua and Felicitas • 39
6. The Trials and Execution of Cyprian • 43
7. The Age of Martyrs in Legend: The Seven Sleepers of Ephesus • 48

CHAPTER TWO: THE DESERT FATHERS AND MOTHERS • 55

8. Christianity in the Desert: St. Antony the Great • 57
9. Antony's Disciples: Paul the Simple • 83
10. The First Hermit: St. Paul of Thebes • 87
11. A Harlot in the Desert: Mary of Egypt • 97
12. A Famous Pillar Saint: Symeon Stylites • 115
13. A Transvestite Saint: Mary/Marina • 127

CHAPTER THREE: BISHOPS, MONKS, AND NUNS • 135

14. St. Martin of Tours • 137
15. *The Life and Miracles of St. Benedict* • 167
16. Venantius Fortunatus's *Life of St. Radegund* • 205
17. Radegund Writes to the Bishops • 218
18. An Irish Missionary: *St. Gall*, by Walahfrid Strabo • 223
19. A Mirror for Monks: The *Life of St. Maiol, Abbot of Cluny*, by Odilo, Fifth Abbot of Cluny • 250

CHAPTER FOUR: ROYAL SAINTS • 265

20. Ælfric's *Life of St. Edmund, King and Martyr* • 267
21. St. Margaret, Queen of Scotland • 273

CHAPTER FIVE: PILGRIMAGE • 295

22. St. Augustine on the Rites at the Martyrs' Tombs • 297
23. Pilgrimage and Miracles in North Africa • 299
24. Sæwulf Makes a Pilgrimage to the Holy Land • 307
25. *The Pilgrim's Guide to St. James of Compostella* • 313
26. Pilgrimage as Metaphor: *The Canterbury Tales* • 328
27. Jerusalem Pilgrimage in 1480: the Tribulations of Brother Felix • 335

CHAPTER SIX: RELICS • 355

28. Gregory of Tours: the Power of Relics • 356
29. The Humiliation of St. Mitrias • 364
30. The Affair of St. Sergius's Fingerbone • 366
31. Criticism of the Cult of Relics: Claudius of Turin • 368
32. Theft of Relics: the Translation of SS. Marcellinus and Peter • 373
33. False Relics and Imposters • 395
34. Fundraising with Relics: the Monks of Laon • 398
35. Fire at the Shrine of St. Edmund • 402

CHAPTER SEVEN: NEW DIRECTIONS • 411

36. The New Hermits: Godric of Finchale • 412
37. Women's Spirituality I: Christina the Astonishing • 436
38. Women's Spirituality II: Umiltà of Faenza • 453
39. The Conversion of St. Francis of Assisi and the Founding of his Order • 470
40. Humanistic Hagiography: the Writings of St. Francis's Companions • 488
41. The Official *Life of St. Francis*: the Stigmata • 497
42. *The Canticle of Brother Sun* • 504
43. The Canonization of St. Francis • 508

CHAPTER EIGHT: HAGIOGRAPHIC ROMANCES • 517

44. St. Ursula and the Eleven Thousand Virgins • 518
45. Four 'Lives' from *The Golden Legend* (Alexis, Mary Magdalene, Eustace, James the Dismembered) • 534
46. 'Lives' of St. Christopher: the Irish *Libar Breac* • 561
47. 'Lives' of St. Christopher: *The South English Legendary* • 568

48. An Old French *Life of St. Margaret of Antioch* • 579

CHAPTER NINE: EPILOGUE • 593

49. A Reformer's View of the Cult of the Saints • 595
50. A Heretic's Confession • 598
51. Erasmus: *A Pilgrimage for Religion's Sake* • 601

Index of Topics • 629
Acknowledgement of Sources in Copyright • 634

LIST OF ILLUSTRATIONS

[Fig. 1]   Martyrdom of St. Ignatius, 1

[Fig. 2]   Funeral lamp from the Catacombs, 3

[Fig. 3]   SS. Cornelius and Cyprian, 6

[Fig. 4]   St. Antony, 8

[Fig. 5]   St. Antony tortured by demons, 8.3

[Fig. 6]   Lives of the Desert Fathers and Mothers, 9

[Fig. 7]   St. Jerome, 10

[Fig. 8]   St. Paul and St. Antony, 10.11

[Fig. 9]   St. Mary of Egypt, 11

[Fig. 10]   St. Symeon Stylites, 12

[Fig. 11]   St. Marina, 13

[Fig. 12]   St. Martin, 14.1

[Fig. 13]   Two events in the 'life' of St. Martin, 14,5, 6

[Fig. 14]   Exorcism of demons, 14.13

[Fig. 15]   Death of St. Martin, 14.b

[Fig. 16]   St. Benedict, 15

[Fig. 17]   St. Benedict and the rebellious monks, 15.3

[Fig. 18]   St. Benedict exorcises the Devil, 15.9

[Fig. 19]   St. Benedict reproves King Totila, 15.15

[Fig. 20]   Benedictine saints: Scholastica, Justina, Maurus, and Placidus with
            St. Benedict, 15.33

[Fig. 21]   Death of St. Benedict, 15.37

[Fig. 22]   St. Radegund, 16

[Fig. 23]   The Long Gospel, St-Gall, 18

[Fig. 24]   St. Edmund of East Anglia, 20

[Fig. 25]   Richard II of England with SS. Edmund, Edward, and John the
            Baptist, 20

[Fig. 26]   Dunfermline Abbey, burial place of St. Margaret, 21

[Fig. 27]   Tomb of St. Elizabeth of Hungary, 21.19

[Fig. 28]   St. Louis of France, 21.29

[Fig. 29]   Pilgrimage to Emmaus, 22

[Fig. 30]   St. James the Great, 25

[Fig. 31]   St. James the 'Moor-slayer,' 25.7

[Fig. 32]   Sufferers from St. Vitus's Dance on a pilgrimage, 25.7

[Fig. 33]   The Canterbury Pilgrims, 26

[Fig. 34]   The island and harbor of Rhodes, 27

[Fig. 35]   A family carrying out a vow, 27

[Fig. 36a] The Crown of Thorns, 28.5

[Fig. 36b]   A fragment of the Lord's Cross, 28.5
 [Fig. 37]   A thirteenth-century reliquary, 32.1.15
 [Fig. 38]   The Crown of Thorns received in Paris, 32.2.3
 [Fig. 39]   A relics procession, 34
 [Fig. 40]   Pilgrims approaching the relics of St. Philip, 35.14
 [Fig. 41]   The marriage of St. Francis to Lady Poverty, 39.24
 [Fig. 42]   St. Francis preaching to the birds, 40.51
 [Fig. 43]   St. Francis receiving the stigmata, 41.2
 [Fig. 44]   St. Francis encounters Poverty, Chastity, and Obedience, 43.122
 [Fig. 45]   A reliquary of St. Ursula, 44
 [Fig. 46]   St. Ursula as patron of young girls, 44.10
 [Fig. 47]   St. Mary Magdalene washes the feet of Christ, 45
 [Fig. 48]   St. Mary Magdalene, 45
 [Fig. 49]   The translation of St. Mary Magdalene, 45
 [Fig. 50]   St. Eustace, 45
 [Fig. 51]   Dogheaded men on a cross at Conchan, Isle of Man, 46
 [Fig. 52]   St. Christopher, 47
 [Fig. 53]   St. Christopher as a giant, 47
 [Fig. 54]   Three images of St. Margaret, 48
 [Fig. 55]   John Wycliffe, 49
 [Fig. 56]   Ruins of the gatehouse at Walsingham Priory, 51
 [Fig. 57]   Plan of Canterbury Cathedral, 51

A CHRONOLOGICAL GUIDE TO THE CONTENTS

(Numbers in brackets refer to selections in the Reader)

c.35	Death of St. Stephen, protomartyr [23]
150–160s	Rise of Montanism [3,4]
c.156	Martyrdom of St. Polycarp [1]
160–220	Tertullian [4]
177	Martyrs of Lyons and Vienne [2]
Early 200s	Tertullian's *Address to the Martyrs* [4]
203	Martyrdom of Perpetua and Felicitas [3]
249–251	Persecution under Decius [6, 7]
250–356	St. Antony the Great [8, 9]
257–258	Martyrdom of Cyprian [6]
260–339	Eusebius of Caesarea [2]
c.290–347	Pachomius [8]
312	Constantine's victory at the Milvian Bridge, and his conversion to Christianity [8]
c.316–397	St. Martin of Tours [14]
325	Council of Nicaea
328–373	Athanasius, Bishop of Alexandria, author of the *Life of St. Antony the Great* [8]
347–419/20	St. Jerome, author of the *Life of Paul of Thebes* [10]
354	Birth of Augustine of Hippo [5, 22, 23]
385	Ambrose's discovery and translation of the relics of Gervasius and Protasius in Milan
393–466	Theodoret of Cyrrhus [12]
396–459	Symeon Stylites [12]
397	Sulpicius Severus's *Life of St. Martin* [14]
c.400–450	Conversion of Ireland by St. Patrick [18]
c.400	Augustine's sermons on the Feast of SS. Perpetua and Felicitas [5]
408–450	Reign of Theodosius, emperor in the east, used as the setting for the second part of the account of the Seven Sleepers of Ephesus [7]
410	Sack of Rome by the Visigoths [22, 23]
413	Augustine begins writing *The City of God* [22, 23]
419	Palladius's *Lausiac History*, including Paul the Simple [9]
430	Death of Augustine of Hippo [5, 22, 23]

c.480–547	St. Benedict of Nursia [15]
450–500s	Early versions of Mary of Egypt [11] and Mary/Marina [13]
518–587	St. Radegund [16, 17]
538–594	Gregory of Tours [7, 28, 29, 30]
c.540–600	Venantius Fortunatus, author of the *Life of St. Radegund* [16]
c.550–645	St. Gall [18]
590–604	Pope Gregory the Great, author of the account of the life and miracles of St. Benedict [15]
634–638	Sophronius Bishop of Jerusalem; *Life of St. Mary of Egypt* attributed to him [11]
673–735	Bede, author of the *Ecclesiastical History of the English People* [20]
c.720	Founding of the Abbey of St. Gall, on the site of the saint's hermitage [18]
c.770–840	Einhard [32]
789	Charlemagne's capitulary, *Admonitio Generalis*, prohibiting the veneration of false or dubious saints [32]
800	Charlemagne crowned Holy Roman emperor
Early 800s	The vision of the star at Compostella [25]
808–849	Walahfrid Strabo, author of the *Life of St. Gall* [18]
813	Synod of Mainz: no recognition of new saints without ecclesiastical licence [32]
c.817–827	Claudius appointed bishop of Turin [31]
c.828	Einhard and the translation of the relics of SS. Marcellinus and Peter [32]
841–869	St. Edmund of East Anglia [20]
910–994	St. Maiol of Cluny [19]
950–1010	Ælfric, author of the *Passion* of St. Edmund [20]
c.969	Earliest account of St. Ursula and the Eleven Thousand Virgins [44]
973	First fully documented papal canonization: St. Udalricus
c.980–1047	Rodolphus Glaber, author of *The Five Books of the Histories* [33]
1000s	Vézelay lays claim to the relics of St. Mary Magdalene [45]
1032–1033	Odilo's *Life of St. Maiol* [19]

1044–1093	St. Margaret of Scotland [21]
1053–1124	Guibert of Nogent [34]
1065–1170	Godric of Finchale [36]
1066	Death of King Edward the Confessor [21]
1100s	Compilation of the Codex Callixtinus, including *The Pilgrim's Guide to Compostella* [25]
c.1100	Composition of the account of St. Ursula and the Eleven Thousand Virgins [44]
1102–1103	Sæwulf's pilgrimage to the Holy Land [24]
1112	Guibert of Nogent's description of fundraising with relics by the monks of Laon [34]
1150–1224	Christina of St-Trond [37]
c.1155–1202	Jocelin of Brakelond [35]
1170	Martyrdom of St. Thomas Becket at Canterbury [26]
c.1170–1240	Jacques de Vitry (Bishop of Acre, 1216-28) [37]
1181–1226	St. Francis of Assisi [39, 40, 41, 42, 43]
1198	Destruction by fire of the shrine of St. Edmund [35]
1200s	The Beguine movement in the low countries, the Rhineland, and northern France [37, 38]; composition of the Old French *Life of St. Margaret of Antioch* [48]
c.1201–1272	Thomas of Cantimpré [37]
1224	St. Francis receives the stigmata on Mount La Verna [41]; *The Canticle of Brother Sun* [42]
1226–1310	Umiltà of Faenza [38]
1228	Canonization of St. Francis [43]; Thomas of Celano's first *Life of St. Francis* [39, 43]
1234	Papal processes of canonization made the only legitimate source of inquiry into a prospective saint's life
1243	Thomas of Celano's second *Life of St. Francis*
1256	St. Bonaventure's official *Life of St. Francis* [41]
1260	Jacobus de Voragine, *The Golden Legend* [45]
1300s	Compilation of *The Little Flowers of St. Francis*; John of Tynemouth's collection of *The Lives of the Saints of England, Ireland, Scotland and Wales* [36]
c. 1300	St. Christopher in *The South English Legendary* [47]
c.1343–1400	Geoffrey Chaucer, author of *The Canterbury Tales* [26]
c.1330–1384	John Wycliffe [49]
1400s	Irish Life of St. Christopher in the *Libar Breac* [46]

1428-1431   Trials of Lollard heretics at Norwich [50]

1453   Capture of Constantinople by the Ottoman sultan Mehmed II

1480   Brother Felix Fabri's pilgrimage to Jerusalem [27]

1526   Erasmus publishes *A Pilgrimage for Religion's Sake* [51]

1563   *The Book of Martyrs* by John Foxe published in English [49]

INTRODUCTION

It satte me wel bet ay in a cave
To bidde and rede on holy seyntes lyves.
(Chaucer, *Troilus and Criseyde*, 2, 117-8, c.1380)

It was the saints that baffled me. So I got to work on them as best I
could, and pretty soon knew that the old fellow with the bell was
Anthony Abbot, and the same old fellow with hobgoblins plaguing him
was Anthony being tempted in the desert. Sebastian, that sanctified
porcupine, was easy, and so was St. Roche, with the dog and a bad leg.
I was innocently delighted to meet St. Martin, dividing his cloak, on a
Swiss coin. The zest for detail that had first made me want to be a
polymath stood me in good stead now, for I could remember the particular attributes and symbols of scores of saints without any trouble,
and I found their legends delightful reading.
(Robertson Davies, *Fifth Business*, 1970)

I

It was as a graduate student at the University of Toronto in the 1960s that I,
like Dunstan Ramsay, the hero of Robertson Davies' novel, first became
interested in the mysterious world of medieval hagiography. It was not then
the vibrant field of research for North American academics that it has since
become, and I had the intoxicating feeling of treading on near-virgin ground
as I read the pioneering Middle English editions of Carl Horstman and the
work of Hippolyte Delehaye. However, I soon realized that in the dusty
stacks of the library I was contending with another borrower, one whose
interests exactly matched my own, and whose depredations reduced me to
the frustrations of book recall and delay familiar to those who do library
research. I never discovered who my fellow-traveler was, though when *Fifth
Business* appeared in 1970 I fancied it might have been Robertson Davies
himself, a prominent figure on the Toronto campus in those years. Gradually
I developed a strong sense of identity with this shadowy soul. Here we were,
the only two people in a major Canadian university so far as I knew who
were preoccupied with one of the strangest, most fascinating, and most complex phenomena of the Middle Ages: the cult of the saints.

The modern study of hagiography has of course been carried forward by scholars in the Roman Catholic Church from the early seventeenth century, but since the 1960s it has also been pursued with ever-increasing zeal by growing numbers of academics, with many important and interesting results. Like the other volumes in this series, my Reader has been designed with an undergraduate audience in mind, as an introduction to the study of primary materials from the late classical and medieval phases of the cult of the saints. I hope that it will also be useful to advanced students as a ready reference. The organization is conceived first chronologically, beginning with the early Christian martyrs and ending with selections from the period of the Reformation. However, some chapters are thematic rather than chronological in focus, and it should be noted, for instance, that while 'lives' of bishops, monks, and nuns appear early in the collection, I do not mean to imply that this group did not continue to dominate in the canonizations of the later Middle Ages.

In an age such as ours, when the word 'hagiography' is often seen as a term of opprobrium equivalent to "a whitewash job" (especially when linked with the writing of modern biography), the question might well be asked, "What do medieval saints' 'lives' have to tell students of the Middle Ages? Why should we read them at all?" We no longer feel, with Chaucer's Criseyde, that reading the legends of holy saints is a moral obligation. These days we want our public figures revealed to us warts and all, if not warts exclusively. There seems little to recommend in a genre where the writers not only dwelt almost exclusively on the virtue of their subjects but also drew largely on the material of miracles and visions. Indeed, often they blatantly ignored opportunities for factual evidence in pursuit of their definition of the higher goal of virtue, a point famously made in Reginald of Canterbury's preface to his *Life of St. Malchus,* where he states that whenever he came across a good story anywhere, he included it: "Since Malchus was just, saintly, loved by Christ, and full of the very essence of righteousness, I do not deviate from the truth, no matter what miracles I ascribe to Malchus, even though they were manifested only in some other saint."[1]

Equally unsympathetic to someone used to the methods of modern biography may be the hagiographers' almost universal preference for the abstract and generalizing idiom of moral and spiritual value over concrete detail. Thus if Christian virtue bores us and we decide to use medieval accounts of saints as a source for the personal and the eccentric, for realism in style, for historical liveliness, or for the bizarre and spectacular in human belief and

---

1   Quoted by Charles W. Jones, *Saints's Lives and Chronicles in Early England* (Ithaca, N.Y.: Cornell University Press, 1947), p. 61.

behavior, we are often disappointed. These features do occur, it is true: Thomas of Cantimpré's *Life of Christina of St-Trond* comes to mind in terms of the bizarre and spectacular, along with 'St. James the Dismembered' in *The Golden Legend*, and there are many isolated examples of vivid historical description, such as those found in Gregory of Tours. Nevertheless it would be misleading to place undue emphasis upon them, not only because what seems strange to us may have appeared otherwise at the time of writing, but also because to emphasize the exceptional would be to ignore another major feature of medieval hagiography: its self-conscious conventionality. It is indeed this characteristic, most apparent in the way writers refer back to earlier examples of the genre, that gives rise to another common complaint: "Once you've read one saint's life, you've read them all."

The study of history offers one kind of response to these objections: hagiography was the most widely-used and long-lived genre of Late Antiquity and the Middle Ages, and students setting out to understand the major figures, the concerns, and the sensibilities of these periods need to be knowledgeable about it. While historians in the past have often been so suspicious of the genre that they decided largely to ignore it, many are now discovering the contributions that a careful reading of hagiography and materials surrounding the cult of the saints can make to the field. There is no better introduction to the Christian civilization of early Europe than through the lives of its most famous men and women. And if the aim is to recover a historical reading of these documents, we need to be reminded also that although descriptions of heroically virtuous lives may seem flat and repetitive to us, it is likely that to a medieval audience they offered an intriguing variety of fine distinctions. Their very conventionality, unprized by us because we value novelty so highly, had the effect of reassurance and so made hagiographies appropriate vehicles for teaching by example and for encouraging others in the faith.

Still, cultivating a sympathetic reading of this genre in the twentieth century is bound to present a challenge, at least in some cases. Chief among the rewards of persistence is the opportunity to see many facets of a moment in history through the impact of a single important person upon the other people, events, and intellectual and spiritual movements that were drawn within his or her orbit. Among these conditions of writing, those of the hagiographer himself (less frequently, herself) are prominent, for despite their strong emphasis on the eternal verities, saints' 'lives' are also occasional works: they derive both from the writers' desire to praise God, venerate the saints, and teach the faithful, and from a particular set of circumstances existing at the time of writing. It was the hagiographers who shaped the way we see their subjects, for although, for convenience's sake, we talk about the saints, we are really speaking of the way their biographers chose to present them. Conditions influencing them might include the need to promote a saint for purposes of local or national repute; to raise money to build a church; to perpetuate a personal relationship or the memory of a leader; to follow the injunctions of pope, king, or patron; to produce evidence for the process of canonization; and any number of other issues. Frequently the saint was at the center of a power struggle between rival social or religious groups, and a 'life' was the means of asserting superior authority and of laying claim to patronage.

Nor is it true that one saint's 'life' is the same as any other, whatever the hagiographers themselves might have thought. Though nominally divided into four categories (apostles, martyrs, confessors, and virgins), the saints assumed roles that ran the gamut of religious experience: they were prophets, reformers, and leaders; mystics and hermits; kings, queens, and popes; teachers; cloistered members of the religious orders; merchants, wives, and serving-girls; and not least, mythical creations who embodied some essential belief or fulfilled a particular spiritual need, like the dogheaded St. Christopher who appears in stories of Christian conversion, or Mary/Marina, through whom the misogynist desert monks expressed their opinion that a woman must put aside her female nature if she were to become truly holy.

If the genre was conventional, the conventions were constantly under pressure for renewal as ideals of sanctity changed. Jerome wrote about Paul of Thebes as the ideal hermit; Sulpicius Severus created in his *Life of St. Martin* the model Frankish bishop who remained at heart a monk and a recluse; Gregory the Great saw in Benedict of Nursia the pattern of the good abbot who cared first and foremost for his monks, a pattern reworked by Odilo in his *Life of St. Maiol* to suit the aspirations of the growing Cluniac community. The accounts of the desert fathers and mothers, of all types of hagiography perhaps the one that had the most enduring impact on Christians and on the genre, influenced the twelfth-century revival of the eremitical tradition, and in works such as Reginald of Durham's account of Godric of Finchale, the tradition achieved a new relevance through the addition of features of native English saints' lives and local settings. The canonization of kings and queens required the adaptation of the virtuous life to a public role. Later, with the advent of the great collections of hagiography, such as Jacobus de Voragine's *Golden Legend* and *The South English Legendary*, the conventions were adapted to the practical needs of preaching and included features designed to appeal to secular audiences.

In addition to their importance as subjects of history, however, the saints have become a focus for modern theoretical approaches. Because women from the outset constituted an important (though still relatively small) group of saints, and one of the few categories of medieval women about which a sizeable body of information exists, they have become a popular subject for scholars using feminist theory. Medieval women mystics in particular have received attention, both in numerous editions and translations of their writings and in the work of feminist critics. Because material about them is so widely accessible, they are not represented in this volume, although mysticism is present as one aspect of the lives of several of the late medieval saints. A second area of modern critical investigation, anthropology, has seen in saints of both sexes important liminal figures effecting social change as radical spiritual leaders and through their association with pilgrimage and the medieval rituals around the dead. For obvious reasons, the saints have also figured prominently in the ongoing discussions of the dialogue between body and intellect or soul. A related theme, the construction of gender and sexuality, is a current theoretical concern that will continue to find interesting material in medieval hagiography. Perhaps most importantly, because the saints were figures of power with special access to God during life and, after death, the ability to influence human affairs through the mediation of relics and prayers, they continue to give scholars an excellent opportunity to study the structures and transactions of power in the institutions of Late Antiquity and the Middle Ages. The complex relationships described by Einhard in the Carolingian world, articulated through the relics of SS. Peter and Marcellinus, offer a political example, and a monastic one is found in Jocelin of Brakelond's account of Abbot Samson's efforts to wrest financial control from the monks of Bury St. Edmunds.

Finally, the study of medieval hagiography continues to produce some surprises. Students of environmentalism can find in the writings stemming from the eremitical movement a steady tradition of sympathy between the saints and nature. The desert fathers and mothers with their string of tame lions and their fierce urge to recreate paradise in arid lands still succeeded in having dominion over all creation, it is true, but they did so in a much kindlier way than is sometimes thought characteristic of Christian tradition. Among their followers were saints who gave shelter to injured deer; shared bread with a bear; considered the implications of a bell-ringing weasel; kept a tame cricket; and, if compelled to prevent a rabbit from ransacking a vegetable garden, tied a bundle of edible greens to its back to help it on its way.

II

Faced with a vast body of medieval hagiography and materials on the cult of the saints, an anthologizer can hardly hope to escape sins of omission. Additional problems are presented by the Reader's limited space measured against the inordinate length of many saints' 'lives,' by my own preference for printing complete works if at all possible, and by the fact that some important 'lives,' though readily accessible in good editions, needed to be included because they are fundamental to a study of the genre. The result is a compromise: well-known but essential writings, such as the accounts of Perpetua and Felicitas, Martin of Tours, and Benedict of Nursia, are included (with some related material such as Augustine's sermon on the feast of SS. Perpetua and Felicitas) along with a variety of lesser-known works such as the 'life' of Maiol of Cluny, Turgot's account of St. Margaret, John of Tynemouth's Godric of Finchale, Umiltà of Faenza, and an Irish 'life' of St. Christopher. The purpose of a partly eclectic selection is to give readers a sense both of a continuous and conscious tradition (Thomas of Celano, for instance, writing the 'life' of St. Francis, refers back to Sulpicius Severus's 'life' of St. Martin of Tours written centuries earlier) and of the variety and responsiveness to new religious movements in the cult of the saints. I have, however, included primarily accounts that could be given in their entirety; where that was impossible (as with St. Antony or St. Francis of Assisi) editorial insertions or the introduction indicate what is missing.

As with other volumes in this series, the texts consist of previously translated works (with modernized diction when appropriate, or – as in the case of St. Martin of Tours – revised against a more recent edition of the Latin original) and of previously unpublished translations. Information in square brackets represents additional clarification by the editor and some of the translators. BHL (*Bibliotheca Hagiographica Latina*) numbers are supplied in the prefaces to selections where appropriate, to identify the version of a 'life' I have used. Although every effort has been made to ensure accuracy in older works and previously unpublished translations, it will quickly be apparent that these are not 'scholarly' texts: references, including biblical ones, have been omitted or reduced to a minimum with the aim of clearing the ground as much as possible between the reader and the text.

The emphasis in this Reader is on hagiography, but since it is hardly possible to study individual saints without some understanding of the cult as a whole, a selection of materials relating to the role of pilgrimages and relics has been included. From the modern reader's point of view, they are among the most interesting. Pilgrimage accounts make up the earliest travel writings, combining the desire for religious knowledge with an eager curiosity about new countries and exotic peoples and behaviors. The cult of relics is both fascinating in its doctrinal aspects – that saints can be at once with God in heaven and also powerfully present in their fragmented body parts on earth – and also gave rise in medieval writings to expressions of the tension between piety and its abuses, as the selections from Gregory of Tours, Guibert of Nogent, and Rodulfus Glaber most notably illustrate. Pilgrimages and the cult of relics as they were practised throughout the Middle Ages comprise the essential background of much medieval hagiography.

III

The gratitude expressed here towards those who have helped me produce this Reader is very far from perfunctory. In particular I wish to thank Paul Dutton, the editor of the Broadview series *Readings in Medieval Civilizations and Cultures,* who cheerfully undertook tasks far exceeding the normal editorial role. It was he who first suggested that I teach for Simon Fraser's Humanities Program a course in medieval hagiography that became a starting point for the Reader. He has contributed two of his own translations (Einhard's account of the theft of the relics of SS. Marcellinus and Peter, and the previously unpublished *Life of St. Maiol of Cluny*), and he made many excellent suggestions both for my translation of *The Life of St. Godric* and for the Reader as a whole. Throughout the process he has taken time unstintingly from his own busy schedule to offer advice and encouragement.

I am also grateful to my colleagues Lawrin Armstrong, who kindly extracted me from the coils of Wycliffe's Latin, and Harvey de Roo, who gave helpful comments on my translation of passages from *The South English Legendary.* Here and elsewhere I am of course responsible for any mistakes that remain. A grant from the Dean of Arts, Simon Fraser University, enabled me to hire researchers Steven Ward, Sharon Alker, and Nadeane Trowse, who, infected with my own enthusiasm for the saints, gave ready assistance with the preparation of texts and pictures. My students in Humanities 305 unearthed some surprising hagiographical resources in Vancouver libraries, and my friend Lynn Simpson visited the site of St. Godric's hermitage on my behalf and brought back useful materials. I owe special thanks to Nancy Blake, Margot Dykstra, and Christine Stojakovic of the S.F.U. Interlibrary Loans Department, headed by Todd Mundle, for their cheerful and efficient help in searching out obscure items; without them this project would not have been possible. Anita Mahoney and Bill Souder gave computer assistance, and Fred Kyba of the Media Center painstakingly prepared the pictures. Barbara Conolly, Julie Smith, and the staff at Broadview Press were unfailingly patient, good-humored, and helpful during the editing process. Finally I wish to thank David, Jordan, and John, who have listened patiently over the years to many stories about the saints.

SUGGESTIONS FOR FURTHER READING:

Attwater, Donald. *The Penguin Dictionary of Saints.* Harmondsworth: Penguin, 1983.

Brown, Peter. *The Cult of the Saints: Its Rise and Function in Latin Christianity.* Chicago: University of Chicago Press, 1981.

———. *The Body and Society: Men, Women and Sexual Renunciation in Early Christianity.* New York: Columbia University Press, 1988.

Bynum, Caroline Walker. *Fragmentation and Redemption: Essays on Gender and the Human Body in Medieval Religion.* New York: Zone Books, 1991.

———. *The Resurrection of the Body in Western Christianity 200-1336.* New York Columbia University Press, 1995.

Delehaye, Hippolyte. *The Legends of the Saints.* Trans. Donald Attwater. New York: Fordham University Press, 1962.

Elliot, Alison Goddard. *Roads to Paradise: Reading the Lives of the Early Saints.* Hanover, NH: Brown University Press, 1987.

Farmer, David Hugh. *The Oxford Dictionary of Saints.* Oxford: Oxford University Press, 1992.

Geary, Patrick. *Furta Sacra: Thefts of Relics in the Central Middle Ages.* Princeton, NJ: Princeton University Press, 1978.

———. *Living with the Dead in the Middle Ages.* Ithaca, NY: Cornell University Press, 1994.

Goodich, Michael. *Vita Perfecta: The Ideal of Sainthood in the Thirteenth Century.* Stuttgart: Anton Hiersemann, 1982.

———. *Violence and Miracle in the Fourteenth Century: Private Grief and Public Salvation.* Chicago: University of Chicago Press, 1995.

Heffernan, Thomas J. *Sacred Biography: Saints and Their Biographers in the Middle Ages.* New York: Oxford University Press, 1988.

Kemp, Eric W. *Canonization and Authority in the Western Church.* London: Oxford University Press, 1948.

Kieckhefer, Richard. *Unquiet Souls: Fourteenth-Century Saints in their Religious Milieu.* Chicago: University of Chicago Press, 1984.

Petroff, Elizabeth Alvilda. *Body and Soul: Essays on Medieval Women and Mysticism.* New York: Oxford University Press, 1994.

Rollason, David. *Saints and Relics in Anglo-Saxon England.* Oxford: Blackwell, 1989.

Sumption, Jonathan. *Pilgrimage: An Image of Medieval Religion.* London: Faber & Faber, 1975.

Turner, Victor, and Edith Turner. *Image and Pilgrimage in Christian Culture: Anthropological Perspectives.* Oxford: Blackwell, 1978.

Van Dam, Raymond. *Saints and their Miracles in Late Antique Gaul*. Princeton, NJ: Princeton University Press, 1993.

Ward, Benedicta. *Miracles and the Medieval Mind: Theory, Record and Event, 1000-1215*. London: Scolar Press, 1987.

Weinstein, Donald, and Rudolph M. Bell. *Saints and Society: The Two Worlds of Western Christendom, 1000-1700*. Chicago: University of Chicago Press, 1981.

CHAPTER ONE:

MARTYRS OF THE EARLY CHURCH

The persecution of Christians in the Roman empire during the first three centuries following the death of Christ constituted for later writers the heroic age of the Church and left an indelible imprint on the collective Christian imagination down through the Middle Ages. Nevertheless, there remains considerable argument about the numbers of Christians who were killed. Official suppression of the new faith was sporadic and even during periods of intense persecution, such as those instituted by the emperors Decius in 248 and by Diocletian in 303, the provincial governors often showed reluctance to execute those who had been arrested. The most common cause of persecution, apart from political or economic conditions, was the Christians' rejection of the Roman gods upon whose favor the success of the empire was seen to depend. Thus Polycarp was accused of being an atheist (and could ironically turn the accusation against his accusers). Under Decius all citizens were required to sacrifice to the gods and to obtain a certificate that they had done so. The persecutions ended with the Edict of Milan in 313 which decreed tolerance towards Christianity. Issues of authentication aside, the documents that record the suffering of the early martyrs remain some of the most moving in all hagiography.

[Fig.1.] The Martyrdom of St. Ignatius of Antioch, from a 9th-century Greek manuscript (copy in Jameson, *Sacred and Legendary Art* [London, 1883], 2, 695]). Of Syrian origin, Ignatius was condemned to be sent to Rome and thrown to the lions under the persecution of Trajan. When brought to the colosseum he is reported to have said, "I am as the wheat of [God's] field, and must be ground by the teeth of the lions that I may become bread worthy of being served up to him."

1. THE MARTYRDOM OF ST. POLYCARP, BISHOP OF SMYRNA

Polycarp holds a particularly important place in the minds of early writers because he was not only one of the first martyrs but also a prominent figure in the early church. According to the second-century theologian Irenaeus of Lyons, as a young man Poly-carp had personally known St. John the Evangelist. He was one of the first to quote in writing parts of the New Testament (in his 'Letter to the Philippians'), thereby giving testimony to the existence of these texts, which he used in his defence of orthodox Christianity against the Gnostic and Marcionite heresies. Thus he provided a vital link between the apostles and the second generation of church theologians. The earliest account of his death, printed below, is found in a letter sent to the Christian church at Philomelium in Asia Minor from the church in Smyrna. It exists in Greek manu-scripts, the oldest of which dates from the 10th century, and is thought to be the earli-est authentic account of a martyr's death. Polycarp's importance in the eyes of his con-temporaries is indicated by the fact that the description of his martyrdom (which took place about 155, although there is disagreement about the exact date), was addressed not only to the church in Philomelium but also to "all the dioceses of the Holy Catholic Church in every place." Unlike his contemporary, Ignatius, Bishop of Anti-och, who described himself as "lusting after [a martyr's] death," Polycarp apparently neither sought martyrdom nor sought to avoid it when he was arrested. His friends' careful disposal of his bones, "being of more value than precious stones and more esteemed than gold," is evidence that the cult of relics had already begun.

Source: trans. E.C.E. Owen, *Some Authentic Acts of the Early Martyrs* (Oxford: Clarendon Press, 1927), pp. 32-41; repr. with permission. BHL 6870.

The Church of God which dwells in Smyrna to the Church of God which dwells in Philomelium [in Asia Minor] and to all the dioceses of the Holy Catholic Church in every place. May the mercy, peace, and love of God the Father and of our Lord Jesus Christ be multiplied.

1. We write unto you, brethren, the story of the martyrs and of blessed Polycarp, who put an end to the persecution, setting his seal thereto by his martyrdom. For almost all that went before so happened, that the Lord might show forth anew an example of martyrdom which is conformable to the Gospel. For he waited to be betrayed, as did also the Lord, that we also might be imitators of him [Christ], looking not only on our own things, but also on the things of others. For it is a mark of true and steadfast love to desire not our own salvation only but that of all the brethren.

2. Blessed and noble are all martyrdoms that happen according to the will of God. For we should act with discretion leaving the power over all events to God. For who can fail to admire their [the martyrs'] nobility and patience

and love of their Master? Who being so torn with scourges that the framework of the flesh was laid bare to the veins and arteries within, showed such patience that the very bystanders felt pity and sorrow, while some reached so high a pitch of nobility that no sound or groan escaped them, making manifest to us all that in the hour of their torture the martyrs of Christ were absent from the flesh, or rather that the Lord was present and of their company. Fixing their thoughts on the grace of Christ they despised the torments of the world, redeeming in one hour eternal punishment. And the fire of their inhuman torturers was cold to them, for their eyes were set on escape from the eternal fire which is never quenched, and with the eyes of the heart they looked upon the good things reserved for them that endure, which ear hath not heard, nor eye seen, neither have they entered into the heart of man, but they were revealed by the Lord unto them who were no longer men, but already angels. Likewise those who were condemned to the beasts endured terrible torments, having harrows laid beneath them, and being tormented with other kinds of manifold tortures, that the Devil, if he could, might through the continual torment turn them to deny their faith; for he devised many things against them.

3. But, thanks be to God, he did not prevail against all. For the noble Germanicus gave strength to their cowardice by his own fortitude, who made a notable fight with the beasts. For when the proconsul [the Roman official] endeavored to prevail upon him, bidding him take pity on his own youth, he with violence dragged the wild beast towards him, wishing to be rid the sooner of their life of unrighteousness and sin.

At this all the multitude, wondering at the nobility of the people of Christ, who were beloved of God and honored him, cried out, "Away with the Atheists! Seek Polycarp!"

4. But one, Quintus by name, a Phrygian just arrived from Phrygia, lost heart when he saw the beasts. He it was who constrained himself and some others to come forward of their own motion. After much entreaty the proconsul persuaded him to take the oath and offer sacrifice. Therefore, brethren, we do not commend those who give themselves up; for this is not the teaching of the Gospel.

5. The excellent Polycarp on hearing the news was not dismayed, but wished to remain in the city; but the greater number urged him to depart secretly. And so he did, to a little farm, not far from the city, and passed the time with a few companions, doing nothing else but pray night and day for all and for the Churches throughout the world, as was his custom. And while praying he fell into a trance three days before he was taken, and saw his pillow being consumed by fire. And he turned and said to those with him, "I must be burned alive."

6. While his pursuers were still waiting for him, he went away to another farm, and immediately they followed close upon him. Not finding him, they laid hands on two young slaves, one of whom confessed under the torture. Now it was impossible Polycarp should escape, since his betrayers belonged to his own household. And the justice of the peace whose lot it was to bear the same name as Herod, was in a hurry to bring him into the stadium, that he, being made partner with Christ, might fulfil his lot, and his betrayers might meet the same punishment as Judas.

7. Taking the young slave with them, the constables and horsemen armed in the usual way went out on the preparation [the day before the Sabbath] about the dinner-hour 'as against a thief' at a run. Coming up in a body late in the day they found him [Polycarp] lying in a cottage in an upper room; he could indeed have escaped from there also elsewhere, but he refused, saying, "The will of the Lord be done." Hearing then that they were come he went down and talked with them, those present marveling at his great age and his constancy, and at their excessive eagerness to take a man so old. So he bade food and drink to be set before them at that hour, as much as they wanted; and besought them to give him an hour to pray undisturbed. On leave being given he stood and prayed, being so full of the grace of God that for two hours he could not once be silent, and the hearers were astonished and many repented for having assailed an old man so godlike.

8. When at length he ended his prayer after remembering all that ever had dealings with him, great and small, well-known and unknown, and the whole Catholic Church throughout the world, the time having now come for his departure, they set him on an ass and brought him to the city, it being a High Sabbath. He was met by Herodes, the High Sheriff, and by Herodes' father, Nicetes, who, having transferred him to the carriage, sat down beside him, and strove to persuade him with these words: "What is the harm of saying, 'Caesar is Lord,' and offering incense," with more to this effect, "and saving your life?" At first he made them no answer, but, when they persisted, he said: "I do not intend to do as you advise me." Failing to persuade him, they reviled him, and made him descend with so much haste that in getting down from the carriage he hurt his shin. He, as though nothing had happened, paid no heed, but went on quickly with much eagerness on his way to the stadium, where the din was so great that none could be so much as heard.

9. As Polycarp entered the stadium, there came a voice from heaven, saying, "Be strong, Polycarp, and play the man." None saw the speaker, but the voice was heard by those of our brethren who were present. When he was brought in, thereupon a great din arose as soon as they heard "Polycarp is taken." So the proconsul asked him whether he were the man. And when he said "Yes," he tried to persuade him to deny his faith, saying: "Have respect to

your age," and other such things as they were used to say: "Swear by the Fortune [divinity] of Caesar, repent, say 'Away with the Atheists.'" Polycarp, gazing with a steadfast countenance on all the crowd of lawless heathen in the stadium, waved his hand to them, sighed, and looking up to heaven said: "Away with the Atheists." When the proconsul pressed him further and said, "Swear and I set you free: curse Christ," Polycarp answered, "Eighty and six years have I served him, and he did me no wrong. How can I blaspheme my King, that saved me?"

10. When the proconsul persevered saying: "Swear by the Fortune of Caesar," Polycarp answered: "If you vainly imagine that I shall swear by the Fortune of Caesar, as you say, and suppose that I know not what I am, hear a plain answer, 'I am a Christian.' If you wish to learn the Christian's reason, give me a day and listen." The proconsul said: "It is the people you must convince." Polycarp answered: "I would have counted you worthy to be reasoned with; for we have been taught to give honor as is fit, where we can without harm, to governments and powers ordained by God, but the people I do not deem worthy to hear any defence from me."

11. The proconsul said: "I have beasts, and to them I will throw you, unless you repent." "Bring them in," he answered, "For repentance from the better to the worse is no change to be desired, but it is good to change from cruelty to justice." The other spoke again to him: "If you despise the beasts, I will have you consumed by fire, unless you repent." "You threaten me," answered Polycarp, "with the fire that burns for an hour and is speedily quenched; for you know nothing of the fire of the judgment to come and of eternal punishment which is reserved for the wicked. Why delay? Bring what you will."

12. While speaking these and many other words he grew full of confidence and joy, and his face was filled with grace, so that it fell out that not only was he not troubled by the things said to him, but on the contrary the proconsul was amazed and sent his own herald to proclaim thrice in the midst of the stadium, "Polycarp has confessed himself to be a Christian." Upon this proclamation of the herald the whole multitude of heathen and Jews that dwelt in Smyrna cried aloud in ungovernable fury: "This is the teacher of Asia, the father of the Christians, the destroyer of our gods, who teaches many not to sacrifice or worship." So saying they shouted beseeching Philip, the Asiarch, to let loose a lion on Polycarp. However, he said it was not lawful for him to do this, as he had concluded the wild beast combat. Then they thought good to cry with one voice that Polycarp should be burnt alive. For it must needs be that the vision revealed to him on his pillow be fulfilled, when in prayer he saw it aflame, and turning to the faithful who

were with him said in prophecy: "I must be burned alive."

13. This then was brought about with great speed, more quickly than words can say, the crowd gathering together forthwith wood and fuel from the shops and baths, the Jews being particularly zealous in the work, as is their custom. When the pyre was ready, he [Polycarp] put off all his upper garments and undid his girdle, and endeavored to take off his shoes, which he had not been used to do before because all the faithful used to contend with one another who should first touch his body. For even before his martyrdom he was treated with all honor for the goodness of his life. So he was immediately girded with the things devised for his burning; but when they were about to nail him to the stake as well, he said: "Leave me as I am; for he that enabled me to abide the fire, will also enable me to abide at the stake unflinching without your safeguard of nails."

14. So they bound him without nailing him. And he, with his hands bound behind him, like a choice ram taken from a great flock for sacrifice, an acceptable whole burnt-offering prepared for God, looked up to Heaven and said: "Lord God Almighty, Father of thy well-beloved and blessed Son, Jesus Christ, through whom we have received the knowledge of thee, God of Angels and Powers and of the whole creation and of all the race of the righteous who live before thee, I bless thee that thou didst deem me worthy of this day and hour, that I should take a part among the number of the martyrs in the cup of thy Christ to the resurrection of life eternal of soul and body in incorruption of the Holy Spirit: among whom may I be accepted before thee today, a rich and acceptable sacrifice, as thou didst fore-ordain and fore-show and fulfil, God faithful and true. For this above all I praise thee, I bless thee, I glorify thee through the eternal and heavenly high priest Jesus Christ, thy well-beloved Son, through whom to thee with him and the Holy Spirit be glory now and for evermore. Amen."

15. When he had offered up the Amen, and finished his prayer, those who had charge of the fire set light to it. And a great flame blazing forth, we to whom it was given to behold, who were indeed preserved to tell the story to the rest, beheld a marvel. For the fire forming a sort of arch, like a ship's sail bellying with the wind, made a wall about the body of the martyr, which was in the midst, not like burning flesh, but like bread in the baking, or like gold and silver burning in a furnace. For we caught a most sweet perfume, like the breath of frankincense or some other precious spice.

16. At last when the impious people saw that his body could not be consumed by the fire they gave orders that a slaughterer should go and thrust a dagger into him. This being done there came out such a gush of blood that it put out the fire, and all the throng marveled that there should be so great a

difference between the unbelievers and the elect, one of whom was the most admirable martyr, Polycarp, an apostolic and prophetic teacher of our time, and bishop of the Catholic Church in Smyrna. For every word that he uttered from his mouth was fulfilled then and shall be fulfilled hereafter.

17. But the Adversary [Satan], that malicious and wicked one who is the enemy of the race of the just, seeing the greatness of his witness, and the blamelessness of his life from the beginning, and that he was crowned with the crown of immortality, and had won a prize beyond gainsaying, made it his business that we might not even recover his body, though many were eager to do so and to touch his sacred flesh. At any rate he suggested to Nicetes, the father of Herodes and brother of Alce, to entreat the proconsul not to give us his body, "Lest," said he, "they should abandon the crucified, and begin to worship him." The Jews made the same suggestions with much vehemence, who also watched the body, when we were about to take it from the fire, not knowing that we can never abandon Christ who suffered for the salvation of those who are being saved throughout the whole world, the sinless for sinners, nor can we worship any other. For him, being the Son of God, we adore, but the martyrs we love as disciples and imitators of the Lord, and rightly for their unsurpassable loyalty to their own king and master; may it be granted us to have partnership and fellow-discipleship with them.

18. So the centurion, seeing the contentiousness of the Jews, set him in the midst and burnt him [Polycarp's body] according to their custom. So we later took up his bones, being of more value than precious stones and more esteemed than gold, and laid them apart in a convenient place. There the Lord will grant us to gather so far as may be and to celebrate with great gladness and joy the birthday of his martyrdom, in memory of those who have fought the good fight before us and for the training and preparation of those to come.

19. Such is the story of the blessed Polycarp, who with the eleven from Philadelphia was martyred in Smyrna, and is more particularly remembered by all, so that he is spoken of in every place even by the Gentiles, having been not only a famous teacher, but also an illustrious martyr, whose martyrdom all desire to imitate, as being after the pattern of the gospel of Christ. Having vanquished by his patience the unjust ruler and thus received the crown of immortality, he rejoices greatly with the apostles and with all the just, and glorifies the almighty God and Father, and praises our Lord Jesus Christ, the savior of our souls, the pilot of our bodies, and the shepherd of the Catholic Church throughout the world.

20. You indeed made request that the events might be described to you at greater length, but we for the present have declared them to you in brief by

our brother Marcion. On receiving this, send on the letter to the more distant brethren that they may glorify the Lord who makes choice of his own servants. To him that is able to bring us all by his grace and bounty to his eternal kingdom through his only begotten son Jesus Christ be glory, honor, power, and majesty for ever and ever. Salute all the saints [the faithful]. Those with us, and Evaristus, the writer of this, with his whole house salute you.

21. The blessed Polycarp was martyred on the second day of the first part of the month Xanthicus [23 February according to the Roman calendar], on a High Sabbath, at the eighth hour [2 p.m.]. He was taken by Herodes, when Philip of Tralles was chief priest [the Asiarch mentioned in 12 above], in the proconsulship of Statius Quadratus, in the everlasting reign of Jesus Christ; to whom be glory, honor, majesty, and a throne eternal, from generation to generation. Amen.

[The following ending appears to have been added to a later recension of the text, ostensibly by Pionius]

22. We pray that you may be of good cheer, brethren, while you walk by the word of Jesus Christ according to the Gospel: with whom be glory to God for the salvation of the elect saints; even as blessed Polycarp suffered martyrdom, in whose footsteps God grant that we may be found in the kingdom of Jesus Christ. This account was copied by Gaius from the papers of Irenaeus [the Bishop of Lyons c.177-203], a disciple of Polycarp, Gaius having been himself a companion of Irenaeus. And I, Socrates, wrote it down in Corinth from the copy of Gaius. Grace be with you all.

I, Pionius, in my turn wrote it from the aforementioned copy, having searched it out, for the blessed Polycarp made it known to me by revelation, as I shall show in what follows. I gathered it together when already almost worn away by time, that the Lord Jesus Christ may gather me also with his elect into his heavenly kingdom, to whom be glory with the Father and the Holy Spirit for ever and ever. Amen.

2. THE MARTYRS OF LYONS AND VIENNE

The harrowing account of the deaths of forty-eight Christians in Lyons in 177 is found in the 'Church History' authored by the fourth-century bishop, theologian, and writer, Eusebius of Caesarea. Situated at the confluence of two major rivers, Lyons was an important Roman administrative town and center for trade. It also had the earliest organized Christian church in Gaul, and the prominence of its members may in part explain the violence and scope of the attack on them, which was extraordinary for its cruelty. The two leaders of the Gallic church – Pothinus, the bishop of Lyons, and Sanctus, the deacon of Vienne – both lost their lives, as well as a mixed company of church members that included slaves, women, Roman citizens, and Greek-speaking Christians from Asia Minor. The account asserts that even those who recanted at the last minute were thrown into prison and accused of other crimes, while charges of cannibalism and incest were lodged against the Christians in addition to the customary accusation of treason for their refusal to adopt the imperial cult. Eusebius's account in Greek is the only source; he claims to be quoting a letter written by the communities of Lyons and Vienne to the churches of Asia and Phrygia.

Source: trans. Arthur Cushman McGiffert, *Eusebius: Church History*, in *A Select Library of Nicene and Post-Nicene Fathers of the Christian Church*, ed. Philip Schaff and Henry Wace (New York: The Christian Literature Company; Oxford and London: Parker and Co., 1890), 1, pp. 211-217. BHL 6839.

5, 1. In the seventeenth year of the emperor Antoninus Verus [in fact, Marcus Aurelius], the persecution of our people was rekindled more fiercely in certain districts on account of an insurrection of the masses in the cities; and judging by the number in a single nation, myriads suffered martyrdom throughout the world. A record of this was written for posterity, and in truth it is worthy of perpetual remembrance. A full account, containing the most reliable information on the subject, is given in my 'Collection of Martyrdoms' which constitutes a narrative [that is] instructive as well as historical. I will repeat here such portions of this account as may be needful for the present purpose.

Other writers of history record the victories of war and trophies won from enemies, the skill of generals, and the manly bravery of soldiers, defiled with blood and with innumerable slaughters for the sake of children and country and other possessions. But our narrative of the government of God will record in ineffaceable letters the most peaceful wars waged on behalf of the peace of the soul, and will tell of men doing brave deeds for truth rather than country, and for piety rather than dearest friends. It will hand down to imperishable remembrance the discipline and the much-tried fortitude of the athletes of religion, the trophies won from demons, the victories over invisible enemies, and the crowns placed upon all their heads. The country in which the arena was prepared for them was Gaul, of which Lyons and Vienne are the principal and most celebrated cities. The Rhône passes through both of them, flowing in a broad stream through the entire region. The most celebrated churches in that country sent an account of the witnesses [the literal meaning of the Greek word for 'martyrs' as those who testified to the truth of Christianity] to the churches in Asia and Phrygia, relating in the following manner what was done among them. I will give their own words:

The servants of Christ residing at Vienne and Lyons, in Gaul, to the brethren throughout Asia and Phrygia, who hold the same faith and hope of redemption, peace and grace and glory from God the Father and Christ Jesus our Lord. Then the others were divided, and the proto-witnesses [first martyrs] were manifestly ready, and finished their confession with all eagerness. But some seemed unprepared and untrained, weak as yet, and unable to endure so great a conflict. About ten of these proved abortions [they recanted], causing us great grief and sorrow beyond measure, and impairing the zeal of the others who had not yet been seized, but who, though suffering all kinds of affliction, continued constantly with the witnesses and did not forsake them. Then all of us feared greatly on account of uncertainty as to their confession; not because we dreaded the sufferings to be endured, but because we looked to the end, and were afraid that some of them might fall away. But those who were worthy were seized day by day, filling up their number, so that all the zealous persons, and those through whom especially our affairs had been established, were collected together out of the two churches.

And some of our heathen servants also were seized, as the governor had commanded that all of us should be examined publicly. These, being ensnared by Satan, and fearing for themselves the tortures which they beheld the saints endure, and being also urged on by the soldiers, accused us falsely of Thyestean banquets and Oedipodean intercourse [cannibalism and incest], and of deeds which are not only unlawful for us to speak of or to think, but which we cannot believe were ever done by men. When these accusations were reported, all the people raged like wild beasts against us, so that even if any had before been moderate on account of friendship, they were now exceedingly furious and gnashed their teeth against us. And that which was spoken by our Lord was fulfilled: "the time will come when whosoever killeth you will think that he doeth God service."

Then finally the holy witnesses endured sufferings beyond description, Satan striving earnestly that some of the slanders might be uttered by them also. But the whole wrath of the populace, and governor, and soldiers was aroused exceedingly against Sanctus, the deacon from Vienne, and Maturus, a late convert, yet a noble combatant, and against Attalus, a native of Pergamus [in Asia Minor; some of the martyrs were Greeks], where he had always been a pillar and foundation, and Blandina, through whom Christ showed that things which appear mean and obscure and despicable to men are with God of great glory, through love toward him manifested in power, and not boasting in appearance.

For while we all trembled, and her earthly mistress, who was herself also one of the witnesses, feared that on account of the weakness of her body, she would be unable to make bold confession, Blandina was filled with such power as to be delivered and raised above those who were torturing her by turns from morning till evening in every manner, so that they acknowledged that they were conquered, and could do nothing more to her. And they were astonished at her endurance, as her entire body was mangled and broken; and they testified that one of these forms of torture was sufficient to destroy life, not to speak of so many and so great sufferings. But the blessed woman, like a noble athlete, renewed her strength in her confession; and her comfort and recreation and relief from the pain of her sufferings was in exclaiming, "I am a Christian, and there is nothing vile done by us."

But Sanctus also endured marvelously and superhumanly all the outrages which he suffered. While the wicked men hoped by the continuance and severity of his tortures to wring something from him which he ought not to say, he girded himself against them with such firmness that he would not even tell his name, or the nation or city to which he belonged, or whether he was bond or free, but answered in the Roman tongue to all their questions, "I am a Christian." He confessed this instead of name and city and race and everything besides, and the people heard from him no other word.

There arose therefore on the part of the governor and his tormentors a great desire to conquer him; but having nothing more that they could do to him, they finally fastened red-hot brazen plates to the most tender parts of his body. And these indeed were burned, but he continued unbending and unyielding, firm in his confession, and refreshed and strengthened by the heavenly fountain of the water of life, flowing from its source in Christ. And his body was a witness of his sufferings, being one complete wound and bruise, drawn out of shape, and altogether unlike a human form. Christ, suffering in him, manifested his glory, delivering him from his adversary, and making him an example for the others, showing that nothing is fearful where the love of the Father is, and nothing painful where there is the glory of Christ. For when the wicked men tortured him a second time after some days, supposing that with his body swollen and inflamed to such a degree that he could not bear the touch of a hand, if they should again apply the same instruments, they would overcome him, or at least by his death under his sufferings others would be made afraid, not only did this not occur, but, contrary to all human expectation, his body arose and stood erect in the midst of the subsequent torments, and resumed its original appearance and the use of its limbs, so that, through the grace of Christ, these second sufferings became to him, not torture, but healing.

But the devil, thinking that he had already consumed Biblias, who was one of those who had denied Christ, desiring to increase her condemnation through the utterance of blasphemy, brought her again to the torture, to compel her, as already feeble and weak, to report impious things concerning us. But she recovered herself under the suffering, and as if awaking from a deep sleep, and reminded by the present anguish of the eternal punishment in hell, she contradicted the blasphemers. "How," she said, "could those eat children who do not think it lawful to taste the blood even of irrational animals?" And thenceforward she confessed herself a Christian, and was given a place in the company of the witnesses. But as the tyrannical tortures were made of no effect by Christ through the patience of the blessed, the devil invented other contrivances – confinement in the dark and most loathsome parts of the prison, stretching of the feet to the fifth hole in the stocks, and the other outrages which his servants are accustomed to inflict upon the prisoners when furious and filled with the devil. A great many were suffocated in prison, being chosen by the Lord for this manner of death, that he might manifest in them his glory. For some, though they had been tortured so cruelly that it seemed impossible that they could live, even with the most careful nursing, yet, destitute of human attention, remained in the prison being strengthened by the Lord, and invigorated both in body and soul; and they exhorted and encouraged the rest. But such as were young, and arrested recently, so that their bodies had not become accustomed to torture, were unable to endure the severity of their confinement, and died in prison.

The blessed Pothinus, who had been entrusted with the bishopric of Lyons, was dragged to the judgment seat. He was more than ninety years of age, and very infirm, scarcely indeed able to breathe because of physical weakness; but he was strengthened by spiritual zeal through his earnest desire for martyrdom. Though his body was worn out by old age and disease, his life was preserved that Christ might triumph in it. When he was brought by the soldiers to the tribunal, accompanied by the civil magistrates and a multitude who shouted against him in every manner as if he were Christ himself, he bore noble witness. Being asked by the governor who was the God of the Christians, he replied, "If thou art worthy, thou shalt know." Then he was dragged away harshly, and received blows of every kind. Those near him struck him with their hands and feet, regardless of his age; and those at a distance hurled at him whatever they could seize; all of them thinking that they would be guilty of great wickedness and impiety if any possible abuse were omitted. For thus they thought to avenge their own deities. Scarcely able to breathe, he was cast into prison and died after two days. Then a certain great dispensation of God occurred, and the compassion of Jesus appeared beyond measure, in a manner rarely seen among the brotherhood, but not beyond the power of Christ. For those who had recanted at their first arrest were imprisoned with the others, and endured terrible sufferings, so that their denial was of no profit to them even for the present. But those who confessed what they were, were imprisoned as Christians, no other accusation being brought against them. But the first were treated afterwards as murderers and defiled, and were punished twice as severely as the others. For the joy of martyrdom, and the hope of the promises, and love for Christ, and the Spirit of the Father supported the latter; but their consciences so greatly distressed the former that they were easily distinguishable from all the rest by their very countenances when they were led forth. For the first went out rejoicing, glory and grace being blended in their faces, so that even their bonds seemed like beautiful ornaments, as those of a bride adorned with variegated golden fringes; and they were perfumed with the sweet savor of Christ so that some supposed they had been anointed with earthly ointment. But the others were downcast and humble and dejected and filled with every kind of disgrace, and they were reproached by the heathen as ignoble and weak, bearing the accusation of murderers, and having lost the one honorable and glorious and lifegiving name. The rest, beholding this, were strengthened, and when apprehended, they confessed without hesitation, paying no attention to the persuasions of the devil.

After these things, finally, their martyrdoms were divided into every form. For plaiting a crown of various colors and of all kinds of flowers, they presented it to the Father. It was proper therefore that the noble athletes, having endured a manifold strife, and conquered grandly, should receive the crown, great and incorruptible.

Maturus, therefore, and Sanctus and Blandina and Attalus were led to the amphitheater to be exposed to the wild beasts, and to give to the heathen public a spectacle of cruelty, a day for fighting with wild beasts being specially appointed on account of our people. Both Maturus and Sanctus passed again through every torment in the amphitheater, as if they had suffered nothing before, or rather, as if, having already conquered their antagonist in many contests, they were now striving for the crown itself. They endured again the customary running of the gauntlet [between two lines of men using whips] and the violence of the wild beasts, and everything which the furious people called for or desired, and at last, the iron chair, in which their bodies, being roasted, tormented them with the fumes. And not with this did the persecutors cease, but were yet more mad against them, determined to overcome their patience. But even thus they did not hear a word from Sanctus except the confession which he had uttered from the beginning. These, then, after their life had continued for a long time through the great conflict, were at last sacrificed, having been made throughout that day a spectacle to the world, in place of the usual variety of combats.

But Blandina was suspended on a stake, and exposed to be devoured by the wild beasts who should attack her. And because she appeared as if hanging on a cross, and because of her earnest prayers, she inspired the combatants with great zeal. For they looked on her in her conflict, and beheld with their outward eyes, in the form of their sister, him who was crucified for them, that he might persuade those who believe on him, that every one who suffers for the glory of Christ has fellowship always with the living God. As none of the wild beasts at that time touched her, she was taken down from the stake, and cast again into prison. She was preserved thus for another contest, so that, being victorious in more conflicts, she might make the punishment of the crooked serpent [Satan] irrevocable; and, though small and weak and despised, yet clothed with Christ the mighty and conquering athlete, she might arouse the zeal of the brethren, and having overcome the adversary many times might receive, through her conflict, the crown of immortality.

But Attalus was called for loudly by the people, because he was a person of distinction. He entered the contest readily on account of a good conscience and his genuine practice in Christian discipline, and as he had always been a witness for the truth among us. He was led around the amphitheater, a tablet being carried before him on which was written in the Roman language 'This is Attalus the Christian,' and the people were filled with indignation against him. But when the governor learned that he was a Roman, he commanded him to be taken back with the rest of those who were in prison concerning whom he had written to Caesar, and whose answer he was awaiting.

But the intervening time was not wasted nor fruitless to them; for by their patience the measureless compassion of Christ was manifested. For through their continued life the dead were made alive, and the witnesses showed favor to those who had failed to witness. And the Virgin Mother [the Church] had much joy in receiving alive those whom she had brought forth as dead. For through their influence many who had denied were restored, and re-begotten, and rekindled with life, and learned to confess. And being made alive and strengthened, they went to the judgment seat to be again interrogated by the governor; God, who desires not the death of the sinner, but mercifully invites to repentance, treating them with kindness. For Caesar commanded that they should be put to death, but that any who might deny should be set free. Therefore, at the beginning of the public festival which took place there, and which was attended by crowds of men from all nations, the governor brought the blessed ones to the judgment seat, to make of them a show and spectacle for the multitude. Wherefore also he examined them again, and beheaded those who appeared to possess Roman citizenship, but he sent the others to the wild beasts.

And Christ was glorified greatly in those who had formerly denied him, for, contrary to the expectation of the heathen, they confessed. For they were examined by themselves, as about to be set free; but confessing, they were added to the order of the witnesses. But some continued without, who had never possessed a trace of faith nor any apprehension of the wedding garment [the white garment worn at baptism], nor an understanding of the fear of God; but, as sons of perdition, they blasphemed the way through their apostasy. But all the others were added to the Church.

While these were being examined, a certain Alexander, a Phrygian by birth and physician by profession, who had resided in Gaul for many years and was well known to all on account of his love to God and boldness of speech (for he was not without a share of apostolic grace), standing before the judgment seat, by signs encouraged them to confess [the faith], and appeared to those standing by as if in travail. But the people were enraged because those who formerly denied now confessed, and cried out against Alexander as if he were the cause of this. Then the governor summoned him and inquired who he was. And when he answered that he was a Christian, being very angry he condemned him to the wild beasts. And on the next day he entered along with Attalus. For to please the people, the governor had ordered Attalus again to the wild beasts. And they were tortured in the amphitheater with all the instruments contrived for that purpose, and having endured a very great conflict, were at last sacrificed. Alexander neither groaned nor murmured in any manner, but communed in his heart with God. But when Attalus was placed in the iron seat, and the fumes arose from his burning body, he said to the people in the Roman language: "Lo! this which ye do is devouring men; but we do not devour men; nor do any other wicked thing." And being asked, what name God has, he replied, "God has not a name as man has." After all these, on the last day of the contests, Blandina was again brought in, with Ponticus, a boy about fifteen years old. They had been brought every day to witness the sufferings of the others, and had been pressed to swear by the idols. But because they remained steadfast and despised them, the multitude became furious, so that they had no compassion for the youth of the boy nor respect for the sex of the woman. Therefore they exposed them to all the terrible sufferings and took them through the entire round of torture, repeatedly urging them to swear, but being unable to effect this; for Ponticus, encouraged by his sister so that even the heathen could see that she was confirming and strengthening him, having nobly endured every torture, gave up the ghost.

But the blessed Blandina, last of all, having, as a noble mother, encouraged her children and sent them before her victorious to the King, endured herself all their conflicts and hastened after them, glad and rejoicing in her departure as if called to a marriage supper rather than cast to wild beasts. And after the scourging, after the wild beasts, after the roasting seat, she was finally enclosed in a net, and thrown before a bull. And having been tossed about by the animal, but feeling none of the things which were happening to her, on account of her hope and firm hold upon what had been entrusted to her, and her communion with Christ, she also was sacrificed. And the heathen themselves confessed that never among them had a woman endured so many and such terrible tortures.

But not even thus was their madness and cruelty toward the saints satisfied. For, incited by the wild Beast [Satan], wild and barbarous tribes were not easily appeased, and their violence found another peculiar opportunity in the dead bodies. For, through their lack of manly reason, the fact that they had been conquered did not put them to shame, but rather the more enkindled their wrath as that of a wild beast, and aroused alike the hatred of governor and people to treat us unjustly; that the Scripture might be fulfilled: "He that is lawless, let him be lawless still, and he that is righteous, let him be righteous still." For they cast to the dogs those who had died of suffocation in the prison, carefully guarding them by night and day, lest any one should be buried by us. And they exposed the remains left by the wild beasts and by fire, mangled and charred, and placed the heads of the others by their bodies, and guarded them in like manner from burial by a watch of soldiers for many days. And some raged and gnashed their teeth against them, desiring to execute more severe vengeance upon them; but others laughed and mocked at them, magnifying their own idols, and imputed to them the punishment of the Christians. Even the more reasonable and those who had seemed to sympathize somewhat reproached them often, saying, "Where is their God, and what has their religion, which they have chosen rather than life, profited them?" So various was their conduct toward us; but we were in deep affliction because we could not bury the bodies. For neither did night avail us for this purpose, nor did money persuade, nor entreaty move to compassion; but they kept watch in every way, as if the prevention of the burial would be of some great advantage to them.

The bodies of the martyrs, having thus in every manner been exhibited and exposed for six days, were afterward burned and reduced to ashes, and swept into the Rhône by the wicked men, so that no trace of them might appear on the earth. And this they did, as if able to conquer God, and prevent their new birth "so that," as they said, "they may have no hope of a resurrection, through trust in which they bring to us this foreign and new religion, and despise terrible things, and are ready even to go to death with joy. Now let us see if they will rise again, and if their God is able to help them, and to deliver them out of our hands."

[Eusebius resumes his narration]

5, 2. Such things happened to the churches of Christ under the above-mentioned emperor, from which we may reasonably conjecture the occurrences in the other provinces. It is proper to add other selections from the same letter, in which the moderation and compassion of these witnesses is recorded in the following words: "they were also so zealous in their imitation of Christ, 'who, being in the form of God, counted it not a prize to be on an equality with God,' that, though they had attained such honor, and had borne witness, not once or twice, but many times, having been brought back to prison from the wild beasts, covered with burns and scars and wounds, yet they did not proclaim themselves witnesses, nor did they suffer us to address them by this name. If any one of us, in letter or conversation, spoke of them as witnesses, they rebuked him sharply. For they conceded cheerfully the appellation of witness to Christ 'the faithful and true witness,' and 'firstborn of the dead,' and prince of the life of God; and they reminded us of the witnesses who had already departed, and said, 'They are already witnesses whom Christ has deemed worthy to be taken up in their confession, having sealed their testimony by their departure; but we are lowly and humble confessors' and they besought the brethren with tears that earnest prayers should be offered that they might be made perfect. They showed in their deeds the power of testimony, manifesting great boldness toward all the brethren, and they made plain their nobility through patience and fearlessness and courage, but they refused the title of witnesses as distinguishing them from their brethren, being filled with the fear of God." A little further on they [the letter-writers] say: "they humbled themselves under the mighty hand, by which they are now greatly exalted. They defended all, but accused none. They absolved all but bound none. And they prayed for those who had inflicted cruelties upon them, even as Stephen, the perfect witness, 'Lord, lay not this sin to their charge.' But if he prayed for those who stoned him, how much more for the brethren!" And again after mentioning other matters, they say:

"For, through the genuineness of their love, their greatest contest with him was that the Beast [Satan], being choked, might cast out alive those whom he supposed he had swallowed. For they did not boast over the fallen [those who recanted under threat of torture], but helped them in their need with those things in which they themselves abounded, having the compassion of a mother, and shedding many tears on their account before the Father. They asked for life, and he gave it to them, and they shared it with their neighbors. Victorious over everything, they departed to God. Having always loved peace, and having commended peace to us, they went in peace to God, leaving no sorrow to their mother, nor division or strife to the brethren, but joy and peace and concord and love."

This record of the affection of those blessed ones toward the brethren that had fallen may be profitably added on account of the inhuman and unmerciful disposition of those who, after these events, acted unsparingly toward the members of Christ.

[Fig. 2] A third-century terra-cotta funeral lamp from the catacombs, showing a young Christian woman holding the palm leaves of martyrdom (reproduced in Lacroix, *Military and Religious Life in the Middle Ages* [London, 1874], 424).

3. THE PASSION OF SS. PERPETUA AND FELICITAS

*This account of the martyrdom of a group of Christians in North Africa in 203 is
exceptional because it is presented largely in the words of two of the martyrs themselves: a man named Saturus and a young married woman of the Roman upper
classes called Vibia Perpetua. Perpetua's reported words account for the major part of
the 'Passion' and take us from the time of her arrest in the town of Thuburbo Minus,
a short distance from Carthage, to the point where she is awaiting imminent death in
the amphitheater. This document, then, may include one of the few writings by women
extant from this period. However, like the previous two selections, the account gives
evidence of complex transmission. An unnamed author narrates the opening and closing sections of the narrative, and places the martyrdoms in the context of Montanism,
an important early Christian movement whose adherents (including Tertullian, see 4
below) believed in the 'parousia,' that is, the imminence of the second coming of
Christ, promoted the importance of prophecy and women's special gifts in this domain,
and took a rigorously ascetic view of earthly life. The 'Passion' is also of great intrinsic
interest because of the visions, narrated in detail, received by Perpetua and Saturus
while in prison. The whole account survives in Latin and Greek in a long version
known as the 'Passio' (the Latin version is given here), and in a short version in Latin
only, known as the 'Acta,' possibly composed to be read aloud in church on the saints'
feast-day.*

Source: trans. H. R. Musurillo, *Acts of the Christian Martyrs* (Oxford: Clarendon Press, 1972), pp.
106-131; repr. with permission. BHL 6633.

1. The deeds recounted about the faith in ancient times were a proof of
God's favor and achieved the spiritual strengthening of men as well; and they
were set forth in writing precisely that honor might be rendered to God and
comfort to men by the recollection of the past through the written word.
Should not then more recent examples be set down that contribute equally
to both ends? For indeed these too will one day become ancient and needful
for the ages to come, even though in our own day they may enjoy less prestige because of the prior claim of antiquity.

   Let those then who would restrict the power of the one Spirit to times
and seasons look to this: the more recent events should be considered the
greater, being later than those of old, and this is a consequence of the extraordinary graces promised for the last stage of time. For *in the last days, God
declares, I will pour out my Spirit upon all flesh and their sons and daughters shall
prophesy and on my manservants and my maidservants I will pour my Spirit, and the
young men shall see visions and the old men shall dream dreams.* So too we hold in
honor and acknowledge not only new prophecies but new visions as well,

according to the promise. And we consider all the other functions of the Holy Spirit as intended for the good of the Church; for the same Spirit has been sent to distribute all his gifts to all, as the Lord apportions to everyone. For this reason we deem it imperative to set them forth and to make them known through the word for the glory of God. Thus no one of weak or despairing faith may think that supernatural grace was present only among men of ancient times, either in the grace of martyrdom or of visions, for God always achieves what he promises, as a witness to the non-believer and a blessing to the faithful.

And so, my brethren and little children, *that which we have heard and have touched with our hands we proclaim also to you, so that* those of you that were witnesses may recall the glory of the Lord and those that now learn of it through hearing *may have fellowship* with the holy martyrs and, through them, *with* the Lord *Christ Jesus,* to whom belong splendor and honor for all ages. Amen.

2. A number of young catechumens [those receiving instruction in preparation for baptism] were arrested, Revocatus and his fellow slave Felicitas, Saturninus and Secundulus, and with them Vibia Perpetua, a newly married woman of good family and upbringing. Her mother and father were still alive and one of her two brothers was a catechumen like herself. She was about twenty-two years old and had an infant son at the breast. (Now from this point on the entire account of her ordeal is her own, according to her own ideas and in the way that she herself wrote it down.)

3. While we were still under arrest (she said) my father out of love for me was trying to persuade me and shake my resolution. 'Father,' said I, 'do you see this vase here, for example, or water pot or whatever?'

'Yes, I do,' said he.

And I told him: 'Could it be called by any other name than what it is?'

And he said: 'No.'

'Well, so too I cannot be called anything other than what I am, a Christian.'

At this my father was so angered by the word 'Christian' that he moved towards me as though he would pluck my eyes out. But he left it at that and departed, vanquished along with his diabolical arguments. For a few days afterwards I gave thanks to the Lord that I was separated from my father, and I was comforted by his absence. During these few days I was baptized, and I was inspired by the Spirit not to ask for any other favor after the water but simply the perseverance of the flesh. A few days later we were lodged in the prison; and I was terrified, as I had never before been in such a dark hole. What a difficult time it was! With the crowd the heat was stifling; then there was the extortion of the soldiers; and to crown all, I was tortured with worry for my baby there. Then Tertius and Pomponius, those blessed deacons who tried to take care of us, bribed the soldiers to allow us to go to a better part of the prison to refresh ourselves for a few hours. Everyone then left that dungeon and shifted for himself. I nursed my baby, who was faint from hunger. In my anxiety I spoke to my mother about the child, I tried to comfort my brother, and I gave the child in their charge. I was in pain because I saw them suffering out of pity for me. These were the trials I had to endure for many days. Then I got permission for my baby to stay with me in prison. At once I recovered my health, relieved as I was of my worry and anxiety over the child. My prison had suddenly become a palace, so that I wanted to be there rather than anywhere else.

4. Then my brother said to me: 'Dear sister, you are greatly privileged; surely you might ask for a vision to discover whether you are to be condemned or freed.' Faithfully I promised that I would, for I knew that I could speak with the Lord, whose great blessings I had come to experience. And so I said: 'I shall tell you tomorrow.' Then I made my request and this was the vision I had.

I saw a ladder of tremendous height made of bronze, reaching all the way to the heavens, but it was so narrow that only one person could climb up at a time. To the sides of the ladder were attached all sorts of metal weapons: there were swords, spears, hooks, daggers, and spikes; so that if anyone tried to climb up carelessly or without paying attention, he would be mangled and his flesh would adhere to the weapons.

At the foot of the ladder lay a dragon of enormous size, and it would attack those who tried to climb up and try to terrify them from doing so. And Saturus was the first to go up, he who was later to give himself up of his own accord. He had been the builder of our strength, although he was not present when we were arrested. And he arrived at the top of the staircase and he looked back and said to me:

'Perpetua, I am waiting for you. But take care; do not let the dragon bite you.'

'He will not harm me,' I said, 'in the name of Christ Jesus.'

Slowly, as though he were afraid of me, the dragon stuck his head out from underneath the ladder. Then, using it as my first step, I trod on his head and went up.

Then I saw an immense garden, and in it a grey-haired man sat in shepherd's garb; tall he was, and milking sheep. And standing around him were many thousands of people clad in white garments. He raised his head, looked at me, and said:

'I am glad you have come, my child.'

He called me over to him and gave me, as it were, a mouthful of the milk he was drawing; and I took it into my cupped hands and consumed it. And all those who stood around said: 'Amen!' At the sound of this word I came to, with the taste of something sweet still in my mouth. I at once told this to my brother, and we realized that we would have to suffer, and that from now on we would no longer have any hope in this life.

5. A few days later there was a rumor that we were going to be given a hearing. My father also arrived from the city, worn with worry, and he came to see me with the idea of persuading me.

'Daughter,' he said, 'have pity on my grey head – have pity on me your father, if I deserve to be called your father, if I have favored you above all your brothers, if I have raised you to reach this prime of your life. Do not abandon me to be the reproach of men. Think of your brothers, think of your mother and your aunt, think of your child, who will not be able to live once you are gone. Give up your pride! You will destroy all of us! None of us will ever be able to speak freely again if anything happens to you.'

This was the way my father spoke out of love for me, kissing my hands and throwing himself down before me. With tears in his eyes he no longer addressed me as his daughter but as a woman. I was sorry for my father's sake, because he alone of all my kin would be unhappy to see me suffer.

I tried to comfort him saying: 'It will all happen in the prisoner's dock as God wills; for you may be sure that we are not left to ourselves but are all in his power.'

And he left me in great sorrow.

6. One day while we were eating breakfast we were suddenly hurried off for a hearing. We arrived at the forum, and straight away the story went about the neighborhood near the forum and a huge crowd gathered. We walked up to the prisoner's dock. All the others when questioned admitted their guilt. Then, when it came my turn, my father appeared with my son, dragged me from the step, and said 'Perform the sacrifice – have pity on your baby!'

Hilarianus the governor, who had received his judicial powers as the successor of the late proconsul Minucius Timinianus, said to me: 'Have pity on your father's grey head; have pity on your infant son. Offer the sacrifice for the welfare of the emperors.'

'I will not,' I retorted.

'Are you a Christian?' said Hilarianus.

And I said: 'Yes, I am.'

When my father persisted in trying to dissuade me, Hilarianus ordered him to be thrown to the ground and beaten with a rod. I felt sorry for father, just as if I myself had been beaten. I felt sorry for his pathetic old age.

Then Hilarianus passed sentence on all of us: we were condemned to the beasts, and we returned to prison in high spirits. But my baby had got used to being nursed at the breast and to staying with me in prison. So I sent the deacon Pomponius straight away to my father to ask for the baby. But father refused to give him over. But as God willed, the baby had no further desire for the breast, nor did I suffer any inflammation; and so I was relieved of any anxiety for my child and of any discomfort in my breasts.

7. Some days later when we were all at prayer, suddenly while praying I spoke out and uttered the name Dinocrates. I was surprised; for the name had never entered my mind until that moment. And I was pained when I recalled what had happened to him. At once I realized that I was privileged to pray for him. I began to pray for him and to sigh deeply for him before the Lord. That very night I had the following vision. I saw Dinocrates coming out of a dark hole, where there were many others with him, very hot and thirsty, pale and dirty. On his face was the wound he had when he died.

Now Dinocrates had been my brother according to the flesh; but he had died horribly of cancer of the face when he was seven years old, and his death was a source of loathing to everyone. Thus it was for him that I made my prayer. There was a great abyss between us: neither could approach the other. Where Dinocrates stood there was a pool full of water; and its rim was higher than the child's height, so that Dinocrates had to stretch himself up to drink. I was sorry that, though the pool had water in it, Dinocrates could not drink because of the height of the rim. Then I woke up, realizing that my brother was suffering. But I was confident that I could help him in his trouble; and I prayed for him every day until we were transferred to the military prison. For we were supposed to fight with the beasts at the military games to be held on the occasion of the emperor Geta's birthday. And I prayed for my brother day and night with tears and sighs that this favor might be granted me.

8. On the day we were kept in chains, I had this vision shown to me. I saw the same spot that I had seen before, but there was Dinocrates all clean, well dressed, and refreshed. I saw a scar where the wound had been; and the pool that I had seen before now had its rim lowered to the level of the child's waist. And Dinocrates kept drinking water from it, and there above the rim was golden bowl full of water. And Dinocrates drew close and began to drink from it, and yet the bowl remained full. And when he had drunk enough of the water, he began to play as children do. Then I awoke, and I realized that he had been delivered from his suffering.

9. Some days later, an adjutant named Pudens, who was in charge of the prison, began to show us great honor, realizing that we possessed some great power within us. And he began to allow many visitors to see us for our mutual comfort.

Now the day of the contest was approaching, and my father came to see me overwhelmed with sorrow. He started tearing the hairs from his beard and threw them on the ground; he then threw himself on the ground and began to curse his old age and to say such words as would move all creation. I felt sorry for his unhappy old age.

10. The day before we were to fight with the beasts I saw the following vision. Pomponius the deacon came to the prison gates and began to knock violently. I went out and opened the gate for him. He was dressed in an unbelted white tunic, wearing elaborate sandals. And he said to me: 'Perpetua, come; we are waiting for you.'

Then he took my hand and we began to walk through rough and broken country. At last we came to the amphitheater out of breath, and he led me into the center of the arena.

Then he told me: 'Do not be afraid. I am here, struggling with you.' Then he left.

I looked at the enormous crowd who watched in astonishment. I was surprised that no beasts were let loose on me; for I knew that I was condemned to die by the beasts. Then out came an Egyptian against me, of vicious appearance, together with his seconds, to fight with me. There also came up to me some handsome young men to be my seconds and assistants. My clothes were stripped off, and suddenly I was a man. My seconds began to rub me down with oil (as they are wont to do before a contest). Then I saw the Egyptian on the other side rolling in the dust. Next there came forth a man of marvelous stature, such that he rose above the top of the amphitheater. He was clad in a beltless purple tunic with two stripes (one on either side) running down the middle of his chest. He wore sandals that were wondrously made of gold and silver, and he carried a wand like an athletic trainer and a green branch on which there were golden apples.

And he asked for silence and said: 'If this Egyptian defeats her he will slay her with the sword. But if she defeats him, she will receive this branch.' Then he withdrew.

We drew close to one another and began to let our fists fly. My opponent tried to get hold of my feet, but I kept striking him in the face with the heels of my feet. Then I was raised up into the air and I began to pummel him without as it were touching the ground. Then when I noticed there was a lull, I put my two hands together linking the fingers of one hand with those of the other and thus I got hold of his head. He fell flat on his face and I stepped on his head.

The crowd began to shout and my assistants started to sing psalms. Then I walked up to the trainer and took the branch. He kissed me and said to me: 'Peace be with you, my daughter!' I began to walk in triumph towards the Gate of Life [the *Porta Sanavivaria* by which victorious gladiators or those spared by the people could leave]. Then I awoke. I realized that it was not with wild animals that I would fight but with the Devil, but I knew that I would win the victory. So much for what I did up until the eve of the contest. About what happened at the contest itself, let him write of it who will.

11. But the blessed Saturus has also made known his own vision and he has written it out with his own hand. We had died, he said, and had put off the flesh, and we began to be carried towards the east by four angels who did not touch us with their hands. But we moved along not on our backs facing upwards but as though we were climbing up a gentle hill. And when we were free of the world, we first saw an intense light. And I said to Perpetua (for she was at my side): 'This is what the Lord promised us. We have received his promise.'

While we were being carried by these four angels, a great open space appeared, which seemed to be a garden, with rose bushes and all manner of flowers. The trees were as tall as cypresses, and their leaves were constantly falling. In the garden there were four other angels more splendid than the others. When they saw us they paid us homage and said to the other angels in admiration: 'Why, they are here! They are here!'

Then the four angels that were carrying us grew fearful and set us down. Then we walked across to an open area by way of a broad road, and there we met Jucundus, Saturninus, and Artaxius, who were burnt alive in the same persecution, together with Quintus who had actually died as a martyr in prison. We asked them where they had been. And the other angels said to us: 'First come and enter and greet the Lord.'

12. Then we came to a place whose walls seemed to be constructed of light. And in front of the gate stood four angels, who entered in and put on white robes. We also entered and we heard the sound of voices in unison chanting endlessly: '*Holy, holy, holy!*' In the same place we seemed to see an aged man with white hair and a youthful face, though we did not see his feet. On his right and left were four elders, and behind them stood other aged men. Surprised, we entered and stood before a throne: four angels lifted us up and we kissed the aged man and he touched our faces with his hand. And the elders said to us: 'Let us rise.' And we rose and gave the kiss of peace. Then the elders said to us: 'Go and play.'

To Perpetua I said: 'Your wish is granted.'

She said to me: 'Thanks be to God that I am happier here now than I was in the flesh.'

13. Then we went out and before the gates we saw the bishop Optatus on the right and Aspasius the presbyter and teacher on the left, each of them far apart and in sorrow. They threw themselves at our feet and said: 'Make peace between us. For you have gone away and left us thus.'

And we said to them: 'Are you not our bishop, and are you not our presbyter? How can you fall at our feet?'

We were very moved and embraced them. Perpetua then began to speak with them in Greek, and we drew them apart into the garden under a rose arbor.

While we were talking with them, the angels said to them: 'Allow them to rest. Settle whatever quarrels you have among yourselves.' And they were put to confusion. Then they said to Optatus: 'You must scold your flock. They approach you as though they had come from the games, quarreling about the different teams.'

And it seemed as though they wanted to close the gates. And there we began to recognize many of our brethren, martyrs among them. All of us were sustained by a most delicious odor that seemed to satisfy us. And then I woke up happy.

14. Such were the remarkable visions of these martyrs, Saturus and Perpetua, written by themselves. As for Secundulus, God called him from this world earlier than the others while he was still in prison, by a special grace that he might not have to face the animals. Yet his flesh, if not his spirit, knew the sword.

15. As for Felicitas, she too enjoyed the Lord's favor in this wise. She had been pregnant when she was arrested, and was now in her eighth month. As the day of the spectacle drew near she was very distressed that her martyrdom would be postponed because of her pregnancy; for it is against the law for women with child to be executed. Thus she might have to shed her holy, innocent blood afterwards along with others who were common criminals. Her comrades in martyrdom were also saddened; for they were afraid that they would have to leave behind so fine a companion to travel alone on the same road to hope. And so, two days before the contest, they poured forth a prayer to the Lord in one torrent of common grief. And immediately after their prayer the birth pains came upon her. She suffered a good deal in her labor because of the natural difficulty of an eight months' delivery.

Hence one of the assistants of the prison guards said to her: 'You suffer so much now – what will you do when you are tossed to the beasts? Little did you think of them when you refused to sacrifice.'

'What I am suffering now,' she replied, 'I suffer by myself. But then another will be inside me who will suffer for me, just as I shall be suffering for him.'

And she gave birth to a girl; and one of the sisters brought her up as her own daughter.

16. Therefore, since the Holy Spirit has permitted the story of this contest to be written down and by so permitting has willed it, we shall carry out the command or, indeed, the commission of the most saintly Perpetua, however unworthy I might be to add any thing to this glorious story. At the same time I shall add one example of her perseverance and nobility of soul.

The military tribune had treated them with extraordinary severity because on the information of certain very foolish people he became afraid that they would be spirited out of the prison by magical spells.

Perpetua spoke to him directly. 'Why can you not even allow us to refresh ourselves properly? For we are the most distinguished of the condemned prisoners, seeing that we belong to the emperor; we are to fight on his very birthday. Would it not be to your credit if we were brought forth on the day in a healthier condition?'

The officer became disturbed and grew red. So it was that he gave the order that they were to be more humanely treated; and he allowed her brothers and other persons to visit, so that the prisoners could dine in their company. By this time the adjutant who was head of the jail was himself a Christian.

17. On the day before, when they had their last meal, which is called the free banquet [the public feast given to the condemned], they celebrated not a banquet but rather a love feast. They spoke to the mob with the same steadfastness, warned them of God's judgment, stressing the joy they would have in their suffering, and ridiculing the curiosity of those that came to see them. Saturus said: 'Will not tomorrow be enough for you? Why are you so eager to see something that you dislike? Our friends today will be our enemies on the morrow. But take careful note of what we look like so that you will recognize us on the day.' Thus everyone would depart from the prison in amazement, and many of them began to believe.

18. The day of their victory dawned, and they marched from the prison to the amphitheater joyfully as though they were going to heaven, with calm faces, trembling, if at all, with joy rather than fear. Perpetua went along with shining countenance and calm step, as the beloved of God, as a wife of Christ, putting down everyone's stare by her own intense gaze. With them also was Felicitas, glad that she had safely given birth so that now she could

fight the beasts, going from one blood bath to another, from the midwife to the gladiator, ready to wash after childbirth in a second baptism. They were then led up to the gates and the men were forced to put on the robes of priests of Saturn, the women the dress of the priestesses of Ceres. But the noble Perpetua strenuously resisted this to the end. 'We came to this of our own free will that our freedom should not be violated. We agreed to pledge our lives provided that we would do no such thing. You agreed with us to do this.' Even injustice recognized justice. The military tribune agreed. They were to be brought into the arena just as they were. Perpetua then began to sing a psalm: she was already treading on the head of the Egyptian. Revocatus, Saturninus, and Saturus began to warn the onlooking mob. Then when they came within sight of Hilarianus, they suggested by their motions and gestures: 'You have condemned us, but God will condemn you' was what they were saying.

At this the crowds became enraged and demanded that they be scourged before a line of gladiators. And they rejoiced at this that they had obtained a share in the Lord's sufferings.

19. But he who said, 'Ask and you shall receive,' answered their prayer by giving each one the death he had asked for. For when ever they would discuss among themselves their desire for martyrdom, Saturninus indeed insisted that he wanted to be exposed to all the different beasts, that his crown might be all the more glorious. And so at the outset of the contest he and Revocatus were matched with a leopard, and then while in the stocks they were attacked by a bear. As for Saturus, he dreaded nothing more than a bear, and he counted on being killed by one bite of a leopard. Then he was matched with a wild boar; but the gladiator who had tied him to the animal was gored by the boar and died a few days after the contest, whereas Saturus was only dragged along. Then when he was bound in the stocks awaiting the bear, the animal refused to come out of the cages, so that Saturus was called back once more unhurt.

20. For the young women, however, the Devil had prepared a mad heifer. This was an unusual animal, but it was chosen that their sex might be matched with that of the beast. So they were stripped naked, placed in nets and thus brought out into the arena. Even the crowd was horrified when they saw that one was a delicate young girl and the other was a woman fresh from child birth with the milk still dripping from her breasts. And so they were brought back again and dressed in unbelted tunics.

First the heifer tossed Perpetua and she fell on her back. Then sitting up she pulled down the tunic that was ripped along the side so that it covered her thighs, thinking more of her modesty than of her pain. Next she asked for a pin to fasten her untidy hair: for it was not right that a martyr should die with her hair in disorder, lest she might seem to be mourning in her hour of triumph.

Then she got up. And seeing that Felicitas had been crushed to the ground, she went over to her, gave her hand, and lifted her up. Then the two stood side by side. But the cruelty of the mob was by now appeased, and so they were called back through the Gate of Life.

There Perpetua was held up by a man named Rusticus who was at the time a catechumen and kept close to her. She awoke from a kind of sleep (so absorbed had she been in ecstasy in the Spirit) and she began to look about her. Then to the amazement of all she said: 'When are we going to be thrown to that heifer or whatever it is?'

When told that this had already happened, she refused to believe it until she noticed the marks of her rough experience on her person and her dress. Then she called for her brother and spoke to him together with the catechumens and said: 'You must all *stand fast in the faith* and love one another, and do not be weakened by what we have gone through.'

21. At another gate Saturus was earnestly addressing the soldier Pudens. 'It is exactly,' he said, 'as I foretold and predicted. So far not one animal has touched me. So now you may believe me with all your heart: I am going in there and I shall be finished off with one bite of the leopard.' And immediately as the contest was coming to a close a leopard was let loose, and after one bite Saturus was so drenched with blood that as he came away the mob roared in witness to his second baptism: 'Well washed! Well washed [an ironic use of the greeting to bathers in the public baths]!' For well washed indeed was one who had been bathed in this manner.

Then he said to the soldier Pudens: 'Good-bye. Remember me, and remember the faith. These things should not disturb you but rather strengthen you.'

And with this he asked Pudens for a ring from his finger, and dipping it into his wound he gave it back to him again as a pledge and as a record of his bloodshed.

Shortly after he was thrown unconscious with the rest in the usual spot to have his throat cut. But the mob asked that their bodies be brought out into the open that their eyes might be the guilty witnesses of the sword that pierced their flesh. And so the martyrs got up and went to the spot of their own accord as the people wanted them to, and kissing one another they sealed their martyrdom with the ritual kiss of peace. The others took the sword in silence and without moving, especially Saturus, who being the first to climb the stairway was the first to die. For once again he was waiting for

Perpetua. Perpetua, however, had yet to taste more pain. She screamed as she was struck on the bone; then she took the trembling hand of the young gladiator and guided it to her throat. It was as though so great a woman, feared as she was by the unclean spirit, could not be dispatched unless she herself were willing.

Ah, most valiant and blessed martyrs! Truly are you called and chosen for the glory of Christ Jesus our Lord! And any man who exalts, honors, and worships his glory should read for the consolation of the Church these new deeds of heroism which are no less significant than the tales of old. For these new manifestations of virtue will bear witness to one and the same Spirit who still operates, and to God the Father almighty, to his Son Jesus Christ our Lord, to whom is splendor and immeasurable power for all the ages. Amen.

4. TERTULLIAN'S ADDRESS TO THE MARTYRS

The son of a centurion and educated in Rome, Tertullian converted to Christianity after his return to Carthage in about 195 and became an important leader in the North African church, a theologian, polemicist, and acerbic arbitrator of Christian morals and manners. His treatise addressed to the martyrs was probably written in the early part of his career, during the intense persecution of Christians under the emperor Septimius Severus, and is therefore roughly contemporary with the martyrdoms of Perpetua and Felicitas and their friends in 203. Here Tertullian writes about the difficulties encountered by the early church under persecution, especially the problem of apostates, those who denied their faith under threat of torture. Not only did these weaken the resolve of others, but whether they should be readmitted to the church was a question which continued to divide Christians. Some bishops gave speedier readmittance to the church to penitents who could produce letters written on their behalf by those about to face martyrdom. In this treatise Tertullian praises the martyrs for contributing in this way to the unity of the church they were leaving behind them, although later, during his more rigorous Montanist phase, he was to condemn such letters, perhaps aware that they were subject to abuse. His encouragement to the martyrs develops military and athletic analogies from the New Testament which became hagiographic conventions: the martyr is compared to the triumphant soldier and the champion athlete. The latter operates already in Perpetua's final vision of her own suffering, and Tertullian has sometimes been claimed as the redactor of her 'Passion.'

Source: trans. Rudolph Arbesmann, *Tertullian: Disciplinary, Moral and Ascetical Works,* in *The Fathers of the Church,* 40 (New York: Fathers of the Church, Inc., 1959), pp. 17-29; repr. with permission.

1. Blessed martyrs elect, along with the nourishment for the body which our Lady Mother the Church from her breast, as well as individual brethren from their private resources, furnish you in prison, accept also from me some offering that will contribute to the sustenance of the spirit. For it is not good that the flesh be feasted while the spirit goes hungry. Indeed, if care is bestowed on that which is weak, there is all the more reason not to neglect that which is still weaker. Not that I am specially entitled to exhort you. Yet, even the most accomplished gladiators are spurred on not only by their trainers and managers but also from afar by people inexperienced in this art and by all who choose, without the slightest need for it, with the result that hints issuing from the crowd have often proved profitable for them.

In the first place, then, O blessed, "do not grieve the Holy Spirit" who has entered prison with you. For, if he had not accompanied you there in your present trial, you would not be there today. See to it, therefore, that he remain with you there and so lead you out of that place to the Lord.

Indeed, the prison is the Devil's house, too, where he keeps his household. But you have come to the prison for the very purpose of trampling upon him right in his own house. For you have engaged him in battle already outside the prison and trampled him underfoot. Let him, therefore, not say: "Now that they are in my domain, I will tempt them with base hatreds, with defections or dissensions among themselves." Let him flee from your presence, and let him, coiled and numb, like a snake that is driven out by charms or smoke, hide away in the depths of his den. Do not allow him the good fortune in his own kingdom of setting you against one another, but let him find you fortified by the arms of peace among yourselves, because peace among yourselves means war with him. Some, not able to find this peace in the Church, are accustomed to seek it from the martyrs in prison. For this reason, too, then, you ought to possess, cherish and preserve it among yourselves that you may perhaps be able to bestow it upon others also.

2. Other attachments, equally burdensome to the spirit, may have accompanied you to the prison gate; so far your relatives, too, may have escorted you. From that very moment on you have been separated from the very world. How much more, then, from its spirit and its ways and doings? Nor let this separation from the world trouble you. For, if we reflect that it is the very world that is more truly a prison, we shall realize that you have left a prison rather than entered one. The world holds the greater darkness, blinding men's hearts. The world puts on the heavier chains, fettering the very souls of men. The world breathes forth the fouler impurities – human lusts. Finally, the world contains the larger number of criminals, namely, the entire human race. In fact, it awaits sentence not from the proconsul but from God. Wherefore, O blessed, consider yourselves as having been transferred from prison to what we may call a place of safety. Darkness is there, but you are light; fetters are there, but you are free before God. It breathes forth a foul smell, but you are an odor of sweetness. There the judge is expected at every moment, but you are going to pass sentence upon the judges themselves. There sadness may come upon the man who sighs for the pleasures of the world. The Christian, however, even when he is outside the prison, has renounced the world, and, when in prison, even prison itself. It does not matter what part of the world you are in, you who are apart from the world. And if you have missed some of the enjoyments of life, remember that it is the way of business to suffer some losses in order to make larger profits.

I say nothing yet about the reward to which God invites the martyrs. Meanwhile, let us compare the life in the world with that in prison to see if the spirit does not gain more in prison than the flesh loses there. In fact, owing to the solicitude of the Church and the charity of the brethren, the flesh does not miss there what it ought to have, while, in addition, the spirit obtains what is always beneficial to the faith: you do not look at strange gods; you do not chance upon their images; you do not, even by mere physical contact, participate in heathen holidays; you are not plagued by the foul fumes of the sacrificial banquets, not tormented by the noise of the spectacles, nor by the atrocity or frenzy or shamelessness of those taking part in the celebrations; your eyes do not fall on houses of lewdness; you are free from inducements to sin, from temptations, from unholy reminiscences, free, indeed, even from persecution.

The prison now offers to the Christian what the desert once gave to the Prophets. Our Lord himself quite often spent time in solitude to pray there more freely, to be there away from the world. In fact, it was in a secluded place that he manifested his glory to his disciples. Let us drop the name 'prison' and call it a place of seclusion. Though the body is confined, though the flesh is detained, there is nothing that is not open to the spirit. In spirit wander about, in spirit take a walk, setting before yourselves not shady promenades and long porticoes but that path which leads to God. As often as you walk that path, you will not be in prison. The leg does not feel the fetter when the spirit is in heaven. The spirit carries about the whole man and brings him wherever he wishes. And where your heart is, there will your treasure be also. There, then, let our heart be where we would have our treasure.

3. Granted now, O blessed, that even to Christians the prison is unpleasant – yet, we were called to the service in the army of the living God in the very moment when we gave response to the words of the sacramental oath [at baptism]. No soldier goes out to war encumbered with luxuries, nor does he march to the line of battle from the sleeping chamber, but from light and cramped tents where every kind of austerity, discomfort, and inconvenience is experienced. Even in time of peace soldiers are toughened to warfare by toils and hardships: by marching in arms, by practising swift maneuvers in the field, by digging a trench, by joining closely together to form a tortoise-shield [Roman soldiers when attacking locked their shields over their heads to form a protective cover like a tortoise-shell]. Everything is set in sweating toil, lest bodies and minds be frightened at having to pass from shade to sunshine, from sunshine to icy cold, from the tunic to the breastplate, from hushed silence to the warcry, from rest to the din of battle.

In like manner, O blessed, consider whatever is hard in your present situation as an exercise of your powers of mind and body. You are about to enter a noble contest in which the living God acts the part of superintendent and the Holy Spirit is your trainer, a contest whose crown is eternity, whose prize is angelic nature, citizenship in heaven and glory for ever and ever. And so your master, Jesus Christ, who has anointed you with his Spirit and has brought you to this training ground, has resolved, before the day of the contest, to take you from a softer way of life to a harsher treatment that your strength may be increased. For athletes, too, are set apart for more rigid training that they may apply themselves to the building up of their physical strength. They are kept from lavish living, from more tempting dishes, from more pleasurable drinks. They are urged on, they are subjected to torturing toils, they are worn out: the more strenuously they have exerted themselves, the greater is their hope of victory. And they do this, says the Apostle, to win a perishable crown. We who are about to win an eternal one recognize in the prison our training ground, that we may be led forth to the actual contest before the seat of the presiding judge well practised in all hardships, because strength is built up by austerity, but destroyed by softness.

4. We know from our Lord's teaching that, while the spirit is willing, the flesh is weak. Let us, however, not derive delusive gratification from the Lord's acknowledgment of the weakness of the flesh. For it was on purpose that he first declared the spirit willing: he wanted to show which of the two ought to be subject to the other, that is to say, that the flesh should be submissive to the spirit, the weaker to the stronger, so that the former may draw strength from the latter. Let the spirit converse with the flesh on their common salvation, no longer thinking about the hardships of prison but, rather, about the struggle of the actual contest. The flesh will perhaps fear the heavy sword and the lofty cross and the wild beasts mad with rage and the most terrible punishment of all – death by fire – and, finally, all the executioner's cunning during the torture. But let the spirit present to both itself and the flesh the other side of the picture: granted, these sufferings are grievous, yet many have borne them patiently, nay, have even sought them on their own accord for the sake of fame and glory; and this is true not only of men but also of women so that you, too, O blessed women, may be worthy of your sex.

It would lead me too far were I to enumerate each one of those who, led by the impulse of their own mind, put an end to their lives by the sword. Among women there is the well-known instance of Lucretia. A victim of violence [rape], she stabbed herself in the presence of her kinsfolk to gain glory for her chastity. Mucius [when threatened with torture] burnt his own right hand on the altar that his fair fame might include this deed. Nor did the philosophers act less courageously: Heraclitus, for instance, who put an end to his life by smearing himself with cow dung [apparently in an attempt to cure a fatal illness]; Empedocles, too, who leaped down into the fires of

Mt. Etna [so that, by leaving no bodily trace behind, he could claim divinity]; and Peregrinus who not long ago threw himself upon a funeral pile [to set an example of contempt of death]. Why, even women have despised the flames: Dido did so in order not to be forced to marry after the departure of the man she had loved most dearly [Aeneas]; the wife of Hasdrubal, too, with Carthage in flames, cast herself along with her children into the fire that was destroying her native city, that she might not see her husband [the Carthaginian commander] a suppliant at Scipio's [the Roman general's] feet. Regulus, a Roman general, was taken prisoner by the Carthaginians, but refused to be the only Roman exchanged for a large number of Carthaginian captives. He preferred to be returned to the enemy, and, crammed into a kind of chest, suffered as many crucifixions as nails were driven in from the outside in all directions to pierce him. A woman voluntarily sought out wild beasts, namely vipers, serpents more horrible than either bull or bear, which Cleopatra let loose upon herself so as not to fall into the hands of the enemy.

You may object: 'But the fear of death is not so great as the fear of torture.' Did the Athenian courtesan [in a story told by Pliny] yield on that account to the executioner? For, being privy to a conspiracy, she was subjected to torture by the tyrant. But she did not betray her fellow conspirators, and at last bit off her own tongue and spat it into the tyrant's face to let him know that torments, however prolonged, could achieve nothing against her. Everybody knows that to this day the most important festival of the Lacedaemonians [the Spartans] is 'the whipping.' In this sacred rite all the noble youth are scourged with whips before the altar, while their parents and kinsfolk stand by and exhort them to perseverance. For they regard it as a mark of greater distinction and glory if the soul rather than the body has submitted to the stripes. Therefore, if earthly glory accruing from strength of body and soul is valued so highly that one despises sword, fire, piercing with nails, wild beasts and tortures for the reward of human praise, then I may say the sufferings you endure are but trifling in comparison with the heavenly glory and divine reward. If the bead made of glass is rated so highly, how much must the true pearl be worth? Who, therefore, does not most gladly spend as much for the true as others spend for the false?

5. I omit here an account of the motive of glory. For inordinate ambition among men as well as a certain morbidity of mind have already set at naught all the cruel and torturing contests mentioned above. How many of the leisure class are urged by an excessive love of arms to become gladiators? Surely it is from vanity that they descend to the wild beasts in the very arena, and think themselves more handsome because of the bites and scars. Some have even hired themselves out to tests by fire, with the result that they ran a

certain distance in a burning tunic. Others have pranced up and down amid the bullwhips of the animal-baiters, unflinchingly exposing their shoulders. All this, O blessed, the Lord tolerates in the world for good reason, that is, for the sake of encouraging us in the present moment and of confounding us on that final day, if we have recoiled from suffering for the truth unto salvation what others have pursued out of vanity unto perdition.

6. Let us, however, no longer talk about those examples of perseverance proceeding from inordinate ambition. Let us, rather, turn to a simple contemplation of man's ordinary lot so that, if we ever have to undergo such trials with fortitude, we may also learn from those misfortunes which sometimes even befall unwilling victims. For how often have people been burned to death in conflagrations! How often have wild beasts devoured men either in the forests or in the heart of cities after escaping from their cages! How many have been slain by the sword of robbers! How many have even suffered the death of the cross at the hands of enemies, after having been tortured first and, indeed, treated with every kind of insult! Furthermore, many a man is able to suffer in the cause of a mere human being what he hesitates to suffer in the cause of God. To this fact, indeed, our present days may bear witness. How many prominent persons have met with death in the cause of a man, though such a fate seemed most unlikely in view of their birth and their rank, their physical condition and their age! Death came to them either from him if they had opposed him, or from his enemies, if they had sided with him.

5. AUGUSTINE PREACHES ON THE FEAST OF SS. PERPETUA AND FELICITAS

The account of Perpetua's martyrdom, because of its autobiographical nature, had a strong impact on the North African Christian community. She and Felicitas became the subject of a flourishing cult, and about two hundred years after her death St. Augustine of Hippo preached three sermons on anniversaries of their feast day (7 March). These were intended to follow the reading aloud to the congregation of Perpetua's account of her sufferings. But Augustine was preaching under much different conditions from those in which Tertullian wrote his 'Address to the Martyrs.' Christianity had by now become the official religion of the empire, and the great persecutions had ceased. The Church was faced with the problem of incorporating the cult of the saints and its various manifestations in institutional form. Thus Augustine is concerned to correct any tendency to interpret Perpetua's account in ways not consonant with contemporary church teachings, especially those which affected the role of women. Rather than dwelling on her personal heroism, he emphasizes the power of God manifested in her actions. His interpretation of Perpetua's behavior may strike readers as rather different from the way she appears to us in the original document.

Source: trans. W. H. Shewring, *The Passion of SS. Perpetua and Felicity MM together with the Sermons of S. Augustine upon these Saints* (London: Sheed and Ward, 1931), pp. 45-59; abridged and repr. with permission.

Sermon 280, 1. Today with its anniversary and return calls into our mind, and in a manner sets anew before us, that day whereon the blessed servants of God, Perpetua and Felicitas, being adorned with the crowns of martyrdom, did achieve the flower of perpetual felicity; bearing in the battle the name of Christ, and in the prize of battle finding their own. Their exhortations in the heavenly visions, and the triumphs of their passion, we heard when they were read to us; and all these, set out and made clear with the light of words, we have received with our ears, pondered with our minds, honored with ceremonies of religion, praised with charity. Yet unto so holy a celebration we are bound to give also a solemn homily; and if I that speak it may not set forth their worthiness as I would, yet I bring a ready affection to the joys of so great a feast. For what thing might there be more glorious than these women, whom men may wonder at sooner than they may imitate? But this is chiefly the glory of Him, in whom they that believe, and they that with holy zeal in his name do contend one with another, are indeed "according to the inward man neither male nor female;" so that even in them that are women in body the manliness of their soul hides the sex of their flesh, and we may scarce think of that in their bodily condition which they suffered not appearing in their deeds. The dragon therefore was trodden down by the chaste foot and victorious tread of the blessed Perpetua, when that upward ladder was shown her whereby she should go to God; and the head of the ancient serpent, which to her that fell was a stone of stumbling, was made a step to her that rose. . . .

Sermon 281, 1. These martyrs, brethren, were companions together; but above them all shines out the name and merit of Perpetua and Felicitas, the blessed handmaids of God; for where the sex was more frail, there is the crown more glorious. Truly towards these women a manly courage did work a marvel, when beneath so great a burden their womanly weakness failed not. Well was it for them that they clove unto one husband, even Him unto whom the Church, being one, is "presented as a chaste virgin." Well, I say, that they clove to that husband from whom they drew strength to resist the devil; that women should make to fall that enemy who by a woman did make a man to fall. He [Christ] appeared in them unconquered, who for their sakes became weak. He filled them with fortitude that He might reap them, who did empty himself so that He might sow them. He led them unto this glory and honor who for their sakes did listen to contumely and rebuke. He made these women to die in manly and faithful fashion who for their sakes did mercifully vouchsafe to be born of a woman.

2. And it rejoices a godly soul to look upon such a sight as the blessed Perpetua has told was revealed to her of herself, how she became a man and strove with the devil. Truly in that strife she also did run "towards the perfect man, to the measure of the age of the fulness of Christ." And that ancient and subtle enemy that would leave no device untried, who once by a woman seduced a man and now felt a woman to play the man against him, did strive by a man to vanquish this woman; not without cause. For he set not her husband before her, lest she that by heavenly thoughts already dwelt in the skies, by disdaining suspicion of fleshly love should remain the stronger; but he gave to her father the words of deceit, that the godly soul which might not be softened by the urging of pleasure, might nevertheless be broken by the assault of filial love. In which matter St. Perpetua answered her father with such temperance that neither did she transgress the commandment which bids honor be paid to parents nor yielded to those deceits wherewith that so subtle enemy tried her. And he, being on all sides overcome, caused that same father to be struck with a rod; that whereas she had condemned his words, she might at the least have compassion upon his stripes. And she grieved indeed at that insult upon her aged father, loving him yet to whom she consented not. For she detested the folly in him and not his nature; his infidelity, and not her own birth. Therefore with the greater glory she resisted so

beloved a father when he counseled ill, whom she could not see smitten without lamentation; and therefore that sorrow took nothing away from the strength of her constancy, but rather it added somewhat to the glory of her passion. For "unto them that love God all things work together for good."

3. As for Felicitas, she was with child in her very dungeon; and in her labor did witness unto her woman's lot with a woman's cry. She suffered the pain of Eve, but she tasted the grace of Mary. A woman's debt was required of her, but He succored her whom a Virgin bore. Lastly her child was brought forth, timely in an untimely month. For God so willed it that the burden of her womb should not be eased in its rightful time, lest in its rightful time the glory of martyrdom should be delayed. God, I say, so willed it, that the babe should be born out of due season, yet so that to all that company should be given their due Felicitas; lest had she been lacking, there should seem to have lacked not a companion only to the martyrs, but the prize of those same martyrs. For that was the name of these two which is the reward of all. For wherefore do martyrs endure all things if not for this, that they may rejoice in perpetual felicity? The women therefore were called that unto which all were called. And therefore although there was in that contest a goodly company, with the names of these two the eternity of all is signified, the solemnity of all is sealed.

Sermon 282, 1. We keep to-day the feast of those two most holy martyrs who not only in their passion shone out with surpassing virtue but also because that great labor of their piety did seal with their names the reward of themselves and of their comrades likewise. For Perpetua and Felicitas are the names of two, but the reward of all. Truly all martyrs would not toil for a while in that strife of passion and confession save that they might rejoice in perpetual felicity. Wherefore by the government of the divine providence it was needful that they should be not martyrs only, but likewise most close companions – as also they were – that they might seal a single day to their glory, and give to them that came after a common solemnity to be kept. For as by the example of their most glorious trial they exhort us to their imitation, so they testify by their names that we shall receive an inseparable reward. Let both in turn hold it, both weave it together. We hope not for the one without the other. For the perpetual without felicity avails not, and felicity fails unless it be perpetual. Now concerning the names of those martyrs to whom this day is dedicate, let these few words suffice.

2. And for those women whose names these are – even as we heard when their passion was read, and as tradition hath delivered to us and we know, these holy and valiant ones were not only of female kind but were very

women. And the one was a mother likewise, so that to the frailty of that sex might be added a more importunate love; so that the Enemy assailing them at all points and hoping they should not bear the bitter and heavy burden of persecution, might think they should straightway yield themselves up to him and be soon his own. But they with the prudent and valiant strength of the inward man did blunt his devices every one and break his assault.

3. In this company of surpassing glory, men also were martyrs; on that selfsame day most valiant men did suffer and overcome; yet did not they with their names commend this day unto us. And this was so, not because women were preferred before men for the worthiness wherewith they bore themselves, but because the weakness of women more marvelously did vanquish the ancient Enemy, and also the strength of men contended to win a perpetual felicity.

6. THE TRIALS AND EXECUTION OF CYPRIAN

Cyprian was an important theologian and bishop of Carthage at the time of the per-secution under the emperor Decius (250), which he spent in hiding. After the death of Decius in 251 there was a period of peace, only to be followed by renewed persecution under the emperor Valerian, whose edict in 257 forbidding Christians to assemble together for any reason, including burials at cemeteries, was especially damaging to the community of converts. Cyprian was first arrested and sent into exile. A year later Valerian's edicts became more severe, and Cyprian was recalled from exile to face his death. The account is important also as an example of the practice of adapting the ear-liest 'lives' from official Roman documents such as those which formed the basis of this one, suitable for reading aloud in church on the anniversary of the saint's death. It records Cyprian's two arrests and interrogations, presented with a few connecting phrases by the writer, and a description in greater detail of his death (perhaps reflecting a different documental source). The trial and interrogation of the saint before the pagan ruler became a conventional trope of certain later types of hagiography, where it is gen-erally the occasion for demonstrating the blatant foolishness of the pagans. Cyprian's exchanges with the proconsul here remain formally polite but with a certain edge, shown in his skill in applying Roman law to protect the very Christians it was attempting to destroy. Readers may sense here also the reluctance of some Roman officials to carry out the letter of the law against well-respected Christians (and Roman citizens) like Cyprian.

Source: trans. E.C.E. Owen, *Some Authentic Acts of the Early Martyrs* (Oxford: Clarendon Press, 1927), pp. 95-99; repr. with permission. BHL 2037.

1, 1. During the consulship of the emperors Valerian and Gallienus, Valerian being consul for the fourth and Gallienus for the third time, on August 30 at Carthage in his private room Paternus the proconsul said to Cyprian the bishop: "The most sacred emperors Valerian and Gallienus have thought fit to send me a letter, in which they have commanded that those who do not observe the Roman religion must recognize the Roman rites. I have therefore made inquiries concerning yourself. What answer have you to give me?"

2. Cyprian the bishop said: "I am a Christian and a bishop. I know no other God but the one true God, who 'made heaven and earth, the sea, and all that in them is.' This God we Christians serve, to him we pray day and night for ourselves, and for all men, and for the safety of the emperors them-selves."

3. The proconsul Paternus said: "Is your will constant in this?"

Cyprian the bishop answered: "A good will, which knows God, cannot be altered."

[Fig. 3] Ninth-century figures of SS. Cornelius (left) and Cyprian, from the cemetery of Callistus on the Appian Way (reproduced in Edward White Benson, *Cyprian: His Life, His Times, His Work* [London, 1897], p. 302).

4. The proconsul Paternus said: "Can you then in accordance with the order of Valerius and Gallienus go into exile to the city of Curubis [about 80 km south east of Carthage]?"

Cyprian the bishop said: "I will go."

5. The proconsul Paternus said: "They have thought fit to write to me not about bishops only, but also about priests. I would know therefore from you who the priests are, who reside in this city."

Cyprian the bishop answered: "It is an excellent and beneficial provision of your laws that informers are forbidden. They cannot therefore be revealed and reported by me. They will be found in their own cities."

6. The proconsul Paternus said: "I will seek them out here to-day."

Cyprian the bishop said: "Since our discipline forbids any one to offer himself [for a martyr's death] unsought, and this is also at variance with your principles, they cannot offer themselves any more than I can report them; but if sought out by you they will be found."

7. The proconsul Paternus said: "They shall be found by me." And added: "The emperors have also given instructions that in no place shall meetings be held, nor shall any enter the cemeteries [which were often used for worship]. If therefore any fail to observe these beneficial instructions, he shall suffer death."

Cyprian the bishop answered: "Do as you are instructed."

2, 1. Then the proconsul Paternus ordered the blessed Cyprian to be banished. And as he stayed a long time in exile, the proconsul Aspasius Paternus was succeeded in the proconsulship by Galerius Maximus, who ordered the holy bishop Cyprian to be recalled from banishment and brought before him.

2. When Cyprian, the holy martyr chosen by God, had returned from the city [of] Curubis, which had been assigned as his place of banishment by command of Aspasius, then proconsul, by divine command he remained in his own gardens, whence he daily expected to be summoned, as had been shown him [in a vision, recorded in the account of his 'Life' by Pontius]. 3. While he still lingered in that place, suddenly on September 13 in the consulship of Tuscus and Bassus there came to him two high officials, one an equerry [cavalry officer] of the staff of the proconsul Galerius Maximus, and the other a member of the same staff, an equerry of the bodyguard. 4. These lifted him into a carriage, placed him between them, and conveyed him to the house of Sextus, whither the proconsul Galerius Maximus had retired to recover his health.

5. And so the same Galerius Maximus the proconsul ordered Cyprian to be remanded till the morrow. For the time being blessed Cyprian withdrew

under guard to the house of a high official, equerry on the same staff of the illustrious Galerius Maximus the proconsul, and remained with him at his house in the street which is called Saturn's between the temple of Venus and the temple of Public Welfare. There the whole congregation of the brethren gathered: when this came to holy Cyprian's knowledge he gave orders that charge should be kept of the young women, for all had remained in the street before the door of the official's house.

3, 1. On the morrow, being September 14, a great crowd gathered in the morning to the house of Sextus in accordance with the command of Galerius Maximus the proconsul. 2. And so the same Galerius Maximus the proconsul ordered that Cyprian the bishop should be brought before him on the morrow where he sat in the Hall Sauciolum. 3. When he had been brought before him, Galerius Maximus the proconsul said to Cyprian the bishop: "Are you Thascius Cyprianus?"

Cyprian the bishop answered: "I am."

4. Galerius Maximus the proconsul said: "Have you taken on yourself to be pope [a term originally applying to all bishops] of persons holding sacrilegious opinions?"

Cyprian the bishop answered: "Yes."

5. Galerius Maximus the proconsul said: "The most sacred emperors have commanded you to perform the rite [of acknowledging Caesar's divinity]."

Cyprian the bishop answered: "I refuse."

6. Galerius Maximus the proconsul said: "Consider your own interest."

Cyprian the bishop answered: "Do as you are bid. In so clear a case there is no need for consideration."

4, 1. Galerius Maximus having conferred with the council gave sentence hardly and reluctantly in these terms: "You have long lived in the holding of sacrilegious opinions, and have joined with yourself very many members of an abominable conspiracy, and have set yourself up as an enemy of the gods of Rome and religious ordinances, nor have the pious and most sacred emperors Valerian and Gallienus, the Augusti, and Valerian, the most noble Caesar, been able to recall you to the observance of their rites. 2. And therefore since you have been convicted as the contriver and standard-bearer in most atrocious crimes, you shall be an example to those whom by your wickedness you have joined with you: discipline shall be vindicated in your blood." 3. With these words he read from his tablets the sentence: "It is our pleasure that Thascius Cyprianus should be executed by the sword."

Cyprian the bishop said: "Thanks be to God!"

5, 1. After this sentence the crowd of brethren cried: "Let us also be beheaded with him." Hence arose an uproar among the brethren, and a great crowd accompanied him. 2. So the same Cyprian was led forth on to the land of Sextus, and there he divested himself of his mantle and kneeled upon the ground, and bowed in prayer to the Lord. 3. And when he had divested himself of his dalmatic [robe indicating high status] and handed it to the deacons, he stood clad in his linen garment, and prepared to await the executioner. 4. When the executioner arrived he charged his friends that they should give to the same executioner twenty-five golden pieces. Napkins and handkerchiefs were strewn before him by the brethren [to catch his blood and be preserved as relics]. 5. Thereafter blessed Cyprian bound his eyes with his own hand, but, as he could not fasten the ends of the handkerchief for himself, the priest Julianus and the sub-deacon Julianus fastened them for him.

6. So the blessed Cyprian suffered, and his body was laid out hard by to content the curiosity of the heathen. Thence it was removed by night, and, accompanied by tapers and torches, was conducted with prayers in great triumph to the burial-ground of Macrobius Candidianus the procurator, which lies on the Mappalian way near the fishponds. A few days later Galerius Maximus the proconsul died.

6. The most blessed martyr Cyprian suffered on the 14th day of September under the emperors Valerian and Gallienus, in the reign of our Lord Jesus Christ, to whom belong honor and glory for ever and ever. Amen.

7. THE AGE OF MARTYRS IN LEGEND: THE SEVEN SLEEPERS OF EPHESUS

Gregory of Tours (born 539), prolific hagiographer and recorder of saints' miracles, is the redactor of this popular medieval story with its source in an early version that circulated in the eastern Mediterranean. The first part of the tale takes place during the same persecution under Decius in which Cyprian died, and the second part in the reign of the eastern emperor Theodosius II (408-450), at a time when controversy concerning the resurrection of the body was at its height. Compared to the vivid contemporary accounts of the martyrs' sufferings, this story has many of the characteristics of folktale: remoteness of time and place, stereotyped treatment of the villain Decius, increased emphasis on the miraculous, subordination of narrative logic to didactic concerns, and a 'Rip Van Winkle' plot which appears in stories in many parts of the world, including the Koran. Fictional or not, however, the legend was immensely popular, and the grotto (on a mountainside near Ephesus) in which the seven were thought to have slept away the years became a famous site of medieval pilgrimage. Archaeological evidence indicates that many other people wanted to be buried as close as possible to a place which had come to symbolize faith in the resurrection of the body.

Source: trans. William C. McDermott, *Monks, Bishops and Pagans: Christian Culture in Gaul and Italy, 500-700*, ed. Edward Peters (reissued 1975; Philadelphia: University of Pennsylvania Press, 1949), pp. 199-206; repr. with permission. BHL 2313.

1. In the time of the emperor Decius, when throughout all the earth the persecution of the Christians was being stirred up and deadly sacrifices were being offered to vain idols, there were in the palace of the king seven important men, born of noble lineage, Achillidis, Diomedis, Diogenus, Probatus, Sambatus, Stephanus, and Quiriacus. They often saw the savage crimes of the emperor when he ordered deaf and dumb idols to be worshiped instead of God Eternal. Stirred by God, they hurried to baptism and from the source of regeneration were named Maximianus, Malchus, Martinianus, Constantinus, Dionisius, Johannis, Serapion. Then Decius, when he arrived at the city of Ephesus, ordered that the Christian race be sought out with such zeal that he might be able, if heaven allowed, to snuff out the very name of the religion. At last sacrifices are prepared and he sacrifices and with beguiling words and with threats of terror stirs up his own men to sacrifice. All were sacrificing victims; the whole city reeked with the smell of the dreadful ceremonies. When the seven champions of Christ saw this, with tears they prostrated themselves in prayer and, sprinkling dust on their heads, urgently called upon the compassion of the Lord, that looking down from his holy heaven he should not allow the people for long to be destroyed in this frowardness.

2. When this was discovered, persecutors of the Christian name came to

the prince saying: "The orders of your realm, O king, traverse the ends of the whole earth, and none dares go against your command, and all taste the daily sacrifices to the immortal gods save seven men whom you foster and cherish with singular affection." To them the emperor said: "And who are these?" They replied: "Maximianus, son of the prefect, with his accomplices." And immediately, while the emperor raged, they were led into his presence loaded with fetters, having their faces suffused with tears and dust on their heads just as they had been while praying in the sight of the Master. Looking at them, the emperor said: "Does such great treachery of an evil mind possess you that you dare infringe upon our dignity and refuse due burnt offerings to the immortal gods? For I say to you on my honor that you will undergo divers kinds of torture for your contempt of our gods." The men replied, saying: "Our God is the one, true God, the Creator of heaven and earth and sea, to whom we offer the due sacrifice of daily praise, for whose honor we are prepared to die. We know that those names which you urge us to worship, under the name of gods, are absolutely nothing, because they are able to make no use of life, since they are fashioned with limbs by the art of artisans. And so those who worship them are by the sanction of the prophets condemned to become like them – both those who made them and those who worship them."

3. Then the emperor raged and, when all men had been removed, said: "Depart, gallows birds, from our presence, until, practising penitence for the crime of this obstinacy, you shall be received in our palace and reconciled by the mercy of the gods. Until then you shall enjoy the flower of youth because it is not fitting that such physical charm and beauty be subjected to torture." And when the iron had been stricken from their necks, he ordered them to go free until he should return to Ephesus. When the seven men had received permission to go and the emperor had departed to another city, they went to their own homes. And when the treasures in their homes had been examined, they took their gold and silver and all their garments and furniture, and having distributed it to the poor, went to a cave in Mount Chilleus, carrying with them a little money for the purchase of the necessities of life. And they chose Malchus to go secretly to the city, buy food, and hear what the emperor was decreeing daily concerning the Christians.

4. Then when the saints freed from prison were enclosed under barriers, and were free for continual prayer, that most worthless emperor returned to Ephesus, and when according to his wont Christians were sought out, he asked about Maximianus and his comrades. Their parents, however, said they were hidden in a certain cave in Mount Chilleus from which they could easily be routed out if a regal order of the emperor should go forth. When the men, at Malchus's announcement, learned this, extremely terrified they pros-

trated themselves on the ground and with tears prayed that the Master, guarding them under his protection, should free them from the sight of that most unjust emperor. While they were praying, God in his providence, because they were needed for the future, heard their prayer and caught up their souls. And they lay on the ground as though sleeping in sweet sleep.

5. Then the emperor, troubled, said to his men: "Go, therefore, and stop up the mouth of the cavern lest those rebels against the gods have a way to go forth." While those men were going who were to stop up the mouth of the cave, two men went ahead of them, Theodorus and Ruben, Christians, who because of the emperor's threats were praying to Christ only in secret. They wrote on lead tablets the whole history of the saints and placed these inside in the entrance to the cavern, without the knowledge of any, saying: "Whenever God wishes to reveal the blessed limbs of his champions to the peoples, let these tablets teach what they have endured in his name." And when those came who had been sent, they rolled up great stones, closed the entrance of the cave, then went away saying: "Let them grow weak with hunger and devour themselves with their own jaws, who considered it of little worth to offer due libations to our gods."

6. After this when Decius was dead, in the following times the height of power came to Theodosius, son of Arcadius. In his time that unclean sect of the Sadducees arose, wishing to destroy the hope of resurrection, saying that the dead do not rise. The fountainheads of this heresy were the bishops Theodorus and Gaius, who wished to join the soul of the emperor himself to this unbelief. Whence it happened that the emperor, much afflicted for this reason and prostrate on the ground, prayed to the Lord that he should make known to him what he should fitly believe. There was at that time in Ephesus a certain Dalius, extremely rich in flocks, who, going around Mount Chilleus, ordered his servants, saying: "Prepare enclosures here for our sheep, because this place is suitable for feeding the flocks." For he did not know what had occurred in the cave. However, while the servants were working and rolling out huge rocks, they came to the mouth of the cave and found great stones. Rolling these away, they constructed a wall. Nevertheless they did not enter the cave.

7. Then the Lord ordered the breath of life to return to the bodies of the saints, and they arose and greeted each other after their custom and, thinking they had slept only one night, they sat down strong and vigorous. For not only were their bodies comely and very beautiful, but even their garments were untouched and unharmed, just as they had been put on by them a great many years before. And turning to Malchus they said: "Tell us, brother, we ask, what the emperor has said this night, or if we have been sought out, that

we might know." To them he said: "You have been sought out that you might sacrifice to the gods." To him Maximianus said: "All of us are prepared to die for Christ. But now take pieces of silver and go to purchase food and listen carefully and report to us what you have heard." And so he took the money and left. For these were silver pieces stamped with the name of Decius. However, approaching the gate of the city he saw the sign of the cross above the gate and thunderstruck he marveled, saying to himself: "Was the heart of Decius changed yesterday after the setting of the sun when I left the city so that he should protect those entering through the gate with the sign of the cross?" And he entered the city and heard men swear by the name of Christ and saw a church and a priest who was hastening to and fro through the city, and he examined new walls, and marveling even more he said to himself, "Think you that you have entered another city?" And approaching the market he brought forth his pieces of silver, asking that they give him food.

8. But they examined the stamp of his silver and said: "This man has found ancient treasures, for, behold, he offers silver from the time of Decius." Malchus, in truth, hearing these things, was turning over his thoughts in his heart, saying: "What mean these things? Do I see a vision?" However the men took him and led him to the bishop Marinus and the prefect. To him the prefect said: "Whence are you and from what region have you come?" He said: "From Ephesus, if indeed this is the city of the Ephesians, which I remember seeing yesterday." The prefect said: "Whence have you these pieces of silver?" He replied: "I took them from the home of my father." The prefect said: "And where is your father?" And he named his parents, but nobody recognized them. The prefect said: "Tell us, whence have you these pieces of silver? For they are from the time of Decius, who has been dead for years. From this it is manifest that you have come to deceive the wise men of the Ephesians and for this reason ought to be subjected to torture until you disclose the truth." And Malchus, moved, said with astonishment and tears: "I would ask you one thing if you think it worthy. Where is the Emperor Decius who persecuted Christians in this city?" Marinus the bishop replied: "Dearly beloved son, there is not a man in this city who recalls the time of Decius; for he died many years ago."

9. Malchus hearing this turned and said to the bishop: "I thought that I with my brothers had slept only one night, but, as I learn, the course of many years has passed during our sleep. And now the Lord has aroused me with my brothers that every age might know that the resurrection of the dead will come to pass. Therefore follow me and I will show you my brothers who have arisen with me." Then the astonished bishop with the prefect and all the people followed Malchus and came to the cave. While Malchus was telling

his brothers what had happened to him in the city, the bishop entered and found a box sealed with two silver seals. He went outside and calling together the whole multitude of the city with the prefect he opened the seals and found the two lead tablets on which had been written the whole passion of these men, as I have related above. And they learned that those things were true which were said by Malchus.

10. Then having entered, they found the blessed martyrs sitting in a corner of the cave, and their countenances were flourishing like the rose and shining in virtue like the sun; for their garments and bodies had not been destroyed. Then Marinus the bishop with the prefect fell at their feet and worshipped them, and all the people glorified God who deemed it proper to show such a miracle to his servants. In truth the saints told the bishop and all the people what had happened to them in the time of Decius. Then the bishop with the prefect sent messengers to the emperor Theodosius, saying: "Hasten quickly if you wish to see a great miracle which is manifest in your times, by the gift of God. For if you come, you will find out that the hope of resurrection is verily so in accordance with the solemn promise of the evangelical covenant."

11. The emperor Theodosius hearing this arose from his couch of mourning and extending his hands to God, said: "I thank you, Lord Jesus Christ, the Sun of justice, who have deemed it proper to sprinkle the shadows of mortals with the light of your truth; I thank you who did not permit the lamp of my confession to be veiled by the vile fog of false advocacy." When he had said these things and his horsemen had mounted, he came with the greatest haste to Ephesus. Then the bishop with the prefect and the whole multitude of the city came out to meet the emperor. Then while they were ascending the mountain, the sainted martyrs came out to meet Augustus [Theodosius], and their faces gleamed with virtue like the sun. And Augustus fell to the earth and worshiped them, glorifying God. And rising he kissed them and wept on the neck of each one of them, saying: "I see your faces as if I saw my Lord Jesus Christ when he called Lazarus from the tomb, to whom I offer unlimited thanks because he has not withdrawn from me the hope of resurrection."

12. Then Maximianus replied: "Know, emperor, that the Lord ordered us to rise again to strengthen your faith. Therefore trusting always in him learn that the resurrection of the dead will come to pass, since today you see us after our resurrection speaking with you and telling the greatness of God." And they spoke many other things with him, and having stretched themselves on the ground again slept, handing over their souls to the immortal King, Almighty God. The emperor seeing these things fell upon their bodies and weeping kissed them, and taking off his own raiment placed it upon

them, ordering golden coffins to be made in which they might be buried. But on that night the saints appeared saying: "Do not do this, but leave us above the earth; whence a second time the Lord will arouse us on the great day of the resurrection of all flesh." Then the emperor built above them a great basilica and constructed there a place of refuge for the poor, ordering that they be fed at public expense. And when the bishops had been called together he celebrated a festival of the saints, and all glorified God in whose Trinity is perfect honor and glory for age upon age. Amen.

Here ends the passion of the seven sainted martyrs sleeping near Ephesus, translated into Latin by the bishop Gregory, with the interpretation of John the Syrian. The day of their passion is observed on the fourth of August.

CHAPTER TWO

THE DESERT FATHERS AND MOTHERS

With the conversion of the emperor Constantine in 312, the immediate threat of persecution was removed. One effect was that martyrdom was no longer a simple way of recognizing and acknowledging saints, and other, less palpable standards had to be relied upon. The extremes of self-deprivation, heroic resistance to temptation, and extraordinary virtue manifested especially in miracles became the new signs of sanctity. Even before the end of the persecutions, however, numbers of Christians had begun to escape from the towns and cities into the deserts of Egypt and Syria. Several reasons have been suggested for this movement, including the pressures of economic hardship, social problems connected with the decline of the late Roman empire, and spiritual tensions within the Church itself. Whatever the reasons, many Christians no longer found it possible to live the life exemplified by Christ and the apostles within their communities, and so fled to the desert to confront privation and temptation as Christ had done before them. Some lived in cells or caves, alone or with one or two companions, meeting in larger groups only to hear Mass. Others joined cenobitical communities like that of Tabennisi, founded by Pachomius in about 315. Whether solitary or communal, the basis of their life was manual labor, prayer, and penance.

[Fig. 4] Two representations of St. Antony: an early stone statue (Lacroix, *Military and Religious Life in the Middle Ages,* p. 301) and a sixteenth-century statue by Caroto (Jameson, *Sacred and Legendary Art,* 2, 749). Both show him in a monk's robe, carrying a Bible (he is said to have learned the scriptures by hearing them read), holding a bell and accompanied by a pig. The bell and pig first appear to have been associated with Antony because of his epic battle with demons. Consecrated bells were thought to drive away the fiend, represented by an unclean animal (the earlier statue shows a pig enveloped in flames). In c.1100, the Order of the Hospitalers of St. Antony was founded at La Motte, which became a center of pilgrimage for sufferers of ergotism, known as St. Antony's Fire. The Hospitalers rang small bells to beg for alms, and were allowed to let their pigs roam freely; the smallest church bell and the smallest pig in a litter both carried the name 'tantony' in popular English speech.

8. CHRISTIANITY IN THE DESERT: ST. ANTONY THE GREAT

The most famous of the desert fathers was Antony (c.250-356), whose 'life' was written in Greek by Athanasius, bishop of Alexandria, shortly after Antony's death. Translated into Latin by Evagrius, it was widely read in both the East and the West, and remained enormously influential: Augustine tells us that his own conversion was initiated by hearing about Antony's life and his influence on others ('Confessions,' 8, 6-12). A short prologue included in Evagrius's version suggests that the 'life' may have been written at the request of western monks who wished to emulate desert asceticism, and it was instrumental in introducing monasticism to the West. More than any other single work, 'The Life of St. Antony' also influenced the form and the content of later hagiographies. Originally an adaptation of classical biography to Christian purposes, it became the primary model for later writers of saints' 'lives,' and Antony the outstanding example for those seeking perfection in the monastic life.

Source: trans. from Migne, *Patrologia Graeca*, 26 (1887), pp. 835-976, by Dom J. B. McLaughlin, *St. Antony the Hermit, by St. Athanasius* (London: Burns Oates and Washbourne, 1924), pp. 1-122, abridged; repr. with permission.

Book 1

Antony's conversion to the ascetic life, his early temptations, and his solitary withdrawal into the desert.

1. Antony was of Egyptian race, his parents of good birth and good means; Christians too, so that he also was brought up [as a Christian]. As a child he lived with his parents, knowing nothing but them and his home; and when he grew to be a boy and was advancing in age, he refused to learn letters, desiring to be away from the company of children; all his wish was, as is written of Jacob, to dwell unspoiled at home.

With his parents he frequented the church, not with a child's inattention, nor with the contempt [of a youth], but obeying his parents, and listening to the lessons that were read, and carefully keeping the fruits of them in his own life. Nor again, though he found himself in a fairly rich home, did he worry his parents for rich and varied food, nor care for the enjoyment of it; he was satisfied with what was there, and asked no more.

After his parents' death he was left alone with one very young sister. He was eighteen or twenty years old, and had charge of the home and of his sister. Less than six months after the death of his parents he was going out to church as usual, and collecting his thoughts he pondered as he went how the apostles, leaving all things, followed the Savior; and the people in the [Book of] Acts who sold their possessions and brought the price and laid it at the feet of the apostles for distribution among the needy – what good and great hope was laid up in heaven for these. With these thoughts in his mind he entered the church; and it so fell that the Gospel was being read then, and he heard the Lord saying to the rich man: "If thou wilt be perfect, go sell all that thou hast and give to the poor, and come follow me and thou shalt have treasure in heaven." Then, as though it was from God that his thoughts of the saints had come, and this reading had been for his sake, as soon as he went out of the church he gave to the villagers the property he had from his parents (it was 300 acres of land, fertile and very beautiful) [so] that they might not interfere with him and his sister. And all else that they had, in personal property, he sold, and raised a fair sum of money, which he gave to the poor, keeping a little because of his sister.

But when, again entering the church, he heard the Lord saying in the Gospel, "Be not solicitous for the morrow," he could not bear to wait longer, but went out and distributed this also to the poor. His sister he commended to known and trusty virgins, and put her with a sisterhood to be brought up; and then he gave himself for the future to the religious life, minding himself and living a life of hardship, in front of his own house. For as yet monasteries were not so universal in Egypt, and no monk yet knew the great desert; but each who wished to attend to his soul exercised himself alone not far from his own village. Now there was at the time in the neighboring village an old man who had practised the solitary life from youth. Antony, seeing him, was eager to imitate him, so he too at first began to stay in the places near the village. From there, if he heard anywhere of an earnest soul, he went forth like a wise bee and sought him out; nor would he return to his own place till he had seen him and got from him what would help him on his way to virtue; then he went back. There, then, he made his first steps, steadying his mind not to turn back to his inheritance nor to think of his kindred, but to give all its desire and all its energy to keeping up the religious life. He worked with his hands, having heard "He that will not work neither let him eat," spending the money partly on bread, partly on the poor. He prayed constantly, having learned that in private we must pray without ceasing. For he so listened to the reading that nothing of what is written escaped him, but he retained everything, and for the future his memory served him instead of books.

Living this manner of life, Antony was beloved by all. He made himself really subject to the devout men whom he visited, and learned for himself the special religious virtues of each of them: the graciousness of one, the continual prayer of another; he observed the meekness of one, the charity of another; studied one in his long watchings, another in his love of reading; admired one for his steadfastness, another for his fasting and sleeping on the ground; watched one's mildness, another's patience; while in all alike he remarked the same reverence for Christ and the same love for each other. Having thus gathered his fill, he returned to his own place of discipline, and thereafter pondered with himself what he had learned from each, and strove to show in himself the virtues of all. He had no contentions with those of his own age, save only that he would not be found second to them in the better things; and this he did in such manner that none was grieved, but they too were glad on his account. Seeing him such, then, all the village people and the devout with whom he had intercourse called him a man of God, and loved him as a son or as a brother.

2. But the devil, the hater and envier of good, could not bear to see such resolution in a young man, but attempted to use against him the means in which he is skilled. First he tried to draw him back from the religious life by reminding him of his property, of the care of his sister, his intimacy with his kindred, the love of money, the love of fame, the many pleasures of the table, and the other relaxations of life; and lastly the hardness of virtue, and how great is the labor of it: suggesting that the body is weak, and time is long. So he raised in his mind a great dust-cloud of arguments, to drive him aside from his straight purpose. But when the enemy saw himself powerless in face of Antony's resolution, and that rather he [the devil] was himself overthrown by his firmness and routed by his great faith and beaten by Antony's constant prayer, then, placing his trust in "the weapons that hang at his waist" and glorying in these (for these are his first snare against the young), he advances against the young man, disturbing him by night, and so besetting him by day that even onlookers could see the struggle that was going on between the two. He suggested evil thoughts; and the other turned them away by his prayers. He roused feelings; and Antony, ashamed, defended himself by faith and prayers and fastings. The wretched fiend even stooped to masquerade as a woman by night, simply to deceive Antony; and he quenched the fire of that temptation by thinking of Christ and of the nobility we have through him, and of the dignity of the soul. Again the enemy suggested the delight of pleasure; but he, angered and grieved, thought over the threat of the fire and the torment of the worm: these he opposed to his temptations, and so came through them unhurt. So all these things turned to the confusion of the adversary; for he who thought to be like to God was now mocked by a youth; and he who gloried over flesh and blood was now defeated by a man clad in the flesh. For with him wrought the Lord who for us took flesh and gave to the body the victory over the devil; so that those who truly strive can each say, "Not I, but the grace of God with me."

As the serpent could not conquer Antony by this means either, but saw himself thrust out of his heart, at length, gnashing his teeth, as it is written, like one in a frenzy, he showed himself in appearance as he is in mind, coming to Antony in the shape of a black boy, and as it were flattering him. He no longer assailed him with thoughts, for the deceiver had been cast out, but now using a human voice he said, "Many have I deceived, and very many have I overthrown; yet now, when I attacked you and your works as I have attacked others, I was not strong enough." Antony asked, "Who are you that say such things to me?" Then at once he answered in piteous tones, "I am the lover of uncleanness, I take charge of the ensnaring and the tempting of the young; and I am called the spirit of fornication. How many have I deceived who meant to be careful! How many that were chaste have I drawn away with temptations! I am he through whom the prophet reproaches the fallen, saying, 'You were deceived by a spirit of fornication'; for it was through me that they were tripped up. I am he that so often beset you and as often was defeated by you." Then Antony thanked God, and taking courage against him said to him, "Then you are much to be despised; for your mind is black, and your strength as a child's. I have not one anxiety left on your account, 'the Lord is my helper, and I will despise my enemies.'" Hearing this the black spirit instantly fled, cowering at his words and fearing even to approach the man.

This was Antony's first victory over the devil; or rather, this was the triumph in Antony of the Savior, "who condemned sin in the flesh that the justice of the law may be fulfilled in us who walk not according to the flesh but according to the spirit."

But thereafter Antony did not grow careless and neglect himself as though the devil were beaten; neither did the enemy cease his wiles, as having failed. For he wandered round again like a lion seeking some chance against him. And Antony, having learned from the scriptures that the craftiness of the enemy are many, gave himself earnestly to the religious life, deeming that though the foe had not been able to beguile his heart with bodily pleasures he would surely try to ensnare him by other means; for the devil is a lover of sin. More and more, therefore, did he repress the body and bring it into subjection, lest after winning at one point he should be dragged down at another. He decided, therefore, to accustom himself to harder ways. And many wondered, but he easily bore the hardship; for the eagerness of the spirit, long abiding with him, [created] in him a good habit, so that a small occasion given by others led him to a great exercise of zeal. For such was his watching that often he passed the whole night unsleeping; and this not once, but it was seen with wonder that he did it most frequently. He ate once in the day, after sunset; and at times he broke his fast only after two days, and often even after four days. His food was bread and salt, his drink only water.

Of meat and wine it is needless to speak, for nothing of this sort was to be found among the other monks either. For sleep a rush mat sufficed him; as a rule he simply lay on the ground. The oiling of the skin he refused, saying that it would be better for young men to prefer exercise and not seek for things that make the body soft, [but] rather to accustom it to hardships, mindful of the apostle's word, "When I am weak then am I strong." For he said that when the enjoyments of the body are weak, then is the power of the soul strong.

He had also this strange-seeming principle: he held that not by length of time is the way of virtue measured, and our progress in it; but by desire, and by strong resolve. Accordingly he himself gave no thought to previous time; but each day, as though then beginning his religious life, he made greater effort to advance, constantly repeating to himself St. Paul's saying, "Forgetting the things that are behind, and reaching out to the things that are before," keeping in mind, too, the voice of Elijah the prophet saying, "The Lord liveth, before whose sight I stand this day." For he observed that, in saying "this day," he did not count the time gone by; but as though always making a beginning, he was earnest each day to present himself such as one ought to appear before God – clean of heart, and ready to obey his will and none other. And he used to say within himself that from the way of life of the great Elijah a religious man must always study his own way of life, as in a mirror.

3. Having thus mastered himself, Antony departed to the tombs that lay far from the village, having asked one of his acquaintances to bring him bread from time to time. He entered one of the tombs, his friend closed the door of it on him, and he remained alone within. This the enemy would not endure, for he feared lest by degrees Antony should fill the desert too with monks; and coming one night with a throng of demons, he so scourged him that he lay on the ground speechless from the pain. For, he declared, the pain was so severe that blows from men could not have caused such agony. By God's providence (for the Lord does not overlook those who hope in him) his friend came the next day bringing him bread, and when he opened the door and saw him lying on the ground, as [if] dead, he lifted him and took him to the village church and laid him on the ground. Many of his kin and the village people watched beside Antony as if he were dead. But towards midnight Antony came to himself and woke, and seeing all asleep and only his friend waking, he signed to him to come near, and asked him to lift him again and carry him back to the tombs without waking anyone. So he was carried back by the man, and the door was closed as before, and he was again alone within. He could not stand because of the blows, but he prayed lying

down. And after his prayer he shouted out, "Here am I, Antony; I do not run away from your blows. For though you should give me yet more, nothing shall separate me from the love of Christ." Then he sang the psalm: "If camps shall stand against me, my heart shall not fear."

The monk, then, thought and spoke in this way. But the enemy of all good, marveling that even after the blows he had courage to go back, called together his hounds [other demons] and burst out in fury, "Do you see that we have not stopped this man either by the spirit of fornication or by blows, but he challenges us; let us attack him another way." For plans of ill are easy to the devil.

Thereupon in the night they made such a crashing that it seemed the whole place was shaken by an earthquake; and, as if they had broken through the four walls of the building, the demons seemed to rush in through them in the guise of beasts and creeping things, and the place was at once filled with the forms of lions, bears, leopards, bulls, serpents, asps, scorpions, wolves. And each moved according to its own likeness. The lion roared, ready to spring, the bull seemed thrusting with its horns, the serpent crept yet reached him not, the wolf held itself in act to strike. And the noise of all the visions was terrible, and their fury cruel. Antony, beaten and goaded by them, felt keener bodily pain. Nevertheless he lay fearless and more alert in spirit. He groaned with the soreness of his body, but in mind he was cool, and said jokingly, "If you had any power in you, it would have been enough that just one of you should come; but the Lord has taken your strength away, and that is why you try to frighten me if possible by your numbers. It is a sign of your helplessness that you have taken the shapes of brutes." Again he said cheerily, "If you can, and if you have received power over me, do not wait, but lay on. But if you cannot, why are you [upsetting] yourselves for nothing? For our trust in the Lord is like a seal to us, and like a wall of safety."

So after making many attempts they gnashed their teeth at him because they were [making fools of] themselves and not of him.

And the Lord in this also forgot not Antony's wrestling, but came to his defence. For looking up he saw as it were the roof opening and a beam of light coming down to him. And the demons suddenly disappeared, and the soreness of his body ceased at once, and the building was again sound.

Antony, seeing that help had come, breathed more freely, being eased of his pains. And he asked the vision, "Where wert thou? Why didst thou not show thyself from the beginning, to end my suffering?" And a voice came to him: "I was here, Antony, but I waited to see thy resistance. Therefore since thou hast endured and not yielded, I will always be thy helper, and I will make thee renowned everywhere." Hearing this he arose and prayed, and he

[Fig. 5] St. Antony tortured by demons, copy of a fifteenth-century engraving by Martin Schongauer (from S. Baring-Gould, *Lives of the Saints* [London and New York, 1898], 1).

was so strengthened that he perceived that he had more power in his body than formerly. He was at this time about thirty-five years old.

4. The next day, going out with still greater zeal for the service of God, he met the old man before mentioned, and asked him to live in the desert with him. He refused, because of his age and because this was not as yet usual; but Antony at once set out for the mountain [at Pispir, east of the Nile, about 50 miles south of Memphis]. Yet once more the enemy, seeing his zeal and wish-

ing to check it, threw in his way the [illusory shape] of a large disc of silver. Antony, understanding the deceit of the evil one, stood and looked at the disc, and confuted the demon in it, saying, "Whence [comes] a disc in the desert? This is not a trodden road, and there is no track of any faring this way. And it could not have fallen unnoticed, being of huge size. And even if it had been lost, the loser would certainly have found it had he turned back to look, because the place is desert. This is a trick of the devil. You will not hinder my purpose by this, Satan; let this thing perish with thee." And as Antony said this, it disappeared like smoke before the face of the fire.

Now as he went on he again saw, not this time a phantom, but real gold lying in the way. Whether it was the enemy that pointed it out or whether it was a higher power training the disciple and proving to the devil that he cared nothing even for real riches, he himself did not say, and we do not know; only that it was gold that he saw. Antony marveled at the quantity, but avoided it like fire and passed on without looking back, running swiftly on till he lost sight of the place and knew not where it was.

So with firmer and firmer resolution he went to the mountain, and finding beyond the river a fort long deserted and now full of reptiles, he betook himself there and dwelt in it. The reptiles fled at once as though chased by someone; and he, closing up the entrance and laying in bread for six months (the Thebans do this, and often it keeps unspoiled for a whole year), and having water in the fort, went down into the inner rooms and lived there alone, not going out himself, and not seeing any who came to visit him. For a long time he continued this life of asceticism, only receiving his loaves twice in the year from the house above.

His acquaintance who came to see him often spent days and nights outside, since he would not let them enter. They seemed to hear a tumultuous crowd inside, making noises, uttering piteous cries, shrieking, "Stand off from our domain. What have you to do with the desert? You cannot stand against our contrivings." At first those outside thought there were men fighting with him who had got in to him by a ladder, but when they bent down through a hole and saw no one, then they thought it was demons, and feared for themselves and called to Antony. He listened to them, though he gave no thought to the demons, and going near to the door he urged the people to go home and fear not, saying that the demons made these displays against the timid. "Do you therefore sign yourselves and go away bravely, and leave them to make fools of themselves." So they went away, protecting themselves with the sign of the cross, and he remained and was [not at all] hurt by them. Nor did he weary of the struggle. For the aid of the visions that came to him from on high, and the weakness of his enemies, brought him much ease from his labors, and prepared him for greater earnestness. His friends used to come constantly, expecting to find him dead; but they heard him singing, "Let God arise and his enemies be scattered, and those who hate him flee from his face. As smoke fades away so may they fade away. As wax melts before the face of the fire so may sinners perish before the face of God." And again: "All the nations surrounded me, and by the name of the Lord I drove them off."

He spent nearly twenty years in this solitary religious life, neither going out, nor being seen regularly by any. After that, many longed and sought to copy his holy life, and some of his friends came and forcibly broke down the door and removed it; and Antony came forth as from a holy of holies, filled with heavenly secrets and possessed by the spirit of God. This was the first time he showed himself from the fort to those who came to him. When they saw him they marveled to see that his body kept its former state, being neither grown heavy for want of exercise, nor shrunken with fastings and strivings against demons. For he was such as they had known him before his retirement. The light of his soul, too, was absolutely pure. It was not shrunk with grieving nor dissipated by pleasure; it had no touch of levity nor of gloom. He was not bashful at seeing the crowd, nor elated at being welcomed by such numbers; but was unvaryingly tranquil, a man ruled by reason, whose whole character had grown firm-set in the way that nature had meant it to grow.

Through him the Lord healed many of those present who were suffering from bodily ills and freed others from evil spirits. And the Lord gave Antony grace in speech so that he comforted many in sorrow; others who were at strife he made friends; charging all not to prefer anything in the world to the love of Christ. And when he spoke and exhorted them to be mindful of the good things to come and of the love of God for us, who "spared not his own son but delivered him up for us all," he induced many to take up the solitary life. And so from that time there were monasteries in the mountains, and the desert was peopled with monks, who went forth from their own [people] and became citizens of the kingdom of heaven.

Book 2
Antony's teachings on the monk's vocation and the assaults of demons.

5. When he had to cross the canal of Arsenoe (the need was his visitation of the brethren), the canal was full of crocodiles. And simply praying, he entered it with all his companions; and they passed through unhurt.

He returned to the monastery and continued the same holy and generous labors. He preached constantly, increasing the zeal of those who were already monks, and stirring many others to the love of the religious life; and soon, as the word drew men, the number of monasteries became very great; and to all he was a guide and a father.

One day, when he had gone out and all the monks came to him asking to hear [a] discourse, he spoke to them as follows in the Egyptian tongue:

"The scriptures are enough for our instruction. Yet it is well that we should encourage each other in the faith, and stimulate each other with words. Do you, therefore, bring what you know and tell it like children to your father; while I, as your elder, share with you what I know and have experienced. First of all, let one same zeal be common to all, not to give up what we have begun, not to be faint-hearted in our labors, not to say we have lived long in this service, but rather as beginners to have greater zeal each day. For the whole life of a man is very short, measured beside the ages to come, so that all our time is nothing compared to eternal life. And in the world, every merchandise is sold at its worth, and men barter like value for like. But the promise of eternal life is bought for a trifle. For it is written, 'The days of our life have seventy years in them; and in the mighty they are eighty years and more, they are a labor and a burden.' If, then, we spend the whole eighty years in the religious life, or even a hundred, we shall not reign in heaven for the same space of a hundred years, but in return for the hundred we shall reign through ages of ages. And if our striving is on earth, our inheritance shall not be on earth; but in heaven is our promised reward. Our body, too, we give up corruptible; we receive it back incorruptible.

Therefore, children, let us not faint, nor weary, nor think we are doing much, 'For the sufferings of this present time are not worthy to be compared to the glory that shall be revealed to us.' Neither let us look back to the world thinking that we have renounced much. For the whole earth is but a narrow thing compared to all heaven. If, then, we were lords of the whole earth, and renounced the whole earth, that, too, would be worth nothing beside the kingdom of heaven. As though a man should make light of one bronze coin to gain a hundred pieces of gold; so he that owns all the earth and renounces it, gives up but little, and receives a hundredfold. If, then, the whole earth is no price for heaven, surely he who has given up a few acres must not boast nor grow careless; for what he forsakes is as nothing even if he leaves a home and much wealth.

There is another thing to consider: if we do not forsake these things for virtue's sake, still we leave them later on when we die; and often, as Ecclesiastes reminds us, to those whom we would not. Then why not leave them for virtue's sake, and to inherit a kingdom?

Therefore let none of us have even the wish to possess. For what profit is it to possess these things which yet we cannot take with us? Why not rather possess those things which we can take away with us – prudence, justice, temperance, fortitude, understanding, charity, love of the poor, gentleness, hospitality? For if we gain these possessions we shall find them going before-hand, to make a welcome for us there in the land of the meek.

With these thoughts let a man urge himself not to grow careless; especially if he considers that he is one of God's servants, and owes service to his master. Now as a servant would not dare to say, 'Today I do not work, because I worked yesterday,' nor would count up the time that is past and rest in the coming days; but each day, as is written in the Gospel, he shows the same willingness, in order to keep his Lord's favor and avoid danger; so let us too daily abide in our service, knowing that if we are slovenly for one day he will not pardon us for the sake of past times, but will be angry with us for slighting him. So have we heard in Ezechiel; so, too, Judas in one night destroyed all his past toil.

Therefore, children, let us hold fast to the religious life, and not grow careless. For in this we have the Lord working with us, as it is written, 'God co-operates unto good with everyone that chooseth the good.' And to prevent negligence, it is well for us to ponder on the apostle's saying, 'I die daily.' For if we also so live as dying daily, we shall not sin. What is meant is this: that when we wake each day, we should think we shall not live till evening; and again when we go to sleep we should think we shall not wake, for our life is of its nature uncertain, and is measured out to us daily by Providence. So thinking, and so living from day to day, we shall not sin, nor shall we have any longing for anything, nor cherish wrath against anyone, nor lay up treasure on the earth; but as men who each day expect to die, we shall be poor, we shall forgive everything to all men. The desire of women and of evil pleasure we shall not meet and master but we shall turn away from it as a fleeting thing, striving always and always looking to the day of judgment. For the greater fear and the danger of torment always breaks the delight of pleasure and steadies the wavering mind.

Having made a beginning, and set out on the way of virtue, let us stretch out yet more to reach the things that are before us. Let none turn back like Lot's wife, especially as the Lord has said, 'No man setting his hand to the plow and turning back is fit for the kingdom of heaven.' Turning back simply means changing one's mind and caring again for worldly things. And when you hear of virtue, do not fear nor feel the word strange; for it is not afar from us, not something that stands without; no, the thing is within us, and the doing is easy, if only we have the will. The Greeks go abroad and cross the sea to study letters; but we have no need to go abroad for the kingdom of heaven, nor to cross the sea after virtue. For the Lord has told us before-hand, 'The kingdom of heaven is within you.' Virtue, therefore, needs only our will, since it is within us, and grows from us. For virtue grows when the soul keeps the understanding according to nature. It is according to nature when it remains as it was made. Now it was made beautiful, and perfectly straight. For this reason Joshua, the son of Nun, commanded the people, 'Make straight your hearts to your ways.' For the straightness of the soul consists in the mind's being according to nature, as it was made; as, on the other hand, the soul is said to be evil when it bends and gets twisted away from what is according to nature. So the task is not difficult; if we remain as God made us, we are in virtue; if we give our minds to evil, we are accounted wicked. If, then, it were a thing that must be sought from without, the task would indeed be hard; but if it be within us, let us guard ourselves from evil thoughts and keep our soul for the Lord, as a trust we have received from him; that he may recognize his work, finding it as it was when he made it.

Let us fight also not to be mastered by anger, nor enslaved by concupiscence. For it is written that 'the anger of man worketh not the justice of God.' And 'concupiscence having conceived bringeth forth sin, and sin when it is completed bringeth forth death.'

6. Living this life, let us watch ceaselessly, and, as it is written, guard our heart with all watchfulness. For we have enemies, terrible and unscrupulous, the wicked demons; and against them is our warfare, as the apostle said, 'not against flesh and blood, but against principalities and powers, against the rulers of the world of this darkness, against the spirits of wickedness dwelling in the high places.' Great is the number of them in the air around us, and they are not far from us. But there is much difference in them. It would be long to speak of their nature and differences, and such a discourse is for others greater than us. The only pressing and necessary thing now is to know their treacheries against us. Let us first understand this, that the demons were not made as demons; for God made nothing bad. But they also were created beautiful, but fell from heavenly wisdom and thenceforward, wandering about the earth, they have deceived the Greeks with their apparitions. They envy us Christians and move everything to hinder us from the way to heaven, lest we mount to where they fell from. Therefore there needs much prayer and self-discipline so that a man may receive from the Holy Ghost the gift of discerning spirits, and may be able to know which of them are less wicked, and which more; and in what kind of thing each of them is interested; and how each is defeated and cast out. For they have many treacheries, and many moves in their plotting. The blessed apostle and his followers knew this, saying, 'we are not ignorant of his contrivings.' And we, from being tempted by them, must guide one another. Therefore, as having in part experience of them, I speak to you as my children.

If, then, they see any Christians, but especially monks, laboring gladly and making progress, they first attack them and tempt them by putting continual stumbling-blocks in their way. These stumbling-blocks are bad thoughts. We must not fear their suggestions for by prayers and fastings and trust in the Lord they are defeated at once. Yet when defeated they do not cease, but come back again wickedly and deceitfully. For when they cannot mislead the heart with plainly unclean delights they attack again in another way and try to frighten it by weaving phantoms, taking the forms of women, of beasts and reptiles, and gigantic bodies, and armies of soldiers. But even so we must not fear their phantoms; for they are nothing, and quickly disappear, especially if one fortifies oneself with faith and the sign of the cross. But they are daring and utterly shameless. For if here too they are beaten, they come on again in another way. They pretend to prophesy, and to foretell things to come; and to show themselves taller than the roof, and of vast width, in order, if possible, to catch by such phantoms those whom they could not beguile with thoughts. And if even so they find the soul firm in faith, and in the hope of its purpose, then they bring in their leader."

"Often," he said, "they appear in shape such as the Lord revealed the devil to Job, saying, 'His eyes are like the look of the dawn. From his mouth come forth burning lamps, and fires are shot forth. From his nostrils comes the smoke of a furnace burning with a fire of coals. His breath is coals, and flame proceeds from his mouth.' When the leader of the devils appears in this way, the wretch causes terror as I said, boasting as the Lord described, saying to Job, 'He esteemed iron as chaff, and bronze as rotten wood; he thought the sea a vessel for ointments, the deeps of hell a captive; he judged the deeps to be a place for walking,' and by the mouth of the prophet, 'The enemy said, I will pursue and will capture'; and by another, 'I will grasp the whole world in my hand like a nest, and as deserted eggs will I seize it.' And all such boastings and threatenings they make, seeking to deceive the devout. Here, again, we faithful must not fear his appearances nor heed his words. For he lies; and there is no truth at all in his speech. For he talks thus and makes so bold, ignoring how he was dragged away with a hook like a serpent by the Savior, was haltered like a beast of burden, was ringed through the nostrils like a runaway, and his lips pierced with an armlet. The Lord has tethered him as a sparrow, to be mocked at by us. He and his demons are put like scorpions and snakes to be trodden under foot by us Christians. A proof of this is our now living this life in spite of him. For he that threatened to wipe up the sea, and to grasp the world, now, behold, cannot hinder our devotion, cannot even stop me speaking against him. Therefore let us not heed whatever he may say, for he lies, nor fear his lying visions. For it is no true light that is seen in them; rather they bring a foretaste and likeness of the fire that was prepared for them. They seek to frighten men with that in which they themselves shall burn. They appear, but at once they disappear again, having hurt no one, and taking with them the likeness of the fire that is to receive them. So we need not fear them on this account either; for by the grace of Christ all their practisings are to no purpose. They are treacherous, and ready to take on them any part and any shape. Often, without appearing, they pretend to sing psalms, and repeat sayings from the scripture. Sometimes when we are reading they will repeat at once like an echo the very words we have read. When we are asleep they wake us to prayers, and this persistently, scarcely letting us get to sleep. At times, too, they take the shape of monks and pretend to talk piously, in order to deceive by the likeness of form, and then lead whither they will those whom they have beguiled. But we must not heed them, though they wake us to pray, though they advise us to fast altogether, though they pretend to accuse and reproach us for things wherein once they were our accomplices. Not for piety nor for truth's sake do they do this, but in order to bring the simple into despair; and to say that asceticism avails not, and to make men disgusted with the monastic life as burdensome and most grievous; and to entangle those whose life is contrary to them.

Against such as these the prophet sent by God pronounces woe, saying, 'Woe to him that giveth his neighbor a troubled drink to turn him back.' For such devices and thoughts turn men back in the way that leads to virtue. And our Lord himself, even when the demons spoke the truth (for they truly said, 'Thou art the Son of God'), yet silenced them and forbade them to speak, lest after saying the truth they should oversow their own wickedness; and also to teach us never to heed them even though they seem to speak truth; for it is unseemly that we who have the holy scriptures, and the freedom of Christ, should be taught by the devil, who kept not his own rank, but is minded now one way, now another. Therefore he forbids him to speak, even to quote the words of scripture: 'To the sinful one God said, "Why do you relate my judgments and take my testament into your mouth?"' For they do everything; they talk, they make an uproar, they pretend, they unsettle the mind, all to deceive the simple; making a din, laughing senselessly, hissing. And if one heeds them not, they weep and wail as defeated.

The Lord, then, silenced the demons, being God. But we, learning from saints, must do as they did and imitate their courage. For they, when they saw these things, said, 'When the sinner stood against me I was dumb, and was humbled, and kept silence from good things.' And again, 'But I, as a deaf man, heard not: and as a dumb man not opening his mouth: and I became as a man that heareth not.' Wherefore let us not listen to them; they are none of ours. Nor let us harken, though they call us to prayer or speak of fastings. But rather let us attend to our own purpose of holy living, and not be cheated by them who do all deceitfully. We must not fear them, though they seem to assault us, or threaten death; for they are powerless, and can do nothing but threaten.

This much I have said of them in passing. But now we must not shrink from a fuller discourse about them; it will be safer for you to be warned."

The chapters of Book 2 omitted here record Antony's continuing discourse on the nature of demons, the problem of distinguishing good visions from bad ones, and the ultimate powerlessness of Satan.

Book 3
The persecution under Maximinus (c.305–311) and Antony's life in the inner mountain, between the Nile and the Red Sea.

11. As Antony made this discourse, all rejoiced. It increased the love of virtue in some, in some it cast out carelessness, and in others it ended self-conceit. All were persuaded to despise the plottings of the devil, admiring the grace which God had given to Antony for the discerning of spirits.

The monasteries in the hills were like tents filled with heavenly choirs, singing, studying, fasting, praying, rejoicing for the hope of the life to come, laboring in order to give alms, having love and harmony among themselves. And in truth it was like a land of religion and justice to see, a land apart. For neither wronger nor wronged was there, nor complaint of tax-gathering; but a multitude of ascetics, all with one aim of virtue; so that, looking back on the monasteries and on so fair an array of monks, one cried aloud saying, "How lovely are thy dwellings, O Jacob, thy tents, O Israel; like shady groves, and like a garden by a river, and like tents that the Lord hath pitched, and like cedars beside the waters."

Antony himself retired as usual to his own monastery by himself, and went on with his holy life, groaning daily at the thought of the mansions of heaven, longing for them, and seeing the shortness of man's life. For when going to food, and sleep, and the other needs of the body, shame came on him thinking of the spirituality of the soul. Often when he was to eat with many other monks the thought of the spirit's food came back on him, and he excused himself and went a long way from them, thinking it shame that he should be seen eating by others. Yet he ate alone, for the needs of the body; and often too with the brethren, ashamed on their account, but emboldened by the words of help he gave them. He used to say that we should give all our time to the soul rather than to the body. A little time indeed we must of necessity allow to the body; but in the main we must devote ourselves to the soul and seek its profit, that it may not be dragged down by the pleasures of the body, but rather that the body be made subject to the soul, this being what the Savior spoke of: "Be not solicitous for your life what you shall eat, nor for your body what you shall put on. And seek not what you may eat or what you may drink, and be not lifted up; for all these things do the nations of the world seek. But your Father knoweth that you have need of all these things. But seek ye first his kingdom, and all these things shall be added to you."

After this, the persecution which then befell under Maximinus overtook the Church. When the holy martyrs were taken to Alexandria, Antony also quitted his monastery and followed, saying, "Let us too go that we may suffer if we are called, or else may look on the sufferers." He had a longing to be martyred; but not wishing to give himself up, he ministered to the confessors in the mines and in the prisons. In the hall of judgment he was full of zeal for those who were called, stirring them to generosity in their struggles, and in their martyrdom receiving them and escorting them to the end. Then the judge, seeing the fearlessness of Antony and his companions, and their zeal in this work, gave orders that none of the monks should appear in the judgment hall, nor stay in the city at all. All the others thought best to be hidden that day, but Antony cared so much for it that he washed his tunic all the more, and on the next day stood on a high place in front and showed himself plainly to the prefect. While all wondered at this, and the prefect saw as he went through with his escort, Antony himself stood fearless, showing the eagerness that belongs to us Christians; for he was praying that he too might be martyred, as I have said. He himself mourned because he was not martyred; but God was keeping him to help us and others, that to many he might be a teacher of the strict life that he had himself learned from the scriptures. For simply at seeing his behavior many were eager to become followers of his way of life. Again, therefore, he ministered as before to the confessors; and as though sharing their bonds, he wearied himself in serving them. When later the persecution ceased, and the bishop Peter of blessed memory had died a martyr [Peter, bishop of Alexandria, executed in 311], Antony departed and went back to his monastery and abode there, a daily martyr to conscience, fighting the fights of the faith. He practised a high and more intense asceticism; he fasted constantly; his clothing was hair within and skin without, and this he kept till his death. He never bathed his body in water for cleanliness, nor even washed his feet; nor would he consent to put them in water at all without necessity. Neither was he ever seen undressed; nor till he died and was buried did any ever see the body of Antony uncovered.

12. When he retired and purposed to pass a season neither going forth himself nor admitting any, a certain captain of soldiers, Martinianus, came and

disturbed him, for he had a daughter beset by a demon. As he stayed long, beating the door and asking him to come and pray to God for the child, Antony would not open, but leaned down from above and said, "Man, why do you cry to me? I am a man like yourself. But if you trust in Christ whom I serve, go, and as you trust so pray to God, and it shall be done." And he at once believing and calling on Christ, went away with his daughter made clean from the demon. Many other things did the Lord through Antony for he says, "Ask and it shall be given to you." For though he opened not the door very many sufferers simply slept outside the monastery, and trusted and prayed sincerely, and were cleansed.

As he saw that many thronged to him, and that he was not suffered to retire in his own way as he wished, and being anxious lest from what the Lord did through him, either he himself should be lifted up, or another should think about him above the truth, he looked around him and set out to go to the upper Thebaid, where he was not known. He had got loaves from the brethren, and was sitting by the banks of the river watching if a boat should pass, that he might embark and go up with them. While he was thus minded, a voice came to him from above: "Antony, where are you going, and why?" He was not alarmed, being used to be often thus called, but listened and answered, "Since the crowds will not let me be alone, therefore I want to go to the upper Thebaid because of the many annoyances here, and especially because they ask me things beyond my power." And the voice said to him, "Though you should go up to the Thebaid, or, as you are considering, down to the pastures, you will have greater and twice as great a burden to bear. But if you wish to be really alone, go up now to the inner desert." Antony said, "And who will show me the way? For I know it not." And at once he was shown some Saracens [desert tribespeople] setting out that way. Advancing and drawing near, Antony asked to go with them into the desert, and they welcomed him as though by the command of Providence. He traveled with them three days and three nights and came to a very high hill. There was water under the hill, perfectly clear, sweet and very cold; beyond was flat land, and a few wild date palms.

Antony as though moved by God, fell in love with the place; for this was the place indicated by the voice that spoke to him at the river-bank. At the beginning he got bread from his fellow-travelers and abode alone on the hill, none other being with him; for he kept the place from then on as one who has found again his own home. The Saracens themselves, who had seen Antony's earnestness, used to travel by that way on purpose and were glad to bring him bread; he had besides a small and frugal refreshment from the date-palms. Afterwards, when the brethren learned the place, they were careful to send to him, as children mindful of their father. But Antony, seeing that by occasion of the bread some were footsore and endured fatigue, and wishing to spare the monks in this matter also, took counsel with himself, and asked some of those who visited him to bring him a pronged hoe, an axe, and some corn. When they were brought he went over the ground about the hill, and finding a very small patch that was suitable, he tilled it and sowed it, having water in abundance from the spring. This he did every year, and had bread from it; being glad that he should trouble no one on this account, but in all things kept himself from being a burden. But later, seeing that people were coming to him again, he grew a few vegetables also, that the visitor might have some little refreshment after the weariness of that hard road. At first the beasts in the desert used often to damage his crops and his garden when they came for water; but he catching one of the beasts said graciously to all, "Why do you harm me when I do not harm you? Begone, and in the name of the Lord do not come near these things again." And thereafter, as though fearing his command, they did not approach the place.

He then was alone in the inner hills, devoting himself to prayer and spiritual exercise. But the brethren who ministered to him asked that they might bring him each month olives and pulse and oil; for he was now an old man.

How many wrestlings he endured while he dwelt there we have learned from those who visited him, not against flesh and blood, as it is written, but against opposing demons. For there also they heard tumults and many voices and clashing as of weapons; and at night they saw the hill full of wild beasts; and they saw him fighting as with visible foes, and praying against them. He comforted his visitors; but he himself fought, bending his knees and entreating the Lord. And it was indeed a thing to admire, that being alone in such a wilderness, he was neither dismayed by the attacks of devils, nor with so many four-footed and creeping things there did he fear their savageness; but according to the scripture he trusted the Lord truly like Mount Zion, with a mind tranquil and untossed; so that rather the devils fled, and the wild beasts kept peace with him, as it is written.

Thus the devil watched Antony and gnashed his teeth against him, as David says in the psalm, while Antony had consolations from the Savior, and abode unharmed by his wickedness and his many arts. He [the devil] set wild beasts on him when watching at night. Almost all the hyaenas in that desert, coming out from their dens, surrounded him. He was in their midst, and each with open mouth threatened to bite him. But knowing the enemy's craft, he said to them all, "If you have received power over me I am ready to be eaten by you, but if you are sent by devils, delay not, but go; for I am Christ's servant." On this they fled, his words chasing them like a whip.

A few days after, while he was working (for he was careful to work), someone stood at the door and pulled the string of his work; for he was weaving baskets, which he gave to his visitors in exchange for what they brought. He rose and saw a beast, resembling a man as far as the thighs, but with legs and feet like a donkey. Antony simply crossed himself and said, "I am Christ's servant; if you are sent against me, here I am," and the monster with its demons fled so fast that for very speed it fell and died. And the death of the beast was the demons' fall; for they were hasting to do everything to drive him back from the desert, and they could not. . . .

14. This was his instruction to those who visited him. To sufferers he gave compassion, and prayed with them, and often the Lord heard him in many ways. He neither boasted when he was heard, nor murmured when not; but always gave thanks to God, and urged the sufferers to be patient and to know that healing belonged not to him nor to any man, but to God who acts when he will and to whom he will. The sufferers took the old man's words in place of healing, since they had learned to suffer with patience and not with shrinking; and the cured learned not to thank Antony, but God alone.

A man named Fronton from Palatium had a terrible disease; for he was biting his tongue, and his eyes were in danger. He came to the hill and begged Antony to pray for him. When he had prayed he said to Fronton, "Depart and you shall be healed." Fronton objected, and for days stayed in the house, while Antony continued saying, "You cannot be healed while you stay here. Go, and when you reach Egypt you shall see the sign that is wrought on you." The man believed and went; and as soon as he came in sight of Egypt he was freed from his sickness and made well, according to the word of Antony which he had learned from the Savior in prayer.

A girl from Busiris in Tripoli had a dreadful and distressing sickness, a discharge from eyes, nose and ears which turned to worms when it fell to the ground; and her body was paralyzed and her eyes unnatural. Her parents hearing of monks who were going to Antony, and having faith in the Lord who healed the woman troubled with an issue of blood, asked to accompany them with their daughter, and they consented. The parents and their child remained below the hill with Paphnutius, the confessor and monk. The others went up, but when they wished to tell about the girl, Antony interrupted them and described the child's sufferings and how they had traveled with them. On their asking that these also might come to him, he would not allow it, but said, "Go, and you will find her cured if she is not dead. For this is not my work, that she should come to a wretched man like me; but healing is the Savior's, who doeth his mercy in all places to them that call on him. To this child also the Lord hath granted her prayer, and his love has made known to me that he will heal her sickness while she is there." So the marvel came to pass; and going out they found the parents rejoicing and the girl in sound health.

Two of the brethren were traveling to him, when the water failed, and one died and the other was dying; he had no longer strength to go, and lay on the ground awaiting death. But Antony sitting on the hill called two monks who happened to be there, and urged them saying, "Take a jar of water and run down the road towards Egypt; for two were coming, and one has just died, and the other will if you do not hasten. This has just been shown me in prayer." The monks therefore went and found the one lying a corpse, and buried him; the other they revived with water, and brought him to the old man; for the distance was a day's journey. If anyone asks why he did not speak before the other died, he asks amiss in so speaking. For the sentence of death was not from Antony, but from God, who so decreed about the one and revealed concerning the other. In Antony this only is wonderful, that while he sat on the hill and watched in heart, the Lord revealed to him things far off.

For another time also, as he was sitting there and looking up, he saw in the air someone borne along, and great rejoicing in all that met him. Wondering at such a choir, and thinking of their blessedness, he prayed to learn what this might be. And at once a voice came to him that this was the soul of the monk Amun in Nitria [a famous monk, Amun had been a wealthy Alexandrian, who founded a series of monastic retreats in the desert of Nitria]. He had lived as an ascetic till old age. Now the distance from Nitria to the hill where Antony was is thirteen days' journey. Those who were with Antony, seeing the old man in admiration, asked to know, and heard from him that Amun had just died. He was well known, because he often visited there, and because through him also many miracles had come to pass, of which this is one. Once, when he had need to cross the river called the Lycus, the waters being in flood, he asked his companion Theodore to keep far from him that they might not see each other naked in swimming the river. Theodore went; but he was again ashamed to see himself naked. While, therefore, he was ashamed, and pondering, he was suddenly carried to the other side. Theodore, himself a devout man, came up; and seeing that Amun was first and unwetted by the water, asked to know how he had crossed. And seeing that he did not wish to speak, he seized his feet, declaring that he would not let him go till he had heard. Amun, seeing Theodore's obstinacy, especially from his speech, asked him in turn not to tell anyone till his death, and then told him that he had been carried across and set down on the other side; that he had not walked on the water, and that this was a thing not possible to men, but only to the Lord and those to whom he granted it, as he did to the great apostle Peter. And Theodore told this after Amun's death. Now the monks to whom Antony spoke of Amun's death noted the day; and when, thirty days later, the brethren came from Nitria they enquired and found that Amun had fallen asleep at the day and hour when the old man saw his soul carried up. And both these and the others were all amazed how pure was the soul of Antony, that he should learn at once what happened thirteen days away, and should see the soul in its flight.

Again, Archelaus the Count once met him in the outer hills and asked him only to pray for Polycratia, the renowned and Christ-like virgin of Laodicea; for she was suffering much in her stomach and side, through her great mortifications, and was weak throughout her body. Antony therefore prayed, and the Count made a note of the day when the prayer was made and departing to Laodicea he found the virgin well. Asking when and on what day she was freed from her sickness, he brought out the paper on which he had written the time of the prayer; and when he heard he immediately showed the writing on the paper, and all recognized with wonder that the Lord had freed her from her pains at the moment when Antony was praying and invoking the goodness of the Savior on her behalf.

Often he spoke days beforehand of those who were coming to him, and sometimes a month before; and of the cause for which they came. For some came simply to see him, some through sickness, some suffering from devils. And all thought the toil of the journey no trouble or loss; for each returned feeling helped. Antony, while he said and saw such things, begged that none should admire him in this regard, but rather should admire the Lord, who grants to us men to know him in our own measure. Another time when he had gone down to the outer monasteries and was asked to enter a ship and pray with the monks, he alone perceived a horrible, pungent smell. The crew said that there was fish and pickled meat in the boat, and that the smell was from them, but he said it was different; and even as he spoke came a sudden shriek from a young man having a devil, who had come on board earlier and was hiding in the vessel. Being charged in the name of our Lord Jesus Christ, the devil went out and the man was made whole and all knew that the foul smell was from the evil spirit.

Another came to him, one of the nobles, having a devil. This demon was so dreadful that the possessed man did not know he was going to Antony; also he used to eat the filth of his own body. Those who brought him begged Antony to pray for him; and Antony, pitying the youth, prayed and watched the whole night with him. Towards dawn the youth suddenly sprang on Antony, pushing him. His friends were indignant, but Antony said, "Do not be angry with the youth; it is not he, but the demon in him, for being rebuked and commanded to depart into waterless places, he became furious, and has done this. Therefore glorify God; for his attacking me in this way is a sign to you of the demon's going." And when Antony had said this the youth was at once made whole; and then, in his right mind, recognized where he was and embraced the old man, thanking God.

The omitted chapters of Book 3 record how Antony taught the monks and the visions he received from God.

Book 4
Antony as the champion of orthodoxy against heresies; his last years and death.

18. The renown of Antony reached even to kings. For on hearing of these things, Constantine Augustus and his sons, Constantius Augustus and Constans Augustus, wrote to him as to a father and begged to receive answers from him. He, however, did not value these writings nor rejoice over the letters, but was just what he had been before the kings wrote to him. When the letters were brought to him he called the monks and said, "Do not admire if a king writes to us, for he is a man; but admire rather that God has written the law for men, and has spoken to us by his own Son." He wished not to receive the letters, saying that he knew not what to answer to such. But being urged by the monks because the kings were Christians, and they might be scandalized as though he made them outcasts, he allowed them to be read. And he wrote back, welcoming them because they worshiped Christ; and advised them, for their salvation, not to think much of things present, but rather to remember the coming judgment; and to know that the only true and eternal king is Christ. He begged them also to be lovers of men, to care for justice, and to care for the poor. And they were glad to get his letter. So was he beloved by all, and so did all wish to hold him as a father.

With this character, and thus answering those who sought him, he returned again to the mount in the interior, and continued his usual life. Often when sitting or walking with visitors he would become dumb, as it is written in Daniel. After a time he would resume his former discourse with the brethren but they perceived that he was seeing some vision. For often in the mountain he saw things happening in Egypt, and described them to the bishop Serapion [bishop of Thmuis, in lower Egypt, a personal friend of Antony also involved in the Arian controversy], who was within and saw Antony occupied with the vision. Once as he sat working he became as in ecstasy, and in the vision he groaned constantly. Then after a time he turned to his companions groaning; and trembling he prayed, bending his knees and abiding a long time, and when he arose the old man was weeping. Then the others trembled and were much afraid and begged him to tell; and they urged him for a long time till he was compelled to speak. Then with a great groan he said, "Ah, my children, better is it to die than that there happen what I have seen in this vision." And when they asked again he said with tears, "Wrath shall overtake the Church, and she shall be delivered up to men who are like to senseless beasts. For I saw the table of the Lord, and around it mules standing on all sides in a ring and kicking what was within, as might be the kicking of beasts in a wild frolic. You heard surely," he said, "how I was groaning; for I heard a voice saying, 'My altar shall be made an abomination.'" So the old man said; and two years after [356, when the imperial government handed over the church buildings of Alexandria to the Arians] came this present onset of the Arians, and the plundering of the churches; wherein, seizing by force the vessels, they had them carried away by pagans; when, too, they forced the pagans from the workshops to their meetings, and in their presence did what they would on the sacred table. Then we all understood that the kicking of the mules had foreshown to Antony what the Arians are now doing, brutishly as beasts. When he saw this vision, he comforted his companions, saying, "Do not lose heart, children; for as the Lord has been angry, so later will he bring healing. And the Church shall quickly regain her own beauty, and shine as before. And you shall see the persecuted restored, and impiety retiring to its own hiding places, and the true faith in all places speaking openly with all freedom. Only, defile not yourselves with the Arians. For this teaching is not of the apostles, but of the demons and their father the devil; and indeed from no source, from no sense, from a mind not right it comes; like the senselessness of mules.". . .

20. The manner of the end of his life I ought also to tell, and you to hear eagerly; for this also is a pattern to imitate. He was visiting as usual the monks in the outer hills; and learning of his end from Providence, he spoke to the brethren saying, "This is the last visiting of you that I shall make; and I wonder if we shall see each other again in this life. It is time now for me to be dissolved; for I am near a hundred and five years." Hearing this they wept, clasping and embracing the old man. But he talked joyously, as one leaving a foreign town to go to his own; and bade them "not to fail in their labors nor lose heart in their strict life, but live as dying daily; and, as I have said before, to be earnest to guard the heart from unclean thoughts; to vie with the holy; not to go near the Meletian schismatics, for you know their wicked and profane heresy; nor to have any fellowship with the Arians, for the impiety of these is plain to all. Be not troubled if you see judges protecting them, for their triumph will end, it is mortal and short-lived. Therefore do ye keep yourselves clean from these, and guard the tradition of the Fathers, and above all the loving faith in our Lord Jesus Christ, which you have learned from the Scriptures and have often been put in mind of by me."

When the brethren pressed him to stay with them and die there, he would not for many reasons, as he implied without saying; but on this account chiefly. To the bodies of religious men, especially of the holy martyrs, the Egyptians like to give funeral honors and wrap them in fine linens, but not to bury them in the earth, but to place them on couches and keep them at home with them; thinking by this to honor the departed. Antony often asked the bishops to tell the people about this; and likewise shamed laymen and reproved women, saying it was not right nor even reverent; for that the bodies of the patriarchs and prophets are preserved even till now in tombs; and the very body of our Lord was put in a sepulcher, and a stone set against it hid it till he rose the third day. He said this to show that he does wrong who after death does not bury the bodies of the dead, holy though they be. For what is greater or holier than the Lord's body? Many therefore, hearing him, buried [the dead] thenceforward in the ground, and thanked God that they had the right teaching.

Now knowing this, and fearing lest they might so treat his body also, Antony hastened and took leave of the monks in the outer hills; and returning to the inner hills where he was used to dwell, he fell sick after a few months. He called those who were there (there were two who lived in the house, who had been fifteen years in the religious life, and ministered to him because of his great age) and said to them: "I am going the way of my fathers, as the Scripture says; for I see myself called by the Lord. Be you wary, and undo not your long service of God, but be earnest to keep your strong purpose as though you were but now beginning. You know the demons who plot against you, you know how savage they are, and how powerless; therefore fear them not. Let Christ be as the breath you breathe; in him put your trust. Live as dying daily, heeding yourselves and remembering the counsel you have heard from me. And let there be no communion between you and the schismatics, nor the heretical Arians. For you know how I also have avoided them for their false and anti-Christian heresy. So do you also be earnest always to be in union first with the Lord and then with the saints; that after death they also may receive you into everlasting tabernacles as known friends. Ponder these things, and mean them. And if you have any care for me, and remember me as your father, do not allow anyone to take my body to Egypt lest they should deposit it in houses; for that is the reason why I entered the mountains and came here. And you know how I have always reproached those who do this, and bade them stop the practice. Therefore care for my body yourselves, and bury it in the earth; and let my words be so observed by you, that no one shall know the place but yourselves only. For in the resurrection of the dead I shall receive it back from the Savior incorruptible. Distribute my garments; the one sheepskin give to

Athanasius the bishop, and the cloak I used to lie on, which he gave me new, but has worn out with me; and the other sheepskin give to Serapion the bishop; and do you have the hair-cloth garment. And now God save you, children; for Antony departs and is with you no more." Having said this and been embraced by them, he drew up his feet; then gazing as it seemed on friends who came for him, and filled by them with joy, for his countenance glowed as he lay, he died and was taken to his fathers. Then they, as he had given them orders, cared for his body and wrapped it up and buried it there in the earth; and no man yet knows where it is laid save only those two. And they who received the sheepskins of the blessed Antony and the cloak that he wore out, each guard them as some great treasure. For to look on them is like looking on Antony; and to wear them is like joyously taking on us his teachings.

This is the end of Antony's life in the body, as that was the beginning of his religious life. And if this is but little to tell of such virtue as his, yet from this little do you judge what manner of man was Antony the man of God, who from youth to such great age held unchanged his keen quest of a better life; who never for old age yielded to the desire of varied meats; nor for failing strength of body changed his form of dress nor even bathed his feet with water. And yet in all respects he was to the end untouched by decay. He saw well, his eyes being sound and undimmed; and of his teeth he had not lost one; only they were worn near the gums, through the old man's great age. In feet and hands, too, he was quite healthy; and altogether he seemed brighter and more active than all those who use rich diet and baths and many clothes.

That he was everywhere spoken of, and by all admired, and sought even by those who had not seen him – these things are proof of his virtue and of a soul dear to God. For Antony was known not for his writings, nor for worldly wisdom, nor for any art, but simply for his service of God. That this is God's gift none could deny. For how was he heard of even to Spain, and to Gaul, to Rome and to Africa, he sitting hidden in the hills, unless it were God who everywhere makes known his own people, who also had in the beginning announced this to Antony? For though they themselves act in secret, and wish to be unnoticed, yet the Lord shows them as lanterns to all; that even from this the hearers may know that the commandments are able to be fulfilled, and so may take courage on the path of virtue.

Now, therefore, read this to the other brethren that they may learn what should be the life of monks, and may believe that our Lord and Savior Jesus Christ glorifies them that glorify him, and not only brings to the kingdom of heaven those who serve him to the end, but even here (though they hide themselves and seek retirement) he makes them everywhere known and spoken of for their own goodness and for the helping of others. And if need arise, read it also to the pagans, that perhaps thus they may learn not only that our Lord Jesus Christ is God and the Son of God, but also that through him the Christians, who serve him sincerely and who piously trust in him, not only prove that the demons whom the Greeks think gods are no gods, but trample on them and drive them out as deceivers and corrupters of men, through Christ Jesus our Lord, to whom is glory for ages of ages. Amen.

Chapters omitted from Book 4 discuss Antony's devotion to the orthodox faith, his response to Greek (pagan) philosophers, and his influence on others.

9. ANTONY'S DISCIPLES: PAUL THE SIMPLE

Of the many stories told about the desert monks, the following narrative illustrates not only their traditional occupations and deprivations, but also, with some humor, the relationship between St. Antony and his often importunate disciples. It is taken from the 'Lausiac History' by Palladius (c.363-431), an Egyptian monk who wrote a Greek account of desert monasticism for Lausus, a chamberlain at the court of the eastern Roman emperor Theodosius II. Palladius's 'History' remains one of our chief sources of information about desert asceticism. His observations were made from his own experience, from the writings of others (he knew Athanasius's 'Life of St. Antony'), and from conversations with other monks. He describes about sixty ascetics, men and women, and his work was famous in both the East and the West for providing a first-hand description of a manner of living which gripped the imagination of Christians throughout the Middle Ages.

Source: trans. W. C. Lowther Clarke, *The Lausiac History of Palladius,* Society for Promoting Christian Knowledge, Series 1, Greek Texts (London and New York: Macmillan, 1918), pp. 96-101; repr. with permission.

1. . . . A certain Paul, a rustic peasant, exceedingly guileless and simple, was wedded to a most beautiful woman of depraved character, who for a very long while concealed her sins from him. However, Paul came in suddenly from work and found his wife and her lover behaving shamefully, Providence thus guiding Paul to what was best for himself. And laughing discreetly he called to them and said: "Good, good I don't mind, truly. By Jesus, I'll take her no longer. Go, you have her and her children, for I am going to become a monk."

2. And saying nothing to anyone he hastened along the eight stages and went to the blessed Antony and knocked at the door. He came out and asked him: "What do you want?" He said to him: "I want to become a monk." Antony answered and said to him: "You are an old man, sixty years old; you cannot become a monk here. But rather go back to your village and work and live an active life giving thanks to God, for you cannot endure the tribulations of the desert." The old man answered again and said: "Whatever you teach me, I will do it."

3. Antony said to him: "I have told you that you are an old man and cannot stand it. If you really want to become a monk, go to a cenobium [monastery] with a number of brethren, who can support your weakness. For I live here alone, eating after a five days' fast, and that without satisfying my hunger." With these and such-like words he tried to frighten Paul away and, since he could not endure him, Antony shut the door and did not go out for

[Fig. 6] The temptations and labors of the desert hermits, depicted in frescoes in the Campo Santo, Pisa (etching in Jameson, *Sacred and Legendary Art*, 2, 757). At the upper left, St. Antony buries St. Paul with the help of two lions; below (9) Mary of Egypt receives the sacrament from Zossima; at left centre (10) the devil in the form of a lady pilgrim tempts a monk (his claw foot is revealed beneath the robe); at right center (16) a desert father weaves a basket of leaves; at bottom left (17) St. Marina sits outside the monastery cradling her foster-child.

three days because of him, not even for necessary purposes. But Paul did not go away.

4. But on the fourth day, necessity compelling him, he opened the door and went out and said to him again: "Go away from here, old man. Why do you annoy me? You cannot stay here." Paul said to him: "It is impossible for me to die elsewhere than here." So Antony looked about and noticed that he had not with him any form of nourishment, neither bread nor water, and that he was now in the fourth day of his fast, and saying: "Lest perchance you die and stain my soul," he received him. And Antony adopted in those days a regime which he had never tried in his youth.

5. And having moistened some palm-leaves he said to him: "Take these, weave them into mats, as I do." The old man wove until the ninth hour, laboriously completing ninety feet. So Antony looked and was displeased and said to him: "You have woven badly, unpick them and weave them over again"- imposing this nauseous task upon him, though he was hungry and aged, in order that he might be disgusted and flee away from Antony. But he both unpicked and wove again the same leaves, though it was more difficult, because they were all shriveled up. And Antony, seeing that he neither murmured nor was discouraged nor angry, felt compunction.

6. And after sunset he said to him: "Would you like us to eat a piece of bread?" Paul said to him: "As you please, father." And this again moved Antony, that he did not rush eagerly at the mention of food, but had thrown the choice upon him. So he laid the table and brought in bread. And Antony, having put out the biscuits, weighing six ounces each, moistened one for himself – for they were dry – and three for Paul. And Antony struck up a Psalm which he knew, and after singing it twelve times he prayed twelve times, to test Paul.

7. But he eagerly joined in the prayer, for he would have preferred being eaten by scorpions, so I think, to living with an adulterous woman. But after the twelve prayers they sat down to eat late in the evening. Now Antony, having eaten the one biscuit, did not touch another. But the old man, eating more slowly, was still at his little biscuit. Antony was waiting for him to finish and says to him: "Eat, father, a second biscuit." Paul says to him: "If you will eat, I will too; if you do not eat, I will not." Antony says: "I have had enough, for I am a monk."

8. Paul says to him: "I too have had enough, for I too want to become a monk." He rises again and prays twelve prayers and chants twelve Psalms. Antony sleeps a little of his first sleep and then gets up to sing Psalms at midnight until day. So when he saw the old man eagerly following his mode of life he said to him: "If you can do thus every day, stay with me." Paul said to

him: "If there is anything more, I do not know [if I can do them]; but I can do easily these things which I have seen." Antony said to him the next day: "Behold, you have become a monk."

9. So Antony, convinced after the required number of months that Paul had a perfect soul, being very simple and grace co-operating with him, made him a cell, three or four miles away, and said to him: "Behold, you have become a monk; remain alone in order that you may be tried by demons." So Paul dwelt there one year and was counted worthy of grace over demons and diseases. Among other cases, a demoniac was once brought to Antony, exceedingly terrifying, possessed by a spirit of high rank, who cursed even heaven itself.

10. So Antony, having examined him, said to those who brought him: "This is not my work, for I have not yet been counted worthy of power over this order of high rank, but this is Paul's business." So Antony went off and led them to Paul, and said to him: "Father Paul, cast out this demon from the man that he may go away cured to his home." Said Paul to him: "What are you doing ?" Antony said to him: "I have no leisure, I have something else to do." And Antony left him and went again to his own cell.

11. So the old man got up, and having prayed an effective prayer, addressed the demoniac: "Father Antony has said, 'Go out from the man.'" But the demon cried out, saying with blasphemies: "I am not going out, bad old man." So Paul took his sheepskin coat and struck the man on the back with it saying: "Father Antony has said, 'Go out.'" Again the demon cursed with some violence both Antony and him. Finally he said to him: "You are going out; or else I'll go and tell Christ. By Jesus, if you don't go out I am going this very minute to tell Christ, and He will do you harm."

12. Again the demon cursed yet more, saying: "I am not going out." So Paul got angry with the demon and went outside his dwelling at high noon. But the heat of the Egyptians is akin to the furnace of Babylonia. And standing on a rock on the mountain he prayed and said: "O Jesus Christ, who wast crucified under Pontius Pilate, thou seest that I will not descend from the rock, I will not eat nor drink till I die, unless thou drive out the spirit from the man and free the man."

13. But before the words were out of his mouth the demon cried out, saying: "Oh violence! I am being driven away. The simplicity of Paul drives me away, and where am I to go?" And immediately the spirit went out and was turned into a great dragon seventy cubits long [a cubit is about 50 cm/20 inches long] and was swept away to the Red Sea, that the saying might be fulfilled: "The righteous will declare the faith that is shown." This is the marvelous tale of Paul who was surnamed Simple by all the brotherhood.

10. THE FIRST HERMIT: ST. PAUL OF THEBES

St. Jerome, author of the 'Life of St. Paul' (also known as Paul of Thebes), was born in north-eastern Italy c.345 but was strongly attracted to the life of the desert ascetics. When he was in his early forties he abandoned the world and went into the Syrian desert near Chalcis, where he spent two years in relative isolation living in a cell and trying to imitate the routine of manual labor, prayer, and contemplation of the desert monks. He found himself unsuited to the life, but remained its strong proponent, and some years later made another pilgrimage to the deserts of Egypt and Palestine before settling in a monastery at Bethlehem where he died c.419-20.

He wrote the 'Life of St. Paul' during or shortly after his period of isolation in the desert, and it provides the only information that we have about this saint. Jerome had already experienced a frightening dream in which he stood accused before God of being a Ciceronian, not a Christian, but the 'Life' is stylistically elegant and contains numerous classical echoes. Compared to the 'Life of St. Antony,' it is a highly roman- ticized view of desert asceticism replete with marvels and strange creatures, and to these features it undoubtedly owed its great popularity.

Source: trans. Marie Liguori Ewald, *Fathers of the Church: Early Christian Biographies,* ed. Roy J. Deferrari (repr. 1964; Washington, D.C.: The Catholic University of America Press, 1952), pp. 225-38; repr. with permission. BHL 6596.

1. Many have often questioned exactly who was the first monk to take up his abode in the desert. Some, indeed, searching quite deep, have gone back as far as blessed Elias [Elijah] and John to find the beginning of monastic life. Elias, however, seems to me to have been more than a monk, and John began to prophesy before he was born. Others, on the contrary, claim that Antony was the founder of this mode of life – an opinion in which the generality of mankind agrees. They are right in part; not so much that he holds prece- dence in time as that all others were inspired by him. In truth, Amathas and Macarius, disciples of Antony, the former of whom buried his master, affirm even to this day that a certain Paul of Thebes was the originator of the prac- tice – though not of the name – of solitary living. I, too, hold this opinion. Some, according to their whims, toss out one absurdity after the other: in an underground cave, for instance, there was a man with hair hanging down to his heels; and they go on to invent many incredible tales which it is useless to recount. Because theirs is an impudent lie, their opinion does not seem worth refuting. The story of Antony has been diligently handed down to posterity in both Greek and Latin. I have therefore determined to write a few words about the beginning of Paul's eremitical life and about his death, more because the account has never been written than because of any con-

[Fig. 7] St. Jerome doing penance in the desert (School of Andrea del Sarto, in the Louvre; copy in Lacroix, *Military and Religious Life in the Middle Ages,* p. 302). The presence of the lion records the popular story in which he rescued a lion by removing a thorn from its paw; the lion in gratitude remained to serve him.

fidence in my ability. As a matter of fact, no one has yet discovered how he lived during his middle life and what snares of Satan he endured.

2. Under the persecutors, Decius and Valerian, at the time when Cornelius at Rome and Cyprian at Carthage [6 above] suffered martyrdom with joyful hearts, a savage tempest ravaged many churches in Egypt and the [area of] Thebes. At that time, the Christians were vowed to fall by the sword in the name of Christ; but the wily enemy, eager to strangle souls, not bodies, sought out lingering tortures. Cyprian himself, who suffered at his hands, said those who wanted to die were not permitted to be killed. That his cruelty may be better known, I add two examples for remembrance's sake.

3. The persecutor commanded one martyr who had persevered in his faith, and had survived being roasted on hot metal plates, to be anointed with honey and prostrated under the burning sun with his hands bound behind his back, in the hope that the victor over the glowing gridiron would yield to the agony of the stings of insect hordes. Another youth, in the first bloom of manhood, was carried off into a most beautiful garden. There, among white lilies and red roses, with the soft murmuring waters of a winding stream nearby, and the wind gently rustling the leaves of the trees in lulled whispers, the persecutor bade him recline on a bed of down. To prevent his escape, an alluringly scented snare of garlands held him captive with entangling coils. When all others had withdrawn, a beautiful harlot came to him, entwined her arms around his neck in tender embraces, and then – oh, sinful even to relate – began to caress him wantonly, in order that she might force

him to yield to her shameless advances. What should a soldier of Christ do? Where could he turn? Lust was on the point of overcoming him whom torture could not conquer. At last, inspired from heaven, he bit off a piece of his tongue and spat it into her face as she kissed him. Ensuing pain prevailed over lustful passion.

4. At the time that such outrages were being perpetrated in the lower Thebaid, Paul, at about the age of sixteen, came into a rich inheritance, upon the death of his parents. His sister was already married. Highly educated not only in Greek but also in Egyptian letters, he was a gentle lad who loved God exceedingly. Until the storm of persecution should cease thundering, [he lived] in seclusion in a more distant villa. But, alas, 'to what dost thou not drive the hearts of men, O accursed hunger for gold!' His own brother-in-law, instead of concealing him, plotted to betray the boy. He heeded not the ears of his wife, not the ties of consanguinity, not God beholding all things from heaven; nothing could deter him from his criminal intent. He came; he threatened; he employed cruelty as if it were piety.

5. When the prudent young man realized what was happening, he fled into the fastnesses of the mountains, where, awaiting the end of the persecution, he made a virtue of necessity. After careful examination of his surroundings, he found a rocky ridge, at the foot of which there was a cave, its opening shut off by a stone of no great size. Eagerly removing the stone — curiosity is human — he came upon a large chamber open to the sky. The spreading branches of an ancient palm tree protected the vestibule. He discovered, too, a clear spring whose gushing waters were almost immediately swallowed up again by the earth which had given them birth. Throughout the hollowed mountain, there were many smaller chambers in which Paul saw rusty forges and mallets of the kind used in coining money. The place, according to Egyptian accounts, was a secret mint during Anthony's stay with Cleopatra.

6. There in this humble dwelling which he grew to love (just as if God himself had given it to him), he passed the rest of his life in prayer and solitude. The palm tree supplied his few needs of food and clothing. Lest anyone should question the possibility of such an existence, I call upon Christ and his holy angels to witness that I have seen, and still see, monks living in that part of the desert which lies between Syria and the land of the Saracens [desert tribespeople]. One monk, in fact, lived in seclusion in that wilderness for thirty years, subsisting on barley bread and muddy water, while another, sustained by five dry figs a day, inhabited an old cistern (which they call *kabba* in the Gentile language of Syria). I know, of course, that all this will seem incredible to those who will not admit that 'all things are possible to them that believeth.'

7. But, to return from my digression. When blessed Paul, already one hundred and thirteen years old, was leading a heavenly life on earth, and Antony, a nonogenarian, was tarrying in another solitude (as he was wont to say), the thought occurred to Antony that no other monk had gone to live in the desert. It was revealed to him in sleep, however, that another more worthy than he dwelt in the deeper recesses of the desert and that it was his duty to seek him out. At the break of dawn, the venerable old man, supporting his weak legs with a sturdy staff, without delay set out on his quest – whither he did not know. Soon, the midday sun was beating down its scorching rays; nevertheless, nothing could hold him back from the journey he had undertaken. "I believe in my God," he prayed, "I believe that he will guide me to his servant, the sight of whom he has promised me." His prayer barely finished, he became aware of a creature, half man and half horse, which the poets call a centaur. Arming himself with the sign of the cross on his forehead, Antony cried: "Ho, there, where does the servant of God live?" The creature, barbarously gnashing its teeth, and mouthing rather than uttering words with its shaggy lips, attempted to answer him respectfully. Then, indicating the proper direction with its right hand, it stretched over the open fields in swift flight and vanished from the sight of the astonished hermit. Whether, indeed, it was the Devil who assumed this form to frighten him or whether the desert, productive of monstrous animals, brought forth this beast, too, we do not know for certain.

8. Mystified, Antony hastened on his way, pondering over the strange event. He had not advanced very far when, in the midst of a little rocky valley, he met a manikin with a hooked nose and a forehead pointed with budding horns, the lower part of his body shaped like a goat. At this startling encounter, Antony, like a good warrior, seized the 'shield of faith' and the breastplate of hope. As if to reassure him, the beast, as a pledge of peace, offered him fruit from a palm tree for refreshment on his journey. Antony recognized the overtures of peace, stopped and asked him who he was, receiving the answer: "I am a mortal and one of the inhabitants of the desert whom the pagans, deluded by all manner of error, worship under the names of fauns, satyrs, and incubi. I serve as the ambassador of my flock. We beseech you to intercede for us with him who is 'Lord over all,' for we know that he came at one time for the salvation of the world and that his 'sound hath gone forth into all the earth.'" The aged traveler wept many tears over these words, tears that told of the great overflowing joy of his heart. He rejoiced over the glory of Christ and the defeat of Satan. At the same time, he marveled that he could understand the creature's speech and, striking the ground with his staff, cried out: "Woe to you, Alexandria, because you worship monsters for

God! Woe to you, meretricious city, in which all the demons of the world find refuge. What now will you answer? Beasts speak the name of Christ." He had not yet finished his lamentation when the horned animal fled away as if borne on wings. If anyone should find it difficult to believe this incident, let him heed the testimony of the whole world under the rule of Constantine, for just such a creature was brought to Alexandria alive and exposed to public view as a great spectacle. Later, they preserved the dead body of the brute from decaying in the summer heat by salting it, and then sent it on to Antioch for the emperor to see.

9. I must return to my story. Antony continued his anxious wandering through the region, intent only on the tracks of wild beasts through the vast waters of the desert. What should he do? Where should he turn his steps? Another day slipped by. Sure of only one thing, that Christ would not abandon him, he prayed without ceasing throughout that second night. In the dim light of early dawn, he discerned not far away a wolf, panting with burning thirst, which crawled to the foot of the mountain. He followed it with his eyes and, when the beast had disappeared from view, he approached closer to the spot and tried to peer within the cave which it had entered. His effort availed him nothing; he could see nothing in the darkness. But, as the Scripture says, 'perfect love casteth out fear,' cautiously and with bated breath, the wary explorer made his way slowly and carefully into the cave, stopping frequently to catch every sound. Finally, through the terrifying darkness, he saw a light in the distance. Eagerly, he hurried toward it and in his haste his foot struck against a stone which made a rattling noise. At the first sound of an intruder, blessed Paul (for this was Paul's hiding-place) quickly closed and firmly barred the entrance to his retreat. Then, indeed, Antony fell in a heap on the ground in front of the door and lay there until the sixth hour and longer, begging and imploring for admission: "Who I am, whence I came, why I came, you know. I know that I am not worthy to behold you; nevertheless, I shall not go away until I have seen you. You who receive beasts, why do you refuse man? I have sought, and I have found; I knock that it may be opened to me. If you do not grant my request, I shall die right here before your very door. Certainly, then, you will bury my body." So he continued in his speech and remained unshaken '... To whom the hero thus made brief reply:' "No one who pleads so earnestly means to threaten. No one with such tears plans mischief. You come when you are about to die and then you wonder why I do not open to you?" Paul laughingly opened wide the entrance. Immediately, they embraced each other, called one another by name, and together offered their thanks to God.

[Fig. 8] St. Paul and St. Antony dividing the loaf which has been brought to them by the raven, shown flying above their heads (copy of a picture by Brusasorci, 1530, in Jameson, *Sacred and Legendary Art,* 2, 754).

10. After the holy kiss, Paul seated himself beside Antony and spoke thus: "Behold whom you have sought with so much fatigue; tangled grey hair covers an old man with wasted limbs. Behold, you see a man soon to return to dust. But, truly as 'Charity . . . endureth all things' tell me, I beg of you, how is man faring in the world? Are there new roofs rising in the ancient cities? What power rules the world? Are there still some who are ensnared by the horror of demons?" While they were discoursing about such matters, they noticed a fleet raven alight upon a branch of a tree. Gently swooping down, to their amazement, it deposited a whole loaf of bread between them. "Ah," said Paul when the bird had flown away, "God has sent us our dinner, God truly good, truly merciful. For sixty years now, I have received a piece of bread every noon. Today, in honor of your arrival, Christ has doubled the rations of his soldiers."

11. Giving thanks to God, they said their grace and sat down at the edge of the clear spring. Here arose a dispute, which lasted almost until evening, over who should break the bread. Paul, as host, urged Antony, while Antony felt that, by right of his seniority, the privilege belonged to Paul. Finally it was decided that each would pick up one end of the bread and pull it toward himself; his own portion would remain in his hand. Afterwards, prone on the ground, they sipped a little water. Then, offering God a sacrifice of praise, they spent the rest of the night in prayerful vigils. When day had already returned to earth, blessed Paul spoke thus to Antony: "For a long time now, brother, I have known that you dwelled in these regions; for a long time, God had promised you to me for a companion. Since my hour of eternal sleep has arrived, and because I have always desired 'to be dissolved and to be with Christ,' having 'finished the course, . . . a crown of justice' remains for me. You have been sent by God to bury my miserable body, to return earth to earth."

12. Antony listened to these words with tears and groans, imploring Paul not to forsake him but to accept him as a companion on that journey. Paul answered: "You ought not seek your own interests but those of another. It is indeed profitable for you to cast off the burden of the flesh, to follow the Lamb, but it is also profitable for the rest of your brethren that they may be the more instructed by your example. I beg of you, hasten if it is not too much to ask, and bring back the cloak which Athanasius the bishop gave you, to wrap about my wretched body." Now, blessed Paul made this request not because he cared at all whether or not his body decayed covered up or naked since for a long time now he had been wearing garments woven from palm leaves, but because he wanted to spare Antony the grief of witnessing his death. Antony was amazed that he had heard about Athanasius and his

cloak and, as if he saw Christ in Paul, worshiping God in his heart dared make no reply. Weeping he silently kissed Paul's eyes and hands and returned to his monastery, which was later seized by the Saracens. His steps could scarcely keep pace with the ardor of his soul, but although his body was wasted from fasting and broken by the years of great age, his spirit triumphed over infirmity.

13. At last, worn out and breathless, his journey ended, he reached his dwelling place. Two disciples who had been serving him for some time hurried out to meet him and inquired: "Where have you delayed so long, father?" "Woe to me a sinner," he replied, "who falsely bear the name of monk! I have seen Elias, I have seen John in the desert, and in truth, I have seen Paul in paradise!" Then, with sealed lips and striking his breast, he brought out the cloak from his cell. To his disciples begging for more detail he said: "There is a 'time to keep silence and a time to speak.'"

14. Without taking even a little food, Antony set out again on the same road by which he had returned. Longing after Paul, ardently desiring to see him, he was absorbed in thinking about him for he feared what actually did happen, that during his absence Paul would give his soul back to Christ. When another day had dawned and he still had a three-hour journey to go, he saw Paul, shining in snowy whiteness, ascend into heaven amid a host of angels and the choirs of Prophets and Apostles. Antony immediately fell prostrate, threw sand upon his head, groaned and wept: "Why do you dismiss me, Paul? Why do you go without a farewell? I have known you so late; why do you depart so quickly from me?"

15. In relating the event later blessed Antony recalled that he ran the rest of the way with such great speed that he seemed like a bird flying. Justly so, for, when he entered the cave, he found Paul kneeling, his head erect and his hands raised toward heaven, his body lifeless. At first, thinking that he was alive, he began to pray with him. When he did not hear the habitual sighing of the praying monk, he fell upon his face, weeping, for he realized that even the lifeless body of the saint rendered by its attitude dutiful homage to God unto whom all creatures live.

16. Thereupon, Antony wrapped up the body and carried it out beyond the entrance, chanting hymns and psalms in the Christian manner. He grieved that he did not have an implement to dig a grave. His mind in a turmoil, he pondered: "If I return to the monastery, it will mean a journey of four days; if I remain here, I shall accomplish nothing. Let me die, as it is fitting, alongside of your warrior, O Christ; falling, let me pour forth my last breath." While he was entertaining such thoughts, behold, there came rushing from the interior of the wilderness two lions with their manes flowing about

their necks. At the first sight of them, he was thoroughly frightened, but, turning his thoughts back to God, he remained as undaunted as if he were looking at doves. They dashed directly to the body of the blessed old man, stopped short, wagging their tails, and dropped down at his feet, roaring with mighty roars to communicate their grief in the only way they could. Then, not far from the corpse, they began to scratch the ground with their paws; vigorously scooping away the sand, they dug out a space that would hold the body of a man. Straightway, as if demanding a reward for their work, with heads hanging but ears twitching, they made for Antony and began to lick his hands and feet. He understood that they were merely begging a blessing from him. His joy burst forth in praise of Christ, that even dumb animals sensed him to be God: "O God, without whose permission not even a leaf flutters, nor a single sparrow falls to the ground, grant unto them as thou knowest how to give" and, making a sign with his hand, he commanded them to go away. After they had gone, he lifted the saint's body, his aged shoulders bending under the burden, deposited it in the grave, and covered it over with the customary mound of earth. On the next day, lest the devoted heir go without something from his possessions who had died without a will, Antony claimed for himself the tunic which, in the manner of a plaited basket, the holy man had woven for himself from the leaves of the palm. He returned to his monastery with his relic and related to his disciples all that had happened. From that time, he always wore Paul's tunic on the solemn feasts of Easter and Pentecost [the seventh Sunday after Easter, when the Holy Spirit descended on the apostles].

17. I should like to close this little work by asking those whose heritage is so vast that they cannot keep account of it, who veneer their houses with marble, who string upon one thread the value of whole estates, if there was anything wanting to this naked old man? You drink from jeweled goblets; he satisfied nature with the hollow of his hands. You wear tunics interwoven with gold; he did not possess even the covering of the meanest of your slaves. On the contrary, paradise opens to him, a pauper; hell awaits you, robed in luxury. He, naked, has preserved the garment of Christ; you, clothed in silks, have cast off the vestment of Christ. Paul, who lies covered with the lowliest dust, will rise again in glory; you, pressed down by mighty sepulchers of stone, will burn with your riches. Have mercy, I beseech you; at least, spare the riches which you love so much. Why do you shroud your dead in vestments of gold? Why does not your ambition cease with grief and tears? Or is it true, perhaps, that the corpses of the rich do not decay unless wrapped in silk?

18. I beg of you, whoever read this, that you remember the sinner Jerome,

who, if God should grant him his greatest desire, would much rather choose the tunic of Paul with his merits than the purple of kings with their kingdoms.

11. A HARLOT IN THE DESERT: MARY OF EGYPT

The image of the reformed prostitute dominated in portrayals of the desert mothers, and like their prototype Mary Magdalene, these women often became powerful liturgical icons of repentance and divine forgiveness. Accounts of Mary Magdalene and Mary of Egypt were sometimes collated, but while the former had a major cult in the West, Mary of Egypt was especially venerated in the East. Her story circulated in eastern monastic circles from the sixth century onwards: an early account was written down by Cyril of Scythopolis who inserted it as a short and rather unspectacular incident in his 'Life of Cyriacus.' The story evolved with the help of accretions from other sources: readers will recognize similarities to Jerome's 'Life of St. Paul' (10 above). The version here is one that circulated in the West and is attributed to Sophronius, bishop of Jerusalem from 634-8.

Source: trans. from Migne, *Patrologia Latina*, 73, 671-90, by Benedicta Ward, *Harlots of the Desert: A Study of Repentance in Early Monastic Sources* (Kalamazoo, Michigan: Cistercian Publications, 1987), pp. 35-56; repr. with permission. BHL 5415.

"It is good to keep close the secret of a king, but to reveal gloriously the works of God." This is what the angel said to Tobit after his eyes had been miraculously healed from blindness after the dangers through which he had led him and from which he had delivered him because of his piety. Not to keep the secret of a king is a dangerous and fearful matter. But to keep silent about the miraculous works of God, that is dangerous to the soul. This is why, moved by dread of keeping silent about the things of God, and remembering the punishment promised to the servant who took a talent from the lord and buried it, fruitlessly hiding what had been given him to work with, I will not be silent about the holy tale which has reached us. No one should have any doubts about believing me, for I am writing about what I have heard, and no one should think in astonishment over the magnitude of the miracles that I am inventing fables. God deliver me from inventing or falsifying an account in which his name comes! But it seems to me unreasonable to think basely and unworthily about the majesty of the incarnate word of God, and not to believe in what is told here. If, however, such readers of this narrative are found, who are so overcome by the miraculous nature of this account that they will not want to believe it, may the Lord be merciful to them! For they consider the infirmity of human nature and think that miracles related about people are impossible. But now I shall start on my tale of events which took place in our own time, as they were revealed to me by good men experienced from childhood in godly words and deeds. They must not try to justify their lack of faith on the grounds that miracles cannot hap-

[Fig. 9] The chief events in the legend of St. Mary of Egypt, recorded in a window in Bourges Cathedral (copy in Baring-Gould, *Lives of the Saints,* 4). The story reads from left to right, starting at the bottom.

pen in our own generation. For the grace of the Father, flowing from generation to generation through holy souls, makes friends of God and prophets, as Solomon teaches. But now it is time to begin on this holy tale. . .

1. Among those who lived as monks in Palestine there was an old man renowned for his way of life and gift of words; from his infancy he was nourished in the monastic way of life and its works. (He was called Zossima but, in spite of his name, no one should think that I am referring to that Zossima who was at one time guilty of doctrinal error; that was one Zossima, this was another Zossima, and they had nothing in common except the same name.) This Zossima lived in one of the monasteries of Palestine from the beginning of his conversion, and having passed through the whole of monastic discipline, he became established in every kind of abstinence. From childhood he observed in everything the rule handed on canonically, carrying out without blame the contest of perfect monastic discipline. And he added much from his own experience, seeking to subdue the flesh to the spirit. Nor was he known to have offended in any way. So perfect was he in all monastic behavior, that many monks from monasteries of the aforementioned region and even from distant parts often came to him, drawn by his example and his teaching, to put themselves under the direction of his greater discipline.

2. While he occupied himself with all this, he never ceased from meditation on the sacred words, whether he was lying down or getting up or holding his work in his hands. If however you want to know on what kind of food he fed, know that he had only one occupation, unflagging and unceasing, always praising God and meditating on the divine word. Often, they say, the old man was found worthy of divine visions, illuminated from on high for, according to the word of the Lord, "Blessed are the pure in heart, for they shall see God." How much more is this true of those who keep their bodies cleansed and ever sober; they will see with the unsleeping eye of the soul visions from on high, having in them the pledge of the bliss that awaits them. Zossima used to tell how when he was hardly weaned he was placed in that monastery, where he lived until his fifty-third year, following an ascetic way of life. It was then that he began to be tormented by the thought that it seemed as if he had attained perfection in everything and needed no teaching from anyone. And so, as he himself said, he began to say to himself: "Is there a monk on earth capable of affording me benefit or passing on to me anything new, some kind of spiritual achievement of which I either do not know or in which I have not succeeded as a monk? Surely there can be found among the men of the desert one surpassing me in his deeds?" While he was turning over this and similar thoughts, some one stood before him and said, "Zossima, you have done as well as any man can, you have done well in the whole of the monastic way. But among human beings, no-one

can attain perfection. A greater ordeal lies ahead of you, although you do not know this. And so that you may know how many and varied are the ways to salvation, leave your native land, go out of your father's house, like Abraham, glorious among the patriarchs, and go to the monastery which lies near the river Jordan."

3. As soon as he had ceased speaking, Zossima left the monastery where he had lived since childhood and having reached Jordan, the holy river, he set out to him who had called him, along the road to the monastery to which he had been ordered to go. He knocked on the door of the monastery and saw first the door-keeper, who took him to the abbot. The abbot received him, and took note of his appearance and behavior, for he made the customary prostration, bowing down according to the monastic rule, and begged him to pray for him. Then the abbot asked him "Where have you come from, brother, and for what purpose have you come to our humble monastery?" Zossima answered, "There is no need to say where I have come from, but I have come in order to make spiritual progress. For I have heard concerning you things worthy of glory and honor, which could draw a soul to intimate familiarity with Christ our God." The abbot said to him, "God alone who heals human infirmity will reveal, brother, his divine will to you and to us and teach us how to do what is right. Man cannot help man unless, soberly and constantly, each brings his attention to bear on what is right and proper and has God as his fellow-worker in his labor. But if, as you say, it was the love of God that moved you to visit us humble old monks, stay with us and the Good Shepherd will feed us all by the grace of his spirit, he who laid down his life to save us and who knows his sheep by name." When the abbot had said this, Zossima again prostrated, asked his prayers, said "amen" and went to live in the monastery.

4. There he saw old men, glorious in the life of action and also of contemplation, fervent in spirit, serving the Lord. They sang Psalms without ceasing, standing all night and they always had some work in their hands and unceasing prayer in their mouths. There was no idle word there, no thought of gold or silver, in that house there was no concern about business. The expenses of the whole year, the profits, or any worry about temporal life was unknown to them even by name. For all of them there was only one aim to which all were hastening: to be in the body as a corpse, to die completely to the world and everything in the world. They were not without the food that fails not, the Word of God; they fed their bodies only with bread and water; for each one burned with the love of God.

5. On seeing this, according to his own words, Zossima was very edified, and strove to advance, hastening in his own race, for he had found companions who were the best of all workers in paradise. Some days passed, and the

time approached when it is the custom for Christians to keep the holy fast, preparing themselves for the day of the divine passion and saving resurrection. The gates of the monastery were always kept closed to allow the monks to work in peace; they were only opened when a matter of real necessity forced a monk to go outside the monastery. The place was a desert and not only out of reach from most of the neighboring monasteries but even unknown. The monks had a rule and I think it was because of this that God had led Zossima there.

6. What the rule was and how it was kept I shall now tell you. On the Sunday which gave its name to the first week of Lent, the divine mysteries [Mass] were celebrated in church as usual and everyone received the most pure and life-giving mysteries. And it was also the custom to eat a little food. After this they all met in church and having prayed fervently with prostrations, the old men kissed each other and the abbot, embracing each other and bowing deeply, and each one asked the others to pray for him, and to support him, as they shared the coming conflict. Then last of all the monastery gates were opened and singing in harmony the Psalm, 'the Lord is my light and my salvation, whom shall I fear? The Lord is the strength of my life, of whom then shall I be afraid?' and so on, they all went out of the monastery. They left one or two brothers in the monastery, not to guard their property (there was nothing there to attract thieves) but so as not to leave the church without services. Each one took with him whatever food he could and wanted. One carried a little bread for his bodily needs, another figs, another dates, and another grain steeped in water. The last one at the end had nothing but his own body and its tattered clothing and when his nature demanded food, he fed on whatever grew in the desert. But for them all there was one rule and command inflexibly observed by all: not to know about each other, or how the others lived and fasted. At once they crossed the Jordan and then parted from each other over the wide expanse of the desert and not one approached another. If one did notice a brother afar off coming towards him, then he turned aside; each lived by himself and with God, singing Psalms all the time and hardly touching food. After they had passed all the days of the fast like this, they returned to the monastery the Sunday before the life-giving resurrection of the Savior from the dead, when the church has ordained that the feast with palms should be celebrated before the feast [of Easter]. Each returned with the fruits of his own conscience, knowing how he had labored and by which labors he had sown seed in the ground. No one asked anyone else how he had succeeded in the trial he had set himself beforehand.

7. This was the rule of the monastery and it was very strictly observed. Each of them fought in the desert against himself before the judge of the

fight, God; and he did not seek to please other people by fasting in front of them. For whatever is done for the sake of other people, to please human beings, is not only of no benefit but can lead to severe punishment. So Zossima, also, according to the rule of the monastery, crossed the Jordan, taking a little food with him for the journey for the needs of the body, and the poor clothes he was wearing. He kept the rule, walking through the desert and allowing only the time for food that nature demanded. He slept at night lying on the ground and sleeping for a short time, wherever he happened to be in the evening. In the morning he set out again on his way burning with the desire that did not grow less, to go further. As he himself said something in his soul urged him to go deep into the desert. He hoped he might find some father there who would fulfil his longing. So he went on tirelessly, as if he were hurrying towards a well-known inn. He had already walked for twenty days when he stopped at the sixth hour and turned towards the East for the customary prayers. He always interrupted his journey at the customary hours of the day and rested a little from his labors, standing, singing Psalms or praying upon his knees. And as he sang, without turning his eyes from heaven, he saw on the right from where he stood the shadow of a human body. At first he was troubled, thinking that he saw the appearance of a devil and he trembled. But he protected himself with the sign of the cross, and chased away fear (his prayers were now over) and he saw that there really was some kind of being walking along at mid-day. It was a woman and she was naked, her body black as if scorched by the fierce heat of the sun, the hair on her head was white as wool and short, coming down only to the neck.

8. On seeing this apparition, Zossima began to run swiftly in the direction in which what he had seen was going, and he rejoiced with unspeakable joy. Throughout those days he had not seen a human face once, nor an animal, nor a bird, not even the shadow of a creature. He longed to know who it was that had appeared to him hoping that some great mystery would be revealed to him. But when the apparition saw Zossima approaching, it began to run quickly into the depth of the desert. Zossima forgetting his age, and not thinking of the difficulties of the route, ran very fast, in order to catch up with the fugitive. As soon as he drew near, it ran away. Zossima ran faster and soon he drew near to the one that fled. When Zossima had run near enough for his voice to be heard, he began to shout, in tears, "Why are you running away from an old man, a sinner? Wait for me, servant of God, whoever you are, in the name of God for whose sake you live in the desert. Wait for me, infirm and unworthy as I am, I beg you, in the name of your hope of reward for your labor. Stop and grant me, an old man, a prayer and blessing for the

sake of God who despises no-one." So Zossima begged with tears and they both ran on to a place that looked like the bed of a dried up stream. (Where could a stream have come from in that land? The ground there had that appearance naturally.) When they reached that place, the fugitive went down and up the other side of the ravine and Zossima, exhausted and unable to run further, stopped on this side, adding tears to tears and increased his sighs with such sighs that his grief might be heard much more since the sound was now nearby.

9. Then the fugitive spoke: "Father Zossima, forgive me, for God's sake, but I cannot turn round and show myself to you, for I am a woman and, as you see, with the shame of my body uncovered. If you wish to answer the prayer of a sinful woman throw me the cloak you are wearing so that I can cover my woman's weakness and turn and have your blessing." At this dread and anxiety fell on Zossima, as he said himself, when he heard her calling him by his name of Zossima. But he was a man of good intelligence and wise in the ways of God so he decided that she would not have called him by his name, when she had never either seen him or heard of him before, unless she was enlightened by the grace of insight. He obeyed her request at once, and took off the old and tattered cloak he was wearing and threw it to her, turning his back. She took it and partially hid the nakedness of her body with it and then turned to Zossima and said, "Why do you want to see a sinful woman, father? What do you want to learn from me or see, that you were not afraid to undertake such a heavy task?" He knelt down and asked her to give him the customary blessing. She also knelt down. So they both remained on the ground asking one another for a blessing.

10. After a long time the woman said to Zossima, "Father Zossima, it is proper for you to give the blessing and say the prayer, for you have the dignity of the office of a priest, and for many years you have stood at the holy table and offered the sacrifice of Christ." These words threw Zossima into greater dread, he trembled and was covered with a sweat of death. But at last, breathing with difficulty, he said to her, "O Mother in the spirit, it is plain from this insight that all your life you have dwelt with God and have nearly died to the world. It is plain above all that grace is given you since you called me by my name and recognized me as a priest although you have never seen me before. But since grace is recognized not by office but by gifts of the Spirit, bless me, for God's sake, and pray for me out of the kindness of your heart." So the woman gave way to the wish of the old man, and said, "Blessed is God who cares for the salvation of souls." Zossima answered "Amen," and they both rose from their knees. The woman said to the old man, "Why have you come to see me, a sinner, sir? Perhaps it was the grace of the Holy Spirit

which brought you to perform a certain service for me in due time? Tell me, how are the most Christian tribunes and emperors ruling now? How does the church care for its flock?" Zossima said to her, "By your holy prayers, mother, Christ has given lasting peace everywhere. But hear the request of an unworthy monk and pray to the Lord for the whole world and for me, a sinner, that my wandering through the desert should not be without fruit." She answered him, "It is only right, Father Zossima, that you who have the office of a priest should pray for me and for all; but we must be obedient so I shall willingly do what you bid me." With these words, she turned to the East and raising her eyes to heaven and stretching up her hands she began to pray moving her lips in silence, so that almost nothing intelligible could be heard. So Zossima could not understand anything of her prayer. As he said, he stood there trembling, looking at the ground and saying nothing. He also swore, calling on God as a witness, that when she seemed to him to be continuing steadfastly in prayer, he raised his eyes a little from the ground and saw that she had risen a cubit [50 cm/20 inches] from the ground and was standing praying in the air. When he saw this, even greater dread seized him and he fell to the ground, covered with sweat and terrified, not daring to say anything, but saying within himself, "Lord, have mercy!"

11. As he lay on the ground, the old man was troubled by the thought that this might be an evil spirit and the prayer an illusion. But the woman turned round and helped the monk up and said, "Why are your thoughts troubling you, father, and deceiving you about me, that I may be an evil spirit and my prayer false? Be assured, sir, that I am just a woman and a sinner, but protected by holy baptism. I am not a spirit but earth and ashes, entirely flesh, in no way calling to mind a spirit of phantasy." With these words, she made the sign of the cross on her brow and eyes, lips and breast, saying, "God deliver us, Father Zossima, from the evil one and his emissaries, for his envy of us is great." When he heard and saw this, the old man fell on the ground and embraced her feet with tears, saying, "I beg you, in the name of the Lord Jesus Christ, who is indeed our Lord, born of a Virgin, for whose sake you clothed yourself in this nakedness, for whose sake you have wasted your flesh in this way, do not hide who you are from your servant or where you came from, when and how you came to this desert; tell me everything, so that the wonderful works of God may be manifest, for as it is written, if wisdom is kept hidden and treasure a secret, what profit is there in them? I beg you to tell me everything, for God's sake. For you will not be telling me out of vainglory or for praise but to satisfy me, a sinner and unworthy. I believe that God, for whom you live and whom you serve, has brought me into the desert for the purpose of revealing to me the things he has done for you. It is

not in our power to oppose God's providence. If it were not pleasing to the Lord Christ to reveal you and what you have achieved, he would not have allowed anyone to see you and he would not have given me the strength to accomplish such a journey, I who never wished nor dared to leave my cell."

12. When he had said this and more, the woman raised him up and said, "I am ashamed, my father, to tell you about the infamy of my deeds. But as you have already seen my naked body, I shall also lay bare before you my deeds, so that you may know with what shame and contrition my soul is filled. It is not because of vainglory, as you have realized, that I want to tell you about myself, for what have I got to be vainglorious about, having been chosen as a vessel of the Devil? I know, too, that when I begin my story you will run away from me, as a man runs from a snake; your ears will not bear to hear the wickedness of my deeds. I tell you, I shall not keep quiet about anything, begging you first of all to pray for me without ceasing, that mercy may be found for me on the day of judgment." The old man wept without restraint. Then the woman began to tell him what had happened to her, thus:

13. "My homeland, father, was Egypt. I lived with my parents but when I was only twelve years old I spurned their care and went into Alexandria. I am ashamed to think how I first lost my virginity there and how I was on fire with untiring and clamorous desire for lust, for it cannot be told briefly. Let me only say this, so that you may understand the insatiable fire within me: for more than seventeen years, I passed my life openly tarrying in the fires of lust. I had not lost my virginity for any gift of money, for I frequently refused what they wanted to give me. I did this with as many as I could get to come to me. Do not think that I was at all rich, for I lived by begging or sometimes by spinning threads of flax. It was just that what I did, I did out of insatiable desire. I wanted to wallow in this trough and that to me was life. I thought any kind of desecration to be natural. While I was living in this way, one summer I saw a great crowd of men, Egyptians and Libyans, going down toward the sea. I stopped one of them and asked him where they were going in such haste. He told me, 'They are all going to Jerusalem for the exaltation of the Holy Cross which is to be celebrated there in a few days time.' Then I said to him, 'Do you think they would take me, if I wanted to go with them?' 'Anyone who has the fare can go,' he replied. I said, 'Indeed, brother, I have neither the fare nor any food, but I will go and get into one of the ships that are going and they will take me even if they do not want to. I have a body and that will serve as both fare and food for me.' For I wanted to go (forgive me, my father) so that I might soon have more lovers for my lust.

14. I beg you, my lord and father, do not force me to say any more about my shame, for I am afraid of the judgment of God and lest my words corrupt

both you and the very air." Then Zossima, watering the ground with tears, said to her, "For God's sake, speak, Mother; go on and do not break the thread of your life-giving narrative." So she took up the story again and continued: "Then the young man who had heard my obscene remarks went away, laughing. I threw away the spindle that I was carrying (for until then I used to have it with me) and I ran down to the sea, whither I had seen the others hurrying; I saw some young men, about ten in number, standing on the shore, with beautiful bodies and graceful movements, and I judged them just right for what I wanted. They were waiting, it seemed, for the rest of their sailing companions, while some had already gone ahead into the ship. So as was my custom, I shamelessly pushed into the midst of them and said, 'Take me wherever you are going and I will not be without my uses for you.' I added more and more shameless things and they were all moved to laughter. When they saw that I was ready for anything shameless, they accepted me and carried me into their ship which was ready to sail, and we set sail at once. How can I tell you, man of God, about what followed? What tongue can say, what ear can hear what happened on that ship and during that voyage, for I compelled into sin even those who were unwilling. There was no kind of perverted and unspeakable lust that I did not perform with them. I am amazed, my father, that the sea carried my lusts and that the earth did not open to take me alive down into hell. But I think my God was seeking my repentance, for he does not desire the death of sinners but guards them in his loving kindness, waiting for them to be converted. So I continued in this way until we reached Jerusalem and for all the days there that preceded the festival, I was occupied in similar or even worse behavior. I was not content to have had the young men with whom I had satisfied my lusts at sea during the voyage, but misused others on land, both the citizens and those who were there as pilgrims.

15. Now when the festival of the exaltation of the precious Cross came round, and I was going about as usual hunting for the souls of young men, I saw at first light that everyone was going to the church. So I went along, running with those who were running there and I came with them into the forecourt of the cathedral. At the hour for the exaltation of the Holy Cross I pushed and was pushed, fighting my way fiercely through the crowd to get in. So somehow, I, unhappy wretch that I was, came near to where the life giving wood [the Cross of the crucifixion] was being displayed. But as soon as I reached the threshold where others were going in without difficulty, I was prevented from entering by a kind of force. I was pushed back and found myself standing alone in the courtyard. I thought it had only happened because of my weakness as a woman, so again I mingled with the others,

struggling and using my elbows to push forward to the same spot, but I labored in vain.

16. All the rest went in without difficulty, with no impediment, but as soon as I set foot on the threshold of the church, it refused to admit me. It was as if a detachment of soldiers stood in the way to prevent me from entering; some unexplained power repelled me and I stood again in the forecourt. I suffered this again three or four times and at last, worn out, I gave up pushing and being pushed back (for I lacked strength of body for such violence). I drew back and stood in a corner of the forecourt. And only then did I begin to see why it was that I was being prevented from going in to see the life-giving wood. For a salutary understanding touched my mind and the eyes of my heart and showed me that it was the sinfulness of my actions that prevented me from going in. So I began to weep and grieve and beat my breast; I drew sighs and tears from the bottom of my heart. And then I saw in the place where I was standing, a picture of the holy Mother of God. Gazing directly into her eyes, I said 'Virgin and Lady, who gave birth to the word of God according to the flesh, I see now that it is not suitable or decent for me, defiled as I am, to look upon this picture of you, ever immaculate Virgin, who always kept your body and soul chaste and clean from all sin. Indeed, it would be right for you in your purity to reject and loathe my impurity. But God to whom you gave birth became man, as I have heard, to save sinners and to call them to repentance; so help me, for I am alone and without any other help. Receive my confession, and give me leave to enter the church and do not deprive me of the sight of that most precious wood upon which was fixed God made man, whom you carried and bore as a Virgin and where he gave his blood for my redemption. O Lady, let the doors be opened to me so that I may adore the divine Cross. I beg you, from whom Christ took flesh, to guarantee my promise, which is, that I will never again defile my flesh by immersing it in horrifying lusts. As soon as I have seen the Cross of your Son, holy Virgin, I will go wherever you as my mediator for salvation shall order and lead.'

17. When I had said this, with burning faith, as if receiving some assurance from some sure source, and trusting in the mercy of heart of the Mother of God, I moved out of the place in which I had been standing to pray, and once more I mingled with those who were going in. There was nothing to push me away or prevent me from approaching the door by which they were going into church. At that point a great terror and stupor came over me, and I trembled all over, but when I came to the door which until then had been closed to me, it was as if all the force that had previously prevented me from entering now allowed me to go in. So I was admitted without hindrance, and

went into the holy of holies and I was found worthy to worship the mystery of the precious and life-giving wood of the Cross. Thus I understood the promises of God and realized how God receives those who repent. I threw myself on the floor and kissed the sacred dust. Then I went out and ran back to her who was my mediator. I came to the place where I had set my signature to the promise I had made to her who guaranteed it and kneeling before the face of the Mother of God, ever Virgin, I spoke thus: 'O most loving Lady, you have always shown merciful loving-kindness; you have not rejected the prayer of an unworthy sinner. I have gazed upon that glory which was rightly kept from the sight of the impure; glory to God, who accepts through you the repentance of sinners. What more can I, a sinner, think or say? It is time, Lady, to keep the pledge which I made with you as my witness and to fulfil that which I promised. Now therefore, lead me wherever you please; lead me to salvation, teach me what is true, and go before me in the way of repentance.' When I had said this, I heard a voice far off which said, 'If you cross over the Jordan you will find rest.' When I heard the voice say this, I believed it had come because of me, and I cried out, weeping, towards the picture of the Mother of God, 'Lady, Lady, Queen of the whole world, by whom salvation came to the human race, do not forsake me.' When I had said this, I went out of the courtyard of the church and at once I hurried away. As I went, someone noticed me and gave me three pennies, saying 'Take these, mother.' So I took them and bought three loaves with them, receiving them as a blessing for my journey. I asked the man who sold me the bread, 'Where is the road to the Jordan and what is it like?' When I was shown the city gates which lead in that direction, I ran out of them, weeping, and set out on my journey.

18. I asked the way from those whom I met and walked for the rest of the day. It had been the third hour [9 o'clock] when I deserved to see the precious and holy Cross. At sunset I saw the church of St. John the Baptist near the Jordan, and having prayed in the church, I went down immediately to the Jordan and washed my hands and face in its holy water. Then I made my communion of the most pure and life-giving sacrament of Christ the Lord, in the church of St. John, forerunner and baptist; I ate half a loaf and drank from the Jordan; all night I lay on the ground. At first light, I crossed over to the other side and again I begged my guide to lead me wherever she pleased. So I came into this desert and from that time until this day, I go further and run on, waiting for my God who saves those who turn to him out of faintness of heart and in tempest." Zossima asked her, "How many years have passed, my lady, since you began to live in the desert?" The woman replied, "I think it is forty-seven years since I left the holy city." Zossima asked her,

"And what have you been able to find to eat, my lady?" The woman replied, "I was carrying two and a half loaves when I crossed the Jordan, and after a while they became hard as stones and I have gone on eating a little of them at a time for all these years." Then Zossima said, "And have you passed this length of time without suffering? Have you felt nothing of the violence of this sudden change?" She said, "Now you are asking me about something which I tremble to speak of, if I am to remember what great dangers I have borne and the evil thoughts that confused me. For I am afraid lest I suffer more tribulation from them again." Zossima said, "Lady, hide nothing from me. Let us speak clearly for once about this in order to learn what we ought."

19. So she said to him, "Believe me, father, I struggled for seventeen years with the wild beasts of huge and irrational desires; when I began to eat, my desire was for meat; I longed for the fish that they have in Egypt, I even desired the wine which had been so sweet to me; for I had enjoyed wine very much and I used to drink so much that I got drunk; and now I craved that which I had used so much in the world. But here I did not even have water when I was burning in the heat and in very great need. Also there came to me a great longing for songs of a lewd kind, troubling me and making me remember the devilish songs I had learned to sing in the world. At once then weeping and beating my breast I brought back to my mind the promise of faithfulness which I had made when I entered this solitude. In imagination, I would come before the picture of the holy Mother of God, who had accepted me on trust, and implore her to chase from me those thoughts which were afflicting my most wretched soul. So when I had wept greatly and grievously, beating my breast courageously, I saw a light which shone around me on every side and soon I became calm and safe. As for the thoughts that would push me into harlotry again, I do not know, father; how can I tell you about those? When such thoughts grew in me, I would fling myself on the ground and flood the earth with weeping, hoping that she would stand by me who had been my guarantor, appearing to me in my disobedience and threatening me with punishment for my crimes. I did not get up from the ground until that most sweet light shone around me and drove away the thoughts raging in me. Often I directed the eyes of my heart to her, my guarantor, praying to her without ceasing to help me in this solitude to repentance. For I have her as my helper whose purity bore our creator. And so for seventeen years, as I told you, I lived among many dangers, until now. From that time till this, my helper the Mother of God has been with me, and she directs me in all things." Then Zossima said, "You had no food or clothing?" And she replied, "As I told you, I used up the loaves seventeen years

ago, and then I ate herbs that I found in the desert. The clothing that I had when I crossed over Jordan tore and fell to pieces with age. I endured much from the freezing of cold and the burning of heat: I was burned by the heat of summer and frozen stiff and shivering in the winter by so much cold; often I fell to the ground and lay there unmoving, without breath, struggling with many and diverse needs and huge temptations but through it all even until this day the power of God has guarded my unhappy soul and body. When I think from what evils the Lord has freed me, I am nourished by incorruptible food, and I cover my shoulders with the hope of my salvation. I feed upon and cover myself with the Word of God, who contains all things. For man does not live by bread alone and all who have no clothing will be clothed in stone having discarded the outer covering of sins.

20. When Zossima heard how she drew her witnesses from the Scriptures, from the books of Moses and Job, with the Psalms, he said to her, "Have you learned the Psalms, then, mother, and read the other books of holy Scripture?" When she heard this she smiled and said to him, "Believe me, I have seen no one since I crossed over Jordan until I saw you today, not even an animal or any kind of creature since I came into this desert. Never in any way did I learn letters nor have I ever heard anyone reading or singing them, but the word of God living and active itself teaches man knowledge. That is enough about me. Now I ask you, by the incarnation of God the Word, to pray to the Lord for me, a sinner." When she had said this, the old man ran to her and knelt at her feet, weeping and saying, "Blessed be the Lord God who does great and wonderful things, glorious and marvelous, without end. You are indeed blessed, O God, for you have shown me how generous you are to those who fear you. O Lord, you do not abandon those who seek you." She restrained the old man and would not let him bow right down but said to him "I implore you, sir, by our Lord and Savior, Jesus Christ, tell no one anything you have heard until God releases me from this flesh. Now you have heard all this, go in peace, and this time next year I will show myself again to you, and you will see me, if God preserves us. And for the Lord's sake, do what I am going to ask: when the holy season of fasting comes round next year, do not cross the Jordan as is usually done in that monastery." Zossima was astonished to hear her talking to him about the custom of the monastery as if she knew it, but he said nothing except to glorify God who gives great things to those who love him. Then she said, "Stay in the monastery, father, as I have told you, and even if you want to go out, you will not be able to do so. But at sunset on the most holy day of the Lord's Supper, take for me a portion of the life-giving body and blood [the Eucharist] in a holy vessel, worthy of such mysteries, and bring it to me on the bank of Jordan, on the

inhabited side, so that when I come I may receive the life-giving gifts. Since the time when I made my communion in the church of the most blessed forerunner [John the Baptist] before crossing the Jordan, never have I received those holy things, and so I implore you not to refuse my request: bring me the life-giving and divine mysteries at that hour when the Lord made his disciples partakers of the holy Supper. And I send this message to Father John, the abbot of the monastery in which you live: look to yourself and to your flock; something is happening there that needs correction. I do not want you to tell him about this now but when the Lord directs you to do so." With these words, she asked him to pray for her, and disappeared very swiftly into the depths of the desert.

21. As for Zossima, he fell on his knees and kissed the ground on which her feet had stood, giving glory to God. Then with great thankfulness he went away, praising and blessing our Lord and God, Jesus Christ. He passed through the desert again and returned to the monastery on the very day when the monks returned there. He remained silent all the year, not daring to tell anyone what he had seen but by himself he prayed to God that he would show him again the face he longed to see. He sighed to think how slowly a year goes by. When the Sunday came which starts the holy fast, at once everyone went out into the desert with customary prayers and singing of psalms. But Zossima was kept back, ill with a fever, and remained in the monastery. And he remembered that the holy one [Mary] had told him that even if he wanted to go out of the monastery, he would not be able to do so. Some days passed and he got up after his illness but stayed in the monastery. When the monks returned and the day came for the holy Supper, he did what he had been told to do and took in a small chalice a portion of the precious body and blood of Christ our God, and he put figs and dates in a basket with some lentils soaked in water. He left late in the evening and sat down on the bank of the Jordan to wait for the holy one to come. When the holy woman was late, Zossima did not fall asleep but watched the desert closely, waiting to see that for which he longed. Then he said to himself, "Perhaps she has already been and not finding me, gone back?" And saying this, he began to weep, raising his eyes to heaven and praying to God, saying, "Do not send me away, O Lord, without seeing that which you once allowed me to behold."

22. While he was praying and weeping in this way, another thought struck him: "What will happen if she does come? How will she cross the Jordan since there is no boat? How can she come to me, unworthy as I am? Alas, I am wretched; who is keeping such beauty from me?" The old man was turning these things over in his mind, when lo, the holy one came, and stood on

the other bank from whence she had come. When Zossima saw her, he arose rejoicing and greatly exulting he glorified God. And again the thought seized him that she could not cross the Jordan, but when he looked he saw her signing the waters of the Jordan with the sign of the Cross. For the darkness was lit by the full splendor of the moon, since it was that time in the month. As soon as she had made the sign of the Cross, she stepped on to the water and walking over the flowing waves she came as if walking on solid land. Zossima was amazed and began to kneel, but she stopped him, calling over the water and saying "What are you doing, father, you who are a priest of God and carrying the holy mysteries?" At once he obeyed her words. When she came up from the water, she said to the old man, "Give me a blessing, father, give me a blessing." He replied with great haste, (for a great stupor had come over him at so glorious a miracle) and said, "Indeed God does not lie when he promises that we shall be like him, insofar as we have been purified. Glory to you, Christ our God, who have shown me by your handmaiden here how much I should consider myself below the measure of true perfection." When he had said this the woman asked him to say the holy creed and then he began the Lord's prayer. When he had finished the 'Our Father,' the holy one, as is the custom, gave the kiss of peace to the old man. And when she received the life-giving gifts of the sacrament, groaning and weeping with her hands held up to heaven, she cried out, "Lord, now let your servant depart in peace, according to your word; for my eyes have seen your salvation." And she said to the old man, "Forgive me, father, and fulfil my other wish: go now to the monastery and may the peace of God keep you. Return in a year to the stream where I first met you. Do not fail me in this but for God's sake, come. It is the will of God that you see me again." He answered her, "Would that it were possible now to follow your footsteps and have the precious fruit of the sight of your face! Tarry, mother, grant a little request of an old man and deign to accept a little food which I have brought." Saying this he showed her the basket he had brought with him. She touched the lentils with the tip of her finger and taking three grains placed them in her mouth, saying that the grace of the Holy Spirit is sufficient to keep whole the substance of the soul. Then she said to the old man, "For God's sake pray for me, and remember me always as a sinner." He touched the feet of the holy one and with tears begged her to pray for the Church, for the kingdom and for himself and so, weeping, he let her go, for he would not detain her any longer if she did not will it.

23. So once again she made the sign of the Cross over the Jordan and crossed over, walking on the element of water in the same way that she had when she came. And the old man went back full of joy and fear, reproaching himself that he had not asked the holy one her name, but he hoped to do so

the following year.

24. So when a year had again passed, he went again into the huge solitude of the desert, having done every thing according to custom, and he hurried towards that marvelous sight. He walked through the desert without finding any indications that this was the place he was looking for, so he looked right and left, turning his gaze in all directions as if he were a huntsman wanting to capture a much coveted animal. But seeing no movement anywhere he began to weep bitterly. And looking up to heaven he began to pray, "Show me, O Lord, that angel in the flesh of whom the world is not worthy."

25. Having prayed in this way, he came to the place which looked like a stream and on the other side he saw the rising sun, and when he looked, he saw the holy one lying dead, her hands folded and her face turned to the East. Running up to her, he watered the feet of the blessed one with tears; otherwise he did not dare to touch her. He wept for some time and said the appropriate Psalms, then the prayer for the dead, and then he said to himself, "Is it right to bury the holy body here?" And then he saw by her head these words written in the earth: "Father Zossima, bury in this place the body of Mary the sinner, return me to the earth of which I am made, dust to dust, having prayed to the Lord for me, who died on the first day of the Egyptian month of Pharmuti called the fifth of the Ides of April by the Romans [9 April], on the self same night as the passion of the Lord after making her communion of the divine and mysterious Supper."

26. When he had read what was written, the old man wondered who it was that had written those words, since she had told him that she was unlettered, but he rejoiced to know the name of the holy one. He realized that as soon as she had received communion from the divine mysteries by the Jordan, in that same hour she had come to the place where at once she had passed from this world. The same journey which had taken Zossima twenty days with difficulty, Mary had covered in an hour and then at once passed on to God. So Zossima glorified God and shed tears on the body, saying, "It is time, Zossima, to fulfil the command. But how, wretched man, are you going to dig out a grave with nothing but your hands?" Then he saw not far away a small piece of wood, thrown down in the desert. Picking it up he set about digging. But the ground was dry and very hard and would not yield to the efforts of the old man. He grew tired, and poured with sweat. He sighed from the depths of his soul and raising his eyes he saw a great lion standing by the body of the holy one and licking her feet. When he saw the lion he trembled with fear, especially because he remembered that Mary had said she had never met any animals. But protecting himself with the sign of the Cross, he believed that he would be kept from harm by the power of the one who lay there. As for the lion, it walked up to him, expressing friendliness in every

movement. Zossima said to the lion, "Greatest of the beasts, you have been sent by God, so that the body of the holy one should be buried, for I am old and have not enough strength to dig her grave. I have no spade and I cannot go back all that distance to fetch suitable tools. So do the work with your paws and we shall be able to give to the earth the mortal tabernacle of the saint."

27. While he was still speaking the lion had already dug out with its front paws a hole big enough to bury the body in. Again the old man watered the feet of the holy one with tears and then, with the lion standing by, he called upon her to pray for everyone, he covered her body with earth; it was naked as it had been before, except for the torn monastic cloak which Zossima had thrown across her and with which Mary, turning away, had partially covered her body. Then they both withdrew. The lion went off into the depths of the desert as meekly as if it were a lamb, and Zossima went home, blessing and praising God and singing hymns of praise to our Lord Christ. When he reached the monastery, he told the monks everything that he had heard and seen, hiding nothing. From the very beginning he told them everything in detail and all marveled to hear of God's wonders and kept the memory of the saint in fear and love. As for Abbot John, he did find a few in the monastery in need of correction, so that none of the saint's words proved useless or inexplicable. Zossima lived in that monastery until he was a hundred, and then he went in peace to God, thanks be to our Lord Jesus Christ, who with the Father is one in power and honor and glory, with the adorable and life-giving Spirit, now and for ever and to the ages of ages, Amen.

The monks preserved this story without writing it down, and offered it to anyone who wanted to hear it as a pattern for edification, but no one had heard of anyone writing it down to this day. But I have told in writing what I heard orally. Perhaps others also have described the life of the saint and much better and more worthily than I have, but this has not come to my notice. As far as lies in my power, I have written down this account, putting truth before everything else. And may God who gives great things to those who seek him, grant benefit to those who read this story, as a reward for the one he ordered to write it. And may he deign to accept him into that same company and assembly where dwells that blessed Mary about whom this story is, together with all those who throughout the generations have pleased him with godly thoughts and labors. And let us all glorify God, king of all generations, that he may vouchsafe his mercy to us also at the day of Judgment in Christ Jesus our Lord, to whom is due all glory, honor and worship together with the Father without beginning, now and forever and to the ages of ages. AMEN.

12. A FAMOUS PILLAR SAINT: SYMEON STYLITES

With the exception of St. Antony, Symeon was the most famous desert ascetic of his own times and is still the best known today, having come (rather misleadingly) to sym- bolize the desert movement as a whole. A modern reader is unlikely to sympathize with his excesses, and many of his contemporaries in the Syrian monasteries also had misgivings about this aspect of his holiness, though perhaps because they felt outdone by it. The tradition of standing on pillars, copied from Symeon by others, may have originated with Syrian shepherd-monks who imposed on themselves the penance of standing out in the open air all their lives. Despite his residence on pillars of increasing height, Symeon fulfilled one of the traditional roles of the holy man by acting as medi- ator for other people in conflict, and his intervention was sought in the doctrinal dis- putes of his day. The description by Theodoret, author of his 'life,' of the behavior of the people from near and far who flocked avidly to see this desert wonder suggests that for them he was not just a great curiosity. They understood his physical mortification as an expression of a powerful inner spirituality.

Theodoret of Cyrrhus (393-466) was born in Antioch and entered a monastery after his parents died. He gained a reputation as an important and controversial the- ologian, exegete, and historian. As bishop of Cyrrhus from 423 until his death, he vis- ited many notable holy men including Symeon, and gave an account of their lives in his Greek 'Religious History.'

Source: trans. R. M. Price, *A History of the Monks of Syria by Theodoret of Cyrrhus* (Kalamazoo, Michigan: Cistercian Publications, 1985), pp. 160-171; repr. with permission.

1. The famous Symeon, the great wonder of the world, is known of by all the subjects of the Roman empire and has also been heard of by the Persians, the Medes, the Ethiopians; and the rapid spread of his fame as far as the nomadic Scythians has taught his love of labor and his philosophy. I myself, though having all men, so to speak, as witnesses of his contests that beggar descrip- tion, am afraid that the narrative may seem to posterity to be a myth totally devoid of truth. For the facts surpass human nature, and men are wont to use nature to measure what is said; if anything is said that lies beyond the limits of nature, the account is judged to be false by those uninitiated into divine things. But since earth and sea are full of pious souls educated in divine things and instructed in the grace of the all-holy Spirit, who will not disbe- lieve what is said but have complete faith in it, I shall make my narration with eagerness and confidence. I shall begin from the point at which he received his call from on high.

2. There is a village lying on the border between our region and Cilicia; they call it Sisa. Originating from this village, he was taught by his parents

[Fig. 10] Symeon Stylites prostrating himself before God (from Hone's *Everyday Book*, Baring-Gould, *Lives of the Saints*, 1).

first to shepherd animals, so that in this respect too he might be comparable to those great men the patriarch Jacob, the chaste Joseph, the lawgiver Moses, the king and prophet David, the prophet Micah and the inspired men of their kind. Once when there was much snow and the sheep were compelled to stay indoors, he took advantage of the respite to go with his parents to the house of God. I heard his sacred tongue recount the following: he told how he heard the Gospel utterance which declares blessed those who weep and mourn, calls wretched those who laugh, terms enviable those who possess a pure soul, and all the other blessings conjoined with them. He then asked one of those present what one should do to obtain each of these. He suggested the solitary life and pointed to that consummate philosophy.

3. Therefore, having received the seeds of the divine word and stored them well in the deep furrows of his soul, he hastened – he said – to a nearby shrine of the holy martyrs. In it he bent his knees and forehead to the ground, and besought the One who wishes to save all men to lead him to the perfect path of piety. After he had spent a long time in this way, a sweet sleep came upon him, and he had the following dream: 'I seemed,' he said, 'to be digging foundations, and then hear someone standing by say that I had to make the trench deeper. After adding to its depth as he told me, I again tried to take a rest; but once more he ordered me to dig and not relax my efforts. After charging me a third and a fourth time to do this, he finally said the depth was sufficient, and told me to build effortlessly from now on, since the effort had abated and the building would be effortless.' This prediction is confirmed by the event, for the facts surpass nature.

4. Getting up from there, he repaired to the dwelling of some neighboring ascetics. After spending two years with them and falling in love with more perfect virtue, he repaired to that village of Teleda which we mentioned above, where the great and godly men Ammianus and Eusebius had pitched their ascetic wrestling-school [monastery]. The inspired Symeon, however, did not enter this one, but another which had sprung from it; Eusebonas and Abibion, having enjoyed sufficiently the teaching of the great Eusebius, had built this retreat of philosophy. Having shared throughout life the same convictions and the same habits, and displayed, as it were, one soul in two bodies, they made many love this life as they did. When they departed from life with glory, the wonderful Heliodorus succeeded to the office of superior over the community. He lived for sixty-five years, and spent sixty-two years immured within; for it was after three years of rearing by his parents that he entered this flock, without ever beholding the occurrences of life. He claimed not even to know the shape of pigs or cocks or the other animals of this kind. I too had often the benefit of seeing him; I admired his simplicity of character and was especially amazed at his purity of soul.

5. After coming to him, this all-round contestant in piety spent ten years contending. He had eighty fellow contestants [monks], and outshot all of them; while the others took food every other day, he would last the whole week without nourishment. His superiors bore this ill and constantly quarreled with it, calling the thing lack of discipline; but they did not persuade him by their words, nor could they curb his zeal. I heard the very man who is now superior of this flock recount how on one occasion Symeon took a cord made from palms – it was extremely rough even to touch with the hands – and girded it round his waist, not wearing it on the outside but making it touch the skin itself. He tied it so tightly as to lacerate in a circle the whole part it went round. When he had continued in this manner for more than ten days and the now severe wound was letting fall drops of blood, someone who saw him asked what was the cause of the blood. When he replied that he had nothing wrong with him, his fellow contestant forcibly inserted his hand, discovered the cause and disclosed it to the superior. Immediately reproaching and exhorting, and inveighing against the cruelty of the thing, he undid the belt, with difficulty, but not even so could he persuade him to give the wound any treatment. Seeing him do other things of the kind as well, they ordered him to depart from this wrestling-school, lest he should be a cause of harm to those with a weaker bodily constitution who might try to emulate what was beyond their powers.

6. He therefore departed, and made his way to the more deserted parts of the mountain. Finding a cistern that was waterless and not too deep, he lowered himself into it, and offered hymnody to God. When five days had passed, the superiors of the wrestling-school had a change of heart, and sent out two men, charging them to look for him and bring him back. So after walking round the mountain, they asked some men tending animals there if they had seen someone of such a complexion and dress. When the shepherds pointed out the cistern, they at once called out several times, and bringing a rope, drew him out with great labor – for ascent is not as easy as descent.

7. After staying with them for a short time, he came to the village of Telanissus, which lies under the hill-top where he now stands; finding a tiny cottage in it, he spent three years as a recluse. In his eagerness to be always increasing his wealth of virtue, he longed to fast forty days without food, like the men of God Moses and Elijah. He urged the wonderful Bassus, who at the time used to make visitations of many villages, as supervisor of the village priests, to leave nothing inside and seal the door with mud. When the other pointed out the difficulty of the thing and urged him not to think suicide a virtue, since it is the first and greatest of crimes, he replied: 'But you then, father, leave me ten rolls and a jar of water; and if I see my body needs nour-

ishment, I shall partake of them.' It was done as he bade. The provisions were left, and the door was sealed with mud. At the end of the forty days, Bassus, this wonderful person and man of God, came and removed the mud; on going in through the door he found the complete number of rolls, he found the jar full of water, but Symeon stretched out without breath, unable either to speak or to move. Asking for a sponge to wet and rinse his mouth, he brought him the symbols of the divine mysteries; and so strengthened by these, he raised himself and took a little food – lettuce, chicory and suchlike plants, which he chewed in small pieces and so passed into the stomach.

8. Overwhelmed with admiration, the great Bassus repaired to his own flock, to recount this great miracle; for he had more than two hundred disciples, whom he ordered to possess neither mounts nor mules, nor to accept offerings of money, nor to go outside the gate whether to buy something necessary or see some friend, but to live indoors and receive the food sent by divine grace. This rule his disciples have preserved to this day. They have not, as they become more numerous, transgressed the injunctions that were given them.

9. But I shall return to the great Symeon. From that time till today – twenty-eight years have passed – he spends the forty days without food. Time and practice have allayed most of the effort. For it was his custom during the first days to chant hymns to God standing, then, when because of the fasting his body no longer had the strength to bear the standing, thereafter to perform the divine liturgy seated, and during the final days actually to lie down – for as his strength was gradually exhausted and extinguished he was compelled to lie half-dead. But when he took his stand on the pillar, he was not willing to come down, but contrived his standing posture differently: it was by attaching a beam to the pillar and then tying himself to the beam with cords that he lasted the forty days. Subsequently, enjoying henceforward still more grace from above, he has not needed even this support, but stands throughout the forty days, not taking food but strengthened by zeal and divine grace.

10. After spending three years, as I said, in this cottage, he repaired to that celebrated hill-top, where he ordered a circular enclosure to be made. After procuring an iron chain of twenty cubits [a cubit is about 50 cm/20 inches], nailing one end to a great rock and fixing the other to his right foot, so that not even if he wished could he go outside these limits, he lived all the time inside, thinking of heaven and compelling himself to contemplate what lies above the heavens – for the iron chain did not hinder the flight of his thought. But when the wonderful Meletius, who had at that time been appointed to supervise the territory of the city of Antioch [as its bishop] and

was a wise man of brilliant intelligence and gifted with shrewdness, told him that the iron was superfluous, since the will was sufficient to impose on the body the bonds of reasoning, he yielded and accepted the advice with compliance: and bidding a smith be called, he told him to sever the chain. When a piece of leather, which had been tied to his leg to prevent the iron injuring his body, had to be torn apart (for it had been sewn together), people saw, they said, more than twenty large bugs lurking in it; and the wonderful Meletius said he had seen this. I myself have mentioned it in order to show from this example as well the endurance of the man: for though he could easily have squeezed the leather with his hand and killed them all, he steadfastly put up with their painful bites, welcoming in small things training for greater contests.

11. As his fame circulated everywhere, everyone hastened to him, not only the people of the neighborhood but also people many days' journey distant, some bringing the paralyzed in body, others requesting health for the sick, others asking to become fathers; and they begged to receive from him what they could not receive from nature. On receiving it and obtaining their requests, they returned with joy; and by proclaiming the benefits they had gained, they sent out many times more, asking for the same things. So with everyone arriving from every side and every road resembling a river, one can behold a sea of men standing together in that place, receiving rivers from every side. Not only do the inhabitants of our part of the world flock together, but also Ishmaelites, Persians, Armenians subject to them, Iberians, Homerites, and men even more distant than these; and there came many inhabitants of the extreme West, Spaniards, Britons, and the Gauls who live between them. Of Italy it is superfluous to speak. It is said that the man became so celebrated in the great city of Rome that at the entrance of all the workshops men have set up small representations of him, to provide thereby some protection and safety for themselves.

12. Since the visitors were beyond counting and they all tried to touch him and reap some blessing from his garments of skins, while he at first thought the excess of honor absurd and later could not abide the wearisomeness of it, he devised the standing on a pillar, ordering the cutting of a pillar first of six cubits, then of twelve, afterwards of twenty-two and now of thirty-six – for he yearns to fly up to heaven and to be separated from this life on earth. I myself do not think that this standing has occurred without the dispensation of God, and because of this I ask fault-finders to curb their tongue and not to let it be carried away at random, but to consider how often the Master has contrived such things for the benefit of the more easy going. He ordered Isaiah to walk naked and barefoot, Jeremiah to put a loin-

cloth on his waist and by this means address prophecy to the unbelieving, and on another occasion to put a wooden collar on his neck and later an iron one, Hosea to take a harlot to wife and again to love a woman immoral and adulterous, Ezekiel to lie on his right side for forty days and on his left for one hundred and fifty, and again to dig through a wall and slip out in flight, making himself a representation of captivity, and on another occasion to sharpen a sword to a point, shave his head with it, divide the hair into four and assign some for this purpose and some for that – not to list everything. The Ruler of the universe ordered each of these things to be done in order to attract, by the singularity of the spectacle, those who would not heed words and could not bear hearing prophecy, and make them listen to the oracles. For who would not have been astounded at seeing a man of God walking naked? Who would not have wanted to learn the cause of the occurrence? Who would not have asked how the prophet could bear to live with a harlot? Therefore, just as the God of the universe ordered each of these actions out of consideration for the benefit of those inured to ease, so too he has ordained this new and singular sight in order by its strangeness to draw all men to look, and to make the proffered exhortation persuasive to those who come – for the novelty of the sight is a trustworthy pledge of the teaching, and the man who comes to look departs instructed in divine things. Just as those who have obtained kingship over men alter periodically the images on their coins, at one time striking representations of lions, at another of stars and angels, and at another try to make the gold piece more valuable by the strangeness of the type, so the universal Sovereign of all things, by attaching to piety like coin-types these new and various modes of life, stirs to eulogy the tongues not only of those nurtured in the faith but also of those afflicted by lack of faith.

13. Words do not testify that these things have this character, but the facts themselves proclaim it; for the Ishmaelites [Arab tribesmen of the Syrian desert], who were enslaved in their many tens of thousands to the darkness of impiety, have been illuminated by his standing on the pillar. For this dazzling lamp, as if placed on a lampstand, has sent out rays in all directions, like the sun. It is possible, as I have said, to see Iberians and Armenians and Persians arriving to receive the benefit of divine baptism. The Ishmaelites, arriving in companies, two or three hundred at the same time, sometimes even a thousand, disown with shouts their ancestral imposture; and smashing in front of this great luminary the idols they had venerated and renouncing the orgies of Aphrodite [perhaps the Syrian goddess Atargatis, sometimes identified with Venus] – it was this demon whose worship they had adopted originally, – they receive the benefit of the divine mysteries, accepting laws from this

sacred tongue and bidding farewell to their ancestral customs, as they disown the eating of wild asses and camels [thus respecting the prohibition in Deut 14:7].

14. I myself was an eyewitness of this, and I have heard them disowning their ancestral impiety and assenting to the teaching of the Gospel. And I once underwent great danger: he told them to come up and receive from me the priestly blessing, saying they would reap the greatest profit therefrom. But they rushed up in a somewhat barbarous manner, and some pulled at me from in front, some from behind, others from the sides, while those further back trod on the others and stretched out their hands, and some pulled at my beard and others grabbed at my clothing. I would have been suffocated by their too ardent approach, if he had not used a shout to disperse them. Such is the benefit that the pillar mocked by lovers of mockery has poured forth; such is the ray of divine knowledge which it has made descend into the minds of barbarians.

15. I know another case of such behavior by these men. One tribe begged the man of God to utter a prayer and blessing for their chieftain; but another tribe that was present objected to this, saying that the blessing ought to be uttered not for him but for their own leader, since the former was extremely unjust while the latter was a stranger to injustice. A long dispute and barbarian quarrel ensued, and finally they went for each other. I myself exhorted them with many words to stay calm, since the man of God had power sufficient to give a blessing to both the one and the other; but these said that man should not get it, while those tried to deprive the other of it. By threatening them from above and calling them dogs, he with difficulty extinguished the dispute. I have told this out of a wish to display the faith in their understanding; for they would not have raged against each other, if they did not believe the blessing of the inspired man to possess the greatest power.

16. On another occasion I witnessed the occurrence of a celebrated miracle. Someone came in – he too was a tribal chieftain of Saracens [the Arab tribesmen] – and begged the godly person to assist a man who on the road had become paralyzed in the limbs of his body; he said he had undergone the attack at Callinicum – it is a very great fort. When he had been brought right to the center, Symeon bade him disown the impiety of his ancestors. When he gladly consented and performed the order, he asked him if he believed in the Father and the only-begotten Son and the Holy Spirit. When the other professed his faith, he said: 'Since you believe in these names, stand up!' When he stood up, he ordered him to carry the tribal chieftain on his shoulders right to his tent, and he was of great bodily size. He at once picked him up and went on his way, while those present stirred their tongues to sing hymns to God.

17. He gave this order in imitation of the Master, who told the paralytic to carry his bed. But let no one call the imitation usurpation, for his is the utterance, 'He who believes in me will himself do the works that I do, and greater than these will he do.' Of this promise we have seen the fulfilment; for while the Lord's shadow nowhere performed a miracle, the shadow of the great Peter canceled death, drove out diseases, and put demons to flight. But it is the Master who through his servants performed these miracles too; and now likewise it is by the use of his name that the godly Symeon performs his innumerable miracles.

18. [This section, the last part of 19 and the final section are interpolations not found in most mss.] It happened that another miracle occurred in no way inferior to the preceding. A not undistinguished Ishmaelite, who was one of those who had found faith in the saving name of Christ the Master, made prayer to God with Symeon as the witness, and a promise as well: the promise was to abstain thereafter till death from all animal food [vegetarianism was a common form of asceticism]. At some time he broke this promise, I know not how, by daring to kill a bird and eat it. But since God chose to bring him to amendment by means of a reproof and to honor his servant [Symeon] who had been the witness of the broken promise, the flesh of the bird was changed in nature to stone, with the result that not even if he wanted to was he now able to eat – for how was it possible, since the body which he had got hold of for eating had been petrified? Astounded by this extraordinary sight, the barbarian repaired to the holy man with great speed, bringing to light his secret sin, proclaiming his transgression to all, asking from God forgiveness for his offence and calling the saint to his aid, that through his all-powerful prayers he might free him from the bonds of sin. Many have been eyewitnesses of this miracle by touching the part of the bird by the breast, which is composed of bone and stone.

19. I have been, not only an eyewitness of his miracles, but also a hearer of his predictions of the future. The drought that occurred, the great crop-failure of that year and the simultaneous famine and plague that followed, he foretold two years beforehand, saying that he had seen a rod threatening mankind and indicating the scourging it would cause. On another occasion he revealed beforehand an attack of what is called the grasshopper, and that it would not cause serious harm, for the mercy of God would follow hard on the punishment. When thirty days had passed a countless swarm so swooped down as to intercept the rays of the sun and create shade; and this we all saw distinctly. But it harmed only the fodder of the irrational animals, while causing no injury to the food of human beings. Also to me, when under attack from someone, he disclosed the death of my enemy fifteen days in advance, and from experience I learnt the truth of his prediction. [The following

interpolation refers to attacks on the Roman Empire in 440-441.] He also saw on one occasion two rods descend from the sky and fall on the land both east and west. The godly man explained it as a rising of the Persian and Scythian nations against the Roman empire; he declared the vision to those present, and with many tears and unceasing prayers stopped the blows with which the world was threatened. Certainly the Persian nation, when already armed and prepared for attack on the Romans, was through the opposition of divine power driven back from the proposed assault and fully engaged in domestic troubles within.

20. Although I know very many other occurrences of this kind, I shall omit them, to avoid length in the account – and the preceding are sufficient to show the spiritual perception of his mind. His reputation is also great with the king of the Persians. As the envoys who came to see Symeon related, he wished to inquire carefully about the man's way of life and the nature of his miracles; and his spouse is said to have asked for oil honored by his blessing and to have received it as a very great gift. All the king's courtiers, struck by his reputation, and despite hearing from the Magians [persecutors of Christians] many calumnies against him, wished to inquire precisely, and on being informed called him a man of God. The rest of the crowd, going up to the muleteers, servants and soldiers, offered them money, begging to receive a share in the blessing attached to the oil.

21. The queen of the Ishmaelites, being sterile and longing for children, first sent some of her highest officials to beg that she become a mother, and then when she obtained her request and gave birth as she had wished, took the prince she had borne and hastened to the godly old man. Since women are not allowed access, she sent the baby to him together with a request to receive blessing from him. 'Yours,' she said, 'is this sheaf; for I brought, with tears, the seed of prayer, but it was you who made the seed a sheaf, drawing down through prayer the rain of divine grace.' But how long shall I strive to measure the depth of the Atlantic ocean? For just as the latter cannot be measured by men, so the daily deeds of this man transcend narration.

22. More than all this I myself admire his endurance. Night and day he is standing within view of all; for having removed the doors and demolished a sizeable part of the enclosing wall, he is exposed to all as a new and extraordinary spectacle – now standing for a long time, and now bending down repeatedly and offering worship to God. Many of those standing by count the number of these acts of worship. Once one of those with me counted one thousand two hundred and forty-four of them, before slackening and giving up count. In bending down he always makes his forehead touch his toes – for his stomach's receiving food once a week, and little of it, enables his back to bend easily.

23. As a result of his standing, it is said that a malignant ulcer has developed in his left foot, and that a great deal of pus oozes from it continually. Nevertheless, none of these afflictions has overcome his philosophy, but he bears them all nobly, both the voluntary and the involuntary, overcoming both the former and the latter by his zeal. He was once obliged to show this wound to someone; I shall recount the cause. Someone arrived from Rabaena, a worthy man, honored with being a deacon of Christ. On reaching the hill-top, he said, 'Tell me, by the truth that has converted the human race to itself, are you a man or a bodiless being?' When those present showed annoyance at the question, Symeon told them all to keep silence, and said to him, 'Why on earth have you posed this question?' He replied, 'I hear everyone repeating that you neither eat nor lie down, both of which are proper to men – for no one with a human nature could live without food and sleep.' At this Symeon ordered a ladder to be placed against the pillar, and told him to ascend and first examine his hands, and then to place his hand inside his cloak of skins and look at not only his feet but also his severe ulcer. After seeing and marveling at the excess of the wound and learning from him that he does take food, he came down from there, and coming to me recounted everything.

24. During the public festivals he displays another form of endurance: after the setting of the sun until it comes again to the eastern horizon, stretching out his hands to heaven he stands all night, neither beguiled by sleep nor overcome by exertion.

25. Despite such labors and the mass of his achievements and the quantity of his miracles, he is as modest in spirit as if he were the last of all men in worth. In addition to his modest spirit, he is extremely approachable, sweet and charming, and makes answer to everyone who addresses him, whether he be artisan, beggar, or peasant. And he has received from the munificent Master the gift also of teaching. Making exhortation two times each day, he floods the ears of his hearers, as he speaks most gracefully and offers the lessons of the divine Spirit, bidding them look up to heaven and take flight, depart from the earth, imagine the expected kingdom, fear the threat of hell, despise earthly things, and await what is to come.

26. He can be seen judging and delivering verdicts that are right and just. These and similar activities he performs after the ninth hour – for the whole night and the day till the ninth hour he spends praying. But after the ninth hour he first offers divine instruction to those present, and then, after receiving each man's request and working some cures, he resolves the strife of those in dispute. At sunset he begins his converse from then on with God.

27. Although engaged in these activities and performing them all, he does not neglect care of the holy churches – now fighting pagan impiety, now

defeating the insolence of the Jews, at other times scattering the bands of the heretics, sometimes sending instructions on these matters to the emperor, sometimes rousing the governors to divine zeal, at other times charging the very shepherds of the churches to take still greater care of their flocks.

28. I have proceeded through all this trying from a drop to indicate the rain, and using my forefinger to give readers of the account a taste of the sweetness of the honey. The facts celebrated by all are many times more numerous than these, but I did not promise to record everything, but to show by a few instances the character of the life of each one. Others, doubtless, will record far more than these; and if he lives on, he will perhaps add greater miracles. I myself desire and beg God that, helped by his own prayers, he may persevere in these good labors, since he is a universal decoration and ornament of piety, and that my own life may be brought into harmony and rightly directed in accordance with the Gospel way of life.

After a further span of life with many miracles and labors – having alone of men of any time remained unconquered by the flames of the sun, the frosts of winter, the fierce blasts of the winds and the weakness of human nature – since he had henceforth to be with Christ and receive the crowns of his immeasurable contests, he proved by his death, to those who disbelieved it, that he is a man. And he remained even after death unshakable, for while his soul repaired to heaven, his body even so could not bear to fall, but remained upright in the place of his contests, like an unbeaten athlete who strives with no part of his limbs to touch the ground. Thus, even after death does victory remain united to the contestants according to Christ. Certainly cures of diseases of every kind, miracles, and acts of divine power are accomplished even now, just as when he was alive, not only at the tomb of the holy relics but also by the memorial of his heroism and long contending – I mean the great and celebrated pillar of this righteous and much-lauded Symeon, – by whose holy intercession we pray both that we ourselves may be preserved and made firm in the true faith, and that every city and country upon which the name of our Lord Jesus Christ is invoked may enjoy protection, untried by every kind of damage and injury from both the sky and their enemies. To Him be glory for ever and ever.

13. A TRANSVESTITE SAINT: MARY/MARINA

The romantic tradition of the disguised female ascetic living as a monk or desert hermit was another dominant image in the biographies of women saints of the fifth and sixth centuries. Though expressly forbidden by scripture (Deut 22.5), the adoption of male clothing may have had its origins in the idea among some Christian sects that male dress signified the adoption of a Christ-like nature and a turning away from the weakness thought to be inherent in the female character. A similar idea may be operating in the final vision of Perpetua (see 3 above). The date and provenance of the story of Marina are uncertain, but similar stories may have been produced by monks living at Scetis in the Egyptian desert, and like them the 'Life' of Marina reflects monastic concerns and biases, especially the monks' preoccupation with sexual temptation. Perhaps partly for this reason her story remained popular and was retold numerous times and in many places throughout the Middle Ages.

Source: trans. Agnes Smith Lewis, *Select Narratives of Holy Women from the Syro-Antiochene or Sinai Palimpsest* (London: C. J. Clay and Sons, Cambridge University Press, 1900), pp. 37-45, revised.

1. Glory and praise and adoration to God the lover of men, he whose door is opened at all times to the repentant; and to him who does not enter, the hindrance is in himself. For God does not reject men as Peter also, the chief of the apostles, says: "Of a truth I have perceived that God is no respecter of persons, but in all nations he who fears him and works righteousness is accepted by him." And Ezekial the prophet: "God says: 'I desire not the death of the wicked' says the Lord of lords, but that he should turn from his wicked way and live.'" And the chosen apostle Paul makes known concerning our Lord, that he wishes every man to repent, saying in the epistle to Timothy, "I entreat you, therefore, that before all things you should offer prayer and supplication and thanksgiving to God on behalf of all men, on behalf of kings and great men, that we may lead a peaceable and quiet life in all godliness and purity." For this is good and acceptable before God our Savior, he who will have all men to be saved, and turn to the knowledge of the truth. For there is one mediator between God and man, our Lord Jesus Christ, he who gave himself as a ransom on behalf of all men. For the door of the house of God is open, as we have said; and every one who will works in the vineyard of righteousness; not only men but also women, must, despite the weakness which attaches to them, enter into the kingdom. Women have been celebrated in all generations, and they have even surpassed men. A few in number will be mentioned by us in this treatise.

2. Miriam the sister of Moses was called a prophetess. She led Israel of old, and by her hands God wrought redemption for Israel. And again by the hand

[Fig. 11] St. Marina and her foster-child (after Cahier; in Baring-Gould, *Lives of the Saints,* 8).

of Judith he delivered them. And Hannah was called the prophetess because of the many years that she sat in the temple of the Lord in holiness until she became worthy to carry the Lord on her arm. By holiness man comes near to God, as the apostle says, "Follow after holiness, without which no man shall see God." By this many women have prospered. One of them was the blessed Mary, who is the subject of the story which we commence. And behold, we begin to narrate the story of her excellent life and her power of endurance, this wonderful blessed one, worthy of praise.

3. There was a certain man in Bithynia, and he had a wife who bore him one only daughter; and he called her Mary. Now after the departure of her mother from this world her father reared her with sedulous teaching, and in honorable life. But when she arrived at full stature, he said to her, "My daughter, behold, everything that I have is given into your hands. For I am going away to care about my soul." But when the girl heard this from her father, she answered and said to him, "Father, you are seeking to save your soul, but to destroy my soul. Do you not know that it was said by our Lord, 'I lay down my life for my sheep?' And again, he said that he who redeems the soul is as he who created it." But when her father had heard these things from her, his love was aroused by her words, the more when he saw her thus weeping and mourning. He spoke thus to her, "My daughter, what is there that I can do for you? You are a woman. I am thinking of entering a monastery, so that I may be removed from the snares of this world, and you, how can you be with us? for the devil will contend with you more readily, and with the servants of God." But when the girl heard this, she returned him an answer, and said, "No sir, I shall not enter the monastery thus as you have said, but I will shave the hair from my head and I will clothe myself in the dress of a man, and then I will enter the monastery with you."

4. Now when he was inclined to be persuaded by the words of his daughter, he distributed and gave everything he possessed to the poor, and he shaved off the hair from the head of his daughter and clothed her, as she had said, in the dress of a man, and changed her name, and called her Marina. Now when all these things were effectually accomplished, he was continually warning her, and saying to her: "Look, my daughter, how you keep yourself. Like straw in the midst of fire, be ready to conduct yourself in the midst of the brethren, and all the more so since no woman has ever entered the monastery. Keep yourself therefore spotless to Christ, that we may finish our confession to him." When he had said these things to her, he led her and entered into the convent.

5. Day by day, as it may be said, this wonderful girl gained the admiration of all, while she was perfect in all virtues, that is to say, in obedience, humil-

ity, and great devotion, with the others. She spent a little while in the monastery. The brothers imagined that she was a eunuch because she had no beard, and also because of the softness of her voice; but others thought that she had hurt herself by too great toils in devotion.

6. Now it happened that her father departed from the world, and she increased the more her deeds, and her obedience and her piety; so that she even received gifts of grace from God, against demons and against various sufferings. And when she placed her hand on the sick, she obtained without delay healing for them by the help of God.

7. Now there were in that convent brothers, holy men, forty in number. And every month four of the brothers were sent on account of the business of the monastery, because there were other monasteries as well as their own, so that they were continually going out visiting and providing for it. Now it happened that there was a certain inn about the middle of the road on which they usually traveled, where those who were sent on the business of the convent entered and lodged. And it was not easy to travel over all the road in a single day. But the innkeeper took them in with great solicitude, serving them well, and gave them a place of refuge apart in the garden.

8. Now on a certain day the abbot called Marina and said to him: "My brother, I am convinced of the sincerity of your life, and I know that you are perfect in it all; namely, in humility and in the sedulousness of your obedience. Turn therefore and go forth on the visiting of the monastery, for even the brothers are perplexed that you are never away on its business. When you do this, and are obedient, and go out, you will receive a yet greater reward from God." And when the humble one heard these things from the abbot, he immediately fell at his feet saying to him: "Pray for me, father, and I will go altogether as you have commanded me."

9. Now when the event occurred, and Marina went forth with three brothers, for the visiting of the monastery, they lodged in the above-mentioned inn. And while they were there it happened that a certain soldier seduced the daughter of the innkeeper, so that she became pregnant by him. And the soldier who did this vile deed said to the daughter of the innkeeper, being instigated by the devil: "If this should become known to your father, say to him: 'That young monk slept with me.'" But day by day she became larger, so that her father became aware that a vile thing had happened to his child. And when he knew it, he demanded it from her hands, and said: "How has this evil happened to you?" Then she threw the blame on Marina, saying: "The monk whom you praise for being holy did this to me, and by him I am with child."

10. Then her father went to the monastery and bursting in, he said:

"Where is the deceitful Christian who you say is holy?" But when one of the superintendents received him, according to their custom, with a greeting, saying to him: "You have done well in coming, brother. What is the matter with you, and why are you so flurried? Tell us what has happened to you," he called out the more, saying, "The hour was an evil one in which I made your acquaintance." But when these things were made known to the abbot, he inquired and was eager to calm the tumult in the heart of the innkeeper, and to learn exactly what the kind of accusation was. But he raised his voice all the more, saying, "May I never again see a monk on the earth!" and many things like these, he said. And when the abbot had interrogated him again, to learn from him what was the reason of the commotion in the business, he [the abbot] said to him, "Tell me, brother, what is the reason of your accusation? so that I also may apologize to you." Then that innkeeper answered and said: "What you request of me I shall tell you. I had one only daughter, with whom I expected my old age to repose, and behold, see what Marina has done to me, he whom you say is blessed. He seduced her and behold! she is with child." But when the abbot had heard these things from him, he was astonished, and said to him, "What can I do for you, my brother, since he is not here, he is away visiting, but nevertheless he is disgraced, so that at his arrival there is nothing for me to do, but to chase him from the monastery."

11. Now when Marina came to the monastery with the three brethren who were with him, the abbot said to him: "Tell me, my brother, are these your manners? is this your piety? is this your humility? Behold, you have disgraced my monastery. This innkeeper came and spoke thus against you. When you lodged in his inn, you seduced his daughter, and, behold! her father has made us a spectacle to the world. Tell me, is this the way in which you confessed Christ? is this your profession? have you shown this way of life to your brothers? is this virtue?"

12. Now when Marina heard these things, he threw himself on his face on the ground, crying out with bitter weeping and with choking tears, and he said to the abbot, "Forgive me, father, for the sake of our Lord, because I have transgressed as a human being." But the abbot, being angry with him, turned him out of the monastery, saying: "Do not enter our monastery again." Then he [Marina] went out of the monastery and sat down outside, enduring the cold and the heat. And those who were going in and out of the monastery inquired of him, saying: "For what cause do you sit outside the door of the monastery?" and he answered, "Because of my sin, for I have committed fornication, and I am driven away from the monastery." But when the time was fulfilled, and the day arrived that the daughter of the innkeeper should give birth, she bore a male child. And the father of the girl took it up

and brought it to the monastery, and when he found Marina sitting outside the door of the monastery, he threw down the baby before him, saying: "Take your son, whom you have wickedly begotten," and he left it with him and went away. Then Marina took up the baby and lamented, saying: "O Lord my God! if I am requited according to my sins, for what reason should this poor baby die here with me?" And Marina, being disturbed in this way, began to bring milk from the shepherds to the baby, that he might rear the boy as its father. But it was not enough for Marina that he had borne this accusation, but the boy stained his clothes with much weeping. And the blessed Marina endured this pain and this grief for three years.

13. Now at the end of three years the brethren took pity on Marina and said to the abbot, "All this indignity has been enough for him, for he confesses his sin before all men. And, moreover, after sitting there for three years, he offers repentance to God, as one who has been led astray by the devil." And when the abbot was not persuaded to receive him, all the brothers spoke, saying: "Unless you will receive him, we also will go forth from the monastery. For we cannot look at him any longer, lying destitute at the door of the monastery, and not take pity on him. We suffer from his distress, and if we did not, how could we implore God about our sins? For we see that, behold, during three years he has been outside the door of the monastery, and he is afflicted and in great want." But when the abbot heard these things he said to them: "Henceforth because of your love I will receive him." And the abbot called Marina and said to him, "You are not worthy ever to enter this monastery because you have spoiled the rule of the monastery by the sin which you have committed. But, nevertheless, on account of the love of the brothers, I will receive you. You shall be the last of them all by the rule of the monastery." But Marina threw himself on the ground and said, "Even that, my lord, will be a great thing for me, that you have deemed me worthy to enter within the door of the monastery. For whereas I transgressed and committed fornication, at least thus while I serve the holy fathers, I may become worthy by means of their prayers of a little forgiveness for what I have done amiss."

14. And after all these things the abbot set him to the ignominious tasks of the monastery. And he fulfilled them with great assiduity. But he called to the boy and he followed him and he wept and cried, "Father, father," with the rest of the things that children have to ask for [such as] their food. But the alms which Marina acquired were not sufficient to feed the boy; he was in great distress because of his nourishment. And when the boy before him attained to full stature, he conducted himself in the monastery with the assiduity of a high order of excellence. For no man remains in the initial

childhood (of mind) in which he is born. But as he is taught he grows up, and this boy became worthy of the monastic garb.

15. But after a little while on a certain day the abbot asked the brethren saying, "Where is Marina? For lo! I have not seen him for three days at the offering." (For he was always found there before every one else at the service). "Go, therefore, into his cell, and see if perchance he is in some sickness." And when the brothers entered, they found him dead. And they told it to the abbot, saying: "Poor Marina is asleep." Then he said: "How is that? How did his poor soul depart? What excuse did he make before God?" And when the abbot had said these things, he commanded that they should dress him. But when the brethren went to dress him, according to the commandment of the abbot, they found that he was a woman. And when they saw her, their limbs became weak, and the light of their eyes was troubled. And immediately when they had rested a little, they began crying, "*Kyrie eleison*" [Lord, have mercy]. But the abbot, when he heard the sound of the crying, inquired in order that he might learn what was the reason of their cry. And they said to him, "Brother Marina is a woman." And when he came and saw her, he was seized with great amazement also, at what endurance she had possessed; and he fell on his face on the ground, and cried with choking tears, saying, "Forgive me: I have sinned against God and against you. I will die here before your holy feet until I receive forgiveness for my sins which I committed against you." And he said other things like these, and more than these, lying on his face at the feet of the saint, with sobs and with weeping for three days. But at the end of three days, a voice came to him, saying: "If you had done these things intentionally to me, this sin would not have been forgiven you. But, nevertheless, the sin is forgiven you, because you committed it unwittingly."

16. Then when the abbot rose from before the feet of the saint, he sent for the innkeeper and they brought him. And when he came the abbot said to him: "Behold, poor Marina is dead." But when the innkeeper heard it, he answered and said: "God forgive him! for he disgraced my house." Then the abbot said to him: "May God forgive you, because you have troubled me also and my monastery. Do not remain henceforth in sin, but repent. For you have sinned before God, and have also made me sin. You incited me with your words and I sinned because of your fault. For although Marina's knowledge and her dress were those of a man, by nature she was a woman." But when the innkeeper heard that she was a woman, he was amazed and was seized with astonishment at these things which were said, and he still remained incredulous. Then the abbot led him by the hand and showed him his unbelief, what he had said to him. Then the innkeeper also began with

many tears to confess his sin, which he had committed unwittingly.

17. And while this commotion was going on, they dressed her sacred body, and laid her in an honorable place with a beautiful service, and with much glory inside of the monastery, and they praised God who had endowed her with such endurance. But at the conclusion of all these things came the daughter of the innkeeper, worried by a demon; and she confessed all the truth, saying, "It was a soldier who committed this impurity with me and made me pregnant, and advised me to wrong the handmaid of God, and the monastery." And while the girl said these things, she was cured [of being possessed by the demon] without delay by the grace of the holy Mary. And they all praised our Lord for the occurrence and for the sign that had happened, he who has given such endurance to those who love him that she persevered thus until death and never revealed herself to any one as a woman.

May we also, my beloved ones, emulate in perseverance and in endurance the manly woman, so that our Lord may give us grace and mercy with her and the portion of the saints in the fearful day of judgment, by our Lord Jesus Christ, to whom with his Father and his living and Holy Spirit be glory and honor and adoration for ever and ever.

CHAPTER THREE

BISHOPS, MONKS AND NUNS

With the spread of monasticism from the Mediterranean world into Gaul and the eventual Christianization of northern Europe, the predominant model of sanctity continued to be that of the confessor who bore witness to the Faith by a life of heroic virtue. However, sanctity now became increasingly the domain of the clergy. The greatest number of saints came from the ranks of the Church, and included particularly bishops, abbots, and abbesses. One reason for the predominance of high-ranking clergy was that positions of power both offered more opportunity for heroic virtue, and also made that virtue more visible to the community, whose veneration might decide whether or not a successful cult developed. However, the qualities of wise administrator had to be linked with a commitment to solitary asceticism. The hagiographers attributed to bishops like Martin and abbots like Maiol and Gall a strong reluctance to take up office, although inevitably they succumbed to entreaties and went on to wage spiritual warfare against deficient monks and backsliding or tyrannical secular rulers. The cult of saints was a vital instrument in the conversion of northern tribes, and although cloistered saints were less likely to be known to the laity, their cults were carefully promoted and preserved in their own monastic houses.

[Fig. 12] The 'life' of St. Martin, told on a thirteenth-century tapestry in the Louvre (Lacroix, *Military and Religious Life in the Middle Ages,* p. 281). Reading from the top left, it shows the famous scene of Martin sharing his cloak with the beggar (1-2); his baptism (3); his restoration of the catechumen at Ligugé and of a slave (4-5); his consecration as Bishop of Tours; various miracles, including exorcism (7-10); his analogy between the birds of prey and fiends of hell (11); his death (12).

14. MARTIN OF TOURS

Sulpicius Severus, author of the 'Life of St. Martin of Tours,' was born in Aquitaine in south-eastern Gaul. He had received a classical education and was trained as a lawyer, but when his wife died prematurely, he retired to his country estate (about 392) and, influenced by his friend Paulinus of Nola, adopted the combined roles of Christian ascetic and man of letters. In about 394 he visited St. Martin at Tours, an encounter that affected him deeply and inspired him to publish the 'life' shortly before Martin's death in 397. The account is dominated by Sulpicius's ideal of the bishop-monk who combines asceticism with involvement in the busy affairs of men, particularly expunging continuing practices of paganism in Gaul. Archaeological evidence does suggest the presence of important pagan cults in the areas cited by Sulpicius, and even their destruction at about the time Martin would have been engaged in his prohibited activities. But Sulpicius does not tell us a number of things we would like to know about Martin, such as his interactions with his strife-ridden fellow-bishops in Gaul, especially over the condemnation and execution of the rebel Spanish bishop Priscillian (though he does explore this issue somewhat in a later work, the 'Dialogues,' c.404). The 'Life of St. Martin' was to have great influence on later medieval hagiographers, as well as on the cult of the saint. Largely on the basis of this work and its fame, the Merovingians adopted Martin as their chief patron saint and, nearly a hundred years after his death, commissioned an impressive new church at Tours in his honor to serve as a center for pilgrimages. Sulpicius's hagiography was held up as a prime example of elegant style in a genre previously admired more for Christian content than graceful writing. As indicated in the prologue and Sulpicius's letters, two of which are included here, he was well aware of his reputation as a writer and anxious that the 'life' should add to it. Nevertheless, the 'life' does seem to have been inspired by his genuine devotion to the saint, and by a desire to be even more closely connected to him after his death than perhaps he was in his lifetime.

Source: trans. Rev. Alexander Roberts, *The Life of St. Martin,* in *A Select Library of Nicene and Post-Nicene Fathers of the Christian Church,* ed. Philip Schaff and Henry Wace (New York: The Christian Literature Company; Oxford and London: Parker and Co., 1890), 11, pp. 3-23, modernized and revised against the Latin text edited by Jacques Fontaine, *Vie de Saint Martin* (Paris: Du Cerf, 1967), I, pp. 248-345. BHL 5610.

Severus to his dearest brother, Desiderius [a monastic friend]:

1. I had decided, brother and soul-mate, to keep hidden in its pages and confined within the walls of my own house the little book which I had written concerning the life of St. Martin. For I am by nature very weak, and wished

to avoid human judgment, lest my somewhat unpolished style should displease my readers (as I think it will), and I should be found worthy of rebuke by everyone for having the audacity to take up a subject which ought to have been reserved for truly eloquent writers. But I have not been able to refuse your request which you have repeated so often. For what could there be which I would not do for your love, even at the risk of my own humiliation? However, I have submitted the book to you trusting that you will reveal it to no one else, since you have promised this. Nevertheless, I do have fears that you will serve as its doorway to the world; and I well know that, once out, it can never be recalled. If this happens, and you see it being read by others, you will kindly ask the readers to take into account the content rather than the language, and to be patient if by chance the style afflicts their ears, because the kingdom of God rests not on eloquence, but upon faith. Let them also remember that salvation was preached to the world not by orators (although certainly if it had been an advantage, the Lord could have made use of that too) but by fishermen. As for me, indeed, when I first felt impelled to write what follows (because I thought it disgraceful that the virtues of so great a man should remain hidden), I resolved in my own mind not to feel ashamed of solecisms: for I had never acquired any great knowledge of such things, and if I had once by chance had a smattering of those studies, I had lost it all over time through neglect. But nevertheless, in order to avoid the need for such an annoying form of self-defence in future, if you think it right, let the book be published but suppress the author's name. In order to do this, kindly erase the title which the book bears on its front, so that the page may be silent; and (for it is quite enough) let the book proclaim its subject-matter, not its author.

Preface

1. Many human beings who have devoted themselves to the vain pursuit of worldly glory believe they have immortalized their own names by writing about the lives of famous men. This plan, although it did not secure for them a lasting reputation, still has undoubtedly brought them a little of the fruits of the hope they cherished, since both by preserving their own memory (though to no purpose), and by having presented to the world examples of great men, they have aroused a considerable imitation among their readers. But their concerns had nothing to do with the blessed and eternal life hereafter. For how does the glory of their writings, destined to perish with the world, profit them? Or what benefit has posterity derived from reading of the battles of Hector or the philosophical treatises of Socrates? Not only is it

foolish to imitate them, but it is absolute madness not to attack them as fiercely as possible, for in truth, those persons who estimate the worth of human life only by present actions have delivered up their hopes to fables, and their souls to the tomb. In fact, they have entrusted the task of perpetuating themselves to the sole memory of mortals, whereas it is the duty of humankind rather to seek after eternal life than an eternal memorial, and not by writing, or fighting, or philosophizing, but by living a pious, holy, and religious life. This human error, transmitted in literature, has prevailed to such an extent that it has found many who emulate either empty philosophy or foolish heroism.

For this reason, I think I will accomplish something well worth the necessary trouble if I write the life of a most holy man, which will serve in future as an example to others, and which indeed will arouse the readers to pursue true knowledge, heavenly warfare, and divine virtue. In so doing, I have regard also to my own interests, so that I may look for no empty remembrance among men, but an eternal reward from God. For, although I myself have not lived in such a way as to be an example to others, nevertheless, I have made it my task to bring out of obscurity one who deserves to be imitated. I shall therefore set about writing the life of St. Martin, and shall narrate both what he did before he became a bishop, and what he accomplished as a bishop. At the same time, I cannot hope to set down all that he was or did. Those excellences of which he alone was aware are completely unknown, because he did not seek for honor from men but desired, as much as he could, to hide all his virtues. And I have even omitted many of the facts known to me, because I believe it is enough to record the most striking and important ones. At the same time, I had to consider the interests of readers, in case they should be averse to an excessive number of incidents. But I implore those who are to read what follows to give complete faith to the things narrated, and to believe that I have written nothing of which I did not have certain knowledge and evidence. I should, in fact, have preferred to be silent rather than to narrate things which are false.

2. Martin, then, was born at Sabaria in Pannonia [modern Hungary], but was brought up at Ticinum [Pavia] which is situated in Italy. In terms of worldly dignity, his parents were not of the lowest rank, but they were pagans. His father was at first simply a soldier, but afterwards a military tribune. He himself took up a military career while a youth and was enrolled in the imperial guard, first under king Constantine, and then under the Caesar Julian. This, however, was not done of his own free will, for, almost from the earliest years of his holy childhood, this distinguished boy aspired rather to the service of God. For, when he was ten years old, against the wish of his

parents, he fled to a church, and begged to become a catechumen [to begin instruction in Christianity]. Soon afterwards, in a wonderful manner he became completely devoted to the work of God, and when he was twelve years old, he longed for a life in the desert [to become a hermit]; and he would have made the necessary vows, if his youthfulness had not been an obstacle. His mind, however, was always intent upon hermitages or the Church, and already meditated in his boyish years on what he later fulfilled as a religious. But since an edict was issued by the rulers of the state that the sons of veterans should be enrolled for military service, his father (who grudged his pious behavior) delivered him up when he was fifteen years old, and he was arrested and put in chains and was bound by the military oath. He was content with only one servant as his attendant, and then, reversing roles, the master waited on the servant to such a degree that, for the most part, it was he who pulled off his [servant's] boots and he who cleaned them with his own hand; and while they took their meals together, it was he who more often served them. For nearly three years before his baptism, he was a professional soldier, but he kept completely free from those vices in which that class of men become too frequently involved. He showed great kindness towards his fellow-soldiers, and wonderful affection, and his patience and humility surpassed what seemed possible to human nature. There is no need to praise the self-denial which he displayed: it was so great that, even at that date, he was regarded not so much as being a soldier as a monk. By all these qualities he had so endeared himself to the whole body of his comrades, that they held him in extraordinary affection. Although not yet regenerated in Christ, by his good works he acted the part of a candidate for baptism. This he did, for instance, by aiding those who were in trouble, by giving help to the wretched, by supporting the needy, by clothing the naked, while he reserved nothing for himself from his military pay except what was necessary for his daily sustenance. Even then, far from being a senseless hearer of the Gospel, he took no thought for the morrow.

3. So it happened one day when he had nothing except his weapons and his simple military dress, in the middle of a winter which had been very bitter and more severe than usual, so that the extreme cold had caused the death of many, he chanced to meet at the gate of the city of Amiens a poor naked man. He [the beggar] was entreating the passers-by to have pity on him, but all passed the wretched man without notice, when Martin, that man full of God, recognized that the beggar to whom others showed no pity was reserved for him. But what should he do? He had nothing except the cloak in which he was dressed, for he had already parted with the rest of his garments for similar purposes. Taking, therefore, his sword which he was wear-

ing, he divided his cloak in half, and gave one part to the beggar, and clothed himself again with what was left. At this, some of the bystanders laughed, because he was now an unsightly object in his mutilated clothing. Many, however, who were of sounder understanding, regretted deeply that they themselves had done nothing similar. They especially felt this because, possessing more than Martin, they could have clothed the poor man without reducing themselves to nakedness.

The following night while he slept Martin had a vision of Christ wearing the part of his cloak with which he had clothed the beggar. He was told to regard the Lord with the greatest care, and to recognize [the Lord's] robe as his own. Before long, he heard Jesus saying in a clear voice to the multitude of angels standing round, "Martin, who is still only a catechumen, clothed me with this robe." Truly the Lord remembered his own words, which he had spoken [while on earth]: "Inasmuch as ye have done these things to one of the least of these, ye have done them unto me," when he declared that he himself had been clothed in that beggar; and he confirmed the testimony he bore to such a good deed by condescending to show himself in that very garment which the beggar had received.

After this vision the sainted man was not puffed up with vain glory, but he acknowledged the goodness of God in his own action, and as he was now twenty years old he rushed off to receive baptism. However, he did not immediately retire from military service, but gave into the entreaties of his tribune, whom he served as one of his private staff. For the tribune promised that, after his term of office had expired, he too would retire from the world. Martin was held back by this expectation, and continued to act the part of a soldier (although only in name) for nearly two years after he had received baptism.

4. In the meantime, the barbarians were invading the two divisions of Gaul, and Caesar brought an army together at the city of Worms, and began to distribute a donative [bonus] to the soldiers. As the custom was, they were called forward, one by one, until it came to Martin's turn. Then, indeed, thinking it a good time to ask for his discharge – for he did not think it would be proper for him to receive a donative, if he did not intend to continue as a soldier – he said to Caesar, "Until now I have served you as a soldier: permit me now to be a soldier for God. Let the man who is to fight for you receive your donative; I am a soldier of Christ: it is not lawful for me to fight." Then the tyrant began to rage at what he said, declaring that [Martin] was withdrawing from military service from fear of the battle which was to take place the next day, and not from any religious motive. But Martin, full of courage, and all the more resolute in the face of this attempt at intimidation,

said, "If this is attributed to cowardice and not to faith, tomorrow I will confront the battle-line unarmed, and in the name of the Lord Jesus, protected by the sign of the cross and not by shield or helmet, I will advance unharmed into the ranks of the enemy." Then he was ordered to be thrown back into prison, so that he might keep his promise by exposing himself unarmed to the barbarians. But the next day, the enemy sent ambassadors to negotiate peace, surrendering themselves and everything they possessed. From these circumstances, who can doubt that this victory was indeed due to the saintly man? For it was granted him that he should not be sent unarmed into battle. And although the good Lord could have preserved his own soldier even from the swords and spears of the enemy, yet he removed all necessity for fighting so that [Martin's] blessed eyes might not have to witness the death of others. For Christ was not bound to present any victory on behalf of his own soldier other than subduing the enemy without bloodshed or the death of anyone.

5. After leaving military service, [Martin] sought out blessed Hilary, bishop of the city of Poitiers whose proven faith in the things of God was highly regarded, and he stayed with him for some time. Now, this same Hilary did his best to attach [Martin] more closely to him by conferring on him the office of deacon, thereby binding him to the divine ministry. But when he constantly refused, claiming that he was unworthy, Hilary, who was a man of deep understanding, saw that he could only be constrained in one way, that is by being given the sort of office which seemed to be somewhat humiliating to him. He therefore appointed him to be an exorcist. Martin did not refuse this appointment, for he did not want to appear to look down on it because it was somewhat humble. Not long after this, he was told in a dream to visit his homeland and his parents from concern for their religion, for they were still held back by paganism. He set out with the full consent of the holy Hilary, who made him promise, with many prayers and tears, that he would return. According to report, Martin undertook the journey sadly, after calling the brothers as witnesses that many sufferings lay before him. The result fully justified this prediction.

For, first of all, having lost his way in the Alps, he fell into the hands of outlaws. One of them lifted up his axe and poised it above Martin's head, when another held back the hand which was about to strike; nevertheless, with his hands tied behind his back, [Martin] was handed over to one of them to be guarded and stripped. The outlaw, having led him further away, began to ask him who he was. Martin replied that he was a Christian. The outlaw next asked him whether he was afraid. Then Martin, full of courage, replied that he had never felt safer, because he knew that the mercy of the Lord would be especially present with him in the midst of trials. He added

[Fig. 13] The baptism of Martin by St. Hilary, and the Devil appearing to Martin in human form on the road from Milan, pictured in a window in the church of St. Florentin, Yonne, c. 1528 (Baring-Gould, *Lives of the Saints*, 13).

that he grieved rather for the man who held him captive, since he was unworthy of the mercy of Christ because he was a thief.

And then Martin began to expound the Scripture, and he preached the word of God to the outlaw. Why make a long tale of it? The outlaw believed; and he accompanied Martin back and sent him once more on his way, entreating him to pray to the Lord for him. Afterwards that same outlaw was seen to lead a religious life; so that, in fact, the narrative I have related is based on his own account.

6. Martin, then, continuing on his way, had passed Milan when the Devil met him on the road in human form and asked him where he was going. Martin replied that he was going where the Lord called him, and the Devil said to him, "Wherever you go, or whatever you attempt, the Devil will resist you." Then Martin in the words of the prophet replied, "The Lord is my helper; I will not fear what man can do to me." At once his enemy vanished from his sight. And so, just as he had planned and intended, he freed his mother from the error of paganism, though his father continued in its evil ways. However, he saved many by his example.

After this, when the Arian heresy [which denied the full divinity of Christ, and had been condemned at the Council of Nicaea in 325] had spread through the whole world and especially into Illyria [the Dalmatian coast, roughly modern Croatia], and when, almost singlehandedly, he was fighting most strenuously against the treachery of the priests, and was often punished – for not only was he publicly whipped, but finally he was compelled to leave the city – he made for Italy again. There he found that in the two divisions of Gaul the departure of holy Hilary, driven into exile by the strength of the heretics, had thrown the Church into turmoil, and so he established a monastery for himself at Milan. There, too, Auxentius, the originator and leader of the Arians, bitterly persecuted him, and after inflicting many injuries upon him drove him out of the city. Thinking, therefore, that it was necessary to submit to circumstances, he withdrew to an island called Gallinaria with a priest, a man of great virtue, as his companion. Here he existed for some time on the roots of plants. While doing so, he ate hellebore, which is said to be poisonous. But when he felt the strength of the poison increasing within him, and was at the point of death, he warded off the imminent danger through prayer and at once all his pain disappeared. Not long afterwards, having discovered that the king had repented and had granted holy Hilary permission to return, he attempted to meet him at Rome and set out for that city.

7. As Hilary had already left, Martin followed in his footsteps to Poitiers; and after he had been most joyfully welcomed by him, he established for himself a monastery not far from the town [Ligugé]. At this time he was joined by a certain catachumen who wished to have instruction in the teachings of the most holy man. Only a few days later, however, the catechumen fell suddenly ill, suffering from a high fever. It so happened that Martin was then away from home. He was absent for three days, and on his return he found the lifeless body; and death had been so sudden, that he had left this world without receiving baptism. The body had been laid out in public, and the grieving brethren were visiting it as their sad duty required, when Martin hurried up, weeping and lamenting. But with his soul completely filled with the Holy Spirit, he ordered the others to leave the cell in which the body was lying; and bolting the door, he stretched himself at full length on the dead limbs of the departed brother. After he had stayed lying there for some time in prayer, and had become aware through the Spirit that the power of God was present, he rose up for a short time, and fixing his gaze on the dead man's face he waited with confidence for the result of his prayer and the mercy of the Lord. And after scarcely two hours had passed he saw the dead man begin to move all his limbs little by little, and his eyes trembling and blinking as he recovered his sight. Then indeed he raised a loud voice to the Lord and gave thanks, filling the cell with cries. Hearing the noise, those who had been standing at the door immediately rushed inside. And truly a marvelous spectacle met them, for they beheld the man alive whom they had left for dead.

Thus restored to life, he immediately received baptism and lived for many years afterwards; and he was the first one among us to give both substantial proof of Martin's virtues and to testify to them. He often related that, when he left the body, he was brought before the tribunal of the Judge [God], and had a dismal sentence pronounced on him which relegated him to the dark places among the crowd of common men. Then, however, he added, it was suggested by two angels of the Judge that he was the man for whom Martin was praying; and so the same angels were ordered to lead him back and to give him to Martin, and restore him to his former life. From this time forward, the name of the blessed man became famous, so that he was treated as if he were already a saint by everyone, and was also held to be powerful and a true apostle.

8. Not long afterwards, while Martin was passing by the estate of a certain man named Lupicinus, who was held in high esteem by everyone, he was greeted with shouting and the lamentations of a wailing crowd. He approached with concern and asked the cause of the weeping, and was told that one of the slaves of the family had put an end to his life by hanging himself. Hearing this, Martin entered the little room in which the body was lying, and, sending the whole crowd outside, he stretched himself upon the body, and prayed for a short time. Before long the dead man began to revive, his face grew animated and his drooping eyes were fixed on Martin's face; he made a slow effort to rise, and then he took hold of the saintly man's hand and stood up. In this way, while the whole crowd looked on, he walked along with Martin to the porch of the house.

9. At about the same time, Martin was sought after to be bishop of the church at Tours but when he could not easily be persuaded to leave his monastery, a certain Rusticius, one of the citizens, pretended that his wife was ill, and by throwing himself down at [Martin's] knees, prevailed on him to leave. A crowd of citizens had previously been posted along the road on which he traveled, and in this way he was escorted to the city as if under guard. In an amazing manner, an incredible number of people not only from that town but also from the neighboring cities had assembled to give their votes. They all had only the same wish, the same desire, the same opinion: that Martin was most worthy of being bishop, and that the Church would be happy with such a priest.

A few impious persons, however, including some of the bishops who had been summoned to appoint the prelate, resisted, asserting strongly that Martin's person was contemptible, that he was unworthy of being a bishop, that he was despicable in appearance, his clothing was shabby and his hair disgusting. This madness of theirs was ridiculed by people of sounder judgment, since even while they attempted to slander him they were proclaiming his extraordinary merits. And in truth, they were not allowed to do anything other than what the people wished for, in accordance with Divine will.

Among the bishops who were there, however, his principal opponent is reported to have been a certain person named Defender; and it was observed that on this occasion he was severely censured by a reading from the prophets. For it happened that the reader whose duty it was to give the reading that day had been stopped by the people and was not there. The officials fell into confusion while they waited for the one who had not come, and one of the bystanders took up the Psalter and seized upon the first verse that he found. Now, the words of the Psalm were these: "Out of the mouth of babes and sucklings thou hast perfected praise because of thine enemies, that thou mightest destroy the enemy and the avenger." With the reading of these words, a shout went up from the people, and the opposition was confounded. It was believed that this Psalm had been chosen by the will of God, so that Defender might hear testimony concerning his own actions, because the praise of the Lord was perfected from the mouths of babes and nursing infants in the case of Martin, while at the same time the enemy was both revealed and destroyed.

10. And now it is beyond my power to describe completely what Martin was like after he became bishop, and how he distinguished himself. For with the utmost constancy he remained the same as he had been before. There was the same humility in his heart, and the same simplicity of clothing. Filled with both authority and courtesy, he kept up the position of a bishop properly, yet in such a way as not to abandon the life and virtues of a monk. For some time he lived in a cell adjacent to the church; but afterwards, when he could not tolerate the disturbance caused by the numbers of visitors, he established a monastery for himself about two miles outside the city.

This spot [Marmoutier] was so hidden and remote that he no longer had to wish for the solitude of a hermit. For on one side it was surrounded by the steep rock of a high mountain, while the rest of the land had been enclosed in a gentle curve of the Loire river; there was only one means of access, and that was very narrow. Here, then, he inhabited a cell built of wood, and a great number of the brothers were housed in the same fashion, but most of them had made themselves shelters by hollowing caves out of the overhanging rock. There were about eighty disciples who were instructed by the example of their holy master. There, no one possessed anything of his own; everything was held in common. No one was allowed either to buy or to sell anything, as is the custom among many monks. No art was practiced there, except that of the scribes, and even this was assigned to the younger brothers while the elder spent their time in prayer. It was rare for any of them to leave his cell, except to gather at the place of prayer. After a period of fasting was over, they all ate their meals together. No one used wine, except when illness compelled them to do so. Most of them wore garments of camel's hair; softer clothing was considered a serious fault there. This must be considered all the more remarkable, because many of them were considered to be of high rank, brought up in a very different fashion, and yet they had forced themselves to accept humility and patience; and we have seen many of these afterwards made bishops. For what city or church would not want a priest from the monastery of Martin?

11. But let me go on to describe the other virtues which Martin displayed as a bishop. Very close to the monastery, not far from the town, there was a place which was thought to be holy because of a popular superstition that some martyrs had been buried together there. For there was also an altar which was believed to have been placed there by former bishops. But Martin did not easily put his faith in uncertainties, and often asked the older priests and clerks to tell him the name of the martyr, or the time when he suffered. He did so, he said, because he was very scrupulous about these issues, since no steady tradition concerning them had come down from antiquity.

Therefore for some time he kept away from the place, not disparaging the cult (because he was still uncertain), but at the same time not lending his authority to the opinion of the masses, lest superstition should increase. Then one day he went out to the place, taking a few brothers with him as companions. There standing above the very sepulcher, Martin prayed to the Lord to reveal who the entombed man was, and what his merits were. Then, turning to the left, he saw standing close by a foul, ferocious ghost. Martin commanded him to reveal his name and nature. He declared his name, and confessed his guilt. He said that he had been a thief, and that he was beheaded for his crimes; that he had been venerated mistakenly by the people; that he had nothing in common with the martyrs, for glory was their reward while his was punishment. Marvelous to relate, those who were present heard the speaker's voice but saw no one. Then Martin revealed what he had seen, and ordered the altar which had been there to be removed, and thus he freed the people from that superstitious error.

12. It happened not long afterwards while Martin was going on a journey that he met the body of a pagan that was being carried to the tomb with superstitious funeral rites. Seeing from a distance a crowd approaching, and not knowing what it was about, he stood still for a little while. For there was nearly half a mile between him and the crowd, so that it was difficult to make out what he was seeing. Nevertheless, because he saw it was a group of peasants, when the linen cloths covering the body were blown about by the wind, he believed that some profane sacrificial rites were being performed. For it was the custom among the peasants of Gaul in their wretched madness

to carry about through the fields the images of demons covered with a white veil.

Therefore he raised the sign of the cross against them and commanded the crowd not to move from the place where they were and to put down what they were carrying. At this, wonderful to relate, you might have seen the wretched creatures first become as rigid as rocks. Next, when they tried with a great effort to move forward, but were not able to take a step farther, they began to whirl themselves about in the most ridiculous fashion until they were defeated and had to put down the dead body. They were thunderstruck and looked at each other, silently wondering what had happened to them. But when the saintly man discovered that the peasants were simply performing funeral rites, and not sacrifices, with raised hand he gave them back the power of leaving and of lifting up the body. Thus when he wished, he made them stand still, and when he pleased, he let them go.

13. On another occasion, in a certain village he demolished a very ancient temple, and set about cutting down a pine-tree that stood close to the temple. The chief priest of that place and a crowd of other pagans began to oppose him. And although these people had, at the Lord's command, been quiet while the temple was being destroyed, they could not endure the cutting-down of the tree. Martin carefully impressed upon them that there was nothing sacred in the trunk of a tree, and urged them instead to honor God whom he himself served; the tree had to be cut down because it was dedicated to a demon.

Then one of them who was bolder than the others said, "If you have any trust in your God, whom you say you worship, we ourselves will cut down this tree, and you stand in its path; for if, as you say, your Lord is with you, you will not be hurt." Then Martin, courageously trusting in the Lord, promised to do so. Upon this, all that crowd of pagans agreed to the condition; for they held the loss of their tree a small matter, so long as they got the enemy of their religion buried under its fall. Since that pine-tree was leaning to one side, so that there could be no question as to which way it would fall when it was cut, Martin was bound to the spot where the tree would certainly fall, as the pagans had stipulated.

Then they began to cut down their own tree, with great delight and rejoicing. A wondering crowd stood some distance away. Little by little the pine-tree began to shake, and, on the point of falling, threatened its own ruin. The monks at a distance grew pale and, terrified by the approaching danger, they lost all hope and faith, expecting only Martin's death. But he, trusting in the Lord, waited courageously, even as the falling pine made a cracking noise, even as it was falling and as it rushed down upon him: simply lifting his hand against it, he held up the sign of salvation. Then, indeed –

[Fig. 14] A fifth-century bas-relief from Pérouse showing the exorcism of a catechumen by four of the clergy, who are holding crosses over him to drive the Devil out of his body (Lacroix, *Military and Religious Life in the Middle Ages,* p. 212).

you would have thought it driven back like a spinning top – it swept round to the opposite side, so that it almost crushed the peasants, who had stood in what seemed to be a safe spot.

Then a shout went up to heaven: the pagans were amazed by the miracle while the monks wept for joy, and the name of Christ was proclaimed by them all together. And as it is well known, on that day salvation came to that region. For there was hardly one of that huge crowd of pagans who did not long for the laying-on of hands [to become a catechumen] and, abandoning their impious errors, they believed in the Lord Jesus. Certainly, before Martin's time, very few, indeed hardly any in those regions had received the name of Christ. Through his virtues and example that name has prevailed to such an extent that now there is no region that is not filled either with crowded churches or monasteries. For wherever he destroyed pagan temples, there immediately he used to build either churches or monasteries.

14. At about the same time and in the same work he showed similar virtue. For when he set fire in a certain village to a very ancient and famous temple, the encompassing flames were carried by the wind to a house which was nearby, in fact connected to the temple. When Martin became aware of this, climbing rapidly he scaled the roof of the house, and posted himself in front of the advancing flames. Then an amazing event took place: you could have seen the fire thrust back against the force of the wind, so that the elements seemed to be fighting against each other. Thus through Martin's power the fire only acted in the place where it was ordered to do so.

In another village called Levroux, Martin wished in a similar way to overthrow a temple which had become very wealthy because of superstitious belief, and a crowd of pagans resisted him to such a degree that he was driven back and did not escape injury. So he withdrew to a place close by. There for three days, clothed in a hair shirt and ashes, he continued to fast and pray, and besought the Lord that as he had not been able to overthrow that temple by human effort, Divine power might destroy it. Then suddenly two angels armed with spears and shields like heavenly warriors appeared to him, saying that they were sent by the Lord to put the mob of peasants to flight, and to give protection to Martin in case anyone should resist while the temple was being destroyed. They told him to return and complete the blessed work which he had begun. And so Martin returned to the village; and while the crowd of pagans looked on in silence, he destroyed the heathen temple down to its foundations and reduced all the altars and images to dust. When they saw this the peasants understood that divine power had struck them with astonishment and terror so that they could not fight against the bishop, and almost all of them believed in the Lord Jesus; and they began to cry out openly and to confess that they ought to worship the God of Martin and despise the idols which were of no help to them.

15. I shall also relate what took place in a village of the Edui [near Autun]. When Martin went there to destroy a temple, a furious crowd of pagan peasants rushed upon him. And when one of them, bolder than the rest, drew his sword and made to attack him, Martin threw back his cloak and bared his neck to the one about to deliver the blow. The pagan did not hesitate to strike, but when he had raised his hand up high, he fell to the ground on his back and, overwhelmed by the fear of God, he begged for mercy. Another event, similar to this, occurred. When a certain man decided to wound him with a knife as he was destroying some idols, at the very moment of delivering the blow, the weapon was struck from his hands and disappeared. Very often, too, when the pagans objected to the overthrow of their temples, [Martin's] holy speech so calmed their hearts that, once the light of truth had been revealed to them, they destroyed their temples themselves.

16. The grace of effecting cures was so powerful in [Martin] that scarcely any sick person came to him who did not at once recover health. The following example will make this clear. At Trèves a certain girl was seized by a paralysis so terrible that for a long time she was unable to make use of her body for any of the normal purposes, and she was, so to speak, already almost dead in every part; only the smallest breath of life fluttered within her. Her grieving relatives stood nearby, expecting only her death, when it was suddenly announced that Martin had come to that city. When the girl's father discovered this, he ran to make a request for his almost lifeless child. It happened that Martin had already entered the church. There, while the people were looking on and many other bishops were present, the old man, lamenting loudly, embraced [Martin's] knees and said: "My daughter is dying of a

miserable illness; and, what is more cruel than death itself, she is alive only in spirit for her flesh is already dead. I beg you to go to her, and give her your blessing; for I believe that through you she will be restored to health." Martin, thrown into confusion by his words was amazed, and shrank back, saying that this was not within his abilities, that the old man's judgment was faulty and that he was not worthy to be the one through whom the Lord should reveal a sign of his power. The father, in tears, vehemently persisted and pleaded with Martin to visit the dying girl. At last, compelled to go by the bishops who were standing by, he went down to the girl's home. An immense crowd was waiting at the doors, to see what the servant of the Lord would do. And first, having recourse to his usual weapons in these matters, he threw himself down on the ground and prayed. Then he examined the sick girl and asked for some oil to be brought to him. After he had blessed it, he poured the powerful sacred liquid into the girl's mouth, and immediately she regained her voice. Then gradually, through contact with him, her limbs began to come alive one at a time until finally as the people looked on she arose and stood up firmly.

17. At the same time a servant of the proconsul Tetradius was possessed by a demon who was torturing him to the point of causing him an agonizing death. Martin, therefore, was asked to lay his hands on him, and he ordered the servant to be brought to him, but the evil spirit could not by any means be made to leave the small room where he was: he raged and bared ferocious teeth at those who approached. Then Tetradius threw himself at the feet of the saintly man, pleading with him to go himself to the house in which the man possessed by the Devil was kept. But Martin said that he could not visit the house of an unconverted pagan. For at that time Tetradius was still imprisoned by the errors of the pagans. He, therefore, pledged his word that if the demon were driven out of his servant he would become a Christian. So Martin laid his hand upon the servant and cast the evil spirit out of him. When he saw this, Tetradius believed in the Lord Jesus and immediately became a catechumen; not long after, he was baptized, and he always felt the greatest affection for Martin who was the author of his salvation.

At about the same time and in the same town, Martin entered the home of a certain householder, and, stopping short at the very threshold, he said that he saw a horrible demon in the courtyard of the house. When he ordered it to leave, it took hold of the family cook, who was inside the house. The poor wretch began at once to be violent and to bare his teeth at everyone he met. The house was thrown into disorder, the family was in confusion, and the people present ran away. Martin threw himself in front of the frenzied creature and first of all commanded him to stand still. But when he continued to gnash his teeth and, with gaping mouth, threatened to bite, Martin put his fingers into his mouth and said "If you have any power, devour these." But then, as if red-hot iron had entered his jaws, the possessed man kept his teeth from biting and avoided touching the saintly man's fingers; and when he was forced by punishments and tortures to flee from the possessed body, since he was permitted no escape through the mouth, he was purged along with the excrement from the stomach, leaving disgusting traces behind him.

18. Meanwhile, a sudden rumor troubled the city with news that the barbarians were moving in for the attack. Martin ordered a person possessed by a demon to be set before him, and commanded him to declare whether this message was true or not. Then he confessed that there were ten demons with him who had spread this rumor among the people, so that from fear of this Martin would be driven from the town; in fact, nothing was further from the barbarians' thoughts than to make any inroad. When the unclean spirit confessed these things in the middle of the church, the city was set free from fear and its present confusion.

At Paris when Martin was entering the gate of the city with large crowds accompanying him, he kissed a leper whose pitiful face struck fear in everyone, and blessed him; he was instantly cleansed from his sickness, and the next day, he appeared in church with a clear skin and gave thanks for the health which he had recovered. Nor should we ignore the fact that threads from Martin's garment or those plucked from the sackcloth which he wore acted as curative powers upon the sick. Either tied round the fingers or placed around the neck, they very often drove away diseases from the afflicted.

19. Arborius, a prefect [senator] and a man of very holy and faithful character, had a daughter who was gravely ill with an intermittent burning fever. When the fever was at its height, he placed in her bosom a letter from Martin which happened to have been brought to him, and at once the fever disappeared. This event made such an impression on Arborius that he at once consecrated the girl to God, and devoted her to perpetual virginity. Then he went to Martin and presented the girl to him, as an obvious living example of his power as a miracle-worker, since she had been cured by him even though he was not present; and he would not allow anyone but Martin to consecrate her or to place on her the robe of virginity.

Paulinus [of Nola], too, a man who was afterwards to be such a great example, had begun to suffer sharp pain in one of his eyes, and already a fairly thick film had grown over it and had covered up the pupil, when Martin touched his eye with a painter's brush and restored it to its former health, with all the pain removed.

Also he himself fell by accident from an upper room and tumbled down a broken, uneven staircase. He received many injuries, and as he lay in his cell at the point of death, tortured with severe pain, that night an angel appeared to him who washed his wounds and applied healing ointment to the bruises on his body. And so the next day he was so completely restored to health that you would not have thought that he had had an accident. But it would be too long to list everything of this kind. These few examples out of the many miracles will suffice, and let it be enough that I have not subtracted from the truth in the most striking cases, while I have avoided boring the reader by multiplying them.

20. And here I will insert some smaller matters among the greater ones (although such is the general decay and corruption of our times, that it is in fact almost an exceptional matter when the priesthood has the firmness not to succumb to royal flattery). A number of bishops from various parts of the world had assembled before the emperor Maximus, a man of fierce character who at that time was elated with the victory he had won in the civil wars. When the disgraceful flattery of all those around the emperor was generally noticed, and priestly merit had with deplorable meekness taken second place to the royal retinue, in Martin alone apostolic authority continued to assert itself. For even if he had to make a supplication to the sovereign for some things, he commanded rather than entreated him; and although often invited to dine with the emperor, he stayed away, saying that he could not sit at the table of one who had deprived one emperor of his kingdom, and the other of his life. At last, Maximus maintained that he had not assumed imperial power of his own accord, but that he had simply defended a sovereign power that, according to divine will, had been forced upon him by his own soldiers; that God's favor was clearly not alienated from one who, by an almost incredible turn of events, had secured the victory, and that none of his adversaries had been killed except in open battle. At length, Martin was convinced either by his reasoning or his entreaties, and came to the royal banquet. The king was wonderfully pleased because he had gained this point.

Moreover, there were guests present who had been invited as if to a celebration, men of the highest and most illustrious rank: the prefect, who was also consul, named Evodius, whose righteousness was surpassed by no one, and two counts wielding immense power, the brother and uncle of the emperor. Between these two, the priest who accompanied Martin had taken his place, but he himself occupied a seat which was immediately next to the king. About the middle of the feast, according to custom, a servant presented a goblet to the king. He ordered it rather to be given to the most holy bishop, expecting and hoping that he [the emperor] would then receive the cup from his hand. But when Martin had drunk he handed the goblet to his own priest, thinking that no one there was worthier to drink next after him, and believing that it would not be right to prefer either the emperor himself or those who ranked next to him over the priest. The emperor and all those present admired this conduct so much, that the very thing that had caused them loss of respect gave them pleasure. The report then ran through the whole palace that Martin had done, at the king's feast, what no bishop had dared to do at banquets given by the lowest magistrates.

Martin also predicted to the same Maximus long before it happened that if he went into Italy, as he then desired to do in order to make war against the emperor Valentinian, he should know that he would certainly be victorious in the first attack, but would perish a short time afterwards. And we have seen that this did in fact take place. For when [Maximus] first arrived, Valentinian was put to flight; but he recovered his strength about a year afterwards, and killed Maximus after he had captured him inside the walls of Aquileia.

21. It is also well known that angels often appeared to Martin and spoke to him, exchanging conversation by turns with him. As for the Devil, Martin held him so distinctly within his gaze that whether he kept himself in his proper shape, or changed himself into different forms of spiritual wickedness, whatever his appearance, Martin recognized him. The Devil knew very well that he could not escape discovery, and therefore frequently heaped insults upon Martin, because he could not deceive him with his tricks.

On one occasion the devil rushed into Martin's cell with a great noise with the bloody horn of an ox in his hand; showing him his blood-stained hand and at the same time exulting in the crime he had committed, he said: "O Martin, where is your power? I have just slain one of your people." Then Martin assembled the brothers, and told them what the devil had said; he ordered them to search the individual cells carefully and to find out who had been stricken with this calamity. They reported that none of the monks was missing, but that one peasant, hired by them, had gone to the forest to bring home wood in his wagon. So Martin instructed some of them to go and meet him, and not far from the monastery the man was found almost dead. As he drew his last breath, he told the brethren the cause of his mortal wound: he said that after yoking the oxen together, he was tightening some loose straps on the yoke holding his oxen together when one of them, throwing his head free, had wounded him in the groin with his horn. And shortly after, the man died.

You may see the Lord's judgment in giving this power to the devil. This was a marvelous ability in Martin: he foresaw events far in advance, not only on the occasion I have described, but also on many similar occasions, in fact as often as such things occurred, and he disclosed to the brothers what had been revealed to him.

22. Now, the devil often tried to mock the holy man by a thousand harmful tricks, and often thrust himself upon his sight in the most diverse shapes possible. For sometimes he presented himself by changing his appearance into that of Jupiter, very often into Mercury, and into Venus and Minerva; Martin, never afraid, protected himself against him with the sign of the cross or by the help of prayers. Often, too, were heard words of reproach, in which the crowd of demons attacked Martin with insults; but knowing that all were false and groundless, he was not moved by their accusations.

Furthermore, some of the brothers testified that they had heard a demon reproaching Martin with insulting cries, and asking why he had taken back certain of the brothers who, having been baptized, had fallen into various kinds of errors but who afterwards had repented – and he listed off the sins of each one; but Martin had resisted the devil firmly, replying that former sins are cleansed away by leading a better life, and that through the mercy of God, those who have given up their evil ways are to be absolved from their sins. The Devil retorted that such guilty men as those referred to did not come within the pale of pardon, and that the Lord extended no mercy to those who had once fallen away. But Martin is said to have cried out with these words: "Wretched creature, if you yourself would only stop attacking mankind, and if, even now when the day of judgment is at hand, you would repent of your deeds, with true confidence in the Lord I would promise you the mercy of Christ."

O what a holy presumption concerning the loving-kindness of the Lord, in which even if he could not assert authority, Martin nevertheless showed his feelings! And since I have spoken here about the Devil and his tricks, it does not seem beside the point – even if I am digressing – to relate the next incident. For a portion of Martin's virtues is shown here, and it is proper to record an event which was worthy of a miracle as a cautionary example in case anything similar should occur later on.

23. There was a certain youth, Clarus by name, of very noble rank, who afterwards became a priest and who is now through his happy ending numbered among the saints. He left all others to be near Martin, and in a short time achieved the utmost faith and every kind of virtue. Now, it happened that when he had built himself a dwelling not far from the bishop's monastery, and many brothers were staying with him, a young man called Anatolius came to him, professing himself to be a monk and falsely assuming every appearance of humility and innocence, and lived for some time in the community with the rest. Then, as time went on, he began to assert that angels regularly came to talk to him. As no one trusted him, he coerced a number of the brothers to believe by certain signs. Finally he went to such lengths as to declare that messengers passed between himself and God, and he

wished now to be regarded as one of the prophets. Clarus, however, could by no means be induced to believe. He then began to threaten Clarus with the anger of God and with imminent punishment, because he did not believe one of the saints. At last it is reported that he cried out with the following declaration: "Behold, tonight the Lord will give me a white robe out of heaven, and clothed in it I will dwell in the midst of you; and that will be a sign to you that I am the Power of God, since I shall have been given the garment of God."

Then indeed there was great anticipation among them all because of this declaration. And so, about the middle of the night, the whole monastery appeared to be disturbed by the noise of people moving eagerly about; and the cell in which the young man was enclosed was seen to be glittering with many lights; and the whisperings of those moving about in it, as well as a kind of murmur of many voices, could be heard. Then it grew silent, and the youth emerged and called one of the brothers named Sabatius to come, and showed him the robe in which he had been clothed. Filled with amazement, Sabatius called the rest together, and Clarus himself also came running; and after a light was brought, they all carefully examined the garment. Now, it was extremely soft, marvelously bright, and of glittering purple, and yet no one could discover what the nature of the fabric was. However, when it was more closely examined by sight or touch, it seemed nothing else than a garment. In the meantime, Clarus urged the brothers to pray earnestly to the Lord to show them more clearly what it really was. So the rest of the night was spent in singing hymns and psalms. But when day broke, Clarus took the young man by the hand and wished to bring him to Martin, being well aware that he could not be deceived by any arts of the Devil. Then, indeed, the miserable man began to resist with all his might and claimed that he had been forbidden to show himself to Martin. And when they forced him to go against his will, the garment vanished from among the hands of those who were pulling him. Who then can doubt that this, too, was due to the power of Martin, so that the Devil could no longer dissemble or conceal his own deception when it was to be laid before Martin?

24. It was noted about the same time that there was a young man in Spain who by many signs had acquired personal authority among the people, and who was so conceited that he claimed openly to be Elijah. When many were ready to believe this, he went on to say that he was actually Christ; and he succeeded so well even in this delusion that a certain bishop named Rufus worshiped him as if he were the Lord. And since then, because of this, we have seen him deprived of his bishopric. Many of the brothers have also reported that at the same time a certain man appeared in the East who boasted that he was John. Since false prophets of this kind have appeared, we

can assume that the coming of Antichrist is at hand; for in these persons he is already practising the mystery of evil.

And truly it appears that I should not pass over the great ruse with which the Devil tempted Martin during this same period. For one day, the fiend stood beside Martin while he was praying in his cell. He had enveloped himself in a brilliant light which preceded him, so that he might more easily deceive people by the brilliance of an assumed splendor, and he was clothed also in a royal robe, with a gold crown of precious stones encircling his head, his shoes too inlaid with gold, and he had a tranquil appearance and joyful expression, so that no one might think he was the Devil. At first Martin was dazzled by his appearance, and both were profoundly silent for a long time. The Devil was the first to speak. He said, "Acknowledge, Martin, who it is that you behold. I am Christ; and since I am about to descend to earth, I wished first to manifest myself to you." When Martin was silent, and gave no response at all, the Devil dared to repeat his audacious announcement: "Martin, why do you hesitate? Believe, since you see! I am Christ." Then the Spirit revealed the truth to Martin, so that he might understand it was the Devil and not God, and he replied: "The Lord Jesus did not predict that he would come clothed in purple, and with a glittering crown upon his head. Unless Christ appears in the shape and form in which he suffered, openly displaying the marks of his wounds upon the cross, I will not believe that he has come." On hearing these words, the Devil vanished like smoke. He filled the cell with such a disgusting smell that he left unmistakable evidence that he was the Devil. This event took place in the way I have just related, and I heard it from the lips of Martin himself; therefore let no one think it is a fiction.

25. Since I had for a long time heard accounts of his faith, life and power, I burned with the desire to know him, and so I undertook what for me was the pleasure of a pilgrimage to see him. At the same time, because my mind was already on fire with the desire of writing his life, I obtained my information partly from himself, to the extent that I could question him, and partly from those who had lived with him, or who were well acquainted with the facts of the case. And at this time it is hard to believe the humility and kindness with which he received me; he was delighted and rejoiced in the Lord that I esteemed him so highly as to undertake a long journey from my desire to see him. Wretch that I am — I hardly dare admit it — he considered me worthy to be admitted to his sacred table, and he himself gave me water to wash my hands. In the evening it was he who washed my feet; and I did not have the courage to oppose or resist — in fact, I was so overcome by the authority he unconsciously exerted, that I would have felt it wrong not to let him do it.

His conversation with me was entirely directed to the necessity of abandoning worldly pleasures and secular responsibilities so that we might freely and without impediment follow the Lord Jesus; and he urged me to follow the excellent contemporary example of that distinguished man Paulinus, whom I have mentioned above, who by parting with his great possessions and following Christ was almost the only person in these times who had fulfilled the Gospel's precepts. He insisted that he was the one we should follow and the one we should imitate, and added that the present generation was fortunate to have such a model of faith and virtue. For Paulinus was rich and had many possessions, and by selling them all and giving them to the poor according to the expressed will of the Lord, he had shown by example that what seemed impossible could in fact be done.

What seriousness and dignity there were in Martin's words and conversation! How eager he was, how effective, and how prompt and ready to solve problems connected with Scripture! And because I know that many are incredulous on this point – because I have met persons who still did not believe them even when I related them – I call to witness Jesus, and our common hope as Christians, that I never heard from any lips other than Martin's such knowledge and genius, or such excellence and purity of speech. But yet, how very insignificant is such praise when compared to Martin's virtues! Still, it is remarkable that in an uneducated man even this gift [of speaking well] was not lacking.

26. But now my book draws to a close, and my discourse must come to an end. This is not because everything there is to say about Martin has been exhausted, but because, just as lazy poets grow careless towards the end of their work, so I must succumb, conquered by the weight of the material. For, although it was possible to set down his external deeds in some sort of language, no language, I truly own, can ever describe his inner life, his daily conduct, or his mind, intent always upon heaven.

No one can adequately describe his perseverance and self-control in abstinence and fastings, or his power in vigils and prayers, or the nights and days spent by him without a moment separated from the service of God, either for leisure or for business, or even for eating or sleeping, except in so far as the necessities of nature required. I freely confess that, if, as the saying is, Homer himself were to rise up from the depths, he could not do justice to this subject, to such an extent did all Martin's qualities surpass the possibility of being expressed in language. Never did a single hour or moment pass in which he did not engage in prayer or apply himself to reading, although even during his reading, or if he was busy with something else, he never relaxed his mind from prayer. In truth, just as blacksmiths at work habitually beat their own anvil as a sort of relief from the labor, so Martin was still engaged in prayer, even when he appeared to be doing something else. O truly blessed man, in whom there was no guile – judging no man, condemning no man, returning evil for evil to no man! He displayed such marvelous patience when he endured injuries, that even when he was chief priest, he allowed himself to be wronged by the lowest clerics with impunity; he neither removed them from their position because of their conduct, or, as far as it lay within him, did he drive them out of his affections.

27. No one ever saw him enraged, or excited, or grieving, or laughing; he was always just the same – displaying a kind of heavenly happiness in his expression, he seemed to have surpassed ordinary human nature. There was never any word on his lips but Christ, and there was never any feeling in his heart except piety, peace, and mercy. Frequently, too, he used to weep for the sins of those who were obviously his detractors – those who, as he led his retired and tranquil life, slandered him with poisoned tongue and a viper's mouth.

And truly I have had experience of some who were envious of his virtues and his life – who really hated in him what they did not see in themselves, and what they lacked the power to imitate. And – a wickedness to be profoundly regretted and lamented – the greater part of his detractors, although they were very few in number, were reported to be bishops! Here, however, it is not necessary to name any one, although a good many of these people are still barking at me. It will be enough if any one of them reads this account and recognizes himself, and has the grace to blush. For if he becomes angry, he will be admitting that he is one of those spoken of, even if I have really been thinking of some other person. Besides, if there are any people of that sort, I shall not object if they include myself in their hatred along with such a man as Martin.

I am very certain of this, however: that this little work will give pleasure to all truly good people. And I shall only say further that, if any one reads this work and does not believe it, he himself will fall into sin. As for myself, I am aware that I have been compelled to write these things by my belief in the facts, and by the love of Christ, and that in doing so I have set down what is well known, and recorded what is true; and, as I trust, there is a reward prepared by God not for the person who reads these things, but for the one who believes them.

A. Sulpicius writes to his friend, the deacon Aurelius

After you left me this morning, I was sitting alone in my cell absorbed in the reflections which often occupy me: hope for the future, weariness with the present world, a terror of Judgment, fear of punishment, and, as a consequence or indeed as the source of my whole train of thought, remembrance of my sins, which had left me overwhelmed with sadness. Then, after I stretched out on my couch, fatigued with mental anguish, sleep crept upon me, as frequently happens from grief – and since such sleep is always somewhat light and uncertain in the morning hours, so it spread through my limbs only in a hesitant way which seemed to hold them in suspense. Thus it happens, in contrast to what occurs in a different kind of slumber, that one can feel he is sleeping while almost awake.

Suddenly I seemed to see St. Martin appear to me in the form of a bishop, clothed in a shining white robe, with a countenance like fire, eyes like stars, and glittering hair. He appeared to me with the features and bodily form which I had known, so that I find it almost difficult to say what I mean – I could not fix my eyes upon him, though I could clearly recognize him. He smiled at me slightly, and held out in his right hand the small treatise which I had written about his life. I embraced his sacred knees, and begged for his blessing according to custom, and I felt him place his hand on my head with the sweetest touch, while among the solemn words of blessing he repeated the name of the Cross so familiar to his lips. When I had fixed my eyes earnestly upon him, for I could not have enough of gazing upon his face, he was suddenly snatched away from me and raised on high. Nevertheless I followed him with my eyes as he was conveyed by a swiftly-moving cloud across the vast expanse of air until the heavens opened up and received him, and I could not see him any longer. And not long after, I saw the holy priest Clarus, a disciple of Martin's who had recently died, ascending by the same path as his master.

Boldly, I wished to follow, but while I tried with all my strength to reach the heights [of heaven], I awoke. Once roused from sleep, I had begun to rejoice over the vision, when a young servant came in with a face sadder than usual and the appearance both of wanting to speak and of suffering. "Why are you sad, and what news do you bring?" I asked. He replied, "Two monks have arrived from Tours, and they have brought word that Lord Martin is dead."

I confess that I was cut to the heart, and bursting into tears, I wept most abundantly. Even now as I write these things to you, brother, my tears are flowing, and I find no consolation for my unbearable sorrow. And when this news reaches you, I should like you to share in my grief, as you shared with me in his love. I beg you, come to me at once, so that we may mourn together the one whom we both love. And yet I am well aware that such a man ought not to be mourned, since at last, after his victory over the world and triumph over the age, he has been given the crown of righteousness. Nevertheless, I cannot master my grief. I have indeed sent my patron on before me, but I have lost my great source of consolation in this present life – even though, if reason had any influence on suffering, I ought to rejoice.

For he is now united with the apostles and prophets, and (I say this with all respect for the saints) in that assembly of the righteous he is second to none; and especially, as I hope, believe, and trust, he is admitted among those who washed their robes in blood: now, immaculate, he follows the Lamb as his guide. For although the conditions of our times could not ensure him the honor of martyrdom, yet he will not be deprived of the glory of a martyr, because by his vowed intention and his courage he was both able and willing to be a martyr. And if he had been permitted [to live] in the times of Nero and of Decius [Roman emperors who persecuted the Christians; see 6 and 7 above], and to take part in the struggle which then took place, I take the God of heaven and earth as witness that he would willingly have climbed upon the torture rack, and readily have thrown himself upon the flames: and, like the young Hebrews, even in the midst of the circling flames in the furnace he would have sung a hymn to the Lord. But if it had pleased the persecutor to inflict on him the punishment which Isaiah endured, he would never have shown himself inferior to the prophet, nor would he have shrunk from having his limbs torn in pieces by saws and red-hot instruments. And if the impious fury [of the persecutors] had preferred to drive the blessed man over precipitous rocks or steep mountains, I maintain that trusting in the testimony of truth he would willingly have fallen. But if, following the example of the teacher of the Gentiles [St. Paul], he had been led along with other victims condemned to die by the sword, as indeed often happened, he would have been first among them all to urge on the executioner so that he might obtain the crown of blood. And, in truth, in the face of all the punishments and tortures to which human weakness most often yields, he would not have gone back on his confession of the Lord, but rather he would have been happy and rejoiced to endure pain and torment; he would have stood his ground immovably and laughed in the midst of his afflictions.

But although he did not endure all these things, nevertheless he gained a bloodless martyrdom. For what agonies of human suffering did he not endure in the hope of eternal life: hunger, vigils, nakedness, fastings, the insults of the envious, the persecutions of the wicked, care of the sick, solicitude for those in danger? For who ever suffered that Martin did not suffer too? Who stumbled and Martin was not hurt? Who died, and Martin did not mourn deeply? To say nothing of the various struggles which he carried on daily against the power of human evil and spiritual wickedness, while in those different temptations invariably fortitude in conquering, patience in waiting, and placidity in enduring always prevailed in him. . . .

B. Sulpicius writes to Bassula, his mother-in-law

Sulpicius Severus sends greetings to Bassula, his respected parent.

If it were lawful for parents to be summoned to court [by their children], I would drag you openly before the magistrate's tribunal with a just grievance, and charge you with robbery and plunder. For why should I not complain of the injury which I have suffered at your hands? You have left me not the smallest bit of writing at home, no book, not even a letter – you steal everything and publish it all to the world. If I write to a friend in confidence, if by way of a joke I happen to dictate anything which nonetheless I would have preferred to keep private, everything reaches you almost before it has been written or dictated. It's no surprise: you have got my stenographers in your debt, and thanks to them any trifles I compose are revealed to you. And yet I cannot be angry with them for obeying you, since it is due to your generosity that they are in my service, and so they are always mindful of the fact that they belong to you rather than to me. You alone are the guilty party, you alone are to blame, for you set traps for me and fraudulently circumvent my scribes in order that my writings – with no distinction at all made between private correspondence or casual missives – are put into your hands quite unelaborated and unpolished. For, to say nothing about other writings, I beg to ask how that letter which I recently wrote to Aurelius the Deacon could reach you so speedily. For I was living at Toulouse, while you were at Trèves, torn far from your native land – to the anxiety of your son; what opportunity, I should like to know, did you have to get hold of that confidential letter? For I have received a letter from you in which you write that in the same correspondence in which I mentioned the death of holy Martin, I ought to have described how he died. As if, indeed, I had either published the letter so that it would be read by someone other than the person to whom it was apparently sent; or as if I in particular had been charged with undertaking the great task of writing all the things which should be known about Martin and making them public. Therefore, if you desire to learn anything about the saintly bishop's death, you should inquire rather among those who were present when his death occurred; for my part, I have resolved to write nothing to you in case you publish me everywhere. Nevertheless if you give your word that you will read what I send you to no one, I shall satisfy your wishes in a few words, and on this condition I shall communicate to you the details which I know at first hand.

Martin predicted the time of his own death long before it occurred, and told the brothers that his departure from the body was at hand. In the meantime, he had reason to visit the church at Cosne [Candes]. For the clergy of that church were quarreling among themselves, and Martin wanted to restore peace, and although he was well aware that the end of his life was at hand, yet he did not refuse to undertake the journey for that reason. He thought that it would be an excellent crown to set upon his virtues if he should leave behind him a church restored to peace. And so after he set out, accompanied as usual by a very large crowd of most holy disciples, he saw water-fowl diving in the river for fishes, and endlessly cramming their prey into their rapacious jaws. "This," he exclaimed, "is an image of how the demons act: they lie in wait for the unwary and capture them before they are aware of it; they devour their victims once they have caught them, and they are never satisfied with what they have devoured." Then Martin with powerful words commanded the birds to leave the pool in which they were swimming, and to head for dry regions and deserts, and he used on the birds the very same authority with which he used to put demons to flight. And so all those birds gathered together and, forming a single body, left the river and made for the mountains and woods, to the amazement of those who observed such power in Martin that he could even command the birds.

He stayed for some time in the village, or rather in the church, to which he had gone. After peace had been restored among the clergy and he was thinking about returning to his monastery, he suddenly began to fail in bodily strength and, assembling the brothers, he told them that he was on the point of dying. Then indeed, sorrow and grief took hold of them all, and they lamented with one voice, saying, "Father, why are you abandoning us? To whom can you commit us in our desolation? Ravenous wolves will attack your flock; who will save us from their bite if the shepherd is struck down? We know indeed that you long to be with Christ, but your rewards above are safe and will not be diminished if they are delayed. Instead, have pity on those whom you are deserting." Then Martin was moved by their weeping, for he always melted with pity in the Lord, and he is said to have burst into tears; and, turning to the Lord, he gave the mourners only this answer: "O Lord, if I am still necessary to your people, I will not shrink from the labor: your will be done." He was truly torn between hope and grief and almost in doubt as to which he should prefer, for he neither wished to leave us, nor to be longer separated from Christ. However, he took no account of his own wishes, nor left anything to his own will, but committed himself entirely to the will and power of the Lord, and he prayed in these words, saying, "O Lord, the struggle of bodily warfare is heavy indeed, and surely I have fought enough by now; but if you command me still to stand at the head of your forces, I will not refuse, nor shall I plead exhaustion due to my age. I will

[Fig. 15] Since Martin died while on a diocesan visit to Candes, the people of Tours vied with those of Candes as to which place should receive his remains. The Tourangeois were successful; this miniature shows them stealing the body and returning it to Tours by boat (copy in Baring-Gould, *Lives of the Saints,* 13).

faithfully fulfil the duties you have assigned to me, and I will serve under your banners as long as you command me. And even though an old man longs for release from toil, yet my courage remains victorious over my years and does not know how to yield to old age. But if you will now spare my years, your will shall seem good to me, O Lord. And as for those for whom I fear, you yourself will watch over them."

O man past describing, unconquered by toil, and unconquerable even by death, who showed no preference for either alternative, and who neither feared to die nor refused to live! And so, although for some days he endured a high fever, he still did not cease from the work of God. By night he forced his exhausted limbs to serve his spirit with prayers and vigils, lying on his noble bed of hair cloth and ashes. And when his disciples begged him at least to allow some ordinary straw to be put beneath him, he replied, "It is only fitting for a Christian to die in ashes; if I leave you any other example, I have sinned." Nevertheless, with his eyes and hands always fixed upon heaven, he never relaxed his unconquered spirit from prayer; and when the priests who had gathered around him asked if he would relieve his body a little by turning onto the other side, he said, "Brothers, let me look upon heaven rather than earth, so that my spirit as it is about to leave on its journey may go straight to God." When he had said this, he saw the Devil standing close beside him. "Bloody monster," he said, "why are you here? Murderer, you will find nothing in me: Abraham's bosom will receive me."

As he uttered these words, he sent his spirit up to heaven. Those who were there testified to me that they saw his face as if it had been the face of an angel; his limbs too seemed to be as white as snow, so that people said, "Who would ever believe that he was covered in haircloth and rolled in ashes?" For he appeared already as he would look in the glory of the resurrection to come, and in the form of the transfigured flesh. But the immense crowd of people who gathered for his funeral rites can hardly be believed: the whole city ran to meet his body; all the inhabitants of the country and the villages and many also from the neighboring cities were there. O how great was the mourning of all, how great especially the lamentation of the sorrowful monks! Almost two thousand of them are reported to have gathered on that day – Martin's special glory, for by his example so many plants had sprung up in the service of the Lord. In all certainty, the shepherd was driving his own flocks before him, the pale crowds and robed legions, whether old men whose labor was finished or young recruits who had just sworn allegiance to Christ. Then came the choir of virgins, and if they refrained from weeping out of modesty, beneath what holy joy they hid their suffering! If faith prohibited weeping, nevertheless affection [for Martin] forced groans from them. For there was as much holy rejoicing over the glory he had attained as there was pious sorrow over his death. You would pardon them for weeping; you would congratulate them for rejoicing, as each one proclaimed suffering for himself and rejoicing for [Martin]. In this way, then, the crowd escorted the saintly man's body to its burial place, singing heavenly hymns.

Compare this, if you wish, with the worldly pomp (I will not say a funeral) of a triumph; and what can be reckoned similar to the funeral rites of Martin? Let worldly men lead their captives with hands bound behind their backs ahead of their chariots; Martin's body was accompanied by those who had conquered the world under his leadership. Insane peoples may honor [worldly men] with confused praises; Martin is praised with divine Psalms, Martin is honored with heavenly hymns. Worldly men after their triumphs here are over will be thrust into cruel Tartarus [hell], while Martin is joyfully received into Abraham's bosom – Martin, poor and insignificant on earth, shall enter heaven a rich man. And from that blessed region, as I trust, he will protect me, as I write these lines, and you as you read them.

15. THE LIFE AND MIRACLES OF ST. BENEDICT

Pope Gregory the Great (c.540-604), who was to become a saint himself, wrote the 'life' of St. Benedict during a chaotic period in Italy. The wars between the emperor Justinian and the invading Goths had devastated the country; the Lombards continued their sporadic attacks; and the last decade of the century was marked by floods, plague, and a series of famines. Gregory's 'Dialogues' (594), of which the 'life' forms the second book, and which was written at the request of members of his household, was intended to encourage people by showing them that saints existed in Italy just as they had in the Egyptian desert and elsewhere, and that through their miraculous powers God continued to protect his people. The first and third books of the 'Dialogues' describe a number of Italian saints, and the last book follows as a treatise on the 'Immortality of the Soul,' for the continuing presence and power of the saints after their deaths was understood to give certain evidence of the resurrection.

Before he became Pope in 590, Gregory had experienced an ascetic conversion: he resigned as prefect of Rome, founded monasteries on his family estates in Sicily, and turned his own home in Rome into the monastery of St. Andrew. He lived there as an ordinary monk under the Benedictine Rule (whose compilation is the major achievement ascribed to St. Benedict) until recalled to serve as the Pope's representative in Constantinople, but he continued to regret his loss of a life withdrawn from the world. His relationship to his subject, Benedict, was thus a close one: Benedict too had had a period of withdrawal before becoming a busy abbot overseeing several monasteries and receiving visits from the temporal powers of the day, and Benedict and his people had, like Gregory's, suffered various natural calamities. Although Gregory tells us that he got his information from other people, it is clear that he was well-read in hagiography too: features of his 'life' (the earliest one we have for Benedict) recall accounts of Antony and Paul the Hermit and, especially, St. Martin of Tours, for like other saints Benedict is to be admired primarily not because of his unique personality (although he does emerge as a memorable individual) but because he conforms to the virtuous ideal represented by the desert fathers and their followers.

Source: trans. Odo John Zimmerman, *St. Gregory the Great: Dialogues* (New York: Fathers of the Church, Inc., 1959), pp. 3-6 and 55-110; repr. with permission. BHL 1102.

Prologue to Book 1

Some men of the world had left me feeling quite depressed one day with all their noisy wrangling. In their business dealings they try, as a rule, to make us pay what we obviously do not owe them. In my grief I retired to a quiet spot congenial to my mood, where I could consider every unpleasant detail

[Fig. 16] St. Benedict, from an engraving by Wierx (Jameson, *Legends of the Monastic Orders,* p. 14). He is traditionally shown with a broken tray recalling his first miracle, a cup representing the attempt by rebellious monks to poison him, the raven who saved him from poisoning by his enemy Florentius, and a book signifying the monastic Rule whose authorship is ascribed to him.

of my daily work and review all the causes of my sorrow as they crowded unhindered before my eyes. I sat there for a long time in silence and was still deeply dejected when my dear son, the deacon Peter, came in. He had been a very dear friend to me from his early youth and was my companion in the study of sacred Scripture. Seeing me so sick at heart he asked, 'Have you met with some new misfortune? You seem unusually sad.'

'Peter,' I replied, 'this daily sadness of mine is always old and always new: old by its constant presence, new by its continual increase. With my unhappy soul languishing under a burden of distractions, I recall those earlier days in the monastery where all the fleeting things of time were in a world below me, and I could rise far above the vanities of life. Heavenly thoughts would fill my mind, and while still held within the body I passed beyond its narrow confines in contemplation. Even death, which nearly everyone regards as evil, I cherished as the entrance into life and the reward for labor.

'But now all the beauty of that spiritual repose is gone, and the contact with worldly men and their affairs, which is a necessary part of my duties as bishop, has left my soul defiled with earthly activities. I am so distracted with external occupations in my concern for the people that even when my spirit resumes its striving after the interior life it always does so with less vigor. Then, as I compare what I have lost with what I must now endure, the contrast only makes my present lot more burdensome. I am tossed about on the waves of a heavy sea, and my soul is like a helpless ship buffeted by raging winds. When I recall my former way of life, it is as though I were once more looking back toward land and sighing as I beheld the shore. It only saddens me the more to find that, while flung about by the mighty waves that carry me along, I can hardly catch sight any longer of the harbor I have left.

'Such, in fact, is generally the way our mind declines. First we lose a prized possession but remain aware of the loss; then as we go along even the remembrance of it fades, and so at the end we are unable any longer to recall what was once actually in our possession. That is why, as I have said, when we sail too far from shore, we can no longer see the peaceful harbor we have left. At times I find myself reflecting with even greater regret on the life that others lead who have totally abandoned the present world. Seeing the heights these men have reached only makes me realize the lowly state of my own soul. It was by spending their days in seclusion that most of them pleased their Creator. And to keep them from dulling their spiritual fervor with human activities, God chose to leave them free from worldly occupations.'

And now I think it will be best if I present the conversation that took place between us by simply putting our names before the questions and the answers we exchanged.

Peter: I do not know of any persons in Italy whose lives give evidence of extraordinary spiritual powers, and therefore I cannot imagine with whom you are comparing yourself so regretfully. This land of ours has undoubtedly produced its virtuous men, but to my knowledge no signs or miracles have been performed by any of them; or, if they have been, they were till now kept in such secrecy that we cannot even tell if they occurred.

Gregory: On the contrary, Peter, the day would not be long enough for me to tell you about those saints whose holiness has been well established and whose lives are known to me either from my own observations or from the reports of good, reliable witnesses.

Peter: Would you do me the favor, then, of saying at least something about them? Interrupting the study and explanation of the Scriptures for such a purpose should not cause grave concern, for the amount of edification to be gained from a description of miracles is just as great. An explanation of holy Scripture teaches us how to attain virtue and persevere in it, whereas a description of miracles shows us how this acquired virtue reveals itself in those who persevere in it. Then, too, the lives of the saints are often more effective than mere instruction for inspiring us to love heaven as our home. Hearing about their example will generally be helpful in two ways. In the first place, as we compare ourselves with those who have gone before, we are filled with a longing for the future life; secondly, if we have too high an opinion of our own worth, it makes us humble to find that others have done better.

Gregory: I shall not hesitate to narrate what I have learned from worthy men. In this I am only following the consecrated practice of the Scriptures, where it is perfectly clear that Mark and Luke composed their Gospels, not as eyewitnesses, but on the word of others. Nevertheless, to remove any grounds for doubt on the part of my readers, I am going to indicate on whose authority each account is based. You should bear in mind, however, that in some instances I retain only the substance of the original narrative; in others, the words as well. For if I had always kept to the exact wording, the crude language used by some would have been ill suited to my style of writing. . . .

Book 2: Life and Miracles of St. Benedict, Founder and Abbot of the Monastery Which Is Known as the Citadel of Campania [Monte Cassino]

There was a man of saintly life; blessed Benedict was his name, and he was blessed also with God's grace. Even in boyhood he showed mature understanding, for he kept his heart detached from every pleasure with a strength of character far beyond his years. While still living in the world, free to enjoy its earthly advantages, he saw how barren it was with its attractions and turned from it without regret.

He was born in the district of Norcia [a little town about 112 km/70 miles northeast of Rome] of distinguished parents, who sent him to Rome for a liberal education. But when he saw many of his fellow students falling headlong into vice, he stepped back from the threshold of the world in which he had just set foot. For he was afraid that if he acquired any of its learning he, too, would later plunge, body and soul, into the dread abyss. In his desire to please God alone, he turned his back on further studies, gave up home and inheritance and resolved to embrace the religious life. He took this step, well aware of his ignorance, yet wise, uneducated though he was.

I was unable to learn about all his miraculous deeds. But the few that I am going to relate I know from the lips of four of his own disciples: Constantine, the holy man who succeeded him as abbot; Valentinian, for many years superior of the monastery at the Lateran [in Rome]; Simplicius, Benedict's second successor; and Honoratus, who is still abbot of the monastery where the man of God first lived [Subiaco].

1. When Benedict abandoned his studies to go into solitude, he was accompanied only by his nurse, who loved him dearly. As they were passing through Affile, a number of devout men invited them to stay there and provided them with lodging near the church of St. Peter. One day, after asking her neighbors to lend her a tray for cleaning wheat, the nurse happened to leave it on the edge of the table and when she came back found it had slipped off and broken in two. The poor woman burst into tears; she had only borrowed this tray and now it was ruined. Benedict, who had always been a devout and thoughtful boy, felt sorry for his nurse when he saw her weeping. Quietly picking up both the pieces, he knelt down by himself and prayed earnestly to God, even to the point of tears. No sooner had he finished his prayer than he noticed that the two pieces were joined together again, without even a mark to show where the tray had been broken. Hurrying back at once, he cheerfully reassured his nurse and handed her the tray in perfect condition. News of the miracle spread to all the country around Affile and stirred up so much admiration among the people that they hung the tray

[handwritten: Another example of worshipping someone besides God]

at the entrance of their church. Ever since then it has been a reminder to all of the great holiness Benedict had acquired at the very outset of his monastic life. The tray remained there many years for everyone to see, and it is still hanging over the doorway of the church in these days of Lombard rule [Italy was ruled by the Lombards, a Germanic people from the upper Danube, from 568 until 774]. Benedict, however, preferred to suffer ill-treatment from the world rather than enjoy its praises. He wanted to spend himself laboring for God, not to be honored by the applause of men. So he stole away secretly from his nurse and fled to a lonely wilderness about thirty-five miles from Rome called Subiaco [8 km/5 miles north of Affile, on the Anio River]. A stream of cold, clear water running through the region broadens out at this point to form a lake, then flows off and continues on its course. On his way there Benedict met a monk named Romanus, who asked him where he was going. After discovering the young man's purpose, Romanus kept it secret and even helped him carry it out by clothing him with the monastic habit and supplying his needs as well as he could. *[handwritten: similar to Antony]*

At Subiaco, Benedict made his home in a narrow cave and for three years remained concealed there, unknown to anyone except the monk Romanus, who lived in a monastery close by under the rule of Abbot Deodatus. With fatherly concern this monk regularly set aside as much bread as he could from his own portion; then from time to time, unnoticed by his abbot, he left the monastery long enough to take the bread to Benedict. There was no path leading from the monastery down to his cave because of a cliff that rose directly over it. To reach him Romanus had to tie the bread to the end of a long rope and lower it over the cliff. A little bell attached to the rope let Benedict know when the bread was there, and he would come out to get it. *[handwritten: Devil taking further interest]* The ancient Enemy of mankind grew envious of the kindness shown by the older monk in supplying Benedict with food, and one day, as the bread was being lowered, he threw a stone at the bell and broke it. In spite of this, Romanus kept on with his faithful service.

At length the time came when almighty God wished to grant him rest from his toil and reveal Benedict's virtuous life to others. Like a shining lamp his example was to be set on a lampstand to give light to everyone in God's house. The Lord therefore appeared in a vision to a priest some distance away, who had just prepared his Easter dinner. 'How can you prepare these delicacies for yourself,' he asked, 'while my servant is out there in the wilds suffering from hunger?'

Rising at once, the priest wrapped up the food and set out to find the man of God that very day. He searched for him along the rough mountainsides, in the valleys, and through the caverns, until he found him hidden in the cave. They said a prayer of thanksgiving together and then sat down to talk about the spiritual life. After a while the priest suggested that they take their meal. 'Today is the great feast of Easter,' he added.

'It must be a great feast to have brought me this kind visit,' the man of God replied, not realizing after his long separation from men that it was Easter Sunday.

'Today is really Easter,' the priest insisted, 'the feast of our Lord's Resurrection. On such a solemn occasion you should not be fasting. Besides, I was sent here by almighty God so that both of us could share in his gifts.'

After that they said grace and began their meal. When it was over they conversed some more and then the priest went back to his church.

At about the same time some shepherds also discovered Benedict's hiding place. When they first looked through the thickets and caught sight of him clothed in rough skins, they mistook him for some wild animal. Soon, however, they recognized in him a servant of God, and many of them gave up their sinful ways for a life of holiness. As a result, his name became known to all the people in that locality and great numbers visited his cave, supplying him with the food he needed and receiving from his lips in return spiritual food for their souls. *Growing in popularity teaching wisdom like Jesus & apostles*

2. One day, while the saint was alone, the Tempter came in the form of a little blackbird, which began to flutter in front of his face. It kept so close that he could easily have caught it in his hand. Instead, he made the sign of the cross and the bird flew away. The moment it left, he was seized with an unusually violent temptation. The evil spirit recalled to his mind a woman he had once seen and before he realized it his emotions were carrying him away. Almost overcome in the struggle, he was on the point of abandoning the lonely wilderness, when suddenly with the help of God's grace he came to himself.

He then noticed a thick patch of nettles and briers next to him. Throwing his garment aside he flung himself into the sharp thorns and stinging nettles. *Body vs. Soul* There he rolled and tossed until his whole body was in pain and covered with blood. Yet, once he had conquered pleasure through suffering, his torn and bleeding skin served to drain the poison of temptation from his body. Before long, the pain that was burning his whole body had put out the fires of evil in his heart. It was by exchanging these two fires that he gained the victory over sin. So complete was his triumph that from then on, as he later told his disciples, he never experienced another temptation of this kind. Soon after, many forsook the world to place themselves under his guidance, for now that he was free from these temptations he was ready to instruct others in the practice of virtue. That is why Moses commanded the Levites to begin their service when they were twenty-five years old or more and to become guardians of the sacred vessels only at the age of fifty.

Peter: The meaning of the passage you quote is becoming a little clearer to me now. Still, I wish you would explain it more fully.

Gregory: It is a well-known fact, Peter, that temptations of the flesh are violent during youth, whereas after the age of fifty concupiscence dies down. Now, the sacred vessels are the souls of the faithful. God's chosen servants must therefore obey and serve and tire themselves out with strenuous work as long as they are still subject to temptations. Only when full maturity has left them undisturbed by evil thoughts are they put in charge of the sacred vessels, for then they become teachers of souls.

Peter: I like the way you interpreted that passage. Now that you have explained what it means, I hope you will continue with your account of the holy man's life.

3. Gregory: With the passing of this temptation, Benedict's soul, like a field cleared of briers, soon yielded a rich harvest of virtues. As word spread of his saintly life, the renown of his name increased. One day the entire community from a nearby monastery came to see him. Their abbot had recently died, and they wanted the man of God to be their new superior. For some time he tried to discourage them by refusing their request, warning them that his way of life would never harmonize with theirs. But they kept insisting, until in the end he gave his consent.

At the monastery he watched carefully over the religious spirit of his monks and would not tolerate any of their previous disobedience. No one was allowed to turn from the straight path of monastic discipline either to the right or to the left. Their waywardness, however, clashed with the standards he upheld, and in their resentment they started to reproach themselves for choosing him as abbot. It only made them the more sullen to find him curbing every fault and evil habit. They could not see why they should have to force their settled minds into new ways of thinking.

At length, proving once again that the very life of the just is a burden to the wicked, they tried to find a means of doing away with him and decided to poison his wine. A glass pitcher containing this poisoned drink was presented to the man of God during his meal for the customary blessing. As he made the sign of the cross over it with his hand, the pitcher was shattered, even though it was well beyond his reach at the time. It broke at his blessing as if he had struck it with stone.

Then he realized it had contained a deadly drink which could not bear the sign of life. Still calm and undisturbed, he rose at once and, after gathering the community together, addressed them. 'May almighty God have mercy on you,' he said. 'Why did you conspire to do this? Did I not tell you

[Fig. 17] Benedict and the rebellious monks, from a fourteenth-century fresco by Spinello d'Arezzo (Lacroix, *Military and Religious Life in the Middle Ages*, p. 305). On the left, the monks ask Benedict to head their monastery; on the right, having decided his rule is too austere, they offer him a poisoned drink.

at the outset that my way of life would never harmonize with yours? Go and find yourselves an abbot to your liking. It is impossible for me to stay here any longer.' Then he went back to the wilderness he loved, to live alone with himself in the presence of his heavenly Father.

Peter: I am not quite sure I understand what you mean by saying 'to live with himself.'

Gregory: These monks had an outlook on religious life entirely unlike his own and were all conspiring against him. Now, if he had tried to force them to remain under his rule, he might have forfeited his own fervor and peace of soul and even turned his eyes from the light of contemplation. Their persis-

early example of no coercion into conversion

tent daily faults would have left him almost too weary to look to his own needs, and he would perhaps have forsaken himself without finding them. For, whenever anxieties carry us out of ourselves unduly, we are no longer with ourselves even though we still remain what we are. We are too distracted with other matters to give any attention whatever to ourselves.

Surely we cannot describe as 'with himself' the young man who traveled to a distant country where he wasted his inheritance and then, after hiring himself out to one of its citizens to feed swine, had to watch them eat their fill of pods while he went hungry. Do we not read in Scripture that, as he was considering all he had lost, he came to himself and said, 'how many hired servants there are in my father's house who have more bread than they can eat'? If he was already 'with himself,' how could he have come 'to himself'?

Blessed Benedict, on the contrary, can be said to have lived 'with himself' because at all times he kept such close watch over his life and actions. By searching continually into his own soul he always beheld himself in the presence of his Creator. And this kept his mind from straying off to the world outside.

Peter: But what of Peter the apostle when he was led out of prison by an angel? According to the Scriptures, he, too, 'came to himself.' 'Now I can tell for certain,' he said, 'that the Lord has sent his angel, to deliver me out of Herod's hands, and from all that the people of the Jews hoped to see.'

Gregory: There are two ways in which we can be carried out of ourselves, Peter. Either we fall below ourselves through sins of thought or we are lifted above ourselves by the grace of contemplation. The young man who fed the swine sank below himself as a result of his shiftless ways and his unclean life. The apostle Peter was also out of himself when the angel set him free and raised him to a state of ecstasy, but he was above himself. In coming to themselves again, the former had to break with his sinful past before he could find his true and better self, whereas the latter merely returned from the heights of contemplation to his ordinary state of mind.

Now, the saintly Benedict really lived 'with himself' out in that lonely wilderness by always keeping his thoughts recollected. Yet he must have left his own self far below each time he was drawn heavenward in fervent contemplation.

Peter: I am very grateful to you for that explanation. Do you think it was right, though, for him to forsake this community, once he had taken it under his care?

Gregory: In my opinion, Peter, a superior ought to bear patiently with a community of evil men as long as it has some devout members who can benefit from his presence. When none of the members is devout enough to give any promise of good results, his efforts to help such a community will prove to be a serious mistake, especially if there are opportunities nearby to work more fruitfully for God. Was there anyone the holy man could have hoped to protect by staying where he was, after he saw that they were all united against him?

In this matter we cannot afford to overlook the attitude of the saints. When they find their work producing no results in one place, they move on to another where it can do some good. This explains the action of the blessed apostle Paul. In order to escape from Damascus, where he was being persecuted, he secured a basket and a rope and had himself secretly lowered over the wall. Yet this outstanding preacher of the Gospel longed to depart and be with Christ, since for him life meant Christ, and death was a prize to be won. Besides being eager for the trials of persecution himself, he even inspired others to endure them. Can we say that Paul feared death, when he expressly declared that he longed to die for the love of Christ? Surely not. But, when he saw how little he was accomplishing at Damascus in spite of all his toil, he saved himself for more fruitful labors elsewhere. God's fearless warrior refused to be held back inside the walls and sought the open field of battle. And if you do not mind continuing to listen, Peter, you will soon discover that after blessed Benedict left that obstinate community he restored to life many another soul that was spiritually dead.

Peter: I am sure your conclusion is correct, after the simple proof you gave and that striking example from sacred Scripture. Would you be good enough to return now to the story of this great abbot's life?

Gregory: As Benedict's influence spread over the surrounding countryside because of his signs and wonders, a great number of men gathered round him to devote themselves to God's service. Christ blessed his work and before long he had established twelve monasteries there, with an abbot and twelve monks in each of them. There were a few other monks whom he kept with him, since he felt that they still needed his personal guidance.

It was about this time that pious noblemen from Rome first came to visit the saint and left their sons with him to be schooled in the service of God. Thus, Euthicius brought his son Maurus; and Senator Tertullus, Placid – both very promising boys. Maurus, in fact, who was a little older, had already acquired solid virtue and was soon very helpful to his saintly master. But Placid was still only a child.

4. In one of the monasteries Benedict had founded in that locality, there was a monk who would never remain with the rest of the community for silent prayer. Instead, he left the chapel as soon as they knelt down to pray, and passed the time aimlessly at whatever happened to interest him. His abbot corrected him repeatedly and at length sent him to the man of God. This time the monk received a stern rebuke for his folly and after his return

took the correction to heart for a day or two, only to fall back the third day into his old habit of wandering off during the time of prayer. On learning of this from the abbot, the man of God sent word that he was coming over himself to see that the monk mended his ways. Upon his arrival at the monastery, Benedict joined the community in the chapel at the regular hour. After they had finished chanting the Psalms and had begun their silent prayer, he noticed that the restless monk was drawn outside by a little black boy who was pulling at the edge of his habit. 'Do you see who is leading that monk out of the chapel?' he whispered to Abbot Pompeianus and Maurus. 'No,' they replied. 'Let us pray, then,' he said, 'that you may see what is happening to him.' They prayed for two days, and after that Maurus also saw what was taking place, but Abbot Pompeianus still could not. The next day, when prayers were over, Benedict found the offender loitering outside and struck him with his staff for being so obstinate of heart. From then on the monk remained quietly at prayer like the rest, without being bothered again by the tempter. It was as if that ancient Enemy had been struck by the blow himself and was afraid to domineer over the monk's thoughts any longer.

5. Three of the monasteries the saint had built close by stood on the bare rocky heights. It was a real hardship for these monks always to go down to the lake to get water for their daily needs. Besides, the slope was steep and they found the descent very dangerous. The members of the three communities therefore came in a body to see the servant of God. After explaining how difficult it was for them to climb down the mountainside every day for their water supply, they assured him that the only solution was to have the monasteries moved somewhere else. Benedict answered them with fatherly words of encouragement and sent them back. That same night, in company with the little boy Placid, he climbed to the rocky heights and prayed there for a long time. On finishing his prayer, he placed three stones together to indicate the spot where he had knelt and then went back to his monastery, unnoticed by anyone.

The following day, when the monks came again with their request, he told them to go to the summit of the mountain. 'You will find three stones there,' he said, 'one on top of the other. If you dig down a little, you will see that almighty God has the power to bring forth water even from that rocky summit and in His goodness relieve you of the hardship of such a long climb.'

Going back to the place he had described, they noticed that the surface was already moist. As soon as they had dug the ground away, water filled the hollow and welled up in such abundance that today a full stream is still flowing from the top of the mountain into the ravine below.

6. At another time a simple, sincere Goth came to Subiaco to become

a monk, and blessed Benedict was very happy to admit him. One day he had him take a brush hook and clear away the briers from a place at the edge of the lake where a garden was to be planted. While the Goth was hard at work cutting down the thick brush, the iron blade slipped off the handle and flew into a very deep part of the lake, where there was no hope of recovering it.

At this the poor man ran trembling to Maurus and, after describing the accident, told him how sorry he was for his carelessness. Maurus in turn informed the servant of God, who on hearing what had happened went down to the lake, took the handle from the Goth and thrust it in the water. Immediately the iron blade rose from the bottom of the lake and slipped back onto the handle. Then he handed the tool back to the Goth and told him, 'Continue with your work now. There is no need to be upset.'

7. Once while blessed Benedict was in his room, one of his monks, the boy Placid, went down to the lake to draw water. In letting the bucket fill too rapidly, he lost his balance and was pulled into the lake, where the current quickly seized him and carried him about a stone's throw from the shore. Though inside the monastery at the time, the man of God was instantly aware of what had happened and called out to Maurus: 'Hurry, Brother Maurus! The boy who just went down for water has fallen into the lake, and the current is carrying him away.'

What followed was remarkable indeed, and unheard of since the time of Peter the apostle! Maurus asked for the blessing and on receiving it hurried out to fulfil his abbot's command. He kept on running even over the water till he reached the place where Placid was drifting along helplessly. Pulling him up by the hair, Maurus rushed back to shore, still under the impression that he was on dry land. It was only when he set foot on the ground that he came to himself and looking back realized that he had been running on the surface of the water. Overcome with fear and amazement at a deed he would never have thought possible, he returned to his abbot and told him what had taken place. The holy man would not take any personal credit for the deed, but attributed it to the obedience of his disciple. Maurus on the contrary, claimed that it was due entirely to his abbot's command. He could not have been responsible for the miracle himself, he said, since he had not even known he was performing it. While they were carrying on this friendly contest of humility, the question was settled by the boy who had been rescued. 'When I was being drawn out of the water,' he told them, 'I saw the abbot's cloak over my head; he is the one I thought was bringing me to shore.'

Peter: What marvelous deeds these are! They are sure to prove inspiring to all who hear of them. Indeed, the more you tell me about this great man, the more eager I am to keep on listening.

8. Gregory: By this time the people of that whole region for miles around had grown fervent in their love for Christ, and many of them had forsaken the world in order to bring their hearts under the light yoke of the Savior. Now, in a neighboring church there was a priest named Florentius, the grandfather of our subdeacon Florentius. Urged on by the bitter Enemy of mankind, this priest set out to undermine the saint's work. And envious as the wicked always are of the holiness in others which they are not striving to acquire themselves, he denounced Benedict's way of life and kept everyone he could from visiting him.

The progress of the saint's work, however, could not be stopped. His reputation for holiness kept on growing, and with it the number of vocations to a more perfect state of life. This infuriated Florentius all the more. He still longed to enjoy the praise the saint was receiving, yet he was unwilling to lead a praiseworthy life himself. At length, his soul became so blind with jealousy that he decided to poison a loaf of bread and send it to the servant of God as though it was a sign of Christian fellowship. Though aware at once of the deadly poison it contained, Benedict thanked him for the gift.

At mealtime a raven used to come out of the nearby woods to receive food from the saint's hands. On this occasion he set the poisoned loaf in front of it and said, 'In the name of our Lord Jesus Christ, take this bread and carry it to a place where no one will be able to find it.' The raven started to caw and circled round the loaf of bread with open beak and flapping wings as if to indicate that it was willing to obey, but found it impossible to do so. Several times the saint repeated the command. 'Take the bread,' he said, 'and do not be afraid! Take it away from here and leave it where no one will find it.' After hesitating for a long while, the raven finally took the loaf in its beak and flew away. About three hours later, when it had disposed of the bread, it returned and received its usual meal from the hands of the man of God.

The saintly abbot now realized how deep the resentment of his enemy was, and he felt grieved not so much for his own sake as for the priest's. But Florentius, after his failure to do away with the master, determined instead to destroy the souls of the disciples and for this purpose sent seven depraved women into the garden of Benedict's monastery. There they joined hands and danced together for some time within sight of his followers, in an attempt to lead them into sin.

When the saint noticed this from his window, he began to fear that some of his younger monks might go astray. Convinced that the priest's hatred for him was the real cause of this attack, he let envy have its way and, taking only a few monks with him, set out to find a new home. Before he left, he reorganized all the monasteries he had founded, appointing priors to assist in governing them, and adding some new members to the communities.

Hardly had the man of God made his humble escape from all this bitterness when almighty God struck the priest down with terrible vengeance. As he was standing on the balcony of his house congratulating himself on Benedict's departure, the structure suddenly collapsed, crushing him to death, though the rest of the building remained undamaged. This accident occurred before the saint was even ten miles away. His disciple Maurus immediately decided to send a messenger with the news and ask him to return, now that the priest who had caused him so much trouble was dead. Benedict was overcome with sorrow and regret on hearing this, for not only had his enemy been killed, but one of his own disciples had rejoiced over his death. And for showing pleasure in sending such a message he gave Maurus a penance to perform.

Peter: This whole account is really amazing. The water streaming from the rock reminds me of Moses, and the iron blade that rose from the bottom of the lake, of Eliseus. The walking on the water recalls St. Peter, the obedience of the raven, Elias, and the grief at the death of an enemy, David. This man must have been filled with the spirit of all the just.

Gregory: Actually, Peter, blessed Benedict possessed the Spirit of only one person, the Savior who fills the hearts of all the faithful by granting them the fruits of his redemption. For St. John says of him, 'There is one who enlightens every soul born into the world; he was the true light.' And again, 'we have all received something out of his abundance.' Holy men never were able to hand on to others the miraculous powers which they received from God. Our Savior was the only one to give his followers the power to work signs and wonders, just as he alone could assure his enemies that he would give them the sign of the prophet Jonas. Seeing this sign fulfilled in his death, the proud looked on with scorn. The humble, who saw its complete fulfilment in his rising from the dead, turned to him with reverence and love. In this mystery, then, the proud beheld him dying in disgrace, whereas the humble witnessed his triumph over death.

Peter: Now that you have finished explaining this, please tell me where the holy man settled after his departure. Do you know whether he performed any more miracles?

Gregory: Although he moved to a different place, Peter, his enemy remained the same. In fact, the assaults he had to endure after this were all the more violent, because the very Master of evil was fighting against him in open battle.

The fortified town of Cassino lies at the foot of a towering mountain that shelters it within its slope and stretches upward over a distance of nearly three miles. On its summit stood a very old temple, in which the ignorant country people still worshiped Apollo as their pagan ancestors had done, and

[Fig. 18] Benedict exorcises the Devil, who is sitting on a rock and preventing the monks from using it to build a section of the abbey (fresco by d'Arezzo, Baring-Gould, *Lives of the Saints,* 3).

went on offering superstitious and idolatrous sacrifices in groves dedicated to various demons.

When the man of God arrived at this spot, he destroyed the idol, overturned the altar and cut down the trees in the sacred groves. Then he turned the temple of Apollo into a chapel dedicated to St. Martin [of Tours, who had also destroyed pagan temples; see 14 above], and where Apollo's altar had stood, he built a chapel in honor of St. John the Baptist. Gradually, the people of the countryside were won over to the true faith by his zealous preaching.

Such losses the ancient Enemy could not bear in silence. This time he did not appear to the saint in a dream or under a disguise, but met him face to face and objected fiercely to the outrages he had to endure. His shouts were so loud that the brethren heard him, too, although they were unable to see him. According to the saint's own description, the Devil had an appearance utterly revolting to human eyes. He was enveloped in fire and, when he raged against the man of God, flames darted from his eyes and mouth. Everyone could hear what he was saying. First he called Benedict by name. Then, finding that the saint would not answer, he broke out in abusive language. 'Benedict, Benedict, blessed Benedict!' he would begin, and then add, 'You cursed Benedict! Cursed, not blessed! What do you want with me? Why are you tormenting me like this?'

From now on, Peter, as you can well imagine, the devil fought against the man of God with renewed violence. But, contrary to his plans, all these attacks only supplied the saint with further opportunities for victory.

9. One day while the monks were constructing a section of the abbey, they noticed a rock lying close at hand and decided to use it in the building. When two or three did not succeed in lifting it, others joined in to help. Yet it remained fixed in its place as though it was rooted to the ground. Then they were sure that the Devil himself was sitting on this stone and preventing them from moving it in spite of all their efforts.

Faced with this difficulty, they asked Abbot Benedict to come and use his prayers to drive away the devil who was holding down the rock. The saint began to pray as soon as he got there, and after he had finished and made the sign of the Cross, the monks picked up the rock with such ease that it seemed to have lost all its previous weight.

10. The abbot then directed them to spade up the earth where the stone had been. When they had dug a little way into the ground they came upon a bronze idol, which they threw into the kitchen for the time being. Suddenly the kitchen appeared to be on fire and everyone felt that the entire building was going up in flames. The noise and commotion they made in their attempt to put out the blaze by pouring on buckets of water brought Benedict to the scene. Unable to see the fire which appeared so real to his monks, he quietly bowed his head in prayer and soon had opened their eyes to the foolish mistake they were making. Now, instead of the flames the evil spirit had devised, they once more saw the kitchen standing intact.

11. On another occasion they were working on one of the walls that had to be built a little higher. The man of God was in his room at the time, praying, when the devil appeared to him and remarked sarcastically that he was on his way to visit the brethren at their work. Benedict quickly sent them word to be on their guard against the evil spirit who would soon be with them. Just as they received his warning, the Devil overturned the wall, crushing under its ruins the body of a very young monk who was the son of a tax collector.

Unconcerned about the damaged wall in their grief and dismay over the loss of their brother, the monks hurried to Abbot Benedict to let him know of the dreadful accident. He told them to bring the mangled body to his room. It had to be carried in on a blanket, for the wall had not only broken the boy's arms and legs but had crushed all the bones in his body. The saint had the remains placed on the reed matting where he used to pray and after that told them all to leave. Then he closed the door and knelt down to offer his most earnest prayers to God. That very hour, to the astonishment of all, he sent the boy back to his work as sound and healthy as he had been before. Thus, in spite of the devil's attempt to mock the man of God by causing this tragic death, the young monk was able to rejoin his brethren and help them finish the wall.

Raising the dead

Meanwhile, Benedict began to manifest the spirit of prophecy by foretelling future events and by describing to those who were with him what they had done in his absence.

12. It was a custom of the house, strictly observed as a matter of regular discipline, that monks away on business did not take food or drink outside the monastery. One day, a few of them went out on an assignment which kept them occupied till rather late. They stopped for a meal at the house of a devout woman they knew in the neighborhood. On their return, when they presented themselves to the abbot for the usual blessing, he asked them where they had taken their meal.

knowing when people are lying

'Nowhere,' they answered.

'Why are you lying to me?' he said. 'Did you not enter the house of this particular woman and eat these various foods and have so many cups to drink?'

On hearing him mention the woman's hospitality and exactly what she had given them to eat and drink, they clearly recalled the wrong they had done, fell trembling at his feet, and confessed their guilt. The man of God did not hesitate to pardon them, confident that they would do no further wrong in his absence, since they now realized he was always present with them in spirit.

13. The monk Valentinian, mentioned earlier in our narrative, had a brother who was a very devout layman. Every year he visited the abbey in order to get Benedict's blessing and see his brother. On the way he always used to fast. Now, one time as he was making this journey he was joined by another traveler who had brought some food along. 'Come,' said the stranger after some time had passed, 'let us have something to eat before we become too fatigued.' 'I am sorry,' the devout layman replied. 'I always fast on my way to visit Abbot Benedict.' After that the traveler was quiet for a while. But when they had walked along some distance together, he repeated his sugges-

tion. Still mindful of his good resolve, Valentinian's brother again refused. His companion did not insist and once more agreed to accompany him a little further without eating.

Then, after they had covered a great distance together and were very tired from the long hours of walking they came upon a meadow and a spring. The whole setting seemed ideal for a much needed rest. 'Look,' said the stranger, 'water and a meadow! What a delightful spot for us to have some refreshments! A little rest will give us strength to finish our journey without any discomfort.'

It was such an attractive sight and this third invitation sounded so appealing that the devout layman was completely won over and stopped there to eat with his companion. Toward evening he arrived at the monastery and was presented to the abbot. As soon as he asked for the blessing, however, the holy man reproved him for his conduct on the journey. 'How is it,' he said, 'that the evil spirit who spoke with you in the person of your traveling companion could not persuade you to do his will the first and second time he tried, but succeeded in his third attempt?' At this Valentinian's brother fell at Benedict's feet and admitted the weakness of his will. The thought that even from such a distance the saint had witnessed the wrong he had done filled him with shame and remorse.

Peter: This proves that the servant of God possessed the spirit of Eliseus. He, too, was present with one of his followers who was far away.

Gregory: If you will listen a little longer, Peter, I have an incident to tell you that is even more astonishing.

14. Once while the Goths [the Ostrogoths, a people from eastern Europe who had established a kingdom in Italy under Theodoric in 493] were still in power, Totila their king [541-52] happened to be marching in the direction of Benedict's monastery. When still some distance away, he halted with his troops and sent a messenger ahead to announce his coming, for he had heard that the man of God possessed the gift of prophecy. As soon as he received word that he would be welcomed, the crafty king decided to put the saint's prophetic powers to a test. He had Riggo, his sword-bearer, fitted out with royal robes and riding boots and directed him to go in this disguise to the man of God. Vul, Ruderic and Blidin, three men from his own bodyguard, were to march at his side as if he really were king of the Goths. To supplement these marks of kingship, Totila also provided him with a swordbearer and other attendants. As Riggo entered the monastery grounds in his kingly robes and with all his attendants, Benedict caught sight of him and as soon as the company came within hearing called out from where he sat. 'Son, lay aside the robes you are wearing,' he said. 'Lay them aside. They do not belong

[Fig. 19] Benedict reproving King Totila and predicting his death (fresco by D'Arezzo, Baring-Gould, *Lives of the Saints,* 3).

to you.' Aghast at seeing what a great man he had tried to mock, Riggo sank to the ground, and with him all the members of his company. Even after they had risen to their feet they did not dare approach the saint, but hurried back in alarm to tell their king how quickly they had been detected.

15. King Totila then went to the monastery in person. The moment he noticed the man of God sitting at a distance, he was afraid to come any closer and fell down prostrate where he was. Two or three times Benedict asked him to rise. When Totila still hesitated to do so in his presence, the servant of Christ walked over to him and with his own hands helped him from the ground. Then he rebuked the king for his crimes and briefly foretold everything that was going to happen to him. 'You are the cause of many evils,' he said. 'You have caused many in the past. Put an end now to your wickedness. You will enter Rome and cross the sea. You have nine more years to rule, and in the tenth year you will die.'

Terrified at these words, the king asked for a blessing and went away. From that time on he was less cruel. Not long after, he went to Rome and then crossed over to Sicily. In the tenth year of his reign he lost his kingdom and his life as almighty God had decreed.

There is also a story about the bishop of Canossa, who made regular visits to the abbey and stood high in Benedict's esteem because of his saintly life. Once while they were discussing Totila's invasion and the downfall of Rome, the bishop said, 'The city will be destroyed by this king and left without a single inhabitant.' Benedict assured him, 'Rome will not be destroyed by the barbarians. It will be shaken by tempests and lightnings, hurricanes and earthquakes, until finally it lies buried in its own ruins.' [Totila captured Rome in 546 but stopped short of destroying the entire city.]

The meaning of this prophecy is perfectly clear to us now. We have watched the walls of Rome crumble and have seen its homes in ruins, its churches destroyed by violent storms, and its dilapidated buildings surrounded by their own debris.

Benedict's disciple Honoratus, who told me about the prophecy, admits he did not hear it personally, but he assures me that some of his own brethren gave him this account of it.

16. At about the same time there was a cleric from the church at Aquino [8 km/5 miles from Monte Cassino] who was being tormented by an evil spirit. Constantius, his saintly bishop, had already sent him to the shrines of various martyrs in the hope that he would be cured. But the holy martyrs did not grant him this favor, preferring instead to reveal the wonderful gifts of the servant of God.

As soon as the cleric was brought to him, Benedict drove out the evil spirit with fervent prayers to Christ. Before sending him back to Aquino, however, he told him to abstain from meat thereafter and never to advance to sacred orders. 'If you ignore this warning,' he added, 'and present yourself for ordination, you will find yourself once more in the power of Satan.'

The cleric left completely cured, and as long as his previous torments were still fresh in his mind he did exactly as the man of God had ordered. Then with the passing of years, all his seniors in the clerical state died, and he had to watch newly ordained young men moving ahead of him in rank. Finally, he pretended to have forgotten about the saint's warning and, disregarding it, presented himself for ordination. Instantly he was seized by the devil and tormented mercilessly until he died.

Peter: The servant of God must even have been aware of the hidden designs of Providence, to have realized that this cleric had been handed over to Satan to keep him from aspiring to holy orders.

Gregory: Is there any reason why a person who has observed the commandments of God should not also know of God's secret designs? 'The man who unites himself to the Lord becomes one spirit with him,' we read in sacred Scripture.

Peter: If everyone who unites himself to the Lord becomes one spirit with him, what does the renowned apostle mean when he asks, 'Who has ever understood the Lord's thoughts, or been his counselor?' It hardly seems possible to be one spirit with a person without knowing his thoughts.

Gregory: Holy men do know the Lord's thoughts, Peter, in so far as they are one with him. This is clear from the apostle's words, 'Who else can know a man's thoughts, except the man's own spirit that is within him? So no one else can know God's thoughts but the Spirit of God.' To show that he actually knew God's thoughts, St. Paul added: 'And what we have received is no spirit of worldly wisdom; it is the Spirit that comes from God.' And again: 'No eye has seen, no ear has heard, no human heart conceived, the welcome God has prepared for those who love him. To us, then, God has made a revelation of it through his Spirit.'

Peter: If it is true that God's thoughts were revealed to the apostle by the Holy Spirit, how could he introduce his statement with the words, 'How deep is the mine of God's wisdom, of his knowledge; how inscrutable are his judgments, how undiscoverable his ways!' Another difficulty just occurred to me now as I was speaking. In addressing the Lord, David the Prophet declares, 'With my lips I have pronounced all the judgments of thy mouth.' Surely it is a greater achievement to express one's knowledge than merely to possess it. How is it, then, that St. Paul calls the judgments of God inscrutable, whereas David says he knows them all and has even pronounced them with his lips?

Gregory: I already gave a brief reply to both of these objections when I told you that holy men know God's thoughts in so far as they are one with him. For all who follow the Lord wholeheartedly are living in spiritual union with him. As long as they are still weighed down with a perishable body, however, they are not actually united to him. It is only to the extent that they are one with God that they know his hidden judgments. In so far as they are not yet one with him, they do not know them. Since even holy men cannot fully grasp the secret designs of God during this present life, they call his judgments inscrutable. At the same time, they understand his judgments and can even pronounce them with their lips; for they keep their hearts united to God by dwelling continually on the words of holy Scripture and on such private revelations as they may receive, until they grasp his meaning. In other words, they do not know the judgments which God conceals but only those which he reveals. That is why, after declaring, 'With my lips I have pronounced all the judgments,' the Prophet immediately adds the phrase, 'of thy mouth,' as if to say, 'I can know and pronounce only the judgments you have spoken to me. Those you leave unspoken must remain hidden from our minds.' So the prophet and the apostle are in full agreement. God's decisions are truly unfathomable. But, once his mouth has made them known, they can also be proclaimed by human lips. What God has spoken man can know. Of the thoughts he has kept secret man can know nothing.

Peter: That is certainly a reasonable solution to the difficulties that I raised. If you know any other miraculous events in this man's life, would you continue with them now?

17. Gregory: Under the direction of Abbot Benedict a nobleman named Theoprobus had embraced monastic life. Because of his exemplary life he enjoyed the saint's personal friendship and confidence. One day, on entering Benedict's room, he found him weeping bitterly. After he had waited for some time and there was still no end to the abbot's tears, he asked what was causing him such sorrow, for he was not weeping as he usually did at prayer, but with deep sighs and lamentation. 'Almighty God has decreed that this entire monastery and everything I have provided for the community shall fall into the hands of the barbarians,' the saint replied. 'It was only with the greatest difficulty that I could prevail upon him to spare the lives of its members.'

This was the prophecy he made to Theoprobus, and we have seen its fulfilment in the recent destruction of his abbey by the Lombards [in 589; it was rebuilt in 720]. They came at night while the community was asleep and plundered the entire monastery, without capturing a single monk. In this way God fulfilled his promise to Benedict, his faithful servant. He allowed the barbarians to destroy the monastery, but safeguarded the lives of the religious. Here you can see how the man of God resembled St. Paul, who had the consolation of seeing everyone with him escape alive from the storm, while the ship and all its cargo were lost.

18. Exhilaratus, a fellow Roman who, as you know, later became a monk was once sent by his master to Abbot Benedict with two wooden flasks of wine. He delivered only one of them, however; the other he hid along the way. Benedict, who could observe even what was done in his absence, thanked him for the flask, but warned him as he turned to go: 'Son, be sure not to drink from the flask you have hidden away. Tilt it carefully and you will see what is inside.' Exhilaratus left in shame and confusion and went back to the spot, still wishing to verify the saint's words. As he tilted the flask a serpent crawled out, and at the sight of it he was filled with horror for his misdeed.

19. Not far from the monastery was a village largely inhabited by people the saintly Benedict had converted from the worship of idols and instructed in the true faith. There were nuns living there too, and he used to send one of his monks down to give them spiritual conferences.

After one of these instructions they presented the monk with a few handkerchiefs, which he accepted and hid away in his habit. As soon as he got back to the abbey he received a stern reproof. 'How is it,' the abbot asked him, 'that evil has found its way into your heart?' Taken completely by surprise, the monk did not understand why he was being rebuked, for he had entirely forgotten about the handkerchiefs. 'Was I not present,' the saint continued, 'when you accepted those handkerchiefs from the handmaids of God and hid them away in your habit?' The offender instantly fell at Benedict's feet, confessed his fault, and gave up the present he had received.

20. Once when the saintly abbot was taking his evening meal, a young monk whose father was a highranking official happened to be holding the lamp for him. As he stood at the abbot's table the spirit of pride began to stir in his heart. 'Who is this,' he thought to himself, 'that I should have to stand here holding the lamp for him while he is eating? Who am I to be serving him?' Turning to him at once, Benedict gave the monk a sharp reprimand. 'Brother,' he said, 'sign your heart with the sign of the Cross. What are you saying? Sign your heart!' Then, calling the others together, he had one of them take the lamp instead, and told the murmurer to sit down by himself and be quiet. Later, when asked what he had done wrong, the monk explained how he had given in to the spirit of pride and silently murmured against the man of God. At this the brethren all realized that nothing could be kept secret from their holy abbot, since he could hear even the unspoken sentiments of the heart.

21. During a time of famine [possibly the great famine of 537-8] the severe shortage of food was causing a great deal of suffering in Campania. At Benedict's monastery the entire grain supply had been used up and nearly all the bread was gone as well. In fact, when mealtime came, only five loaves could be found to set before the community. Noticing how downcast they were, the saint gently reproved them for their lack of trust in God and at the same time tried to raise their dejected spirits with a comforting assurance. 'Why are you so depressed at the lack of bread?' he asked 'What if today there is only a little? Tomorrow you will have more than you need.'

The next day 200 measures of flour were found in sacks at the gate of the monastery, but no one ever discovered whose services almighty God had employed in bringing them there. When they saw what had happened, the monks were filled with gratitude and learned from this miracle that even in their hour of need they must not lose faith in the bountiful goodness of God.

Peter: Are we to believe that the spirit of prophecy remained with the servant of God at all times, or did he receive it only on special occasions?

Gregory: The spirit of prophecy does not enlighten the minds of the prophets constantly, Peter. We read in sacred Scripture that the Holy Spirit breathes where he pleases, and we should also realize that he breathes when he pleases. For example, when King David asked whether he could build a temple, the prophet Nathan gave his consent, but later had to withdraw it. And Eliseus once found a woman in tears without knowing the reason for her grief. That is why he told his servant who was trying to interfere, 'Let her alone, for her soul is in anguish and the Lord his hidden it from me and has not told me.'

All this reflects God's boundless wisdom and love. By granting these men the spirit of prophecy he raises their minds high above the world, and by withdrawing it again he safeguards their humility. When the spirit of prophecy is with them they learn what they are by God's mercy. When the spirit leaves them they discover what they are of themselves.

Peter: This convincing argument leaves no room for doubt about the truth of what you say. Please resume your narrative now, if you recall any other incidents in the life of blessed Benedict.

22. Gregory: A Catholic layman once asked him to found a monastery on his estate at Terracina. The servant of God readily consented and, after selecting several of his monks for this undertaking, appointed one of them abbot and another his assistant. Before they left he specified a day on which he would come to show them where to build the chapel, the refectory, a house for guests, and the other buildings they would need. Then he gave them his blessing.

After their arrival at Terracina they looked forward eagerly to the day he had set for his visit and prepared to receive the monks who would accompany him. Before dawn of the appointed day, Benedict appeared in a dream to the new abbot as well as to his prior and showed them exactly where each section of the monastery was to stand. In the morning they told each other what they had seen, but, instead of putting their entire trust in the vision, they kept waiting for the promised visit. When the day passed without any word from Benedict, they returned to him disappointed. 'Father,' they said, 'we were waiting for you to show us where to build, as you assured us you would, but you did not come.'

'What do you mean?' he replied. 'Did I not come as I promised?' 'When?' they asked. 'Did I not appear to both of you in a dream as you slept and indicate where each building was to stand? Go back and build as you were directed in the vision.' They returned to Terracina, filled with wonder, and constructed the monastery according to the plans he had revealed to them.

Peter: I wish you would explain how Benedict could possibly travel that distance and then in a vision give these monks directions which they could hear and understand while they were asleep.

Gregory: What is there in this incident that should raise a doubt in your mind, Peter? Everyone knows that the soul is far more agile than the body.

Yet we have it on the authority of holy Scripture that the prophet Habacuc was lifted from Judea to Chaldea in an instant, so that he might share his dinner with the prophet Daniel, and presently found himself back in Judea again. If Habacuc could cover such a distance in a brief moment to take a meal to his fellow prophet, is it not understandable that Abbot Benedict could go in spirit to his sleeping brethren with the information they required? As the prophet came in body with food for the body, Benedict came in spirit to promote the life of the soul.

Peter: Your words seem to smooth away all my doubts. Could you tell me now what this saint was like in his everyday speech?

23. Gregory: There was a trace of the marvelous in nearly everything he said, Peter, and his words never failed to take effect because his heart was fixed in God. Even when he uttered a simple threat that was indefinite and conditional, it was just as decisive as a final verdict.

Some distance from the abbey two women of noble birth were leading the religious life in their own home. A God-fearing layman was kind enough to bring them what they needed from the outside world. Unfortunately, as is sometimes the case, their character stood in sharp contrast to the nobility of their birth, and they were too conscious of their former importance to practise true humility toward others. Even under the restraining influence of religious life they still had not learned to control their tongues, and the good layman who served them so faithfully was often provoked at their harsh criticisms. After putting up with their insults for a long time, he went to blessed Benedict and told him how inconsiderate they were. The man of God immediately warned them to curb their sharp tongues and added that he would have to excommunicate them if they did not. This sentence of excommunication was not actually pronounced, therefore, but only threatened.

A short time afterward the two nuns died without any sign of amendment and were buried in their parish church. Whenever Mass was celebrated, their old nurse, who regularly made an offering for them, noticed that each time the deacon announced, 'The non-communicants [the unbaptized and the excommunicated] must now leave,' the nuns rose from their tombs and went outside. This happened repeatedly, until one day she recalled the warning Benedict had given them while they were still alive, when he threatened to deprive them of communion with the Church if they kept on speaking so uncharitably.

The grief-stricken nurse had Abbot Benedict informed of what was happening. He sent her messengers back with an oblation and said, 'Have this offered up for their souls during the Holy Sacrifice [communion], and they will be freed from the sentence of excommunication.' The offering was made and after that the nuns were not seen leaving the church any more at the deacon's dismissal of the non-communicants. Evidently, they had been admitted to communion with our blessed Lord in answer to the prayers of his servant Benedict.

Peter: Is it not extraordinary that souls already judged at God's invisible tribunal could be pardoned by a man who was still living in the mortal flesh, however holy and revered he may have been?

Gregory: What of Peter the apostle? Was he not still living in the flesh when he heard the words, 'Whatever thou shalt bind on earth shall be bound in heaven, and whatever thou shalt loose on earth shall be loosed in heaven'? All those who govern the Church in matters of faith and morals exercise the same power of binding and loosing that he received. In fact, the Creator's very purpose in coming down from heaven to earth was to impart to earthly man this heavenly power. It was when God was made flesh for man's sake that flesh received its undeserved prerogative of sitting in judgment even over spirits. What raised our weakness to these heights was the descent of an almighty God to the depths of our own helplessness.

Peter: Your lofty words are certainly in harmony with these mighty deeds.

24. Gregory: One time, a young monk who was too attached to his parents left the monastery without asking for the abbot's blessing and went home. No sooner had he arrived than he died. The day after his burial his body was discovered lying outside the grave. His parents had him buried again, but on the following day found the body unburied as before. In their dismay they hurried to the saintly abbot and pleaded with him to forgive the boy for what he had done. Moved by their tears, Benedict gave them a consecrated Host with his own hands. 'When you get back,' he said 'place this sacred Host upon his breast and bury him once more.' They did so, and thereafter his body remained in the earth without being disturbed again. Now, Peter, you can appreciate how pleasing this holy man was in God's sight. Not even the earth would retain the young monk's body until he had been reconciled with blessed Benedict.

Peter: I assure you I do. It is really amazing.

25. Gregory: One of Benedict's monks had set his fickle heart on leaving the monastery. Time and again the man of God pointed out how wrong this was and tried to reason with him but without any success. The monk persisted obstinately in his request to be released. Finally, Benedict lost patience with him and told him to go.

Hardly had he left the monastery grounds when he noticed to his horror that a dragon with gaping jaws was blocking his way. 'Help! Help!' he cried out, trembling, 'or the dragon will devour me.' His brethren ran to the rescue, but could see nothing of the dragon. Still breathless with fright, the monk was only too glad to accompany them back to the abbey. Once safe within its walls, he promised never to leave again. And this time he kept his word, for Benedict's prayers had enabled him to see with his own eyes the invisible dragon that had been leading him astray.

26. I must tell you now of an event I heard from the distinguished Anthony. One of his father's servants had been seized with a severe case of leprosy. His hair was already falling out and his skin growing thick and swollen. The fatal progress of the disease was unmistakable. In this condition he was sent to the man of God, who instantly restored him to his previous state of health.

27. Benedict's disciple Peregrinus tells of a Catholic layman who was heavily burdened with debt and felt that his only hope was to disclose the full extent of his misfortune to the man of God. So he went to him and explained that he was being constantly tormented by a creditor to whom he owed twelve gold pieces. 'I am very sorry,' the saintly abbot replied. 'I do not have that much money in my possession.' Then, to comfort the poor man in his need, he added, 'I cannot give you anything today, but come back again the day after tomorrow.'

In the meantime the saint devoted himself to prayer with his accustomed fervor. When the debtor returned, the monks, to their surprise, found thirteen gold pieces lying on top of a chest that was filled with grain. Benedict had the money brought down at once. 'Here, take these,' he told him. 'Use twelve to pay your creditor and keep the thirteenth for yourself.'

I should like to return now to some other events I learned from the saint's four disciples who were mentioned at the beginning of this book.

There was a man who had become so embittered with envy that he tried to kill his rival by secretly poisoning his drink. Though the poison did not prove fatal, it produced horrible blemishes resembling leprosy, which spread over the entire body of the unfortunate victim. In this condition he was brought to the servant of God, who cured the disease with a touch of his hand and sent him home in perfect health.

28. While Campania was suffering from famine, the holy abbot distributed the food supplies of his monastery to the needy until there was nothing left in the storeroom but a little oil in a glass vessel. One day, when Agapitus, a subdeacon, came to beg for some oil, the man of God ordered the little that remained to be given to him, for he wanted to distribute everything he had to the poor and thus store up riches in heaven.

The cellarer listened to the abbot's command, but did not carry it out. After a while, Benedict asked him whether he had given Agapitus the oil.

'No,' he replied, 'I did not. If I had, there would be none left for the community.' This angered the man of God, who wanted nothing to remain in the monastery through disobedience, and he told another monk to take the glass with the oil in it and throw it out the window. This time he was obeyed.

Even though it struck against the jagged rocks of the cliff just below the window, the glass remained intact as if it had not been thrown at all. It was still unbroken and none of the oil had spilled. Abbot Benedict had the glass brought back and given to the subdeacon. Then he sent for the rest of the community and in their presence rebuked the disobedient monk for his pride and lack of faith.

29. After that the saint knelt down to pray with his brethren. In the room where they were kneeling there happened to be an empty oil-cask that was covered with a lid. In the course of his prayer the cask gradually filled with oil and the lid started to float on top of it. The next moment the oil was running down the sides of the cask and covering the floor. As soon as he was aware of this, Benedict ended his prayer and the oil stopped flowing. Then, turning to the monk who had shown himself disobedient and wanting in confidence, he urged him again to strive to grow in faith and humility.

This wholesome reprimand filled the cellarer with shame. Besides inviting him to trust in God, the saintly abbot had clearly shown by his miracle what marvelous power such trust possesses. In the future who could doubt any of his promises? Had he not in a moment's time replaced the little oil still left in the glass with a cask that was full to overflowing?

30. One day, on his way to the chapel of St. John at the highest point of the mountain, Benedict met the ancient Enemy of humankind, disguised as a veterinarian with medicine horn and triple shackle. 'Where are you going?' the saint asked him. 'To your brethren,' he replied with scorn. 'I am bringing them some medicine.' Benedict continued on his way and after his prayer hurried back. Meanwhile, the evil spirit had entered one of the older monks whom he found drawing water and had thrown him to the ground in a violent convulsion. When the man of God caught sight of this old brother in such torment, he merely struck him on the cheek, and the evil spirit was promptly driven out, never to return.

Peter: I should like to know whether he always obtained these great miracles through fervent prayer. Did he never perform them at will?

Gregory: It is quite common for those who devoutly cling to God to work miracles in both of these ways, Peter, either through their prayers or by their own power, as circumstances may dictate. Since we read in St. John that 'all those who did welcome him he empowered to become the children of God,' why should we be surprised if those who are the children of God use this power to work signs and wonders? Holy men can undoubtedly perform miracles in either of the ways you mentioned, as is clear from the fact that St. Peter raised Tabitha to life by praying over her, and by a simple rebuke brought death to Ananias and Sapphira for their lies. Scripture does not say that he prayed for their death, but only that he reprimanded them for the crime they had committed. Now, if St. Peter could restore to life by a prayer and deprive of life by a rebuke, is there any reason to doubt that the saints can perform miracles by their own power as well as through their prayers?

I am now going to consider two instances in the life of God's faithful servant Benedict. One of them shows the efficacy of his prayer; the other the marvelous powers that were his by God's gift.

31. In the days of King Totila one of the Goths, the Arian heretic Zalla, had been persecuting devout Catholics everywhere with the utmost cruelty. No monk or cleric who fell into his hands ever escaped alive. In his merciless brutality and greed he was one day lashing and torturing a farmer whose money he was after. Unable to bear it any longer, the poor man tried to save his life by telling Zalla that all his money was in Abbot Benedict's keeping. He only hoped his tormentor would believe him and put a stop to his brutality. When Zalla heard this, he did stop beating him, but immediately bound his hands together with a heavy cord. Then, mounting his horse, he forced the farmer to walk ahead of him and lead the way to this Benedict who was keeping his money.

The helpless prisoner had no choice but to conduct him to the abbey. When they arrived, they found the man of God sitting alone in front of the entrance reading. 'This is the abbot Benedict I meant,' he told the infuriated Goth behind him.

Imagining that this holy man could be frightened as readily as anyone else, Zalla glared at him with eyes full of hate and shouted harshly, 'Get up! Do you hear? Get up and give back the money this man left with you!' At the sound of this angry voice the man of God looked up from his reading and, as he glanced toward Zalla, noticed the farmer with his hands bound together. The moment he caught sight of the cord that held them, it fell miraculously to the ground. Human hands could never have unfastened it so quickly. Stunned at the hidden power that had set his prisoner free, Zalla fell trembling to his knees and, bending his stubborn cruel neck at the saint's feet, begged for his prayers. Without rising from his place, Benedict called for his monks and had them take Zalla inside for some food and drink. After that he urged him to give up his heartless cruelty. Zalla went away thoroughly humbled and made no more demands on this farmer who had been freed from his bonds by a mere glance from the man of God.

So you see, Peter, what I said is true. Those who devote themselves wholeheartedly to the service of God can sometimes work miracles by their own power. Blessed Benedict checked the fury of a dreaded Goth without even rising to his feet, and with a mere glance unfastened the heavy cord that bound the hands of an innocent man. The very speed with which he performed this marvel is proof enough that he did it by his own power.

And now, here is a remarkable miracle that was the result of his prayer.

32. One day, when he was out working in the fields with his monks, a farmer came to the monastery carrying in his arms the lifeless body of his son. Brokenhearted at his loss, he begged to see the saintly abbot and, on learning that he was at work in the fields, left the dead body at the entrance of the monastery and hurried off to find him. By then the abbot was already returning from his work. The moment the farmer caught sight of him he cried out, 'Give me back my son! Give me back my son!'

Benedict stopped when he heard this. 'But I have not taken your son from you, have I?' he asked. The boy's father only replied, 'He is dead. Come! Bring him back to life.' Deeply grieved at his words, the man of God turned to his disciples. 'Stand back, brethren!' he said. 'Stand back! Such a miracle is beyond our power. The holy apostles are the only ones who can raise the dead. Why are you so eager to accept what is impossible for us?' But overwhelming sorrow compelled the man to keep on pleading. He even declared with an oath that he would not leave until Benedict restored his son to life. The saint then asked him where the body was. 'At the entrance to the monastery,' he answered.

When Benedict arrived there with his monks, he knelt down beside the child's body and bent over it. Then, rising, he lifted his hands to heaven in prayer. 'O Lord,' he said, 'do not consider my sins but the faith of this man who is asking to see his son alive again, and restore to this body the soul you have taken from it.'

His prayer was hardly over when the child's whole body began once more to throb with life. No one present there could doubt that this sudden stirring was due to a heavenly intervention. Benedict then took the little boy by the hand and gave him back to his father alive and well. Obviously, Peter, he did not have the power to work this miracle himself. Otherwise he would not have begged for it prostrate in prayer.

Peter: The way facts bear out your words convinces me that everything you have said is true. Will you please tell me now whether holy men can always carry out their wishes, or at least obtain through prayer whatever they desire?

33. Gregory: Peter, will there ever be a holier man in this world than St.

Paul? Yet he prayed three times to the Lord about the sting in his flesh and could not obtain his wish. In this connection I must tell you how the saintly Benedict once had a wish he was unable to fulfil.

His sister Scholastica, who had been consecrated to God in early childhood, used to visit with him once a year. On these occasions he would go down to meet her in a house belonging to the monastery, a short distance from the entrance.

For this particular visit he joined her there with a few of his disciples and they spent the whole day singing God's praises and conversing about the spiritual life. When darkness was setting in, they took their meal together and continued their conversation at table until it was quite late. Then the holy nun said to him, 'Please do not leave me tonight, brother. Let us keep on talking about the joys of heaven till morning.'

'What are you saying, sister?' he replied. 'You know I cannot stay away from the monastery.' The sky was so clear at the time that there was not a cloud in sight. At her brother's refusal Scholastica folded her hands on the table and rested her head upon them in earnest prayer. When she looked up again, there was a sudden burst of lightning and thunder, accompanied by such a downpour that Benedict and his companions were unable to set a foot outside the door.

By shedding a flood of tears while she prayed, this holy nun had darkened the cloudless sky with a heavy rain. The storm began as soon as her prayer was over. In fact, the two coincided so closely that the thunder was already resounding as she raised her head from the table. The very instant she ended her prayer the rain poured down.

Realizing that he could not return to the monastery in this terrible storm, Benedict complained bitterly. 'God forgive you, sister!' he said. 'What have you done?' Scholastica simply answered, 'When I appealed to you, you would not listen to me. So I turned to my God and he heard my prayer. Leave now if you can. Leave me here and go back to your monastery.' This, of course, he could not do. He had no choice now but to stay, in spite of his unwillingness. They spent the entire night together and both of them derived great profit from the holy thoughts they exchanged about the interior life.

Here you have my reason for saying that this holy man was once unable to obtain what he desired. If we consider his point of view, we can readily see that he wanted the sky to remain as clear as it was when he came down from the monastery. But this wish of his was thwarted by a miracle almighty God performed in answer to a woman's prayer. We need not be surprised that in this instance she proved mightier than her brother; she had been looking forward so long to this visit. Do we not read in St. John that God is love? Surely it is no more than right that her influence was greater than his,

[Fig. 20] Benedictine saints: Scholastica, Benedict's sister, is on the left; next to her is Justina, a virgin martyr (c.300) whose relics were translated to Padua, where she became the patron of an important Benedictine monastery. On the right are Maurus and Placidus who, as Gregory relates, were brought to Benedict as boys to become his monks and disciples (Jameson, *Legends of the Monastic Orders,* p. 14).

since hers was the greater love.

Peter: I find this discussion very enjoyable.

34. Gregory: The next morning Scholastica returned to her convent and Benedict to his monastery. Three days later as he stood in his room looking up toward the sky, he beheld his sister's soul leaving her body and entering the court of heaven in the form of a dove.

Overjoyed at her eternal glory, he gave thanks to God in hymns of praise. Then, after informing his brethren of her death, he sent some of them to bring her body to the monastery and bury it in the tomb he had prepared for himself. The bodies of these two were now to share a common resting place, just as in life their souls had always been one in God.

35. At another time, the deacon Servandus came to see the servant of God on one of his regular visits. He was abbot of the monastery in Campania that had been built by the late Senator Liberius, and always welcomed an opportunity to discuss with Benedict the truths of eternity, for he, too, was a man of deep spiritual understanding. In speaking of their hopes and longings they were able to taste in advance the heavenly food that was not yet fully theirs to enjoy. When it was time to retire for the night, Benedict went to his room on the second floor of the tower, leaving Servandus in the one below, which was connected with his own by a stairway. Their disciples slept in the large building facing the tower.

Long before the night office began, the man of God was standing at his window, where he watched and prayed while the rest were still asleep. In the dead of night he suddenly beheld a flood of light shining down from above more brilliant than the sun, and with it every trace of darkness cleared away. Another remarkable sight followed. According to his own description, the whole world was gathered up before his eyes in what appeared to be a single ray of light. As he gazed at all this dazzling display, he saw the soul of Germanus, the Bishop of Capua, being carried by angels up to heaven in a ball of fire.

Wishing to have someone else witness this great marvel, he called out for Servandus, repeating his name two or three times in a loud voice. As soon as he heard the saint's call, Servandus rushed to the upper room and was just in time to catch a final glimpse of the miraculous light. He remained speechless with wonder as Benedict described everything that had taken place. Then without any delay the man of God instructed the devout Theoprobus to go to Cassino and have a messenger sent to Capua that same night to find out what had happened to Germanus. In carrying out these instructions the messenger discovered that the revered bishop was already dead [the year was 541]. When he asked for further details, he learned that his death had occurred at the very time blessed Benedict saw him carried into heaven.

Peter: What an astounding miracle! I hardly know what to think when I hear you say that he saw the whole world gathered up before his eyes in what appeared to be a single ray of light. I have never had such an experience. How is it possible for anyone to see the whole universe at a glance?

Gregory: Keep this well in mind, Peter. All creation is bound to appear small to a soul that sees the Creator. Once it beholds a little of his light, it finds all creatures small indeed. The light of holy contemplation enlarges and expands the mind in God until it stands above the world. In fact, the soul that sees him rises even above itself, and as it is drawn upward in his light all its inner powers unfold. Then, when it looks down from above, it sees how small everything is that was beyond its grasp before.

Now, Peter, how else was it possible for this man to behold the ball of fire and watch the angels on their return to heaven except with light from God? Why should it surprise us, then, that he could see the whole world gathered up before him after this inner light had lifted him so far above the world? Of course, in saying that the world was gathered up before his eyes I do not mean that heaven and earth grew small, but that his spirit was enlarged. Absorbed as he was in God, it was now easy for him to see all that lay beneath God. In the light outside that was shining before his eyes, there was a brightness which reached into his mind and lifted his spirit heavenward, showing him the insignificance of all that lies below.

Peter: My difficulty in understanding you has proved of real benefit; the explanation it led to was so thorough. Now that you have cleared up this problem for me, would you return once more to your account of blessed Benedict's life?

36. Gregory: I should like to tell you much more about this saintly abbot, but I am purposely passing over some of his miraculous deeds in my eagerness to take up those of others. There is one more point, however, I want to call to your attention. With all the renown he gained by his numerous miracles, the holy man was no less outstanding for the wisdom of his teaching. He wrote a Rule for monks that is remarkable for its discretion and its clarity of language. Anyone who wishes to know more about his life and character can discover in his Rule exactly what he was like as abbot, for his life could not have differed from his teaching.

37. In the year that was to be his last, the man of God foretold the day of his holy death to a number of his disciples. In mentioning it to some who were with him in the monastery, he bound them to strict secrecy. Some others, however, who were stationed elsewhere he only informed of the special sign they would receive at the time of his death.

Six days before he died he gave orders for his tomb to be opened. Almost immediately he was seized with a violent fever that rapidly wasted his remaining strength. Each day his condition grew worse until finally, on the sixth day, he had his disciples carry him into the chapel, where he received the Body and Blood of our Lord to gain strength for his approaching end. Then, supporting his weakened body on the arms of his brethren, he stood with his hands raised to heaven and as he prayed breathed his last [21 March, 547 is the generally accepted date of Benedict's death].

That day two monks, one of them at the monastery, the other some distance away, received the very same revelation. They both saw a magnificent road covered with rich carpeting and glittering with thousands of lights. From his monastery it stretched eastward in a straight line until it reached up into heaven. And there in the brightness stood a man of majestic appearance, who asked them, 'Do you know who passed this way?' 'No,' they replied. 'This,' he told them, 'is the road taken by blessed Benedict, the Lord's beloved, when he went to heaven.' Thus, while the brethren who were with Benedict witnessed his death, those who were absent knew about it through the sign he had promised them. His body was laid to rest in the chapel of St. John the Baptist, which he had built to replace the altar of Apollo.

38. Even in the cave at Subiaco, where he had lived before, this holy man still works numerous miracles for people who turn to him with faith and confidence. The incident I am going to relate happened only recently.

A woman who had completely lost her mind was roaming day and night over hills and valleys, through forests and fields, resting only when she was utterly exhausted. One day, in the course of her aimless wanderings, she strayed into the saint's cave and rested there without the least idea of where she was. The next morning she woke up entirely cured and left the cave without even a trace of her former affliction. After that she remained free from it for the rest of her life.

Peter: How is it that, as a rule, even the martyrs in their care for us do not grant the same great favors through their bodily remains as they do through their other relics? We find them so often performing more outstanding miracles away from their burial places.

Gregory: There is no doubt, Peter, that the holy martyrs can perform countless miracles where their bodies rest. And they do so in behalf of all who pray there with a pure intention. In places where their bodies do not actually lie buried, however, there is danger that those whose faith is weak may doubt their presence and their power to answer prayers. Consequently, it is in these places that they must perform still greater miracles. But one whose faith in God is strong earns all the more merit by his faith, for he realizes that the martyrs are present to hear his prayers even though their bodies happen to be buried elsewhere.

It was precisely to increase the faith of his disciples that the eternal Truth told them, 'If I do not go, the Advocate will not come to you.' Now certainly the Holy Spirit, the Advocate, is ever proceeding from the Father and the Son. Why, then, should the Son say he will go in order that the Spirit may come, when, actually, the Spirit never leaves him? The point is that as long as the disciples could see our Lord in his human flesh they would want to keep on seeing him with their bodily eyes. With good reason, therefore, did he tell them, 'If I do not go, the Advocate will not come.' What he really meant was,

[Fig. 21] The death of St. Benedict, surrounded by his monks. The saint is shown both in death and again in the after-life, as seen by two of his monks in a vision, traveling the road leading to the presence of God (fresco by d'Arezzo, Lacroix, *Military and Religious Life in the Middle Ages,* p. 497).

'I cannot teach you spiritual love unless I remove my body from your sight; as long as you continue to see me with your bodily eyes you will never learn to love me spiritually.'

Peter: That is a very satisfying explanation.

Gregory: Let us interrupt our discussion for a while. If we are going to take up the miracles of other holy men, we shall need a short period of silence to rest our voices.

[Fig. 22] St. Radegund receiving the habit of a nun from the hands of St. Médard, Bishop of Vermandois (*Histoire et Cronique de Clotaire,* [Paris, 1513], reproduced in Lacroix, *Military and Religious Life in the Middle Ages,* p. 309).

16. VENANTIUS FORTUNATUS'S
LIFE OF ST. RADEGUND

Although women saints were in the minority thoughout the Middle Ages (according to the historian David Herlihy, the overall ratio up to 1500 was about one woman for every five men), from 476 to 750 they were more likely than at any other time to hold powerful positions as abbesses and to be sanctified as a result. These women were also generally from aristocratic families. Radegund was a Frankish queen and might properly be included among the 'Royal Saints' in this Reader, but it was as a nun, founder and abbess of an important convent at Poitiers, that she achieved fame. When still a child she was carried off as war booty by Clothar I, king of the Franks, after his forces had virtually annihilated her family, the ruling house of Thuringia, in a feud. Clothar sent her to his villa in Picardy until she was old enough for him to marry, in about 540. The feuding continued, however, and after Clothar killed her surviving brother ten years later, Radegund left him, as described in Fortunatus's 'life' below, and pursued her religious vocation singlemindedly until her death in 587, though not without having to evade at least one attempt by Clothar to get her back. Her life is well-documented by Gregory of Tours, by the poet and bishop Venantius Fortunatus, who was also her close friend, and by a nun, Baudonivia, who lived in the convent founded by Radegund at Poitiers. There is also a poem, 'The Thuringian War,' that laments the destruction of the Thuringian royal house and that may have been written by Radegund herself. Fortunatus's account tells us little about Radegund's management of her convent; his aim was rather to prove that her great charity and extreme suffering (often self-inflicted) made her worthy of the same status as a martyr. That she herself was concerned not to let worldly affairs detract from her spiritual life is evident from the fact that she soon established her protégée Agnes as Mother Superior. The convent at Poitiers followed the rule for nuns set down by Caesarius of Arles, which emphasized reading Scripture and meditation, constant prayer, charity to the poor, moderation in ascetic practices, and strict claustration, although the latter did not mean that the nuns could not receive visitors, including men. Later on, the convent suffered more than its share of problems, as described by Gregory of Tours in his 'History of the Franks' (9, 39-44 and 10, 15-17), and the period of Radegund's life was to be regarded as something of a golden age.

Source: trans. Jo Ann McNamara and John E. Halborg, with E. Gordon Whatley, *Sainted Women of the Dark Ages* (Durham and London: Duke University Press, 1992), pp. 70-86; repr. with permission. BHL 7048.

1. Our Redeemer is so richly and abundantly generous that he wins mighty victories through the female sex and, despite their frail physique, he confers glory and greatness on women through strength of mind. By faith, Christ makes them strong who were born weak so that, when those who appeared

to be imbeciles are crowned with their merits by him who made them, they garner praise for their Creator who hid heavenly treasure in earthen vessels. For Christ the king dwells with his riches in their bowels. Mortifying themselves in the world, despising earthly consort, purified of worldly contamination, trusting not in the transitory, dwelling not in error but seeking to live with God, they are united with the Redeemer's glory in Paradise. One of that company is she whose earthly life we are attempting to present to the public, though in homely style, so that the glorious memory that she, who lives with Christ, has left us will be celebrated in this world. So ends the Prologue.

Here begins the 'Life.'

2. The most blessed Radegund was of the highest earthly rank, born from the seed of the kings of the barbarian nation of Thuringia. Her grandfather was King Bassin, her paternal uncle, Hermanfred and her father, King Bertechar. But she surpassed her lofty origin by even loftier deeds. She had lived with her noble family only a little while when the victorious Franks devastated the region with barbaric turmoil and, like the Israelites, she departed and migrated from her homeland. The royal girl became part of the plunder of these conquerors and they began to quarrel over their captive. If the contest had not ended with an agreement for her disposition, the kings would have taken up arms against one another. Falling to the lot of the illustrious king Clothar, she was taken to Athies in Vermandois, a royal villa, and her upbringing was entrusted to guardians. The maiden was taught letters and other things suitable to her sex and she would often converse with other children there about her desire to be a martyr if the chance came in her time. Thus even as an adolescent, she displayed the merits of a mature person. She obtained part of what she sought, for, though the church was flourishing in peace, she endured persecution from her own household. While but a small child, she herself brought the scraps left at table to the gathered children, washing the head of each one, seating them on little chairs and offering water for their hands, and she mingled with the infants herself. She would also carry out what she had planned beforehand with Samuel, a little cleric. Following his lead, carrying a wooden cross they had made, singing Psalms, the children would troop into the oratory as somber as adults. Radegund herself would polish the pavement with her dress and, collecting the drifting dust around the altar in a napkin, reverently placed it outside the door rather than sweep it away. When the aforementioned king, having provided the expenses, wished to bring her to Vitry, she escaped by night from Athies

through Beralcha with a few companions. When he settled with her that she should be made his queen at Soissons, she avoided the trappings of royalty, so she would not grow great in the world but in him to whom she was devoted and she remained unchanged by earthly glory.

3. Therefore, though married to a terrestrial prince, she was not separated from the celestial one and, the more secular power was bestowed upon her, the more humbly she bent her will – more than befitted her royal status. Always subject to God following priestly admonitions, she was more Christ's partner than her husband's companion. We will only attempt to publicize a few of the many things she did during this period of her life. Fearing she would lose status with God as she advanced in worldly rank at the side of a prince, she gave herself energetically to almsgiving. Whenever she received part of the tribute, she gave away a tithe of all that came to her before accepting any for herself. She dispensed what was left to monasteries, sending the gifts to those she could not reach on foot. There was no hermit who could hide from her munificence. So she paid out what she received lest the burden weigh her down. The voice of the needy was not raised in vain for she never turned a deaf ear. Often she gave clothes, believing that the limbs of Christ concealed themselves under the garments of the poor and that whatever she did not give to paupers was truly lost.

4. Turning her mind to further works of mercy, she built a house at Athies where beds were elegantly made up for needy women gathered there. She would wash them herself in warm baths, tending to the putrescence of their diseases. She washed the heads of men, acting like a servant. And before she washed them, she would mix a potion with her own hands to revive those who were weak from sweating. Thus the devout lady, queen by birth and marriage, mistress of the palace, served the poor as a handmaid. Secretly, lest anyone notice, at royal banquets, she fed most deliciously on beans or lentils from the dish of legumes placed before her, in the manner of the three boys [a reference to the behavior of Daniel and his companions at the court of King Nebuchadnezzar]. And if the singing of the hours [church services] started while she was still eating, she would make her excuses to the king and withdraw from the company to do her duty to God. As she went out, she sang Psalms to the Lord and carefully checked what food had been provided to refresh the paupers at the door.

5. At night, when she lay with her prince she would ask leave to rise and leave the chamber to relieve nature. Then she would prostrate herself in prayer under a hair cloak by the privy so long that the cold pierced her through and through and only her spirit was warm. Her whole flesh prematurely dead, indifferent to her body's torment, she kept her mind intent on

Paradise and counted her suffering trivial, if only she might avoid becoming cheap in Christ's eyes. Re-entering the chamber thereafter, she could scarcely get warm either by the hearth or in her bed. Because of this, people said that the King had yoked himself to a *monacha* [a nun] rather than a queen. Her goodness provoked him to harsher irritation but she either soothed him to the best of her ability or bore her husband's brawling modestly.

6. Indeed, it will suffice to know how she bore herself during the days of Quadragesima [the period before Easter], a singular penitent in her royal robes. When the time for fasting drew near, she would notify a *monacha* named Pia, who, according to their holy arrangement, would send a hair cloth sealed carefully in linen to Radegund. Draping it over her body through the whole of Quadragesima, the holy woman wore that sweet burden under her royal garment. When the season was over, she returned the hair cloth similarly sealed. Who could believe how she would pour out her heart in prayers when the king was away? How she would cling to the feet of Christ as though he were present with her and satiate her long hunger with tears as though she was gorging on delicacies! She had contempt for the food of the belly, for Christ was her only nourishment and all her hunger was for Christ.

7. With what piety did she care solicitously for the candles made with her own hands that burned all night long in oratories and holy places? When the king asked after her at table during the late hours, he was told that she was delayed, busy about God's affairs. This caused strife with her husband and later on the prince compensated her with gifts for the wrong he did her with his tongue.

8. If she received a report that any of God's servants was on his way to see her, either of his own accord or by invitation, she felt full of celestial joy. Hastening out in the night time, with a few intimates, through snow, mud or dust, she herself would wash the feet of the venerable man with water she had heated beforehand and offer the servant of God something to drink in a bowl. There was no resisting her. On the following day, committing the care of the household to her trusted servants, she would occupy herself wholly with the just man's words and his teachings concerning salvation. The business of achieving celestial life fixed her attention throughout the day. And if a bishop should come, she rejoiced to see him, gave him gifts and was sad to have to let him go home.

9. And how prudently she sought to devote everything possible to her salvation. If the girls attending her when she dressed praised a new veil of coarse linen ornamented with gold and gems in the barbarian fashion as particularly beautiful, she would judge herself unworthy to be draped in such

fabric. Divesting herself of the dress immediately, she would send it to some holy place in the neighborhood where it could be laid as a cloth on the Lord's altar.

10. And if the king, according to custom, condemned a guilty criminal to death, wasn't the most holy queen near dead with torment lest the culprit perish by the sword? How she would rush about among his trusty men, ministers and nobles, whose blandishments might soothe the prince's temper until the king's anger ceased and the voice of salvation flowed where the sentence of death had issued before!

11. Even while she remained in her worldly palace, the blessed acts which busied her so pleased Divine Clemency that the Lord's generosity worked miracles through her. Once at her villa in Péronne, while that holiest of women was strolling in the garden after her meal, some sequestered criminals loudly cried to her from the prison for help. She asked who it might be. The servants lied that a crowd of beggars were seeking alms. Believing that, she sent to relieve their needs. Meanwhile the fettered prisoners were silenced by a judge. But as night was falling and she was saying her prayers, the chains broke and the freed prisoners ran from the prison to the holy woman. When they witnessed this, those who had lied to the holy one realized that they were the real culprits, while the erstwhile convicts were freed from their bonds.

12. If Divinity fosters it, misfortune often leads to salvation. Thus her innocent brother was killed so that she might come to live in religion. She left the king and went straight to holy Médard at Noyon. She earnestly begged that she might change her garments and be consecrated to God. But mindful of the words of the Apostle: "Art thou bound unto a wife? Seek not to be loosed," he hesitated to garb the Queen in the robe of a *monacha*. For even then, nobles were harassing the holy man and attempting to drag him brutally through the basilica from the altar to keep him from veiling the king's spouse lest the priest imagine he could take away the king's official queen as though she were only a prostitute. That holiest of women knew this and, sizing up the situation, entered the sacristy, put on a monastic garb and proceeded straight to the altar, saying to the blessed Médard: "If you shrink from consecrating me, and fear man more than God, Pastor, he will require his sheep's soul from your hand." He was thunderstruck by that argument and, laying his hand on her, he consecrated her as a deaconess.

13. Soon she divested herself of the noble costume which she was wont to wear as queen when she walked in procession on the day of a festival with her train of attendants. She laid it on the altar and piled the table of divine glory with purple, gems, ornaments and like gifts to honor him. She gave a

heavy girdle of costly gold for the relief of the poor. Similarly, one day she ornamented herself in queenly splendor, as the barbarians would say – all decked out for *stapione* [probable meaning may be 'stepping out']. Entering holy Jumerus's cell, she laid her frontlets, chemise, bracelets, coif and pins all decorated with gold, some with circlets of gems on the altar for future benefit. Again, proceeding to the venerable Dato's cell one day, spectacularly adorned as she should have been in the world with whatever she could put on, having rewarded the abbot, she gave the whole from her woman's wealth to the community. Likewise going on to the retreat of holy Gundulf, later Bishop of Metz, she exerted herself just as energetically to enrich his monastery.

14. From there her fortunate sails approached Tours. Can any eloquence express how zealous and munificent she showed herself there? How she conducted herself around the courts, shrines, and basilica of St. Martin, weeping unchecked tears, prostrating herself at each threshold! After mass was said, she heaped the holy altar with the clothing and bright ornaments with which she used to adorn herself in the palace. And when the handmaid of the Lord went from there to the neighborhood of Candes whence the glorious Martin, Christ's senator and confidant, migrated from this world, she gave him no less again, ever profiting in the Lord's grace.

15. From there, in decorous manner, she approached the villa of Saix near the aforesaid town in the territory of Poitiers, her journey ever prospering. Who could recount the countless remarkable things she did there or grasp the special quality of each one? At table she secretly chewed rye or barley bread which she had hidden under a cake to escape notice. For from the time she was veiled, consecrated by Saint Médard, even in illness, she ate nothing but legumes and green vegetables: not fruit nor fish nor eggs. And she drank no drink but honeyed water or perry and would touch no undiluted wine nor any decoction of mead or fermented beer.

16. Then, emulating St. Germanus's custom, she secretly had a millstone brought to her. Throughout the whole of Quadragesima, she ground fresh flour with her own hands. She continuously distributed each offering to local religious communities, in the amount needed for the meal taken every four days. With that holy woman, acts of mercy were no fewer than the crowds who pressed her; as there was no shortage of those who asked, so was there no shortage in what she gave so that, wonderfully, they could all be satisfied. Where did the exile get such wealth? Whence came the pilgrim's riches?

17. How much did she spend daily on relief? Only she who bore it to the beggars ever knew. For beyond the daily meal which she fed to her enrolled paupers, twice a week, on Thursday and Saturday, she prepared a bath.

Girding herself with a cloth, she washed the heads of the needy, scrubbing away whatever she found there. Not shrinking from scurf, scabs, lice or pus, she plucked off the worms and scrubbed away the putrid flesh. Then she herself combed the hair on every head she had washed. As in the Gospel, she applied oil to their ulcerous sores that had opened when the skin softened or that scratching had irritated, reducing the spread of infection. When women descended into the tub, she washed their limbs with soap from head to foot. When they came out, if she noticed that anyone's clothes were shoddy with age, she would take them away and give them new ones. Thus she spruced up all who came to the feast in rags. When they were gathered around the table and the dinner service laid out, she brought water and napkins for each of them and cleaned the mouth and hands of the invalids herself. Then three trays laden with delicacies would be carried in. Standing like a good hostess before the diners, she cut up the bread and meat and served everyone while fasting herself. Moreover, she never ceased to offer food to the blind and weak with a spoon. In this, two women aided her but she alone served them, busy as a new Martha [the type of active religious life, opposed to her sister Mary, symbol of the contemplative life] until the "brothers" were drunk and happily satisfied with their meal. Then, leaving the place to wash her hands, she was completely gratified with her well-served feast. And if anyone protested, she ordered that they sit still until they wished to get up.

18. Summer and winter, on Sundays, she followed a praiseworthy rule. She would provide an undiluted drink of sweet wine to the assembled paupers. First she doled it out herself and then, while she hurried off to Mass, she assigned a maid to serve everyone who remained. Her devotions completed, she would meet the priests invited to her table for it was her royal custom not to let them return home without a gift.

19. Doesn't this make one shudder, this thing she did so sweetly? When lepers arrived and, sounding a warning, came forward, she directed her assistant to inquire with pious concern whence they came or how many there were. Having learned that, she had a table laid with dishes, spoons, little knives, cups and goblets, and wine and she went in herself secretly that none might see her. Seizing some of the leprous women in her embrace, her heart full of love, she kissed their faces. Then, while they were seated at table, she washed their faces and hands with warm water and treated their sores with fresh unguents and fed each one. When they were leaving she offered small gifts of gold and clothing. To this there was scarcely a single witness, but the attendant presumed to chide her softly: "Most holy lady, when you have embraced lepers, who will kiss you?" Pleasantly, she answered: "Really, if you won't kiss me, it's no concern of mine."

20. With God's help, she shone forth in diverse miracles. For example, if anyone was in desperate straits because of pus from a wound, an attendant would bring a vine leaf to the saint speaking with her about what was to be done with it. As soon as the saint made the sign of the cross over it, the attendant would take it to the desperate one, placing it on the wound which would soon be healed. Similarly an invalid or someone with a fever might come and say that he had learned in a dream that to be healed he should hasten to the holy woman and present one of her attendants with a candle. After it had burned through the night his disease would be killed while the invalid was healed. How often when she heard of someone lying bedridden would she sally forth like a pilgrim bearing fruit, or something sweet and warm to restore their strength? How quickly would an invalid who had eaten nothing for ten days take food when she served it herself and thus receive both food and health together? And she ordered these things herself lest anyone tell tales.

21. Weren't there such great gatherings of people on the day that the saint determined to seclude herself that those who could not be contained in the streets climbed up to fill the roofs? Anyone who spoke of all the most holy woman had fervently accomplished in fasting, services, humility, charity, suffering and torment, proclaimed her both confessor and martyr. Truly every day except for the most venerable day of the Lord, was a fast day for that most holy woman. Her meal of lentils or green vegetables was virtually a fast in itself for she took no fowl or fish or fruit or eggs to eat. Her bread was made from rye or barley which she concealed under the pudding lest anyone notice what she ate. And to drink she had water and honey or perry and only a little of that was poured out for her, however thirsty she was.

22. The first time she enclosed herself in her cell throughout Quadrages-ima, she ate no bread, except on Sundays but only roots of herbs or mallow greens without a drop of oil or salt for dressing. In fact, during the entire fast, she consumed only two *sestaria* [about four cups] of water. Consequently, she suffered so much from thirst that she could barely chant the Psalms through her desiccated throat. She kept her vigils in a shift of hair cloth instead of linen incessantly chanting the offices. A bed of ashes served her for a couch which she covered with a hair cloth. In this manner, rest itself wea-ried her but even this was not enough to endure.

23. While all the *monachas* [nuns] were deep in sleep, she would collect their shoes, restoring them cleaned and oiled to each. On other Quadragesi-mas, she was more relaxed, eating on Thursday and again on Sundays. The rest of the time when health permitted, except for Easter and other high holy days, she led an austere life in sackcloth and ashes, rising early to be singing Psalms when the others awoke. For no monasterial offices pleased her

unless she observed them first. She punished herself if anyone else did a good deed before she did. When it was her turn to sweep the pavements around the monastery, she even scoured the nooks and crannies, bundling away whatever nasty things were there, never too disgusted to carry off what others shuddered to look upon. She did not shrink from cleaning the privies but cleaned and carried off the stinking dung. For she believed that she would be diminished if these vile services did not ennoble her. She carried firewood in her arms. She blew on the hearth and stirred the fire with tongs and did not flinch if she hurt herself. She would care for the infirm beyond her assigned week, cooking their food, washing their faces, and bringing them warm water, going the rounds of those she was caring for and returning fasting to her cell.

24. How can anyone describe her excited fervor as she ran into the kitchen, doing her week of chores? None of the *monachas* but she would carry as much wood as was needed in a bundle from the back gate. She drew water from the well and poured it into basins. She scrubbed vegetables and legumes and revived the hearth by blowing so that she might cook the food. While it was busy boiling, she took the vessels from the hearth, washing and laying out the dishes. When the meal was finished, she rinsed the small vessels and scrubbed the kitchen till it shone, free of every speck of dirt. Then she carried out all the sweepings and the nastiest rubbish. Further she never flagged in supporting the sick and even before she took up the Rule of Arles did her weekly tour of service preparing plenty of warm water for them all. Humbly washing and kissing their feet, the holy one prostrated herself and begged them all to forgive her for any negligence she might have committed.

25. But I shudder to speak of the pain she inflicted on herself over and above all these labors. Once, throughout Quadragesima, she bound her neck and arms with three broad iron circlets. Inserting three chains in them she fettered her whole body so tightly that her delicate flesh, swelling up enclosed the hard iron. After the fast was ended, when she wished to remove the chains locked under her skin, she could not for the flesh was cut by the circlet through her back and breast over the iron of the chains, so that the flow of blood nearly drained her little body to the last drop.

26. On another occasion, she ordered a brass plate made, shaped in the sign of Christ. She heated it up in her cell and pressed it upon her body most deeply in two spots so that her flesh was roasted through. Thus, with her spirit flaming, she caused her very limbs to burn. One Quadragesima, she devised a still more terrible agony to torture herself in addition to the severe hunger and burning thirst of her fast. She forced her tender limbs, already suppurating and scraped raw by the hard bristles of a hair cloth, to carry a

water basin full of burning coals. Then, isolated from the rest, though her limbs were quivering, her soul was steeled for the pain. She drew it to herself so that she might be a martyr though it was not an age of persecution. To cool her fervent soul, she thought to burn her body. She imposed the glowing brass and her burning limbs hissed. Her skin was consumed and a deep furrow remained where the brand had touched her. Silently, she concealed the holes, but the putrefying blood betrayed the pain that her voice did not reveal. Thus did a woman willingly suffer such bitterness for the sweetness of Christ! And in time, miracles told the story that she herself would have kept hidden.

27. For example, a noble matron of Gislad named Bella, who had suffered from blindness for a long time, had herself led from Francia to Poitiers into the saint's presence. Though won over with difficulty, she had her brought in during the silence of a foul night. Prostrate at the saint's knees, the woman could barely ask her to deign to sign her eyes. As soon as she impressed the sign of the cross on them in the name of Christ, the blindness fled; the light returned. Daylight shone on the orbs so long darkened beneath the shades of night. Thus she who had been led there, went home without a guide.

28. Similarly, a girl named Fraifled, whom the Enemy [Satan] vexed, was violently contorted and most wretched. Without delay, she was found worthy of a cure at the saint's hands at Saix. Nor should we omit to mention the following miracle, revealed through the blessed woman at this time. The next day a woman named Leubela, who was gravely vexed in the back by the Adversary, was publicly restored to health when the saint prayed for her and Christ worked a new miracle of healing. For a rustling sound came from under the skin of her shoulder blades and a worm emerged. Treading it underfoot, she went home liberated.

29. What she did secretly was to become known to all people. A certain *monacha* shivered with cold by day and burned with fire by night through an entire year. And when she had lain lifeless for six months, unable to move a step, one of her sisters told the saint of this infirmity. Finding her almost lifeless, she bade them prepare warm water and had the sick woman brought to her cell and laid in the warm water. Then she ordered everyone to leave, remaining alone with the sick woman for two hours as a doctor. She nursed the sick limbs, tracing the form of her body from head to foot. Wherever her hands touched, the sickness fled from the patient and she who had been laid in the bath by two persons got out of it in full health. The woman who had been revolted by the smell of wine, now accepted it, drank and was refreshed. What more? The next day, when she was expected to migrate from this world, she went out in public, cured.

30. Let us increase her praise by recounting another miracle that has rightly not been forgotten. A certain woman labored so heavily under an invasion of the Enemy that the struggling foe could scarcely be brought to the saint. She commanded the Adversary to lie prostrate on the pavement and show her some respect. The moment the blessed woman spoke, he threw himself down for she frightened him who was feared. When the saint, full of faith, trod on the nape of her neck, he left her in a flux that poured from her belly. Also from small things great glory may accrue to the Creator. Once, a ball of thread which the saint had spun was hanging from the vault, when a shrew mouse came to nibble it. But, before he could break the thread, he hung there dead in the very act of biting.

31. Let our book include another event worthy to be called a miracle. One of the saint's men named Florius was at sea fishing when a whirlwind appeared and a mass of billows surged. The sailor had not even begun to bail when a wave came over the side, the ship filled and went under. In his extremity, he cried out, "Holy Radegund, while we obey you, keep us from shipwreck and prevail upon God to save us from the sea." When he said this, the clouds fled away, serenity returned, the waves fell and the prow arose.

32. Goda, a secular girl who later served God as a *monacha*, lay on her bed for a long time. The more she was plied with medicine, the more she languished. A candle was made to the measure of her own height, in the name of the holy woman, and the lord took pity on her. At the hour when she expected the chills, she kindled the light and held it and as a result, the cold fled before the candle was consumed.

33. The more we omit for brevity's sake, the greater grows our guilt. Therefore, as we dispose quickly of the remainder, our relief is slowed. A carpenter's wife had been tormented by diabolic possession for many days. Jokingly, the venerable abbess [Agnes, whom Radegund had made head of the convent] said of her to the holy woman: "Believe me, Mother, I will excommunicate you if the woman is not purged of the Enemy and restored in three days." She said this publicly but she made the holy woman secretly sorry that she had been so slow to heal the afflicted. To be brief, at the saint's prayer on the next day, the Adversary went roaring out of her ear and abandoned the little vessel he had violently seized. Unhurt, the woman returned to the hospice with her husband. Nor should we neglect a similar deed. The most blessed one asked that a flourishing laurel tree be uprooted and transferred to her cell so she could enjoy it there. But when this was done all the leaves withered because the transplanted tree did not take root. The abbess jokingly remarked that she had better pray for the tree to take root in the ground, or she herself would be separated from her food [exclusion from

community meals was a common monastic punishment]. She did not speak in vain for, through the saint's intercession, the laurel with the withered root grew green again in leaf and branch.

34. When one of the *monachas* closest to her suffered because her eye was flooded with a bloody humor, she laid hold of some wormwood which the saint had about her breast for refreshment. When she placed it on her eye, the pain and blood soon fled and, from the freshness of the herb, the eye was suddenly clear and bright again. And that reminds me of something I almost passed by in silence. Children were born to the blessed one's agent, Andered, but he scarcely saw them before he lost them and the sorrowing mother had to think about burying her child even while birthing it. During the preparations, the tearful parents wrapped the lifeless babe in the saint's hair cloth. As soon as the infant's body touched that most medicinal garment and those noble rags, he came back from the dead to normal life. Blushing away his tomblike pallor, he rose from the mantle.

35. Who can count the wonders that Christ's merciful kindness performs? A *monacha* Animia suffered so with dropsical swelling that she seemed to have reached her end. The appointed sisters awaited the moment when she would exhale her spirit. While she was sleeping, however, it seemed to her that the most venerable blessed Radegund ordered her to descend nude into a bath with no water in it. Then, with her own hand, the blessed one seemed to pour oil on the sick woman's head and cover her with a new garment. After this strange ritual, when she awakened from her sleep, all trace of the disease had disappeared. She had not even sweated it away for the water was consumed from within. As a result of this new miracle, no vestige of disease was left in her belly. She who was thought to be ready for the tomb rose from her bed for the office. Her head still smelled of oil in witness of the miracle but the pernicious disease was no longer in her belly.

36. Let us now tell a tale in which the whole region may rejoice. One evening as twilight cast its shadows, the layfolk were singing noisy songs near the monastery as they danced around accompanied by musicians with cithars. The saint had spent some time exhorting two listeners. Then one *monacha* said, joking: "Lady, I recognize one of my songs being preached by the dancers." To which she responded: "That's fine if it thrills you to hear religion mingled with the odor of the world." Then the sister stated: "Truly, lady, I have heard two or three of my songs which I have bound together in this way." Then the saint said: "God witness that I have heard nothing of any worldly song." Thus it was obvious that though her flesh remained in the world, her spirit was already in Heaven.

37. In praise of Christ, let us proclaim a miracle from our own time patterned after an ancient model in the tradition of the blessed Martin [see 14.7

above]. When the most blessed female was secluded in her cell, she heard a *monacha* crying. At the signal, she entered and asked what was the matter. She answered that her infant sister was dead, and though still warm she was laid out and ready to be washed in cold water. Condoling with her, the saint bade her bring the corpse to her in her cell. There she took it into her own hands, closing the door behind her and ordering the other to withdraw to a distance lest she sense what she was doing. But what she did secretly could not be concealed for long. By time the services for the dead were prepared, she had handled the corpse of the dead little girl for seven hours. But seeing a faith he could not deny, Christ utterly restored her health. When the saint rose from prayer, the infant rose from the dead. The old woman got up when the infant revived. When the signal was repeated, she joyfully restored alive the one who was dead when she had tearfully received her.

38. And this noble deed should be commemorated. On the day the holy woman migrated from earth, a tribune of the fisc [treasury] named Domnolenus who was wasting away with a suffocating disease dreamed that he seemed to see the saint approach his town in state. He ran out and saluted her and asked what the blessed one wished. Then she said that she had come to see him. And since it was the wish of the people to establish an oratory for blessed Martin, the most blessed one seized the tribune's hand, saying: "There are venerable relics of the Confessor here with which you could build a shrine which he would consider most fitting." Behold the mystery of God! The foundation and the pavement where a basilica had been built were revealed. Then, in addition, in his slumber she drew her hand over his jaws and stroked his throat for a long time, saying: "I came that God might confer better health on you." And he dreamed she asked: "On my life, because of me, release those whom you have in prison." Waking, the tribune recounted what he had seen to his wife, saying: "Indeed, I believe that at this hour the saint has gone from this earth." He sent to the city to confirm the truth of this. He directed the prison that the seven prisoners held there should be admonished and released. The messenger, returning, reported that she had migrated from the world in that very hour. And the saint's oracle was proved by a triple mystery: the relief of the prisoners, the restoration of the tribune's health, and the temple building.

39. But let this small sample of the blessed one's miracles suffice, lest their very abundance arouse contempt. And even this should in no way be reckoned a small amount, since from these few tales we may recognize in the miracles the greatness with which she lived in such piety and self-denial, affection and affability, humility and honor, faith and fervor, with the result that after her death wonders also ensued upon her glorious passing.

17. RADEGUND WRITES TO THE BISHOPS

*After the death of Radegund and Agnes, the convent at Poitiers was ruled by
Leubovera, and during her tenure a group of nuns led by Clotild (who claimed to be
the daughter of King Charibert) rose in rebellion against her. They left the convent and
wandered at large, eventually taking over the church of St. Hilary at Poitiers, while
making their complaints known to the king and the bishops. Before the quarrel was
settled the abbess herself had been dragged from sanctuary and imprisoned by her
opponents while numbers of followers on both sides were killed in the outbreaks of violence. By the time the case reached this point, however, Leubovera was circulating
among the bishops a copy of a letter written by Radegund at the time of the founding
of the convent. Leubovera's intention was evidently to invoke the power of the
foundress's own words to condemn Clotild and her followers for breaking the rule of
claustration, but the letter also reveals an administrative side of Radegund that Fortunatus does not show us: her farsighted concerns for her convent and her understanding
of the difficulties to which such institutions were liable in the troubled times.*

Source: trans. O.M. Dalton, *The History of the Franks, by Gregory of Tours* (Oxford: Clarendon
Press, 1927), 2,418-21. Repr. with permission.

42. The abbess also read out the letter which the blessed Radegund addressed
to the bishops of her own time. Of this letter she now again sent copies to
the bishops of the neighboring cities. It ran as follows:

'To the holy fathers in Christ and most worthy occupants of their apostolic seats, the bishops, Radegund of Poitiers.

'The first steps of a meet project can only move strongly to fulfilment
when the matter is brought to the ears of our common fathers, the physicians and the shepherds of the fold, and commended likewise to their hearts.
For the active sympathy proceeding from their love, the sage counsel proceeding from their power, the support proceeding from their prayers all unite
to give it furtherance.

'Since in time past, delivered from the chains of secular life by the providence and inspiration of the divine mercy, I turned of my own will to the
Rule of religion under Christ's guidance, and with ardent mind also considered how I might help forward others, that with the approval of the Lord my
desires might become profitable to the rest, I established at Poitiers a
monastery for nuns, founded and enriched by the most excellent lord King
[C]lothar; this monastery after its foundation I myself endowed by the gift of
all the property which the royal munificence had bestowed upon me. Moreover, I appointed for this community gathered together under Christ's
protection the Rule according to which the holy Caesaria lived, and which

the care of the blessed Caesarius, bishop of Arles, had compiled to suit her needs from the institutions of the holy Fathers. With the approval of the most blessed bishops of Poitiers and the other sees, and by the choice of our own community, I appointed as abbess the lady Agnes, my sister, whom I have loved and brought up from her earliest youth; and I submitted myself in regular obedience to her authority next to that of God. And following the apostolic example, I myself and my sisters, when we entered the monastery, made over by deed all our substance in earthly possessions, reserving nothing for ourselves, from fear of that which befell Ananias and Sapphira [in *Acts* 5, 1–11, a husband and wife who kept back part of the money for property they had sold while claiming to give the entire amount to Christ's apostles]. But since the moments and times of man's lot are uncertain, and the world runneth to its end, and there be those who rather seek the fulfilment of their own than the divine will, I remit to you, apostolic fathers, in my lifetime, and with all due devotion, this page containing my prayer to you, in the name of Christ.

'And since I cannot in person throw myself at your feet, I make prostration vicariously through this letter, and by the Father, Son, and Holy Spirit, and by the tremendous day of Judgment, I adjure you, as if you stood before me, to protect us from any tyrant, and secure to us the favor of our rightful king. And if haply after my death any one, whether the bishop of the city, or a royal officer, or any other person shall, as I trust shall never befall, either by suggestion of wicked men or by action of law, seek to trouble the sisterhood, or to break the Rule, or appoint any other abbess than my sister Agnes, whom the most blessed Germanus in the presence of his brethren consecrated with his benediction; or if the community itself, which I may not think possible, shall murmur and seek change; or if any person, were it even the bishop of the city, shall seek to claim, by new privileges over and above those enjoyed by his predecessors or any other persons in my lifetime, either power in the monastery or over its property; or if any shall essay against the Rule to go forth thence; or if any prince or bishop or other powerful person, or any of the sisters, shall with sacrilegious intent diminish or appropriate the property which the most excellent lord [C]lothar or the most excellent kings his sons bestowed upon me, and I, by his injunction and permission, transferred to the monastery to have and hold, of which transmission I obtained confirmation by letters of the most excellent lords the kings Charibert, Guntram, Chilperic, and Sigibert under their oath and signature, or the gifts which others have given for the good of their souls or the sisters have bestowed out of their own possessions; may they through my prayer and the will of Christ in such wise be confronted with God's wrath, and that of yourselves and your successors, that as robbers and despoilers of the poor they may be shut out from your grace. Resist in such wise that none may ever avail to diminish or to change in anything either our Rule or the possessions of the monastery. This also I pray, that when it shall be the will of God that the aforesaid lady Agnes, my sister, shall pass away, an abbess shall be appointed out of our congregation, who shall find favor in God's sight, who shall safely guard the Rule, and in nothing diminish the intent of holy living; let neither her own will nor that of another person be suffered to ruin them. If any, which God forbid, contrary to the command of the Lord and the authority of our kings, shall do aught against the conditions heretofore cited and commended to your protection by prayer before the Lord and his saints, or against the welfare of the monastery, either as regards its occupants or its possessions, or shall in any way vex my above-named sister Agnes, the abbess, may he incur the judgment of God and of the Holy Cross and of the blessed Mary, and may he have as his enemies and pursuers the blessed confessors Hilary and Martin, to whom, after God, I have entrusted the protection of my sisters.

'Thou also, holy bishop, and thy successors, whom I haste to take as my patrons in the cause of God, if there should be found any (which God forbid) to make attempts against these my dispositions, shrink not from appeal to the king who then shall rule over this place, or to the city of Poitiers, on behalf of that which hath been commended to your guardianship before the Lord, or from toil in shielding and defending justice against the unjust attack of others, that the enemy of God may be confounded and driven back. So shall no Catholic king in his own times brook such infamy, or suffer to be destroyed that which hath been founded firm by God's will and mine intent, and the will of the kings themselves. Likewise also I conjure the princes that live after me, whom God shall ordain to rule the people when I am no more, in the name of the King whose reign shall have no end and by whose nod kingdoms consist, who hath given them their very life and their dominion: them I conjure to take under their ward the abbess Agnes and this monastery which, with permission and assistance of the lords and kings their father and grandfather, I have built and duly ordered and endowed. Let them not suffer it, that this our abbess, so many times herein named, be by any man harassed or molested, or aught pertaining to our monastery be hereafter diminished, or in any wise changed; but rather see that all these be defended and secured, which cause I commend to them, for the sake of God, our lords the bishops working with them, and in accordance with my prayer to the Redeemer of all peoples; that they may be forever united in the eternal kingdom with the defender of the poor and the spouse of virgins, in whose honor they protect the handmaids of God. And I conjure you, holy bishops, and our most excellent lords and kings, and the whole Christian people, by the Catholic faith in which you are baptized, when God shall ordain that I pass from the light of this world, let my poor body be buried in that basilica, be it at the time completed or unfinished, which I have begun to build in honor of the holy Mary, the mother of the Lord, and wherein many of our sisters are already laid to rest. May it be that if any shall desire or attempt aught contrary, by virtue of the Cross of Christ and of the blessed Mary, he may incur divine vengeance, and that I, by your mediation, be held worthy to obtain a resting-place in that church among the congregation of my sisters. And I beseech with many tears that this my petition, signed by my own hand, be preserved among the archives of the cathedral church; and that if the action of the wicked shall compel my sister the abbess Agnes, or her community, to entreat your succor and protection, having the pious solace of your pity and the present aid which belongeth to good shepherds, they shall not proclaim themselves forsaken of me, when God hath prepared for them the protection of your grace.

'This request I lay before your eyes, omitting nothing, through the grace of him who from his glorious Cross did commend his virgin mother to the blessed apostle John; that as by him the Lord's commendation was fulfilled, so by you may be fulfilled that which I in my unworthiness and humility commend to you my lords, the fathers of the Church, who now bear the apostolic name. And when you shall have kept this trust which I leave you as beseems your high estate, you shall be partakers in his merits whose apostolic charge you fulfil, and worthily renew his example.'

Fig. 23] Carved ivory cover of the *Evangelium Longum,* or *Long Gospel,* in St-Gall library, showing in the bottom panel the story of St. Gall and the bear related in Chapter 11 of Walahfrid's account (M. Joynt, *The Life of St. Gall,* [New York and Toronto, 1927]).

18. AN IRISH MISSIONARY: *ST. GALL*, BY WALAHFRID STRABO

The distinctively ascetic form of Christianity practised in Ireland from the time of its conversion by St. Patrick in the fifth century produced a number of great leaders, among them the 'wandering monks' of the sixth and seventh centuries who, from motives of penance as well as evangelism, crossed to Britain and the continent and established monasteries there. Two of the most famous monastic houses were Bobbio in northern Italy and St-Gall in Switzerland, the former founded by St. Columbanus and the latter by his disciple St. Gall. Such was the reputation of St-Gall's schools and library that at least three early 'lives' of its founder were commissioned, two of them by the abbot Gozbert in the early ninth century. Walahfrid Strabo (d. 849), author of one of these accounts, was educated at the abbey of Reichenau on Lake Constance and at Fulda, in West Germany, another great center of monastic learning. Later he became tutor to Charles the Bald, son of the emperor Louis the Pious, and subsequently was appointed abbot of Reichenau, a reward for his services at the imperial court. This did not prevent him from being caught up in the ensuing power struggle between Louis's sons in the 830s. A prolific writer on a wide range of subjects including theology, biography, and horticulture, Walahfrid in his 'Life of St. Gall' follows the pattern of edification expected of hagiography and at the same time conveys a vivid impression of the difficulties encountered by the 'wandering monks' as they sought to establish monasteries in hostile lands.

Source: trans. Maud Joynt, *The Life of St. Gall* (London: Society for Promoting Christian Knowledge; New York and Toronto: Macmillan, 1927), pp. 58-111; abridged with modernized vocabulary and repr. with permission. BHL 3247.

Prologue

Were it not that I am constrained to obey you, holy fathers, by the authority of the sacred Scriptures and especially by that saying of the truthful prophet wherein obedience is preferred to sacrifice, I should meet your commands with the following excuse: if that prophet who was chosen of the Lord before yet he was formed in the womb and sanctified before he was born [Jeremiah] nevertheless pleaded ignorance and the infirmity of age when the Lord enlightened him with his spirit and laid upon him the service of proclaiming the word, what shall I do, a transgressor, conceived in sin and brought forth in iniquity, uncircumcised in heart and ears because of the foulness of my life? I, who can neither fitly apprehend the things I ought to know, nor bear in mind the things I hear? How shall I tell of the manifold righteousness of the Lord or take his testimony on my lips, who am neither ripe in years nor have knowledge to commend me, so that my words are supported neither by learning nor experience – especially since you bid me treat of matters whose passing worth I can but faintly grasp? Nevertheless, there are three considerations that lead me to attempt the task. In the first place, I believe I shall be sustained by the Lord, since it is at his command and relying on his promise that I have undertaken with ready obedience an enterprise I should have shrunk from had I considered my own strength only. In the next place, I trust to be aided by the intercession of St. Gall and by your prayers, since it is owing to my reverence and love for you that I have laid this heavy burden on my weak shoulders. Finally, I am treading in the footprints of others and all I have to do is to measure with my own paces the path of truth already marked out for me to follow.

Since the life of our patron St. Gall the Confessor of Christ, over whose precious relics you keep faithful watch, is written in a manner unworthy of the exalted nature of the subject, you desire me to correct and improve the style and to disentangle the confused sequence of the narrative by arranging it in chapters; and as I have no sufficient excuse for declining this task, I will rather incur censure by my incapacity than be condemned for my disobedience.

Some time ago when reading the work I have spoken of [the earlier 'life'], I observed that the country which we Alemannians or Sueves inhabit is frequently called Altimania by the author; and on looking for the source of this name, I did not find it mentioned in any of the writers with whom I have hitherto been able to form acquaintance. If I mistake not, it is a modern invention suggested by the elevated situation of the province. For according to writers of warrant, that part of Alemannia or Suevia [territory that is now modern Switzerland and part of south Germany] which lies between the Pennine Alps and the southern bank of the Danube is called Rhaetia [the area between Lake Constance and the Danube], what extends beyond it on the northern bank of the Danube being counted as part of Germany. Lest it should be thought that I am stating an opinion of my own, I will cite some witnesses on the point. . . . [Walahfrid then quotes from Orosius, a 4th/5th-century writer, and Solinus, a 3rd-century grammarian, to prove his point] . . . If Rhaetia is wholly below the Alps, as many assert, what reason is there for us, when going from Gaul to Noricum, to cross the rugged Alpine heights instead of proceeding directly to Noricum through greater Rhaetia? It is in Rhaetia also, according to the statement above quoted, that the town of Brigantium [modern Bregenz] is situated, now fallen into decay through age, which gives its name to the lake formed by the Rhine, known also by another name of Greek origin as Lake Pontamicus [Lake Constance]. Since then the Sueva, commingling with the Alemannians, occupy part of Germany

beyond the Danube, part of Rhaetia between the Alps and the Danube, and that part of Gaul which lies around the river Arar [Aare], let us stick to the old names as being more accurate and call the country after its inhabitants Alemannia or Suevia. For as there are two names to denote the one people, the surrounding nations who use the Latin tongue call us by the former (that is, Alemannians), while the latter is given us by those who have the German idiom. In like manner, as we know, the Franks have not only brought certain parts of Germany or Gaul under their sway, but have imposed on them their own name as well.

Since I have entered on the description of these provinces, let me also, following the same authorities, say a few words about the situation of the island of Hibernia [Ireland], from which so great a glory has shone upon us. 'The island of Hibernia', says Orosius, 'lies between Britain and Spain and stretches a greater distance northward than Britain. It is nearer to Britain and of more limited area, but on account of its temperate climate and the nature of its soil more productive.' According to Solinus 'it is so rich in pasture that unless the cattle were sometimes in summer shut out from their pastures, they would be in danger from over-feeding. There are no snakes and few birds.' As for the shocking accounts which Solinus and others give of the manners of the inhabitants [that the Irish are warlike and inhospitable, and have the custom of smearing their faces with the blood of fallen enemies], now that the faith of Christ has shone upon them, those may be regarded as obsolete; for where sin abounded, grace more exceedingly abounds, and from the rising of the sun – in India or Ethiopia – to its setting – among the Britons and Scots – the name of the Lord is now praised. For the Lord is exalted above all the peoples and his glory above the heavens.

I beg you therefore, beloved Gozbert, abbot of the monastery of St. Gall, and all the brothers who wage spiritual warfare under your command, to assist me with your prayers, that I may be enabled to execute this work, and other works hereafter in a manner pleasing to God. For if I am encouraged by your approval when I set down anything aright, and corrected with indulgence when I stumble, I will, if the Lord permit, hereafter season with some relish of verse the rustic fare I now offer. It is indeed fitting that he whom the Lord chose from the farthest ends of earth to bring us salvation, should be made known throughout the world by our praises. May the holy Trinity vouchsafe to preserve your Fatherhood ever in health and to keep me in your memory.

O Father, O Son of the Father, O life-giving Spirit, God One and Three, rule us with compassion. I am bound by your commands and directed by your promises; may your light, I beseech you, shine forth in all I say. In you,

O Gall, I will confess God, even as in the Lord I acknowledge you, O Gall; pour forth your holy prayers to the Lord on my behalf, that he may pardon my faults and control my utterance, expunge whatever offends and enlarge whatever is profitable.

1. In the days when the holy Columbanus, who is also called Columba, was famed throughout all Ireland for the sanctity of his life and, like a bright ray of the fiery sun, called forth the love of all men by his signal grace, even as had been foretold of him before his birth (as the book of his deeds sets forth in full [the *Life of Columbanus* by Jonas]): among those who were drawn by the report of his virtues were the parents of the blessed Gall, persons devout in the sight of God and honorable in the sight of men. They, offering their son in the flower of early youth as a sacrifice to the Lord, entrusted him to the teaching of Columbanus that he might be trained in the religious life and might follow examples of obedience and singleness of purpose in the midst of others engaged in spiritual warfare. Being a youth of great promise, he was nurtured by Columbanus with tender affection and grew apace in virtues. Guided by divine grace, he drank in the holy Scripture with such eagerness that he was able from his stores to produce things new and old; and he also mastered the rules of grammar and the intricacies of prosody with able intellect. With such wisdom did he open the obscure passages of Scripture to those who wished to learn, that he won the admiration and praise of all who heard him speak. Being thus ripe in wisdom, by the advice of all and the command of Abbot Columbanus, after passing through the several degrees of divine orders, he at last received the rank of priesthood, though against his will. While engaged in the duties of his sacred calling he sought day and night to propitiate the Lord with prayers and tears; and while seeking only to be found pleasing in the eyes of him who sees above, he gained the love and favor of his fellow men by his gifts and virtuous life.

2. Meantime St. Columbanus, earnestly desiring to attain that perfection spoken of in the Gospel – namely, to leave all he had, take up his cross and follow the Lord, stripped of all possessions – succeeded in persuading those of his brothers whose souls were inflamed with a like fervor, to make good their zeal by action, by renouncing the joys of kindred and home.

Taking ship therefore, they came to Britain and from there crossed the channel to Gaul. When the man of God and his followers reached king Sigebert [in fact Childebert; Sigebert had died in 575, and Columbanus left Ireland c. 590], the king begged him to settle in Gaul and not leave it to go to other nations, promising that he would provide all that the holy father required. To this request the man of God replied: 'We who have left our

homes to follow the Lord, as it is commanded in the Gospel, may not cleave to external riches, lest we may be found transgressors of the divine command.' The king in answer to his objection said: 'If you desire to take up your cross and follow Christ, seek the tranquility of some wide wilderness; only leave not the land beneath my rule to go to neighboring peoples; thus you can both heap up reward for yourself and provide for our salvation.' Columbanus yielded to the persuasions of the king, and being given his choice of a retreat, repaired with his disciples to the wilderness called Vosegus [the Vosges mountains]. There they found a place, commonly called Luxovium [Luxeuil] where there were hot springs and which, though now in ruins, had in former times been enclosed by walls. Here they built a small church in honor of St. Peter the apostle as well as huts to dwell in, and pursued their religious calling, at the same time cultivating the soil; and many not only of the Burgundians but also of the Franks, won by the merit of their lives, flocked to them and by their spiritual teachings were moved to such effectual repentance that some of them brought all their belongings to the place and having shorn their locks, took on them the monastic habit and embraced voluntary poverty.

3. While they abode thus, making such happy progress in the religious life, the great holiness of Columbanus being proved by many miracles came at last to be famed throughout the whole of Gaul and even the provinces of Germany. He was praised and revered by all, even the king himself: Theuderic son of Childebert [d. 595] and grandson of Sigebert, who was then reigning in Burgundy, used often to visit him and implore the aid of his prayers most devoutly. And when the holy father reproved him because he defiled himself with concubines instead of wedding a lawful spouse, the king yielded to his admonitions and promised to forsake all illicit connections. But when the king's grandmother Brunehild, saw him obeying the counsels of the man of God, she was stirred up to enmity and armed her mind with fury as with a serpent's poison; for she feared that, if the king discarded his concubines and chose a queen to be his consort in the realm, her own position would lose its honor and be held cheap.

Oppressed by this fear, she began to cherish enmity against the man of God and after contriving many means to injure him (as the narrative of his holy life attests), she entered into a plot with the king to banish him; and she sent her agents with a letter to him, forbidding him to remain longer in the kingdom. To escape the machinations of this second Jezebel, Columbanus journeyed with his followers to King Clothair [of Neustria, brother of Sigebert] . . .

3-5. [The wandering monks eventually settled on the shores of Lake Zurich, where they destroyed pagan temples and incurred the wrath of the

local inhabitants. They were then welcomed by Willimar, the priest at Arbon, who suggested they settle at Bregenz on Lake Constance.]

6. As they were eager to go there, the priest got ready a small vessel and manned it with rowers; and the venerable abbot, taking with him Gall and a deacon, embarked after calling on the name of the Lord, and steered a straight course for the spot. On landing, they made their way to an oratory which had been dedicated to St. Aurelia and was afterwards restored by St. Columbanus to its pristine honor. After engaging in prayer, they surveyed their surroundings and were well pleased with the situation and aspect of the place. In the oratory they found three images of gilt bronze fixed to the wall; for the people had forsaken the sacred rites of God's altar and used to worship these images instead, saying, as they offered their sacrifices, 'These are the old gods, the former guardians of this place, and it is by their aid that we and ours have been kept alive to this day.' Columbanus laid on Gall the duty of preaching to the people and calling them back from the errors of idolatry to the worship of God; for Gall had received this favor from the Lord, that he had no small knowledge of the native idiom as well as of Latin. It was just then the time for holding a festival in the temple, and a large crowd of men and women of all ages assembled, desiring not only to celebrate the festival but to see the strangers of whose arrival they had heard. When therefore all were gathered together at the hour of prayer, Gall, in obedience to his abbot's command, began to show to the people the way of truth and to exhort them to turn to the Lord, to cast aside vain superstitions and worship God the Father, the Creator of all things, and his only begotten Son in whom is salvation, life and the resurrection of the dead. And laying hold of the images in the sight of all, he broke them to pieces with stones and threw them into the lake. When the people saw this, some of them were converted and confessed their sins, giving glory to God for having enlightened them; others were moved to wrath by the breaking of the images and departed, swelling with rage and resentment. But St. Columbanus had water brought and having blessed it, he sprinkled the temple and dedicated it anew as a church, the monks meantime going round it in procession and chanting Psalms. Then, after calling on the name of the Lord, he anointed the altar, placed within it the relics of St. Aurelia and laid upon it an altar-cloth, after which he celebrated Mass in due order. When all these holy rites had been performed, the people returned to their homes rejoicing. St. Columbanus and his fellow-soldiers stayed in this place for three years and built a small cloister there, where some of them laid out a garden and others cultivated fruit trees. St. Gall used to weave nets and by the mercy of God he caught such quantities of fish that the brothers were never in any want; he was even able to provide for any

stranger who chanced to come and bestowed many a blessing on the people by his toil.

7. It happened once in the silence of the night, as Gall was casting his nets into the lake, he heard a demon calling with loud voice from the summit of the nearest mountain to some fellow of his who seemed to inhabit the water. The one who was called answered (as it were out of the lake) that he was there. 'Rise and come to my aid,' said the other, 'that we may cast out these strangers who have come from afar; for they have driven me from my temple and shattered my image and drawn away after themselves the people who used to follow me. Be not indifferent to my wrongs, but let us with united strength drive our common enemies from our borders.' 'Alas,' replied the second demon, 'what you tell me of your wrongs I know from my own experience. For one of them holds me in subjection in the lake and lays waste my domains, and I can neither damage his nets nor foil him, for the divine name is ever on his lips and by its protection and his ceaseless vigilance he sets my snares at nought. No cunning of ours will get the better of such wary combatants.' On hearing these words, the man of God secured himself on every side with the sign of the holy cross, and said to them: 'In the name of our Lord Jesus Christ I adjure you to depart from this place, nor dare to injure anyone here.' Then he made for the shore with speed and went to tell his abbot what he had heard. When Columbanus heard it, he went to the church and striking the bell, summoned the brothers together. But before they had finished chanting the Psalms, they heard the awful voices of the demons passing from crest to crest of the mountains, in mingled tones of despair and fear as though they were taking their departure. Then the servants of God prostrated themselves in prayer, beseeching the Lord to protect them and offering him praise and thanks because he had vouchsafed to deliver them from the terrors of the fiends.

8. Meantime some of the townsmen, chafing at the overthrow of their idols and spurning the teaching of the monks, began to stir up hatred and frame plots against them. To this end, they went to the duke of those parts, Gunzo by name, and laid charges against the holy men before him, saying that the public hunting in the district had been hindered by the interference of the strangers. When the duke heard this he was inflamed with wrath and sent messengers to order the servants of God to quit the neighborhood. Even this, however, was not enough for the devil-worshipers, for they stole a cow belonging to the monks and drove it into the pathless recesses of the forest. Two of the brothers followed their track and came up with them; but the robbers rose and slew them and made off with their spoils. The monks, wondering why these two so long delayed their return, sent others to seek them,

who, following their footsteps, found them slain. They laid the bodies on their shoulders and carried them back to the cloister. While they were thus overwhelmed with a tide of troubles, the messengers of the duke [Gunzo] arrived and ordered them to depart; nor was this unnatural, seeing there is no fellowship between lightness and darkness. Thus by his craft the devil brought to pass that the people who were slipping from his power in presence of the light were plunged back into their former darkness by the withdrawal of its rays. So the holy men, grieving sorely that they were driven from their pleasant abode, determined with one accord to set out for Italy; and while they were weighed down with sorrow, the holy father Columbanus began to comfort them, saying: 'We have indeed, my brothers, found here a golden shell, but one that harbored venomous reptiles. Nevertheless, dispel the sadness which enfeebles you, for our trust is sure in the aid of our Defender. The God whom we serve will send his angel with us to lead us to Agilof king of the Lombards, and in his realm, if he bestows his favor on us, we shall meet with kindly feelings and find a peaceful spot for our habitation.'

9. When the time for their departure was at hand, St. Gall was seized with a sudden fever; therefore, throwing himself at the abbot's feet, he told him that he was suffering from severe illness and was unable to undertake the journey before them. But Columbanus, thinking that Gall was held back by love of a spot endeared to him by many labors and was shirking the fatigue of a long journey, said to him: 'I know, brother, that now it seems to you a heavy burden to endure toil and weariness for my sake. Nevertheless, this I enjoin on you before I depart, that so long as I am alive in body you shall never take upon you to celebrate Mass.'

After his master and his comrades had gone, Gall placed his nets, big and little, in a boat and went to Willimar the priest; he offered the nets to him and told him with sighs and tears all that had befallen the monks; then he disclosed the causes of his own malady and begged Willimar to take him under his care. Willimar received him with every kindly attention, assigning him a dwelling close to the church and charging two of his clerics, Magnoald and Theodore, to tend him and do their utmost for his recovery. After some days had elapsed, the Lord, who is the true physician, vouchsafed a cure; Gall began to take food and grew stronger day by day till he regained his full health. Surely that was a weakness passing all human strength, a fever for which we should be devoutly thankful, an illness to be counted rather as health and cause of rejoicing! For like his Lord, Gall suffered for us that he might banish the diseases of our souls by his holy preaching; he was unable to go with his master so that he might show us the way of truth. Truly the Lord is long-suffering and merciful, for though so long despised in the persons of his preachers, he waits patiently for the conversion of the sinners and holds back a teacher for them lest they should be abandoned to their errors.

10. Now the deacon of the priest Willimar, whose name was Hiltibod, was well acquainted with every nook and cranny of the wilderness, for he was accustomed to roam through it in order to catch fish and snare hawks, and by daily habit had come to know its inmost recesses. The holy man, who had by this time admitted the deacon to his intimacy, asked him if he had ever found in the wilderness any spot abounding in pure and wholesome water, level and adapted for tillage; 'for I am filled with a burning desire,' said he, 'to pass the days allotted to me on this earth in some retreat, according to that which the psalmist says: "Lo, I have gotten me away far off and remained in the wilderness. I waited for him to deliver me."' The deacon replied: 'This wilderness, my father, has many waters flowing through it, but it is a wild and fearsome place, full of high mountains with narrow winding glens and haunted by savage beasts; for besides stags and such harmless animals it breeds bears and boars and wolves beyond number and exceeding fierce; were I to lead you there, I fear they would devour you.' 'The apostle,' rejoined the holy man, 'has said: "If God be for us, who can be against us?" and again: "We know that all things work together for good to them that love God." He who delivered Daniel from the den of lions can save me also from the clutches of wild beasts.' Whereupon the deacon answered: 'Put some food into your wallet [pilgrim's bag for food] and the smallest of your fishing-nets, and tomorrow I will lead you into the wilderness; and if you find in it a spot that suits you, give thanks to God and fulfil the divine command in all its strictness. For God who has brought you from a far country, will himself send his angel with us, even as he gave a companion from heaven to his servant Tobias, and will show us some spot suited to our pious desires.' The saint accordingly remained fasting for that day and spent the night in prayer until the dawn. For it was fitting that he should by fervent prayer commend to the Lord the enterprise to which he was impelled by divine love.

11. When at last Lucifer in his ascent had laid bare the hidden tracts of darkness and the sun, leaving the lower world, returned in his usual course to visit the upper regions of the earth and displayed to mortals his fiery beams in the eastern quarter of the heavens, the athlete of God, taking with him the things his guide had told him, set out on his way after offering prayer, the deacon going before him. They pursued their journey throughout the day, till at about the ninth hour [3 p.m.] the deacon said: 'Father, it is now time to break our fast; let us refresh ourselves with a little bread and water that we may be better able for the rest of our way.' 'Do you, my son,' replied the man

of God, 'take what food your body needs; I will taste nothing till the Lord shows me the abiding place I seek.' 'If we be partners in suffering,' said the other, 'we shall be partners likewise in consolation.' After these words they hastened on their way, for the day was already declining and the sun was near its setting. They came to the stream called Steinaha [the Steinach] and followed its course till they reached the cliff from which it descends with violence, forming a fine pool below. Here they saw a quantity of fish and they threw their nets into the water and caught some. Then they kindled a fire and the deacon boiled the fish and laid out the bread on the top of the wallet. St. Gall meantime retired a short distance to pray, and as he was walking through the tangled thorn-brake, his foot caught and he fell to earth. The deacon ran to lift him up; but the man of God, filled with the spirit of prophecy, said: 'Let me be; this shall be my rest for ever; here will I dwell, for I have chosen it.' And after praying, he rose to his feet, and taking a hazel-twig he formed it into a cross and fixed it in the ground. He had hanging round his neck a satchel that contained relics of the blessed Mary the mother of God and the holy martyrs Maurice [a famous soldier-saint, martyred with his legion for refusing to sacrifice to pagan gods] and Desiderius [Didier of Vienne, later especially honored in the monastery of St. Gall]. He suspended this satchel from the cross and called the deacon; both prostrated themselves in prayer and the saint uttered the following petition: 'O Lord Jesus Christ, who for the salvation of mankind did vouchsafe to be born of a virgin and to suffer death, spurn not my desire because of my transgressions, but for the honor of your holy mother and your martyrs and confessors prepare in this place a habitation fit for your service.' When he had ended his prayer, as the sun was now setting and the day near its close, they partook at last of food, giving thanks to God before and after meat, and then spread couches for themselves on the ground to rest awhile. But as soon as the saint thought his companion was sound asleep, he arose and prostrating himself (with outstretched arms) in the form of a cross before the satchel, poured forth fervent prayers to the Lord. While he was thus engaged, a bear came down from the mountains and began stealthily to pick up the crumbs and broken morsels which they had let fall during their meal. When the man of God saw this, he said to the beast: 'In the name of the Lord, I command you to take up a log and throw it on the fire.' The monster turned at his bidding and brought a stout log and threw it into the fire. Thereupon the kind-hearted saint went to his wallet and drawing forth a loaf still untouched from his scanty store, gave it to his servitor, saying: 'In the name of my Lord Jesus Christ, depart from this valley; you are free to range the hills and mountains around at will so long as you do no harm to man or beast in this spot.' The deacon meantime, feigning sleep, had watched how the beloved of God dealt with the beast; at last he rose and threw himself at the saint's feet, saying: 'Now I know of a truth that the Lord is with you, since even the beasts of the wilderness obey you.' But the saint answered him: 'Take heed that you tell no man of this till you see the glory of God.'

12. When the night was spent and the golden light of day illumined the forest shades, the deacon said: 'My father, what are we to do to-day?' 'I beg you, my son,' replied Gall, 'take not amiss what I say: since the Lord has caused us to find what we sought, let us pass this day also in this place. Take your net and go to the pool, and I will follow you as soon as I can. It may be the Lord will show us his accustomed bounty, so that on our return to the town we may have to offer the priest our father some gift which the Lord has granted us to find.' 'I am well content with your bidding,' answered the deacon, and rose without delay, calling on the name of the Lord; then taking the little fishing net, he went to the river. As he was about to throw it into the water, two fiends in the shape of women appeared standing on the bank, naked as though they were going to take a bath; and after flaunting their indecency in his face, they took up stones and began to pelt him, saying: 'It is you that has led that man into the wilderness – one full of iniquity and malice, who has always foiled us by his evil practices.' The deacon returned to the man of God and told him what he had seen and heard. Then that chosen warrior of God threw himself on his knees (as did also the deacon) and besought the Lord, saying: 'O Almighty God, whose goodness is past telling and whose majesty is beyond all measure; not according to my merits but according to your mercy, hearken with favor to my prayer and bid these fiends quit this spot that it may be consecrated to your glory.' Then rising they approached the pool and at once the fiends turned and fled along the course of the stream to the neighboring mountain and St. Gall said to them: 'By the boundless might of the Trinity I charge you, phantasms, to leave this spot and withdraw to the uninhabited mountains, and never henceforth dare return hither.' After this they let down their net into the pool and caught as much fish as they wanted. As they were disentangling the fishes from the meshes of the net, they heard from the mountain-top voices like the voices of two women bewailing the dead, saying one to another: 'Alas! what shall we do? where shall we go? This stranger will not suffer us to dwell among men nor even to abide in the wilderness.' Nor was that the only time such voices were heard; but on three occasions afterwards, when the deacon had entered the valley to catch hawks, he heard the demons shouting from a mountain which is called Himilinberg asking one another whether Gall was still in the wilderness or had gone away.

13. After the departure of the fiends, these two faithful lovers of the wilderness continued their way through the valley and espied at last between two streams a spot which they judged well fitted for a settlement, for it offered much that they desired, a fine wood and mountains enclosing a small plain. Then the saint, recalling the words of Jacob after he had beheld the vision of the ladder and the angels ascending and descending thereon, said, 'Truly the Lord is in this place!' Up to that time there had been a great many serpents in that valley, but from that day forth they vanished so completely that not one was ever after seen there. This miracle was like those that went before; for when the devil had been driven from the spot, it was fitting that the creature by whose means he had deceived mankind should also withdraw and make way for the habitation of holiness.

14. On their return to their first halting-place, where the man of God had planted the little cross, the deacon said to him: 'Let us take the wallet and net and go back to the town.' 'Do you, my son,' answered Gall, 'return home at your pleasure; I will stay here a while and follow you in three days' time.' Said the deacon: 'I will by no means go back to our father without you, lest perhaps he say I have killed you for the sake of your spoils or, if I deny the charge, he may reproach me: "Why then have you left him in the wilderness? Return with speed and bring him to me"; and so I shall have double toil and be put to open shame.' The saint replied, 'Go, my son, and I will follow in your steps as soon as may be.' When the deacon had gone, the athlete of God remained for three days fasting from all bodily sustenance, that by his abstinence he might consecrate the spot which he desired for the warfare of the spirit. On the fourth day he left the wilderness and returned to the house of the priest, on whom he bestowed a cordial greeting, giving due thanks and praise to God for all the goodness shown to him. The priest received him joyfully and bade the table be set, and they sat down to meat after blessing and giving thanks to God. In the course of the meal the deacon said to the priest: 'If the bear were here, it is likely Gall would have given him something to eat;' and on the priest's inquiring the meaning of his words, he related all that had happened in the wilderness. From that day they looked upon Gall as a prophet and a saint daily measuring his deserts by the austerity of his life and his zeal in goodness.

While they dwelt together in this way a messenger came to the priest to say that Gaudentius, the bishop of Constance, had departed this life. On hearing the news they began with one accord to offer fervent prayers and tears for his repose.

15. On the seventh day following there came a message from Duke Gunzo to the priest, bidding him come in twelve days' time to the town of

Iburnungae [Uberlingen] and bring the man of God with him. For his only daughter, who was named Fridiburga, a girl of remarkable beauty, was possessed by an evil spirit which tormented her in different ways, so that she remained almost wholly without food and would often roll on the ground, foaming at the mouth and in such dire frenzy that four men could scarcely hold her with all their efforts. When a month had elapsed from the time this malady attacked her, the fiend who had taken up his abode in her began to utter words of ill omen through her lips. Her father sent messengers to Sigebert, son of Theuderic, who was betrothed to her, to tell him how it stood with the girl. The king with all dispatch sent two bishops, from whose merits he looked for great results, with royal gifts to the girl so that they might cure her of her madness through the medicine of prayer. The priest Willimar, wishing to reach the duke at the time appointed in the letter, said to St. Gall, 'You know the duke's command; let us go to him.' 'This journey,' answered Gall, 'is your business, not mine; you go. What have I to do with the princes of this world? I will return to the wilderness whence I came.' 'Do not do so,' said the other, 'but come with me, lest perhaps the duke, being overly afflicted by the sufferings of his daughter, be moved to wrath and send his servants to bring you to him in bonds.' The saint, filled with the spirit of God, replied: 'I will first go to my cloister to make provision for the needs of the brothers who will serve God there in time to come.' (But this he said so that he might avoid going to the duke.) And rising, the brave soldier of the Lord went his way to the place long chosen for his habitation. The next day he charged the brothers who were with him not to tell anyone where he was going but if they should be closely questioned to say that he had been summoned to Italy by a letter from his master Columbanus. Then taking with him two of his disciples he journeyed through the wastes of Rhaetia Curiensis. Crossing the nearest mountain, they came to the wilderness called Sennia [Sennwald], where they turned aside to the neighboring village of Quaradaves [Grabo]. Here they found one Johannes, a deacon, a righteous and God-fearing man who received them with every office of hospitality and kindness; for they pretended they had just come from a great distance. They stayed with him for a week.

16. When the host of the holy men, the priest Willimar, heard that the man of God had left the cloister, he crossed the lake in a boat to the duke and told him what had happened. The duke bade him return immediately and send messengers after St. Gall to entreat him to come, adding: 'If the Lord in answer to his prayers delivers my daughter from the fiends, I will make him bishop of the church of Constance and will bestow on him abundant rewards as well.' The priest promised to do as he was bid, provided he

could find the saint, and returned home in his boat. Meantime the bishops sent by the king arrived and found the girl in a violent frenzy and her parents and kinsfolk and all her household weeping over her and weighed down with grief; the whole house seemed smitten by a common affliction, the girl being tormented with madness, the rest distracted with sorrow. The bishops on entering presented the gifts sent by the king and then poured out prayers to the Lord in the girl's presence. But she, wrestling herself from the hands of those who held her, snatched a sword from one of them and tried to kill the bishops, but failed; whereupon the unclean spirit [that possessed her] addressed one of them, saying: 'If you would cast me out of this vessel, as you have promised the king, why have you not brought the daughter begotten by you on a nun?' Then turning to the other – 'You too have committed fornication with three women. I will never go forth at your command, seeing you have no holiness to strengthen your words. But there is a man of great virtue in the sight of God, that Gall who by his power drove me from Tucconia, where I had gained the repose I long desired, and was so bold as to destroy my dwelling-places; and who afterwards, finding me settled at Brigantium, dispossessed me of my estate by that same power of his. And because your duke banished him from Brigantium, I, to avenge him, have taken possession of this girl and unless he himself comes, nothing shall induce me to quit.' Thereupon one of the bishops struck the raving girl in the face, saying 'Hold your peace, Satan, you enemy of truth, lover and inventor of falsehood.' For he supposed that the fiend was speaking of a barndoor cock [*gallus* is the Latin for rooster; the bishop assumes the devil is making an indecent pun on St. Gall's name]. As the evil spirit assailed them with continual abuse, the bishops remained for three days only, then returned home and acquainted the king with all that had taken place.

17. Meantime the priest, in obedience to the duke's command, followed in the trace of the man of God and found him at last in a cave, refreshing his soul by reading. Going up to him, he saluted him humbly, saying, 'Fear not, servant of God, to come to the duke; for he has promised on his oath to do you no hurt; nay, if you will lay your hand on his daughter's head and the unclean spirit departs from her through your prayers, he will raise you to the rank of bishop in the See of Constance.' While they were discussing the matter, the deacon Johannes arrived, bringing, as he was wont, loaves of unleavened bread for the saint and a small flask of wine and vessels with oil and butter and milk, together with some boiled fish. The man of God was filled with joy at his coming and gave thanks to God; and the three faithful guests sat down to meat and partook of their Lord's gifts after offering thanks. While they were eating, St. Gall said to the priest: 'Spend this night with me

and tomorrow I will go with you if it be the Lord's will.' The priest consented, and the deacon said to the man of God: 'Tomorrow at early dawn I
will come and bring my mule ready saddled so that you may depart together;
and I will meantime take charge of the cave.' 'You have spoken well, my son,'
answered St. Gall. 'I will return the way I came through the wilderness to my
cloister and visit my brothers, and after that I will hasten to the town
[Arbon] as quickly as I can.' The priest earnestly adjured him not to break his
promise. They set out together and Johannes after receiving their blessing
returned home. The saint went straight to his cloister and rested there that
night with the brothers, and next morning, taking two of them with him, he
went to the town, where he found the priest and also a messenger from the
duke urging him to come with all speed; for the girl (so the messenger told
them) had been now for three days without food. They set out in a small
boat, putting forth their utmost speed, so that their vessel cleft the surface of
the deep, and they arrived that night at the duke's abode.

18. When the darkness of night was vanquished and the sun was restoring
the cheerful light of day to the earth, the duke summoned them to the
chamber where the demoniac girl was lodged. She was lying in her mother's
lap with closed eyes, gaping mouth and limbs dazed, like one already dead;
and so foul a stench issued from her lips that the place seemed to reek with
fumes of sulphur. Her father and the members of his household entered the
room to see what the man of God would do. He, trusting in the Lord's
bounty, fell humbly on his knees and with many tears uttered the following
prayer: 'O Lord Jesus Christ, who for the salvation of mankind did condescend to take on you our flesh and be born of a virgin; who commanded the
wind and sea and bade the devil himself begone when he would have overcome you by his wiles; who pledged by your passion to redeem the world
and set it free: for the glory of your name, bid the unclean spirit depart from
this girl, that she, the work of your hands, may be delivered from the proud
foe who has taken possession of her and your creature may joyfully serve
you, her Creator.' Then arising from prayer, he took her right hand and raised
her, for she was very distraught because of the fiend; and laying his hand on
her head, he said: 'In the name of our Lord Jesus Christ, O unclean spirit, I
bid you come forth and leave this creature of God.' On these words she
opened her eyes and gazed at him, and the fiend addressed him thus: 'Are
you that Gall who before now has driven me from my habitation? It was to
avenge the wrong which that duke did you and your fellows that I took possession of his daughter, and are you now casting me out? If I depart from
here, where shall I go?' 'There,' said Gall, 'where everlasting torment awaits
you, prepared for you by the Lord in the abyss.' Straightway in the sight of all

there issued from the girl's mouth the semblance of a bird, black and hideous. That same hour she arose cured, and was restored rejoicing by the man of God to her rejoicing mother.

19. After this, the duke ordered the gifts sent by the king to his daughter to be presented to St. Gall and besought him moreover to accept the high rank of bishop. But the saint replied: 'As long as my lord and father Columbanus lives, the ministry of the altar is forbidden me, nor will I usurp it without his leave; therefore the authority you wish to bestow is a weight I may not bear. But if it is in very truth your will, wait awhile till I send a letter to my abbot to tell him of your wish, and if I have his permission, then I will undertake the charge offered me.' 'You have spoken well' said the duke; 'be it according to your word,' and he dismissed him in peace. St. Gall took the gifts and rowed back across the lake; and the duke, deeply moved by so manifest a proof of his holiness, sent word to the governor of Arbona to go with his staff of officials to the monastery and construct any buildings needed as the man of God would direct.

After the rowers had plied their oars in line to the rowing chant, the holy father reached the town of Arbona; there he called together all the poor and needy and distributed among them the gifts he had brought. One of his disciples, named Magnoald, on seeing this said to him: 'My father, I have here a costly silver vessel, richly chased, which, if it be your will, I will keep back so that we may make vessels out of it for the divine office.' 'My son,' answered Gall, 'remember the words which the blessed apostle Peter spoke to the palsied man who had looked for money: "Silver and gold have I none"; and lest you be found disobedient to his wholesome example, see that you give the vessel you have to the poor. For my blessed teacher Columbanus is accustomed to offer the sacrifice of the Mass in vessels of iron, because it is said that our Savior was nailed to the cross with iron nails.'

20. After all this had taken place, St. Gall returned to the beloved wilderness which was to him a court, and shortly after sent a letter to the deacon Johannes asking him to come to him. On receiving his beloved master's missive, Johannes came at once, bringing such offerings as he could; and after presenting his gifts, he greeted his father and received a father's welcome. He asked the saint how he had fared on his journey. 'Through the divine mercy which went before and followed us,' replied Gall, 'all has turned out well. The duke received us joyfully and God delivered his daughter from the fiend; and he himself bestowed on us gifts of no small value and moreover offered me the rank of bishop, which however I would not accept till I had learned my abbot's pleasure. Now then, my son, be governed by my counsel; stay with me and study the books of divine lore, and with God's grace helping me, I

will teach you to interpret the Scriptures.' The deacon fell at his feet and thanked him; and sending home the attendants who had come with him, he himself stayed with the saint; and Gall became his guide through the storehouses of Scripture and revealed to him the hidden treasures both of the New Testament and the Old. And being illumined by divine favor, he made such progress under his master's zealous teaching, that before long he showed the results of the pains bestowed on him, being proficient in the whole range of the Scriptures.

21. When king Sigebert heard that the duke's daughter was restored to health, he sent word to her father desiring to see her. The duke, taking with him gifts of great value and a number of youths and maidens, besides a numerous retinue of his own, brought her to the Rhine and thence sent her on with an escort to the king [at Metz]. Sigebert received her with joy and inquired how she had been cured of her malady, since the bishops who were sent to heal her had failed to do so. 'My lord,' she replied, 'in the province I have just quitted there is a man named Gall of Scottish [Irish] race, who dwells in a wilderness and who has such merit in the sight of God that he has power even over demons. When I, your handmaiden, was sore beset by the foe, so that my life hung in the balance and I was near death, this man of God came at my father's request, and making over me the sign of the Cross, with voice of authority he bade my oppressor depart. Then in the sight of all there issued from my mouth as it were a crow, black as pitch and hideous as hell; and after I had been strengthened by receiving the divine Sacrifice, I was restored to my former health.' Then falling at the king's feet, she added: 'I beseech you, my lord, to grant this man your special favor and be not slow to pay him fitting thanks on my behalf.' The king asked in what wilderness this excellent man dwelt. 'In the mountain pass,' she answered, 'which borders on the territory of Arbona; it is common land and lies between the Rhaetian Alps and the shore of the Brigantine lake.' When the king heard that Gall was settled on common land, he ordered a charter to be drawn up by which the saint would hold his dwelling-place by virtue of royal authority. Together with this charter he sent two pounds of gold and the same weight of silver by his messengers to the man of God, commending himself to the saint's prayers; and he commanded Duke Gunzo to supply him with all that was needful for building a cloister in the wilderness if he so desired.

22. After the lapse of a few days, the king, wishing to wed the girl, issued an order that the assembly of priests and nobles should be present at the marriage ceremony; and entering the place where she was lodged, with a throne of high dignitaries, he said to her: 'Let us go up to the palace, for everything is ready for the wedding, and the priests and heads of the people have arrived

with fitting gifts.' On hearing these words, she fell at his feet, saying: 'My lord, I am weak after all I have suffered, my strength is exhausted and my limbs refuse their office; grant me at least a week's respite that I may somewhat recover my strength before I present myself to your sight.' The king yielded to this request and returned to the palace, while she remained in her own apartment; and in both places great preparations were made for the festivity. Many indeed were surprised that these two, after being kept so long apart, should have deferred their union. When the week had passed, about the time of morning service, the maiden, accompanied by two men and two female attendants, entered the church of St. Stephen Protomartyr [the first martyr: see *Acts* 6, 8-60]. There she withdrew behind the door, and unknown to her companions, took off her regal attire and donned the habit of a holier calling. Having thus laid aside the garb of earthly grandeur and sought the splendor of holiness by her self-abasement, she approached the altar and falling on her face, prayed earnestly to the Lord; then rising to her feet she laid hold of the horn of the altar and uttered these words: 'Blessed Stephen, you who witnessed for Christ with your blood, let my prayer find favor with the Lord through your merits; that through your intercession he may this day turn the heart of my lord the king to my will and that the veil which I have put on for love of God may not be taken from my head.' On seeing this, the men who were with her went to the king and told him what had occurred. He summoned the priests and some of his nobles and asked them what they thought should be done. Then Cyprian bishop of Arles answered the king: 'It is plain that the girl bound herself with the vow she has carried out, at the time when she was freed from the evil spirit; beware therefore lest, if you render her vow of no effect, she be assailed anew by the demon and her last state be worse than the first; so you would incur great guilt.' The king, being a man of steadfast justice and full of the fear of God, gave devout assent to this counsel, and entering the church, sent for the robe which had been prepared for the bride and the diadem which was to crown her splendor; and when they were fetched, he bade the girl come to him. But she, already the bride of God and enrolled among the followers of the Lamb, clung yet faster to the horn of the altar and would not let herself be torn from it, for she was afraid of being removed from the church. Then the king told her not to fear, saying: 'To-day you shall see your wish fulfilled in all things.' She, wavering between hope and fear, laid her head on the altar and said: 'Behold the handmaid of the Lord; be it unto me according to his will.' The king told the priests to raise her and bring her to him and at his command she was clad with the royal robe and crowned with the sacred veil. And looking on her, the pious monarch said: 'Behold! you are arrayed to be my bride, but I yield you to the embraces of a heavenly bridegroom, our Lord Jesus Christ,' and taking her right hand he laid it on the altar. Then going outside the church, he gave vent to his hidden love in tears. Afterwards he sent for the maiden and made her remain in the palace; and after bestowing costly gifts on her, he placed her over the convent of nuns built in honor of St. Peter, chief of apostles, in the city of Metz, where all the events related above took place. In all that she did on this occasion, the girl followed the counsel of St. Gall who with the Lord's aid had delivered her from the evil spirit.

23. In the meantime the deacon Johannes remained with the holy father, eagerly drinking in the heaven-bestowed wisdom which St. Gall so richly possessed in solving the problems of holy Scripture and laying the foundations of sound belief. He also learned to master and to find pleasure in the daily labors which St. Gall, following the austere discipline of the apostles, used to perform with unflagging zeal and promptness. Illumined by divine grace, whatever he did but see or hear he committed to the depths of his memory or, if I may use the phrase, stored up in the coffer of his heart. Thus he passed three years under St. Gall's tutelage in the constant exercise of meekness and humility.

24. At the end of this time, the duke sent a letter to the man of God, asking him to come to Constance to choose a bishop for the See. He likewise summoned the bishops of Autun and Verdun with a large number of their clergy and the bishop of Nemidona (now called Speier), and sent moreover messengers and letters throughout Alemannia bidding the priests, deacons and clergy in general assemble at Constance on the day appointed, that is, the Sunday next after Easter. He himself with his leading nobles and counts was present at the gathering. Attended by this vast concourse the Synod was opened and it was announced that it would last for three days. St. Gall, guided by divine counsel, took with him Johannes and Magnoald, both of whom had been raised to the office of deacon, and arrived at the town; and on his entering the place of assembly, the duke pronounced the following words: 'May God Almighty, by whose providence the whole body of the Church is governed and increased, through the merits and intercession of blessed Mary ever Virgin, to whom this place is dedicated, pour out his spirit upon us this day that we may choose a bishop fit to rule the flock of the faithful and to guide the Church of God with a shepherd's care.' Then he called upon the bishops and clergy to elect a ruler for the church in accordance with the canon law. Whereupon all the clergy began with one voice to say: 'That Gall is well spoken of by all who know his life. He has attained the highest degree of proficiency in holy Scripture; he shines in beauty of life and in the light of wisdom; in him are joined uprightness and chastity, gen-

tleness and humility, self-restraint and long-suffering. He is a generous alms-giver, a father to the orphan and prompt to succor the widow in her distress. It is fitting that one who practises every virtue should be the pastor of the people.' On hearing this, the duke said to Gall: 'Do you hear what they say of you?' 'They say well indeed,' answered the holy father; 'would that their words were true. But in treating of this matter, they forget that it is forbidden in the canons that anyone who has left his own country should without more ado be ordained bishop in another. There is, however, here with me a deacon named Johannes on whom the praises they have given me may deservedly be bestowed. Believing him to be chosen by the divine judgment I now commend him to you for election to the bishopric.'

25. The saint's testimony won for Johannes the favor of all, for they could not but believe what one so beloved of God asserted concerning him; and the duke called Johannes into the midst, saying: 'Are you the deacon Johannes?' 'I am,' replied he. 'Of what race are you?' inquired the duke. 'I was born in Rhaetia Curiensis of a family of humble rank,' said Johannes. 'Can you bear the weight,' asked the duke, 'of a bishop's miter [liturgical head-dress]?' Here St. Gall interposed, saying that he would answer for Johannes as for a son. While they were discussing the matter, the deacon slipped away and went and hid himself in the church of St. Stephen Martyr outside the town. But priests and people followed him there and laid hold of him, and he was brought back to the presence of the bishops and the duke, protesting indeed, but shedding tears of joy at the same time; and all lifted up their voice with one accord, saying: 'The Lord has chosen Johannes to be his bishop this day.' And all the people answered 'Amen!' Then the bishops led him to the altar and consecrated him with solemn benediction; and when the ceremony was ended, they asked him to celebrate Mass. When the divine sacrifice had been offered in due form and the Gospel lesson read, they begged St. Gall to minister to the assembled crowd the food of sacred doctrine. He mounted on a step, taking with him the bishop Johannes, in order that the latter might interpret for the benefit of those who understood no Latin the matters which he himself expounded for their edification. He began his discourse with the Creation and the sin for which Adam was driven from Paradise; then passing on to the Deluge [Noah's Flood], he dealt in order with the times of the patriarchs and their doings. He told how the children of Israel left Egypt and passed through the Red Sea, how they received the Law from Moses and were miraculously fed from heaven. Then after touching briefly on the kings in their order and the times of the prophets, he told of the coming of the Savior, of his baptism and his glorious miracles, of the wicked persecutions he endured and his shameful death on the Cross. As the pastors

of the church and the assembled throng listened, they were moved to tears and said one to another, 'Truly the Holy Spirit has spoken today by the mouth of this man.' Then St. Gall continued his discourse to the resurrection of Christ and finished by telling of the Last Judgment. All his hearers were lifted up in spirit and returned to their homes full of joy and blessing the Lord.

The venerable teacher remained with the bishop Johannes for the space of a week, during which he gave him much salutary advice and encouragement, constantly repeating these words: 'Whom God has chosen, man shall not despise; whom the divine judgment commends, he shall be exalted in the esteem of all.' Then he returned to his cloister after receiving Johannes's benediction; and the bishop ordered the stewards of the See to go to the man of God and obey all his commands. Thereafter so strong a mutual affection was maintained between these two that they seemed to cleave together in spirit and be divided in body only. The master with a father's tenderness continually supported the disciple by his prayers and wholesome counsel; the disciple paid his teacher the honor due to a father and provided for all his needs; and their holy fellowship grew ever stronger through their increasing respect and love for one another.

26. In course of time this eminent cultivator of virtues built a small church and round it cells for the accommodation of his brothers; for he had now twelve followers, in whom his teaching and example had kindled the desire to seek those things which are eternal, fortified by the monastic life. One day, when the monks had returned to their beds after matins [the service held in the middle of the night], as dawn was breaking the man of God called his deacon Magnoald and said to him, 'Make all ready for the service of Mass, that I may celebrate the divine mysteries without delay.' 'Will you then yourself celebrate Mass?' inquired Magnoald. 'After vigils this night past,' answered Gall, 'I learnt in a vision that my lord and father Columbanus had passed from the miseries of this life to the joys of Paradise today [23 November, 615]; therefore it behoves me to offer Mass for his repose.' The bell was accordingly sounded, the monks entered the oratory and prostrated themselves in prayer, Mass was said and earnest petitions were offered on behalf of St. Columbanus. After the service, St. Gall said to the deacon Magnoald: 'My son, think it not too much if I make a request of you. Set out straightway for Italy and journey till you come to the monastery of Bobbio; there make diligent inquiry concerning all that happened to my abbot, and if you find he is dead, note well the day and hour, that you may know whether my vision is true; and when you have ascertained all, come back and tell me.' The deacon threw himself at his master's feet, pleading that he did not know the way; but

the saint in reassuring tones told him not to be afraid, saying, 'Go and the Lord will direct your steps.' Strengthened by these words of comfort, the disciple obeyed his holy teacher's command and after receiving a blessing to sustain him on the road set out with speed. When he reached the monastery of Bobbio, he found that all had happened just as had been revealed to his father Gall in the vision. He stayed there for a night and the monks gave him a letter for St. Gall recounting the final passing of St. Columbanus, and also sent by him the staff of Columbanus (which is commonly called the *cambota*), saying that the holy abbot before his decease had given orders that Gall should receive his absolution by means of this familiar token. Taking his leave of them, the deacon sped on his way and faring well on his journey reached his lord and father on the eighth day, bringing the letter and the token of absolution. St. Gall, who still cherished a warm affection for his father Columbanus, shed copious tears on reading the letter and told the assembled brothers the reason of his grief; and thereafter they offered up continual prayers and Masses in memory of that sainted father.

27. One day while Gall and his brothers were engaged in building the Church, a plank which was destined for one of the walls was found to be shorter than its fellows by the length of four palms. The workmen would have thrown it away, but St. Gall, conscious of the power he possessed in the Lord, bade them stop work and enter the house with him, to partake of the meal which the Lord had provided. They obeyed and he blessed the bread and distributed it with his own hands. On returning to their unfinished work after the meal, they found the plank which they were about to throw away because of its shortness, now longer than all the rest by half a foot, and marveling at its miraculous growth, they fixed it in its proper place in the wall. This same plank used long after to be much resorted to by the faithful and through the Lord's doing proved an effective cure for toothache, thus enhancing the glory of the original miracle by a succession of new ones. From this incident we may estimate the greatness of St. Gall's merits and the power of his intercession; for, in the first place, contrary to nature a piece of dry wood grew longer; and lest this miracle should fall into oblivion, it was continually recalled to memory by fresh portents.

28. After a time Eustasius, abbot of the monastery of Luxeuil, who had been appointed by Columbanus of blessed memory, passed from the exile of this life to the fatherland on high. The monks held counsel and decided to recall St. Gall and commit themselves to his rule; and they sent six of their number who had originally come from Ireland to bear him a letter setting forth their wishes. The messengers traveled by direct route to the cloister of the man of God; as soon as their arrival was announced, they were con-

ducted to prayers, after which they entered the house and presented the letter. When the saint had read it, he said to them: 'My brothers, being earnestly
desirous to imitate that prophet who said: I am become a stranger unto my
brothers and an alien unto my mother's children, I left my kinsfolk and
acquaintance and even sought the recesses of the wilderness that I might
have more leisure and freedom to serve the Lord; yes, and besides renouncing
my family and patrimony, I refused the rank of bishop and the riches of this
world; and how, after giving up so much and embracing poverty, shall I again
be entangled in the affairs of this life, uplifted by its honors and weighed
down by its burdens? Far be it from me that having put my hand to the
plough I should now look back on what I have left, like a dog which returns
to its vomit. You yourselves know that when I was among you I always took
special care to be humble and obedient; and do you think now to urge me to
a position so exalted? Make your plans anew and turn elsewhere, for the
Lord will not suffer me to change the purpose I have formed.' With these
and like words he dispelled from their minds all hope of obtaining their
request. Then he called one of his monks and asked what they were to have
for their next meal. On hearing that there was only a small measure of flour
for them all, he bade them make it into loaves and gather some vegetables,
saying: 'The Lord is able to prepare a table in the wilderness.' Then he himself took his net and accompanied by one of his disciples and the brothers
who had just arrived, he went to the pool in the stream, saying, 'Let us see
whether the Lord of his mercy will grant us some little fishes for our needs.'

On reaching the pool in which the waters of the stream were collected,
they saw a big fish swimming in it, chased by two otters. They threw in their
net, caught the fish and brought it to land; they found it measured twelve
palms in length and four in breadth. The otters meantime plunged into the
depths; but when the holy fishermen had thrown their net a second time and
were driving the fishes from their hiding places by beating the water, they
came again to the surface and drove such a multitude of fishes into the net
that it burst in several places. As soon as they had landed their booty, the saint
(who had plenty of practical wisdom) with the help of his companions threw
back some of the fish into the water, and said to the brothers: 'It is because of
your coming today that the Lord has vouchsafed us this wondrous sign of his
bounty.' They, on the other hand, declared it was due to his own merits; and
thus conversing they returned home, he leading the way at a brisk pace. And
behold! as they neared the entrance to the cloister, there appeared a man
who brought with him as a proof of his devotion two skins full of wine and
three pecks of flour. The gifts were thankfully received and they all ate the
food; and when their bodies were refreshed, they were eager to feast their

souls also with converse on spiritual themes. St. Gall kept them for some days and because of his regard for them bestowed on them every attention. He also told them much which he had learnt on sure authority concerning their common father Columbanus. Then he dismissed them with the kiss of peace and armed with his blessing they returned home.

29. The time was now at hand when the Author and Increaser of all good things meant to take his champion from the wrestling-ground of this world and crown him with lasting laurels. Not long after the events related, the priest Willimar came to the saint and asked him to return with him to the town of Arbon, saying in tone of humble and piteous entreaty: 'My father, why have you forsaken me and deprived me of your wholesome instructions, seeing I depend on your words and hearken to you willingly? I know of no reason save the foulness of my sins; for surely you would not deprive me of the comfort of your teaching, if my life did not displease you. Now then, do not cast us off because of our sins, but come at the Lord's bidding and bestow on us your usual kindness, opening the way of truth to those who seek it.' Touched by his supplication, the saint went down to the town with him; and on a festival day, when a large audience had gathered, he refreshed their hungry hearts with his eloquence, and the wisdom which shone in his discourse filled them all with joy and veneration. After he had stayed two days in Arbon, on the third he was attacked by a fever which rapidly increased to such a pitch that he could neither return to his cloister nor take any nourishment. He lay ill for a fortnight; and on the sixteenth day of October (that is, the seventeenth Calends of November), having completed the ninety-fifth year of his age, he was delivered from this house of bondage and yielded up his soul full of merits to cleave henceforth to abiding joys.

30. When Johannes, the head of the church of Constance, heard that St. Gall was ill at Arbon, he set out in a boat to cheer his faithful friend with a visit, taking with him such kinds of food and drink as he judged suited for the invalid. As he drew near the landing-place, he heard the sound of wailing proceeding from the priest's house and inquired the cause; and on being told that St. Gall, the truest and most intimate friend he possessed, had departed from the perils of this life, he plunged into the water – for his grief was so great that he could not wait till the boat touched the shore – and landing with his attendants entered the priest's house, giving vent to his sorrow in word and gesture. He found the saint's body already wrapped in a shroud and placed in a coffin; and opening the coffin and gazing on his friend's corpse, he shed bitter tears and said: 'Alas, beloved father! best of teachers! Why did you bring me from my father's house to leave me an orphan in the midst of dangers? Why have you by your untimely death shattered the hope with

which I looked forward to your counsels? To you indeed death is a gain, for it has brought you the reward you so earnestly desired; but to us, still beset by the storms of this world, it is a source of great woe. But though we grieve that your life in the body is cut short, we ought rather to rejoice that your immortal soul is set free, being assured that you will not cease to aid with your prayers those whom you were accustomed to strengthen with your advice and example.' While he was speaking, the priest urged him to rise and make supplication in more formal manner to the Lord for the repose of the departed. So they entered the church and the bishop offered up Mass for his beloved friend. After this tribute of brotherly affection, looking round, he saw the grave in which the saint was to be buried; and taking a cross and all things customary in a funeral service, they returned to the house to bear the treasured remains to the burial-place. But when they had placed the coffin on the bier and were going to carry it to the grave, they could not move it with all their efforts. They were amazed at a portent so unusual, and while they were debating the matter, the bishop said, 'In truth I perceive that my father Gall is not satisfied with this spot for his burial.' Then he bade the priest find two horses yet unbroken and have them brought. This was done; with much difficulty the horses were saddled and led to the place where the body was lying; and the bishop along with the clergy offered the following prayer: 'O God, who, by the power of your majesty are present in all places at the one time; it was for love of you that this man left his country, that he might obey your commands; grant that his body may be born by these untamed horses to the spot assigned by your will to his merits.' To this prayer all present responded 'Amen.'

31. This seems the proper place to tell of a miracle which the Lord vouchsafed to work during the funeral of his confessor, in order to show plainly to all that his servant, freed from the prison of the flesh, was now at last enjoying true life with him. Among those present was a certain beggar who among other painful effects of disease was so crippled in all his joints that he was wholly unable to walk. When the priest was distributing the saint's clothes among the poor, he gave this man his shoes and leggings. Delighted with the gift, the cripple lost no time in fitting the sacred spoils to his own legs and feet; no sooner had he done so than his joints were loosened, and leaping up, he cried out with a loud voice, giving thanks unto the Lord and to St. Gall, to whose merits he perceived his cure to be due. On beholding this miracle, the bishop and all present glorified God with one voice, saying, 'The Lord has this day vouchsafed to declare the glory of his servant present by a manifest token of his power.' They gave a wax taper to the man who was healed and he followed the funeral procession with the rest. This was the

first miracle which the Lord wrought in memory of the saint after his decease.

32. During the funeral of the blessed pastor, another proof, and that no small one, of his holiness came to light. He had a case made of leather which he always kept carefully locked, never allowing the key to pass out of his own possession, so that none of his disciples as long as he lived could ever find out what was in it; and wherever he went, he used to carry this case slung over his shoulder. Now that he had passed away, they took the key and opened the case and found in it a small hair shirt and an iron chain stained with blood. Upon this they examined their master's body and found the marks made by the chain where it used to gird him, the flesh being deeply furrowed in four places, so that the hair shirt was here and there stained through by the blood which oozed from the wounds. They placed the case with its contents at the head of the bier and carried it with the body to the burial-place, where they hung the three tokens of his self-mortification at the head of his tomb. There, in after days, the Lord, working many miracles through them, revealed the saint's merits to those who came with devout intent. From this we may gather that though St. Gall did not shed his blood as a victim of persecution, yet as a confessor, by offering himself a living sacrifice in the odor of sanctity to the Lord and daily taking up his cross to follow the Savior, he endured the sufferings of martyrdom and earned its reward.

33. After the sanctity of their revered father had been thus openly revealed to all present at the funeral both by miracle and by these other proofs, the bishop approached the bier and raising one end, while the priest lifted the other, placed it across the horses' backs, saying to the bystanders: 'Take the bridles from the horses' heads and leave them free to go wherever the Lord wills.' Then they took cross and candles and set out, chanting Psalms and hymns. The horses, swerving neither to right nor left, made in a straight line for the saint's cloister. There the bier was taken down and placed in front of the oratory, and his disciples, lifting the remains of their holy teacher, carried them in and laid them before the altar. There they joined the bishop in prayer on his behalf and after offering petitions suitable to the occasion, dug a grave between the wall and the altar and buried him; and when all had been done in due order, the crowd which had gathered for the funeral received the bishop's benediction and returned to their homes.

34. When the precious remains had thus been consigned in peace to that favored spot, the Lord, wishing to comfort the grief of the mourners, wrought a miracle of very unusual nature to show that the spirit of their friend was with him in glory. When taking up the body before leaving the town, they lit two wax tapers which were carried burning to the burial place

and set one at the head and the other at the foot of the grave. Wondrous to relate, for thirty days following the tapers continued to burn without being one bit diminished. And in proof that the melting wax was endued with this power of lasting from heaven, many prodigies were wrought by it in after days. For any one suffering from toothache or inflammation of the eyes or stoppage of the ears had only to take a piece of wax from the tapers and apply it to the part affected, and he instantly received the coveted gift of health. Later such effective power in the healing of different disorders was manifested at the saint's tomb to all who came and implored his intercession in faith, so that the report went out to all the neighboring regions, and their inhabitants resorted there in numbers.

And now, holy fathers, seeing that if the life and miracles of St. Gall were compressed into a single book, they might cause the reader some weariness by their length, I have decided to divide this work into two books, the first giving a truthful account of his life and deeds up to his burial, the second dealing with the miracles which the Lord afterwards wrought on account of his merits: that is, in the first place, those which have been handed down to us by previous writers, and secondly, those which in our own time were taken down from the lips of unimpeachable witnesses by our beloved brother Gozbert [monk of St. Gall, nephew of Abbot Gozbert]. This I have done in order that the events may not be scattered and disconnected through their having been written down at various times, but those which are related by their nature may also be joined in the order of the narrative. And now let me bring my first book to an end, leaving for the following one all that yet remains to be told.

19. A MIRROR FOR MONKS:
THE LIFE OF ST. MAIOL, ABBOT OF CLUNY,
BY ODILO, FIFTH ABBOT OF CLUNY.

In the early eleventh century Gaul was undergoing religious reform, and the monastery of Cluny was the driving force behind it. Cluny's former abbot, Maiol (c.910-994), received much of the credit for its success, and a cult emerged. Not only did the great and powerful abbot Odilo — mocked as King Odilo by his adversaries — compose the 'Life of St. Maiol,' translated below, but the monk Syrus composed another account of the saint's life, a colorful hagiography that was much excerpted and soon turned into verse. Odilo's hagiographic account of Maiol does not follow the normal chronological biography and gives relatively little factual information, because Syrus's 'life' was already available and because its aims were different. Odilo's composition is important for what it tells us about Cluny around 1032-33, for the career of Odilo himself, and especially for its reflection of contemporary Cluniac ideology and attitudes towards holiness. It is an example of a house hagiography, a monastic mirror, as it were, to be gazed into by the monks of Cluny and their powerful supporters.

Source: trans. P.E. Dutton from *Sancti Odilonis abbatis Cluniacensis V De vita beati Maioli abbatis libellus,* ed. M. Marrier and A. Duchêne in *Bibliotheca Cluniacensis* (Brussels and Paris, 1614), cols. 279-290 and repr. in J.P. Migne, *Patrologia Latina,* vol. 142, cols. 943-962; repr. with permission. BHL 5182.

Preface

1. Odilo, the priest, sends his greetings to Hugh [who succeeded him as sixth abbot of Cluny, 1049-1109] and to his dearest brother Alaman.

When I was staying last Easter in the cloister of the Romainmôtier [over which Odilo was abbot], on the day before the Mass of our father Maiol [10 May 1033], one of the brothers by the name of John, who, in keeping with the appropriate meaning of his name, is endowed with the gift of the Lord's grace, began to inquire in what book he ought that night to find [suitable] readings. I said to him that it was proper for the words of that most blessed father Gregory [the Great] to be recited in memory of this father, because that same father [Maiol] while he lived [had] listened to and read those very words often and with the greatest attention, and, when he could, had spoken of them at great length. After the evening service finished a short time later and the time had been set for the day service, both normal custom and necessity led me to go to bed. I was then worried by the times and fretting greatly not only about the loss of property, but also about the immense danger of unexpected calamity and unheard of suffering [he refers here to the dire famine that struck Gaul in 1033]. What troubled [me] more were the great and lamentable losses suffered by the entire land and all the poor. [My] anxious thoughts about this great crisis and my great distress had already stolen sleep from me for many nights. But finally, on that very night, when as usual disturbing thoughts were aggressively trying to force themselves upon me, I began to ask the blessed Maiol to seek the remedy of consolation from the Lord for me. After a little while, the dear memory of that great father came to me and spoke in the following way, assuring me that if I took the trouble to fill my soul with his praises, I would soon surely gain the help of divine consolation. For that reason, dearest elders and brothers, I labored – not as the greatness of [Maiol] himself [deserved], but as the smallness of my ability [allowed] – to write the book you will find below. Indeed, whatever kind of work it might [prove to] be, my fraternal hope and prayer is that the flame of your spiritual sense might examine, discern, and correct it.

Here Begins the Little Book

2. After the holy, divine, and health-giving teachings of the apostles and evangelists, and the most victorious, unconquered, and glorious struggles of the blessed martyrs, in the third place, as I might put it, the divine honor of [Christ's] own church provided a new solace, namely lights burning with love [and] shining in speech. [For] I say that apostolic priests and outstanding men were endowed, not in a vain, but in a healthy way, with human knowledge and were filled with divine wisdom. Through their spiritual understanding and far-sighted research into divine writings the shadow of the law was transformed into light; the prophetic speech [of the Bible], in profundity the highest [sign] of him and in height the profoundest, spiritually came to the light of understanding; and the glory, power, and majesty of the evangelical light also drove off the darkness of the whole world.

3. For through the forthright labors of those men the acts of the apostles are revealed and recommended to the faithful. Through the careful studies of those men, the victories and merits of the blessed martyrs are recommended to the holy church. For with the faith, wisdom, and presence of the preaching of those men, the murmur of those whispering and barking against the catholic faith is checked and overcome; the noise of the schismatics is quieted and the empty talk of those speaking [in this way] is shut up; the power of idols is smashed; the cruelty of the gentiles is surpassed; the folly of the philosophers is condemned, is spat upon, and negated; the untruthfulness, faithlessness, infidelity, wrongness, and madness of all the heretics is blown away like [some] smoky stench and stinking smoke so that it might never more appear, and is released and exhaled into nothing.

4. Afterwards the joyful heavenly court took up these great men and men of this sort as though they were its own citizens, the servants of the King himself. In keeping with that highest and heavenly republic, divine judgment wished to look after the interests of the meek of the church in a suitable gathering in a fourth place, so that he might now bestow that grace, which is normally bestowed by means of the high and mighty, by means of the humble, innocent and simple [of the Church]. It was then that the monastic movement began to sprout and, to put it more accurately, to come back to life. We know that the order proceeded from blessed Elias and John the Baptist. Hence we rejoice that through their apostolic teaching and lives the increase of virtues and the labors of the holy spiritual fathers have come down to us. Indeed, the perfection of that one and clear evangelical [way], indeed the very precept of the Lord [himself], was fulfilled perfectly through them and by them. That [way] was unknown to one young man who asked the Savior about how to possess the eternal life. The Lord Christ himself responded and said to him: "If you would be perfect, go and sell all that you have, and give it to the poor, and you shall have treasure in heaven, and come and follow me."

5. Among the most avid listeners and most devout followers of this salvific command that most blessed father, who was worthily called Benedict [of Nursia], shone as if he were some brilliant heavenly star. He was so great in his life, habits, and miracles, that the most holy pope Gregory – in all things an apostolic man and the bishop of the apostolic see – described his birth, life, and death and bore testimony to him [see 15 above]. Among the chief primates of the church he is distinguished, both by his life and teachings, to hold an honorable place and privileged position. With the passage of time, namely after the death of that most devoted father [Benedict], almost all of Gaul took up the beginnings of his institution [monasticism] and religion through blessed Maurus, his disciple. Then through him and the men whom he himself lifted up to truth, and after much time, the same [species of] religion grew to its height of perfection. [But] when they died, the truth grew rarer, wickedness flourished, and monastic discipline, the source of all good virtue, waned. The study of the devout fathers [of the Church] began to fail, and just as by means of religious men full of the fervor of the Holy Spirit the rule of holy monasticism [had] gradually received a measure of perfection, so by means of negligent and lazy men it little by little declined. Therefore this sickly failure of the formerly healthy [state of monasticism] crept in stealthily until Berno, an abbot of blessed memory [from 909 to 926], with the help of the most Christian duke William of Aquitaine, began to construct a monastery in Burgundy, in the land of Mâcon, in a village called Cluny [in

909]. As much as [Berno] could, he strove to work on that very construction and with immense effort he brought the goal of his pious devotion to a laudable end. By the merit and example of that one, many who came to the tranquil gates of the monastery turned away from the world. For their sake we cherish by specifically mentioning [him] and we specifically mention in cherishing that one [Berno] who we know came forth for the salvation of many.

6. There was a man, Odo by name, a man praiseworthy in all things, a very devout and faithful follower of blessed St. Martin, the bishop of Tours, and a cleric and canon of his church. In fact, this noble and [yet] humble man, [was] thoroughly learned in strict devotional practices, [and] after the father [Berno] died, succeeded to the rule of the abbey [between 926 and 944] by the election of the many faithful. Afterwards the Roman world learned through his writings how he came to the height of virtue.

7. Aymard, a son of blessed simplicity and innocence, succeeded this man of happy memory [in 944]. He was very attentive to increasing the estates and temporal resources [of Cluny] and was careful to oversee [them]. He bore the loss of his sight and whatever adversity came his way very patiently without any grumbling or complaining. Indeed, because of the merit of his simple patience and the innocence of his life, this man was rewarded with a very great gift by Christ for it was during his time [as abbot, 944-964] that he was deemed worthy to summon the source of our well-being, blessed Maiol, to the love of the monastic order.

8. In the work of converting this one, the kind advice and spiritual ideas of that venerable man Hildebrand were very helpful. This man, since he was one of the chief monks of Cluny and the provost of that monastery, was twice invited to take up the office of abbot, but declined, because he always wanted more to obey than to command, more to follow than to lead. Some may, perhaps, think that I am foolish because, though I set out to write about the blessed Maiol, as it turns out I have [instead] set down all of the above. [But] no one should believe that this was an accident, because it was done on purpose. For whatever I said above about just and holy people, I [also] knew was entirely, completely, or for the most part present in that man about whom I wish to speak.

9. That man, our blessed father Maiol, descended from illustrious stock [c.910-994] and was nobly reared from infancy under the watchful eyes of his noble parents. In his youth, he devoted himself to ecclesiastical studies in order to become steeped in spiritual learning. Therefore, by a higher will and divine providence it happened that this boy, who had such outstanding promise, was then [so] firmly committed to holy living that he passed the

whole of his adolescence without jeopardizing his chastity; and so it happened that he maintained the virginal dignity of his body throughout the entire course of his life. As he became a young adult, he did not put off learning higher and better things in divine letters [or] more turbulent and earthly things in human literature, and thus, having been trained in both [kinds of learning], he was not afraid to approach the altar of Lyons [an altar to Augustus, but here, perhaps, a reference to Lyons' pagan past and educational expertise]. Then, in that city, which was the nurse and mother of philosophy, and not unworthily held by ancient custom and ecclesiastical law to be the chief place in all Gaul, he wished to obtain [the services of] Antony, a learned and wise man, as his teacher in the liberal arts. Later on he was to follow the examples of that great Antony [the desert father; see 8 above], the disciple of Christ alone, even more than the teachings of that Antony [of Lyons, who was] a philosopher by secular training. Next, from that city [of Lyons] he came to the city of [the region of] Mâcon. He had been invited there, since he was a religious man, by the leaders of that land and by its citizens, namely by his relatives and friends. He remained religiously among them for a little while, [but] his praiseworthy life and admirable devotion could not remain hidden to the bishop of that city [of Besançon]. With the advice of its clerics and citizens, [the bishop] humbly asked him not to say no to taking up the office of archdeacon in that church. As he was endowed with the gift of humility, that man did not, of course, hesitate to obey one who was a bishop and by whom he knew himself to be divinely ruled. And, as things later clearly showed, that whole business was directed towards the accumulation of further training.

10. At last, after taking up this great and dignified office, he showed himself that he might please [both] God and the world, not a world fixed in malignancy, but a world reconciled to God the Father through the blood of Christ. For that city [of Besançon] has a monastery nearby that was appropriately and richly committed, it seems to many, to spiritual work, to which the said seignior [Maiol] was now frequently summoned by the abbot and monks of the monastery for frequent meetings and [for the purpose of] spiritual retreat. Finally, after those pleasant meetings and shared work of pure charity, the brothers of that monastery saw in the reflection of his mind his angelic appearance and heard the sweet eloquence in the instructions of his heart. They wanted to obtain him as one of their brothers, that afterwards they might deserve to have him as their father. The entire flock of the Lord was determined on this point, but that senior [monk] Hildebrand, about whom I spoke above, worked hardest toward bringing it about. For now according to the prayers of the brothers of that monastery the grace of the Lord engen-

dered in him [Maiol] a contempt of the world. What more can I say? He resigned his high ecclesiastical office, spurned the arrogance of worldly nobility, and rejected the worldly company of friends and family, so that he might freely serve the true King, Christ. He subdued himself entirely to the rule of heaven. Before long, on a certain day he came to the monastery and was officially received, regularly led in, and, as is customary, was honorably and charitably treated. My account cannot fully relate how great was the joy of the brothers over his arrival, how surpassing their happiness, how constant their rejoicing. In him there was an immediate desire to reject the world, a very firm commitment to the love of God, a dear fraternity toward the love of his fellows, no resistance toward learning by heart the rule of regular observance, and a swiftness to exhibit the virtue of obedience not only toward the abbot, but also toward his brothers. Pure simplicity led him to supply an example to all. How great was his conduct among the brothers from the very start of his entry into the community was apparent from the affection of those brothers at the time of his much celebrated election [as abbot]. For then it was not necessary for anyone to instruct him in the rules of observance. Of him, as the holy evangelist says, "the anointing of the heavenly grace teaches of all things." Meanwhile the life and teaching [of Maiol] began to shine so perfectly, that he deserved, with the praise of all the faithful, to gain the first and most distinguished place in the house of God. For he so pleased God that he rose through the various steps of humility to the pinnacle of monastic perfection and he seemed now not one among many, but outstanding among all and above all [in holiness].

11. It is reported that in the sixth year of his conversion from the world that abbot of happy memory, the lord and devout father, Aymard, whose blessed monk Maiol was and whose advice and commands [Maiol] obeyed and always determined to obey with the full attention of his mind and with his body permitting, began to be completely forsaken by the strength of his worldly body and became blind. This was very hard on him, although he bore it patiently. Since he had already foreseen his death and knew that he could not long assume the care of so great a monastery and of such a large spiritual flock, he began to consider with his spiritual and religious brothers in a spiritual way the governance of the monastery and the election of his successor, and he began patiently and calmly in his mind to make arrangements. A search was made by all and it led to that one among the monks, namely the lord Maiol, who was chosen. Indeed, I am not able, because of the greatness of him, to speak of the matter of his election, but let me briefly try. Not there or any place else could or will [anyone] more outstanding be found [for election] than blessed Maiol. What more can I say? The elected

one was summoned, the summoned one resisted, the implored one refused, the sworn one trembled, the one so ordered submitted. For this reason I should praise God, since the praiseworthy proof of obedience overcame his protestation of refusal. Finally he was elected by the monks, acclaimed by the people, blessed by the bishops, placed with greatest celebration by the said father of the monastery in the highest place, greeted respectfully by the monks, and was honored and cherished by all as lord and abbot. And he was held, not only by those, but even by all who were able to see and know him, in higher honor and veneration than all the men of his age.

12. Concerning his birth, life, habits, miracles, and death, let the reports of our predecessors, which were put forth in a clear way, suffice. Those who were able to say the greatest things about great things have magnificently described his distinguished deeds and the merits granted to him by God. But I, the least little servant of [all] the servants of that one, have dared to record in [my] poor way and summarily with the briefest points not other things, but those that they themselves said before. I have imitated Alcuin, the master of the emperor Charlemagne, [but I am] as unequal to that one as a sinner is to a just man, as an ignorant fellow is to a learned one, and as one not knowing how to speak to one who is very eloquent. That man brought to my attention and to the attention of our [monks] the life of the highest and incomparable man, the holiest priest Martin, which was described in the purest style by Severus Sulpicius and illustrated with many stories [see 14 above]. For just as no one after the apostles equals blessed Martin, so I profess that I am not nearly the equal of Alcuin. That one said, inasmuch as he was great, great things about the great; I, being little, shall say little things about the great. That one spoke of St. Martin as the greatest priest and an incomparable man; I shall speak of Maiol as the most pious father and holiest abbot, a most distinguished and catholic man.

13. Thus that man descended from the most distinguished background and he shone with the double nobility of both his parents. This man, as if he were a brilliant star, was destined by the very eternal light of lights to be born for the enlightenment of many. For he himself, as he was noble, was nobly reared and wisely trained. Let us rise from lower to higher things, [for] that man was even said [to be] and was often to be spoken of and described [as] serious in gait, refined in voice, eloquent in speech, joyful in appearance, angelic in countenance, serene in demeanor, showing himself to be virtuous in every act, gesture, and movement of his body. He seemed to me in the fine arrangement of his limbs to be appropriately elegant, the handsomest of all mortals. He was steady in his faith, sure in his hope, full of its twin charity, pure in his wisdom, remarkable in his intelligence, prudent in his advice,

robust in strength, a constant cultivator of spiritual knowledge, and a true lover of charitable devotion. He was filled with the spirit of the fear of the Lord, who, as the prophet David said, is known to be the "beginning of wisdom," namely of that wisdom with whose clarity blessed Maiol was filled.

14. He deserved to take up the reward of the heavenly beatitudes. Our Maiol, burning with the light of this reward, wanted in his spirit to stand a poor man alongside the other poor, so that he might deserve to be rewarded by the King of heaven in his heavenly kingdom. He was anxious to be meek with the blessed meek, so that he might possess the land of the living with them. With those blessed ones who wail, he wanted to wail over the ignorance of their children and to mourn over the disasters of the whole world, so that he might come to the eternal consolation with all of them. To those hungering and thirsting for justice, he was anxious to share that same justice [with them] in eating and drinking, and to banquet with those hungry and thirsty ones in a heavenly banquet and always to be sated [with them] in spiritual delights. And he was anxious to be merciful towards the wretched so that with those blessed with mercy he might receive mercy from the lord. To the extent that a human is constantly filled with heavenly desire, he deserved to obtain divine contemplation through his just merits and the invocation of submission, so that he might stand worthily with those blessed ones who have a pure heart and [enjoy] a vision of the Lord. And, that he might more truly be worthy to be called and [actually] to be a son of God, he learned to be perfectly peaceful, so that not only might he possess the patience to control his own soul, but so that he might return all troubled ones, as much as he could, to peace and happiness. For the sake of justice, he learned to endure with patience the persecutions and emotions of the ancient enemy [the Devil] and evil people, so that he might, because of his justice, become blessed with the patient and stand with the poor in spirit in order to receive and possess the kingdom of Heaven.

15. Adorned with the three virtues [faith, hope, and charity] and everywhere surrounded and supported by the eight blessings of the Gospels, the most blessed father Maiol anxiously and fervently desired to acquire the four cardinal virtues and to live [by] these acquired virtues with just works. Thus, by his own prudence and the prudence of those who had lived earlier he might gain salvation. Thus, by means of temperance, which is also known as moderation, he might with moderation dispose of the spiritual business imposed upon him with a temperament of just discretion. By means of fortitude, he might be able to resist the devil and his vices and with this resistance and by battling rightly he might powerfully overcome that author of wickedness. By means of justice, which is spread through all the types of virtues and

which seems to be the basis of those same virtues, by living soberly, piously, and justly, and by fighting the good fight, and by seeing things through to the end, and by serving the faith, he might be worthy to receive the crown of justice reserved for him by that one who is the giver and author of all virtues, God the one blessed before all things and above all things throughout the ages, whose gift of blessing and clement kindness came to us in reward that we might enjoy such and so great a pastor [Maiol]. In him we have an example we should follow, and in him there was a form implanted for us [to see and] with which we should be stamped, just as blessed Gregory says about our head, Jesus Christ, our lord, in the spread of whose body the blessed Maiol deserved to obtain the best place, as if his healthiest member.

16. If anyone dares to deny the assertions put forth [here] about the life and the powers of his soul, he should take the trouble to check out the manifest miracles and physical signs through which the faith of those who are inclined to doubt the merits and gifts of the elect will be supported and strengthened. It should be explained to them in the words of the blessed Gregory [the Great]: "There is no need for faith in matters that human reason proves by experience." And lest anyone have doubts about [Maiol's] holiness and glory, let him learn from those who saw and heard how he lived, how he taught, and how, full of days and adorned with virtues, he died. Since he will have learned from the statements of the faithful that he lived in a holy manner and that he taught rightly, he should believe that [Maiol] had certainly through Christ's guidance come to [enjoy] the glory of all the saints. How great were the miracles the Lord deigned to demonstrate through him, both before and after his death, very orthodox books composed by very learned men bear witness, books written with rhetorical polish [such as the one by Syrus] and, in some places, enlivened with dactylic verse [as was the account by Rimbald]. And because the almighty Lord suffers no time to pass without witness to his kindness, he constantly renews the examples of his holiness in order to correct the flaws of our [human] weakness. That happened even more often than usual during [Maiol's] time.

17. Among all those bearing the label of holiness who have shone in our times, blessed Maiol showed himself to be the most outstanding. I should briefly say a few things about his distinguished habits and the virtues of his distinguished life. Let me first state that he was in everything skilful and praiseworthy. For he was [a model of] distinction in action, sobriety in custom, humility in prosperity, patience in adversity. He was affable to the gentle, frightening to the proud, thrifty when he needed to be, generous when it was appropriate. He was not erratic in his behavior, nor confused in his actions. To every person, no matter how great, he was always one and the

same. He was a devoted imitator of the saints. In order to obey and serve, he listened carefully to those to whose servitude and instruction he submitted himself. By hearing, that is, not with a deaf ear, he learned more about that sevenfold bond clearly set out by Peter [in 2 *Pet.* 1] in the marvelous order of the numbers three and four. So that others might also learn [this way], he taught it through speech and writing, demonstrating virtue in faith, knowledge in virtue, abstinence in knowledge, patience in abstinence, piety in patience, fraternal love in piety, and charity in fraternal love. For he preferred the laudatory witness of apostolic simplicity to dialectical syllogisms, to rhetorical arguments, and to all the cleverness of all the philosophers. He said with Paul, "for I have learned, in whatsoever state I am, therewith to be content. I know both how to be abased, and I know how to abound: everywhere and in all things I am instructed both to be full and to be hungry, both to abound and to suffer need. I can do all things through Christ which strengthen me." He learned from the wisdom of such doctors and divine philosophers and he was enriched by the teachings and virtues of complete ecclesiastical instruction, as Ecclesiasticus says about Moses: "He was made beloved to God and people, and thus his memory is in the blessing." Father Maiol was beloved to God and to his people, because through the love of God and his neighbors, which he firmly maintained, he was pleasing to both God and his people. He attempted to please the people in order not to displease God, and thus to please God so that he might help the people. He pleased God by living well and by teaching correctly. He was pleasing to people because of his ability to show them spiritual and temporal benefits. Truly we acknowledge his memory in blessing, while we cherish and especially recognize that the buildings of the heavenly mansion had grown, grew, and continue to grow because of him and those whom he reared in Christ.

18. Let me speak with reverence of those spiritual builders who were working on the same structure, [among whom] one especially shone, the lord abbot William, who recently departed from human life [on 1 January 1031]. He had labored more than all of us. I am not able because of my smallness and eagerness to report in full his pure acts, praiseworthy life, and remarkable conversion.

19. How clearly the memory of the very blessed Maiol and his disciples survives in blessing, let both those monasteries constructed from their foundations by those people [and] those returned from a corrupted state to a better one through an increase in their virtue answer. How much that man, about whom I am speaking, pleased God it is right to show openly to people through the signs and miracles that God worked on account of his merit. Since, as the most faithful witness of many faithful people shows, those bur-

dened by many and diverse illnesses, even some despairing of life, were visited by him and brought back to [a state of] pristine health by the grace of God. Many, once the fog over their eyes had been cleared away, began to see clearly again because of his merit. Many people afflicted with fevers of different kinds, with the onset of the grace of God, were freed by his prayers. Many people, as it is reported, were thought worthy to receive a full cure from snakebites, from attacks by wolves and dogs, and from the invasion and illusions of demons because with his right hand he made the sign of the Lord's cross [over them]. Many people were freed through his intercession from the danger of drowning, from being struck by lightning, and from other disasters. When candles, either from the negligence of a chamberlain or because of some chance event, went out in the night in front of his bed, as those who were present witnessed, they divinely came back to light. Once when he was in the monastery of the most holy St-Denis [in Paris] and was reading one night, as was his habit, the book on the *Celestial Hierarchy* [written] by that same admirable martyr in both languages [Latin and Greek] and in both modes of the philosopher, a deep sleep stole over him and the candle in his hand flowed down onto the page of the book. Then a certain remarkable and unusual thing happened. The fire, following its nature, consumed the wood and wax, but left the page unharmed.

20. If he did not bring the dead back to life, there are other better and clearer miracles which the Lord worked through him. "If the soul is more than the body," the restoration of souls to eternal life is much greater than the resuscitation of bodies to the troubles of this life and to the dangers to those returning [to this life]. How many people he saved from the death of the soul and from the pit of vices, and brought back to the paths of [true] life by his example, the very number of them, which is known to God alone, cannot be counted. By these things and virtues of this sort he was distinguished by God and was loved by humans.

21. Many catholics and honorable clerics, religious monks and reverend abbots venerated that man as the holiest of fathers. Holy and wise bishops regarded him as their dearest brother. He was called seignior and lord by emperors and empresses, by the kings and rulers of the world. He was honored by the popes of the holy see, and truly was at that time the leader of the monastic movement. That famous man, the lord Caesar, Otto the Great [962-973] loved him with his whole heart. The wife of the same Caesar, the holy empress Augusta Adelaide, loved him with sincerest and dearest devotion. Their son, the emperor Otto [II, 967-983], loved him with humble devotion, with fondness, and likewise with love. Conrad [the Peaceful, king of Burgundy, 937-993], the noble and peaceful brother of the same empress, and his

most noble wife, Mathilda, [also loved him]. As often as they looked upon his visage, they loved him that much more. What can I say about that most noble ruler Henry of Burgundy? What can I say about Lambert, a most illustrious man and most noble count? What can I say about William, and about Richard, the powerful dukes of Aquitaine and Normandy? What can I say about the princes and march lords of Italy? How much William the ruler of Provence loved that one, his life and death show, for because of [Maiol's] merit and also in faithful obedience [to him] he took up the habit of blessed Benedict [he became a Benedictine monk]. Archeanbald, the faithful bene- factor of Souvigny [where Maiol died], was dearest among his people, the father of the adjoining land, and a powerful protector of the poor. How greatly and how devoted he was to blessed Maiol, that place proclaims in many ways for it was adorned and embellished by him, [both] before and after the death of that father, with buildings, riches, and different kinds of ornaments, so that it seemed that some king had done this. That man, who now exists as the inheritor of his office and name, treats that place well, and still takes nothing away from its inhabitants. Thus blessed Maiol was made greater and was glorified by the oncoming grace of God in the sight of kings and princes, in the presence of all the people, so that we can say about him without doubt what Ecclesiasticus said about Moses, the servant of God: "he glorified that one in the sight of kings, and revealed his glory to them." Hugh [Capet], the king of the Franks [987-996], as often as he saw him, received him with humble devotion and regarded him with great honor. At the time of his rise [to kingship], he asked [Maiol] to come to him so that, with his advice and help, the monastery of St-Denis might be better arranged than it was. [Maiol], knowing the saying of the Lord, said: "Return unto Caesar the things of Caesar and unto God the things of God." And he also knew the precept of the apostle "Fear God, honor the king." To carry out that business, he joyfully undertook a journey that took him to Souvigny. There, with God calling him, and being full of days and holiness, he died, on the fifth [day before] the Ides of May, on the sixth day of the week [on 11 May 994], after the celebration of that most holy and solemn day on which Jesus Christ our Lord, with the prince of death defeated, ascended to the right hand of the Father. He showed himself to his faithful and ascendent Maiol after his journey.

22. After his death, King Hugh [Capet], honored his funeral and tomb with his presence and royal gifts. [At his tomb], with the Lord's presence, many miracles were and are being done, and many beneficial things are per- formed for many and continue to be performed. [My] memory does not suffice to record in detail the number and importance of all these things. But

let me bring about a briefer conclusion. At the tomb of that one about whom I am speaking and whose life and merits I am striving to impress upon the charitable kindness of the faithful, many held in the grips of whatever kind of deformity were and are cured by the grace and mercy of Christ. There the paralyzed are lifted up, and the lame, feverish, and blind, and those possessed by demons are healed, and we know that those terribly and miserably burned by fire are released [from pain]. Anyone coming there full of devotion who faithfully seeks his help in any [such] matter, will return home safe and sound with his prayers answered. This our lord Jesus Christ, who lives and rules in the unity of the holy spirit, [and is] God through all the ages of ages, commands. Amen.

23. I wanted here to bring my account of the life and habits of blessed Maiol, in which I tried to speak with faithful timerity and humble presumption, to a close. But I have [in the meantime] remembered a certain memorable portent concerning this father, which I had heard about from the accounts of some faithful men. Some say that father [Maiol] himself used to refer to [this incident] frequently in happy terms, but I was afraid to insert it in this work, since it might seem unbelievable to some people. Later on I began to recall certain events that occurred in the time of that man that revealed the apparent reason for that portent. For that reason I have confidently decided to say something about it. But new material of this unusual sort spoke against beginning [my account all over again], because I feared that on account of the magnitude of [the task] I could not accomplish it. When I was thinking about these things, a thought came to me: could anyone who has the nature of a gentle man suitably describe the furious and savage attack of a wolf as that one, who wrote the 'Life' of St. Jerome, the translator of the Bible and a most learned, erudite, and catholic man, portrayed the softness and obedience of a lion [see Fig. 7 above]?

24. At that time a great and extremely violent group of Saracens came to a boil in the far reaches of Spain and came by the sea almost to the ends of Italy and Provence. Massacres were visited upon every kingdom and upon people of both sexes and every age. They destroyed monasteries, depopulated cities, villages, and estates, and so came rapidly through the Julian Alps to the summit of the Apennine Alps. There they threw off any restraints on their impiety and afflicted the Christian population for a long time with various assaults and calamities. For they killed some, captured others, and stole all the possessions of others, and so fulfilled their impious vows by means of brutal warfare. Among the other evils that most wicked race brought about, they captured by fraud and trickery the blessed father Maiol who was returning from Rome [in 971 or 972]. They stole everything [from him], bound him in

chains, and abused him with hunger and thirst. But [Maiol] was freed by heaven and at last ransomed with the money of his own monastery, and with the Lord's protection he escaped from their hands unharmed. His unjust capture was the cause of their expulsion and everlasting damnation. But just as after the passion of Christ the Jews were exiled from their own lands, so after the capture of that slave of [Christ], his most faithful servant, Maiol, the Saracens were expelled from Christian lands. And just as by means of Titus and Vespasian, the Roman rulers, the Lord took his vengeance upon the Jews, so by means of that most illustrious man and Christian ruler William, [and] by means of the merits of blessed Maiol, the yoke of the Saracens fell from the shoulders of the Christians. Many lands unjustly possessed by them tore [themselves] away with a powerful force from their brutal domination.

25. But, having said this, it is important for us to return to the suggested plan. What did I suggest? That a certain remarkable portent foreshadowed the events that occurred in the time of blessed Maiol. What were those events? The unexpected arrival of the Saracens, the suffering of the Christians, the destruction of monasteries and cities, the capture, ransom, and freeing of blessed Maiol, and the ejection, with God's help, of that extremely violent people from Christian lands. Why and in what way was that portent remarkable? An unheard of and savage attack of wolves preceded that extremely cruel invasion of the Saracens, chiefly in those very regions where the invasion of the Saracens occurred after they had crossed the sea. I have spoken for [good] measure of how the multitude of the faithful was freed from the persecution of the Saracens; let me [now] speak according to my ability about how the land was freed from an [earlier] infestation of wolves.

26. There was at that time a certain knight in those parts by the name of Fulcher who was an excellent warrior, extremely wealthy by inheritance, and, as I said of his most noble son, he shone with the twin nobility of both his parents. He was a man of great counsel, was prudent and wise by nature, and was the father of our most holy father Maiol, about whom I am speaking. In his lands and neighborhood, the savage attacks of these wolves were overwhelming. In the vast horde of these wolves there was one that seemed physically stronger than the others. It was faster in running, crueller in attack, and more excited to devour [humans than the others]. Indeed, in its greed it used to swallow the whole limbs of human bodies. When that man heard and saw that this problem, this great disaster, was daily growing worse, he began to think not only about his own interests, but also about those of others. And he began to wonder how he could free himself and his neighbors from this great danger. Then, advised by the divine will from above and comforted by heavenly advice, he began to erect fences and to construct sheepfolds. He

introduced rams, sheep, and lambs into them. At that time no one [else] dared to do such a thing because of the savage attacks of the wolves. Then fitted out with military arms, that is, with breastplate and helmet, and entirely covered above with sheep's skin, he began to spend his nights in a sheepfold.

27. One night the wolves attacked the sheepfolds. By the will of God it happened that the wolf who was crueller [than all the rest] fell upon the waiting man. The wolf jumped on his back and placed both his feet upon the man's shoulders and began to look all around to see how he could more easily kill the ram, but there was no ram there. He found that [his victim's] throat and neck were protected by iron-plate, its head was covered by a helmet, and its body was magnificently protected. He could not injure it in any place. That strong man suddenly stretched out both his hands, seized the wolf's feet, and grasped the limbs of the wolf with his [own] limbs, and quickly returned to his companions. Those men had been waiting for him for a long time and had doubted his plan. To their [amazed] eyes he [now] offered up that great wolf as a great gift. The wolf was kept alive until morning and was shown to the people to whom he had been such a threat. He was killed, cut up, and in his guts the whole limbs of human bodies were found. The body of that slaughtered wolf was [then] strung up and, with him dead, all the other wolves fled from those lands.

28. Anyone who wants to understand these things wisely should be able to perceive something spiritual in that [incident]. By the savage attack of the wolves I believe the fury of the Saracens was foretold. By that man [Fulcher] who was praiseworthy in many ways in his lay state and who tricked the wolf and by tricking [him] killed him, I understand his foreshadowed son [Maiol]. For through the power of Christ [Maiol] overcame an invisible wolf, namely the ancient Enemy [the devil]. He spurned all his vices and illusions, which were overcome through celestial virtue and spiritual arms. And he saved the souls of many faithful people by his power, example, teaching, and his merits, and he introduced [them] to the one way of salvation, life, truth, and justice.

[Thus it is] that the Lord Jesus Christ, who is the way, the truth, and the life, who is God, and who lives and reigns through all the ages of ages, precedes, accompanies, and follows [us]. Amen.

CHAPTER FOUR

ROYAL SAINTS

A small percentage of saints from the ranks of the nobility came from royalty. Most European and Scandinavian countries had cults of royal saints from an early period: they include Sigismond king of the Burgundians (516-23); Oswald of Northumbria (633-43); Wenceslas of Bohemia (early tenth century); and Olaf of Norway (1015-30). Early royal saints achieved their status by instituting or spreading Christianity in their realms, or by defending it from unbelievers; they were likely to die violently as martyrs, either in battle or as the result of dynastic strife or treachery. Later royal saints, such as Elizabeth of Hungary (1207-31) and Louis IX of France (1214-70), were sometimes associated with reform movements, achieved sanctity as confessors or thaumaturges rather than martyrs, and were more likely to be women than in the early phase. The state of being a king (or even a consort) presupposed divinity to some extent, and this may partly explain the cult of royal saints. Also, as with high prelates, royalty possessed the greatest material wealth and temporal power, and any voluntary rejection of these goods for a life of charity and asceticism made a strong impression. Their cults were by no means confined to their own countries, for locations were dictated by the migration of relics and their reputations for miraculous cures: Oswald of Northumbria, for instance, had cults in Switzerland, Germany, Austria, and northern Italy.

[Fig. 24] St. Edmund pierced by Viking arrows, with the wolf who later guarded his head sitting by him (after Cahier; Baring-Gould, *Lives of the Saints,* 14).

20. ÆLFRIC'S *LIFE OF ST. EDMUND, KING AND MARTYR*

King Edmund of East Anglia became the center of an important English cult at Bury St. Edmunds, where his body was translated in the early tenth century, shortly after his martyrdom. As the text below explains, Abbo of Fleury first wrote the 'Passio' in about 987, and it was translated into Old English by Ælfric, abbot of Eynsham (near Oxford), as one of a number of homilies intended for reading aloud on saints' feast days. Ælfric's aim was to give his English countrymen access to Christian writings in Latin, and thus to strengthen their faith. He used a variety of Latin sources for his saints' 'lives,' and as comparison with Abbo's own account of St. Edmund shows, his idea of translation was not a literal rendering of the text: he readily omits content, paraphrases, summarizes, changes the order and adds material from other sources, and reworks the Latin in rhythmical Old English prose. He was one of the earliest writers in a flourishing hagiographical tradition of translating Latin saints' 'lives' into the European vernaculars.

Source: trans. M. A. Stouck, from the Old English text edited by G. I. Needham, *Ælfric: Lives of Three English Saints* (London: Methuen, 1966), pp. 43-59.

1. In the days of Æthelred the king a certain very learned monk came from the south across the sea, from St. Benedict's monastery at Fleury, to archbishop Dunstan three years before he died [in 985], and this monk was called Abbo. They spoke together, until Dunstan recounted the history of St. Edmund, just as Edmund's sword-bearer told it to king Æthelstan when Dunstan was a young man and the sword-bearer was very old. Then this monk [Abbo] set down the whole account in a book and afterwards, when the book reached us a few years later, we translated it into English as it now stands. After two years this monk, Abbo, went home to his monastery and was at once appointed abbot of that same monastery [Fleury, at St-Benoît-sur-Loire, where the remains of St. Benedict had been taken from Monte Cassino in about 673].

2. Blessed Edmund, king of East Anglia, was wise and worthy and always glorified almighty God in his way of life. He was humble and faultless and continued so steadfast that he would not submit to shameful sins, and he did not swerve in his conduct to either side, but was always mindful of the true teaching, "are you set on high as ruler? Do not exalt yourself, but be among men as if you were one of them." He was charitable to the needy, and like a father to widows, and always guided his people benevolently in the ways of righteousness and punished the cruel and lived happily in the true faith.

3. Finally [in 865] it happened that the Danes came with a naval force, laying waste and slaughtering far and wide throughout the land as their custom

is. In that fleet were Hinguar and Hubba, their chief leaders, united in the Devil, and they landed in Northumbria with their warships and devastated that region, and killed the people. Then Hinguar turned east with his ships and Hubba stayed behind in Northumbria, having won the victory by means of his great cruelty. Hinguar came by sea to East Anglia, in the same year that prince Alfred (who later became the famous king of Wessex) was twenty-one years old; and the forementioned Hinguar stole up suddenly upon the countryside like a wolf, and slaughtered the people, men, women and innocent children, and shamefully mistreated the guiltless Christians.

4. Soon afterwards he sent an arrogant message to the king saying that he should yield and do homage if he valued his life. The messenger came to Edmund the king and quickly delivered Hinguar's message: "Hinguar our king, bold and victorious on sea and on land, conqueror of many peoples, has now landed here suddenly with an army to set up his winterquarters with his troops. He commands you now to share your hidden gold-hoard and the treasures of your ancestors with him at once, and to be his under-king if you want to live, for you have not the strength to withstand him."

5. So then king Edmund summoned to him a bishop who was nearby and consulted with him how to reply to the fierce Hinguar. The bishop was afraid of the sudden disaster, and feared for the king's life, and said that he thought it best for him to submit to Hinguar's demands. The king was silent, and bent his gaze upon the ground; and finally he said as befits a king, "Behold, bishop, the poor people of this land have been shamefully mistreated, and now I would rather fall in the fight if only my people might be the owners of their own land;" and the bishop said, "Alas, beloved king, your people lie dead, and you lack the forces to enable you to fight, and the pirates will come and capture you alive unless you save your life by fleeing, or else save yourself by yielding to him." Then said King Edmund, full of courage as he was, "With all my heart I desire and wish not to be left behind alone by my dear thanes, who were suddenly murdered in their beds with their children and wives by these pirates. It was never my custom to take flight, but I would rather die, if I must, for my own country; the almighty God knows that I will never swerve from worshiping him nor from his true love, whether I die or live."

6. With these words he turned to the messenger whom Hinguar had sent to him and said to him fearlessly, "Truly, you deserve to be killed now, but I will not defile my clean hands with your foul blood because I follow Christ who set us the example; and I will gladly be slain by you, if it is the will of God. Go now, swiftly, and tell your cruel lord, 'as long as he lives, Edmund will never yield to Hinguar, commander of the heathen, unless first in this

[Fig. 25] Richard II of England (1367-1400) with his patron saints, from left, King Edmund of East Anglia, King Edward the Confessor (1003-66), and John the Baptist. Both Edmund and Edward were famous in England as the country's patron saints: their replacement by St. George began only in the fourteenth century. In this picture from the Wilton Diptych, the saints are shown presenting Richard to the Virgin Mary who is depicted in the facing panel holding the infant Christ and surrounded by angels (Jameson, *Legends of the Monastic Orders,* p. 100).

land he will yield to Christ the Savior by believing [in him].'"

7. Then the messenger went off swiftly and met the fierce Hinguar on the way with his whole army, hastening towards Edmund, and told the wicked man how he had been answered. So Hinguar resolutely gave orders to his naval force that they should all seize only the king, who had scorned his orders, and instantly tie him up. When Hinguar arrived, King Edmund stood

in his hall, and remembering the Savior, threw down his weapons: he wanted to follow Christ's example, for he forbade Peter to take up arms against the bloodthirsty Jews. Then the impious men bound Edmund and shamefully mistreated him and beat him with cudgels, and then they led the Christian king to a tree made firm in the earth and tied him to it with strong bonds, and afterwards they scourged him for a long time with whips; and he contin-ued to call out in complete faith between the blows to Christ our Savior; and the heathen grew furiously angry at his faith, because he called on Christ to help him. Then they shot at him with javelins, as if for sport, until he was completely covered with their missiles, like the bristles of a hedgehog, just as [St.] Sebastian was. Then the cruel pirate Hinguar realized that the noble king would not forsake Christ, but with steadfast faith continued to call upon him: so he ordered him to be beheaded, and the heathen did so. Even as he called upon Christ, the heathen dragged the blessed man away to kill him, and with one stroke they cut off his head, and his holy soul jour-neyed to [be with] Christ. There was a certain man nearby, kept safe by God's [will] and hidden from the heathen, who heard all this and afterwards recounted it just as we are describing it here.

8. So then the pirates returned to their ships, hiding the blessed Edmund's head in thick brambles so that it should not be entombed. Then after some time, when they had gone away, the country-dwellers arrived (those who remained there) at the place where their lord's body lay, all except for the head, and they were deeply distressed at heart because of his murder, and especially because they did not have the head of his corpse. Then the spy who had seen it happen told them that the pirates had [taken] the head with them, and that he thought (as it was certainly true) that they had hidden the head somewhere in the wood. Then they all went with one accord to the wood, searching everywhere in the bushes and brambles to see if they could find the head anywhere.

9. And a great miracle occurred: a wolf was sent, by God's guidance, to guard that head from other wild animals by day and by night. The people continued searching, always calling out (as those accustomed to going into the woods usually do) "Where are you now, comrade?" and the head answered them "Here! Here! Here!" calling out often and answering them all in response to each one of their cries, until they all came upon it because of the calls. There lay the grey wolf protecting the head and clasping it between his two paws, and though greedy and hungry, because of God he did not dare to taste the head, but guarded it against wild animals. Then they were amazed at the wolf's protectiveness, and they carried the sacred head home with them, giving thanks to almighty God for all his wonders; but the wolf

followed after the head until they reached the town, just as if he were tame, and afterwards he returned again to the woods. Then the people laid the head with the sacred body and buried it as best they could in such haste, and at once built a church above [the tomb].

10. Then afterwards, when many years had passed and the raiding had ceased, and peace was granted to the afflicted people, they gathered together and reverently built a church for the saint, because miracles often occurred at his tomb in the chapel where he was buried. They wished to carry the holy body with the people honoring it and lay it in the church. Then there was great wonder that Edmund's body was as whole as if he were alive, his corpse uncorrupted, and his neck which had been cut through was healed, except for a mark like a red silk thread around his neck, as if to show people how he had been killed. And in the same way, the wounds which the cruel heathen had inflicted on his body with their many javelins were healed through the might of heavenly God; and he lies uncorrupted to this present day, awaiting the resurrection and the everlasting glory. His uncorrupted body tells us that he lived chastely in this world, and because of his pure life he went to be with Christ.

11. A certain widow called Oswyn lived at the saint's tomb in prayer and fasting for many years afterwards; she would cut the saint's hair every year and trim his nails lovingly and chastely, and keep them at the shrine as relics on the altar.

Then the land-dwellers venerated the saint faithfully, and bishop Theodred endowed the church abundantly with gifts of gold and silver to honor him. Once, eight wicked thieves in one night came to the venerable saint; they wanted to steal the treasures that people had brought there, and tried to force their way in. One of them struck the door-bolt hard with a hammer, another filed around it with a file, a third also dug under the door with a spade, and another tried to open the window by means of a ladder; but they labored in vain and made wretched progress, for the saint miraculously struck them motionless, each one as he stood working with his tool, so that none of them could commit that sinful deed nor stir from the spot but stood that way until morning. People were astonished to see how the wretches hung there, one on a ladder, one bending to dig, and each one bound fast in his task. Then they were all brought to the bishop, and he ordered them all to be hung high on the gallows; but he forgot how merciful God spoke these words through his prophet: "Always deliver up those who are led to death;" and also holy law forbids clerics, whether bishops or priests, to concern themselves with thieves, because it is not fitting for those who are the chosen of God to consent to any man's death, if they are the Lord's servants. Afterwards when bishop Theodred examined his book, he regretted and lamented that he had given the wicked thieves such a harsh judgment, and repented of it ever afterwards, to his life's end, and he bade the people earnestly to fast with him for three whole days, praying the Almighty to have mercy on him.

12. There was a certain man in that land called Leofstan, rich in the sight of the world and foolish before God, who rode in great arrogance to the saint's shrine and insolently commanded them to show him the holy saint, to see whether he was incorrupt; but as soon as he saw the saint's body, at once he went mad and roared horribly, and ended wretchedly with an evil death. This is similar to what the orthodox pope Gregory [see 15 above] said in his treatise about St. Lawrence, who lies in Rome – both good and evil people kept wanting to examine how he lay; but God put a stop to them, because some seven people died there together while they were looking at his body; then the others ceased their human foolishness in inspecting the martyr.

13. We have heard about many miracles spoken of among the people concerning the blessed Edmund which we do not wish to set down in writing here, but everyone knows them. Through this saint and others like him it is clear that almighty God can raise humankind again on the day of Judgment, incorrupt from the earth, he who keeps Edmund's body whole until the great day, even though he was made of earth. That place [the shrine] is worthy of being venerated for the glorious saint's sake, and deserves to be well provided with God's undefiled servants in Christ's service, because the saint is more glorious than people can conceive.

14. Nor is the English nation deprived of the Lord's saints when in England lie buried such saints as this holy king, and blessed Cuthbert, and Æthelthryth at Ely, and also her sister [Sexburgh], incorrupt in body, to strengthen the faith. And there are also many other saints in England who work many miracles – as it is known far and wide – to the glory of the Almighty in whom they believed. Christ reveals to humankind through his glorious saints that he is almighty God who brings such miracles to pass, although the wretched Jews entirely rejected him, because they are damned, as they themselves know. No miracles are worked at their tombs, because they do not believe in the living Christ; but Christ reveals to humankind where the true faith is, when he brings to pass such wonders far and wide over the earth. Therefore glory be to him forever, with his heavenly Father and the Holy Ghost. Amen.

21. ST. MARGARET, QUEEN OF SCOTLAND

Margaret's early life was closely entwined with the chief political events taking place in England and Scotland in the eleventh century. Her grandfather, Edmund Ironside, ruled England briefly in 1016 but was killed by Cnut the Dane, who then succeeded him. Her father Edward Ætheling was dispatched first to Sweden and then to Hungary, where he was married (though not, as sometimes claimed, to the daughter of St. Stephen of Hungary) and raised three children, Margaret (born about 1044), Christina, and Edgar. The family returned to England in 1054; after Edward Ætheling's death, they remained there under the protection of King Edward the Confessor until his death in 1066, when young Edgar's claim to the throne was passed over and Harold was elected king. For two years after the Norman Conquest the family remained in England, and might have continued to live there had trouble not arisen among the northern barons who in 1068 rebelled against King William. The rebellion was unsuccessful and many of the barons fled to Scotland to take refuge at the court of the king, Malcolm III. Margaret and her family were among them, perhaps aware that the rebellion would make William unlikely to tolerate the presence of a rival Saxon contender for the throne at his court. A second rebellion in Northumbria in 1070 made Margaret's return to Scotland permanent.

Raised in the devoutly Christian Hungary of Andrew I and the equally pious court of Edward the Confessor, Margaret had intended to become a nun. Under the pressure of political events, however, she consented to marry Malcolm III, king of Scotland from 1058 after the defeat of Macbeth (who, as readers of Shakespeare know, murdered Malcolm's father Duncan). Malcolm had also been raised partly at the court of Edward the Confessor, and may have absorbed some of its piety. He had been married once before, had three children by his first wife, and was nearly forty when he married Margaret, who was about twenty-four. She bore him six sons, three of whom became kings of Scotland, and two daughters, one of whom, Matilda (to whom the 'life' is addressed), married Henry I of England. Unlike Radegund (see 16 above), and despite her earlier vocation to be a nun, Margaret saw her duty in terms of her husband's kingdom. Historians argue about the extent to which she reformed the Scottish church, but it seems clear that she was instrumental in moving it into the mainstream of continental Christianity from a loose Celtic system, largely directed by powerful 'culdees,' or 'companions of God,' who lived in scattered religious cells and were out of touch with the institutional Church. In this work she was aided by archbishop Lanfranc with whom she corresponded, who sent monks from the Benedictine foundation at Canterbury to help with the work of reorganizing the Scottish church and founding monastic houses. The 'Turgot' cited as the author of Margaret's 'life' was her friend and confessor. Like many hagiographers he rejects strict chronological organization and avoids specific names of people or geographical locations, relying instead upon the time-

less language of virtue and faith. His portrayal of Margaret combines the conventional characteristics of lives of saintly queens with striking personal glimpses.

Source: text edited by Papebroch in the *Acta Sanctorum*, June 10, 2, 328, trans. William Forbes-Leith, *The Life of St. Margaret of Scotland, by Turgot, Bishop of St. Andrews* (3rd ed.; Edinburgh: David Douglas, 1896), pp. 19–81. BHL 5325.

The Prologue

To the honorable and excellent Matilda, queen of the English, Turgot, a servant of the servants of St. Cuthbert, sends the blessing of peace and health in this present life, and in the life which is to come the blessing of all good things.

1,1. You have, by the request you made, commanded me (since a request of yours is to me a command) that I should narrate for you the particulars of the life of your mother, whose memory is held in veneration. How acceptable that life was to God you have often heard by the concordant praise of many. You remind me how in this matter my evidence is especially trustworthy, since (thanks to her great and familiar intercourse with me) you have understood that I am acquainted with most of her secrets. These your commands and wishes I willingly obey; nay, more, I venerate them exceedingly, and I respectfully congratulate you – whom the King of the Angels has raised to the rank of Queen of England – that you desire not only to hear about the life of your mother, who always yearned after the Kingdom of the Angels, but further: to have it continually before your eyes in writing, so that, although you were only a little familiar with her face, you might at least have a perfect acquaintance with her virtues [Matilda was raised at the convent of her aunt Christina at Romsey, in England]. For my part, my own wish inclines me to do what you ask, but I have, I confess, a lack of ability, as the materials, in truth, for this undertaking are more than my writing or my words can avail to set forth.

2. So I am in two minds, and drawn two ways at once. On the one hand, the greatness of the subject makes me shrink from obeying; on the other, I dare not refuse because of the authority of you who command me, and the memory of her of whom I am to speak. I cannot do justice to my subject, yet my duty is to make it known so far as I can. I owe this to the love I have for her, and to the obedience which is due from me to you. I trust that the grace of the Holy Spirit, which gave her such powers for good, will give me also the ability to recount them. "The Lord shall give the word to them that preach good tidings with great power."

[Fig. 26] Dunfermline Abbey, burial place of Margaret of Scotland. In 1250 her remains were translated to a splendid new tomb in the choir, but in the sixteenth century the church fell into disrepair and the site of the tomb is outside the present church (from Forbes-Leith, trans. *The Life of St. Margaret by Turgot,* p. 22).

3. In the first place, then, it is my wish that you should know, and others through you, that were I to attempt to recount all I could tell to her honor, I might be suspected, while praising your mother, to be really flattering your own queenly dignity. But far be it from my grey hairs to mingle falsehood with the virtues of such a woman as she was, in unfolding which I profess – as God is my witness and my judge – that I add nothing to the truth. On the contrary, I suppress many things, fearing that they might appear incredible, and I might be charged (as the orator says) with decking out the crow in the feathers of the swan.

I, 4. Many, as we read, have got their name from a quality of their mind, so that in their regard there is shown a correspondence between the word forming their name and the grace they have received. Peter was so named from "the rock," that is Christ, in token of the firmness of his faith; John, which means "the grace of God," from his contemplation of the Divinity and his prerogative of Divine love; and the sons of Zebedee were named Boan-erges, that is, "the sons of thunder," because they thundered forth the preach-ing of the Gospel. The same thing was true of this virtuous woman, for the fairness which was pre-shadowed in her name was eclipsed by the surpassing beauty of her soul. She was called Margaret, and in the sight of God she showed herself to be a pearl, precious in faith and works. She was indeed a pearl to you, to me, to all of us, yes, to Christ himself, and being Christ's she is all the more ours now that she has left us, having been taken to the Lord. This pearl, I repeat, has been removed from the dunghill of the present world, and now she shines in her place among the jewels of the eternal King. Of this no one, I think, will doubt, who reads the following narrative of her life and death. When I call to mind her conversations with us, seasoned as they were with the salt of wisdom; when I remember her tears wrung from the compunction of her heart; when I regard her staidness and the even balance of her manners; when I remember her affability and prudence, I rejoice while I lament, and in lamenting I rejoice. I rejoice, because she has passed away to God, after whom she yearned; and I grieve because I am not rejoicing along with her, in the heavenly places. I rejoice for her, because she now sees, in the land of the living, those good things of the Lord in which she had believed; but for myself I mourn, because so long as I suffer the miseries of this mortal life in the land of the dead, so long am I constrained to exclaim day by day: "Unhappy man that I am, who shall deliver me from the body of this death!"

5. Since, then, I am about to speak of that nobility of the mind which she had in Christ, it is fitting that something should be stated as to her nobility according to this world. Her grandfather was that King Edmund who had earned an honorable surname from his matchless valor, for he was staunch in fight and not to be overcome by his enemies; and therefore he was called in English "the ironside." His brother on his father's side, but not on his mother's, was the most religious and meek Edward [the Confessor; see Fig. 25 above], who proved himself a father to his country, which, like another Solomon (that is, a lover of peace), he protected rather by peace than arms. His was a spirit which overcame anger, despised avarice, and was utterly free from pride. And no wonder; for as from his ancestors he drew the glory of his kingly rank, so from them too he inherited his nobility of life. He was descended from Edgar, King of the English, and Richard, Count of the Normans, his grandfathers on either side; not only most illustrious, but also most religious men. Of Edgar it may briefly be said (if we would do justice to his worth as well in this world as in Christ), that he was marked out beforehand as a king both just and peaceful. For at his birth St. Dunstan heard the holy angels rejoicing in heaven and singing with great joy: "Let there be peace, let there be joy in the Church of the English as long as this new-born child shall hold his kingdom and Dunstan run the course of this mortal life."

6. Richard also, father to Emma the mother of this Edward, was an ancestor worthy of so illustrious a grandchild; he was a man of energy and worthy of all praise. None of his forefathers had attained greater prosperity and

honor in his earldom of Normandy, nor was any of them more fervent in religion. Though of great wealth, he was poor in spirit, like a second David; though raised to be lord over his people, he was the most humble servant of the servants of Christ. Among other memorials of his love of religion, this devout worshiper founded the noble monastery of Fécamp, in which it was his frequent custom to stay with the religious. There, in habit a secular but in heart a monk, he placed the food of the brethren on the table where they were eating their silent meals and served them with drink; so that, according to the Scriptures, "The greater he was, by so much the more did he humble himself to all." If anyone wishes to be more fully acquainted with his works of magnificence and virtue, let him read the book called "The Acts of the Normans," which contains his history. Edward, the grandchild of such forefathers, did in no way degenerate from their renown and excellence. As already has been said, he was the brother of King Edmund on the father's side only, from whose son came Margaret, who by the splendor of her merits completes the glory of this illustrious pedigree.

7. While Margaret was still in the flower of youth, she began to lead a very strict life, to love God above all things, to employ herself in the study of the divine writings, and to exercise her mind in them with joy. Her understanding was keen to comprehend any matter, whatever it might be; to this was joined a great tenacity of memory, enabling her to store it up, along with a graceful flow of language to express it.

8. While she was meditating upon the law of the Lord day and night, and, like another Mary sitting at his feet, delighted to hear his word, rather in obedience to the will of her friends than to her own, by the appointment of God she was married to Malcolm, son of King Duncan, the most powerful king of the Scots. But although she was compelled to do as the world does, she thought it beneath her dignity to fix her affection upon the things of the world, and thus good works delighted her more than riches. By means of her temporal possession she earned for herself the rewards of heaven; for there, where her heart was, she had placed her treasure also. And since before all things she sought the kingdom of God and his justice, the bountiful grace of the Almighty freely added to her honors and riches in abundance. This prudent queen directed all such things as it was fitting for her to regulate; the laws of the realm were administered by her counsel; by her care the influence of religion was extended, and the people rejoiced in the prosperity of their affairs. Nothing was firmer than her fidelity, steadier than her favor, or juster than her decisions; nothing was more enduring than her patience, graver than her advice, or more pleasant than her conversation.

9. She had no sooner attained this eminent dignity, than she built an eter-

nal memorial of her name and devotion in the place where her nuptials had been held [Dunfermline]. The noble church which she erected there in honor of the Holy Trinity was to serve a threefold purpose; it was intended for the redemption of the king's soul, for the good of her own, and for securing to her children prosperity in the present life and in that which is to come. This church she beautified with rich gifts of various kinds, amongst which, as is well known, were many vessels of pure and solid gold for the sacred service of the altar, about which I can speak with the greater certainty since, by the queen's orders, I myself, for a long time, had all of them under my charge. She also placed there a cross of priceless value, bearing the figure of our Savior, which she had caused to be covered with the purest gold and silver studded with gems, a token even to the present day of the earnestness of her faith. She left proofs of her devotion and fervor in various other churches, as witness the Church of St-Andrews, in which is preserved a most beautiful crucifix erected by her there, and remaining even at the present day. Her chamber was never without such objects, I mean those which appertained to the dignity of the divine service. It was, so to speak, a workshop of sacred art: in which copes for the cantors, chasubles, stoles, altar-cloths, together with other priestly vestments and church ornaments of an admirable beauty, were always to be seen, either already made, or in course of preparation.

10. These works were entrusted to certain women of noble birth and approved gravity of manners, who were thought worthy of a part in the queen's service. No men were admitted among them, with the exception only of such as she permitted to enter along with herself when she paid the women an occasional visit. No giddy pertness was allowed in them, no light familiarity between them and men; for the queen united so much strictness with her sweetness of temper, so great pleasantness even with her severity, that all who waited upon her, men as well as women, loved her while they feared her, and in fearing loved her. So it came to pass that when she was present no one ventured to utter even one unseemly word, much less to do anything that was objectionable. There was a gravity in her very joy, and something stately in her anger. With her, mirth never expressed itself in fits of laughter, nor did displeasure kindle into fury. Sometimes she rebuked the faults of others – her own always – using that commendable severity tempered with justice which the Psalmist directs us unceasingly to employ, when he says, "Be ye angry, and sin not." Every action of her life was regulated by the balance of the finest discretion, which impressed its own distinctive character upon each single virtue. When she spoke, her conversation was seasoned with the salt of wisdom; when she was silent, her silence was filled with good

thoughts. So thoroughly did her outward bearing correspond with the staid-ness of her character that it seemed as if she had been from her very birth the pattern of a virtuous life. In fact, I may say, every word which she uttered, every act which she performed, showed that she was meditating upon the things of heaven.

11. Nor was she less careful about her children than she was about herself. She took great care that they should be well brought up, and especially that they should be trained in virtue. Knowing that it is written: "he that spareth the rod hateth his son," she charged the governor who had the care of the nursery to curb the children, to scold them, and to whip them whenever they were naughty, as frolicsome children will often be. Thanks to their mother's religious care, her children surpassed in good behavior many who were their elders; they were always affectionate and peaceable among them-selves, and everywhere the younger paid due respect to the elder. Thus it was that during the solemnities of the Mass, when they went up to make their offerings after their parents, never on any occasion did the younger venture to precede the elder; the custom being for the elder to go before those younger according to the order of their birth. She frequently called them to her, and carefully instructed them about Christ and the things of Christ, as far as their age would permit, and she admonished them to love him always. "O, my children," said she, "fear the Lord; for they who fear him shall lack nothing and if you love him, he will give you, my dear ones, prosperity in this life, and everlasting happiness with all the saints." Such were this mother's wishes for her children, such her admonitions, such her prayers for them, poured out night and day with tears. She prayed that they might confess their Maker through the faith which works by love, that confessing they might worship him, worshiping might love him in all things and above all things, and loving might attain to the glory of the heavenly kingdom.

2, 12. Nor need we wonder that the queen governed herself and her household wisely when we know that she acted always under the wisest of masters, the guidance of the holy Scriptures. I myself have had frequent opportunities of admiring in her how, even amidst the distractions of law-suits, amidst the countless cares of state, she devoted herself with wonderful assiduity to the study of the word of God, respecting which she used to ask profound questions from the learned men who were sitting near her. But just as no one among them possessed a deeper intellect than herself, so none had the power of clearer expression. Thus it very often happened that these doc-tors went from her much wiser men than when they came. She sought with a religious earnestness for those sacred volumes, and oftentimes her affection-ate familiarity with me moved me to exert myself to obtain them for her use. Not that in doing this she cared for her own salvation only; she desired that of others also.

13. First of all in regard to King Malcolm: by the help of God she made him most attentive to the works of justice, mercy, almsgiving, and other virtues. From her he learned how to keep the vigils of the night in constant prayer; she instructed him by her exhortation and example how to pray to God with groanings from the heart and abundance of tears. I was astonished, I confess, at this great miracle of God's mercy when I perceived in the king such a steady earnestness in his devotion, and I wondered how it was that there could exist in the heart of a man living in the world such an entire sorrow for sin. There was in him a sort of dread of offending one whose life was so venerable; for he could not but perceive from her conduct that Christ dwelt within her; nay, more, he readily obeyed her wishes and prudent counsels in all things. Whatever she refused, he refused also; whatever pleased her, he also loved for the love of her. Hence it was that, although he could not read, he would turn over and examine books which she used either for her devotions or her study; and whenever be heard her express especial liking for a particular book, he also would look at it with special interest, kissing it, and often taking it into his hands. Sometimes he sent for a worker in precious metals, whom he commanded to ornament that volume with gold and gems, and when the work was finished, the king himself used to carry the book to the queen as a loving proof of his devotion.

14. The queen on her side, herself a noble gem of royal race, much more ennobled the splendor of her husband's kingly magnificence, and contributed no little glory and grace to the entire nobility of the realm and their retainers. It was due to her that the merchants who came by land and sea from various countries brought along with them for sale different kinds of precious wares which until then were unknown in Scotland. And it was at her instigation that the natives of Scotland purchased from these traders clothing of various colors, with ornaments to wear; so that from this period, through her suggestion, new costumes of different fashions were adopted, the elegance of which made the wearers appear like a new race of beings. She also arranged that persons of a higher position should be appointed for the king's service, a large number of whom were to accompany him in state whenever he either walked or rode abroad. This body was brought to such discipline that, wherever they came, none of them was permitted to take anything from anyone, nor did they dare in any way to oppress or injure country people or the poor. Further, she introduced so much state into the royal palace, that not only was it brightened by the many colors of the apparel worn in it, but the whole dwelling blazed with gold and silver; the vessels employed for serving

the food and drink to the king and to the nobles of the realm were of gold and silver, or were, at least, gilded and plated.

15. All this the queen did, not because the honors of the world delighted her, but because duty compelled her to discharge what the kingly dignity required. For even as she walked in state, robed in royal splendor, she, like another Esther, in her heart trod all these trappings under foot, and bade herself remember that beneath the gems and gold lay only dust and ashes. In short, in her exalted dignity she was always especially watchful to preserve humility. It was easy for her to repress all vain glory arising from worldly splendor, since her soul never forgot how transitory is this frail life. She always bore in mind the text which describes our condition in this our unstable humanity: "Man, born of a woman, living for a short time, is filled with many miseries. He comes forth as a flower and is destroyed, and flees as a shadow, and never continues in the same state." She meditated without ceasing upon that passage of the blessed apostle James, where he asks: "What is our life? It is a vapor which appears for a little while, and afterwards shall vanish away." And because, as the Scripture says, "blessed is the man that is always fearful," this worthy queen made it easier for her to shun sin by placing ever before her soul's eye, tremblingly and fearfully, the terrible day of Judgment. With this thought she frequently entreated me to rebuke her without any hesitation in private whenever I saw anything worthy of blame either in her words or her actions. As I did this less frequently and sharply than she wished, she urged the duty on me, and rebuked me for being drowsy (so to speak) and negligent in her regard, "for," as she said, "the just man shall correct me in mercy and shall reprove me; but let not the oil," that is, the flattery, "of the sinner fatten my head. Better are the wounds of a friend than the deceitful kisses of an enemy." She could speak thus because she courted censure as helping her progress in virtue, where another might have reckoned it a disgrace.

16. Journeying thus onwards towards the heavenly country in thought and word and deed, this devout and spiritually worthy queen called on others to accompany her in the undefiled way, so that they with her might attain true happiness. When she saw wicked men she admonished them to be good, the good to become better, the better to strive to be best. The zeal of God's house (that is, of the Church) had so consumed her that with apostolic faith she labored to root up all weeds which had lawlessly sprung up therein. Observing that many practices existed among the Scottish nation that were contrary to the rule of the right faith and the holy customs of the universal Church, she caused frequent councils to be held, in order that by some means or other she might, through the mercy of Christ, bring back into the

way of truth those who had gone astray.

17. Among these councils the most important is that in which for three days she, with a very few of her friends, combated the defenders of a perverse custom [certain of the *culdees*] with the sword of the Spirit, that is to say, with the word of God. It seemed as if a second Helena [mother of the emperor Constantine and legendary finder of the true cross] were there present, for as that queen in former days overcame the Jews by citing passages from the Scriptures, so in our times did Queen Margaret overcome those who were in error. In this discussion the king himself took part as an assessor and chief actor, being fully prepared both to say and do whatever she might direct in the matter at issue. And as he knew the English language quite as well as his own [Gaelic], he was in this council a very exact interpreter for either side.

18. The queen introduced the subject under discussion by premising that all who serve one God in one faith along with the Catholic Church ought not to vary from that Church by new or far-fetched usages. She then laid it down, in the first place, that the fast of Lent was not kept as it ought to be by those who were in the habit of beginning it on the Monday of the first week in Lent, thus differing from the holy Catholic Church which begins it on the fourth day of the previous week at the commencement of Lent. The opponents objected: "The fast which we observe we keep according to the authority of the Gospel, which reports that Christ fasted for six weeks." She replied by saying: "Here you differ widely from the Gospel, wherein we read that our Lord fasted for forty days, a thing which notoriously you do not do. For seeing that during the six weeks you deduct the six Sundays from the fast, it is clear that thirty-six days only remain on which to fast. Plainly, then, the fast which you keep is not that fast of forty days which is commanded by the Gospel, but consists of six and thirty days only. It comes then to this, you ought to do as we do. Like us, you should begin your fast four days before the first Sunday of Lent; that is, if you wish, according to our Lord's example, to observe an abstinence of forty days. If you refuse to do this, you will be the only persons who are acting in opposition to the authority of our Lord himself and the tradition of the entire holy Church." Convinced by this plain demonstration of the truth, these persons began henceforth the solemnities of the fast as Holy Church observes them everywhere.

19. The queen now raised another point; she asked them to explain why it was that on the festival of Easter they neglected to receive the sacrament of the body and blood of Christ according to the usage of the holy and apostolic Church? They answered her thus: "The apostle, when speaking of persons who eat and drink unworthily, says that they eat and drink judgment to

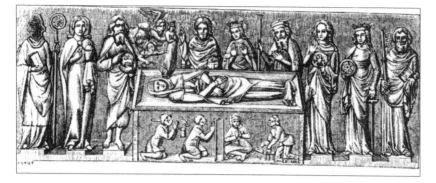

[Fig. 27] A bas-relief in the church of St. Elizabeth at Marburg, Hesse, showing the tomb of St. Elizabeth of Hungary, a famous thirteenth-century royal saint. Daughter of Andrew II of Hungary, she was married at an early age to Louis IV of Thuringia, and gave birth to three children. After Louis died of plague while on crusade, she settled at Marburg and devoted herself to charitable works and a life of extreme privation. She died at the age of twenty-four. The relief shows the infirm on the side of her tomb coming to her shrine in search of healing miracles. Behind the tomb stand (left to right) a bishop; Mary Magdalene; John the Baptist; Christ and the Virgin; Elizabeth's husband Louis; John the Evangelist; Catherine of Alexandria and the apostle Peter (Lacroix, *Military and Religious Life in the Middle Ages,* p. 461).

themselves. Now, since we admit that we are sinners, we fear to approach that mystery, lest we should eat and drink judgment to ourselves." "What!" said the queen to them; "Shall no one that is a sinner taste that holy mystery? If so, then it follows that no one at all should receive it, for no one is pure from sin; no, not even the infant who has lived but one day upon the earth. And if no one ought to receive it, why did the Lord make this proclamation in the Gospel: 'Except you shall eat the flesh of the Son of Man and drink his blood, you shall not have life in you'? But if you would understand the passage which you have quoted from the apostle according to the interpretation of the fathers [of the Church], then you must give it quite a different meaning. The Evangelist does not hold that all sinners are unworthy of the sacraments of salvation; for after saying 'He eats and drinks judgment to himself,' he adds, 'not discerning the body of the Lord' – [that is,] not distinguishing it by faith from bodily food. It is the man who, without confession and penance, and carrying with him the defilements of his sins, presumes to approach the sacred mysteries, such a one I say it is who eats and drinks judgment to himself. Whereas we who many days previously have made confession of our sins and have been cleansed from their stains by chastening penance, by trying fasts, by almsgiving and tears, approaching in the Catholic faith to the Lord's table on the day of his resurrection, receive the body and blood of Jesus Christ, the immaculate Lamb, not to judgment but to the remission of our sins, and as a health-giving preparation for eternal happiness." To these arguments they could not answer a word, and knowing now the meaning of the Church's practices, observed them ever after in the sacrament of salvation.

20. Again, there were certain places in Scotland in which Masses were celebrated according to some sort of strange rite, contrary to the usage of the whole Church. Fired by the zeal of God, the queen attempted to root out and abolish this custom, so that henceforth, in the whole of Scotland, there was not one single person who dared to continue the practice.

It was another custom of theirs to neglect the reverence due to the Lord's day by devoting themselves to every kind of worldly business upon it just as they did upon other days. That this was contrary to the law, she proved to them as well by reason as by authority. "Let us venerate the Lord's day," said she, "because of the resurrection of our Lord, which happened upon that day, and let us no longer do servile works upon it; bearing in mind that upon this day we were redeemed from the slavery of the Devil. The blessed pope Gregory affirms the same, saying: 'We must cease from earthly labor upon the Lord's day and we must devote ourselves entirely to prayer, so that upon the day of our Lord's resurrection we may make expiation for such negligences as we may have committed during the six days.' The same father, Gregory [the Great], after censuring with the greatest severity a certain piece of worldly business which had been done on the Lord's day, decreed that the persons who had advised it should be excommunicated for two months." The arguments of the queen were unanswerable; and from this time forward those prudent men paid such respect to her earnestness that no one dared on these days either to carry any burden himself or to compel another to do so.

21. Next, she proved how utterly abominable, even more to be shunned by the faithful than death itself, was the unlawful marriage of a man with his step-mother, as also that the surviving brother should take the widow of his deceased brother as his wife; both of which customs had heretofore prevailed in the country. In this council she succeeded in condemning and expelling from her realm many other inveterate abuses that had gained a footing in it, contrary to the rule of faith and the institutions and observances of the Church. For everything that she proposed she supported so strongly by the testimony of the sacred Scriptures and the teaching of the holy fathers, that no one on the opposite side could say one word against them; indeed, rather, giving up their obstinacy and yielding to reason, they willingly consented to adopt all she recommended.

3, 22. Thus it came to pass that this venerable queen, who by God's help had so desired to cleanse his house from all filth and error, was found day by day worthier of becoming his temple, as the Holy Spirit shone ever brighter in her heart. And I know truly that she was such, because I not only saw the works which she did outwardly, but besides this, I knew her conscience, for she revealed it to me. It was her good pleasure to converse with me on the most familiar terms, and to open her secret thoughts to me; not because there was anything that was good in me, but because she thought there was. When she spoke with me about the salvation of the soul and the sweetness of the life which is eternal, every word she uttered was so filled with grace that the Holy Spirit, who truly dwelt within her breast, evidently spoke by her lips. So deep was her contrition that while she was talking, she seemed as if she could melt away in tears, so that my soul, pierced like her own, wept also. Of all living persons whom I know or have known she was the most devoted to prayer and fasting, to works of mercy and almsgiving.

23. Let me speak first of all about her prayerfulness. In church no one was so silent and composed as she, no one so wrapped in prayer. While she was in the house of God she would never speak of worldly matters, or do anything which savored of the earth; she was there simply to pray, and in praying to pour forth her tears. Only her body was then here below, her spirit was near to God, for in the purity of her prayer she sought nothing but God and the things which are God's. As for her fasting, I will say this alone, that the strictness of her abstinence brought upon her a very severe infirmity.

24. To these two excellent gifts of prayer and abstinence she joined the gift of mercy. For what could be more compassionate than her heart? Who could be more gentle than she towards the needy? Not only would she have given to the poor all that she possessed; but if she could have done so she would have given her very self away. She was poorer than any of her paupers; for they, even when they had nothing, wished to have something; while all her anxiety was to strip herself of what she had. When she went out of doors, either on foot or on horseback, crowds of poor people, orphans and widows flocked to her, as they would have done to a most loving mother, and none of them left her without being comforted. But when she had distributed all she had brought with her for the benefit of the needy, the rich who accompanied her or her own attendants used to hand to her their garments, or anything else they happened to have by them at the time, that she might give them to those who were in want; for she was anxious that none should go away in distress. Nor were her attendants at all offended but rather each strove who should first offer her what he had, since he knew for certain that she would pay it back two-fold. Now and then she helped herself to some-

thing or other out of the king's private property, it did not matter what it was, to give to a poor person; and this pious plundering the king always took pleasantly and in good part. It was his custom to offer certain coins of gold upon Maundy Thursday [the Thursday before Easter] and at High Mass, and some of these coins the Queen often devoutly pillaged, and gave to the beggar who was petitioning her for help. Although the king was fully aware of the theft, he generally pretended to know nothing of it, and felt much amused by it. Now and then he caught the queen in the very act, with the money in her hand, and laughingly threatened that he would have her arrested, tried, and found guilty. Nor was it only towards the poor of her own nation that she exhibited the abundance of her cheerful and open-hearted charity, but those persons who came from almost every other nation, drawn by the report of her liberality, shared in her bounty. Of a truth then this text may be applied to her, "He has dispersed abroad, he has given to the poor, therefore his justice remains for ever."

25. But who can tell the number of English of all ranks, carried captive from their own land by violence of war and reduced to slavery, whom she restored to liberty by paying their ransom? Spies were employed by her to go secretly through all the provinces of Scotland and ascertain what captives were oppressed with the most cruel bondage, and treated with the greatest inhumanity. When she had privately ascertained where these prisoners were detained, and by whom ill-treated, commiserating with them from the bottom of her heart she took care to send them speedy help, paid their ransom and set them at liberty immediately.

26. At the period of which we are speaking, there were in many places throughout the realm of Scotland persons shut up in different cells, and leading lives of great strictness; in the flesh, but not according to the flesh, for being upon earth, they led the life of angels. These the queen busied herself in often visiting and conversing with, for in them she loved and venerated Christ, and would recommend herself to their prayers. As she could not induce them to accept any earthly gift from her, she urgently entreated them to be so good as to bid her to perform some charitable deed or work of mercy, and this devout woman at once fulfilled whatever was their pleasure, either by helping the poor out of their poverty or by relieving the distressed in their troubles, whatever these might be.

27. Since the church of St-Andrews was much frequented by the devout, who flocked to it from all quarters, she erected dwellings on either shore of the sea which divides Lothian from Scotland, so that the poor people and the pilgrims might shelter there and rest themselves after the fatigues of their journey. She had arranged they should there find all that they needed for the

refreshment of the body. Servants were appointed, whose special duty it was to see that everything which might be required for these wayfarers should always be in readiness, and who were directed to attend upon them with all diligence. Moreover, she provided ships for the transport of these pilgrims both coming and going, nor was it lawful to demand any fee for the passage from those who were crossing.

28. Having spoken of the daily manner of life of this venerable queen, as well as of her daily works of mercy, it is fitting that I should now attempt to say a few words as to the way in which she habitually spent the forty days before Christmas, and the entire season of Lent. After taking rest for a short period at the beginning of the night, she went into the church, and there, alone, she completed first of all the Matins of the Holy Trinity, then the Matins of the Holy Cross, and lastly the Matins of Our Lady. Having ended these, she began the offices of the Dead, and after these the Psalter; nor did she cease until she had reached its conclusion. When the Priests were saying the Matins and Lauds at the fitting hour, she in the meantime either finished the Psalter she had begun or if she had completed it, began saying it a second time. When the office of Matins and Lauds was finished, returning to her chamber, along with the king himself, she washed the feet of six poor persons, and used to give them something with which to relieve their poverty. It was the chamberlain's special duty to bring these poor people in every night before the queen's arrival, so that she might find them ready when she came to wait upon them. Having done this, she went to take some rest in sleep.

29. When it was morning she rose from bed and devoted a considerable time to prayer and the reading of the Psalms, and while thus engaged, she performed the following work of mercy. She ordered that nine little orphans, utterly destitute, should be brought in to her at the first hour of the day, and that some soft food such as children like at that tender age should daily be prepared for them. When the little ones were carried to her she did not think it beneath her to take them upon her knee, and to get their food ready for them, and this she put into their mouths with the spoon which she herself used. The queen, who was honored by all the people, did this act of charity for the sake of Christ, and as one of Christ's servants. To this most loving mother might be applied with great propriety that saying of the blessed Job, "From my infancy mercy grew with me, and it came forth with me from my mother's womb."

30. While this was going on, it was the custom to bring three hundred poor people into the royal hall, and when they were seated round it in order, the king and queen entered; whereupon the doors were shut by the servants, for with the exception of the chaplains, certain religious and a few atten-

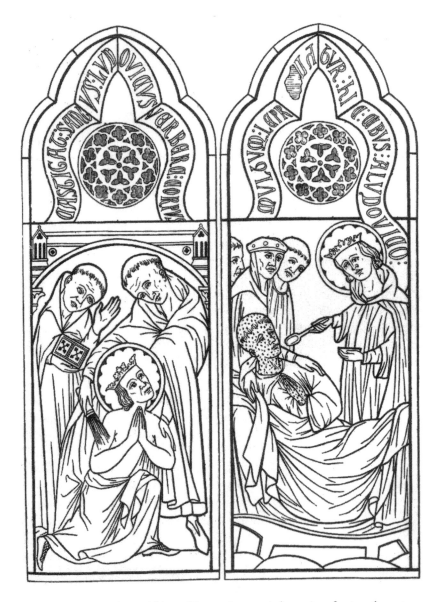

[Fig. 28] Louis IX, saint and king of France (1214–70) shown in a fourteenth-century window at St-Denis submitting himself to penitential flagellation and feeding a leper. His eventful life, which included two crusades, was chronicled by the Sieur de Joinville. Louis was famous for his charitable deeds, his founding of churches, hospitals and monasteries, his justice and his role as peace-maker. He died of fever while on crusade, and was canonized in 1297 (Baring-Gould, *Lives of the Saints*, 9).

dants, no one was permitted to be present at the giving of these gifts. The king on the one side and the queen on the other waited upon Christ in the person of his poor, and served them with food and drink which had been prepared for this special purpose. When the meal was finished, the queen's custom was to go into the church, and there with long prayers and with tears and sighs to offer herself as a sacrifice to God. Upon holy days, in addition to the hours of the Holy Trinity, the Holy Cross, and Holy Mary, recited within the space of a day and a night, she used to repeat the Psalter two or three times; and before the celebration of the public Mass she had five or six Masses sung privately in her presence.

31. These concluded, it was time for the queen's meal. But before this was served she herself humbly waited upon twenty-four poor people whom she fed; for without reckoning the charitable deeds which I have already mentioned, throughout the course of the year she supported twenty-four poor as long as she lived. It was her will that wherever she lived they also should be living in the neighborhood; wherever she went they were to accompany her. Not until after she had devoutly waited upon Christ in these his poor was it her habit to refresh her own feeble body. In this meal she hardly allowed herself the necessities of life, since the apostle teaches us that we ought not to make provision for the flesh in its desires. She ate no more than sufficed for the preservation of her life, and not to gratify her palate. Her meal – frugal and scanty – rather excited hunger than allayed it. She seemed to taste her food, not to take it. From this let it be understood, I pray you, how great was her abstinence when she fasted, remembering what it was when she feasted. Her whole life was one of exceeding temperance, but during the fasts (that is during the forty days before Easter and Christmas), the abstinence she was accustomed to afflict upon herself was incredible. By reason of this excessive severity she suffered to the end of her life from an acute pain in the stomach; yet the weakness of her body did not impair her strength in good works. During this period she was assiduous in reading the sacred volumes, she was instant in prayer, her charity was unceasing, and she exercised herself wholly and watchfully in all the things of God. And knowing, as she did, that it is written "whom the Lord loves he chastises, and he scourges every son whom he receives," she willingly accepted with patience and thanksgiving the pains of the flesh, regarding them as the stripes of a most loving Father.

32. Devoted as she was to such works as these, and burdened by constant infirmities, God's power was made perfect in her weakness. Thus passing onwards from strength to strength, each day made her better. And now forsaking all things earthly with her whole soul, she longed for the things of heaven, indeed, thirsted after them, exclaiming with the Psalmist in the lan-

guage both of her heart and lips, "my soul has thirsted after God, the living fountain; when shall I come and appear before the face of God?" I leave it to others to admire the tokens of miracles which they see elsewhere; I admire much more the works of mercy which I perceived in Margaret; for signs are common to the good and the bad, whereas works of piety and true charity belong to the good only. The former sometimes are the proof of holiness, the latter are that which constitutes it. Let us then, I repeat, admire in Margaret the actions which made her a saint, rather than the miracles which, had we any record of them, would have proved that she was one. In her character let us observe with admiration the works of the ancient saints rather than their miracles – her justice, her piety, her mercy, and her love. Yet it will not be out of place if I narrate here one incident which may go to prove what the holiness of her life was.

33. She had a book of the Gospels beautifully adorned with gold and precious stones, and ornamented with the figures of the four Evangelists, painted and gilded. All the capital letters throughout the volume were radiant with gold. She had always felt a particular attachment for this book; more so than for any of the others which she usually read. It happened that as the person who carried it was once crossing a ford, he let the book, which had been carelessly folded with a wrapper, fall into the middle of the river. Unconscious of what had happened, the man quietly continued his journey; but when he wished to produce the book, suddenly it dawned upon him that he had lost it. Long was it sought, but nowhere could it be found. At last it was discovered lying open at the bottom of the river. Its leaves had been kept in constant motion by the action of the water and the little coverings of silk, which protected the letters of gold from becoming injured by contact with the opposite page, were carried off by the force of the current. Who would fancy that the book could afterwards be of any value? Who would believe that even a single letter would have been visible? Yet in truth, it was taken up out of the middle of the river so perfect, so uninjured, so free from damage, that it did not seem to have even been touched by the water. The whiteness of the leaves and the form of the letters throughout the volume remained exactly as they had been before it had fallen into the river, except that in part of the end leaves the least possible mark of damp might be detected. The book was conveyed to the queen, and the miracle was at the same time related to her; and she, having thanked Christ, valued it much more highly than she had done before.

Whatever others may think, I for my part believe that this wonder was worked by our Lord out of his love for the venerable queen.

4, 34. While Almighty God was preparing everlasting rewards for her works of devotion, the queen was preparing herself with more than her usual assiduity for entering another life. Her own words made this more obvious shortly afterwards. It would seem that her departure from this world, as well as certain other events which were impending, had been known by her long beforehand. Therefore, summoning me to come to her privately, she began to recount to me in order the history of her life, and as she proceeded with it she shed floods of tears. In short, so deep was her compunction, and out of this compunction sprang such abundant tears, that — as it seemed to me — there was nothing whatever which at that time she might not have obtained from Christ. When she wept, I wept likewise; and thus we wept and at times were silent altogether, since by reason of our sobs we could not give utterance to words. For the name of that compunction which consumed her heart reached my soul also, borne into it by the spiritual fervor of her words. And when I heard the language of the Holy Ghost speaking by her tongue, and could thoroughly read the tenderness of her conscience by what she said, I judged myself unworthy of the grace of so exalted a familiarity.

35. When she had ended what she had to say about matters which were pressing, she then addressed herself to me, saying: "I now bid you farewell. I shall not continue much longer in this world, but you will live after me for a considerable time. There are two things which I beg of you. One is, that as long as you survive you will remember me in your prayers; the other is, that you will take some care about my sons and daughters. Lavish your affection upon them; teach them before all things to love and fear God; never cease instructing them. When you see any one of them exalted to the height of an earthly dignity, then, as at once his father and his master in the truest sense, go to him, warn him lest through means of a passing honor he become puffed up with pride, or offend God by avarice, or through prosperity in this world neglect the blessedness of the life which is eternal. These are the things," said she, "which I ask you — as in the sight of God, who now is present along with us both — to promise me that you will carefully perform." At these words I once more burst into tears, and promised her that I would carefully perform her wishes; for I did not dare to oppose one whom I heard thus unhesitatingly predict what was to come to pass. And the truth of her prediction is verified by present facts, since I survive her death, and I see her offspring elevated to dignity and honor. Thus, having ended the conference, and being about to return home, I bade the queen my last farewell; for after that day I never saw her face in the flesh.

36. Shortly afterwards she was attacked by an infirmity of unusual severity, and was purified by the fire of a tedious sickness before the day on which God called her to himself. I will describe her death as I heard it narrated by a priest of hers, whom she loved more intimately than the others on account of his simplicity, his innocence, and his purity. After the queen's death he

made an oblation in perpetual service for her soul, and having put on the monk's habit offered himself up as a sacrifice for her at the tomb of the uncorrupt body of the most holy father Cuthbert [at the shrine of St. Cuthbert at Durham]. He was continually beside the queen during the last days of her life, and with his prayers recommended her soul to Christ when it was leaving the body. He gave me more than once a connected narrative of her decease as he saw it, for I frequently asked him to do so; and in doing this he was moved to tears.

37. "For a little more than half a year," said he, "she was never able to ride on horseback, and seldom to rise from her bed. On the fourth day preceding her death, while the king was absent on an expedition [the invasion of Northumbria], and at so great a distance that it was impossible for any messenger, however swift, to bring her tidings of what was happening to him, she became sadder than usual. Then she said to me, for I was seated near her, 'Perhaps on this very day such a heavy calamity may befall the realm of Scotland as has not been for many ages past.' When I heard these words I paid no great attention to them, but a few days afterwards a messenger arrived who told us that the king was slain on the very day [12 November, 1093] on which the queen had spoken the words narrated. As if foreseeing the future, she had been most urgent with him not to go with the army, but it came to pass – how, I know not – that he failed to follow her advice.

38. "On the approach of the fourth day after the king's death, her weakness having somewhat abated, the queen went into her oratory to hear Mass; and there she took care to provide herself beforehand for her departure, which was now so near, with the holy viaticum of the body and blood of our Lord. After partaking of this health-giving food she returned to her bed, her former pains having assailed her with redoubled severity. The disease gained ground, and death was imminent. Her face was already covered with a deadly pallor, when she directed that I, and the other ministers of the sacred altar along with me, should stand near her and commend her soul to Christ by our Psalms. Moreover, she asked that a cross, called the Black Cross, which she always held in the greatest veneration, should be brought to her. There was some delay in opening the chest in which it was kept, during which the queen, sighing deeply, exclaimed, 'O unhappy that we are! O guilty that we are! Shall we not be permitted once more to look upon the Holy Cross!' When at last it was got out of the chest and brought to her, she received it with reverence, and did her best to embrace it and kiss it, and several times she signed herself with it. Although every part of her body was now growing cold, still as long as the warmth of life throbbed at her heart she continued steadfast in prayer. She repeated the whole of the fiftieth Psalm, and placing

the cross before her eyes, she held it there with both her hands.

39. "It was at this point that her son who now, after his father, holds the reins of government in this realm, having returned from the army entered the queen's bedroom. Conceive his distress at such a moment! Imagine to yourself how his heart was racked! He stood there in a dilemma; everything was against him, and he did not know which way to turn. He had come to announce to his mother that his father and brother were both slain [Margaret's eldest son Edward had died in the same battle as his father], and he found that mother, most dearly beloved by him, at the point of death. He knew not whom first to lament. Yet the loss of his dearest mother, when he saw her lying nearly dead before his eyes, stung him to the heart with the keenest pang. Besides all this, the condition of the realm caused him the deepest anxiety, for he was fully aware that the death of his father would be followed by an insurrection. Sadness and trouble beset him on every side.

40. "The queen, who seemed to the bystanders to be rapt in an agony, suddenly rallied and spoke to her son. She asked him about his father and his brother. He was unwilling to tell the truth, and fearing that if she heard of their death she herself would immediately die, he replied that they were well. But, with a deep sigh she exclaimed, 'I know it, my boy, I know it. By this holy cross, by the bond of our blood, I adjure you to tell me the truth.' Thus pressed, he told her exactly all that had happened. What could she do, think you? To murmur against God was for such a one impossible. At the same moment she had lost her husband and her son, and disease was bringing her to a cruel death, yet in all these things she sinned not with her lips, nor spoke foolishly against God. Raising her eyes and her hands towards heaven, she glorified God, saying, 'All praise be to you, Almighty God, who has been pleased that I should endure such deep sorrow at my departing, and I trust that by means of this suffering it is your pleasure that I should be cleansed from some of the stains of my sins.'

41. "Feeling now that death was close at hand, she at once began the prayer which is usually uttered by the priest before he receives the body and blood of our Lord, saying, 'Lord Jesus Christ, who according to the will of the Father, through the co-operation of the Holy Ghost, have by your death given life to the world, deliver me.' As she was saying the words, 'Deliver me,' her soul was freed from the chains of the body, and departed to Christ, the Author of true liberty; to Christ whom she had always loved, and by whom she shared in the happiness of the saints, as she had followed the example of their virtues. Her departure was so calm, so tranquil, that we may conclude her soul passed at once to the land of eternal rest and peace. It was remarkable that her face, which, when she was dying had exhibited the usual pallor

of death, became afterwards suffused with fair and warm hues, so that it seemed as if she were not dead but sleeping. Her corpse was shrouded as became a queen, and was borne by us to the Church of the Holy Trinity [Dunfermline Abbey], which she had built. There, as she herself had directed, we committed it to the grave opposite the altar and the venerable sign of the Holy Cross which she had erected. And thus her body at length rests in that place in which, when alive, she used to humble herself with vigils, prayers, and tears."

CHAPTER FIVE

PILGRIMAGE

The importance of pilgrimage as an institution that grew out of the cult of the saints can hardly be overestimated for its influence on medieval trade, communications, art, architecture, and spirituality. Pilgrimages were undertaken for a number of legitimate reasons: to receive a healing miracle at the shrine of the saint was probably the most common, given the prevalence of disease and the inadequacy of medical knowledge to effect cures, but they were also undertaken voluntarily in order to visit the holy places referred to in the Bible, or from a desire to renounce the world and adopt a life of asceticism, or as an act of expiation for sin, either one's own or another's (inheritors of beneficiaries were sometimes enjoined to go on pilgrimage on behalf of the deceased). Compulsory pilgrimages might also be imposed on criminals, especially members of the clergy or nobility who were found guilty of serious crimes. But there is no doubt that many people went on pilgrimage for less legitimate purposes. Some went because they had fallen out with their parish priests and wanted entry into a different but still legitimate spiritual jurisdiction; and there must have been many who, like the fifteenth-century writer quoted by Jonathan Sumption, went for no better reason than "curiosity to see new places and experience new things, impatience of the servant with his master, of children with their parents, or wives with their husbands." Pilgrim accounts are among the earliest travel writings that we have, appealing strongly to a sense of curiosity and an interest in the exotic, and often including the lives of saints in either abbreviated or full-length versions. These accounts range from simple logs and practical travel guides to literature of the highest imaginative order. The largest group extant (including accounts of the Crusades, a kind of armed pilgrimage) concerns journeys to the Holy Land, and on medieval maps Jerusalem was situated at the center of the known world.

[Fig. 29] In this panel from a thirteenth-century French altarpiece, the two disciples who encountered Christ on the way to Emmaus after his crucifixion (*Luke* 24:13-31) are shown wearing typical late medieval pilgrim dress: a broad-brimmed hat and simple robe, with a long staff and 'scrip' or wallet (Lacroix, *Military and Religious Life in the Middle Ages*, p. 374).

22. ST. AUGUSTINE ON THE RITES AT THE MARTYRS' TOMBS

From very early times, Christians visited the graves of the martyrs on the anniversaries of their deaths and observed certain rites which, because they were to some degree spontaneous and unregulated, gave rise to misunderstanding among both converts and pagans. In 'The City of God,' written after the sack of Rome by the Goths in 410, Augustine gives evidence of the developing cult of the saints and responds to some of its difficulties. In Book 8 he defends Christian rituals at the burial sites of the saints by differentiating between the pagan worship of the gods in their temples and the Christian practices at the tombs of the martyrs.

Source: trans. Gerald G. Walsh and Grace Monahan, *Saint Augustine: The City of God Books 8-16* (New York: Fathers of the Church, Inc., 1952), 8, 27, pp. 74-76; repr. with permission.

27. . . . we do not construct shrines, consecrate priests and render rites and sacrifices for these martyrs. The simple reason is that it is not they but God who is our God. It is true that we honor their shrines because they were holy men of God who fought for truth, even unto death, so that true religion might be made known and falsehoods and fictions be overcome. Others before them who knew the truth were too afraid to express their convictions.

Certainly, no Christian ever heard a priest, standing before an altar built for the honor and service of God over the holy body of a martyr, say in his prayers: 'I offer this sacrifice to thee, Peter, or Paul, or Cyprian.' No! Before the monuments of these martyrs, the sacrifice is offered to God alone, who made them first men and then martyrs and finally associated them with his holy angels in heavenly honor. In celebrating this sacrifice we thank this true God for their victories and, while renewing our memory of them and calling on God to help us, we encourage ourselves to imitate them in seeking like crowns and palms. Thus, any signs of veneration paid by pious people at the tombs of martyrs are mere tributes to their memory, not sacred ceremonies nor sacrifices offered to the dead, as to gods. This is true, even of the custom of bringing food to these places – something, by the way, which is not done by more enlightened Christians and in most countries is entirely unknown. However, those who do it bring their food to the tombs and pray that it be sanctified by the merits of the martyrs in the name of the Lord of martyrs. Afterwards, they carry it away, either to eat it themselves or to distribute it to the needy. Anyone who knows that there is only one sacrifice offered by Christians, here or elsewhere, knows that this custom is not a sacrifice to the martyrs.

We revere our martyrs, therefore, with neither divine homage nor the human vices which the pagans offer to their gods. We neither offer them sacrifices nor do we convert their sins into sacred rites. Consider, for example, Isis, the wife of Osiris, the Egyptian goddess and her ancestors, all of whom were kings according to tradition. (While offering a sacrifice to her forebears, she discovered a field of barley and carried some of the ears to the king, her husband, and to his councilor, Mercury, and so she has come to be identified with Ceres.) Now, anyone who wants to find out how many and monstrous were their wickednesses, as reported by poets and the mystic writings of the Egyptians, can get an idea from the letter which Alexander wrote to his mother, Olympias, describing the facts as revealed to him by the priest Leo. Let anyone who likes it and can stand it read it, but then let him pause and reflect in honor of what kind of man, guilty of what monstrous sins, sacred rites were offered to the dead as to gods. It is unthinkable that the pagans, even though they hold such men to be divine, should be rash enough to compare them in any way with our holy martyrs whom we do not consider gods.

If, then, we do not ordain priests for the purpose of offering sacrifices to our martyrs, for that would be incongruous, improper, and unlawful, since worship is due to God alone, still less do we regale our martyrs with their crimes or with disgraceful plays as the pagans do when they commemorate the sins of their gods – either real sins committed by their deities when they were men or, if their gods were never human, fabricated for the delight of wicked demons. The god of Socrates, if he had one, could never have belonged to this class of evil spirits, unless, perhaps, some magicians, desiring to excel in this kind of art, may have managed to impose such a deity on a man who was an utter stranger to and innocent of this art of making gods. What more need I say? Can anyone, however slight his intelligence, imagine that such demons are to be worshiped in order that we may attain to an eternal felicity after death? . . .

23. PILGRIMAGE AND MIRACLES IN NORTH AFRICA

In the concluding book of 'The City of God,' as part of his argument that miracles continue to take place in the world and are evidence of God's ongoing concern for his people, Augustine also gives us a picture of some of the earliest kinds of pilgrimage. While some, like St. Jerome and his disciple, Paula, undertook long pilgrimages to the Egyptian desert and to the Holy Land, Augustine shows us that many others made journeys to local shrines which contained relics of the martyrs, usually just a few miles distant from their homes. These pilgrimages took place particularly on the saint's feast day when miracles of healing and exorcising demons were eagerly anticipated by the crowd of onlookers. Augustine describes the miracles that took place at shrines dedicated to St. Stephen, deacon of the church and protomartyr, whose death by stoning at the hands of an angry mob, c.35, is described in Acts 6-7. Stephen's tomb was discovered in 415 and his remains were translated to Constantinople and then to Rome, but some of his relics found their way to shrines in North Africa.

Source: trans. Gerald G. Walsh and Daniel J. Honan, *Saint Augustine: The City of God Books 17-22* (New York: Fathers of the Church, Inc., 1954), 22, 8, 9, pp. 440-451; repr. with permission.

8, 1. . . . There is an estate in the country less than thirty miles from Hippo Regius, called Victoriana. The shrine there is dedicated to the martyrs of Milan, Protasius and Gervasius. To this shrine there was brought a youth who had become possessed by a devil, one summer's day at noon, when he was cooling his horse in the flowing waters of a river. This demoniac was lying near the altar of the shrine as though he were as dead as a corpse, when the lady of the villa came to vespers and evening prayers, as was her wont, along with her maids and some nuns. As soon as they began to sing, the demoniac, as though struck by the sound, came to and, trembling all over, took hold of the altar. Unable or not daring to move, there he remained, as though he had been tied or fastened to the altar. The demon, crying out at the top of his voice, began to beg for mercy, and to confess where and when he had taken possession of the young man. Finally, the demon declared that he would depart. He did so, but not before threatening to work havoc with certain parts of the young man's body. These parts the demon named. There upon, an eye was found torn from its socket, resting on the cheek and hanging by a tiny vein as by a root. The pupil, which was black, turned white.

Those who had witnessed all this, and others who had been attracted by the screaming, prostrated themselves in prayer. They were overjoyed by the youth's return to sanity, but grieved by the dislocation of the eye. Some insisted that a doctor be called, but the youth's brother-in-law, who had brought him to the shrine, said simply: 'God who put this demon to flight is able, through the prayers of his saints, to restore the sight of this eye.' There-upon, as best he could, he pushed the eye back into its socket, bandaged it with his handkerchief, and said that the bandage must not be removed for at least a week. A week later, the bandage was removed. The eye was found to be in perfect condition. Many other miracles occurred at that shrine, but I need not mention them here.

2. I know of another demoniac, a young girl of Hippo, who was freed from possession as soon as she anointed herself with some oil into which the tears of a priest who was praying for her had fallen. I also know of a bishop who prayed for a demoniac, a young man whom he had never seen, but who was at once delivered from the devil.

3. There is a good story of the poor old man, Florentius, who lived here in Hippo. He was a man of prayer who eked out a living by repairing old clothes, but when he lost his own cloak he had no money to buy another. So, he betook himself to the Shrine of the Twenty Martyrs, the most famous shrine in these parts, and there, in a loud voice, he prayed for a new cloak. Of course, some of the young people who were there could not help laughing; and, even when the old man left, they went after him, teasing him for asking the martyrs to give him fifty *folles* [pennies] to buy a cloak. The old man said nothing. He just went along the beach. What should he see there but an immense fish, tossed up by the waves and still squirming. The good-natured young fellows helped the old man to catch it, and he went right off to Cato-sus, a good Christian and the cook at the Restaurant Conditaria, told him what happened, and sold him the fish for 300 *folles*. Florentius had in mind to buy enough wool to have his wife make him a complete outfit. In the mean time, however, the cook, while cutting up the fish, found in its gullet a gold ring. Partly out of pity and partly out of religious scruples, he gave the ring to the old man, saying: 'Look, this is the way the Twenty Martyrs have put a suit on your back!'

4. At Aquae Tibilitanae, there was once a procession in which Bishop Praejectus was carrying a relic of the glorious martyr, St. Stephen, and, while an immense crowd was milling around him, a blind woman begged to be led to the bishop. She handed him the flowers she had in her hand. He took them and applied them to her eyes. Immediately she was able to see. Full of joy, she took her place in the procession, needing no one to lead her, and the people followed in amazement behind her.

5. There is a relic of the same martyr reserved in the town ship of Synita, not far from the city of Hippo. Once it was being carried by Bishop Lucillus of Synita in a procession, with the line of people stretching out before him and behind him. The bishop was suffering – as he had been for a long time –

from a fistula, and had already arranged for an operation to be performed by a doctor who was a great friend of his. Suddenly, during the procession of the relic, the fistula dried up and not a trace of it was ever after found on his body.

6. Here is another miracle wrought by a relic of the same saint. Eucharius, a Spanish priest stationed in Calama, had long been suffering from stone. Bishop Possidius applied the relic and the priest was cured. Sometime later, however, he fell a victim to another sickness and was so near death that they had already bound his hands. Then his tunic was taken to touch the relic of the saint. It was brought back and placed over the apparently dead body. The priest was at once restored to life.

7. In the same town of Calama, there lived a man of the highest social distinction, named Martial. He was elderly, a pagan, and strongly opposed to Christianity, although his daughter was a Catholic and his son-in-law was a recent convert. Martial fell sick. The two young people begged him, with tears in their eyes, to turn Christian. He refused emphatically and indignantly dismissed them from his presence. The son-in-law decided to go to the shrine of St. Stephen, and there he prayed with his whole soul that God might give Martial the grace not to put off his conversion to Christ. He prayed and prayed, with groans and tears and the deepest feelings of ardent piety. As he left, he took a few flowers from the altar and, at night when Martial was asleep, put the flowers on his pillow. Sure enough, before dawn the next day, Martial called out for someone to run for the bishop, who, as it happened, was visiting me in Hippo. Martial then asked for the priests. They arrived. He said: 'I believe.' To the joy and astonishment of all, he was baptized. He continued to live for some time, but never did he stop from repeating the words: 'Christ, receive my spirit,' although he had never heard that these were the last words of the blessed Stephen as he was being stoned to death. These were the last words of Martial, too, for, before long, he died.

8. It was also in Calama that three victims of the gout were healed through the intercession of the same martyr, Stephen. Two were natives and another had come there on pilgrimage. The natives were at once cured, but the pilgrim heard a voice telling him what means he should take when the pain was acute. He followed the instruction and he, too, was at once cured.

9. There is another shrine of St. Stephen in a village called Audurus. Once, when a child was playing in the square before the church, a cart drawn by oxen left the road and one of the wheels ran over the child. While he was breathing his last, his mother snatched him up and placed him on the altar of the relic. The child not only returned to consciousness, but showed no sign of the crushing he had suffered.

10. Near Audurus, there is an estate called Villa Caspaliana. There, a consecrated virgin fell sick and was on the brink of death. Her parents took her habit to touch the relic, but, before they could return, she died. However, the moment the corpse was clothed with the habit, the breath of life returned and the nun was restored to health.

11. There was a Syrian named Bassus living in Hippo. He had a sick daughter in danger of death. So he took her robe to touch the relic of St. Stephen. There at the shrine he prayed for the health of his daughter. He was still praying when some of his servants came running from his home to tell him that the girl was dead. However, some of his friends who were also praying there received the news first, and forbade the servants to tell the father for fear he might break down in public. However, when he reached home, he found the house filled with wailing. He threw the girl's dress on the corpse. Her life was restored.

12. It was in Hippo, too, that the son of a neighbor of mine, Irenaeus, a tax collector, died. The corpse was laid out; the funeral was arranged; everyone was grieving and sorrowing. One of the friends who had come to console the family suggested that the body be anointed with oil from the shrine of St. Stephen. This was no sooner done than the boy came back to life.

Here I am in a fix. I promised to hurry on with the writing of this work. How can I delay to tell all the miracles I know? On the other hand, I know that many of my fellow Catholics, when they come to read what I have written, will complain that I have left out any number of miracles which they hap pen to know as well as I do. All I can do is to ask them now to forgive me, and to remember how long a task it would be to tell them and how impossible it would be to do both that and also my duty of bringing this work to an end. Actually, if I kept merely to miracles of healing and omitted all others, and if I told only those wrought by this one martyr, the glorious St. Stephen, and if I limited myself to those that happened here at Hippo and Calama, I should have to fill several volumes and, even then, I could do no more than tell those cases that have been officially recorded and attested for public reading in our churches. This recording and attesting, in fact, is what I took care to have done, once I realized how many miracles were occurring in our own day and which were so like the miracles of old and also how wrong it would be to allow the memory of these marvels of divine power to perish from among our people. It is only two years ago that the keeping of records was begun here in Hippo, and already, at this writing, we have nearly seventy attested miracles. I know with certain knowledge of many others which have not, so far, been officially recorded. And, of course, at Calama, where the recording began much earlier and where miracles are more frequent, the number of attested cases is incomparably greater. So, too, at Uzalum, a town near the city of Utica, there have been, to my knowledge, many notable miracles wrought through this same martyr. Thanks to Bishop Evodius, there was a shrine there dedicated to St. Stephen long before ours was established. But the custom of taking formal depositions from witnesses was not there in vogue, nor is it now – unless, perhaps, it has been very recently introduced. Not long ago when I was there, a lady of great social distinction, Petronia by name, was miraculously cured of a serious and long standing sickness which had baffled the doctors. I urged her, with Bishop Evodius concurring, to have a written deposition drawn up which could be read in church to the people, and she obediently accepted the suggestion.

13. One detail of this deposition I must mention here, in spite of the urgency to return to the main theme of this work. It is this. Petronia states that she had been persuaded by a certain Jew to wear, as a remedy for her complaint, under her clothes and next to her skin, a belt made of braided hair on which was to be strung a ring. Underneath the jewel of this ring, she was to place a stone, taken from the kidney of an ox. Thus begirdled, she set out on pilgrimage from Carthage to the shrine of the martyr. She rested for a while at her villa on the river Bagrada, but, on rising one morning to resume her journey, what was her astonishment to find the ring lying on the floor at her feet. She at once felt for the braided belt she was wearing and there it was tied as firmly as ever. Then she thought that the ring must have snapped and fallen off, but it was perfectly solid as before. This she took as a miraculous token that she was to be cured at the shrine. So, she tore off the belt and threw it, along with the ring, into the river.

Perhaps it may be too much to expect that people will believe this who refuse to believe that the Lord Jesus was born without any lesion in the maidenhead of his mother and that he passed through closed doors into the presence of his disciples. But, at least, such people should investigate facts and, if they find them true, should accept them. The lady in question is of the highest distinction both by birth and by marriage and she lives in Carthage. In regard to a person so outstanding, living in a city so important, anyone who really wants to find out the facts can do so. And as for the martyr by whose intercession the lady was restored to health, certainly he believed in the Son of the Virgin Mother, and believed in him who passed through closed doors to reach his disciples, and believed in him who ascended into heaven with the flesh in which he rose from the dead – and this is the miracle on account of which I have been relating all these attesting miracles. Moreover, the reason why so many miracles are wrought through this blessed martyr is that he laid down his life for this faith.

14. It is a simple fact, then, that there is no lack of miracles even in our day. And the God who works the miracles we read of in the Scripture uses any means and manner he chooses. The only trouble is that these modern miracles are not so well known as the earlier ones, nor are they sufficiently pounded into people's memory by constant reading, so that they may stick, as it were, like gravel in cement. Even where pains are taken, as is now the case in Hippo, to have the written depositions of the beneficiaries of these graces read to the people, only those in church hear the stories, and that only once, and the many who are not present hear nothing, and those who have listened forget in a day or so, and you hardly ever hear of a person who has heard a deposition telling it to someone else who was not in church for the reading.

15. However, this is not the case with one miracle that happened here in Hippo. It was no more remarkable than others I have mentioned, but it was so clear and obvious to everyone that no one who lives here could have failed to see it or, at least, to hear about it, and certainly no one could ever forget it. It involved seven brothers and three sisters belonging to a noble family of Caesarea in Cappodocia. When their father died, they did some injustice to their widowed mother. This was so bitterly resented that she put a curse on them. Whereupon, God so punished the children that all of them were afflicted by a dreadful convulsion of their whole bodies. The humiliation in the eyes of their neighbors became unbearable, and all of them scattered in different directions and began to wander throughout the Roman world. Of these ten, two, Paul and Palladia, turned up at Hippo, after their plight had made them notorious in ever so many other places. They arrived here about two weeks before Easter, and day after day they came to church to pray before the shrine of the glorious martyr, St. Stephen. They prayed that God would forgive their sins and give them back their health. Both in church and wherever they went throughout the city they were a spectacle for all to see. Some of our people had seen them in other cities and knew the cause of the convulsions and told their friends the story.

Well, Holy Week passed; Easter Sunday dawned. The basilica was crowded. There at the shrine, grasping the bars of the latticework around the reliquary, stood the young man, praying. Of a sudden, he fell prostrate and lay there as if in a trance. However, the convulsions, that ordinarily continued even in his sleep, stopped. The crowd around him were filled with awe and fear. Many wept. Some wanted to lift him to his feet, but others prevented this, thinking it better to wait for him to die. Just as suddenly, he arose. The trembling had stopped. He was cured. There he stood, perfectly normal, looking at the crowd who kept gazing at him. Then everyone burst into a prayer of thankfulness to God. The whole church soon rang with the clamor of rejoicing.

One after another, people rushed to where I was sitting, ready to begin the processional entrance into the basilica. Each of them told me again the news I had just been told. Then, as I was rejoicing and thanking God, the young man himself, followed by the rest of the crowd, broke in upon me. He knelt down before me, then rose to receive the kiss of peace.

16. In the crowded church, cries of joy rose up everywhere: 'Thanks be to God.' 'Praise be to God.' No tongue was silent. When I held up my hand in salutation, the cries broke out afresh, louder than ever. Only when silence was finally restored could the Scriptural selections appointed for Easter be read. When the time came for the sermon, I said very little, in spite of the joyousness of what had happened. I wanted to allow the people to meditate in their own minds on the divine eloquence of the divine deed rather than to listen to any mere words of mine. The man stayed for dinner, and told me the whole tragic story both of his mother and of his brothers and sisters. Next day, after my sermon, I announced that, on the following day, the written record of the miracle would be read in public. And so, on the third day after Easter, I had the brother and sister stand on the steps of the choir, where I was accustomed to speak, and there listen to a reading of the deposition. Every eye of every man and woman in the audience was fixed on the pair – the sister still shaken by convulsions and the brother perfectly calm. Thus, those who had not seen the brother before the cure could gauge the measure of God's mercy by looking at his sister. They saw in him so much to thank God for, and in her so much that called for prayer. When the recital was finished, I asked the brother and sister to remove themselves from the gaze of the congregation. Then I began to speak at length of the whole affair. I was still speaking when, all of a sudden, from the shrine of the martyr, new cries of rejoicing could be heard. The people who were listening to me first turned in that direction, and then began rushing to the shrine. What the girl had done when she left the choir was, in fact, to go straight to the shrine to pray to the holy martyr. And as soon as she touched the metal grating she collapsed, just as her brother had done, into a kind of trance. From this she rose up cured.

17. I was just asking what had happened to cause all this hubbub and happiness when in came the people bringing the recovered girl back from the shrine to the basilica. Such a clamor of wonderment then went up and such sobbing for joy that I thought it would never end. She was led to the very spot where just before she had stood full of convulsions. They hailed her now for being like her brother, just as they had grieved for her when she was so unlike him. They had hardly had time to utter a prayer for her, and here she was, with the prayer of their hearts already answered. The exultation contin-

ued, and the wordless praise to God was shouted so loud that my ears could scarcely stand the din. But, of course, the main point was that, in the hearts of all this clamoring crowd, there burned that faith in Christ for which the martyr Stephen shed his blood.

9, 18. Now, the faith to which all these miracles bear witness is the faith that holds that Christ rose bodily from the dead and ascended with his flesh into heaven, because, of course, the martyrs were witnesses. That, in fact, is what the word 'martyr' means. The martyrs were witnesses to this faith. It was because they bore witness to this faith that they found the world hostile and cruel. Yet, they overcame the world, not by defending themselves, but by preferring to die for Christ. Those whose intercession has the power from the Lord to work these miracles were killed on account of his name and died for faith in him. First came the miracle of their fortitude in dying for this faith, and then came, as a consequence, the power revealed in these miracles.

19. This question, then, calls for an answer: If the resurrection of the flesh into eternal life did not occur in the case of Christ and is not to occur hereafter in our case, in accordance with the promises made by Christ and those in the Old Testament which likewise foretold the coming of Christ, then how explain these great wonders wrought by dead martyrs? For, they were put to death precisely for that faith which proclaims this resurrection. It makes no difference whether we say that it is God himself who works these miracles in the marvelous way that the Eternal operates in the temporal order, or whether we say that God works these miracles through his servants. And, in regard to what he does through his servants, it is all one whether he does these things through the spirits of martyrs, as though they were still living in their bodies, or whether he uses angels and effects his purposes by his orders, which are given invisibly, inaudibly, immutably. In that case, miracles which we think are done by martyrs are the result, rather, of their prayers and intercession, and not of their actions. Or God may have varying means to his different ends and these means may be altogether incomprehensible to the minds of men. But the main point is that all miracles are witnesses to that faith which proclaims the supreme miracle of the resurrection of the flesh into life everlasting.

24. SÆWULF MAKES A PILGRIMAGE TO THE HOLY LAND

'The Pilgrimage of Sæwulf' (1102-3) is the only account we have by an Englishman (or so he is presumed to be, from his name) before the fifteenth century. We know nothing for certain about him: perhaps he was a sailor or an ecclesiastic, or he may have been the same English merchant mentioned by William of Malmesbury who entered the abbey of Malmesbury in old age. If so, his experiences might suggest a comparison to Godric of Finchale's at a slightly later date [see 36 below]. Pilgrimage accounts tend to be impersonal catalogues of places to visit and detailed descriptions of what the pilgrim can expect to find, rather like the most factual modern tourist guides. But Sæwulf does not just give us a logbook, for he reports things he has heard about as well as seen, is conversational in style, and is interested in both classical and biblical antiquity. His description breaks off as he approaches Constantinople on the way home, like most accounts that omit the return journey because reaching the goal of the saint's shrine was usually thought of as the end of the pilgrimage. From his account it is clear that Jerusalem pilgrims retraced not only the places associated with the life and passion of Christ, but were also eager to see those sites connected to Old Testament patriarchs and well-known saints: Sæwulf, for instance, notes on a chapel wall the picture of the Virgin that so moved Mary of Egypt 'when with her heart all full of compunction she earnestly begged the aid of the same Mother of God, in whose image the picture was painted, speaking to her by the Holy Ghost, as is read in her life' (see 11 above).

Source: trans. by Lord Bishop of Clifton, *Sæwulf* (London: The Library of the Palestine Pilgrims Text Society, 1887-1897), Vol. 4, pp. 1-11, abridged.

1. I, Sæwulf, unworthy sinner as I am, was on my way to Jerusalem for the purpose of praying at our Lord's Sepulcher. And, although I went on the direct route with others who were going thither, yet either through being oppressed with the burden of my sins, or through the poorness of the ship, I was not able to cross over the open sea; [so] I determined to note down merely the names of the islands by which I directed my course.

Some embark at Bari, some at Barletta, some at Zaponeta, or Trani, and some even at Otranto, at the most southerly port of Apulia [all located in south-eastern Italy]. We, however, went on board ship at Monopolis, a day's journey from Bari, on Sunday the 13th July, the feast of St. Mildred Virgin. It was an unlucky time, as it afterwards proved for us, and if the mercy of God had not protected us, we should have all been drowned. For the very same day, when we were on the sea, a long way from the harbor, we suffered shipwreck from the violence of the waves. But by the favor of God we returned back safe to shore.

2. We then went on to Brindisi, and there again, on an unlucky day, we went aboard the same ship, but somewhat repaired, and so landed on an island of Greece, at the city which together with the island is called Corfu, on the vigil of St. James the Apostle [24 July]. From thence we came to the island which is called Cephalonia, driven by a great storm, on the first of August. There Robert Guiscard died [in 1085 while preparing to attack Constantinople], and there also our companions died, which caused us great sorrow. We afterwards sailed thence, and steered for Polipolis, and then we came to the beautiful island of Patras, and entered its city for the sake of praying to blessed Andrew the apostle, who suffered and was buried there, but was afterwards translated to Constantinople. From Patras we came on the vigil of St. Laurence [9 August] to Corinth. There it was that blessed Paul the apostle preached the word of God, and wrote an Epistle to some [of his converts]. There we suffered many hardships. We crossed from thence to the Port of Livadostro, and thus, some on foot and some on asses, we went two days' journey to Thebes, which city is commonly called Stinae. The following day we reached Nigrepont, on the vigil of St. Bartholomew the apostle. There we hired another ship. Athens, where Paul the apostle preached, is distant two days' journey from the neighborhood of Corinth. There blessed Dionysius was born and educated, and afterwards converted to the Lord by blessed Paul. There is a church of the blessed Virgin Mary, in which there is oil in a lamp which is always burning yet never runs short. We afterwards came to the island of Petali, and then to Andros, where they make precious thread and samite [cloth made of gold and silver threads], and cloths embroidered with silk. From thence we came to Tinos, next to Syra, and then to Myconos, and so to Naxos; beside which is the memorable island of Crete. From thence we passed by Carea, Omargon, Samos, Scyo, and Metelina. Afterwards we arrived at Patmos, where Blessed John the apostle and evangelist was banished by Domitian, and where he wrote the Apocalypse. Ephesus is on one side, near to Smyrna, a day's journey off, where the same [evangelist] afterwards went alive into his sepulcher. The apostle Paul also wrote an Epistle to the Ephesians. We then came to the islands of Leros and Calimno, and then to Anshos, where was born Galienus, the most highly esteemed physician among the Greeks. Thence we crossed over by the harbor of the ruined city of Lydo, where Titus the disciple of St. Paul the Apostle preached. From this we came to Asum, which is called Argentea.

3. We next reached Rhodes, where is said to have been one of the seven wonders of the world – that is the Colossus, an idol a hundred and twenty-five feet in height, which the Persians destroyed, together with almost the whole Roman province, when they were on their way to Spain [in fact the Colossus had already fallen, damaged by an earthquake in about BC 225; it

was broken up and the bronze sold for scrap by the Arabs in the seventh century]. It was to these Colossians that the blessed apostle Paul wrote an epistle [actually, Paul wrote to the Colossians in Asia Minor]. A day's journey from thence brought us to Patara, the city where blessed Nicholas the Archbishop was born [St. Nicholas], and where we were driven in by a great storm late in the evening. The next morning we set sail, and arrived at a city all in ruins, which is called St. Mary Mogronissi, which means Long Island, and here the Christians – who have been driven out of Alexandria by the Turks – used to live, as appears by the churches and other buildings. Thence we came to the city of Myra, where St. Nicholas ruled as the head of the archiepiscopate. Myra is the port of the Adriatic Sea, as Constantinople is the port of the Aegean Sea. Having worshiped at the holy tomb in honor of the saint [his remains in fact had been translated to Bari in 1087, so the tomb was empty when Sæwulf visited it], we came with a favorable wind to the island which is called Xindacopo, which in Latin means the 'sixty oars' on account of the force of the sea. Near it is the port which, with the country around it, is called Finica. From that place we came after three days across the broadest part of the Adriatic Sea to the city of Paphos, a portion of the island of Cyprus. It was here that, after our Lord's Ascension, the apostles all assembled, and held a council concerning things that were to be settled, and thence sent St. Barnabas the apostle to preach; and after his death, St. Peter came thither from Joppa, and there scattered the seed of the word of God, before he mounted the episcopal chair of Antioch. From the island of Cyprus we shifted our course for seven days, and were tossed about by storms at sea before we were able to reach the harbor, insomuch that, one night, being violently driven by a contrary wind, we were being carried back to Cyprus; but by the mercy of God – who is near at hand to all who call upon him in truth – we were stirred with much contrition, and returned again to our desired course. But for seven nights we were overwhelmed with such storm and peril that we were almost all destitute of hope. However, in the morning when the sun arose, there appeared also before our eyes the coast of the port of Joppa; and, as the exceeding trouble of our danger had cast us down in desolation, so the unexpected and unhoped-for joy multiplied our gladness a hundredfold. Therefore, after the lapse of thirteen weeks – as on a Sunday we embarked at Monopolis, and had been always either on the waves of the sea, or on islands in huts and empty hovels, for the Greeks are not hospitable – so on a Sunday with great gladness and giving of thanks did we disembark at the port of Joppa.

4. Now I beseech you, all of you, my most beloved friends, stretch forth your hands on high, and clap them; sing joyfully to God with one voice with me in one cry of exultation, because in all my journey he who is mighty has

confirmed his mercy upon me. Blessed by his name from henceforth, even for ever! Incline your ears, dearest friends, and hear the mercy which the loving-kindness of God manifested towards me and mine, although I am the least of his servants. On the very same day that we anchored, someone said to me, God prompting him as I believe: 'Sir, go on shore today, lest perhaps tonight or early in the morning, a storm may come on and you may not be able to land.' When I heard this, I was at once seized with a desire to go ashore. I hired a boat and, with all my belongings, landed. While I was landing, the sea became troubled, the tossing increased, and a violent tempest arose, but by the gracious favor of God I arrived unharmed. What further took place? We went into the city to seek for lodging, wearied and overcome with our long toil; we took some refreshment, and rested. However, early in the morning, as we came out from church, we heard the noise of the sea, the cries of the people, and all were running together, and wondering at such things as they had never heard before. We ran, full of fear with the rest, and came to the shore. When we got there, we saw the storm running mountains high, and beheld the bodies of men and women without number drowned and miserably lying on the beach. We saw also ships dashed against each other and broken into small pieces. Who could listen to anything but the roaring of the sea and the crashing of the ships? It was even louder than the cries of the people and the shouting of all the crews. Our ship, however, being very large and strongly built, and several others laden with corn and other merchandise, and with pilgrims outward or homeward bound, still held by their anchors and cables, although they were sorely tossed about by the waves. Oh, what fear of evil did they fall into! What eye of those who beheld them was so hard and stony that it could refrain from tears? We had not been gazing long, when, by the violence of the waves or the currents, the anchors gave way, the cables were broken, and the ships were given up to the fierceness of the waves, all hope of escape being cut off. They were now lifted up on high, now drawn down to the depths, and quickly were thrown up out of the deep upon the sand or upon the rocks. There they were miserably dashed from side to side, and gradually torn to pieces by the tempest. The fierceness of the storm would not suffer them to return sound to the sea, and the steepness of the beach would not allow them to reach the shore in safety. But what boots it to tell how lamentably sailors and pilgrims, when all hope was gone, still clung, some to the ships, some to the masts, some to the spars, some to the cross-timbers? What more shall I say? Some, stupefied with terror, were drowned; some, as they were clinging, were decapitated by the timbers of their own ship. This may seem incredible to many, yet I saw it. Some, washed off from the decks of their ships, were carried out again to the deep.

Some, who knew how to swim, voluntarily committed themselves to the waves, and thus many of them perished. Very few, who had confidence in their own strength, arrived safe on shore. Thus, out of thirty very large ships . . . all laden with pilgrims or merchandise, scarcely seven remained unwrecked by the time I had left the shore. More than a thousand persons of either sex perished on that day. A greater misery on one day no eye ever saw. But from all these [dangers] our Lord delivered me by his grace. To him be honor and glory, world without end. Amen.

5. We went up from Joppa to the city of Jerusalem, a journey of two days, along a mountainous road, rocky, and very dangerous. For the Saracens, always laying snares for the Christians, lie hidden in the hollow places of the mountains, and the caves of the rocks, watching day and night, and always on the look out for those whom they can attack on account of the fewness of the party, or those who have lagged behind their party through weariness. At one moment they are seen all around everywhere, and all at once they disappear entirely. Anyone who makes that journey may see this. Oh, what a number of human bodies, both in the road and by the side of it, lie all torn by wild beasts! Some may perhaps wonder that the bodies of Christians should lie there unburied. But it is not to be wondered at all; for there is very little earth, and the rocks do not easily lend themselves to be dug into; and besides, if there was earth, who would be so foolish as to leave his party, and, as it were alone, dig a grave for his companion? If he did so, he would be making ready a grave for himself rather than for his companion. On that road not only the poor and the weak, but even the rich and the strong, are in danger. Many are cut off by the Saracens, but more by heat and thirst; many through scarcity of drink, but many more perish from drinking too much. We, however, with our whole party arrived unhurt at our longed-for destination. Blessed be the Lord, who has not cast out my prayer, nor turned away his mercy from me. Amen.

6. The entrance of the city of Jerusalem is at the west, under the tower of King David, by the gate that is called the Gate of David. The Church of the Holy Sepulcher, which is called the *martyrium*, is the first spot to be visited, not only because of the direction of the streets, but because it is more celebrated than all the other churches. And fittingly so, for all things which were foretold by the holy prophets all over the world concerning our Savior Jesus Christ were there all truly accomplished. The church itself, when our Lord's cross was found, was built by Maximus the Archbishop, by the aid of the Emperor Constantine and his mother Helena [she who, as one of the earliest pilgrims to the Holy Land, was credited with finding the true cross], royally and magnificently. In the middle of that church is our Lord's Sepulcher, sur-

rounded by a very strong wall, and covered over, lest, when it rains, the rain should fall upon the Holy Sepulcher; for the church above it lies open without a roof.

7. . . . In the atrium of the Church of our Lord's Sepulcher some most holy places are visited. First, the prison where our Lord Jesus Christ, after his betrayal, was confined, as the Assyrians bear witness. Next, a little higher, is seen the place where the Holy Cross was found, together with the other crosses; and where afterwards a great church was built in honor of Queen Helena, but was subsequently entirely destroyed by the pagans. Lower down, and not far from the prison, a marble column is seen, to which Jesus Christ our Lord was bound and beaten with most cruel scourges. Close by is the place where our Lord was stripped of his garments by the soldiers. Then there is the place where he was clothed with a purple robe by the soldiers, and crowned with the crown of thorns, and they parted his garments, casting lots. Afterwards you go up to Mount Calvary, where . . . the Son of God . . . was sacrificed to God the Father as the victim for the redemption of the world. The rock of the same mountain is a witness of our Lord's passion, being rent greatly close to the hole in which the cross of our Lord was fixed, because it could not bear without rending the slaying of its Creator . . .

25. THE PILGRIM'S GUIDE TO ST. JAMES OF COMPOSTELLA

The tradition that the body of the apostle St. James was returned to Spain (where he had preached the Gospel) after his execution in Palestine may have begun as early as the sixth century, but it was not until much later that Compostella achieved its fame. In the early ninth century a hermit claimed to have had a vision in which the tomb of the saint was revealed to him by a bright star shining above the hill where the city of Compostella ('field of the star') now stands. The local bishop, Theodomir, searched for the tomb on the strength of the hermit's vision, and found it in the place indicated by the star; a church was built above it and pilgrims began to arrive. Soon one of the most venerated sites in the Christian world, it was linked with the legendary names of Charlemagne and Roland and became the great bulwark of Christianity against the Mozarabic domination of Spain. In due course roads and bridges were improved and religious houses built to accommodate the throng of pilgrims, while trade of all kinds increased and other saints' shrines (such as those at Vézelay and Conques), fortunate enough to be situated on one of the major routes, also flourished. 'The Pilgrim's Guide,' from which the following excerpt is taken, is found in the famous 'Codex Callixtinus,' a twelfth-century compilation of materials that promoted pilgrimage to Compostella. Although the 'Guide' appears to have been written by more than one hand and at different dates, it is usually ascribed to Aimery Picaud, a French cleric from Poitou who may also have served as a papal chancellor. His account differs from Sæwulf's in being intended primarily as a guide for other pilgrims rather than a narration of his own travels, but the writer's personal concerns and prejudices make it lively and colorful. He is especially interested in the saints and shrines encountered on the way to Compostella, as demonstrated by his long lists of them and by his inclusion of a fully-fledged, though dubious, 'Life,' (omitted here), of St. Eutrope of Saintes.

Source: trans. James Hogarth, *The Pilgrim's Guide: A 12th-Century Guide for the Pilgrim to St. James of Compostella* (London: Confraternity of St. James, 1992), pp. 3–88; abridged and repr. with permission.

1. Of the Roads to St. James

There are four roads leading to St. James which join to form one road at Puente la Reina, in the territory of Spain. One runs by way of St. Giles [St-Gilles du Gard] and Montpellier and Toulouse and the Somport pass; another by St. Mary of Le Puy and St. Faith of Conques and St. Peter of Moissac; the third by St. Mary Magdalene of Vézelay and St. Leonard of Limousin [St-Léonard de Noblat] and the town of Perigueux; and the fourth by St. Martin of Tours and St. Hilary of Poitiers and St. John of Angély [St-Jean d'Angély] and St. Eutropius of Saintes and the town of Bordeaux.

[Fig. 30] St. James the Great, pictured in pilgrim's dress; on his hat is a badge consisting of a scallop shell, symbol of the saint that pilgrims who made the long journey to Compostella were entitled to wear (from the Vienna Missal, in Baring-Gould, *Lives of the Saints*, 8).

The roads which go by St. Faith, by St. Leonard and by St. Martin join at Ostabat and after crossing the pass of Cize [through the Pyrenees] meet the road over the Somport pass at Puente la Reina; and from there a single road leads to St. James.

[*Chapters 2 and 3 list the stages and places encountered on the road "so that pilgrims setting out for St. James may be able to estimate the expenses involved in their journey."*]

4. Of the World's Three Hospices

The Lord established in this world three columns most necessary for the support of the poor: the hospice in Jerusalem, the hospice of Mont-Joux [on the Great St. Bernard pass] and the hospice of Santa Cristina on the Somport pass. These hospices were sited in places where they were necessary: they are holy places, houses of God, places of refreshment for holy pilgrims, of rest for the needy, of comfort for the sick, of salvation for the dead, of help for the living. Those who built these most holy places will without doubt possess the kingdom of God.

5. Of the Names of those who repaired the Road to St. James

These are the names of those who, in the time of Diego [Gelmirez] archbishop of St. James, and Alfonso, emperor of Spain and Galicia, and Pope Callistus, repaired the road to St. James, from Rabanal to Puertomarin, for the love of God and his apostle, before the year 1120, in the reign of Alfonso [I] of Aragon and Louis [VI] the Fat, king of France: Andrew, Roger, Avitus, Fortus, Arnold, Stephen and Peter, who rebuilt the bridge over the Mino which had been demolished by Queen Urraca. May the souls of these men and those who worked with them rest in eternal peace!

6. Of the Good and the Bad Rivers on the Road to St. James

These are the rivers on the road to St. James from the pass of Cize and the Somport pass. From the Somport pass there flows down a river of pure water, the Aragon, which irrigates Spain. From the pass of Cize there flows a river of pure water which many call the Runa and which flows down towards Pamplona. At Puente la Reina there are both the Arga and the Runa. At a place called Lorca, to the east, there flows a stream known as the Salt River. Beware of drinking from it or of watering your horse in it, for this river brings death. On its banks, while we were going to St. James, we found two Navarrese sitting there sharpening their knives; for they are accustomed to flay pilgrims' horses which die after drinking the water. In answer to our question they lied, saying that the water was good and drinkable. Accordingly we watered our horses in the river, and at once two of them died and were forthwith skinned by the two men.

Through Estella flows the river Ega, the water of which is sweet, pure and excellent. At the village of Los Arcos is a stream which is death, and between Los Arcos and the first hospice beyond the village is another stream which is fatal to both horses and men who drink it. At the village of Torres del Rio, in Navarrese territory, is a river which also is fatal to horses and men, and there is another river that brings death at the village of Cuevas.

At Logrono is a large river called the Ebro, with pure water and an abundance of fish. All the rivers between Estella and Logrono have water which brings death to men and beasts who drink it, and the fish in these streams are likewise poisonous. Do not eat, in Spain or Galicia, the fish commonly known as *barbus* [barbel] or the one which the Poitevins call *alose* [shad] and the Italians *clipia,* or an eel or a tench: if you do you will assuredly die or fall sick. And anyone who eats any great quantity of these and does not fall sick must have a stronger constitution than other people or must have lived in the country for a long time; for all kinds of fish, beef and pork in Spain and Galicia make foreigners ill.

Those rivers which are sweet and good for drinking are the following: the Pisuerga, which flows at the Puente de Itero; the Carrion, at Carrion de los Condes; the Cea at Sahagun; the Elsa at Mansilla de las Mulas; the Porma, at the large bridge [the Puente de Villarente] between Mansilla and Leon, the Torio, which flows through Leon, below the Jewish quarter; the Bernesga, on the far side of Leon in the direction of Astorga; the Sil at Ponferrada, in a green valley; the Cua at Cacabelos; the Burbia at the bridge of Villafranca del Bierzo; the Valcarce, which flows down the valley of that name; the Mino at Puertomarin; and a river in wooded country two miles from the city of St. James, at a place called Lavacolla, in which French pilgrims traveling to St. James are accustomed, for love of the apostle, to take off their clothes and cleanse not only their private parts but the whole of their body. The river Sar, which flows between the Mount of Joy [Monte del Gozo] and the city of St. James, is held to be clean; so too is the Sarela, which flows on the other side of the town, to the west.

I have described these rivers so that pilgrims going to St. James may take care to avoid drinking bad water and may choose water that is good for them and for their horses.

[Fig. 31] St. James depicted as the 'Moor-slayer,' the defender of Christianity against the Moors in Spain (copy of a painting by Careno de Miranda in Jameson, *Sacred and Legendary Art*, 1, 217).

7. Of the Names of the Countries and the Characteristics of the Peoples on the Road to St. James

Going to St. James on the Toulouse road we come first, after crossing the Garonne, into Gascony, and then, going over the Somport pass, enter Aragon and then Navarre, which extends as far as the bridge over the Arga [Puente la Rienna] and beyond. If, however, we take the road over the pass of Cize we come, after Tours, into Poitou, a fertile and excellent region, full of all delights. The men of Poitou are strong and warlike, skilled in the use of bows and arrows and of lances in war, valiant in battle, swift runners, elegant in their attire, handsome of face, ready of tongue, generous and hospitable. Then comes Saintonge; and from there, after crossing an arm of the sea and the river Garonne, we come into the territory of Bordeaux, which has excellent wine and an abundance of fish but an uncouth manner of speech. The speech of Saintonge is also uncouth, but that of Bordeaux is more so.

Then, for travelers who are already tired, there is a three days' journey through the Landes of Bordeaux. This is a desolate country, lacking in everything: there is neither bread nor wine nor meat nor fish nor water nor any springs. There are few villages on this sandy plain, though it has honey, millet, panic [a kind of millet] and pigs in plenty. If you are going through the Landes in summer be sure to protect your face from the huge flies, called *guespe* [wasps] and *tavones* [horse flies], which are particularly abundant in this region. And if you do not watch your feet carefully you will sink up to your knees in the sea sand which is found everywhere here.

After passing through this region you come into Gascony, a land well supplied with white bread and excellent red wine, woods and meadows, rivers and springs of pure water. The Gascons are loud-mouthed, talkative, given to mockery, libidinous, drunken, greedy eaters, clad in rags and poverty-stricken; but they are skilled fighters and notable for their hospitality to the poor. They take their meals without a table, sitting round the fire, and all drink out of the same cup. They eat and drink a great deal and are ill clad; nor do they scruple to sleep all together in a scanty litter of rotting straw, the servants along with the master and mistress.

Leaving this country, the road to St. James crosses two rivers near the village of St-Jean de Sorde, one on the right and the other on the left; one is called a *gave*, the other a river, and they must both be crossed by boat. Accursed be their boatmen! For although the rivers are quite narrow these men are in the habit of taking a piece of money for each person, rich or poor, whom they ferry across, and for a horse they exact four, unworthily and by force. Their boat is small, made from a single tree-trunk, ill-suited to carry horses; and so when you get into the boat you must take care not to fall into the water. You will do well to hold on to your horse's bridle and let it swim behind the boat. Nor should you go into a boat that has too many passengers, for if it is overloaded it will at once capsize.

Often, too, having taken their passengers' money, the boatmen take such a number of other pilgrims on board that the boat overturns and the pilgrims are drowned; and then the wicked boatmen are delighted and appropriate the possessions of the dead.

Then, round the pass of Cize is the Basque country with the town of Bayonne, on the coast to the north. Here a barbarous tongue is spoken; the country is wooded and hilly, short of bread, wine and all other foodstuffs, except only apples, cider and milk. In this country there are wicked toll-collectors – near the pass of Cize and at Ostabat and St-Jean and St-Michel-Pied-de Port – may they be accursed. They come out to meet pilgrims with two or three cudgels to exact tribute by improper use of force; and if any traveler refuses to give the money they demand they strike him with their cudgels and take the money, abusing him and rummaging in his very breeches. They are ruthless people, and their country is no less hostile, with its forests and its wildness; the ferocity of their aspect and the barbarousness of their language strike terror into the hearts of those who encounter them. Although they should levy tribute only on merchants they exact it unjustly from pilgrims and all travelers. When custom requires that the duty to be paid on a particular object is four or six pieces of money they charge eight or twelve – double the proper amount.

We urge and demand, therefore, that these toll-collectors, together with the king of Aragon and the other rich men who receive the proceeds of the tolls and all those who are in league with them, to wit Raymond de Soule, Vivien d'Aigremont and the Vicomte de St-Michel, with all their posterity, and also the ferrymen already mentioned and Arnauld de la Guigne, with his posterity, and the other lords of the two rivers, who unjustly receive the money collected by the ferrymen, and also the priests who, knowing what they do, admit them to confession and the Eucharist, celebrate divine service for them and receive them in church – we demand that all these men should be excommunicated until they have expiated their offences by a long and public penance and have moderated their demands for tribute, and that the sentence of excommunication should be made public not only in their own episcopal see but also in the basilica of St. James, in presence of the pilgrims. And if any prelate should pardon them, either from benevolence or for his own profit, may he be struck with the sword of anathema!

It should be said that the toll-collectors are not entitled to levy any kind of tribute on pilgrims and that the ferrymen are properly entitled to charge only an *obol* [half a penny] for taking over two men – that is, if they are rich

— and for a horse a piece of money; for a poor man they may charge nothing at all. Moreover the ferrymen are required to have boats amply large enough to accommodate both men and horses.

Still in the Basque country, the road to St. James goes over a most lofty mountain known as the Portus Cisere tribute [Pass of Cize], so called either because it is the gateway of Spain or because necessary goods are transported over the pass from one country to the other. It is a journey of eight miles up to the pass and another eight down from it. The mountain is so high that it seems to touch the sky, and a man who has climbed it feels that he could indeed reach the sky with his hand. From the summit can be seen the Sea of Brittany and the Western Sea, and the bounds of the three countries of Castile, Aragon and France. On the highest point of the mountain is the place known as the Cross of Charles, because it was here that Charlemagne, advancing into Spain with his armies, cleared a passage with the aid of axes and picks and mattocks and other implements, set up the Lord's cross and, kneeling with his face turned towards Galicia, prayed to God and St. James. And so pilgrims are accustomed to kneel here in prayer, looking towards the country of St. James, and each then sets up a cross. Sometimes as many as a thousand crosses are to be seen here, and so the place is known as the first station for prayer on the road to St. James.

On this mountain, before Christianity was fully established in Spain, the impious Navarrese and the Basques were accustomed not only to rob pilgrims going to St. James but to ride them like asses and kill them. Near the mountain, to the north, is a valley known as the Valley of Charles [Valcarlos] in which Charlemagne was encamped with his armies when his warriors were killed at Roncesvalles. This is the road used by many pilgrims who do not wish to climb the mountain.

Below the pass on the other side of the mountain are the hospice and the church containing the rock which Roland, that most valiant hero, split from top to bottom with a triple stroke of his sword. Beyond this is Roncesvalles, scene of the great battle in which King Marsile [the Moslem king of Spain in the French poem *Chanson de Roland*], Roland, Oliver and forty thousand other warriors, both Christians and Saracens, were killed.

After this valley comes Navarre which is well supplied with bread and wine, milk and livestock. The Navarrese and the Basques resemble one another in appearance, diet, dress and language; but the Basques have a fairer complexion than the Navarrese. The Navarrese wear short black garments reaching only to the knee, after the manner of the Scots. Their shoes, which they call *lavarcas*, are made of hairy untanned leather; they are tied on with thongs, and cover only the sole of the foot, leaving the upper part bare. They wear dark-colored woollen cloaks, fringed like traveling cloaks, which reach to the elbow and are known as *saias*. Coarsely dressed, they also eat and drink coarsely: in Navarre the whole household – master and servant, mistress and maid – eat from the same pot, in which all the food is mixed together, using their hands instead of spoons, and drink from the same cup. Watching them eat, you are reminded of dogs or pigs greedily gulping down their food; and when you hear them speaking it is like the barking of dogs. Their language is utterly barbarous: they call God *Urcia*, the Mother of God *Andrea Maria*, bread *orgui*, wine *ardum*, meat *aragui*, fish *araign*, a house *echea*, the master of the house *iaona*, the mistress *Andrea*, a church *elicera*, the priest *belaterra* (which means 'good earth'), corn *gari*, water *uric*, the king *ereguia* and St. James Jaona *domne Jacue*.

This is a barbarous people, different from all other peoples in customs and in race, malignant, dark in color, ugly of face, debauched, perverse, faithless, dishonorable, corrupt, lustful, drunken, skilled in all forms of violence, fierce and savage, dishonest and false, impious and coarse, cruel and quarrelsome, incapable of any good impulses, past masters of all vices and iniquities. They resemble the Getae [the people who lived around the mouth of the Danube, and whose name was synonymous in Roman times for ferocity] and the Saracens in their malignance, and are in every way hostile to our French people. A Navarrese or a Basque will kill a Frenchman for a penny if he can. In some parts of the region, in Biscay and Alava, when the Navarrese are warming themselves, men show their private parts to women and women to men. The Navarrese fornicate shamelessly with their beasts, and it is said that a Navarrese will put a padlock on his she-mule and his mare lest another man should get at them. He also libidinously kisses the vulva of a woman or a she-mule.

The Navarrese, therefore, are condemned by all right-minded people. But they are good in battle, though not in besieging fortresses; and they are regular in the payment of tithes and accustomed to make offerings to the altar. Every day, when a Navarrese goes to church, he makes an offering to God of bread, wine, corn or some other substance. Wherever a Navarrese or Basque goes he has a horn round his neck like a hunter and carries two or three javelins, which he calls *auconas*. When he goes into his house or returns there he whistles like a kite; and when he is hiding in secret places or in some solitary spot with robbery in mind and wants to summon his companions without attracting notice he hoots like an owl or howls like a wolf.

It is commonly said that the Basques are descended from the Scots; for they resemble them in customs and in appearance. Julius Caesar is said to have sent three peoples – the Nubians [perhaps the Numiani, another British

[Fig. 32] Sufferers from St. Vitus's Dance (chorea, a nervous disease) going on a pilgrimage to the shrine of St. Willibrod at Echternach (now in Luxembourg) which was famous for its miraculous cures of this illness (from a drawing by Breugel in Lacroix, *Military and Religious Life in the Middle Ages,* p. 392).

tribe], the Scots and the tailed men of Cornwall – into Spain to make war on the peoples of Spain who refused to pay him tribute, telling them to kill all males and to spare only the women. These peoples came to Spain by sea and after destroying their ships devastated the country by fire and sword, from Barcelona to Saragossa and from Bayonne to Mount Oca. They were unable to advance any further, for the Castilians united and drove them out of their territory. In their flight they came to the coastal mountains between Najera and Pamplona and Bayonne, on the seaward side in Biscay and Alava, where they settled down and built many fortresses. Having killed all the men, they took their wives by violence and had children by them, who later became known as Navarrese – the name being interpreted as *non verus* ['not true'], that is not engendered of a pure race or legitimate stock. The Navarrese also used to derive their name from a town called Naddaver [possibly Nadabar, in Ethiopia] in the country from which they originally came: a town which was converted to the Lord in early times by the preaching of Matthew, the apostle and evangelist. Leaving Navarre, the route runs through the forest of Oca and continues through Spanish territory – Castile and the

Campos — in the direction of Burgos. This is a country full of treasures, of gold and silver, fortunate in producing fodder and sturdy horses and with an abundance of bread, wine, meat, fish, milk and honey. It is, however, lacking in trees and the people are wicked and vicious.

Then, after crossing the territory of Leon and going over the passes of Monte Irago [Foncebadon] and Cebrero, you come into Galicia, a well wooded and well watered region with rivers and meadows and fine orchards, excellent fruit and clear springs, but with few towns and villages or cultivated fields. There is little wheaten bread or wine but ample supplies of rye bread and cider, cattle and horses, milk, honey and sea fish both large and small. The country is rich in gold, silver, cloths, animal furs from the forests and other riches, as well as precious Saracen wares.

The Galicians are more like our French people in their customs than any other of the uncultivated races of Spain, but they have the reputation of being violent-tempered and quarrelsome.

8. Of the Bodies of Saints which rest on the Road to St. James and are to be visited by Pilgrims

Pilgrims going to St. James by way of St-Gilles must in the first place pay honor to the body of the blessed Trophimus the Confessor in Arles [Trophime, first-century bishop, but not the one referred to by St. Paul]. St. Paul refers to him in his epistle to Timothy; he was consecrated as a bishop by Paul and sent by him to preach the Gospel in Arles for the first time. It was from this most clear spring, we are told by Pope Zosimus, that the whole of France received the waters of the faith. His feast is celebrated on 29th December.

Also to be visited in Arles is the body of the blessed Caesarius [the sixth-century archbishop of Arles], bishop and martyr, who instituted a Rule for nuns in that city. His feast is celebrated on 1st November. In the cemetery of Arles pilgrims should seek out the relics of the blessed bishop Honoratus [of Arles, d. 429], whose feast is celebrated on 16th January. In his venerable and magnificent basilica rests the body of the Blessed Genesius, that most precious martyr [d. Arles, 303 or 308]. In the village of Trinquetaille near Arles, between two arms of the Rhône, is a magnificent tall marble column, standing behind the church of St. Genesius, to which it is said he was tied by the faithless people before being beheaded; it is still stained red with his blood. Immediately after his execution the saint took his head and threw it into the Rhône; his body was carried down by the river to the basilica of St. Honoratus, where it was given honorable burial. His head floated down the river to the sea and was conveyed under angelic guidance to Cartagena in Spain, where it now gloriously rests, performing numerous miracles. The saint's feast is celebrated on 25th August.

The pilgrim must then visit the cemetery near Arles known as Aliscamps and, as the custom is, intercede for the dead with prayers, psalms and alms. The cemetery is a mile long and a mile wide, and in no other cemetery can be found so many and such large marble tombs. They are of different forms and bear ancient inscriptions in Latin script but in unintelligible language. The further you look the more sarcophagi you see. In this cemetery there are seven churches. If, in any one of them, a priest celebrates the Eucharist for the dead, or a layman has a mass said for them, or a clerk reads the Psalter, they will be sure on the day of resurrection before God to find these pious dead helping them to obtain salvation; for many are the holy martyrs and confessors who rest here, and whose souls dwell amid the joys of Paradise. Their memory is celebrated, according to custom, on the Monday after the Easter octave. A visit must also be paid, with a most attentive eye, to the venerable body of the blessed Aegidius the most pious confessor and abbot [St. Giles, an eighth-century hermit and one of the most popular saints of the Middle Ages]; for this most blessed saint, famed in all the countries of the world, must be venerated by all, worthily honored by all and loved, invoked and supplicated by all. After the prophets and the apostles none among the blessed is worthier than he, none is more holy, none is more glorious, none is readier to help. It is he, more than any of the other saints, who comes most rapidly to the help of the needy and the afflicted and the suffering who call on his aid. What a fine and profitable act it is to visit his tomb! Anyone who prays to him with all his heart will assuredly be granted his help that very day. I have had personal experience of what I say: once in this saint's town I saw a man who, on the very day that he had invoked this blessed confessor, escaped from an house belonging to a cobbler named Peyrot just before it collapsed and was reduced to rubble. Who will spend most time at his place of burial? Who will worship God in his most holy basilica? Who will most frequently embrace his sarcophagus? Who will kiss his venerable altar or tell the story of his most pious life?

[A detailed description of the shrine follows.]

Such is the tomb of the blessed Aegidius, confessor, in which his venerable body rests with honor. May they blush with shame, those Hungarians who claim to have his body; may they be dismayed, those monks of Chamalières, who think they have his whole body; may they be confounded, those men of St-Seine who assert that they possess his head; may they be struck with fear, those Normans of Coutances who boast that they have his whole body; for his most holy bones, as many have borne witness, could not be removed from his own town. Certain men once attempted by fraud to carry off the venerable arm of the blessed confessor to distant lands, but were quite unable to remove it. . . .

Those Burgundians and Germans who go to St. James by the Le Puy road should venerate the relics of the blessed Faith [Foy], virgin and martyr, whose soul, after her beheading on the hill town of Agen, was borne up to heaven in the form of a dove by choirs of angels and crowned with the laurels of immortality. When the blessed Caprasius [Caprais], bishop of Agen, heard this while hiding in a cave to escape the rage of persecution he found the courage to face martyrdom, hastened to the place where the blessed virgin had suffered and himself gained the palm of martyrdom, bearing himself most valiantly and even reproaching his executioners for their slowness.

Thereafter the most precious body of the blessed faith, virgin and martyr, was honorably buried by Christians in the valley commonly known as Conques [in fact, her remains were stolen from Agen in the late ninth century]. Over her tomb was built a handsome basilica, in which the Rule of St. Benedict is strictly observed to this day for the glory of God. Many benefits are granted both to the sick and to those who are in good health. In front of the basilica is an excellent spring, the virtues of which are too great to be told. The saint's feast is celebrated on 6th October. Then, on the road to St. James by way of St-Léonard [de Noblat], the most holy body of the blessed Mary Magdalene is above all to be venerated [at Vézelay]. This is that glorious Mary who in the house of Simon the Leper watered the Savior's feet with her tears, wiped them with her hair, kissed them and anointed them with a precious ointment [see 45 below]. Accordingly her many sins were forgiven her, for she had greatly loved Jesus Christ her redeemer, who loves all men. It was she who after the Lord's ascension left Jerusalem with the blessed Maximinus and other disciples of the Lord, sailed to Provence and landed at the port of Marseilles. She lived the life of a hermit in that country for some years and was then buried in Aix by Maximinus, who had become bishop of the town. Much later a sanctified monk named Badilo translated her most precious relics to Vézelay where they now rest in an honorable tomb. There a large and beautiful basilica and an abbey were built; there sinners have their faults remitted by God for love of the saint, the blind have their sight restored, the tongues of the dumb are loosed, the lame are cured of their lameness, those possessed by devils are delivered and ineffable benefits are granted to many of the faithful. The saint's feast is celebrated on 22nd July. . . .

Pilgrims traveling on this road should also pay honor, on the banks of the Loire to the venerable body of the blessed Martin [of Tours], bishop and confessor, who gloriously brought three dead men back to life and is reported to have restored lepers, men possessed by devils, the sick, the lunatic and the demoniac, and sufferers from other diseases, to the health they desired. The shrine containing his most sacred remains, in the city of Tours, is resplendent with a profusion of gold, silver and precious stones and is graced by numerous miracles. Over it a great and splendid basilica, in the likeness of the church of St. James, has been built. The sick come to it and are made well, the possessed are delivered, the blind see, the lame stand upright, all kinds of sickness are cured and all those who ask for the saint's intercession are fully satisfied. His glorious renown, therefore, is spread throughout the world in well merited eulogies, for the honor of Christ. His feast is celebrated on 11th November. . . .

Also to be visited is the venerable head of the blessed John the Baptist, which was brought by certain religious men from Jerusalem to a place called Angély in Poitou. There a great and magnificent basilica was built and dedicated to him, and in this his most sacred head is venerated night and day by a choir of a hundred monks and has wrought countless miracles. While the head was being transported by sea and by land it gave many proofs of its miraculous power: on the sea it warded off numerous perils, and on land it brought dead men back to life. Accordingly it is believed to be indeed the head of the venerable Forerunner. It was found on 24th February in the time of the emperor Marcian, when the Forerunner first revealed to two monks the place where his head was concealed. . . .

[An account of the life and martyrdom of Eutropius of Saintes follows, and a continuing list of other saints to be honored on the way to St. James.]

Finally and above all pilgrims are to visit and pay the greatest veneration to the most holy body of the blessed apostle James in the city of Compostella.

May the saints mentioned here and all the other saints of God intercede for us, through their merits and their prayers, with our Lord Jesus Christ, who lives and reigns with the Father and the Holy Ghost, God from eternity to eternity.

Amen. . . .

9. Of the body and the altar of St James

. . . So far we have spoken of the characteristics of the church: we must now consider the venerable altar of the apostle. In this venerable basilica, according to tradition, the revered body of the blessed James rests under the magnificent altar set up in his honor. It is enclosed in a marble tomb which lies within a fine vaulted sepulcher of admirable workmanship and fitting size. That the body is immutably fixed there we know from the evidence of St.

Theodomir, bishop of the city, who discovered it and was unable to move it from the spot. May they blush for shame, therefore, those envious people beyond the mountains who claim to have some part of it or to possess relics of it [Toulouse, and a number of places in France and Italy claimed such possession]! For the body of the saint is here in its entirety – divinely illuminated by paradisiac carbuncles, constantly honored by divine fragrances, radiant in the light of celestial candles and devoutly attended by watching angels. . . .

11. Of the Reception to be given to Pilgrims of St. James

Pilgrims, whether poor or rich, returning from St. James or going there must be received with charity and compassion; for whosoever receives them and gives them hospitality has for his guest not only St. James but our Lord himself. As the Lord says in his Gospel 'He that receiveth you receiveth me.' Many are those who have incurred the wrath of God because they would not take in the pilgrims of St. James and the needy.

A weaver in Nantua, a town between Geneva and Lyons, refused bread to a pilgrim of St. James who asked for it; and at once he saw his cloth fall to the ground, rent asunder. At Villeneuve a poor pilgrim of St. James asked for alms, for the love of God and the blessed James, from a woman who was keeping bread under hot ashes. She told him that she had no bread: whereupon the pilgrim said, 'May the bread that you have turn into stone!' The pilgrim had left the house and gone some distance on his way when the wicked woman went to take her bread out of the ashes and found a round stone in the place where the bread had been. Struck with remorse, she set out to look for the pilgrim, but could not find him.

At Poitiers two valiant French pilgrims, returning from St. James in great need, asked for hospitality, for the love of God and St. James, in the street running from the house of Jean Gautier to the church of St-Porchaire, but found none. Finally, at the last house in the street, by the church, they were taken in by a poor man; and that night, by the operation of divine vengeance, a fierce fire broke out and quickly destroyed the whole street, beginning with the house where they had first asked for hospitality and going right up to the house where they were taken in. Some thousand houses were destroyed, but the one where the servants of God were taken in was, by grace, spared.

Thus we learn that the pilgrims of St. James, whether rich or poor, should be given hospitality and a considerate reception.

Here ends the fourth book of the apostle St James. Glory be to him who has written it and to him who reads it.

26. PILGRIMAGE AS METAPHOR: *THE CANTERBURY TALES*

The idea of pilgrimage as a metaphor for human life is as old as the institution itself, and in the late Middle Ages no one embodied it more imaginatively than Geoffrey Chaucer in his unfinished collection, 'The Canterbury Tales.' Writing in the late four- teenth century, Chaucer chose as the goal for his fictional pilgrimage the shrine of Thomas à Becket at Canterbury, famous throughout Christendom as the site of Becket's murder at the instigation of Henry II in 1170. Unlike non-figurative accounts of pilgrimage, which center primarily upon the outward circumstances of travel, Chaucer makes the pilgrim travelers (including himself) the initial focus of his ironic descriptive powers. As the pilgrims go on to tell their stories the reader may sometimes forget that they are meant to be traveling the road to Canterbury, but Chaucer reminds us of the central metaphor in the linking passages between the tales, while the tales themselves suggest the broad and varied world of human experience which comprises 'the pilgrim- age of this life.' At the end of the collection, the last speaker, the Parson, invokes "that perfect glorious pilgrimage that is called the heavenly Jerusalem." His 'tale,' a sermon on repentance, places the focus finally on pilgrimage as metaphor: it is based upon the biblical text "Stand at the cross-roads, and look for the ancient paths, and ask of them which is the way of righteousness, and walk in it, and you will find rest for your souls."

Source: Chaucer's rhyming verse is here translated into modern prose by David Wright, *The Canterbury Tales* (London: Fontana Press, 1964), pp. 5-21; repr. and abridged with permission.

The General Prologue to **The Canterbury Tales** *[Selections]*

When the sweet showers of April have pierced the dryness of March to its root and soaked every vein in moisture whose quickening force engenders the flower; when Zephyr [the warm west wind] with his sweet breath has given life to tender shoots in each wood and field; when the young sun has run his half-course in the [Zodiacal] sign of the Ram; when, nature prompt- ing their instincts, small birds who sleep through the night with one eye open make their music – then people long to go on pilgrimages, and pious wanderers to visit strange lands and far-off shrines in different countries. In England especially they come from every shire's end to Canterbury to seek out the holy blessed martyr St. Thomas à Becket, who helped them when they were sick.

It happened one day at this time of year, while I was lodging at the Tabard in Southwark, ready and eager to go on my pilgrimage to Canterbury, a company of twenty-nine people arrived in the hostelry at nightfall. They

[Fig. 33] The Canterbury Pilgrims set out from the Tabard Inn in Southwark, with the Miller in the lead playing on his bagpipes (from an engraving in John Urry's 1722 edition of Chaucer).

were of various sorts, accidentally brought together in companionship, all pilgrims wishing to ride to Canterbury. The rooms and stables were commodious and we were very well looked after. In short, by the time the sun had gone down I had talked with every one of them and soon became one of their company. We agreed to rise early to set out on the journey I am going to tell you about. But nevertheless before I take the story further it seems right to me to describe, while I have the time and opportunity, the sort and condition of each of them as they appeared to me: who they were, of what rank, and how dressed. I shall begin with the Knight.

The KNIGHT was a very distinguished man. From the beginning of his career he had loved chivalry, loyalty, honorable dealing, generosity, and good breeding. He had fought bravely in the king's service, besides which he had traveled further than most men in heathen as well as in Christian lands. Wherever he went he was honored for his valor. He was at Alexandria when it fell. When he served in Prussia he was generally given the seat of honor above the knights of all other nations; no Christian soldier of his rank had fought oftener in the raids on Russia and Lithuania. And he had been in Granada at the siege of Algeciras, fought in Benmarin and at the conquests of Ayas and Attalia, besides taking part in many armed expeditions in the eastern Mediterranean. He had been in fifteen pitched battles and fought three times for the faith in the lists at Tramassene, and each time killed his foe. This same distinguished Knight had also fought at one time for the king of Palathia against another heathen enemy in Turkey. He was always outstandingly successful; yet though distinguished he was prudent, and his bearing as modest as a maid's. In his whole life he never spoke discourteously to any kind of man. He was a true and perfect noble knight. But, speaking of his equipment, his horses were good, yet he was not gaily dressed. He wore a tunic of thick cotton cloth, rustmarked from his coat of mail; for he had just come back from his travels and was making his pilgrimage to render thanks. . . .

There was a remarkably fine-looking MONK, who acted as estate-steward to his monastery and loved hunting: a manly man, well fitted to be an abbot. He kept plenty of fine horses in his stable, and when he went out riding people could hear the bells on his bridle jingling in the whistling wind as clear and loud as the chapel bell of the small convent of which he was the head. Because the Rule of St. Maur or of St. Benedict was old-fashioned and somewhat strict, this Monk neglected the old precepts and followed the modern custom. He did not give two pins for the text which says hunters cannot be holy men, or that a monk who is heedless of his Rule – that is to say a monk out of his cloister – is like a fish out of water. In his view this saying was not worth a bean; and I told him his opinion was sound. Why should he study and addle his wits with everlasting poring over a book in cloisters, or work with his hands, or toil as St. Augustine commanded? How is the world to be served? Let St. Augustine keep his hard labor for himself! Therefore the Monk, whose whole pleasure lay in riding and the hunting of the hare (over which he spared no expense) remained a hard rider and kept greyhounds swift as birds.

I saw that his sleeves were edged with costly grey fur, the finest in the land. He had an elaborate golden brooch with a love-knot at the larger end to fasten his hood beneath his chin. His bald head shone like glass; and so did his face, as if it had been anointed. He was a plump and personable dignitary, with prominent, restless eyes which sparkled like fire beneath a pot. His boots were supple and his horse in perfect condition. To be sure he was a fine-looking prelate, no pale and wasting ghost! His favorite dish was a fat roast swan. The horse he rode was a brown as a berry. . . .

Among the rest were a HABERDASHER, a CARPENTER, a WEAVER, a DYER, and a TAPESTRY-MAKER, all dressed in uniform livery belonging to a rich and honorable Guild. Their apparel was new and freshly trimmed; their knives were not tipped with brass but finely mounted with wrought silver to match their belts and purses. Each seemed a proper burgess worthy of a place on the dais of a guildhall; and every one of them had the ability and judgment, besides sufficient property and income, to become an alderman. In this they would have the hearty assent of their wives – else the ladies would certainly be much to blame. For it's very pleasant to be called 'Madam' and take precedence at church festivals, and have one's mantle carried in state.

They had taken a COOK with them for the occasion, to boil chickens with marrowbones, tart flavoring-powder and spice. Well did he know the taste of London ale! He knew how to roast, fry, seethe, broil, make soup and bake pies. But it was the greatest pity, so I thought, that he'd got an ulcer on his shin. For he made chicken-pudding with the best of them. . . .

There was among us a worthy WIFE from near Bath, but she was a bit deaf, which was a pity. At cloth-making she beat even the weavers of Ypres and Ghent. There was not a woman in her parish who dared go in front of her when she went to the offertory; if anybody did, you may be sure it put her into such a rage she was out of all patience. Her kerchiefs were of the finest texture; I daresay those she wore upon her head on Sundays weighed ten pounds. Her stockings were of the finest scarlet, tightly drawn up above glossy new shoes; her face was bold, handsome, and florid. She had been a respectable woman all her life, having married five husbands in church (apart from other loves in youth of which there is no need to speak at present.) She had visited Jerusalem thrice and crossed many foreign rivers, had been to Rome, Boulogne, the shrine of St. James of Compostella in Galicia, and Cologne; so she knew a lot about traveling around – the truth is, she was gap-toothed [a sign of luck, travel, and a lascivious disposition]. She rode comfortably upon an ambling horse, her head well covered with a wimple and a hat the size of a shield or buckler. An outer skirt covered her great hips, while on her feet she wore a pair of sharp spurs. In company she laughed and rattled away. No doubt she knew all the cures for love, for at that game she was past mistress. . . .

With him [the Summoner] rode a worthy PARDONER [a seller of papal indulgences] of Rouncival at Charing Cross, his friend and bosom companion, who had come straight from the Vatican at Rome. He loudly carolled 'Come hither, love, to me,' while the Summoner sang the bass louder than the loudest trumpet. This pardoner's hair was waxy yellow and hung down as sleek as a hank of flax; such locks of hair as he possessed fell in meager clusters spread over his shoulders, where it lay in thinly scattered strands. For comfort he wore no hood; it was packed in his bag. With his hair loose and uncovered except for a cap, he thought he was riding in the latest style. He had great staring eyes like a hare's. Upon his cap he'd sewn a small replica of St. Veronica's handkerchief. His wallet lay on his lap in front of him, chockful of pardons hot from Rome. He'd a thin goatlike voice and no vestige or prospect of a beard; and his skin was smooth as if just shaven. I took him for a gelding or a mare. But as for his profession, from Berwick down to Ware there was not another pardoner to touch him. For in his wallet he kept a pillow-slip which, he said, was Our Lady's veil. He claimed to have a bit of the sail belonging to St. Peter when he tried to walk on the waves and Jesus Christ caught hold of him. He had a brass cross set with pebbles and a glass reliquary full of pigs' bones. Yet when he came across some poor country parson he could make more money with these relics in a day than the parson got in two months, and thus by means of barefaced flattery and hocus-pocus he made the parson and the people his dupes. To do him justice, in church at any rate he was a fine ecclesiastic. Well could he read a lesson or a parable; but best of all he sang the offertory hymn, because after it was sung he knew he must preach, as he well knew how, to wheedle money from the congregation with his smooth tongue. Therefore he sang all the louder and merrier.

Now I have told you in a few words the class of person, dress, and number of our party and the reason why it assembled in this excellent inn at Southwark, the Tabard hard by the Bell. And now it's time to tell you how we comported ourselves the night of our arrival at the inn; and afterwards I'll speak of our journey and the rest of our pilgrimage. But first I must beg you to be good enough not to put it down to my lack of refinement if in this matter I use plain language to give an account of their conversation and behavior and when reporting their actual words. For you know as well as I do that whoever repeats a story told by another must reproduce as nearly as he can every word entrusted to him, no matter how uncouth or free the language; or else falsify the tale, or invent, or find new words for it. Be the man his brother, he may not shrink, but whatever words are used he also must use. In the Bible the language of Christ himself is outspoken; but as you well know, it's no breach of taste. Besides Plato says (as anyone who can read him may see), 'The words must relate to the action.' Also I beg you to forgive me if in this account I have not paid due attention to people's rank and the order in which they should appear. My wits aren't too bright, as you may suppose.

Our HOST welcomed each of us with open arms and soon led us to our places at the supper-table. He served us with the finest viands; the wine was strong and we were in a mood to drink. Our Host was a striking-looking fellow, a fit master of ceremonies for any hall. He was a big man with prominent eyes (there's no better-looking burgess in Cheapside), racy in his talk, shrewd yet civil; a proper man in every respect. What's more, he was a bit of a wag, for after supper, when we'd settled our bills, among other things he began to talk of amusing us, saying: 'Ladies and gentlemen, you're all most heartily welcome, for on my honor I'm telling you no lie when I say I've not seen such a jolly company as this under my roof at any one time this year. I'd like to provide you with some entertainment if I knew how to set about it. And I've just thought of a game that will amuse you and not cost a penny.

'You're off to Canterbury – Godspeed, and the blessed martyr reward you! And you mean to entertain yourselves by telling stories on the way, I'll be bound; for there's certainly no sense or fun in riding along as dumb as stones; and so, as I said before, I'll devise a game that'll give you some amusement. If it pleases you all to accept my decision unanimously and to do as I'll tell you when you ride off tomorrow, then I swear by my father's soul you can have my head if you don't enjoy yourselves! Not another word – hands up, everyone!'

It did not take us long to make up our minds. We saw no point in deliberating, but agreed to his proposal without further argument and asked him to give what commands he liked.

'Ladies and gentlemen,' began the Host, 'do yourselves a good turn and listen to what I say, and please don't turn up your noses at it. This is the point in a nutshell: each of you, to make the road seem shorter, shall tell two stories on the journey – I mean two on the way to Canterbury and two others on the way home – tales of once upon a time. Whoever tells his story best – that's to say whoever spins the most edifying and amusing tale – is to be given a dinner at the expense of the rest of us, here in this inn and under this very roof, when we return from Canterbury. And just to make it the more fun for you I'll gladly ride with you myself at my own cost and be your guide. Anybody who gainsays my judgment shall pay all our expenses on the road! Now if you agree, let me know here and now without more ado, and I'll make my arrangements early.'

The matter was agreed; we gave our promises gladly, begging him to do as he proposed and be our leader, judge and arbiter of our tales, and arrange a dinner at a set price. We agreed to be ruled by his decision in every respect; and thus we unanimously submitted ourselves to his judgment. Thereupon more wine was fetched, and when we had drunk it we all went to bed without further delay.

Next morning our Host rose up at break of day, roused us all and gathered us together in a flock. We rode off at little more than a walking-pace until we came to the watering-place of St. Thomas, where our Host reined his horse and said, 'Attention, please, ladies and gentlemen! You know what you promised; remember? If you're of the same mind this morning as you were last night, then let's see who's to tell the first tale. Whoever rebels against my ruling must pay for everything we spend upon the road, or may I never drink another drop! Now let's draw lots before going further. Sir Knight,' said he, 'will your honor draw lots, for that is my decree. Come nearer, my lady Prioress, and you too, Master Scholar; lay aside that diffidence and come out of your brown study – all hands draw lots.'

Upon this everybody began drawing lots, and in fine, whether by luck, or fate, or chance, the truth is that to everyone's delight the lot fell to the Knight. Now he must tell his tale, as was right and proper according to the bargain I've described. What more can I say? And when that good man saw how things were, he very sensibly obeyed the promise he had freely given and said, 'Since I must begin the game, why, then, welcome be the luck of the draw, in God's name! Now let us ride on; and listen to what I say.' With that we began to ride forward on our way, and at once he cheerfully began his tale, which went like this. . . .

27. JERUSALEM PILGRIMAGE IN 1480: THE TRIBULATIONS OF BROTHER FELIX

In 1484 a Dominican friar from Ulm, Brother Felix Fabri, wrote a lengthy account of two pilgrimages he had made to the Holy Land. The first, in 1480, proved both dangerous and unsatisfactory, and Brother Felix soon decided to make it a practice run for a second journey in which he could benefit from his earlier mistakes. These included leaving too little time to visit the sites he had come so far to see – a predicament easily understood by the modern traveler who has experienced an accelerated tour of the "six countries in five days" variety. Brother Felix might justly be accused of an obsession with circumstantial detail – he finds it very hard to omit anything – but at the same time his account tells us more about his personal attitude to his experiences than do the earlier writings. Skeptics like Erasmus might scoff at pilgrims and their journeys, but Brother Felix's account is evidence that at the close of the Middle Ages pilgrims could still be spiritually motivated. The following excerpt describes his first pilgrimage.

Source: trans. Aubrey Stewart, *The Wanderings of Felix Fabri*, Part 1 (London: The Palestine Pilgrims Text Society, 1887-1897), 7, pp. 7-47, abridged.

At the time of the celebration of Easter, in the year of our Lord 1480, on the ninth day of the month of April . . . whereon also is celebrated the feast of the dedication of the church of the Dominicans in Ulm, on that same day after dinner, as is the custom, I ascended the pulpit, and preached to the people who were present in great numbers, both to hear the sermon and to obtain indulgences. When I had finished my sermon, before the general confession made by the people on such occasions, I told them all of the pilgrimage which I was on the point of beginning, bidding them, and beseeching them, to importune God with prayers for my safe return, at the present time to sing with me in gladness the hymn of the Lord's resurrection, which the people are wont to sing, together with the hymn for pilgrims by sea. . . .

All the people then sang after me the hymns that I had begun with loud and pleasant voices, and repeated them many times over; nor did they refrain from tears, and some broke out into sobs instead of into song. For many persons of both sexes were anxious and alarmed, fearing, even as I myself feared, that I should perish among such terrible dangers. When the singing was over, I commended them to God by bestowing upon them the general absolution, and, strengthening them by the sign of the cross, I bade them farewell, and descended from the pulpit.

Now, on the fourteenth day of April, early in the morning, after I had received the blessing which is given to those who travel, and after I had kissed and embraced my brethren, we mounted our horses, I and the

reverend Master Ludwig, with a servant from the city of Ulm, and rode to
Memmingen, where, according to my appointment, I met the Lord Apollinaris von Stein, with his son George, and with many men-at-arms; and
straightway on the morrow we prepared to depart, and the noble youth bade
farewell to his father and to all his retainers, and mounted his horse not
without sorrow and fear. I also rushed into the arms of my most kind and
beloved spiritual father, begging his leave to depart and his paternal blessing,
not without deep grief and sorrow, as was shown by the abundant tears and
sobs of us both; nor was there anything to wonder at in this, for the forced
parting of son from his father, and of a true man from his sincere friend, is
naturally grievous. During my embraces and sobs I heard my most beloved
father's last words of advice, that I was not to forget him in the Holy Land,
but that, should a messenger present himself, I was to send a letter from the
sea telling how I was, and to be sure to return soon. And so he sorrowfully
left me, and returned with his servant to Ulm to his children, my brethren.
After my father's departure, a great and almost irresistible temptation assailed
me, for the delightful eagerness to see Jerusalem and the holy places, with
which I had until that time been glowing, altogether died within me, and I
felt a loathing for travel; and the pilgrimage, which had appeared so sweet
and virtuous, now seemed wearisome, bitter, useless, empty, and sinful. I was
angry with myself for having undertaken it, and all those who had dissuaded
me from it I now thought to be the wisest of counselors and the truest of
friends; while I considered that those who had encouraged me were enemies
of my life. I had more pleasure in beholding Suabia than the land of Canaan,
and Ulm appeared to me pleasanter than Jerusalem. Moreover, the fear of the
sea increased within me, and I conceived so many objections to that pilgrimage that, had I not been ashamed, I should have run after Master Ludwig and
re-entered Ulm with him, and I should have had the greatest delight in
doing so. This accursed temptation remained present with me throughout the
whole voyage, and was most troublesome to me, because it took away all the
delight and joy and zeal wherewith a pilgrim supports his labors and is urged
to persist in his work, and caused me to be dull and stupid both in viewing
places of note by sea and land, and also in writing accounts of them. What I
have written was done against the grain, but I sometimes succeeded in conquering my dullness by hard work.

So young Master George and I, with one servant whom he had chosen
from his father's household, set forth from Memmingen, and in a few hours
he began to make my acquaintance and I began to make his, and we and our
several dispositions agreed very well together, which is a great comfort for
those who are making that pilgrimage together. For if a man has a comrade

with whom he cannot agree, woe betide them both during their pilgrimage. So thus we entered the Alps with joy as far as Innsbruck, and after leaving that place, rode hurriedly forward, in order that we might arrive the sooner at Venice. . . .

At Mestre we bade the land farewell, and put to sea in a barque, wherein we sailed as far as Venice to the Fondaco de' Tedeschi. At the Fondaco itself we inquired about inns for knights and pilgrims, and were conducted by a certain German to the inn of St. George, which is a large and respectable one. There we found many noblemen from various countries, all of whom were bound by the same vow as ourselves, and intended to cross the sea and visit the most Holy Sepulcher of the Lord Jesus. There were also in the other inns many pilgrims, both priests, monks, and laymen, gentle and simple, from Germany, from Gaul, and France, and especially two bishops, my Lord of Orleans and my Lord of Le Mans, with a very large retinue of companions and attendants, were there, awaiting the sailing of a ship; and, moreover, certain women well-stricken in years, wealthy matrons, six in number, were there together with us, desiring to cross the sea to the holy places. I was astonished at the courage of these old women, who through old age were scarcely able to support their own weight, yet forgot their own frailty, and through love for the Holy Land joined themselves to young knights and underwent the labors of strong men.

The proud nobles, however, were not pleased at this, and thought that they would not embark in the ship in which these ladies were to go, considering it a disgrace that they should go to receive the honor of knighthood in company with old women. These haughty spirits all endeavored to persuade us not to take our passage in the ship in which the old women meant to sail; but other wiser and more conscientious knights contradicted those proud men, and rejoiced in the holy penitence of these ladies, hoping that their holiness would render our voyage safer. On account of this there arose an implacable quarrel between those noblemen, which lasted until it pleased God to remove those proud men from among us. However, those devout ladies remained in our company both in going thither and in returning.

Now, Master Augustine Contarini, whose name means 'Count of the Rhine,' a noble Venetian, was going to take a cargo of pilgrims, and we agreed with him about the fare, and hired his galley, and received from him berths and cots – that is, places for each of us to lie in the galley – and we hoped for a quick passage, for we had waited for many days while the galley was being fitted for sea. But when everything was ready and there was nothing left to be done but set sail, as we longed to do, there came a ship which brought the bad news that the emperor of the Turks, Mahomet the Great, was besieging the island of Rhodes, with a great fleet by sea and a fully-equipped army of horse and foot by land, and that the whole of the Aegean and Carpathian and Malean seas swarmed with Turks, and that it was impossible during this year to take pilgrims across to the Holy Land. It would not be easy for me to tell with what sorrow the pilgrims heard this news, and the troubles and discord and quarrels to which they gave rise among the pilgrims would weary me to tell of. . . .

[Eventually the pilgrims obtain permission from the Venetian authorities to set sail for the Dalmatian coast.]

Now these contrary winds rose higher and higher, and for three days and nights we lay among these rocks, and whenever we put out, we were driven back again by the force of the wind, to the great discomfort of us all. However, this discomfort saved us; for when three days afterwards a fair wind blew out of that place, and we were making for the high sea, we met a Venetian war-galley, which as it passed us asked our officers if 'anything had happened to us at sea yesterday or the day before.' When we answered 'Nothing, except foul winds which had driven us to shelter under the mountains,' they answered, 'Blessed be those winds which drove you into hiding-places. For if you had been on the open sea yesterday, you would have fallen in with an armed Turkish fleet, which is sailing to Apulia to plunder the Christians there.' On hearing this, we praised God, who had for this time saved us from the hands of the Turks. . . .

We thus arrived at a place where a city stands on a mountain overlooking the sea. It is well walled, but is entirely deserted on account of the breath of a dragon, as will be afterwards explained; and next, after a tedious voyage among lofty mountains, we came to a part of the sea, where the galley remained fixed on the surface of the waters, nor could it be moved by the oars to the right nor to the left; but, as I have said, it stood stock still, because beneath it was the whirlpool called the 'abyss,' or opening into the earth, which there sucks up a great part of the sea, and where the waters sink down into that abyss. Wherefore the waters stand still above it, awaiting their descent into the abyss; and when the sea in that region has not much water in it, the water is whirled round, and whatever swims upon it is in danger of being drawn down. And indeed ships would be swallowed up there if their steersmen did not avoid it. So in this place we stood still, and our sailors endeavored with loud cries and much labor to row the galley away from this gulf, but their labors were in vain. However, the people of Corcyra, when they saw this – for we were within sight of the island and city of Corcyra – came to our aid from Corcyra, or Corfu, with two small galleys. They made ropes fast to our galley, brought them to their own sterns, and then by rowing their own galleys they, with great force, dragged our galley out of the jaws of the abyss, lest the deep should swallow us up. Being thus saved, we proceeded to the island of Corcyra, and after sunset entered the harbor of the city, which was full of ships of war, because, as the lords of the Venetian Senate had told us, the Captain of the Sea was there with an armed fleet to keep the peace at sea. So we slept until morning. At daybreak we went ashore to the city in small boats, and found it full of people, and many Turks were walking about among the Christians. After hearing Mass, we Suabian and Bavarian pilgrims hired a small cottage in the suburbs, and there cooked, ate, drank and slept. This cottage was small, and built of beams of very old and very dry wood: wherefore it happened, in consequence of the enormous fire which we made up for cooking, that the place twice actually caught fire; however, we always put out the fire, so that we did not get into any trouble about it. But the second time that this happened, the neighbors, seeing that the roof was on fire, ran together with clamor and lamentation, while we mounted the roof with ladders and took away the food of the flames.

On this occasion we were in no small danger, for if the fire had gathered strength the whole place would have been burned, and the Greek inhabitants of Corcyra would have sacrificed our lives to revenge themselves for the loss of their houses; indeed, they are very unfriendly to Germans, and are easily roused to attack them. After we had eaten, we respectfully presented the letter which we had received from the Venetian Senate to the Captain of the Sea, begging for his advice and assistance to further our pilgrimage. He, after reading it, advised us to return to Venice with our galley; but when he perceived that this advice was grievous, he said in a sort of rage, 'What folly possesses you, that you should wish to expose yourselves to such risks both of body and soul, of life and property? Behold, the sea is covered with cruel Turks, from whose hands there is no chance of your escaping. Go back to Venice, or stay in some seaport, until better news comes. But if you are utterly determined to go to the East, you must manage your passage yourselves, for I will not permit the galley in which you came to sail thither, because she belongs to St. Mark.' When we heard this, we were much disturbed, and left his presence, asking for time to take counsel. Hereupon the minds of many, especially those of the two bishops, were so wrought upon by the words of the captain, that they determined to return to Venice with all their retinue. Some even of our knights were fearful, and ready to go back; but others were brave and unmoved. I joined these latter, and, as far as I was able, heartened and encouraged the timid ones by preaching to them and quoting such passages of Holy Scripture as might raise in them hopes of divine protection. It befell on one day, when I was absent, that my lords the knights of our company were talking about the perils of our pilgrimage, and some were for going on with it, while others were timid and held back. One of them said, 'You ought not to pay any heed to the words of encouragement which Brother Felix says to you. What is life or death to him? He is a professed monk, and has no property, no friends, no position in life, nor anything else in the world, as we have. It is easier for him to die quickly by the sword of a Turk or Saracen than to grow old in his convent, dying daily.' And he said much more, trying to prevent the lords from listening to me. All this was told me, and I afterwards turned the tables by putting such courage into that same knight that he could not be persuaded into turning back. The captain kept us in Corcyra for eight days, and every day told us more and more frightful news; but we Germans had all agreed together that we would not go back, but that in the name of the Lord we would go on to Jerusalem. At last, when the captain saw that we were determined to carry out our intention, he left off interfering with our pilgrimage; and we made ready to start, removing ourselves into another galley, which we had bought. When all who wished to make this voyage were together on board of this galley, and we were joyfully talking to one another as we stood on deck beside the mast, one of the elders asked that silence should be made, and thus addressed us: 'My lords and brother pilgrims, we are undertaking a great, difficult, and arduous matter in making this pilgrimage by sea. And I say to you of a truth that, humanly speaking, we are acting foolishly in exposing ourselves to so great a danger against the advice and persuasion of the Captain of the Sea, and of everyone else. Wherefore the lords bishops and all the most noble, powerful, dignified, and perhaps the wisest of our company have given it up, and are on their way back to their own country, following the advice which has been given them, while we are setting out in the opposite direction. Now, therefore, so that our attempt may not be a mere act of sinful foolhardiness, we must needs reform our life on board of this galley, and must more frequently invoke the protection of Almighty God and his saints, that we may be able to make our way through the hosts of our enemies and their fleet.'

On hearing these words, we unanimously decided that no more games of cards or dice should be played on board of the galley, that no quarrels, oaths, or blasphemies should be allowed, and that the clerks and priests should add litanies to their usual daily prayers. Indeed, before this decree was made much disorder took place in these matters, for men were gambling morning noon, and night, especially the bishop of Orleans with his suite; and withal they swore most dreadfully, and quarreled daily, for the French and we Germans were always at blows. Thus it happened that one of the followers of the bishop of Orleans struck a devout priest of our company, and incurred excommunication. For the French are proud and passionate men; and, therefore, I believe that it was by an act of divine providence that they were separated from us, and our galley cleared of them; for we should scarcely have reached Jerusalem in their company without bloodshed and the murder of some of us. We stayed one night in Corcyra, sleeping on board ship; and that same night we had a terrible fright; for when it was late and had grown dark, as we still stood round the mast gossiping, we discovered a strange boat alongside of us, wherein were Turks, spies who were trying to listen to what we were saying. We at once betook ourselves to stones, which we hurled after them as they rowed away; however the boat straightway glided away out to sea and escaped. Next morning our trumpeters blew their horns or trumpets to show that we were about to start, and we cast off the moorings of the galley, and with joy and singing turned our backs to the harbor. The other pilgrims who stayed behind stood on the quay and laughed at us, saying that we were desperate men. For it was the common talk in Corcyra that we should be taken before we came to Modon. So thus we passed out of sight of Corcyra, and went on our way with joy mixed with fear. . . .

On the second day we reached Cyprus, and entered the harbor of Limasol, because a contrary wind forced us to make for a harbor. From thence, when the wind dropped, we sailed to the port of Larnaca, intending to remain there for several days, because the master of our ship had a brother at Nicosia in the service of the queen of Cyprus, and had some business to transact with him and bade us wait until it was finished. When his business was settled, we cast off our moorings and desired eagerly to reach our next port, for we had now no place to stop at short of the Holy Land. Sailing along we sighted the Holy Land on the third day, and out of the joy of our hearts we sang 'Te Deum Laudamus' ['We praise thee, O God'] with loud voices, and directed our prow towards Joppa, commonly called Jaffa, and came to an anchor off the rock of Andromeda. Here the master straightway sent a slave to run to Jerusalem and announce our arrival to the Father Warden of Mount Sion, that he might come with his brethren and with asses and their drivers to bring us to Jerusalem. So we abode in our galley for seven days, waiting for our guides, after which we were landed in small boats, and lodged in very old vaulted rooms, which were both ruinous and foulsmelling, wherein we remained for one night only; after this, we mounted the asses which had been brought for us, and thus, escorted by Saracens, we left the sea and came to the town of Ramleh, wherein we abode for some days, and then entered Jerusalem, where we were taken, not to a hospice, but to a house in Millo, wherein we ate, slept, and so forth.

We did not spend more than nine days in the Holy Land, during which we went the round of all the usual holy places in a great hurry, working day and night at the accomplishment of our pilgrimage, so that we were hardly given any time for rest. Having perfunctorily visited the holy places, and after my Master George von Stein and the other nobles had received knighthood in the Church of the Holy Sepulcher, our guides brought us out of the holy city along the road by which we came down to the sea, where our galley lay at anchor. None of the pilgrims remained in Jerusalem save two Englishmen, who wished to go across the desert to St. Catherine's [a famous monastery built on Mount Sinai], with whom I would willingly have stayed had they known either the German or Latin tongue, but as I could not talk with them their company would have been valueless to me; nevertheless, in spite of all these difficulties, I would have stayed in Jerusalem with them, and would have endured the want of a common language with patience, had I not firmly determined that I would return again to Jerusalem. For from that hour when our time came to leave the holy city, I determined and vowed that I would return as speedily as possible, and I regarded this pilgrimage as merely the preamble to that which I intended to make. As a student who means to commit some passage to memory first reads it over carelessly, and then reads it again slowly and leisurely, taking sufficient time to impress it on his mind, so I did with regard to my determination; and I was far from being satisfied with what I saw, nor did I commit the things which I saw to memory, but kept them for a future pilgrimage.

Now, when we reached the sea, we were all weak with our labors, worn out with the heat, the night-watching, and the hardships which we had endured, and, sick as we were, we were put on board our galley, which became like a hospital full of wretched invalids. After many days we returned to Cyprus, and after a prosperous voyage reached the harbor which is called Salina. Here we took the more weakly pilgrims to a neighboring village; but the healthier ones hired horses, and rode together with the captain of the ship to Nicosia, which is the metropolis of Cyprus and the royal residence, and is six German miles distant from the sea. There is an ancient custom that those who have been made knights at the Holy Sepulcher should present themselves to the king of Cyprus, and make a kind of treaty with him, and he calls them his brethren, and enrols their names in his books, giving them each a silver dagger with a sheath and belt. At the end of the dagger hangs a silver-wrought flower, resembling a violet, which is the symbol of the Order.

So my Master George von Stein, whom I never left, rode into Nicosia with me and with the other nobles, and we stayed there three days. Now, as there is no king in Cyprus, the nobles begged the queen to admit them to the Order of the Kings of Cyprus. She invited them into the great hall, and having ranged them in front of her, communicated to them through an interpreter the laws of this Order, which are, that in time of need they should

strive to defend the realm of Cyprus, seeing that it lies in the midst of Saracens, Turks, and Tartars. After they had pledged their faith to the queen with
their hands, she gave them their daggers, and permitted them to depart.

After this we rode back again to the sea. On our way we passed the foot
of an exceedingly high mountain, on the summit whereof is a chapel, in
which they told us was the cross of the good thief, wondrously suspended. I
should have liked to have seen it, but had not the time, so I put off this also
for my next pilgrimage. When we reached the sea and our galley, we found
that two pilgrims were dead, one of whom was a priest of the Minorite
Order, a brave and learned man, and the other was a tailor from Picardy, an
honest and good man. Several others were in the death-agony. We, too, who
had come from Nicosia cast ourselves down on our beds very sick; and the
number of the sick became so great, that there was now no-one to wait
upon them and furnish them with necessities. However, those ancient
matrons, seeing our miseries, were moved with compassion, and ministered to
us, for there was not one of them that was sick. Herein God, by the strength
of these old women, confounded the valor of those knights, who at Venice
had treated them with scorn, and had been unwilling to sail with them. They
moved to and fro throughout the galley from one sick man to another, and
ministered to those who had mocked and scorned them as they lay stricken
down on their beds. . . . During this time one of the knights ended his days
most piteously. We wound a sheet about him, weighted his body with stones,
and with weeping cast him into the sea. On the third day after this another
knight, who had gone out of his mind, expired in great pain and with terrible screams. Him we took ashore for burial in our small boat, for we were
then near the shore of Cyprus at Paphos. All this while we were making no
way, and were in want of water, bread, and other things. A foul wind carried
us out of sight of Cyprus, and for three days and nights we saw no land; then
after this we were carried back again to the harbor of Paphos, which is mentioned in the thirteenth chapter of *Acts*. In that port we bought necessary
stores, left it hurriedly, and were carried along the coast of Cyprus without
making any progress on our journey. Besides these misfortunes another great
one befell us, for that same night, while the officers of the ship were engaged
in managing the sails and tackling of the galley, lo! of a sudden a block fell
from the masthead, which struck and killed our best officer, a man whose
slightest sign was obeyed by all the sailors and galley-slaves. There was
exceedingly great lamentation in the galley at this man's death, nor was there
his like on board to take his place.

For many days we sailed slowly and tediously, hoping to arrive at some
port in Crete and to get clear of Rhodes, but being unable to do so. One day

we saw, a long way off at sea, a war-galley coming swiftly after us, and we
were terribly afraid, thinking that the Turks were coming; but when it came
nearer we saw that it was a Venetian galley, and laying aside the arms which
our captain had ordered to be brought out to defend us against the Turks, we
awaited the approach of the galley that we might hear her news. When she
came near, we learned that the Turks had been defeated, and had raised the
siege of Rhodes and retired in confusion. On hearing this news we were
filled with unspeakable joy, and turning the head of our galley away from its
former course, we pointed it towards the Isle of Rhodes. However, we did
not reach it for many days, being delayed by contrary winds. Moreover, we
were carried into the country of the Turks, and passed through a channel
where we had Turkish land and mountains on either side of us. Here our terrors were renewed, and we feared that perhaps the Turks, if they saw us,
would wreak their vengeance upon us for their defeat at Rhodes. We had no
wind, too, and passed the Turkish land in most wearisome fashion by the
slow labor of the oars. At last there came a wind which took us clear of the
land, and suddenly brought the galley to the Isle of Rhodes; but we came
along by a mountainous coast far from the city of the Colossae. However, we
came to a place where a fountain of living water flows from the foot of a
mountain, to which the sailors launched a boat and rowed with barrels and
brought fresh water on board our galley. When they returned on board, all
the passengers ran from their berths and beds, carrying dishes, pots, basins,
flasks, glasses, and bottles, to beg water from the sailors and boatmen. There
was more struggling and pushing to get water than I ever saw for wine or
bread. The men willingly and cheerfully gave some to each of us, and by the
taste of that fresh water we were revived, and seemed to come to life again,
even as plants and trees, which have been scorched and stricken down by the
heat of the sun, grow green again when sprinkled by the rain and dew. The
whole galley was exhilarated by the taste of this water, and those who before
had scarcely been able to breathe now began to sing, for water when drunk
after one has been long athirst makes a man as merry as a moderate draught
of wine.

What miseries and hardships we had undergone since we left the harbor
of Joppa in the Holy Land until we reached this place, I am not able to tell.
During those days of suffering I often wondered how any man can be so
luxurious as to be troubled well nigh throughout the year by the thought of
the forty days' fast of Lent and the bread-and-water fast on Good Friday. . . .
Nay, what seems even more strange to those who have not experienced such
a voyage, and more piteous to those who have, we were in such a state of
want and wretchedness that even putrid, stinking water was precious, and
the captain and all the ship's officers were in great anxiety lest we should run

Fig. 34] Plan of the island and harbor of Rhodes, from Breydenbach's *Saintes Pérégri-nations de Hiérusalem,* Lyons, 1488 (Lacroix, *Military and Religious Life in the Middle Ages,* facing p. 176).

out of even such water as that. The captain, therefore, gave orders that the steward should no longer give drinking-water of this sort to the animals which were kept on board to be slaughtered for food, but that it should be kept for the human beings, because it was more cruel that they should die of thirst than the brutes. So there the sheep, goats, mules, and pigs, stood for several days without water perishing of thirst. During those days I often saw these creatures licking the planks and the spars, sucking off them the dew which had gathered in the night. And although we had an infinite expanse of waters all around us, yet sea water is not drinkable either for man or beast, for to drink that water kills a man or a beast instead of refreshing him. I do not tell you of the stale bread, the biscuit full of worms, the tainted meat, and the abominable cookery, with all of which we should have been content if we had had wholesome water in good measure, if not for the sound men, at least for the unhappy sick ones. Oftentimes I have suffered so dreadfully from thirst and have had such a longing for cool water that I have thought that, when I got back to Ulm, I would go up straightway to Blaubüren and sit down beside the lake which rises there out of the depths until I had satiated my desire. There was no lack of wine in the galley – indeed, one could easily obtain it in abundance and very good – but we took no pleasure in it without mixing it with water, because of its strength and lukewarmness. So much for this matter. . . .

On the morrow, before we had risen, there came some of the lords of Rhodes to us to examine the galley and to see the pilgrims. We rowed into the city with them, passing through the bodies of dead Turks cast up by the sea, wherewith the shore was covered. When we entered the city we found it terribly ruined, full of stone cannon-balls, great and small, which the Turks had fired into it, of which there were said to be eight thousand and one scattered about the streets and lanes. The walls and towers were sadly ruinous, and we saw many other things, of which I will tell you when I come to this place again in my second pilgrimage. We remained at Rhodes four days, and spent a great deal of money, for everything was exceedingly dear because the Turks had plundered and laid waste the island. I bought two fowls for my Master George for a ducat, because he was in weak health, as I myself was likewise, for I was at that time suffering from dysentery, and almost despaired of my life. At last the time came when we had to leave Rhodes, and there embarked with us on board of our galley some of the Knights of St. John, and some who had for a long time been captives among the Turks, who had been sent to Rhodes with the Turkish army, and had deserted to that city during the siege. We also carried with us some Jews who had fought bravely during the siege. Among those who had escaped from captivity among the Turks was an Austrian nobleman, whom we found in a miserable condition, and whom my Master George took under his protection and brought back to Germany. By the embarking of so many people our galley became crowded and uncomfortable, and during our voyage we were driven hither and thither by contrary winds, and suffered much want before we reached a harbor in Crete. When we arrived there we entered the city of Crete [Candia], and stayed there for a few days, after which we went on board the galley one day late in the evening, bringing our purchases with us, and intending to sail the same night. When day broke and the galley was loosed from the mooring-posts, as they were violently directing the head towards the wind, the helm or rudder struck upon the rocks and broke under water; and the ship was within a little of striking the beak-head upon the rocks which ran out from the shore, in which case the whole galley would have broken up and we should have perished.

Therefore, a loud shout was raised, and people came running from the city to help us. As the rudder was broken we could not sail, but brought back our galley into the harbor to the place where she lay before. Here a waterman made arrangements for the repair of our rudder, which he did as follows, while we looked on. He stripped to his drawers, and then taking with him a hammer, nails, and pincers, let himself down into the sea, sank down to where the rudder was broken, and there worked under water, pulling out nails and knocking in others. After a long time, when he had put everything right, he reappeared from the depths, and climbed up the side of the galley to where we stood. This we saw; but how that workman could breathe under water, and how he could strike with his hammer there, and how he could remain so long in the salt water, I cannot understand. But this much I know, that the human mind has dominion over fire and water, even as the stars have dominion over the human mind. When our rudder was mended and we were thinking of getting away, there rose a contrary wind, so that the galley could not so much as get out of the harbor; so we returned to our former lodgings in the city, and ate and drank there.

This is one of the best and richest of sea-ports, and is full of all manner of good things; the speciality of the place, however, is the Cretan wine, which we call Malvoisie, which is renowned throughout the world, and everything is cheap there. So we did not mind staying there, but enjoyed it. When about the time of vespers we were called on board the galley, some came soon and others late. I myself was one of the first on board, and stood on the poop of the galley to watch whether any strangers besides those who had joined us at Cyprus or Rhodes would come on board; and there came two Greek bishops, with many others. As for what other things I saw there I would not write them down if I wished these 'wanderings' to be a grave narrative; but, as I promised my brethren in my epistle dedicatory, I often mix fun and amusement with serious matters. So while I was standing there watching those who were coming on board, I saw many of our pilgrims standing by the sea-side on the edge of the quay, with their heads dizzy, and afraid to come down into the boats, for the Cretan wine, which is sweet and pleasant to drink, makes the head dizzy when drunk in large quantities. Now, there were stone steps on the shore leading up to the city wall, down which those who wished to come on board the galley had to walk, and get into a small boat, in which they were brought alongside of the galley, and then again they had to get out of the boat and climb up some more steps into the galley. That evening many of them found it so difficult to do this that they had to be carried from the steps down the city wall into the boat, and from the boat into the galley, and right into their berths. Among the rest there came a pilgrim, who was the servant of some grandees in that city, and who was carrying his masters' baggage, together with some flasks of wine and a bag full of new bread, so that he was bowed down by his burden, besides being far gone in drink. When he came upon the steps and began to walk down them to the waterside to reach a boat there, he suddenly pitched headlong into the deep sea with all that he was carrying. At the cry which was raised by the bystanders, boatmen straightway rowed their skiffs to the place where he fell in, and, as he rose, dragged him out; but the loaves of bread and all that he was carrying floated over him, and were all utterly ruined.

There was a pilgrim, a Dalmatian priest, whom I knew very well, who also had drunk too much sweet wine, so that he had much trouble to get on board the galley as far as the mast, where he stood talking to another Dalmatian until dark. He stood near a hatchway, through which people do not go below by night, but only in the daytime, for as soon as night comes on the ladder is taken down, so that those who sleep on that side of the ship may not be disturbed by people coming and going. So when this good pilgrim had finished his talk, and we on the lower deck were all lying in our beds gossiping, he wished to get into his berth through the nearest hatchway, and, being unsteady on his legs, he fell down through the hatchway on to the lower deck with such a crash that his fall shook the whole galley, for he was a big fat man. We all lay silent and terrified, and waited to hear who it was that had fallen. He straightway arose unhurt, and angrily began in a stammering voice, 'There now! I had the ladder under my feet, and had come down three steps, when somebody pulled it from under my feet, and I fell down.' To this someone answered that the ladder had been taken down an hour before, but he replied, 'That is not true, because I had come down three steps, and while I was standing on the third step it was pulled away from me.' On hearing this we all burst out laughing, as we knew that the ladder had been taken away an hour before, and I, being glad that my friend had not been hurt by so high and dangerous a fall, laughed most immoderately. When he heard me laughing he was furiously angry with me. 'So,' said he, 'now I see clearly that it was you, Brother Felix, who pulled the ladder from under me. You shall assuredly not leave this galley before I have my revenge upon you!' When I tried to clear myself he became all the more angry, and cursed me, swearing that on the morrow he would take vengeance on me. However, the sleep which followed cured all these sick and dizzy men who had been the worse for Cretan wine, and on the morrow they had forgotten all about this. But if that pilgrim had suffered that fall sober, without being in liquor, he would very likely have broken his legs or his neck, for it commonly happens that in dangerous feats drunken men are more lucky, though not wiser, than others. . . .

[After leaving Corfu, the ship encounters a fierce storm.]

But while it was yet dark, and no stars could be seen, as we tacked to windward there arose a most frightful storm, and a terrible disturbance of the sea and air. Most furious winds tossed us aloft, lightning flashed, thunder roared dreadfully; moreover, on either side of us fearful thunder bolts fell, so that in many places the sea seemed to be on fire. The rain, too, fell in such torrents as though entire rain-clouds had burst and fallen upon us. Violent squalls kept striking the galley, covering it with water, and beating upon the sides of it as hard as though great stones from some high mountains were sent flying along the planks. I have often wondered when at sea in storms how it can be that water, being as it is a thin, soft and weak body, can strike such hard blows against whatever it meets, for it makes a noise when it runs against the ship as though mill stones were being flung against her; and one cannot wonder at its breaking up a ship even though she were built of iron. Waves of sea-water are more vehement, more noisy, and more wonderful than those of other water. I have had great pleasure in sitting or standing on the upper deck during a storm, and watching the marvelous succession of gusts of wind and the frightful rush of the waters. Storms are endurable by day, but at night they are too cruel, especially when they are violent ones like that of which I am now speaking: for this was a very fierce storm, and the darkness was intense, nor was there any light save the continual flashes of lightning. So fierce a wind kept tossing the galley up and down, rolling it from side to side and shaking it about, that no man could lie in his berth, much less sit, and least of all stand. We were obliged to hang on to the pillars which stood in the middle of the cabin supporting the upper works, or else to crouch on our bended knees beside our chests, embracing them with our hands and arms, and so holding ourselves still; and while doing so, sometimes big heavy chests would be upset, together with the men who were clinging to them. For the galley moves so violently, and in such different directions, that it upsets everything that stands, and, although this sounds miraculous but is perfectly true, even things which were hanging up against the bulk-heads came off their hooks and fell down. Although the ship was everywhere dressed with pitch and the other things which are used to prevent leakage and to keep out the water, yet during this storm the water came in through unsuspected leaks every where, so that there was nothing in the whole ship which was not wet; our beds and all our things were sopping, our bread and biscuit all spoiled by the sea water. On the lower deck was terror and misery; on the upper deck toil and trouble. The wind blew our mainsail all to pieces, so the sailors lowered the yard, and bent to it another sail, for use in storms, which they call 'papafigo'; but after they had hoisted up the yard with the sail furled along it, while the sailors were sitting along the yard letting the ties go, and the sail was falling down, and the sailors on deck were holding in their hands the 'polistrelum,' that is, the rope by which the lower corners of the sail are held, lo! the wind rushed into the sail and filled it with such force that it tore the sheet out of the hands of the sailors, and blew it and the sail itself above the mast-head and above the 'keba,' or 'top,' high into the air: and it blew out so strongly in the wind that the yard bent like a bow, and the very mast itself, although it was big and strong, formed of many beams fastened together, creaked loudly as though it was already split and broken. At this time we were in the greatest danger, for had the mast broken during such a storm, we should soon have been overwhelmed by the sea, galley and all. As a bird cannot fly without its feathers and wings, even so a ship of the greatest burden cannot move without sails, which are its wings and feathers. So when the poets speak of winged horses, they merely mean ships, as, for instance, Perseus came from Greece on a winged horse, and saved Andromeda from the rock at Joppa, and so forth. So our mast made many dreadful noises, and the yard likewise; and every joint in the whole galley seemed to be coming to pieces. Nothing ever frightened me in storms so much as the loud groans of the ship, which are so intense that one thinks that the ship must be broken somewhere. Nor can a man refrain from crying out, because of the sudden and dreadful noise of these groans. So there we stood, beholding a sad sight and in imminent danger. As the sail flapped thus in the air, the galley-slaves and other sailors ran to and fro with as much noise and shouting as though they were just about to be run through with swords; some climbed up the shrouds on to the yard, and tried to draw the sail down to them; some on deck below ran about trying to catch hold of the sheet again; some drove ropes through blocks and put brails round the sail.

Meanwhile the pilgrims and those who were useless at this work prayed to God and called upon the saints. Some made their confessions as though already at the very point of death; some made great vows that they would travel from hence to Rome, to St. James [at Compostella, see 25 above], or to the house of the Blessed Virgin [at Loretto], if only they might escape from this death; for it is only when death is present before our eyes that we fear it. I thought of the aphorisms of Anacharsis the philosopher, who said that those who are at sea cannot be counted among either the living or the dead. Moreover, he said that they were only removed from death by the space of four fingers, four fingers being the thickness of the sides of a ship. Also, when asked which ships were the safest, he replied: 'Those which lie on dry ground, and not in the sea,' declaring that there was no safety at sea, because of its numerous and sudden perils. In the course of this terrible storm, lo! of a sudden there came an unhoped-for help from heaven. Amid the flashing of the lightning there appeared a light which stood fixed in the air above the prow for some time. Thence it slowly moved throughout the whole length of the galley as far as the stern, where it vanished. This light was a ray of fire about a cubit in width. As soon as the officers, the galley-slaves, and the other sailors, and such of the pilgrims as were on deck, saw this light, they all left off working, ceased their noise and shouting, and kneeling down with their hands raised to heaven, cried out in a low voice nothing except 'Holy, holy, holy.' We who were below, not knowing what was happening, were scared at the sudden quiet and silence, and the unwonted prayer. We imagined that they had given up working in despair, and were crying 'holy' because they were on the point of death, and we stood astonished, waiting to see what should be the end of this. So someone opened a door which covered the main hatchway of the galley, through which men come down from the deck into the cabin, and called to us in Italian, saying: '*O, Signori pellegrini, non habeate paura que questo note non avereto fortuna,*' which is, being interpreted: 'Pilgrims, my masters, fear not, for this night and in this storm we shall suffer no evil, for we have received help from heaven.' After this, as the storm continued, the galley-slaves returned to their accustomed labors, and now they no longer howled as before, but worked with joyous shouts; for they never work without shouting. Let no man suppose that what I have told about the light is false, for it is as true as possible, and I could prove it by the oaths of more than two hundred witnesses who are alive at this day; for the arm of the Lord is not shortened that he should be unable to save those who are in distress. . . . At last we reached the city of Venice and broke up our company, every man going to his own home.

Meanwhile, I had become sick, not so that I was bed ridden; but I was too ill to walk or to ride a horse, until I recovered. So my Master George and the other nobles went home; but I remained at Venice in the hands of physicians for about fifteen days, after which, having recovered my health, I set out from Venice in company with a merchant, bought a horse at Treviso, and traveled with my comrade as far as Trent. From Trent I came alone to Nassereit. Arriving there in the afternoon, I found in the inn four of my brother pilgrims from the Holy Land – Englishmen, and we greeted one another with joy. They were making ready to start, wishing to cross the mountain which is called Sericius that same day; but I begged them to wait till the morrow, that we might journey to Ulm together; for I was weary, and did not wish to start on that day. They asked me to ride with them, which I did not wish to do; but begged them to stay with me in the name of our fellowship and friendship. But they would not, because they told me that they had heard for certain that on that very day a great company of armed knights of the court of the Duke of Austria was coming to that village and inn; and they wished to avoid them, as it was not safe to live among men-at-arms. So we parted from one another again, for they went on, and I stayed behind. In the evening there came to the inn many armed noble men with their retainers, who had been sent by the Duke of Austria to defend the castle of Kregen, which Count Eberhard the elder of Wurtemburg was besieging and trying to destroy. So the inn was full of fierce men-at-arms; but when they heard that I had come from the Holy Land they treated me with respect as a priest and monk, and also as a soldier of the Holy Land and the Holy Sepulcher, and invited me to say Mass for them on the morrow, and travel with them. On

[Fig. 35] A family carrying out a vow in a chapel of pilgrimage; note the reliquary of a foot placed behind the altar. Pilgrimages might be undertaken on behalf of those unable to go themselves, and heirs were sometimes requested to make pilgrimages on behalf of the deceased (from a fifteenth-century French illustration, Lacroix, *Military and Religious Life in the Middle Ages,* p. 384).

the morrow I celebrated Mass, and breakfasted with them; and when we set out they paid my bill for me, and took me with them in the midst of their force with pleasure and comfort. When we arrived at Kempten I found there at the Crown Inn the four aforementioned English pilgrims, wounded, beaten, and robbed of all their property, in the greatest sorrow and shame and wretchedness. For in a wood near Kempten robbers had fallen upon them, stricken them from their horses with swords, and when they attempted to repel force by force and defend themselves, had wounded them with cuts of their swords, bound them, and dragged them away from the public road into the inner part of the wood to a lonely field, where they plundered them with many insults, searched their wallets, emptied their purses and scrips, stripped them quite naked, and searched their clothes with great care to find whether they had sewn any money into them. At last they gave them some worse clothes in exchange, and forced them to swear an oath that for the space of three days they would tell no one what had befallen them. I was very sorry for my brethren, but I congratulated myself at not having remained in their company; for if so I should, like them, have fallen into the hands of those robbers. On the morrow I arrived at Memmingen with those knights, and I spent that day there. On the following day, which was the feast of St. Othmar [25 October], I traveled from Memmingen to Ulm in company with a priest. On entering my convent I was gladly and kindly received, and so I betook me to my wonted labors in my cell. I may say with truth that this first pilgrimage of mine was a hundredfold more toilsome and grievous to me than my second one, and much more dangerous both by sea and by land. Our company of pilgrims during my first pilgrimage was more disorderly, for there were among them many very passionate men, and there were daily quarrels, and some thievish Picards, and some were always sick; indeed, in every way this my first journey was much more grievous, albeit my second journey was much more toilsome, more distant, more expensive, and more dangerous; yet I endured more and more deadly perils on my first journey than I did on my second. By this all men may see clearly how untrue is the common saying, that the pilgrimage by sea from Venice to the Holy Land is a mere pleasant excursion with little or no danger. O my God, what a hard and tedious excursion: with how many sufferings was it spoiled. During this excursion I saw many vigorous young noblemen perish, who once had thought in their own conceit that they could rule the waves of the sea and weigh the lofty mountains in scales; but who at last died by the just judgment of God, broken down by hard ships and lamentably humbled in spirit. May God give those who call this pilgrimage an easy excursion the power of feeling its sorrows, that they may learn to have the compassion for pilgrims to the Holy Land which they deserve. It requires courage and audacity to attempt this pilgrimage. That many are prompted to it by sinful rashness and idle curiosity cannot be doubted; but to reach the holy places and to return to one's home active and well is the special gift of God.

Here ends Brother Felix Fabri's first wandering to the Holy Land.

CHAPTER SIX

RELICS

The veneration of relics – bodily parts of the saints, or objects connected with them such as cloths that had been dipped in the blood of a martyr – began as early as the second century (see the account of Polycarp, 1 above). By the fifth century the cult of relics had spread to northern Europe, and there was a constant trafficking in bodily parts between Rome and Gaul. Because the saints were understood to be actually present in their bodily remains, and thus able to act as powerful mediators in human affairs on a continuing basis, both secular and religious authorities saw in relics a means of promoting their political aims and their prestige. The custom of placing relics in church altars as a condition of consecration gave further impetus to the trade and enhanced their appeal to wealthy and powerful individuals who wished to obtain them. Relics might be purchased, given as gifts, included in war booty or simply stolen. Their miraculous powers were intensely coveted by all members of society.

From the beginning the cult had its critics, but more influential were the church fathers who wrote in its defence. They argued that as the earthly reminders of holy men and women, relics provided a model of holy living for other Christians and deserved at least as much respect as had their owners when alive. Relics, it was argued, should receive the same love and respect as the remains of one's ancestors, since the saints are the friends of all Christians; further, the Holy Spirit worked not only through their souls (now in heaven) but also through their physical bodies which remain on earth. The ultimate justification lay in the miraculous: since God performed miracles through the relics of the saints, he clearly intended that they should be venerated.

28. GREGORY OF TOURS: THE POWER OF RELICS

Gregory, bishop of Tours from 573 until his death in 594 or 595, inhabited a post-Roman world of casual brutality, treason, bloodshed, and murder into which, as the bishop of an important Christian center, he was periodically drawn. He is best known for his vivid, gossipy 'History of the Franks' in which this world is superlatively described, but he was also a prolific hagiographer and wrote several collections of saints' 'lives,' paying particular homage to Julian of Brioude, a saint from his native Auvergne, and Martin of Tours, both of whom he adopted as his chief patrons. He also wrote seven books of miracles, describing numerous saints and their powers, especially the saints of Gaul and foreign saints whose relics had been brought to Gaul where they continued to work miracles. In the embattled world of Gregory and his contemporaries it is little wonder that people turned to the relics of the saints to punish their enemies, reveal perjurers, protect themselves and their crops, and obtain healing from their afflictions. Gregory's writings provide a useful introduction to the ways in which relics were understood to work in Merovingian Gaul.

Source: trans. Raymond Van Dam, *Gregory of Tours: Glory of the Martyrs,* Translated Texts for Historians, Latin Series III (Liverpool: Liverpool University Press, 1988), pp. 22-4; 26-7; 52-3; 69; 86-7; 106-9; 123-4; repr. with permission.

5. [Christ's] Cross and his miracles at Poitiers.

The Cross of the Lord that was found by the empress Helena at Jerusalem is venerated on Wednesday and Friday. Queen Radegund [see 16-17 above], who is comparable to Helena in both merit and faith, requested relics of this Cross and piously placed them in a convent at Poitiers that she founded out of her own zeal. She repeatedly sent servants to Jerusalem and throughout the entire region of the East. These servants visited the tombs of holy martyrs and confessors and brought back relics of them all. After placing them in the silver reliquary with the holy Cross itself, she thereafter deserved to see many miracles. Of these miracles I will first mention this one that the Lord deigned to reveal during the days of his suffering. On the [Good] Friday before holy Easter when [the nuns] were spending the night in vigils without any light, about the third hour of the night a small light appeared before the altar in the shape of a spark. Then it was enlarged and scattered bright beams here and there. Slowly it began to rise higher, and after becoming a huge beacon it offered light for the dark night and for the congregation that was keeping vigil and praying. As the sky began to brighten it gradually faded until, upon the return of daylight to the lands, it vanished from the sight of the onlookers.

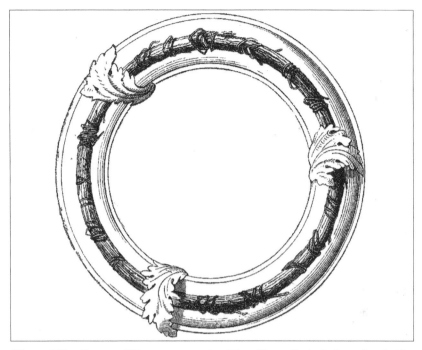

[Fig. 36a] The Crown of Thorns, preserved at Notre Dame, Paris. A ring of reeds (the thorns are not visible), it is enshrined in gold with gold acanthus leaves (Lacroix, *Military and Religious Life in the Middle Ages,* p. 393).

[Fig. 36b] A fragment of the Lord's Cross preserved in the Church of Santa Croce di Gerusalemme, Rome. The fragment, said to have been given to the Pope by St. Helena, is of cedarwood and appears to carry the inscription, 'Jesus of Nazareth, King of the Jews' written backwards in both Greek and Latin (Lacroix, *Military and Religious Life in the Middle Ages,* p. 377).

Often I heard how even the lamps that were lit in front of these relics bubbled up because of the divine power and dripped so much oil that frequently they filled a vessel underneath. But because of the foolishness of my closed mind I was never motivated to believe these stories until that power which is at present being revealed reproved my slow-witted hesitation.

For that reason I will describe what I saw with my own eyes. While visiting the tomb of St. Hilary [at Poitiers], I happened out of respect to arrange a conversation with this queen [Radegund]. I entered the convent, greeted the queen, and bowed before the venerable Cross and the holy relics of the saints. Then, at the conclusion of my prayer, I stood up. To my right was a burning lamp that I saw was overflowing with frequent drips. I call God as my witness, I thought that its container was broken, because placed beneath it was a vessel into which the overflowing oil dripped. I turned to the abbess [Agnes] and said: "Is your thinking so irresponsible that you cannot provide an unbroken lamp in which the oil can be burned, but instead you use a cracked lamp from which the oil drips?" She replied "My lord, such is not the case; it is the power of the holy Cross you are watching." Then I reconsidered and remembered what I had heard earlier. I turned back to the lamp [that was now] heaving in great waves like a boiling pot, overflowing in swelling surges throughout that hour, and (I believe in order to censure my incredulity) being more and more replenished, so that in the space of one hour the container produced more than four times the oil that it held. Stunned, I was silent, and finally I proclaimed the power of the venerable Cross. . . .

The nature of the power of this wood became apparent to me in this way. A man arrived who showed me a small robe that was made of silk and that was very old. He claimed that the Lord's Cross had been wrapped in this robe at Jerusalem. Because of my ignorance this claim seemed outrageous, and I immediately asked how he had received such favor there that he was worthy [to acquire] these relics. For I knew not only that no one was ever judged worthy when this sacred wood was adored, but also that whoever approached improperly was kept away with whips. In reply he said: "As I was leaving Jerusalem, I met the abbot Futes, who had great favor with the empress Sophia [wife of Justin II, emperor at Constantinople from 565 until 578]; for they had entrusted the entire East to this man as if it were his prefecture. I attached myself to this man, and when I was returning from the East I received from him both these relics of saints and this robe in which the holy Cross was then always wrapped." After this man told me this story and gave me this robe, I confess, I dared to wash the robe and allow people with fevers to drink [the water]. But soon, as the divine power brought aid,

Healing

they were healed. Then I even cut off some pieces and gave them to monks as a blessing. I gave one piece to an abbot who returned two years later and claimed under oath that it had healed twelve possessed people, three blind people, and two paralytics. He had placed [his piece of] the robe in the mouth of a mute man, and as soon as it touched his teeth and tongue, it restored his voice and speech. The promise of the Lord convinces us trustfully to believe this story; for the Lord said "Believe that you will receive everything which you have asked in my name and they will come to you."

33. The relics of the martyr St. Stephen.

Stephen was the first deacon of the holy church and the first martyr at Jerusalem, as the sacred history of the apostles relates. He was stoned to death for the holy name of Christ whom he saw at the right hand [of God] in a spiritual vision of power; he begged the mercy [of God] for his persecutors.

Near Tours there is an oratory that people long ago dedicated in Stephen's name and that I ordered to be enlarged a bit. When the reconstruction was completed, we moved the altar forward, exactly as it had been before. But while we were looking in its reliquary, we found none of the holy relics that tradition claimed [to be there]. I sent one of the abbots to fetch relics of Stephen for us from the oratory of the church house, but I forgot to give him the key for the reliquary, which was hanging on my belt. Once the abbot arrived, he removed the seal from the cupboard but found the reliquary locked. He was uncertain about what to do or how to act. If he returned to me, it would require much time to go and come back; if he brought the entire reliquary, he knew I would be annoyed, because in it were the relics of many saints; if he did nothing, he would not obey the order he had received. Why say more? When he took the reliquary hesitantly in his hand, the bolts clicked back and he saw that it was unlocked. He gave thanks, took the relics, and with great amazement brought them to me. At God's command I transferred them [to the altar] during the celebration of mass. Many days later I returned to Tours; there I found the reliquary just as I had left it, locked and again bolted.

unlocks the reliquary

There is a relic of the blood of this holy deacon, as is popularly claimed, in the altar of a church at Bourges. During the episcopacy of Felix a man accused his neighbors of some crime. After he had at length abused his neighbors with provocative words and had challenged them to a public hearing, it was decreed by a mandate of the leading men of the city that the neighbors would clear themselves of this crime for which they were accused by an oath. They approached the altar of the aforementioned church, raised

sinners punished

their hands, and swore their oath. The accuser in the case insisted in a loud voice that they had perjured themselves. Suddenly his feet were jerked up, he was tossed into the air, and his head struck the pavement. To the surrounding crowd he seemed almost lifeless. Almost two hours later when he was thought to be clearly dying, he opened his eyes and confessed his misdeed; he admitted that he had unjustly harassed these men and unjustly proclaimed them to be guilty. In this way, by disclosing the innocent and exposing the guilty the power of the blessed Stephen was clearly apparent.

46. The bodies of St. Gervasius and St. Protasius

In the city [of Milan] there are the victorious bodies of the blessed martyrs Gervasius and Protasius. According to the history of their suffering, for a long time their bodies were concealed underground. Their location was revealed to the blessed Ambrose, who found the bodies [in 386]. After a display of miracles, the bodies were buried in a church that Ambrose had built from his own zeal. Tours in particular has some older churches distinguished with relics of these saints, although by God's grace their relics were also scattered throughout the entire compass of Gaul. Once some monks were talking about these saints, [and wondered] why the aforementioned relics had been so thickly distributed to various places. I do not think it irrelevant to insert in this selection what I heard someone say on this matter, because it is not found in the history of their suffering. For this man said that when their glorious bodies were moved into the church, during the celebration of Mass in honor of the martyrs a board fell from the vault. The board struck the heads of the martyrs and drew a flow of blood. The holy blood was collected after linen cloths, robes, and even the curtains of the church were stained with it. The blood was said to have continued flowing until linen cloths were found to soak it up. Thereafter, since so many relics [of the blood] of the martyrs were gathered, they were sent throughout the whole of Italy and Gaul. St. Martin received many of these relics, as the letter of the most blessed Paulinus [of Nola] states.

62. The martyr Mallosus.

Finding martyrs

Bishop Eberigisilus discovered the body of the martyr St. Mallosus in this way. Although it was reported that Mallosus had consummated his martyrdom in the village of Birten, men were uncertain where he had been buried. There was, however, an oratory there, in which his name was invoked. The aforementioned bishop Eberigisilus built a church in honor of Mallosus so that whenever he received some revelation about the martyr he might, with the Lord's approval, transfer his holy body to the church. Finally, in the side of the church, that is, in the wall which was next to the oratory he built an arch and included the oratory in an apse. He beseeched the pity of the Lord that he reveal whatever he might order concerning the martyr. Later a deacon at Metz was guided by a vision and learned where the martyr was buried. A short time later he came to bishop Eberigisilus. Although he had never been there before, it was as if he were reciting familiar landmarks that he had seen in his vision. He said to the bishop: "Dig here, and you will find the body of the saint," that is, in the middle of the apse. When the bishop had dug about seven feet down, the scent of an overpowering perfume reached his nose and he said: "Since this sweet fragrance surrounds me, I believe in Christ, because he has revealed his martyr to me." Digging further, he found that the holy body was intact. In a loud voice he cried out, "Glory to God in the highest," and he had the entire clergy chant Psalms with him. After singing a hymn he transferred the holy body to the church, and with the conventional laudations he buried it. . . .

82. The power of the relics that were brought to me from Rome.

Through their confession the glorious martyrs have earned the unspeakable benefits of gifts that are always salutary. To petitioners they have revealed themselves by this power that the Lord Creator shared with them. I know that this happened just as my deacon recently told me. This deacon received relics of some martyrs and confessors from pope Pelagius of Rome. A large chorus of monks who were chanting Psalms and a huge crown of people escorted him to Ostia. After he boarded a ship the sails were unfurled and hoisted over the rigging of a mast that presented the appearance of a cross. As the wind blew, they set out on the high seas. While they were sailing to reach the port of Marseilles, they began to approach a certain place where a mountain of stone rose from the shore of the sea and, sinking a bit, stretched into the sea to the top of the water. As the wind forced them on, the ship was lifted by a mighty blast into danger. When the ship was shaken as if struck by the rock, the sailors recognized their peril and announced their death. The deacon lifted the reliquary with the holy relics. He groaned and in a loud voice began to invoke the names of the individual saints. He prayed that their power might liberate from danger those who were about to die. The ship, as I said, sailed closer and closer to the rock. Suddenly, out of respect for the holy relics, a wind blew from that spot with great force against the other wind. It crushed the waves and repulsed the opposing wind. By recalling the

calling wind

ship to the deep sea, the wind freed everyone from the danger of death. So they circumvented this impending danger, and by the grace of the Lord and the protection of the saints they arrived at the port they had hoped for. For these were relics of the saints whose sacred feet had been washed by the hands of the Lord. [There were also relics] of Paul, Lawrence, Pancratius, Chrysanthus, the virgin Daria, and John and his brother, the other Paul. Rome, the capital of the world, piously celebrates their struggles and the prizes of their victories.

83. The relics that my father owned.

I will now narrate what happened with the relics that my father once carried with him. At the time when Theudebert ordered the sons of Clermont to be sent off as hostages [to guarantee the safety of his own family; Gregory's father Florentius was presumably one of the hostages], my father had been recently married. Because he wished himself to be protected by relics of saints, he asked a cleric to grant him something from these relics, so that with their protection he might be kept safe as he set out on this long journey. He put the sacred ashes in a gold medallion and carried it with him. Although he did not even know the names of the blessed men, he was accustomed to recount that he had been rescued from many dangers. He claimed that often, because of the power of these relics, he had avoided the violence of bandits, the dangers of floods, the threats of turbulent men, and attacks from swords.

I will not be silent about what I witnessed regarding these relics. After the death of my father my mother carried these relics with her. It was the time for harvesting the crops, and huge piles of grain had been collected on the threshing floors. Just like the Limagne [a fertile plain in the southern Auvergne], which is clothed with crops but stripped of its trees, so during those days when the seeds were already threshed there was no place to light a fire when a frost appeared. So the threshers kindled fires for themselves from the straw. Then everyone retired to eat. And behold, the fire gradually began to be spread through the straw bit by bit. Quickly, fanned by the wind, the fire spread to the piles of grain. The fire became a huge blaze and was accompanied by the shouts of men, the wails of women, and the crying of children. This happened in our field. When my mother, who was wearing these relics around her neck, learned of this, she rushed from the meal and held the sacred relics in front of the balls of flames. In a moment the entire fire so died down that no sparks were found among the piles of burned straw and the seeds. The grain the fire had touched had suffered no harm.

Many years later I received these relics from my mother. While I was traveling from Burgundy to Clermont, a huge storm appeared in my path. The storm frequently flashed with lightning in the sky and rumbled with loud crashes of thunder. Then I took the holy relics from my pocket and raised my hand before the cloud. The cloud immediately divided into two parts and passed on by the right and the left; it threatened neither me nor anyone else. Then, as a presumptuous young man is expected to behave, I began to be inflated by the arrogance of vain glory. I silently thought that this concession had been made especially for me, rather than because of the merits of the saints. I boasted to my traveling companions and insisted that I had deserved that which God had bestowed upon my naiveté. Immediately my horse suddenly slipped beneath me and threw me to the ground. I was so seriously bruised during this accident that I could hardly get up. I understood that this accident had happened because of my pride; and it was sufficient to note that afterwards the urge of vain glory did not bother me. For if it happened that I was worthy to observe some manifestations of the powers of saints, I have proclaimed that they were due to the gift of God through the faith of the saints.

100. The martyr Georgius.

I know many miracle stories about the martyr Georgius, of which I will narrate a few. Some people were carrying his relics along with the relics of other saints. When these couriers came to a place in the territory of Limoges where a few clerics had already constructed an oratory from wood planks and were constantly praying to the Lord, they requested lodging. They were received with kindness and they spent the night chanting Psalms with the other brothers. At daybreak they took the reliquary but could not lift it at all. Since they completely refused to travel without the holy relics, a great grief came into their hearts. They understood, by the inspiration of God, that they ought to leave some of their relics in this place. They searched in the fastenings [around the relics] and cut off some pieces; they presented them to the elder [cleric] who presided at the oratory. By leaving a part of their protection they received the opportunity of departing to where they wished to go. . . .

29. THE HUMILIATION OF ST. MITRIAS

Like his 'Glory of the Martyrs,' Gregory of Tours's 'Glory of the Confessors' is mainly concerned with Gallic saints grouped around the cities where they were honored. Gregory relied for his information largely on oral traditions and his own experience (he was an inveterate visitor to shrines); thus we have little corroboration from written sources for some of his saints, like Mitrias, whose historicity is uncertain. The story describes a practice associated with relics known as the 'humiliation' of the saint as punishment for a failure to protect those who prayed to him or her. The saint was considered to have been dishonored by what had happened, and would in turn be physically dishonored by being abandoned by supplicants until justice was restored. In most cases this amounted to significant but passive pressure upon the perpetrator to put matters right, but in this story the pressure proves to be fatal.

Source: trans. Raymond Van Dam, *Gregory of Tours: Glory of the Confessors*, Translated Texts for Historians, Latin Series IV (Liverpool: Liverpool University Press, 1988), pp. 73–75; repr. with permission.

70. The Confessor Mitrias of Aix.

The famous athlete [warrior of God] Mitrias was granted to Aix-en-Provence. According to a history of his life, while in his body he was a man of magnificent holiness. Although he was a slave by rank, he was a free man through his righteousness. Those who read the account of his [life's] struggle say that he completed the course of [his life's] good works and departed from this world as a victor. Through his public miracles he often reveals that he lives in heaven. Once, when bishop Franco administered the church of Aix, Childeric, who was then an important man at the court of King Sigibert, seized a villa belonging to the church. Childeric said that the church of Aix improperly possessed it. More swiftly than can be said the bishop was summoned. He gathered oath-takers and stood in the presence of the king, crying out and begging that the king separate his presence from hearing this case lest he be condemned by the judgment of heaven. He added: "I know about the power of the blessed man Mitrias, because he quickly imposes his vengeance against someone who invades [his property]." Then the judges met and discussed the case. Childeric stood up, taunted the bishop, and heaped accusations on him. [He claimed] that the bishop had kept for his own unjust order the possessions that were owed to the sovereignty of the [royal] treasury, and he ordered the bishop to be dragged forcibly from the judicial hearing. Once the bishop was bound, Childeric fined him three hundred gold pieces after the judgment of those present had removed the villa [from his control]. Everyone agreed with Childeric, and no one dared to vote against his wish unless he had approved it.

After Bishop Franco was sentenced and despoiled, he returned to Aix. He knelt in prayer before the tomb of St. Mitrias, recited the verses of a Psalm, and said: "Most glorious saint, no more lights will be lit here, no more melodies of Psalms will be sung, until you first avenge your servants from their enemies and restore to the holy church the properties that have been violently taken from you." He wept as he said this. Then he threw briers with sharp thorns on top of the tomb; after he left, he shut the doors and put other briers likewise in the entrance. Immediately the man who had invaded [the church property, that is, Childeric] was struck with a fever. He lay on his bed, rejected food, refused to drink, and in his fever continually panted. Even if he occasionally became thirsty because of the burning of his fever, he drank only water and nothing else. Why say more? He spent an entire year in this illness, but his evil mind was not changed. Meanwhile all his hair and his beard fell out, and his entire head was so naked that you might think he had once been buried and then recently taken from his tomb after a funeral. After the wretched man was afflicted with these and other similar misfortunes, he reconsidered at a late hour and said: "I have sinned because I plundered the church of God and I brought insult upon the holy bishop. Now, however, go as quickly as possible and, after restoring the villa, place six hundred gold pieces on the tomb of the saint. For I hope that after the property has been returned he might grant a cure to a sick man." His men listened to what he said, took the money, and did as had been commanded of them. They restored the estate and placed the gold coins on the tomb of the servant of God. But when they did this, immediately Childeric exhaled his spirit in the place where he was. Because he had unjustly seized this acquisition, he earned the loss of his soul. The bishop obtained from this enemy of the church the revenge that he had predicted would result from the power of the athlete of God.

30. THE AFFAIR OF ST. SERGIUS'S FINGERBONE

So much were saints' cults and relics a part of the texture of Merovingian life, that Gregory of Tours seamlessly weaves many stories about them into his 'History of the Franks.' The following account concerns Gundovald, who was a rival for the throne of the Frankish king Guntram, Mummolus, the unscrupulous and time-serving count of Auxerre, and the attempt by both men to yoke the power of relics to their political schemes.

Source: trans. O. M. Dalton, *Gregory of Tours: History of the Franks* (Oxford: Clarendon Press, 1927), Vol. 2, 7, 31, pp. 308-309; repr. with permission.

7, 31. At this time Gundovald was at Bordeaux, for Bishop Bertram showed him friendship. Seeking every means of helping forward his cause, he was told by some one that a certain king in the East had possessed himself of a thumb of the holy Sergius the martyr, that he had inserted it in his right arm, and that whenever he was in straits how to drive back his enemies, putting his trust in this protection, he lifted up his right arm, and the multitude of his adversaries fled away, as though vanquished by the power of the martyr. Hearing this, Gundovald began diligently to inquire if there were any one in that place who had succeeded in getting relics of Sergius the Martyr. Thereupon the bishop Bertram told him of one Eufronius, a merchant, because he had a grudge against this man. He [Bertram] had once caused him to be tonsured against his will, because he [Eufronius] coveted his possessions; but Eufronius, disdaining the act, migrated to another city, and when his hair had grown again, he returned. The bishop therefore said: 'There is here a Syrian, Eufronius by name, who has made his house a church, and placed there relics of this saint, and by the saving virtue of the martyr he has been witness of many miracles. Once the city of Bordeaux burned with a great fire, but his house, surrounded though it was by flames, was nowise touched of them.' At these words, Mummolus at once hurried to the Syrian's house, accompanied by Bishop Bertram; they pressed upon the man, and bade him show the sacred relics. He refused; but reflecting that a trap was perhaps being laid for him through some grudge, he added: 'Trouble not an old man, nor do wrong to the saint, but take these hundred gold pieces to depart.' When Mummolus still insisted on seeing the relics, he offered two hundred pieces; but even so he could not obtain his withdrawal unless the relics were displayed. Mummolus now ordered a ladder to be set against the wall (for they were hidden in a casket in the upper part of the wall over against the altar), and commanded his [the bishop's] deacon to go up. He mounted the steps and grasped the casket, but was shaken with such trembling that none thought he would reach the ground again alive. But, as I have said, he laid hold of the casket, which was hanging from the wall, and took it down. Mummolus searched the contents, and found a bone from the saint's finger, which he did not fear to strike with a knife; first he hacked it on the upper side, then on the lower. After many fruitless blows, the small bone remained unbroken; at length it split into three parts, which vanished in different directions; I think it little pleased the martyr that such treatment befell it. Eufronius now wept bitterly, and all prostrated themselves in prayer, beseeching God of his grace to restore to them that which had been removed from their mortal sight. After the prayer, the fragments were found, and Mummolus, taking one of them, departed, though not with the favor of the martyr, as the sequel shall declare. . . .

[Following a siege at the city of Comminges, in Gascony, Mummolus agreed to betray Gundovald and swear loyalty to King Guntram; Gundovald was handed over to the king and pushed to his death over a cliff, but Mummolus was nevertheless stabbed to death on Guntram's orders.]

31. CRITICISM OF THE CULT OF RELICS: CLAUDIUS OF TURIN

Writings critical of the cult of relics make up a small minority of extant documenta-tion, perhaps because, like other expressions of heterodoxy, they tended to be out of favor or were suppressed. Claudius, bishop of Turin from about 816, was a sharp critic of the cult, and it is clear from the opening paragraph of the following selection that his contemporaries thought him little better than a heretic. The historical context is that of ongoing controversy in the Eastern church concerning both relics and icons. The icono-clastic position on images and relics had been condemned at the Council of Nicaea in 787, but there were still those in the West who sympathized with it, especially certain heretical groups in Spain. Claudius's views were condemned by a synod in Paris in 825. Part of his vigorous self-defence in his response to the French abbot Theodemir, who had denounced him, is presented here.

Source: trans. A. Cabaniss, *Early Medieval Theology*, ed. G. E. McCracken and A. Cabaniss, Library of Christian Classics 9 (Philadelphia: Westminster Press, 1957), pp. 241-248; repr. with permission.

Your letter of chatter and dullness, together with the essay subjoined to it, I have received from the hands of the bumpkin who brought it to me. You declare that you have been troubled because a rumor about me has spread from Italy throughout all the regions of Gaul even to the frontiers of Spain as though I were announcing a new sect in opposition to the standard of catholic faith – an intolerable lie. It is not surprising, however, that they have spoken against me, those notorious members of the Devil who proclaimed our head himself [Christ] to be a diabolical seducer. It is not I who teach a sect, I who really hold the unity and preach the truth. On the contrary, as much as I have been able, I have suppressed, crushed, fought, and assaulted sects, schisms, superstitions, and heresies, and, as much as I am still able, I do not cease to do battle against them, relying wholeheartedly on the help of God. For which reason, of course, it came to pass that as soon as I was con-strained to assume the burden of pastoral duty and to come to Italy to the city of Turin, sent there by our pious prince Louis, the son of the Lord's holy catholic church, I found all the churches filled, in defiance of the precept of truth, with those sluttish abominations – images. Since everyone was wor-shiping them, I undertook singlehandedly to destroy them. Everyone there-upon opened his mouth to curse me, and had not God come to my aid, they would no doubt have swallowed me alive.

Since it is clearly enjoined that no representation should be made of any-thing in heaven, on earth, or under the earth, the commandment is to be understood, not only of likenesses of other gods, but also of heavenly crea-tures, and of those things which human conceit contrives in honor of the creator. To adore is to praise, revere, ask, entreat, implore, invoke, offer prayer. But to worship is to direct respect, be submissive, celebrate, venerate, love, esteem highly.

Those against whom we have undertaken to defend God's church say, "We do not suppose that there is anything divine in the image which we adore. We adore it only to honor him whose likeness it is." To whom we reply that if those who have abandoned the cult of demons now venerate the images of saints, they have not deserted their idols but have merely changed the name. For if you portray or depict on a wall representations of Peter and Paul, of Jupiter, Saturn, or Mercury, the latter representations are not gods and the former are not apostles, and neither the latter nor the former are men, although the word is used for that purpose. Nonetheless the selfsame error always persists both then and now. Surely if men may be venerated, it is the living rather than the dead who should be so esteemed, that is, where God's likeness is present, not where there is the likeness of cattle or (even worse) of stone or wood, all of which lack life, feeling, and reason. But if the works of God's hands must not be adored and worshiped, one should ponder carefully how much less are the works of men's hands to be adored and worshiped or held in honor of those whose likenesses they are. For if the image which one adores is not God, then in vain should it be venerated for honor of the saints who in vain arrogate to themselves divine dignities.

Above all, therefore, it should be perceived that not only he who worships visible figures and images, but also he who worships any creature, heavenly or earthly, spiritual or corporeal, in place of God's name, and who looks for the salvation of his soul from them (that salvation which is the prerogative of God alone), that it is he of whom the apostle speaks, "They worshiped and served the creature rather than the Creator."

Why do you humiliate yourselves and bow down to false images? Why do you bend your body like a captive before foolish likenesses and earthly structures? God made you upright, and although other animals face downward toward the earth, there is for you an upward posture and a countenance erect to heaven and to God. Look thither, lift your eyes thither, seek God in the heights, so that you can avoid those things which are below. Exalt your wavering heart to heavenly heights.

Why do you hurl yourself into the pit of death along with the insensate image which you worship? Why do you fall into the Devil's ruin through it and with it? Preserve the eminence which is yours by faith, continue to be what you were made by God.

But those adherents of false religion and superstition declare, "It is to recall our Savior that we worship, venerate, and adore a cross painted in his honor, bearing his likeness. "To them nothing seems good in our Savior except what also seemed good to the unrighteous, namely the reproach of suffering and the mockery of death. They believe of him what even impious men, whether Jews or pagans, also believe who doubt that he rose again. They have not learned to think anything of him except that they believe and hold him in their heart as tortured and dead and always twisted in agony. They neither heed nor understand what the apostle says: "Even though we once regarded Christ according to the flesh, we now regard him thus no longer."

Against them we must reply that if they wish to adore all wood fashioned in the shape of a cross because Christ hung on a cross, then it is fitting for them to adore many other things which Christ did in the flesh. He hung on the cross scarcely six hours, but he was in the Virgin's womb nine lunar months and more than eleven days, a total of two hundred and seventy-six solar days, that is, nine months and more than six days. Let virgin girls therefore be adored, because a Virgin gave birth to Christ. Let mangers be adored, because as soon as he was born he was laid in a manger. Let old rags be adored, because immediately after he was born he was wrapped in old rags. Let boats be adored, because he often sailed in boats, taught the throngs from a small boat, slept in a boat, from a boat commanded the winds, and to the right of a fishing boat ordered them to cast the net when that great prophetic draught of fish was made. Let asses be adored, because he came to Jerusalem sitting on an ass. Let lambs be adored, because it was written of him, "Behold, the Lamb of God, who takes away the sins of the world." (But those infamous devotees of perverse doctrines prefer to eat the living lambs and adore only the ones painted on the wall!)

Still further, let lions be adored, because it was written of him, "The Lion of the tribe of Judah, the Root of David, has conquered." Let stones be adored, because when he was taken down from the Cross he was placed in a rock-hewn sepulcher, and because the apostle says of him, "The Rock was Christ." Yet Christ was called a rock, lamb and lion tropologically, not literally; in signification, not in substance. Let thorns of bramble-bushes be adored, because a crown of thorns was pressed upon his head at the time of his passion. Let reeds be adored, because with blows from them his head was struck by the soldiers. Finally, let lances be adored, because one of the soldiers at the Cross with a lance opened his side, whence flowed blood and water, the sacraments by which the church is formed.

All those things, of course, are facetious and should be lamented rather than recorded. But against fools we are compelled to propose foolish things, and against stony hearts to hurl, not verbal arrows and sentiments, but stony blows. "Return to judgment, you liars," you who have departed from the truth, who love vanity, and who have become vain; you who crucify the Son of God anew and hold him up for display and thereby cause the souls of wretched ones in disordered masses to become partners of demons. Estranging them through the impious sacrilege of idols, you cause them to be cast away by their own Creator and thrown into eternal damnation.

God commanded one thing; they do otherwise. God commanded them to bear the cross, not to adore it; they wish to adore what they are spiritually or corporally unwilling to bear. Yet thus to worship God is to depart from him, for he said, "He who wishes to come after me, let him deny himself and take up his cross and follow me." Unless one forsake himself, he does not approach the One who is above him; nor is he able to apprehend what is beyond himself if he does not know how to sacrifice what he is.

If you say that I forbid men to go to Rome for the sake of penance, you lie. I neither approve nor disapprove that journey, since I know that it does not injure, nor benefit, nor profit, nor harm anyone. If you believe that to go to Rome is to do penance, I ask you why you have lost so many souls in so much time, souls whom you have restrained in your monastery, or whom for the sake of penance you have received into your monastery and have not sent to Rome, but whom you have rather made to serve you. You say that you have a band of one hundred and forty monks who came to you for the sake of penance, surrendering themselves to the monastery. You have not permitted one of them to go to Rome. If these things are so (as you say, "To go to Rome is to do penance"), what will you do about this statement of the Lord, "Whoever causes one of these little ones who believe in me to stumble, it is expedient for him that a millstone be hung around his neck and that he be drowned in the deep, rather than cause one of these little ones who believe in me to stumble"? There is no greater scandal than to hinder a man from taking the road by which he can come to eternal joy.

We know, indeed, that the Evangelist's account of the Lord Savior's words are not understood, where he says to the blessed apostle Peter "You are Peter, and on this rock I will build my church, and I will give you the keys of the kingdom of heaven." Because of these words of the Lord, the ignorant race of men, all spiritual understanding having been disregarded, wishes to go to Rome to secure eternal life. He who understands the keys of the kingdom in the manner stated above does not require the intercession of blessed Peter in a particular location, for if we consider carefully the proper meaning of the Lord's words, we find that he did not say to him, "Whatever you shall loose in heaven shall be loosed on earth and whatever you shall bind in heaven shall be bound on earth." One must know hereby that that ministry has been granted to bishops of the church just so long as they are pilgrims here in this mortal body. But when they have paid the debt of death, others who succeed in their place gain the same judicial authority, as it is written, "Instead of your fathers, sons are born to you; you will appoint them princes over all the earth."

Return, O you blind, to the true light that enlightens every man who comes into this world, because the light shines in darkness, and the darkness does not envelop it. By not looking at that light you are in the darkness. You walk in darkness and you do not know whither you are going, because the darkness has blinded your eyes.

Hear this also and be wise, you fools among the people, you who were formerly stupid, who seek the apostle's intercession by going to Rome; hear what the same oft-mentioned most blessed Augustine utters against you. In *On the Trinity,* book 8, he says, among other things, "Come with me and let us consider why we should love the apostle. Is it because of the human form, which we hold to be quite ordinary, that we believe him to have been a man? By no means. Besides, does not he whom we love still live although that man no longer exists? His soul is indeed separated from the body, but we believe that even now there still lives what we love in him."

Whoever is faithful ought to believe in God when he makes a promise, and by how much the more when he makes an oath. Why is it necessary to say, "O that Noah, Daniel, and Job were present here." Even if there were so much holiness, so much righteousness, so much merit, they, as great as they were, will not absolve son or daughter. He therefore says these things that no one may rely on the merit or intercession of the saints, for one cannot be saved unless he possess the same faith, righteousness, and truth which they possessed and by which they were pleasing to God.

Your fifth objection against me is that the apostolic lord was displeased with me (you state that I displease you as well). You said this of Paschal [I], bishop of the Roman church, who has departed from the present life [in 824]. An apostolic man is one who is guardian of the apostle or who exercises the office of an apostle. Surely that one should not be called an apostolic man who merely sits on an apostle's throne but the one who fulfils the apostolic function. Of those who hold the place but do not fulfil the function, the Lord once said, "The scribes and pharisees sit on Moses's seat; so keep and perform whatever things they tell you. But be unwilling to act according to their works, for they talk but they do not practise."

32. THEFT OF RELICS: THE TRANSLATION OF SS. MARCELLINUS AND PETER

Einhard, the Frankish historian and scholar at the court of Charlemagne and his suc-
cessor, Louis the Pious, has left us (besides his famous biography of Charlemagne) a
startling account of the relics trade as it was practised in early ninth-century Gaul.
Charlemagne and his immediate successors emphasized the cult of the saints and the
role of relics, reinvoking the original decree that altars should contain relics, and requir-
ing that all oaths, whether secular or religious, should be sworn upon them. There was
official encouragement for the adoption of the saints as a focus of devotion, for the dis-
covery of relics to place in new churches, and for pilgrimages in their honor. Relics were
therefore at a premium, and in particular the corporeal relics of martyrs that were
mostly available in Rome, where many martyrdoms had occurred. The need for relics
was made more acute by an increase in the number of religious foundations and by the
competition among them (inspired by both spiritual and economic interests) to obtain
prestigious relics. This in turn created a need for documents that authenticated the
movement of relics from one place to another, known as 'translationes.' Such documents
both honored the saints, like the accounts of their lives, and commemorated a particular
historical event, the movement of their remains from a lowly tomb to a more elevated
one, or from one place to another. In some cases this was accomplished with the express
approval of the bishop; in others the translation was effected by more furtive and elab-
orate means, as in the account that follows. The first two books of Einhard's account
only are presented here; two further books detail the miracles performed by the saints
through their relics.

Source: trans. B. Wendell, *The History of the Translation of the Blessed Martyrs of Christ Marcellinus and Peter: the English Version* (Cambridge: Harvard University Press, 1926); revised by P. E. Dutton against the Latin edition of C. Waitz, in *Monumenta Germaniae Historica: Scriptores,* vol. 15.1 (Hanover, 1888), pp.239 -264; abridged and repr. with permission. BHL 5233.

The Translation and Miracles of the Saints Marcellinus and Peter

Preface

To true worshipers and lovers of the true God and of our Lord Jesus Christ and of his saints, Einhard, a sinner. Those who have committed to letters and to memory the lives and deeds of the just, and of men who obey divine commands, seem to me to have wished little else than by such examples to encourage others to correct bad habits and to join in praising the omnipotence of God. And they have done this not only because they were free from malice but because they abounded in charity which desires the good of all. Now since their worthy purpose is so very clearly only to bring about the ends which I have mentioned, I see no reason why they should not be imitated by many. And since I am sure that the pages which I have written, as well as I could, about the translation of the bodies of the blessed martyrs of Christ, Marcellinus and Peter, and about the signs and wonders that God wanted to be made manifest through them for the good of those believing, were composed with the same wish and purpose, I have decided to revise them and to offer them to those readers who love God. For I not only think that this work should not seem empty and purposeless to any of the faithful, but I also venture to believe that I shall have worked fruitfully and usefully, if I shall have succeeded in stirring any reader to the praise of the Creator.

Book 1

1. When still at court and busy with daily business, I used often to think in many different ways about the rest that I some day hoped to enjoy. Then I came across a secret place, far removed from the vulgar crowd and, by the generosity of Louis, the prince whom I then served, I obtained possession of it. This place is in the German forest, lying midway between the Neckar and Main rivers, and in our times is called Odenwald by the inhabitants and their neighbors. When, according to my powers and means, I had built there not only houses and other buildings for permanent dwelling, but also a church suitably designed for the celebration of the divine service, I began to wonder in the name and honor of what saint or martyr it should be dedicated. And when I had spent a great deal of time in this state of doubt, it happened that a certain deacon of the Roman church by the name of Deusdona, who desired to request the help of the king in some problem of his own, came to court. After he had stayed there for some time and the business on which he had come was settled and he was arranging to return to Rome, he was, as a visitor, invited by me one day, out of politeness, to come and share a frugal dinner with me. There, while talking a good deal at table, we happened in our conversation to reach a point where mention was made of the translation of the blessed Sebastian [Hilduin of St-Denis had acquired the relics of Sebastian in 826], and of the many neglected tombs of the martyrs in Rome. Then, our conversation turned to the dedication of my new church and I began to ask him how I could obtain some piece of the true relics of the saints who lie buried in Rome. At this he at first hesitated a little, and answered that he did not know how this could be managed. Then when he perceived that I was eager and anxious about the matter, he promised that he would answer my question on another day. After that evening, when he was invited by me again, he took from the folds of his garment a written note

and requested that I read it when I was alone, and that I would be so good as
to tell him whether I liked what was written there. I took the note and, as he
requested, I read it in secret. The contents were as follows: he had at home
many relics of the saints, and he was willing to give them to me, if I could
help him get back to Rome. He knew that I had two mules. If I would give
him one of these, and send with him a reliable man of my own, who could
receive the relics from him and bring them back to me, he would send them
to me immediately. The general tone of his request pleased me, and I made
up my mind to test the value of his uncertain promise without delay; so, having given him the animal he asked for, and added money for his journey, I
ordered my notary, whose name is Ratleig, who had himself made a vow to
visit Rome for the purpose of prayer, to accompany him. So setting out from
Aachen – for at that time the emperor was there with his court – they came
to Soissons and there they talked with Hilduin, the abbot of the monastery
of St-Médard. The deacon [Deusdona] had promised the abbot that he would
arrange for him to secure possession of the body of the holy martyr Tiburtius. Excited by these promises, the abbot sent along with them a certain
priest, a crafty man by the name of Lehun, with orders to bring back the
body of this martyr when he had received it from the deacon. Thus the journey began as they made their way toward Rome as fast as they could.

2. Now it happened, after they had reached Italy, that the servant of my
notary, whose name was Reginbald, was overcome by a tertian fever
[malaria], and this led, because of its repeated attacks, to a serious delay in
their journey, for when he was gripped by intense fever they could not
travel. There were few of them and they did not wish to be separated from
each other. At this time, when the trip had been much slowed by the inconvenience and they were trying to accelerate their pace as much as they could,
three days before they came to the city, there appeared in a vision to him
who was sick with the fever a man in the dress of a deacon who asked him
why his master was hurrying to Rome. And when he told him all he knew
about the promises the deacon had made to send me relics of the saints and
those made to the abbot Hilduin, he said: "This will not come to pass as you
suppose, but very differently, yet the final outcome of the mission for which
you came shall be fulfilled. That deacon who asked you to come to Rome
will do little or nothing of what he promised you. Therefore I want you to
follow me and carefully remember the things that I am about to show and
relate to you."

Then taking him, as it seemed to him, by the hand, he made him climb
with him to the summit of a very high mountain. And when they stood
there together: "Turn," he said, "to the east, and observe the country lying

before your eyes." When he did so, and observed the country spoken of, he saw buildings of vast size, built close together like some great city, and asked by his companion if he knew what it was he replied that he did not know. Then his companion said: "It is Rome that you see." And he presently added: "Direct your eyes to the remote parts of the city, and see if any church appears to you in those regions." After he said that, he saw one church clearly. "Go and tell Ratleig," said his companion, "for in the church that you have just seen lies hidden the thing that he should carry back to his master: and so let him get to work, so that he might lay his hands on it as quickly as possible and carry it back to his master." And when he said that none of those who had come with him would put any faith in what he said about things such as these, his companion answered and said: "You know that those traveling with you are troubled because for many days you have suffered from a tertian fever that has not yet abated." And he said: "It is as you say." "Therefore," said his companion, "I want this to be a sign to you and to those to whom you shall relate the words I have spoken to you, for from this hour you shall be so cured, by the loving kindness of God, from the fever by which until now you have been detained, that it will not affect you at all for the rest of this journey." Awakened by these words, he made haste to report to Ratleig everything that he seemed to have seen and heard. When Ratleig reported these things to the priest who was traveling with him, it seemed to both of them that the proof of the dream would be whether the promise of health came true. For on that very day, following the nature of the disease from which he had been suffering, a fever should have attacked the one who had seen the [visionary] dream. And that it was not a vain fancy but rather a true revelation was clear, for neither on that day nor on any of those that followed did he experience in his body any trace of the fever that he had been suffering. So it came to pass that they believed in the vision and no longer had faith in the promises of Deusdona, the deacon.

3. When they arrived in Rome, they took up residence near the church of the blessed apostle Peter, which is called Ad Vincula, in the house of the deacon with whom they had come, and they remained with him for some days, awaiting the fulfilment of his promises. But he, who was quite unable to make good on his promises, excused himself for not doing so by various strategies of delay. At last, when they spoke to him about it, they asked him why he wanted to mock them so. At the same time they requested that he not hold them up any longer by deceiving them, thus preventing with vain hopes their return home. When he had heard them out, and perceived that he could no longer cheat them with trickery of this sort, he first informed my notary that he could not have the relics promised to me, because his

brother, to whom on his departure from Rome he had entrusted both his house and all he possessed, had gone to Benevento on business and he had no idea when he would return. Since he had given him those relics for safe-keeping, along with his other moveable property, he could not find them anywhere in the house; therefore, he was [not] able to see what he should do, because for his part there was nothing sure to hope for. After he had said this to my notary, who complained of being deceived and tricked by him, he talked in I know not what empty and misleading terms with the priest of Hilduin, who had cherished the same hopes, and so got rid of him. But the next day, when he saw them in low spirits, he urged them to come with him to the cemeteries of the saints; for it seemed to him that they might find something there that would satisfy their wishes, and that there was no need for them to go home empty-handed. But, although this proposal pleased them and they wished to set about what he had urged them to do as soon as they could, he put off the business, in his usual way, and by this delay cast their minds, which for a little while had been more cheerful, into such despair that, giving up on him altogether, they decided, although their business was completely unfinished, to return home.

4. But my notary, remembering the dream that his servant had had, began to urge his companions to go, without their host, to the cemeteries which he had promised to show them. So, having found a guide who regularly con-ducted travelers to those holy places, they first came to the church of the blessed martyr Tiburtius, on the Via Labicana, three miles away from the city, and examined the tomb of the martyr as carefully as they possibly could; and discussed with the greatest secrecy whether it could be opened so that no one would notice the fact. Then they descended into the crypt connected to this church, in which the bodies of the blessed martyrs of Christ, Marcellinus and Peter, were buried. Having examined the nature of this monument also, they went home, thinking that they could hide what they had been up to from their host. But it turned out otherwise than they expected. For, although they did not know how, knowledge of what they had done quickly reached him. Worried that they might achieve their desires without him, he made up his mind to figure out their intention as quickly as possible. And since he had a full and detailed knowledge of those holy places, he politely told them that they should all go there together, and, if God should deign to favor their wishes, they should make a common decision to do whatever seemed best to them.

They agreed to his plan, and by common consent fixed on a time for set-ting out. Then, after fasting for three days, they went by night, unnoticed by any of the inhabitants of Rome, to the place I have mentioned. Once in the church of St. Tiburtius, they first attempted to open the altar under which his holy body was believed to lie. But the strenuous nature of the work they began was little to their liking, for the monument, built of very hard marble, easily resisted the inexpert hands of those who were trying to open it. So leaving the burial place of that martyr, they went down into the tomb of the blessed Marcellinus and Peter, and there, having invoked our Lord Jesus Christ and having prayed to the holy martyrs, they managed to raise from its place the stone with which the top of the tomb was covered. When they had taken this off, they saw the most holy body of St. Marcellinus set in the upper part of the tomb and close to his head a marble tablet with an inscription on it which gave them clear proof of just which martyr's limbs lay in that place. So, as was proper, they lifted up the body with the greatest reverence, and, having wrapped it in a clean fine linen, they handed it over to the deacon to carry and to keep for them. Then they put the stone back into place, lest some trace of the body's removal should remain visible. Then they returned to their dwelling place in the city. But the deacon declared that in the house where he lived, near the church of the blessed apostle Peter which is called Ad Vincula, he would and could safely guard the body of the most blessed martyr of which he had taken charge. So he gave it to a monk by the name of Luniso to guard. Thinking that this would satisfy my notary he began to urge him, now that he had obtained the body of the blessed Marcellinus, to return to his own country.

5. But Ratleig was thinking and turning over in his mind a very different scheme. For, as he afterwards told me, it seemed to him by no means acceptable that he should go home with the body of the blessed Marcellinus alone, for it would be a great shame if the body of the blessed martyr Peter, who had been his fellow in suffering, and for five hundred years or more had lain with him in the same tomb, should be left there when [Marcellinus] was departing. And this idea having caught hold in his mind, he so struggled with it as it dawned on him and tormented him that neither food nor the approach of sleep would seem enjoyable or good to him until the bodies of the martyrs, who had been joined together in suffering and in the tomb, were joined together on that journey which he was about to make. But in what way this [reunification of the relics] could be achieved, he did not know, for he knew that he could not find a Roman to give him help in this matter, nor was there anyone to whom he would dare reveal his secret plans. Laboring under this anxiety, he happened to meet a foreign monk by the name of Basil who two years before had traveled from Constantinople to Rome. He lived on the Palatine hill with four disciples in a house with other Greeks, who were of the same religious persuasion as he was. He went to

him and explained the nature of his troubles. Then, encouraged by his advice and trusting in his prayers, he discovered such strength in his own heart that he determined to attempt the deed as soon as he could, despite the danger to himself. He sent for his companion, the priest of Hilduin, and first proposed to him that they should once again go secretly, as they had done before, to the church of the blessed Tiburtius, and try again to open the tomb in which the body of the martyr was believed to be buried.

This plan pleased [both of them] and, in the company of their servants, they set out secretly at night, their host having no idea where they were going. When they had come to the church, and prayed for success before its doors, they entered the church. They split up; the priest with one group went to hunt for the body of the blessed Tiburtius in his church and Ratleig with the others descended into the crypt connected to the church to [search for] the body of the blessed Peter. Having opened the tomb without any difficulty, he took out the sacred limbs of the holy martyr, with no opposition, and put them, once they were in his possession, into a silken bag, which he had made ready to hold them. Meanwhile, the priest who was searching for the body of the blessed Tiburtius, having spent a great deal of time in useless work and seeing that he could make no progress, gave up on his efforts, and joined Ratleig in the crypt, and began to ask him what he should do. Ratleig answered that he thought that the relics of St. Tiburtius were [already] found, and then explained what he meant. A little while before the priest had arrived in the crypt, he had found in the same tomb in which the bodies of the saints Marcellinus and Peter lay, a hole, round in form and dug three feet deep and one foot wide, and placed inside it was a substantial quantity of fine dust. It seemed to both of them that this dust might have been left by the body of the blessed Tiburtius if his bones had been removed from there. So that it might be harder to find, this dust might have been placed just between the blessed Marcellinus and Peter in the same tomb. [Thus] they agreed that the priest should take the dust and carry it away with him as the relics of the blessed Tiburtius. Having thus considered and disposed of this business, they returned to their lodgings with the things that they had found.

6. After this, Ratleig spoke to his host and requested the return of the holy ashes of the blessed Marcellinus that he had entrusted to his safe-keeping. Since he now wished to return to his own country, he did not want to suffer any unnecessary delay. [Deusdona] not only restored at once what was asked for, but also presented [Ratleig with] a substantial quantity of saints' relics, tied up in a bundle, which was to be carried to me. When asked what their names were, he answered that he would tell me himself when he came to see me. He advised, however, that these relics should be treated with the

same respect as that shown to the other holy martyrs, because they had acquired as much merit in the sight of God as the blessed Marcellinus and Peter and that I would realize this as soon as I knew their names. Ratleig took the gift that was offered, and, as he was advised, placed the bundle with the bodies of the holy martyrs. Having consulted with his host, he arranged that the holy and much-desired treasure, placed and sealed up in caskets, should be carried as far as Pavia by the host's brother Luniso, of whom we made mention before, and also by Hilduin's priest who had come with him. As for Ratleig, he remained with his host in Rome, watching and listening for seven successive days, to see if anything about the removal of the bodies of the saints came to the notice of the Romans. When he heard no stranger talking about this deed and when he judged that this business was still unknown, he set out after those whom he had sent ahead, taking his host along with him. They found them waiting for them in [the region of] Ticino, in the church of the blessed John the Baptist, which is commonly called Domnanae, and which was at the time, through a benefice of the kings [Louis and Lothar], in my possession. They decided that they too would stop there for a few days, both to refresh the beasts on which they were riding and to prepare themselves for the longer journey ahead.

7. At the time of this delay, a story arose that ambassadors of the holy Roman church, sent by the pope to the emperor, would soon arrive there. Thus, worried that, if they were found there when they arrived, some inconvenience for themselves or even an obstacle might arise, they decided that some of their party should hurry to depart before the embassy arrived. The rest, however, would stay there and, after the matter over which they were anxious had been carefully investigated and the embassy had proceeded on its way, they would make haste to follow their friends, whom they had sent on ahead. So when they had thus settled things among themselves, Deusdona and Hilduin's priest left before the ambassadors from Rome arrived, and made what haste they could for Soissons, where Hilduin was believed to be. But Ratleig, with the true treasure which he carried with him, remained at Pavia to wait until the ambassadors of the Apostolic See had come and gone, so that when they had crossed the Alps he might make his own journey more safely. Still he feared that Hilduin's priest, who had gone with Deusdona and who had full and complete knowledge of all that had been done and arranged between them, and who seemed so cunning and slimy, might attempt to place some obstacle along the route by which he had planned to travel. So he made up his mind that he had best go another way. He first sent on to me the servant of our steward Ascolf with letters in which he informed me both of his own return and that he was bringing the treasure which with

divine assistance he had discovered. Then, after determining the resting places made ready for the others and believing that they must have now passed the Alps, he left Pavia and in six days came to St-Maurice [a distance of approximately 240 kms or 150 miles]. There, having procured what seemed necessary, he placed those holy bodies, enclosed in their casket, upon a bier and from that point on he carried them publicly and openly, with the help of the people who flocked to meet him.

8. When he had passed the place which is called the Head of Lake [that is, Villeneuve in Switzerland] he found a fork in the road by which the ways leading to Francia are divided in two. Taking the path to the right he came through the territory of the Germans to Soleure, a town in Burgundy. There he met the people whom, after the news of his return had reached me, I had sent from Maastricht to meet him. When the letters from my notary were brought to me by my steward's servant [Reginbald], of whom I spoke before, I was at the monastery of St. Bavo on the River Scheldt. Informed by reading these letters of the advent of the saints, I ordered one of my household to go from St-Bavo to Maastricht, there to collect a company of priests and other clergy, as well as laymen, and then to hurry to meet the approaching saints at the very first place he could find them. Thus, with no delay, he and his party, in a few days, met up with those who were transporting the saints at the place I mentioned above. They joined together and were accompanied from that point on by an ever increasing crowd of chanting people. Soon they came, with the great rejoicing of all, to the city of Argentoratus, which is now called Strasbourg. From there they sailed down the Rhine until they came to a place called Portus where they disembarked on the east bank of the river, and, after a journey of five days and with a great crowd of people rejoicing in praise of God, they came to the place called Michelstadt. That place lies in that German forest which today is called Odenwald, and is about six leagues distant from the River Main. When they found there the church newly built by me, but not yet dedicated, they bore the holy ashes into it, and there set them down, as if they were to remain there forever.

9. When this news was brought to me, I hurried there as fast as I could. Three days after my arrival, at the end of the evening service, a servant of Ratleig, acting on his orders, remained alone in the empty church and with closed doors sat next to those holy bodies in a small chapel, as though guarding them. Suddenly he was overcome by sleep and saw, as it were, two doves come flying in through the right window of the apse and land on the top of the bier above the bodies of the saints. One of the doves was all white, the other dappled with the colors white and gray. When they had walked up and down on top of the bier for a good while and had made again and again the

cooing sound made by doves, as if they were talking, they flew out through the same window, and were to be seen no more. Immediately afterwards a voice was heard above the servant's head: "Go," the voice said, "and tell Ratleig to inform his master that those holy martyrs are unwilling to have their bodies rest in this place, for they have chosen another place to which they want to be taken at once." The speaker of this message could not be seen by him, but when the sound ceased he awoke, and roused from sleep he told Ratleig when he came back to the church what he had seen. The next day, as soon as he could come to me, Ratleig reported to me what his servant had told him. Now, although I did not dare to spurn the sacred secret of this vision, I nevertheless decided that it must be confirmed in some more definite fashion. In the meantime I had the holy ashes removed from the linen packages wrapped with cords in which they had traveled, and had them sewn up in new cushions made of silk. When I examined them and noticed that the relics of the blessed Marcellinus were smaller in quantity than those of St. Peter, I thought that [perhaps St. Marcellinus] had been smaller in stature and in the dimensions of his body than the holy Peter. That this was not the case was later made clear by the discovery of a theft; where, when, by whom, and how this theft was accomplished and uncovered I shall tell you at the proper time. For the time being the sequence of the story as I have begun to tell it must be structured and held to without any diversion.

10. Now after I had examined that great and marvelous treasure, more precious than any gold, the casket in which it was contained began to displease me a great deal, because of the poorness of the material out of which it was made. Desiring to improve it, I directed one of the sacristans, one day when the evening service was over, to find out for me the dimensions of the casket as measured in rods. To do this he lit a candle and lifted up the hanging clothes with which the casket was covered; then he noticed that the casket was, in a wondrous way, dripping all over with a bloody liquid. Alarmed by the strangeness of the thing, he took the trouble to inform me at once of what he had seen. Then I went there with the priests who were present and, full of wonder, saw for myself that astonishing miracle. For as columns, slabs, and marble statues are accustomed to sweat and drip when rain is coming on, so that casket with its most sacred bodies was found to be wet with fresh blood and sprinkled all over with it. The unusual, indeed unheard of, nature of the miracle alarmed us. Thus, after speaking of the matter, we decided to spend three days fasting and praying, so that we might be worthy to know by divine revelation what that great and ineffable sign meant and what it urged us to do. When the three days' fast was over and evening was already growing late, that liquid composed of frightening blood began suddenly to dry up. In

a wondrous fashion the liquid that had dripped for seven successive days without stopping, as if it were an incessant stream, dried up so quickly in a few hours that when the bell called us to the night service (for it was Sunday and we celebrated before dawn) and we went into the church, no trace of the blood could still be found on the casket. But the linen cloths that hung about the casket had been so sprinkled with fluid that they were stained with spots like blood-stains. I ordered them to be preserved. To this day considerable evidence of that great, unheard-of prodigy remains on those linens. It is agreed that the fluid had a somewhat salty taste similar to the quality of tears, that it was thin like water, but that it possessed the color of true blood.

11. In the quiet of that same night, two youths were seen standing beside him by one of our servants by the name of Roland, and, as he himself bore witness, they urged him to tell me many things concerning the need to translate the bodies of the saints. They showed him where and how this should be done, and, with terrifying threats they demanded that I should be told without delay. As soon as he could see me, he carefully told me everything that he had been commanded to tell. When I had learned of these things, I began to fill with anxiety and to turn over in my mind what I ought to do: whether fasting and prayers should again be observed, and God once more appealed to for the resolution of our questions or whether some devout and faultless servant of God should be sought, to whom we could make plain the worry in our hearts and the degree of our perplexity, and from whom we might request that, by his prayers, he should discover for us a clear direction from God concerning this matter. But where and when could such a servant of Christ's household be found by us, particularly in those parts? For although certain monasteries had been established not far from the place where we were, nevertheless, by reason of the rude customs common in the region, there were few men or, perhaps, none about whom anything of this sort or even the slightest rumor was reported. Meantime, while I was so troubled and was praying for the assistance of the holy martyrs, and eagerly requesting all who were there with us to do the same, it happened that for several days no night passed in which it was not revealed in dreams to one, two, or even three of our companions that those bodies of the saints must be translated from that place to another. At last, as he himself acknowledges, there appeared in a vision to a priest by the name of Hiltfrid, who was among those gathered there, a certain man in priestly garment, remarkable for the venerable whiteness of his hair, and clothed in white, who accosted him with words like these: "Why," he said, "is Einhard so hard of heart and so obstinate that he will not put faith in so many revelations, and thinks that these many divinely inspired counsels, which have been sent him, may be

despised? Go and tell him that what the blessed martyrs desire to be done with their bodies cannot remain undone. Since until this moment he has put off satisfying their wish in this matter, let him now, if he does not wish the merit of this deed to pass to another, make haste to obey their command and carry their bodies to the place which they have chosen."

12. After these warnings and others of various sorts had been brought to me, it seemed to me that the new translation of the holy ashes must not be postponed any longer. And so, having sought advice, we decided that we should hasten to accomplish the thing as fast as it could be done. Thus, at dawn one day, after the morning service was finished, after making ready quickly but with the greatest of care everything that seemed necessary for this convoy, we took up that holy and priceless treasure, amid very great grief and lamentation from those who were to remain in that place, and starting on our way we began to carry it, accompanied by a multitude of the poor who in those days had flocked there from all sides for the purpose of receiving alms. The people who lived around that place knew nothing about our plans and purpose. The sky was heavy with dark clouds, which would soon turn into heavy rain if a divine power did not prevent it, for all night long it had rained so hard without stopping that it had seemed hardly possible to begin our journey next day. But that doubt of ours, which came from the weakness of our faith, was resolved, by the grace which is on high through the merits of his saints, very differently from what we had expected, for we found that the way by which we were traveling had been transformed into quite another state than the one we had anticipated. We found little mud and discovered that the streams, which are apt to rise in such heavy and continuous rain as had fallen that night, were hardly swollen at all. When leaving the forest, we came close to the nearest villages and were met on our way by multitudes giving praise to God. They accompanied us for a distance of about eight leagues, devoutly helping us to carry our holy burden and singing God's praise they diligently joined their voices with ours.

13. But when we saw that we could not arrive that day at our destination, we turned aside at a village called Ostheim, which could be seen from the road. Just as evening was falling we bore those holy bodies into the church of St. Martin which is found in that village, and, leaving there most of our company to keep watch over the relics, I myself, with a few others, hurried towards the place to which we were destined. Throughout the night, I made ready all those things that custom demands for the reception of the bodies of saints.

But to the church where we left the sacred treasure of those remains came a nun by the name of Ruodlang who was shaken with palsy. She belonged to the convent of Machesbach [Mosbach], which is distant from that church by the space of one league, and had been brought there in a cart by friends and neighbors. She had passed the whole night among the people gathered there to watch and pray beside the bier of the saints, and she recovered the strength in all her limbs. On her own feet, with no one supporting or assisting her at all, she walked back the next day to the place from which she had come.

14. But we, stirring at daybreak, went out to meet our companions who were coming, having with us a numberless throng of our neighbors, who excited by the news of the approach of the saints had gathered before our doors even at the first gleam of dawn, so that they might journey with us to meet the saints. We came upon them at the place where the brook Gernsprinz empties into the River Main [near Aschaffenburg]. Thence, traveling together and singing in unison the praise of the mercy of our Lord Jesus Christ, we bore those holy remnants of the most blessed martyrs, amid the great joy and exultation of all who could be there, to Upper Mulinheim, for so that place is called in modern times. But, because of the great throng of people who had gone before us and who had filled up the town, we could neither make our way to the church nor carry the bier into it. And so in a field near by, on rising ground, we set up an altar under the open sky. After setting the bier down beside the altar, we celebrated the solemn offices of the Mass. When these were finished and the multitude had gone back to their work, we bore those most holy bodies into the church as demanded by the blessed martyrs, and there, having placed the bier before the altar, we carefully celebrated the Mass once again. While the celebration was going on there, a boy of about fifteen years, by the name of Daniel, from the Portian region, who had come there with other poor people to beg and who was so bent over that unless he lay down on his back he could not see the sky, approached the bier. All of a sudden, as if struck by a blow, he fell down. After he lay there for a long time, like one sleeping, all his limbs were straightened, and regaining the strength of his muscles he got up before our eyes and was sound. These things came to pass on the sixteenth day before the Kalends of February [17 January], and the light of that day was so great and so clear that it equaled the splendor of the sun in summer and the calmness of the air was so gentle and sweet that it seemed with soft sunshine to surpass the season of spring.

15. The next day we placed the holy bodies of the blessed martyrs, enclosed in a new shrine, in the apse of the church, and, as is the custom in Francia, we erected over it a wooden frame and covered it with cloths of fine linen and silk for the sake of beauty. Nearby we set up an altar. Beside the altar, one on each side, we placed the two standards of our Lord's Passion which had been carried before the bier on our journey. We took pains, within the limits imposed by the poorness of our means, to make that place

fitting and suitable for the celebration of divine services and we appointed clergy who would keep wakeful watch there night and day, and carefully and continually sing the praises of the Lord. When these had been called to their posts, not only by my mandate but by a royal diploma that had been sent to us along the way, I was summoned to the palace and, with the Lord making my journey a successful one, I returned in a spirit of great exultation.

Book 2

1. Only a few days after I had come to court, having risen early as is the custom of court officials, I went to the palace first thing in the morning. There I found Hilduin, of whom I made mention in the former book, sitting by the door of the royal bedchamber awaiting the appearance of the emperor. Having greeted him as is customary, I asked him to rise and to come over to a certain window from which there is a view of the lower parts of the palace. Leaning against it side by side, we talked a great deal about the translation of the holy martyrs Marcellinus and Peter and about that wondrous miracle which was revealed in the flow of blood with which, as I have recorded, that casket sweated for seven days. When we came to that part of our conversation in which mention was made of the garments which were found with the bodies, and I said that the robe of the blessed Marcellinus was of wondrously fine texture, he answered, like one who knew the object as well as I did, that what I said about the robes was true. Astonished and perplexed by this, I proceeded to ask him how this knowledge of garments that he had never seen could have reached him. Staring at me, he kept silent for a little while, and then said "It is better, I think, for you to hear from me what, if I do not speak, you will soon learn from others. I should inform you fully about a matter which any other informer would not tell you about as fully, nor indeed can, for it is so provided by nature that no one can speak the whole truth about a thing he knows not by experience but by the accounts of others. I trust so greatly in your character that I believe you will deal justly with me when, by my story, you know the whole truth about what has happened."

And when I had answered him in a few words [to the effect] that I would not deal with him otherwise than was appropriate, he said: "The priest, who on my orders went to Rome for the purpose of bringing me the relics of the blessed Tiburtius, found that he could not accomplish the goal for which he had come. After your notary received the relics of the holy martyrs about which we have been talking and had decided to return home, he formed a plan that he should remain in Rome a little longer, while the priest himself

[Fig. 37] A thirteenth-century reliquary, preserved in the Convent of the Sisters of the Sacred Heart at Mons, France. Made of copper with moveable panels, it contains relics of apostles, church fathers, and martyrs around the crucifixion scene and in the space between the columns (Lacroix, *Military and Religious Life in the Middle Ages,* p. 372).

along with Luniso, the brother of Deusdona, and with the men who were to carry those holy ashes, should go on before him as far as Pavia, and should there await his arrival with Deusdona. The plan pleased them both, and leaving the two of them at Rome, the priest, with Luniso and the servants who bore the relics, set out for Pavia. When they arrived there, the caskets containing the holy ashes were placed in your church behind the altar, and in that church were guarded by clergy and laity with constant vigilance. But one night, when the priest himself along with others was on watch in the church, it happened, as he maintains, that, around the middle of the night, sleep gradually stole over every single person who was gathered there to guard [the relics], except the priest. Then he fell to pondering and it seemed to him that without some great cause it could not have come to pass that so sudden a slumber should overcome so many men. And so, deciding that he ought to avail himself of the opportunity placed before him, he rose up, and with a lighted candle made his way silently to the caskets. Then, burning the cords of the seals by putting the flame of the candle close to them, he quickly opened the caskets without a key and took a small portion of each body. Then he fastened the seals together again, as if they had been unbroken, with the ends of the burnt cords. When no one saw what he had done, he went back to his own seat. Afterwards, when he had returned to me, he gave me the relics of the saints thus obtained by theft, and at first declared that they were not the relics of St. Marcellinus or St. Peter, but of St. Tiburtius. Then, out of some fear unknown to me, he told me in secret from which saints the relics had come, and fully explained to me by what means he had got hold of them. We have placed these relics in St-Médard's in a place where honor is formally shown to them and where they are worshiped with great reverence by all who come there, but whether it is right for us to have them is for you to decide."

When I heard these words, I remembered what I had heard from a certain man with whom I had spent some time during my recent journey to the palace. In conversing with me, he said, among other things: "Have you not heard the rumor about the holy martyrs Marcellinus and Peter which is floating about in these parts?" And when I answered that I knew nothing of it, he said, "Those who come from St. Sebastian [at St-Médard] tell us that a certain priest of the abbot Hilduin, who made the journey to Rome with your notary, when they were on their way back and had in a certain place lodgings in common, and all your men were heavy with drink and sleep, and completely ignorant of what was going on, opened the caskets in which the bodies of the saints were enclosed, and took them out, and going his way carried them to Hilduin, and that they are now at St-Médard's. Apparently little of the holy dust remained in the caskets that were brought to you by your notary." Remembering these words, and comparing them with those which were spoken to me by Hilduin, I was gravely disturbed, especially because I had not as yet found the way to destroy that abominable rumor spread abroad by the wiles of the Devil or to remove it from the hearts of the deceived masses. Nevertheless I judged it best that I should request Hilduin to return to me the very thing which, after that voluntary admission, he could not deny had been taken from my caskets, carried to him, and received by him. This I took care to do as soon as I possibly could, and although he was a little harder and slower than I might have wished in coming to an agreement, he was nevertheless overcome by the earnestness of my prayers, and yielded to my insistence, though a little while before he had declared that, particularly in this matter, he would yield to the demands of no one.

2. Meanwhile, having sent letters to Ratleig and Luniso – for they were in the place where I deposited the bodies of the martyrs [Upper Mulinheim] – I carefully informed them about what kind of rumor concerning the martyrs was spreading through most of Gaul, admonishing them to consider whether they could recall or remember any such moment on their journey, or anything like what Hilduin claimed concerning his priest's actions. Coming to me at once at the palace, they related a story that was very different from the one that Hilduin told. For first they declared everything which that priest had told Hilduin to be false, for after they left Rome no opportunity had been given either to that priest or to anyone else to commit a crime of that sort. Yet at the same time it was clear that this very thing had happened to the holy ashes of the martyrs, but at Rome in the house of Deusdona through the greed of Luniso and the cunning of Hilduin's priest, at that time when the body of the blessed Marcellinus, removed from its tomb, was hidden in the house of Deusdona. This they declared was the nature of the theft. That priest of Hilduin, disappointed in the hope he had of obtaining the body of St. Tiburtius, undertook, in order not to return completely empty-handed to his lord, to obtain by deceit what he could not come by honestly. So approaching Luniso, for he knew him to be poor and, therefore covetous, and offering him four gold and five silver coins, he seduced him into committing this bit of treachery. Accepting the proffered money, he opened the chest in which the body of the blessed Marcellinus had been placed and locked up by Deusdona, and gave that good-for-nothing scoundrel full power to take from it what he chose, as he had hoped would be the case. In that robbery he was not moderate, for he took away as much of the holy ashes of the blessed martyr as could be contained in a vessel holding a pint. That the deed was done in this way, Luniso himself, who had plotted it with the priest, admitted, throwing himself at my feet, crying and sobbing. When the truth of the matter was discovered, I ordered Ratleig and Luniso to go back to the place from which they had come.

3. After I had talked with Hilduin and an agreement had been reached between us about when the holy relics should be returned to me, I ordered two clerics of our household, namely Hiltfrid and Filimar, one a priest, the other a subdeacon, to go to venerable Soissons for the purpose of receiving the relics. By means of those two I sent to the place from which those same relics were to be carried away, for the sake of blessing, one hundred gold coins. When they came on Palm Sunday to the monastery of St-Médard, they stayed there for three days and once they had received that incomparable

[Fig. 38] The Crown of Thorns received in Paris by St. Louis: the top scene commemorates Louis's crusades, showing the island of Cyprus, the Crusaders' fleet, and a battle with Saracens; the panels from left to right show the king visiting the Sainte Chapelle, built to receive the relic; Louis receiving the Crown from Baldwin II, emperor of Constantinople; and the king and his mother worshiping before the relic (Lacroix, *Military and Religious Life in the Middle Ages*, p. 375).

treasure for which they had been sent, they returned, accompanied by two monks from that same monastery, with all the speed they could manage to the palace. Nevertheless they delivered the relics not to me, but to Hilduin. Having received them, he placed them in his private chapel, to be kept there until, after the many engagements of Easter were over, he would have spare time in which to show me what was to be returned before he returned it.

When a week or more after holy Easter had passed and the king had left the palace to go hunting, Hilduin, according to what had been agreed upon between us, took those relics from his oratory where they had been kept safe and carried them into the church of the holy Mother of God [Charlemagne's chapel at Aachen] and there placed them on the altar. Then he caused me to be fetched to receive them. Opening up the box in which the relics were contained, he showed it to me, that I might see what it was that he was giving back to me and what it was that I was receiving.

Then, lifting that same box from the altar he placed it in my hands, and having offered up suitable prayer, he took it upon himself to lead the choir and ordered those of the clergy who were skilled in psalmody to chant an anthem befitting the praise of the martyrs. And so singing he followed us, bearing off that priceless treasure, as far as the doors of the church.

From there, in slow procession with crosses and candles, we made our way, praising the mercy of God, to an oratory that had been built with crude hands in our house, and into it – for no other place was to be found there – we bore the holy relics.

4. But in that procession of ours, which I have said we made from the church to our oratory, something miraculous happened, which I think I should not neglect to mention. For when we were coming out of the church, and singing praise to our Lord God with loud voice, such a great and sweet scent filled all that part of the city of Aachen that looks westward from the church that almost all the inhabitants of that part of the city, and all those at the same time who for any reason or business found themselves in that part of the city, were so divinely moved by the fragrance that, putting down all the work they had in hand, they all made haste, running as fast as they could, first to the church, and then, as it were following the scent, to our oratory into which they had heard that those relics had been carried. So within our gates there was an immense crowd of people, at once professing joy and wonder. Though many of those who had gathered together did not know what was happening, nevertheless with gladness and exceeding joy they offered up praise together to the mercy of almighty God.

5. But after, with spreading fame, it was proclaimed far and wide that the relics of the holy martyr Marcellinus had been brought to that place, there gathered together, not only from the city of Aachen itself and neighboring or adjacent towns, but also from places and villages much further away, such a constant and huge crowd that, except for evenings and at night, there was no easy access for us to that oratory to celebrate divine service. The infirm were brought from all over, and those who suffered from various disorders were set down by their kinsfolk and friends beside the walls of the oratory. You could see there almost every kind of bodily affliction in both sexes and in all ages

being cured, by the virtue which comes from Christ the Lord and by the merit of the most blessed martyr. Sight was given to the blind, gait to the lame, hearing to the deaf, speech to the dumb; even paralytics and those deprived of all strength in their bodies were brought there by the hands of others, and, made sound, they returned home on their own feet.

6. When word of these events was carried by Hilduin to the ears of the king [Louis the Pious], he first resolved that on returning to the palace he would without delay visit our oratory, where these things were wrought, and there do reverence to the martyr. But advised by Hilduin not to do so, he ordered that the relics should be carried to the larger church, and when they were taken there he paid reverence to them with humble prayer, and after the solemnities of the Mass had been celebrated he made an offering to the blessed martyrs, Marcellinus and Peter, of a certain manor, situated near the river Ahr, named Ludovesdorf, having fifteen farms and nine arpents of vine yards. And the queen [Judith] made an offering of her girdle, made of gold and jewels, and weighing three pounds. When these things were done, the relics were carried back again to their proper resting place, that is into our oratory, and there they stayed for forty days or more, until the emperor left the palace to go hunting in the forest, as is his yearly custom. When this was done, we too, after making ready whatever seemed necessary for our journey, set out with those same relics from the town of Aachen.

7. Now at the very moment when we were starting out a certain old woman, very well known at the palace, of about eighty years of age and laboring under a contraction of the sinews, was cured within our very sight. As we later learned from her own statement, she had been burdened with this disease for fifty years and had performed the business of walking by crawling about like a quadruped on her hands and knees.

8. So having begun our journey, aided by the merits of the saints, we came with the help of the Lord, on the sixth day to the village of Mulin-heim, where when we set out for court we had left the holy ashes of the blessed martyrs. On that journey how much joy and how much happiness was brought by the coming of those relics to the people gathered along our way I cannot pass over in silence, and yet no account can fully do justice to it. Yet I must try to tell it, lest a thing that very greatly praises God, should seem, as if by laziness, to be swallowed up in silence. First, indeed, my mind moves me to tell you what we ourselves saw when we went out from the palace, in the presence of many. There is a stream called the Wurm [which flows into the Ruhr], lying about two thousand paces from the palace of Aachen, with a bridge across it. We stopped there for a time, so that the multitude which had followed us to that point from the palace and now desired to go back might have a place to pray. And there a certain man from among

those who were praying came close to the relics with another, and, looking his companion in the face, said, "For the love and honor of this saint, I free you from the debt which you know you owe me." For he owed him, as the man himself admitted, half a pound of silver. Again, another man, leading to the relics a fellow whom he had taken by the hand, said "You killed my father and, therefore, we have been having a blood-feud, but now, for the love and honor of God and of this saint, with all hatred put aside, I wish to join and pledge faith to you that from this time forth there shall forever be friendship between us. Let this saint be the witness of this love agreed upon by you and me, and let him work vengeance upon any who shall attempt to break this peace."

9. At this point the crowd that had started out from the palace with us, after worshiping and kissing the holy relics, with many tears which from excess of rejoicing they could not keep back, returned home. And with another great company which met us there, singing *Kyrie eleison* [Lord have mercy] without interruption, we proceeded on our way to a place where we were joined in a similar manner by others rushing towards us. Then the second great crowd, like the first, having made a prayer, returned again to their daily duties. In this manner, day after day, we were accompanied from the break of dawn until dusk by crowds of people singing praises to Christ the Lord, and so made our way from the palace of Aachen to the village of Mulinheim, the Lord guarding the success of our journey. And there upon the altar, behind which the casket containing the holy ashes of the martyrs had been placed, we set down those relics in a jeweled box.

10. There they stayed in place until the month of November, when, getting ready to go back to the palace, we were warned by a vision that we should not leave that place before we had rejoined the relics once again to the body from which they had been stolen. How it was revealed that this ought to be done should not be passed over in silence, because not only in a dream, as is usual, but also by certain signs and warnings it was made clear to those charged with the duty of keeping watch that the blessed martyrs were entirely determined in this matter that their commands should be obeyed exactly.

11. There was a cleric by the name of Landolf who was appointed to keep watch in the church. It was also his job to strike the bell and he had his bed near the eastern door of the church. When, after the custom of vigils and matins, he had risen in his usual manner and had struck the bell, and the service being finished before daybreak, he wanted to go back to sleep, he prostrated himself for the purpose of supplication before the holy ashes of the martyrs. There, as he claims, when he began to repeat the fiftieth Psalm, he heard close to him on the pavement, as it were, the sound of the feet of a

man walking back and forth. Stricken with no small fear, he raised himself a little on his knees and began to look about in every direction, because he suspected that one of the poor, with the doors of the church shut, was skulking about in some corner. But when he saw that no one else but he was within the walls of the church, he readied himself again for prayer and started to recite the Psalm he had begun before. But, before he could finish a single verse, the jeweled box, containing the holy relics of the blessed Marcellinus, which had been placed on the altar made such a loud ringing noise that you would have thought it had been smashed open, as if by the blow of a hammer. Two doors of the church also, that is the western and the southern, as if some one were shaking and pounding them, made the same sound.

Frightened and greatly perplexed by these things, for he had no idea what he ought to do, he rose from the altar and threw himself in great fear on his bed. Soon overcome with sleep, he saw a man, with a face he had never seen, standing by his side, who addressed him with words like these: "Is it true," he asked, "that Einhard so wishes to rush back to the palace that before he goes he will not rejoin the relics of St. Marcellinus which he has brought here, in the place from which they were removed?" And when he answered that he knew nothing of this matter, that one said: "Arise at first light and tell Einhard by order of the martyrs not to dare to go from here or to start off in any direction until he has restored those relics to their proper place." He sat up wide awake, and was careful to impart to me, as soon as he could, that which he had been ordered to tell me. And I, thinking that in business of this kind nothing should be done carelessly, and indeed judging that what was commanded should be carried out without any delay, gave orders on that very day to make ready what seemed necessary for that purpose. On the next day, with the most anxious care, I delicately joined those relics once again to the body from which they had been separated. For which the blessed martyrs were thankful, as can be seen by the plain witness of the miracle that followed. For the next night, while we were sitting in the church for the solemn office of matins, a certain old man, deprived of the use of his legs, came to prayer, painfully crawling on his hands and knees. In the presence of us all, by the strength of God and the merits of the most blessed martyrs, he was so perfectly cured at the very hour when he came in, that when he walked he no longer needed the use of a crutch. He also declared that he had been deaf for five successive years, and that together with the use of his feet hearing had been restored to him. And so, when all these things had come to pass, I set out, as I said above I wished to do, for court, there to pass the winter pondering many things in my mind.

33. FALSE RELICS AND IMPOSTERS

If opposition to the cult of relics was rare, the abuses to which it was vulnerable were certainly recognized, especially the creation of false relics and the tricksters who promoted them. Gregory of Tours tells a story about an imposter who claimed to have the relics of saints Felix and Vincent, and who carried along with them in his pouch "moles' teeth, the bones of mice, bears' claws and bear's fat" ('History of the Franks,' 9, 6), while Chaucer's Pardoner carries pigs' bones and a piece of sail from St. Peter's fishing boat (see 26 above). Rodolphus Glaber, who tells a similar story, was born c.980 near Auxerre and became a monk, spending time in a number of abbeys influenced by the Clunaic reforms, as well as at Cluny itself. 'The Five books of the Histories,' written mostly while he was at the abbey of St-Germain-d'Auxerre, was dedicated to the abbot of Cluny, Odilo (see 19 above). The following story illustrates not only the corruption to which the cult of relics was susceptible but also the eagerness of lay rulers to acquire relics for their foundations. Manfred built his abbey to encourage resettlement in the Val di Susa, an important Alpine valley which had been depopulated by a Saracen attack. The false relics of St. Justus of Beauvais remained in the monastery but were under such strong suspicion that by the end of the eleventh century, in a move to quench the controversy, the relics received a new identity, and became known as those of St. Justus of Oulx.

Source: trans. John France, *Rodolphus Glaber: The Five Books of the Histories* (Oxford: Clarendon, 1989), pp. 181-185; repr. with permission.

Book 4

3. *To punish the sins of men, God sometimes permits evil spirits to perform miracles.*

6. Through Moses, divine authority gave to the Jews this warning: 'If there arise amongst you a prophet speaking in the name of one of the gods of the Gentiles, and foretells something to come, and by chance it takes place, do not believe him, for the Lord your God is testing you, to know whether you love him or not.' In our own times we have seen a similar kind of thing, though relating to a different matter. In those days there was a common fellow, a cunning pedlar whose name and country of origin were unknown because in the many lands where he sought refuges he took false names and lied about his origins lest he be recognized. Furthermore, in secret he dug bones out of graves, taking them from the remains of the recently dead, then put them into coffers and sold them widely as the relics of holy confessors and martyrs. After he had perpetrated many frauds of this kind in Gaul, he

fled to the Alpine regions where ignorant people very often live scattered amongst the high mountains. Once there he called himself Stephen, though he had been known in other places as Peter or John. At dead of night, in his usual way, he dug out the bones of some obscure man from their humble grave, put them in a box on a bier, and said that by an angelic vision a holy martyr, Justus by name, had (as he pretended) been revealed to him. Soon the vulgar crowd and the idle amongst the rustic population came flocking together at the news, as they are wont to do in such cases, even regretting if they had no illness from which they could ask to be cured. They brought the sick, gave miserable little presents, and kept watch all night expecting sudden miracles, which, as we have said, evil spirits are sometimes allowed to perform, tempting men because of their sins. In the present case we find a clear example. Frequent indeed was the healing of limbs witnessed at that place, and many and various the votive effigies of bones hanging there [a reference to the practice of hanging representations of the cured limb at the shrine]. The bishops of Maurienne, Uzès, and Grenoble, in whose dioceses such profanities were occurring, failed to enquire with any diligence into the affair. They preferred to hold public meetings where they wrongfully took money from the people, at the same time demanding patronage for the trickery.

7. Meanwhile Manfred [marquess of Turin], wealthiest of the marquesses, hearing news of this business, sent some of his men to seize and bring back to him the pretended relic which people were worshiping, believing it to be that of the venerable martyr. The marquess had begun the construction of a monastery at Susa, the oldest of Alpine towns, which was to be dedicated to God Almighty and his Mother, the ever-Virgin Mary; he wanted the supposed martyr to be placed there along with the relics of many other saints after the completion of the work. After a while, when the work on the church was finished and the day of consecration fixed, he invited the neighboring bishops; with them came Abbot William (of whom we have so often spoken) [see 19 above] and some other abbots. The pedlar was also present; he was held in high esteem by the marquess because he had promised that soon he would reveal far more precious relics of saints, whose acts, names, and passions he used to invent just as he invented all the rest. When some learned elders asked him how he had come by such knowledge, he made loud protestations of an unconvincing kind. Now I was there, having traveled in the company of an abbot. The pedlar said: 'An angel appears to me at night and he teaches and tells me all that he knows I wish to learn. He stays with me until I force him to go.' When we replied by asking whether he saw all this while he was awake or asleep, he added: 'Almost every night the angel snatches me from my bed without my wife's knowing; after a long conversa-

tion he leaves, saluting and embracing me.' We knew this for a polished and cunning lie, for this creature was no frequenter of angels, but rather a minister of treachery and evil.

8. The bishops, while celebrating duly the rite of consecration for which they had come, put the bones discovered by that cunning imposter in with the other relics of saints, to the great joy of both kinds of people [the clergy and the laity] who had gathered there in large numbers. All this happened on 17 October [1028]. This date was chosen because the partisans of this pretended relic asserted that these were the bones of St. Justus, who suffered martyrdom on that day in the city of Beauvais in Gaul [Justus was allegedly a child martyr under Diocletian]. His head was taken to Auxerre, where he was born and bred, and is kept there. I, who knew the truth of the matter, treated what they said as rubbish. The more discerning recognized this as a trick and supported what I said. The following night some of the monks and other religious saw monstrous visions in the church, black Ethiopians coming out of the box in which the bones were kept and leaving the church. Although many men of sound judgment denounced the detestable invention as an abomination, the mass of the rustic population, corrupted by the pedlar, venerating the name of the unjust for Justus persisted for a long time in their error. We have recounted all this to give a warning against the many deceits of demons and men which abound all over the world, especially in springs and trees that are rashly venerated by the sick.

34. FUNDRAISING WITH RELICS:
THE MONKS OF LAON

On the Thursday after Easter, 1112, the burghers of Laon rose up against their bishop, Gaudry, in rebellion against his arrogance and high taxes, and murdered him in the street in front of his palace. In the ensuing riot the cathedral of Laon caught fire and was partially destroyed along with many of its reliquaries and tapestries. The monks of Laon then organized a fundraising tour to help rebuild and refurbish the cathedral, as described in the following account taken from the autobiography of Guibert, abbot of the nearby monastery of Nogent. Guibert was also the author of a treatise 'On the Relics of the Saints,' in which he criticized the cult of such corporeal relics as Christ's milk-tooth, which the monks of St-Médard at Soissons claimed to possess. Guibert thought that stricter standards should be applied to relics, and argued that the claim to the existence of Christ's body parts on earth offended not only commonsense (since Christ did not seem remarkable until the beginning of his ministry, no one would have collected relics of his childhood) but also the doctrine of the resurrection of the body. Guibert confined his attack largely to relics whose dubiety was indicated by the frequent claims of rival institutions to possess them – such as the two heads of St. John the Baptist – and was not opposed to an authentic cult of relics; barely a hint of skepticism is present in the account that follows.

Source: trans. Paul J. Archambault, *A Monk's Confession: The Memoirs of Guibert of Nogent* (University Park, Pennsylvania: Pennsylvania State University Press, 1996), pp. 174-181, abridged and repr. with permission.

Meanwhile, in keeping with the customary way, such as it is, of raising money, the monks began carrying round the relics of saints as well as their reliquaries. As a result the great Judge, who chastises with one hand but shows mercy with the other, accomplished miracles everywhere the relics passed. Now they were carrying, along with some box that is barely memorable, a magnificent reliquary containing parts of the robe of the Virgin Mother, of the sponge that was presented to the Savior's lips, and of his Cross. (Whether it really contained some of the hair of Our Lady I don't know.) This reliquary is made of gold and decorated with precious stones; and it has a verse inscription engraved in the gold that praises the wonderful things inside.

On the second trip with the relics they came to a town in the district of Tours called Buzançais, which is held by a robber baron. There our clerics spoke to the people about, among other things, the sorry state of their church. Soon they began to realize that the baron and his townspeople were listening to them with evil in their hearts and planning to attack them whenever they would try to leave town. So the cleric whose mission it was to speak to the crowd found himself in a predicament; and though he did not believe in what he was promising he said to the people standing there: "If there is someone sick among you let him come up to these holy relics and drink the water they have touched, and he will surely be cured." The baron and the townspeople were delighted by the possibility of proving our clerics were lying by taking them at their word, so they brought forward a boy of about twenty who was deaf and dumb. The danger that our clerics were exposing themselves to, and the anxiety they felt at that moment, is impossible to describe. They prayed with heavy sighs to the Lady known to all of us, and her only Son, Jesus. The deaf-mute drank the holy water and was then asked some question or other by the trembling cleric. The boy responded immediately, not exactly by answering the question but by repeating the cleric's very words (since he had never heard anything said to him he was ignorant of everything except what had just been said). To make a long story short: in this poor town, the hearts of the townspeople suddenly became larger than ever before. The baron, who was lord of the town, immediately gave the clerics his only horse, while the generosity of the townspeople went well beyond their means. They became the defenders of those whom they had wanted to attack, and shedding abundant tears, they praised God for the help received. As to the boy who had been cured, he was made keeper in perpetuity of the holy relics. I have seen the boy in our church at Nogent: he was a simple-witted boy, clumsy in speech and slow in comprehension. He faithfully kept relating the great miracle, and he died not long afterward discharging his function . . . .

13. The tour of relics in England.

From here the relic bearers headed for lands overseas. While they were sailing in the Mediterranean, they found themselves on the same ship as some wealthy merchants. They were enjoying favorable winds and a calm sea when suddenly they saw, coming straight toward them, galleys filled with fearsome pirates. They were terrified. As the pirates' oars chopped through the water, the galleys' prows barged through the masses of waves. Soon they were no more than two hundred yards' distance from us, and the relic bearers were as terrified as the crew of their ship. At that moment one of our priests stood up in their midst, and raising the box that contained the relics of the Queen of Heaven, in the name of Christ and his Mother he forbade the pirates to come any closer. At this command the galleys turned around and headed away as speedily as they had approached. You can imagine the shouts of praise and glory that were raised among those who had just been delivered. As a token of gratitude the merchants offered many gifts to the gracious Mary.

[Fig. 39] A relics procession: the remains of St. Veronica being carried to church, from a fifteenth-century manuscript of the *Chroniques de Hainault* (Lacroix, *Military and Religious Life in the Middle Ages,* p. 366).

The relic bearers made their way safely to England and came to the city of Winchester, where they worked a great number of miracles. The same thing happened at Exeter, which also produced an abundance of gifts. Let us pass over the ordinary healings of the sick and speak of the exceptional cases. For we are not recording their itinerary – they can write that themselves – nor considering each individual fact, but are picking out examples useful for sermons.

They were received almost everywhere with the reverence they deserved; but in one village they were refused admittance by the priest in his church, and by the peasants in their homes. Finding two uninhabited houses they stored all their baggage in one and used it for their lodgings, while the other was used to shelter the holy relics. The loathsome peasants persisted, however, in their obstinate refusal of things divine, and the clerics left the village the very next day. As they were leaving, suddenly, with a terrific clap of thunder, a bolt of lightning burst out of the clouds and struck the village, reducing all of its houses to ashes. And – a sign of God's marvelous sense of discrimination! – those two houses, which were situated in the midst of the others that were on fire, were spared. God wanted to give a very clear sign that if these wretches had been afflicted with fire it was because of their irreverence toward the Mother of God. As for the wicked priest, who had merely increased the cruelty of these barbarians he was supposed to educate, he gathered up household goods that he was delighted to think had escaped heaven's fire, and came to the edge of a river (or of the sea, I'm not sure which) hoping to get across. But there everything he had collected to move elsewhere was annihilated on the spot by lightning. Thus, this savage band of rustics who were uninstructed in the mysteries of God were taught to understand through their sufferings.

They came to another town where the evidence of the miracles and the faith of the observers elicited many fervent donations to the holy relics. It happened that one Englishman, standing in front of the church where the relics were venerated, said to a companion: "Let's go have a drink." "I have no money," said the other. "I'll go get some," said the first. "How will you do that?" asked his friend. "Well," said the first, "I've noticed that these clerics have been pumping all kinds of money from these clods with their lies and tricks. I'm going to find some way of siphoning some of that money for my own entertainment." Then he entered the church, walked right up to the platform where the relics had been placed, and giving the impression that he was bending over to venerate them with a kiss, he drew his lips close to some coins that had been left there as offerings and sucked them into his mouth. Then he turned to his friend and said, "Now let's go and drink; I'm sure we have enough money for that now." His friend said, "Where did you get that money? You had nothing a while ago." "I sucked it with my mouth out of the offerings that are given to these impostors in the church." "You have done an evil thing," said the friend, "because you've taken what belongs to the saints." "Shut up," said the first, "and let's go into this nearby tavern."

To make a long story short they drank until the sun went down. Then at nightfall the one who had stolen the money from the holy altar got on his mare and wanted to head home; but when he reached a nearby wood, he made a noose and hanged himself to a tree, thereby expiating his sacrilegious act with a shameful death. I believe these few instances suffice to show the many miracles the powerful Virgin performed among the English. . . .

During that critical phase of the city's history, which I have already recounted, the king, whose greed had contributed to it, did not come back to visit the city. As for the royal provost, when he realized what evils were about to be perpetrated there, he sent his concubine and children on ahead and left town just a few hours before the uprising was to paralyze the city. He was no more than three or four miles away when he saw the city in flames.

35. FIRE AT THE SHRINE OF ST. EDMUND

Early in the tenth century the relics of St. Edmund (see 20 above) were moved to the site of the present Bury St. Edmunds, but when the marauding Danes landed at nearby Ipswich in 1010, a layman named Ailwin carried the body to London for safety and placed it in a church near St. Paul's, where it remained for three years. When the Danish threat had receded, Ailwin tried to return the body to East Anglia, but the bishop and citizens of London wanted to move the coffin to St. Paul's instead, since the relics had proved to work many miracles. The coffin, however, refused to be moved when the citizens of London tried to lift it, thus indicating the saint's desire to return to his home. The abbey which flourished around the shrine of this national saint became immensely wealthy and important, for it was granted all of the region now known as West Suffolk, including the town of Bury St. Edmunds itself. In 1182 Samson was elected abbot, and his chaplain was Jocelin of Brakelond, who wrote the 'Chronicle' of Samson's abbacy from which the following account is taken. Besides giving us an insider's view of the quarrels which might develop between an abbot and his monks, it demonstrates the importance of the saint's relics and the income derived from pilgrims even for an abbey which drew much of its wealth from other sources. The miracle of the joining of Edmund's head to his body seems to have been so well-known that it occasioned no comment from Jocelin when the saint's corpse was uncovered anew; an earlier abbot, Leofstan, had tested its truth by pulling upon the saint's head while a monk pulled upon his feet. The head remained joined to the body, but the abbot's hands were afflicted with palsy from that day forward until he died.

Source: trans. Ernest Clarke, *The Chronicle of Jocelin of Brakelond: A Picture of Monastic Life in the Days of Abbot Samson* (London: De La More, 1903), pp. 162–177; revised from the Latin text in H. E. Butler, ed., *The Chronicle of Jocelin of Brakelond concerning the Acts of Samson, Abbot of the Monastery of St. Edmund* (London: Thomas Nelson and Sons Ltd., 1949).

14. The Shrine of St. Edmund

In the year of grace 1198 the glorious martyr Edmund wished to strike terror into our convent, and to instruct us that his body should be kept more reverently and carefully than it had been up to this point.

There was a wooden platform between the feretory [tomb] and the high altar, on which stood two tapers, which the keepers of the shrine used to renew and stick together by placing one candle upon the stump of another in an unsuitable manner. Under this platform there were many things irreverently huddled together, such as flax and thread and wax, and various utensils. In fact, whatever fell into the hands of the keepers of the shrine was put there, for there was a door with iron gratings.

Now, when these keepers of the shrine were fast asleep on the night of St. Etheldreda [23 June], part of a candle that had been renewed and was still burning fell, as we suppose, upon the aforesaid platform covered with rags. Consequently, all that was near, above or below, began to burn rapidly, so much so that the iron gratings were white hot. And lo! the wrath of the Lord was kindled, but not without mercy, according to that saying, "In wrath remember mercy;" for at the same time the clock struck before the hour of Matins [the service held in the middle of the night], and the master of the vestry got up, and observed and saw the fire. He ran at once, and striking the gong as if for a dead person, cried at the top of his voice that the feretory was consumed by fire.

Then we all came running and found the fire incredibly fierce, and encircling the whole feretory, and almost reaching the beams of the church. Our young men ran for water, some to the well, some to the clock [a mechanical water-clock with a large tank], while others with great difficulty extinguished the force of the fire with their cowls, having first carried off certain pyxes [containing the Holy Sacrament]. And when cold water was poured upon the front of the feretory, the stones fell, and were reduced almost to powder. Moreover, the nails by which the plates of silver were affixed to the feretory fell away from the wood, which had been burnt underneath to the thickness of my finger, and the plates of silver were left dangling one from the other without nails. However, the golden image of the Majesty on the front of the feretory, together with certain stones, remained firm and unharmed, and brighter after the fire than it was before, for it was all of gold.

It so happened, by the will of the Highest, that at that time the great beam which used to be behind the altar had been removed, in order to be adorned with new carving. It also happened that the cross, the small statue of [the Virgin] Mary and St. John, the chest with the shirt of St. Edmund, and the reliquaries which used to hang from the same beam, and other pyxes which also stood upon the beam, had every one of them been previously taken away. Otherwise we believe that all these would have been burnt, as was a painted cloth which hung in the place of this beam. But what would it have been had the church been hung with curtains? When, therefore, we had assured ourselves by carefully inspecting any chinks and crannies that the fire had in no way penetrated the feretory, and had perceived that all was cold, our grief in a great measure subsided, but all at once some of our brethren cried out with a great wailing that the cup of St. Edmund had been burnt. When many of them were searching here and there for stones and plates among the coals and cinders, they pulled out the cup entirely unharmed, lying in the middle of burning embers, which were then put out, and found the same wrapped up in a linen cloth, half burnt. But the oaken box in which the cup was usually placed had been burnt to ashes, and only the iron bands and iron lock were found. When we saw this miracle, we all wept for joy.

Now, as we observed that the greater part of the front of the feretory was stripped off, and abhorring the unsightliness of the burning, we consulted together and sent secretly for a goldsmith, and caused the metal plates to be joined together and fixed to the feretory without the least delay, to avoid the scandal of the matter. We also caused all traces of the fire to be covered over with wax or in some other way. But the Evangelist testifies that "there is nothing covered which shall not be revealed": for some pilgrims came very early in the morning to make their offerings, and although they could have perceived nothing of the damage, nevertheless, certain of them, peering about, inquired where was the fire that they had just heard had been close to the feretory. And since it could not be entirely concealed, these inquirers were told that the candle had fallen down and that three napkins had been burnt, and that by the heat of the fire some of the stones in front of the shrine had been destroyed. Yet for all this a false rumor went out that the head of the saint had been burnt. Some indeed contented themselves with saying that only the hair was singed; but after the truth was known, "the mouth of them that speak lies was stopped."

All these things came to pass by God's providence so that the places round about the shrine of his saint should be more decently kept, and that the purpose of the lord abbot should be sooner and more speedily put into effect, that is to say, that the feretory itself, together with the body of the holy martyr, should be placed with greater security, and with more pomp, in a more dignified position. For before this misfortune occurred, the crest of the feretory was half finished, and the marble blocks on which the feretory was to be elevated and was to rest were for the most part ready and polished.

The abbot [Samson], who at this time was absent, was exceedingly grieved at these reports; and on his return home, going into the chapter-house, he declared that these and even greater perils might befall us for our sins, especially because of our grumbling about our food and drink, thus turning the blame somewhat upon the whole body of the convent, rather than upon the avarice and carelessness of the keepers of the shrine. And in order to induce us to do without our pittances [the extra food provided on special occasions] for at least one year, and to put the revenue of the pittancy towards repairing the front of the feretory with pure gold, he himself first showed us an example of generosity by giving, in our presence, all the gold treasure he possessed, namely, fifteen golden rings, worth, it was believed, sixty marks, towards the restoration of the feretory. Furthermore, we all agreed to give

[Fig. 40] Pilgrims approaching the relics of St. Philip, from a fresco by Andrea del Sarto in the cloister of the Church of the Annunziato, Florence (Lacroix, *Military and Religious Life in the Middle Ages,* p. 378).

our pittancy for this purpose; but our decision was changed because the sacristan said that St. Edmund could very well repair his own feretory without such assistance.

At this time there came a man of great account, but who he was I do not know, who told the abbot about a vision he had seen, and at this the abbot was much moved. Indeed, he related the same in full chapter [before all the monks], with a very bitter speech. "It is indeed true," he said, "that a certain great man has seen a vision in which the holy martyr St. Edmund seemed to be lying outside his feretory, and with groans to say that he was stripped of his clothes and was wasting away with hunger and thirst; and that his cemetery and the porches of his church were negligently kept."

This dream the abbot expounded to us all publicly, laying the blame upon us in this fashion: "St. Edmund alleges that he is naked, because you defraud the naked poor of your old clothes, and because you give with reluctance [only] what you are bound to give them, and it is the same with your food and drink. Moreover, the idleness and negligence of the sacristan [the monk designated to look after services to the altar] and his associates are apparent from the recent misfortune by fire which occurred between the feretory and the altar." On hearing this the convent was very sorrowful; and after chapter several of the brethren met together, and interpreted the dream in this way: "We," said they, "are the naked limbs of St. Edmund, and the convent is his naked body; for we are deprived of our ancient customs and privileges. The abbot has everything – the chamberlainship, the sacristy, the cellary; while we perish of hunger and thirst, because we have not our victuals, save [at the pleasure of] the abbot's clerk and by his ministration. If the keepers of the shrine have been negligent, let the abbot take responsibility for it himself, for it was he who appointed such careless fellows."

Many in the convent spoke in this way. But when this interpretation of the dream was communicated to the abbot in the forest of Harlow, on his way back from London, he was very angry and concerned, and replied, "They will turn that dream against me, will they? By God's face! as soon as I reach home I will restore to them the customs that they say are theirs. I will withdraw my clerk from the cellary, and will leave them to themselves; and I shall see the fruits of their wisdom at the end of the year. This year I remained at home, and kept their cellary in such a way as to incur no debt; and is this the way they thank me?" When the abbot returned home, since he wished to translate the blessed martyr, he humbled himself before God and man, meditating inwardly how he might reform himself and make himself at peace with all men, and especially with his own convent. Therefore, sitting in chapter, he commanded that a cellarer and sub-cellarer should be chosen with the consent of us all, and withdrew his own clerk, saying that whatever he had done, he had done it for our good, and he called upon God and his saints as his witnesses, and justified himself in various ways.

"Hear O Heaven! the things that I speak; give ear, O earth!" to what Abbot Samson did. Since the feast of St. Edmund was now approaching, the marble blocks were polished, and everything was made ready for raising up the feretory. The feast day was kept on the sixth day of the week, and on the following day a three days' fast was proclaimed to the people, and the occasion of the fast was publicly explained. The abbot also announced to the convent that they should prepare themselves to transfer the body on the night following the second day of the week, and to transfer the feretory and place it upon the high altar until the masons' work was finished; and he appointed the time and the manner for doing this work.

When we came to Matins that night, there stood the great feretory upon the altar, empty within, adorned with white deer skins above and below and round about, and all fixed to the wood by silver nails; but one panel stood below, by a column of the church, and the sacred body still lay in its accustomed place. When we had sung Lauds, we all proceeded to receive our disciplines [penances given for sins committed]. When this was done, the lord abbot and those with him dressed themselves in albs and approaching reverently, as was fitting, they hastened to uncover the coffin.

First there was an outer cloth of linen, enclosing the coffin and all the rest. This was found tied on the top with cords of its own. Within this was a cloth of silk, and then another linen cloth, and then a third. And so at last the coffin was uncovered, standing upon a tray of wood, so that the bottom of it might not be damaged by the stone. Fixed to the outside, over the breast of the martyr, lay an angel of gold, about the length of a man's foot, holding in one hand a golden sword and in the other a banner. Underneath it, there was a hole in the lid of the coffin, where the custodians of the martyr in earlier times used to lay their hands in order to touch the sacred body. And over the figure of the angel was inscribed this verse: "Behold! St. Michael's image guards the holy body." At either end of the coffin were iron rings, as there used to be on Danish chests.

So, raising up the coffin with the body, they carried it to the altar and I lent my sinful hand to help in carrying it, although the abbot had strictly commanded that no one should approach unless he was called. The coffin was placed within the feretory, and the panel was put back and fastened down. Now we all began to think that the abbot would show the coffin to the people on the octave of the feast, and would replace the sacred body before all of us. But we were sadly deceived, as the sequel will show; for on Wednesday, while the convent was singing Compline [before retiring for the night], the abbot spoke with the sacristan and Walter the physician, and it was resolved that twelve brethren should be appointed who were strong enough to carry the panels of the shrine, and skilful in fixing and unfixing them.

The abbot then said that it had been the object of his prayers to see his patron saint, and that he wished the sacristan and Walter the physician to go with him when he looked upon the body; and there were also nominated the abbot's two chaplains, the two keepers of the feretory, and the two masters of the vestry, with six others: Hugh the sacristan, Walter the physician, Augustine, William of Diss, Robert and Richard. The convent being all asleep, these twelve robed themselves in albs and drawing the coffin out of the feretory, carried it and placed it upon a table near where the feretory used to be, and commenced unfastening the lid, which was joined and fixed to the coffin with sixteen very long iron nails. When they had done this with considerable difficulty, all were ordered to go further away, except the abbot's two forenamed associates.

Now the coffin was so filled with the sacred body, both in length and width, that even a needle could hardly be put between the head and the wood or between the feet and the wood. The head lay united to the body, somewhat raised by a small pillow. The abbot, standing close by, looked carefully and then found a silk cloth veiling the whole body, and then a linen cloth of wondrous whiteness, and upon the head a small linen cloth, and after that another small and very fine silken cloth, like a nun's veil. Lastly, they discovered the body, wound round with a linen cloth, and then at last all the lineaments of the saint's body were laid open to view.

At this point the abbot stopped, saying he did not dare proceed further, or view the holy body naked. Taking the head between his hands, he sighed and said: "Glorious martyr, St. Edmund, blessed be the hour when you were born! Glorious martyr, turn not my boldness to my perdition, because I, miserable sinner, [presume to] touch you, for you know my devotion and my intention!" And he went on to touch the eyes and the nose, which was very large and prominent. Then he touched the breast and arms and raising the left hand he touched the fingers, and placed his own fingers between the fingers of the saint. Proceeding further, he found the feet standing up stiffly, like the feet of a man who had died that day, and he touched the toes, and counted them as he touched them.

It was then proposed that the other brethren should be called forward, in order that they might see these wonders; and six, who were called, approached and also six other brethren with them, who had stolen in without the abbot's assent and saw the saint's body, namely, Walter of St. Alban's, Hugh the infirmarer, Gilbert the brother of the prior, Richard of Hingham, Jocellus the cellarer, and Thurstan the Little, who alone put out his hand and touched the feet and knees of the saint. And by the providence of the Most High, so that there might be plenty of witnesses, one of our brethren, John of Diss, sitting high up in the roof of the church with the servants of the vestry saw all these things plainly enough.

When all this was done, the lid was fastened down on the coffin with the same and the same number of nails, and in like manner as before, the martyr was covered up with the same cloths and in the same order as he was when first discovered. Finally, the coffin was placed in the accustomed place, and there was laid upon the coffin near to the angel, a certain silken bag in which was placed a small parchment written in English, containing, it is believed, certain salutations of Ailwin the monk, for this parchment was found close by the golden angel when the coffin was uncovered. By the abbot's order, another short piece of writing was . . . also deposited in the same bag, with the following words: "In the year of the Incarnation of our Lord, 1198, the abbot Samson, inspired by devotion, saw and touched the body of St. Edmund on the night after the feast of St. Catherine, these being witnesses." And written below were the names of eighteen monks.

Then the brethren wrapped up the whole coffin in a suitable linen cloth, and over the same placed a new and most valuable silken cloth, which Hubert, archbishop of Canterbury, had offered at the shrine that very year, and they placed lengthwise a certain linen cloth doubled under it and next to the stone, to prevent the coffin or the tray on which it stood from being damaged by the stone. Afterwards the panels were brought forward, and properly joined together on the feretory.

But when the convent assembled to sing Matins, and understood what had been done, all who had not seen these things were very sorrowful, saying among themselves, "We have been sadly deceived." However, after Matins had been sung, the abbot called the convent together in front of the high altar, and briefly recounted what had been done, alleging that he neither should nor could have called all of them to be present on such an occasion. Hearing this, with tears we sang "Te Deum laudamus," [*We praise thee, O God*] and hastened to ring the bells in the choir. Four days later, the abbot deposed the keepers of the shrine and the keeper of St. Botolph [whose feretory was near that of St. Edmund], appointing new ones and establishing rules so that the holy places should be more carefully and diligently kept. He also caused the great altar, which before this was hollow, and in which many things were irreverently stowed away, and also that space which was between the feretory and the altar to be filled in with stone and cement, so that no danger from fire could arise because of the negligence of the keepers as had already been the case; according to the saying of the wise man: "Happy is he who learns caution from the danger of others."

CHAPTER SEVEN

NEW DIRECTIONS

In the eleventh and twelfth centuries increasing numbers of lay people were recognized as saints, and there was growing awareness of the opportunities for living a life of perfection outside established ecclesiastic institutions. This movement had several aspects, including the growth of lay initiatives, mysticism, and women's spirituality. There was also a revival of the eremitical tradition. People from many walks of life looked back to the desert fathers to find a way of accommodating their desire to live perfectly. Among the new hermits, many also wanted to emulate the apostles by adopting poverty and manual labor, and caring for the poor and sick. Some went on to form communities together, in a conscious movement of monastic reform. An early leader in the eremitical movement was St. Romuald (c.950-1027), founder of the monastery of Camaldoli in Tuscany. Camaldoli became the mother house of a new order, the Camaldolese Benedictines, whose Rule combined strictness with eremitical and cenobitic elements. They were supported by the eminent Italian monk and cardinal, Peter Damian (1007-72), author of a 'life' of St. Romuald and one of his disciples. The individualistic approach of the new hermits, mystics, and spiritual women gave rise to deep suspicion as well as admiration. There were a number of efforts to regulate those who were not part of communities, including the creation of the Order of St. Paul the Hermit (see 10 above), in which lay people who wished to live chaste, reclusive lives might be invested by the bishop. The movement towards individualism coincided with the centralization of canonization procedures in the Vatican, and thus many of the new 'saints,' lacking powerful supporters, received only local recognition.

36. THE NEW HERMITS: GODRIC OF FINCHALE

Godric of Finchale (c.1065-1170) was not officially recognized as a saint, but those who knew him were convinced that he exemplified the ideals of sanctity within the eremitical tradition. A full account of his life exists, written by a contemporary, the monk Reginald of Durham. In the fourteenth century an Englishman, John of Tynemouth, made an abridged version of Reginald's account, condensing Godric's experiences as a worldly merchant before he settled at Finchale and emphasizing the penitential and miraculous elements of his life. John included it in his Latin legendary, modeled perhaps on the 'Legenda Aurea,' (see 45 below). It records the lives of over one hundred and fifty saints of the British Isles contained in accounts he consulted during his extensive travels around the country. John may have had a special interest in Godric of Finchale. His own priory of Tynemouth was founded by a group of Benedictine monks from Durham in 1075 and until 1090 it came under the authority of the prior of Durham, as Godric had during his lifetime. John of Tynemouth's collection was revised twice in the fifteenth century and printed by Wynkyn de Worde and (in an abbreviated English version) by Richard Pynson in 1516.

Source: trans. M. A. Stouck from the text edited by Carl Horstman in *Nova Legenda Angliae* (Oxford: Clarendon, 1901), 1, pp. 475-500, abridged. BHL 3603.

1. Godric's Early Life

1. The father of St. Godric was called Ailward and his mother Edwenna; they were poor but full of justice and virtue. They were born in Norfolk and lived in the town of Walpole for a very long time; righteous and free from sin, they passed their lives simply in God's presence. Since they had no offspring, they prayed earnestly that they might bring forth a child fit to worship God. The woman then conceived and bore a son by the name of Godric, which means 'good kingdom' or 'the kingdom of God.' Some years later, a son, William, and a daughter, Burwenna, were born to them. After he had passed his childhood in innocence, [Godric] became a merchant, and at first traded in merchandise of small value in the villages and countryside nearby, and later began to visit cities and markets for the sake of profit.

2. There is a place in the sea called The Wash, beside a town called Spalding, where the tide leaves almost four miles of the beach exposed. There one day, walking alone, Godric came across three beached dolphins: he left the two living ones alone, and cut off a portion of the dead one for himself, and carried it off. Quickly the incoming tide followed him as he hurried away, and first soaked his feet and legs, then "the waters swept over his body and

covered his head." Strong in his faith but burdened [with the dolphin meat], Godric walked beneath the waters all the way to the shore; he gave the fish to his parents, recounted everything, and invited them to praise God.

3. In Lindsey [in Lincolnshire] he traded for four years in smaller wares, then first went to St. Andrews in Scotland and then set out for Rome. After his return he joined some traders and went by ship to Brittany, Flanders and Dacia; he accumulated wealth, half shares in one ship, and part of another; and for his skill he was considered worthy of being made ship's captain. For he had a vigorous disposition [and was] energetic and robust in strength, of moderate height, with broad shoulders, a broad chest, a long face, grey-green eyes sparkling brightly, a wide forehead, bristling eyebrows, long and wide nostrils, a nose nicely curved at the end, a narrow chin, and a full and some-what long beard. His mouth was graceful with moderately full lips; the hair of his head and beard was black when he was young and white in old age; he had a short but heavy-set neck, quite large arms, arched soles to his feet, and knees that were calloused and hard from frequent kneeling.

4. He often used to visit St. Andrews in Scotland to fulfil his vows. He spent sixteen years in trade, traveled to Jerusalem and visited the tomb of our lord. Shortly afterwards he traveled to [the shrine of] Saint Egidius [St. Giles, an early hermit in Provence], and then to Rome. Upon his return, moved by fitting devotion, he went with his mother to London. There, his mother removed her shoes and went to Rome barefoot with her son. Godric humbly supported his mother and carried her on his shoulders whenever the diffi-culty of the journey made it necessary.

5. While they were on the way to Rome a woman of great beauty unex-pectedly approached them and humbly begged to be their companion; she remained diligent and devoted in her support of them, for she washed and kissed their feet. They never asked her who she was or where she came from. On their return, when they drew near to London, she said: "Behold, by the grace of God you have escaped the dangers of this entire journey and you are now at the borders of your own land: it is time for me to return to the place I left. Above all, praise God, who will not fail those who trust in him, and he will bring about what you requested of the apostles in Rome." After these words she departed, and he never learned where she had come from or where she went. Moreover she was invisible to their fellow travelers.

6. After these events, he sold everything he had acquired and gave it to the poor, and coming to Carlyle he remained there, a poor man unknown to all. He learned the Psalms so carefully that in a short time he had memorized the whole Book of Psalms [the Psalter was traditionally the basis of the hermit's devotional life]. Then, feeling that the honor which many paid him there was

a drain on his soul, he withdrew alone into the forest and lived on herbs and fruits from the woods. There was no safe retreat for him [there], but he spent the night in prayer wherever [he was when] darkness stole over him, as much as his human weakness allowed. When snakes and wild beasts drew near, they gazed at him attentively for a while, and soon withdrew in complete tameness. He went scarcely a hundred feet without praying, either kneeling down with his hands raised or prostrate on the ground. Finally, as he walked about [in the forest] he came upon a solitary man [Aelric, who had spent his youth in a monastery at Durham]; as he entered his cave this old man said to him, "Welcome, brother Godric." Although they had never met before and were completely unknown to one another, he replied "May you live well, father Aelric." Falling into a mutual embrace, they wept for joy [see the meeting of St. Paul and St. Antony, 10 above). Said the old man, "You were sent to this place by God, to teach lessons of salvation, and to bury this old body." They had no servant or friend, but they served each other in turn. And when the old man became ill, Godric served him devotedly and sat beside the sick man.

7. He [Godric] said to himself, "I wish to know, by the grace of God [that is in Aelric], what death is like." And he added, "O spirit, you who were created in the likeness of God, and who have so far kept [Aelric's] body invigorated, I beseech you by Almighty God not to leave this little body without enlightening me." And then [Godric] saw all the bonds of the body dissolve, and the soul freed from the body's fetters. When asked [afterwards] about its form or nature, Godric replied in this way: "The essence of the soul cannot be seen by anyone. However, I observed it to be like a hot, burning wind, with a spherical, round shape, which gleamed all over like the clearest glass, and an incomparable brilliance surrounded [Aelric] everywhere. But no one will [ever] be able to explain the dimensions of [the soul's] particular nature. Nevertheless I was sure whose soul this was, and so I could not doubt it." The holy man was buried in Durham's cemetery.

8. After this Godric was unsure what the divine will had in store for him. While he was in constant, earnest prayer to God about this, a voice which came from heaven thundered and said, "It is necessary for you to go to Jerusalem and [then] return." Then, directing his prayer to St. Cuthbert, [Godric] said: "Now come forth, most blessed Cuthbert, confessor of Christ, and graciously reveal to me what I ought to do." At once the same voice thundered: "Go to Jerusalem, to be crucified [suffer] with the Lord; and when you return, seek out a place in the woods around Durham called Finchale." And almost at once he saw [standing] to his right a man with a venerable countenance, clothed in bishop's robes, who said "I am Cuthbert, and I will

be your helper and patron in all things; when you have completed the labor of this journey, you will serve God as his soldier under my protection at Finchale." He finished speaking and at once disappeared.

9. On that pilgrimage, [Godric's] food was dry barley bread and a small amount of water, [taken only] when severe need compelled him. He carried the fresh bread which he had purchased untouched in his pack until with the passage of time it turned stale. He did not change his clothes, nor would he wash, until he reached the holy shrines; nor did he mend his shoes or remove them for the duration. Because of this as he traveled he endured great torment to his feet from pebbles and sand which got into [his shoes]; nevertheless daily he traveled just as far as his companions. He often left the road and prayed, on bent knees or prostrate [on the ground]. On reaching the river Jordan, he washed his penitent's robe, and then for the first time took off his garments and removed his shoes. Because of the sand and pebbles, the skin of his feet was worn away, and the bleeding flesh scarcely clung to the bones; and from then on he did not wear shoes on his feet.

2. Godric Becomes a Hermit at Finchale

10. On returning to England, he reached Finchale at last with great difficulty. There a fierce wolf of enormous size rushed upon him as if it meant to attack the man of God and swallow him alive. [Godric] made the sign of the cross against him, saying, "I order you in the name of the most holy Trinity not to injure me and, if this sign of my submission to God is accepted, to withdraw at once." Immediately the beast prostrated itself at his feet, and when permission was given, it withdrew peacefully, often glancing back at him.

11. Godric built a little dwelling place close to the bank of the river Wear and lived there alone, rarely seeing a human face; and he did not exchange speech with those he encountered, but remained silent. In that place there was a great and terrifying multitude of snakes; nevertheless they were gentle and could be touched by the holy man, and were obedient to his commands. They came into his little house in winter, and while the man of God sat by the fire on one side, a host of them lay down on the other. When some were warm, he brought the rest [close to the fire]. Among the snakes were two who were larger than the rest, and they clung more closely to the man of God. When Godric sat before the hearth they often stretched themselves out at his feet, and when they were warm, they coiled themselves up. Nevertheless it seemed to Godric that sometimes they distracted his thoughts from prayer; and after many years he said to them: "I do not want you to divert me

any more from my commitment to prayer." And he ordered them not to re-enter his home. At once they all departed and did not presume to cross the threshold of his dwelling again.

12. For a long time Godric stayed there unknown, fearing nothing more than the sight and speech of men, lest he fall into sin through flattery or too much conversation. Therefore, when he knew in advance of the arrival of some people, he fled deeper into the woods and took refuge. For several years he ate no human food, but sustained [his] poor body on ferns, leaves and roots. When he was finally recognized, certain people brought him food, but he rejected their gifts and fled from them. Some set down little gifts for him and, withdrawing, left them behind there as [Godric] fled. When [Godric] found them afterwards he lifted them up to heaven with tears and commended them to the Lord, saying "Receive, good Jesus, the gifts of your faithful, and repay them with your kindness." And bearing that food onto a hill, he knelt and said, "Almighty and merciful God, you who give food to the ravens' young when they call out to you, and to the cattle, bestow this food on those creatures who you know are in need of it." Setting it down, he did not worry about what became of it afterwards.

13. A certain woman brought him bread, cheese and butter; and he, not wanting to make her sad, received her gifts. When she had gone, he ascended the hill carrying her gifts in his hands; and when on bent knee he had commended the woman and her gifts to God, he arose and found nothing left. So he rejoiced and understood that the sacrifice had been acceptable to God. This happened to him very often afterwards, and his fame was spread abroad, and people of both sexes brought him presents and he at once gave them out to the poor or commended them to the Lord, for he did not want to take up anything for his own use.

14. Nevertheless, in order to find food by his own labor, he undertook to till the soil and sow seeds, and to produce a plentiful harvest. When the peasants saw this they were angry because their pastureland [was] reduced, and they injured him in whatever way they could. At the feast of St. John, when the crop pushed up ears of corn, the peasants sent a herd of cattle over it by which it was so completely destroyed that no hope of harvest remained. Moreover they very often mocked the man of God, and frequently picked quarrels with him. But he did not respond to their abuse, nor was he irritated by their injuries. The following autumn, the field that had been destroyed was filled with such a great harvest that it seemed to have multiplied its yield three times. When the peasants saw this they did not dare to harm him or his land any further.

3. *Temptations and Privations*

15. When he was gravely assaulted by the temptation to fornication, he wept and fasted so much that he abstained from food not just for the space of two or three days but often for as many as six days. He devoted himself to unceasing vigils, and while the moon shone he rose from prayer and labored at the heaviest manual work. But if the sting of lust persisted, he threw his naked body into brambles and thorns in order to turn pleasure into pain. After the powerful temptations of lust, the Devil tried to frighten him with shapes of different wild animals, but his faith was strong, and he spurned them all. So that he might extinguish the fires of the flesh he subdued his body with the roughest of hair shirts, and he wore a coat of chain-mail on his naked body for nearly fifty years. Not only was the robe hard and heavy, but it produced lice in summer's sweat and the hairy roughness of the shirt nurtured a host [of them]. He wore out three chain-mail coats in his lifetime and countless hair shirts.

16. Finally he built a small hut of rough wood and sticks which he called 'the chapel of the blessed Mary,' and a larger building to the west of it in which he constructed a mill, where he ground grain into flour and made it into loaves in the following way: he reduced branches and the roots of plants to ashes, which he mixed with the flour so that ashes formed a third of it; and thus he baked loaves which he called 'delicacies.' He let those loaves harden for six months so that they would one day become horrible and tasteless in their hardness and dryness. They were made of barley or oats because he did not want to taste wheat at the time. But if they turned mouldy because of their age, he did not care. He cooked the forest plants, with stones or wood mixed in, in water without salt and after four or six weeks he made [the mixture] into small round balls, and dissolved [these] in that same smelly water, and ate them instead of beans when he was starving. He kept this preparation ready for cooking until vermin grew out of it and he rejected it.

17. In his cell he had a broad stone for a table upon which he ate nothing that he had killed [he ate no meat]. He often rebuked himself as if speaking to someone else, saying "O most wicked, demanding stomach, why do you so often inflict worldly suffering on me, why do you so often tempt me with the delights of wickedness? When I give in to you, I deceive myself. You are insatiable and greedy; the more you get, the more you want. You are always unhappy with me and you only repay my attention with pain and regret." He rarely took food in the daytime, but rather prayed all day or else tilled the earth and labored, and took food at night. His drink was a small amount of water, and unless compelled by a very great thirst, he did not [even] take that.

He never lay in a bed, but on the bare ground with his hair shirt as a cover on top [of him]; he lay down exhausted with toil, and beneath his head was the stone which served as his table. He did not allow [himself to] sleep unless sleep came upon him against his will, and then he reclined by leaning against a wall or a stone, or hunched over. When the moon shone he went fearlessly out of doors and pursued his labors, and once he had chased away the drowsiness of sleep, he returned home and devoted himself to prayer. He applied himself to prayers on bent knees all day and all night; he shunned leisure above all, and was always intent upon prayer or meditation.

18. In freezing winter's frost and snow he entered the river naked and all night immersed himself as a living sacrifice to God. But if the water was frozen on the surface, he broke the ice and all night or half of it he endured in it. He did not omit this exercise because of heavy rain or snow. Very often, when the bitter cold lasted for a month, he immersed himself all night in the waters, and stood there right up until the dawn came. When his whole body was stiff from an excess of cold and he shook from the chattering of his teeth, then he said: "These things seem terrible, but more terrible [by far] is the torture of hell."

19. Once when he was standing in the water, the Devil appeared to him spewing fire from his mouth, with ass's teeth, eyes almost a cubit long [approx. 46 cm. or 18 inches], crooked feet and twisted limbs. When he was about to rush upon him, the man of God made the sign of the Cross against him, saying, "The Lord is my helper, and I shall despise my enemies." And so that pestilential creature departed in confusion, but he carried off the clothes that the holy man had left on the bank. When Godric noticed this, he stopped him with a shout. The Devil, terrified, put everything back in its place and fled. Then when the holy man was sitting by his hearth, suddenly [it seemed] as if a hand came out and struck him with such a fierce blow that he almost fell flat on the ground. But the holy man said, "Thanks be to God who has supplied me with an overseer [the Devil] who never permits me to rest." And he went into his chapel at once and stayed there until he knew that the Evil One had left. But since the tempter knew by this that he could not overcome [Godric], he enflamed him with the fire of violent lust. Perceiving this, [Godric] subdued his body with even longer vigils and fasts, so that he passed four nights together without sleep and for an entire week he took no food at all; and he rolled his body in thorns until it flowed with blood, so that his clothes were stained with [it]; and he endured temptations of this sort with grave difficulty for several years, and [even] after forty years the fire [of lust] was scarcely extinguished. He also buried a large jar beneath the earthen floor of the chapel of the blessed Mary and filled it with water, and in time

of temptation he immersed himself in it right up to his chin, and overcame that fire with cold.

20. One day when he was chanting Psalms at the hour of vespers, the Devil standing outside mocked him and began to sing, and said "O you peasant, I know how to sing Psalms just as well as you." And once, when he was on his knees praying, the Enemy entered the chapel and tried to hinder him from his purpose. But he was not afraid, and so despised him that he would not look at him. Angry at this, the [Devil] threw the pyx which contained the host at him. And when [Godric was] still so unperturbed that he would not look at him, [the Devil] threw the chalice [containing] the wine, and poured over him all that it contained. Similarly, he threw at him the water pitcher and everything which stood on the table, one by one. And when the man of God [still] did not rise from his prayer, he threw down the beam on which the cross had been nailed with everything which it supported. And since the man of God could not be moved, all night long the Wicked One raged against him but got nowhere; at last, put to confusion, he departed, leaving such a great stink behind that hardly anyone could bear it. Nevertheless, all the things he had thrown were unharmed, and the image of the crucifix was completely undamaged. The man of God, being a layman, did not presume to touch it, but Prior Roger was called from Durham, and he told him everything, and through [Roger] all things were restored to their places. On the following night when the prior was sleeping the Devil stood beside him saying "You have taught this foolish peasant Godric that I use illusions and tricks, and you have turned him [against me] with your warnings. Take this payment for your trouble!" As he said these things and left, he overwhelmed [the prior] with such a bad smell that he could hardly stand it.

21. In summertime the animals of the forest approached and often tore up Godric's tender plants. Coming close to a stag who was gnawing at some small trees, [Godric] ordered him not to run away. The animal stood still and trembled, and fell down at the saint's feet as if begging pardon for his sin. Godric unfastened his girdle and put it around the animal's neck, and leading him to the garden fence, bade him depart. After this a great herd of animals came, and were busy eating the young shoots in the garden, breaking them off and devouring them. [Godric] came up and ordered the herd not to leave that place. He struck one of them three times with a stick on its flank, and led it through the garden, showing it the damage that they had caused. Then with hand and voice raised he said "In the name of Jesus Christ of Nazareth depart at once, and do not dare to come here before harvest time." As those [animals] at once went out the man of God with gentle hand lifted an infirm deer across the garden fence. The wild beast did not damage his trees further,

nor did it cross over the set boundary. When Godric related this to the brothers [the monks of Durham], he reproved those hard-hearted men who despise the commands of God, since even brute animals receive the words of the servants of God with respect.

22. In fierce winter he always went with bare feet; from this you might have seen his feet gaping with open wounds so that a finger could easily be inserted [in them], and many tracks of scars flowing with putrid blood and split open all the way to the bone. He admitted wild beasts fleeing from bands of hunters into his house, and, when the hunters had gone, he sent them off at once to their usual places.

4. Visions, Apparitions and Miracles

23. While he was singing the Psalms, Godric saw the crucified Christ and the cross in his chapel both move, and after a short time he saw a small child emerge from the mouth of the crucified Christ, the limbs [coming out] little by little: and [this child] descended to the image of the blessed Virgin standing on the same beam of wood and came to rest on her breast. She reached out her hands towards him as he approached and embraced him and held him in her arms for almost three hours. Then the small child returned into the mouth of the crucified Christ, in the same way in which he had come, not walking or moving his feet but smoothly passing through an open space of air. For as long as the boy rested on his mother's breast he acted as if he were alive in the flesh. At his coming and again at his departure, the entire image of the holy Virgin trembled so that it seemed at any moment about to fall from the beam.

24. The Devil in human form presumed to tear up with his hands and destroy a certain old fence [belonging to] the holy man. When he saw that, he restrained him by quickly thrusting out his right hand. At once the Devil transformed himself into the shape of a poor man and begged the man of God for mercy; but when he was ordered, he fled at once without delay. Godric was used to seeing the tricks and treacheries of demons, with which they mock humans; and he often used to reveal how they disturb many people in the quiet of the night.

25. When Godric was praying in his cell, the water of the river Wear became swollen and flowed over all his buildings, and his neighbors came running and wept for the man of God as if he were dead. After a few days the water receded; and his house appeared again undamaged. His friends gathered and asked Godric how he had remained unharmed in this danger. He told them that from inside [his house] he had known nothing of the

flood, but he said that he had devoted himself to prayers throughout that time. Everything was so dry, that inside the house no sign of a single drop [of water] was evident.

26. When, weary from toil, he stopped [to rest], a certain stranger was there who had been watching him for a long time and said, "Is this how the fathers of old, whom you believe you are following, toiled in the desert, fasting and pale? Behold, from morning to noon you have scarcely dug the space of fifty feet of earth, when you ought to demonstrate the devotion of [your] mind to God by the amount of work [you do]." The man of God, smiling, said to him, "As a worker leading the way, therefore, show [me] an example of good work." For [Godric] thought that [the other] was a good man, [who had been] sent by God for his instruction. Passing him the shovel, [Godric] said "The time to fulfil my customary [religious] obligations has come and requires that I return to the chapel; when I come back I shall listen to you, and what you rightly teach I shall willingly accept." Then the other snatched the shovel quickly and began to turn the earth vigorously. When Godric returned he found more work completed than he himself used to accomplish in eight days. Then the man said, "See! You should follow the examples of the fathers with great exertion." Understanding this, the holy man shuddered, because he realized that [the other] was not a real man. Moreover he was all black and hairy, and very tall in stature, and despite the heavy work of digging, no sign of sweat or toil was evident [on him]. Godric returned to his cell, and taking up a little book in his garment, he came back and said, "Tell me who you are and why you have come here." And the other said: "Do you not see that I am a human being like you?" "If you are human," said Godric, "tell me whether you believe in the Father, the Son and the Holy Spirit, and adore the Mother of my Lord with me." That man said: "Do not concern yourself with my belief; this kind of questioning is not your business." Drawing near to him, Godric pulled out the little book containing pictures of the Savior and of blessed Mary and of St. John, and he quickly placed it over his mouth and said, "Behold, if you believe in God, kiss these pictures with reverence." But [the Devil] was unable to endure more and projected a sort of spittle onto the book, disappearing with a grimace. Godric left the earth which he had dug uncultivated for seven years, but he often sprinkled it with holy water, and after seven years he cultivated it.

27. When Godric went about his work outside, a ringing sound sent from heaven vibrated throughout his body whenever he forgot the passage of time. When he heard that sound he hurried to the chapel, and when he had begun to recite the office, the bell would at once cease to vibrate. This miracle was heard even more often by many others, and so he asked God to let him alone

hear that sound and none of the others. And it was so.

28. When the river Wear suddenly began to flood, and threatened to destroy Godric's buildings, he went to the river channel, and stretching out a rod in his right hand, said: "In the name of Jesus Christ, whom I serve, I command you, water, not to rise any further towards my buildings than the normal limits, but rather rise up as far as you can in a jutting projection on the other side." At once the river grew into the shape of a mountain, raised up almost to the middle of the hill lying on the other side. It carried down a great mass of stones into the torrent, from which afterwards the church of St. John the Baptist was built.

29. Once again the Wear in flood approached Godric's buildings. Fearless, he stood in its way and measuring out three paces from his house, he erected there a cross [made] from wood and said, "In the name of him who suffered for us on the Cross, I order you, waters, not to go beyond this point." And the flooding water stood still, raised up like a wall, and not daring to go beyond the set limit. And although the raging water on that day over-whelmed bridges, houses and trees, it did not harm anything that belonged to Godric's little home. Carrying a cross, he had purified the boundaries of his land, so that by the will of God the water stood still, and did not pass over it.

30. David, the king of the Scots [David I, son of St. Margaret and Malcolm Canmore; see 21 above. The raid took place in about 1138], led an army into England and devastated the region with plundering and fire. Certain of the invaders rushed upon Godric's church, and tore down everything, and ate and drank the offerings with the wine, and after they had beaten the man of God severely with a stick twisted with cords, they intended to execute him. As he prepared for death, [fully] expecting it and willingly stretching out his neck, a certain powerful man snatched him from their hands lest he be killed. Then they said to [Godric], "Where is your treasure?" He did not answer them, but turning to the crucifix said, "Lord Jesus, you know that I have no treasure on earth but you, my Lord and God." Furious, they struck him even more. Then one of them withdrew, but before he had gone a third of a mile he became mad and ate his tongue with his own teeth, and threw himself into a lake. Another one [went] insane and threw himself into the river Wear and died. Not [a single] one who had harmed the saint reached Newcastle alive, but different ones perished through different disasters. Often Godric patiently endured injuries, capture, and blows at the hands of thieves, and when they departed, if they happened to have left anything behind, he ran after them and begged them to take that, too.

31. When Godric was gazing upon the altar of blessed Mary, he saw two virgins standing at either end of the altar. Their form was most beautiful, their

garments resplendent like shining snow, and they regarded each other for a long time. Godric, marveling and amazed, was afraid; and soon he was filled with such great joy, that it almost seemed to him as if he was freed from the earthly weight of his body; and without speaking, he continuously turned his eyes upon them. When one stood, so did the other; when one moved, the other moved. At last they approached Godric, and standing [before him] remained silent for some time. Then the one who was on the right addressed him in this way: "Do you not recognize me, Godric?" And he said, "Lady, no-one can, except [the one] to whom you wish to reveal [yourself]." "You have spoken well," said she, "for I am the Mother of Christ, and through me you will obtain his grace. That one [on the left] is Mary Magdalene, a woman apostle among male apostles. We shall be your patrons, and we shall prove to be your comfort in every trouble." He threw himself at the feet of the Virgin and said "I dedicate myself to you, my Lady, so that you will find me worthy to protect forever." Then each of them placed their hands upon his head, and, stroking his hair, they filled the building with a sweet smell. After this the Mother of God sang a song to him, as if she were instructing a child, and taught him to sing [it]; and he sang it often after her and committed it firmly to memory. Moreover it was composed in English meter; and it can be translated into Latin in this way: "Holy Virgin Mary, mother of Jesus Christ of Nazareth, receive, protect and aid your Godric; take him quickly into the kingdom of God [to be] with you." She commanded him that, whenever he feared giving in to temptation, he should comfort himself with this song. "Whenever you call upon me," she said, "you will at once have my help." And she made the sign of the Cross upon his head, and the other woman did the same; and as he watched they ascended on high, leaving behind a marvelous smell. Their garments were so fragile that they could not stand up to the touch of any human being: they were like the membrane contained within the shell of an egg.

32. Godric had just one cow, and he said to her, "In the name of God, I bid you go off to pasture [without a herdsman], and return to me at milking time wherever you can find me." From that day [forward], she obeyed his order just as if she acted rationally. And if at milking time Godric was in the chapel, she stood outside and called to him by mooing. . . .

5. Godric's Gift of Prophecy

33. By divine inspiration the man of God used to gaze upon distant things as well as those near at hand. Therefore on occasion he used to say: "A little while ago I was at Jerusalem, and there I saw buildings razed to the ground

that I had once seen built to lofty heights." He pointed out the shape and position of different regions, of cities and of places. On one occasion he saw ships venturing forth on the sea, and he related how the sails of the ship and the oars were arranged. He named the harbors that were life-threatening to them, and foretold where they would later sink. And once he interrupted those talking to him, saying, "Let us pray, brothers, because a ship is in danger on the sea," and, once the prayer was made, he said "It has just steered [towards land] and has escaped the dangerous storm." For he said that, from the inner vision of his heart, he saw clearly those sailing on the sea, just as with the eyes of his body [he saw people] walking on the land. For ten years before his death he saw everything that happened for ten miles around him. Very often he used to see everything that was [happening] in the world. . . .

34. He chose as his teachers the priors of Durham, to whose rule he subjected himself; thus he would not speak to anyone unless [so] commanded by the prior; whoever tried [to speak] to him, did so in vain, if he did not carry a note from the prior. For four days of the week he kept himself entirely from speaking, that is to say, on the Lord's day and on the second, third and sixth days of the week. But on the Lord's day he always devoted himself to prayer. And when there was any feast day, he observed [the rule of] silence. He abstained from speech from the first Sunday of Advent to the fifth day of the Nativity, and also from Septuagesima [the seventh Sunday before Easter] until after Easter, and on the feast of Pentecost. . . .

35. When his sister went the way of all flesh, he was greatly afflicted and he did not cease to weep and pray for her absolution. He also begged the Virgin Mary earnestly to look favorably on the atonement of her soul. One night while sleeping he saw two men in white garments following the blessed Virgin. They entered the chapel of St. Mary, bearing the spirit of his sister and set her upon the foundation of the altar. And when Godric was rejoicing over this vision, she [the soul of his sister], who was standing in the middle of the altar, began to sing this charming song in English: "Christ and St. Mary have led me forth to [eternal] life, so that I may not [any longer] tread on this earth with bare feet." Then the two men, or angels, singing with their own voice responded: "Lord have mercy, Christ have mercy, Lord have mercy." They held little books covered as it were with red leather and as they sang they beat their hands together in clapping, and scattered the pages of the books. When they had sung this way for a long time, they departed and ascended into the air. The man of God rejoiced and praised Christ's mercy, knowing that the spirit of his sister had been freed from torment. . . .

36. When Roger, prior of Durham, departed this life, Godric said to a citizen who was lamenting his passing, "Truly, my son, four days have passed in

which I have seen no-one at all, and yet I know when that man died. For he died on the evening of the day before yesterday, and he traveled to the joys of eternal light [heaven], and wretched Godric saw and recognized his spirit passing at that very hour, and is sure that he has been granted perpetual rest."
. . .

37. Once when Godric was talking to a guest, he saw the cross upon the altar move, and warned the visitor to watch it closely and to pray. Then they saw the cross with the crucified figure rise off the beam on which it [had] been fixed, and come to rest upon the altar. Then it set itself down in front of the altar on the stone pavement, and then it descended to the lower steps and there it rested for almost an hour, and the image quivered and stirred as if it were alive. Then it rose up in the same way in which it had come, and was reattached to the opening in the beam. So the bishop [probably Ranulph Flambard, bishop of Durham from 1089 to 1128, who had originally given Godric permission to build his hermitage at Finchale] was called and Godric told him about this event. [The bishop] said to him, "I think that this amazing and strange miracle is a sign of your approaching death." The man of God said to him, "This strange happening foretells not the approach of my death, but yours: for you will not see the end of this year." Although that reply did not please the bishop, nevertheless it proved to be true. . . .

38. A certain man, a pilgrim in appearance and dress, knocked at his door saying that he was a hermit living nearby and had come to speak to the man of God. Once inside, before the threshold of the church he threw himself down upon bent knees. Godric first sprinkled him with holy water, raised him up and led him in. Then they both knelt in prayer, and afterwards both arose and having sat down, they consoled one another in turn with spiritual counsel. And this man was tall and shaggy, with black hair and rough clothing, [that is,] a sort of hooded cloak; and underneath it his body appeared to be naked, except for the part which the cloak covered; and he said "Since I have heard of your reputation for holiness, I have long wanted to see you, but I was prevented until now by my duties. Now be so good as to listen: I am very poor, and I live in a cell in Northumbria, but I receive almost no assistance; and so I am asking you to agree to relieve my poverty in some way." The man of God was moved by compassion, and he approached the altar and gave him the bread found there and a coin, saying "Take the little that I have; and if I had more, I would give you more." And he took it and said with tears, "I beg you, my lord, do not scorn to touch my ulcerous body. For I hope that from your touch some relief will come to me; and you will be able to feel those hardships which I have suffered in the name of God." The compassionate man of God reached out his hand and touched his body; and it

was like the body of a goose [that has been] plucked, and where he pressed his hand, the flesh receded as if fleeing from [his] touch. Then the holy man shuddered and withdrew his hand. Then the other said, "I am stricken incessantly with such strong pains that I can scarcely live because of my pain; and you would experience the same if you were a true hermit. I suffer with the continual work of fasting and vigils; I endure dangers by day and night. Often I immerse my body in hellish torments, and sometimes, flying above the heavens, I behold the angels in the sight of the divine majesty. I never refresh myself with food, and I never sleep or rest." Understanding who he was, the man of God commanded him in the name of the Lord to depart immediately. And he fled away at once with the gifts he had received, leaving behind a terrible stench. From having touched him, Godric experienced such great fires of temptation that his virtue was nearly defeated and [he] almost succumbed to obscene pleasures; but through constant prayer, he received the shield of divine protection. Often he tearfully regretted that he had given him gifts, and for that reason he underwent heavy penance. And he was very much amazed that that One had not fled when sprinkled with holy water, but rather had later prayed with him, and knelt, and entered the church.

39. Then the man of God fell sick, so that bleeding blisters covered his entire skin. Within the tenderness of the stinging flesh, the distress of his suffering ran throughout his members one after the other, almost unbearably, while on the outside through the open sores the hot, corrupt blood poured forth. But he did not want to apply anything that would bring relief, but said "If God punished the evil in me that I have done, it is right that I should also chastise [myself for] what I have done." Then summoning an attendant he ordered the open sores to be sprinkled with salt, and to be rubbed with a twist of straw; and he would not permit him to stop until the entire surface of his skin was wet with flowing blood. Whenever the attendant was exhausted, he urged him with renewed strength to return even more vigorously to his work. And if the attendant worked too gently, he himself snatched the twist of straw in his hand and did not spare himself. In this way he bore these torments for a long time until through God's mercy all the force of his pain left him. . . .

40. Ethelwold, bailiff of the bishop of Durham, was denounced to him for having squandered his goods. About to clear himself of the crime of which [he was] accused by the ordeal of combat, he entrusted himself to Godric in [his] prayers. The next day he entered combat and was slain, even though he had been innocent of the crime. At the exact same time that man of God struck a bell and ordered officials to be present, and he said to them "Pray for the soul of Ethelwold, because now he has just been struck down." He said,

"I have heard the unexpected shouts of devils, and I have seen Ethelwold breathe his last. An altercation broke out between the good and evil spirits over where his soul should proceed. Raising my eyes on high I saw a priest covered, as it seemed, all in white and standing before the judgment of Christ. He entrusted the soul of the dead man to the Lord. Thus did the angels of God prevail, and the evil spirits fled; and now the purgatorial fire will purify his soul for a time for certain other sins of his. But he did not commit that crime of which he was accused, but was brought to the infamy of his shameful death by another's ill-will."

41. A certain man, a pilgrim in appearance, came to him and said, "Godric, you should give alms to me and those like me from your labors, just as the most blessed hermits of old once did, for they gave food to others [while] they themselves observed fasts." Godric said, "I give aid willingly to the poor according to my ability." The other was angry and added "Rather, you are a false hermit and an ignorant man, and you deserve to be called dung-heap rather than God-ric [a play on the meaning of Godric's name, explained at the beginning of chapter 1], for you imagine that you are holy and clean, whereas you are abominable and filthy." At this the man of God, smiling, said, "I command you, evil spirit, to depart swiftly from here, and do not presume to bother me, a servant of Christ, any longer." At once that blasphemous spirit vanished into thin air.

42. When he was seated alone in his cell, the evil tempter came to him in the form of a very beautiful woman, and sitting beside him she said "O Godric, why do you shun and abhor women, considering that you were born of a woman? You present yourself as holy, but you are a hypocrite; and as a hermit, but your [way of] life is disgraceful." [Godric] turning to her said "I shun the company of no good woman, but rather consider such women precious, and I often speak to them. I refuse however to speak with evil women. Therefore I beg you in the name of the Lord Jesus Christ, if you are other than you seem, to depart from here, as quickly as possible." At these words she disappeared. . . .

43. In autumn when he was gathering fruit, a certain tall and broad man passed his fence. On the outside he wore a cloak of a sort of green tree-bark, unstitched from the shoulders to the loins, and inside [he was] hairy like the hide of an ox. He cried out, "Hermit, give me some fruit." At first [Godric] was silent, but when the churl persisted, he turned to him and said, "You are striving in vain unless you are asking for charity." Then with partial pronunciation of the word he said "For char..., for char..., I ask and beg." In response the holy man offered the fruit and said, "Receive in the name of charity and give thanks to God." [But] he spurned the offerings and began slowly to

withdraw, revealing his smelly behind, and dragging after him his long, crude genitals. The holy man was so repelled by this ugly sight that he felt all the hairs of his body rise up and stiffen like boars' bristles. And as that tempter withdrew farther off, so much the greater grew both his stench and deformity.

44. One night a certain man came to him in his dreams and said, "Godric, tomorrow when you are digging [the soil], you will find a great treasure, which has until now been hidden from others, and will now be revealed because of your merits." For some time the holy man turned over this vision in his mind, judging that it would be good if this treasure was distributed to the poor. Therefore on the next day when he was digging there and had dug deep, he saw coming out of the ground what looked like black boys with shaved heads, half a cubit tall like pygmies. Laughing loudly they repeatedly threw at him smoky, stinking pellets. [Godric] recognizing them as fantastic illusions said "May the money of your treasure go to hell along with you," and he threw back into the pit the earth which he had dug up. From that day onwards he never wanted to keep anything of gold or silver for himself. . . .

6. Godric's Old Age

45. When Godric had reached the age when he walked with another's help, he endured grievous insults of demons.

Sometimes the Enemy turned himself into a bear, sometimes into a crow, or an eagle, a monkey, a ram and the like. Some raised their heads above the beams of the building, some stretched their necks to the sky, some walked on one foot. Once [a demon] appeared as a sack filled with straw, having no limbs at all. Another time, one threw dust at the man of God, and on still another occasion one hurled stones on the outer wall of [his] cell. Often in the evening a huge crowd of evil spirits entered his cell, and they were very black, and short in stature. Some laughed derisively at him, some raged with loud hissing, some attacked him with burning darts. But the holy man said that nothing was more irritating to them than when he averted his gaze from them; and that their madness was not deflected by any better means than by scorning them with closed eyelids. "For when they are looked at, the judgment of the soul is easily turned to evil." For the man of God said that, strengthened by the sign of the cross, he did not fear their noises any more than he did the movement of the air around him.

46. When the holy man lay down on his bed, the Devil was there, and with a shout brandished a spear in his direction. From his mouth fire came out as if from the mouth of a furnace, and his eyes were more than two

cubits in width. He said, "Behold, Godric, I, the Prince of demons, have come and I will cut you in half. Up to now you have mocked my attendants, but now you will not mock me." The servant of God, who for a period of five years had not stood up except with the aid of another, suddenly rose up alone to resist him. His body was entirely naked, but armed with the sign of the Cross, he spoke in a loud voice: "O dismal prince of demons, why do you rage in vain against me? I have the Lord Jesus Christ, who is your conqueror and judge, as my defender: with such a protector, I do not fear your lies." Their angry voices could be heard outside, and so a servant came running and looked in, trembling. That extraordinary struggle lasted from the first hour of the day to the ninth. Three times the Devil attacked him, and each time he was overcome by the soldier of Christ. Many and loud were the words of the combatants, and the contest [was] severe, until [finally] the wicked enemy departed in confusion. . . .

47. Once at the feast of Easter in the middle of the night [Godric] began to sing in a very high voice; and in the morning when he was questioned by a brother, this is what he said: "I saw angels descending to the tomb of the Lord and rejoicing there with the sweetest melodies. Among them was the blessed Nicholas who reminded me to sing with them, as he said that the voice[s] of men of good will sounded well with the voices of angels." And [Godric] added: "Woe to me, that my life goes on too long, and my longed-for death is delayed! O holy Jesus, how long shall I be separated from you, weighed down by this mass of corruption?" . . .

48. When he was asked about the departure of souls from this world, this is what he replied: "The virtuous soul departs lightly from the body, just as a bean, when it is ripe, pops freely from the husk; but the sinful soul, like an unripe [bean], is forced out with many blows. But once out, it immediately flies high in the air; there [too] [the wicked soul] delays for a time, waiting to see what God wishes to be done with it. There is a kind of narrow iron doorway watched over here and there by the guardians of the good and evil spirits: through this door the souls of the just proceed with rapid passage, but the unjust are confined and harshly tormented, and are dragged down miserably to the lower regions. Today," he said, "I saw the liberated soul of a just man pass quickly through it, and on his account I sang for joy with the angels transporting him." . . .

49. After he began to live in that place [Finchale], he went beyond its boundaries only three times. A certain brother of Westminster came to the man of God; Godric asked him if he knew whether Thomas [Becket; see 26 above] was the new [arch]bishop of Canterbury. [The monk] replied that it was so; and added accordingly: "[My] lord, do you know him?" [Godric] said,

"I have not seen him with my own eyes, but nevertheless I know him so well that I could pick him out from among many men without being told by anyone. I shall entrust certain secrets to him, if you are willing to be my messenger for this purpose." [The monk] willingly assented, and [Godric] said "I command you to greet him on behalf of Godric, and to advise him to persevere steadfastly in his purpose since what he proposes to accomplish is pleasing to God. Nevertheless, he will endure many adversities, and will be forced soon [to go] into exile [in France]. He will travel among strangers until the end of his penance is decreed, and afterwards he will return to England to his See, more powerful and more distinguished than when he left. He himself and Malcolm, the king of the Scots, from among the powerful men who live from the Alps all the way to the boundaries of the kingdom of Scotland, are greatly pleasing to God; but the king will soon receive money as his recompense [Malcolm IV, 1153-65, a great-grandson of St. Margaret, had a reputation for holiness. The reference may be to Henry II's gift of Huntingdon in return for Malcolm's surrender of Northumbria in 1157]. Tell him [Thomas] these things: and you will ask for his written absolution for me, for my sins." The monk returned to [his] country, and diligently carried out the commands. He asked the archbishop whether he knew Godric. "I know that man well," he said, "and I know that he has the spirit of prophecy and is accustomed to foretell the future to many." The next day the archbishop wrote letters to [Godric] with an absolution, and commended himself particularly to [Godric's] prayers. Three months later the archbishop was driven into exile [in 1154].

50. When several years had passed, the same monk came to the man of God, and among other [matters] he began to speak in this way concerning the archbishop: "[My] lord, the archbishop of Canterbury has been kept in exile for a long time now, nor is there any hope that he will return again to England, since we see so many hostile [conditions] threatening him." Godric said, "For a short time he will endure exile, and then, when [his] period of penance is finished, he will return with more honor than when he left." . . .

51. [Godric] was attacked by a severe disease, and a livid tumor extended over the surface of [his] body, [while] a consuming pain from within, like worms feeding on his inward parts, attacked him. One night, when he lay as if lifeless, he began to rejoice in a loud voice for a long time, while everyone marveled, and [he was] so much restored to health [that] he looked very cheerful. When he was asked by a monk why he had been singing, he said, "[My] son, the things I saw were delightful, and truly I could not stop myself from singing. Such a great light shone upon me through the window, and a smell of such great sweetness came over me [along] with that light, that it seemed to me that I had recovered [my] former health. I heard 'Lord have

mercy, Christ have mercy' being sung by celestial inhabitants, and thus I sang those same words." . . .

52. Three men appeared to him descending from heaven, and the one who stood on the left spoke to the one in the middle: "Lord, how long shall Godric suffer here in this way and be separated from our company?" He said "There is still in him something to be atoned for, and his time to leave this world has not yet come." They regarded him with calm expressions, and [Godric] heard from them words which the speech of man cannot express. The middle one of them was the Lord Jesus, on the right was the keeper of the keys of heaven [Peter], to the left John the Baptist. Then [Godric] began to weep earnestly, so that his sobs and sighs deprived him of the faculty of speech.

53. One day he was seized by ecstasy from the first hour of the day up to the ninth [hour], and he kept his hands raised to heaven, and with tears flowing he invoked the most holy mother of God as if she were in his presence. Often he sang the Psalms, frequently he prayed, and always he lamented aloud; very often he sang the sweetest melody. And he added, "Holy Mary have mercy, succor and help and protect [me]; lead me to you, [when I am] rescued from this prison, and gather me up with you in eternal glory. Do not leave me any longer in [my] present wretchedness, because I shall cling to you, and I shall not let you depart elsewhere." After this he spoke as if with someone secretly for a long time. Then, when certain brothers had been called, he said, "The strife of this corporal struggle is hard for me, and [it would be] much better to be released and to be with Christ. For, weighed down by the feebleness of age, I cannot render up the customary prayers, nor can I keep [my] thoughts for long in suspense through inspirational and cheerful meditation. I have spoken," he said, "with the blessed Virgin, who sitting beside me told me many things concerning our heavenly homeland. She also promised that she would not desert me, but that she was preparing a dwelling-place of eternal life for me at the right time."

54. On another occasion he saw the heavens opened, and a multitude of blessed spirits praising the highest Trinity, and praying for the well-being of humankind. He saw present there the Father, Creator of all, and the Son, Redeemer of all, and the Spirit, Comforter of all; and he could not restrain voice and speech for his great joy. Afterwards, beating his chest, he said with tears, "Have mercy, Lord, have mercy! How long, left in this misery, shall I be separated from such great glory?" So great was the earnestness of his remorse that it could not be expressed [any] further.

55. A certain monk sent from holy Archbishop Thomas to Godric said, "Why, lord, has the quarrel between the king and the lord of Canterbury not been settled by reconciliation for so many years?" Godric said, "Since each of

them has sinned in the granting of this office [of archbishop], divine judgment punishes both with scourging. Yet God very often draws out good from evil, and those things which begin badly [sometimes] have a good end." He said, "Tell the archbishop, not to bear these things very hard, lest he might suffer still worse things before long. For his crown will be so much the more glorious, the longer his punishment is. Certainly within six months of my words he shall be reconciled, but Godric will not then be alive; and within nine months, he will return to his own dwelling with everything that had been taken away restored. There he will obtain an end of the whole affair to the honor of God, and salvation for himself, and comfort for many. Let the archbishop ponder well these latest words and their hidden meaning [the reference is to Becket's martyrdom in 1170]."

56. Again, he said to a monk who was accustomed to celebrate Mass for him: "Son, I have often seen angelic spirits, and exchanged speech with them, and I have frequently received help, counsel and comfort from them. But I have lost their frequent visits after the anxiety of this illness, because I am constrained by pressing worries to speak about vain things and to meditate upon temporal matters." He said that their kind could not be understood by the human mind; that recently he had been present at their conversation; and that he was not permitted to disclose to any the secret things which they had said. On another day suddenly he sang out with an elevated voice and sweet melody and repeated often these words: "Welcome, Simon." He did not say many words, but often repeated them, and often changed the melodies of singing. At last in a gentle voice he said, smiling, "Welcome, Simon." They talked together for a very long time; and at last Godric raised his eyes to heaven as if he saw something, and after that, he asked if anyone were present. And others approaching him saw that his expression was more serene than usual. And he said, " My sons, I saw from afar Simon Peter, the keeper of the keys of heaven, approaching, and I sang at his arrival. He sat next to me, spoke with me, and revealed to me many secrets which the human mind cannot grasp, nor can these [secrets] be explained in human words. I saw him leaving, first for other regions, then entering heaven."

7. How Godric's Life Came to Be Written

57. A certain priest, very devoted to the blessed Godric, approached him and sitting at his feet tried to persuade him with many words that it would be very advantageous for posterity to receive an account of his fame. Finally he said that if [Godric] agreed, he would willingly write down his life following his instructions. [Godric] fell silent, and turned his gaze upon the priest; at

last after a long silence he said: "Indeed, you may do this, but you will not by any means follow it up now." When the priest, very curious, insisted that he instruct him as to what he might write, the man of God replied in this way: "You [should] know that the life of Godric was like this: first, Godric was an ignorant man, rich, a fornicator, unclean, a usurer, a counterfeiter, a deceiver, a perjurer, a sycophant, a run-about, a lecher and a glutton; now [he is] a dead flea, a stinking dog, a vile worm, not a hermit but a hypocrite; not a solitary, but a scatter-brain; a devourer of alms, fussy about delicacies, avaricious and neglectful, slothful and sluggish, vainglorious and wasteful, one who is not worthy to be a servant to others, [but who] daily scolds and chastises those who serve him. This, and worse than this, you shall write about Godric." With these words he fell silent, as if angry, and the priest left in confusion.

58. When some years had passed, the man of God took pity on the priest, and of his own accord began to tell him what he wanted [to know]. When [the priest] was about to depart, he took up the book which he had written, and holding it in his hand, knelt before the saint and said: "I hope, father, that you will find this little book worthy of blessing and of commending to God, for the honor of God and the use of the faithful." Then turning to him [Godric] said, " My son, what is that book about?" And he said: "[It is] about the deeds of a certain religious man, who suffered much for God in this life: I have told the truth in it." When [Godric] had examined the little book, he held it up in his hands, and raising his eyes to heaven, said, "Omnipotent Father, and you, my Lord Jesus Christ, and you, Holy Spirit the Comforter of all, and you, most holy Mother of God and perpetual Virgin, and you, St. John the Baptist, with all the saints, I beseech you to find this little book worthy of blessing, inasmuch as it may be acceptable to you and a benefit to posterity." And consecrating it with the sign of the Cross he blessed it, and kissed the priest, saying, "I adjure you, my son, through the name of Jesus Christ and through the love by which you are joined to me, not to disclose this to anyone while I am alive, nor to reveal this writing. For I know that because of this book you will suffer sharp and bitter things from rivals: but you should not be shaken, because the truth will set you free."

8. Godric's Death

59. When Godric had passed sixty years in [his] hermitage, such a large tumor filled his face and limbs that he scarcely appeared like his former self. He experienced great inner pain, as if live worms were running about and consuming everything to the very marrow. But he gave thanks to God, because he considered him worthy of being cleansed from [his] sins, and he said:

"These worms are rightly consuming my body in this life, so that the Eternal Worm [will] not destroy my soul in hell."

60. For almost eight years he lay in bed without strength, and he did not rise up except with the help of another's hand. Meanwhile two devils came bearing a couch and saying, "We have come here to carry you off to hell, since you are a crazy old man, and have become foolish in understanding." [Godric] strengthened himself by making the sign of the Cross, and through prayer he quickly put the demons to flight. Later his testicles became swollen like the breasts of women, and from them almost every day a kind of poisonous fluid was expelled by the hands of [his] servants. For an old abscess [had] broken and had made an ulcer of an open sore from which fluid ran continuously; and he could not be cured before his death.

61. Meanwhile the ancient Enemy, seeing that he felt somewhat warm after a peaceful sleep, and that he turned away from the dampness of his bed and sought a dry place, suddenly hurled him unexpectedly from his bed, and struck his head against a bench. [Godric] had a lump on his head the size of a dove's egg, and he spoke these words: "[The Devil] approached me so quickly that I could not defend myself with the sign of the Cross, and he said, 'O Godric [you] fool, over whom, acting through my agents, I was never strong enough to prevail, now you will be killed by me, while you seek out a soft dry [part] of [your] bed.' What safety is left to us, therefore, when the Enemy has such great powers to bring against us? Let us consider carefully how dangerous it is to cling to the pleasures of the flesh, and to be delighted by comfort, when God cannot be found in the land of those who live comfortably."

62. As his illness worsened, at dawn he said to [his] servant, "Quickly arouse the brothers, so that they may come to give a blessing to my departing spirit." They came running quickly, and laid him on a hair-cloth covered with ashes, and dressed him in a robe and cowl since he had already for some time been a monk of Durham. He died on 20 June, in the year of our Lord 1170, and he crossed into the brightness of perpetual light, about to possess the joy of eternal happiness.

63. When high-born people asked for relics from the saintly body, the brothers were compelled to cut off the nails and filings from his feet. As someone was doing this without sufficient care, he cut a piece of the flesh, and at once the blood flowed out and soaked the hand of the one doing the cutting. In every surrounding grove the leaves and foliage were filled with a sweet moisture and for two months together they preserved a wonderful odor. At the hour when [Godric] departed from the world, a certain young girl, who was driving the sheep to pasture, heard the most melodious singing

in the air, ascending from Finchale to the heavens. After the man of God's death, within a few years the Lord deemed it worthy to bring about two hundred and twenty-eight miracles on behalf of the man of God, Godric; these, for the sake of brevity, I have decided to omit. The perplexed scholars of Durham in their school spoke by turns of the saints Thomas [Becket] and Godric in this way: "Behold, in how short a time the blessed Thomas acquired such great glory; and how Godric the saintly hermit, who in the course of so many years was a soldier for God and endured so much, receives no honor." The following night the holy Godric appeared to the master of scholars while he slept, saying: "You spoke yesterday of many things in your school concerning me and my companion St. Thomas, [and said] that great miracles are done for him but none for me. In fact, since he was archbishop and the custodian of many souls, for whom he willingly died, it is fitting that he should bring help and health to many. For Godric, however, who was the guardian only of his own soul, it is enough [for him] to be with God, so that just as he lived unknown, so he should not be famous after his death. Yet St. Thomas and the blessed Cuthbert and I will come to Finchale, so that we may bring help to the poor and the infirm." After these words he disappeared, and the next day that master revealed his vision to his pupils.

37. WOMEN'S SPIRITUALITY I: CHRISTINA THE ASTONISHING

Twelfth-century reform movements in the church stimulated the growth of new religious ideals and practices, and in the low countries, the Rhineland, and northern France arose a new type of religious life which offered devout women an alternative to becoming a nun or a recluse. This movement, whose members were called the Beguines, largely consisted at first of well-to-do women living communally in private houses under the guidance of a sympathetic clergyman. Given partial recognition by Pope Gregory IX in 1233, the Beguines were never officially recognized as a religious order, though they came increasingly under clerical control. Their religious ideals included the emulation of apostolic life, a return to the scriptural foundations of the church, concern for the conversion and salvation of souls throughout the world, and devotion to poverty and manual labor. The movement was marked by an intense spirituality and by ascetic practices that were often more extreme than those allowed in convents. Its most influential early supporter was Jacques de Vitry (d. 1240), who began his career as a parish priest in the low countries and eventually became the Bishop of Acre and the friend and adviser of Gregory IX. He wrote the 'Life of Mary of Oignies' (d. 1213), the prototypical Beguine. Christina 'the Astonishing,' as she was known (1150-1224), exemplifies the extremes of the new spirituality. She apparently rejected all outward forms of spiritual regulation, though she was attached at different times to at least one recluse and to the nuns at the convent of St. Catherine's where she eventually died. The author of her 'life' was Thomas of Cantimpré, a Dominican who also wrote accounts of three other women who, like Christina, were not Beguines but exemplified aspects of the new movement. Of these, Christina is certainly the most startling. Her historical existence is testified by Jacques de Vitry in the preface to his 'Life of Mary of Oignies,' but Thomas's description of Christina's behavior has been viewed with skepticism. The early part of her 'life' appears to be based on the torments of purgatory as outlined in stories of visions of the other world, such as the famous 'Purgatory of St. Patrick,' and it has also been argued that Thomas's account describes well-recognized stages in the development of a mystic.

Source: trans. Margot H. King, *The Life of Christina of St-Trond by Thomas of Cantimpré* (Saskatoon: Peregrina Publishing Co., 1986), pp. 1-33; repr. with permission. BHL 1746.

Prologue

1. When we were planning to write the life of the unforgettable virgin Christina, we first decided to put at the beginning of our discourse what the revered bishop of Acre (he who later became a Cardinal in the Roman Curia

[Jacques de Vitry]) related about her in these words [in his 'Life of Mary of Oignies']: "I saw another woman [he means Christina] in whom God wrought so wondrously that when she had lain dead for a long time, but before her body had been buried in the ground, she lived again and her soul returned to her body, and God granted that she endure purgatory in the world while still living in the body. Wherefore for a long time she was wondrously afflicted by the Lord so that sometimes she would turn herself around and around in fire, at other times in the winter she would linger in icy water for a long time, and at still other times she was compelled to enter the graves of the dead. Finally, after she had completed her penance with great serenity, she earned so much grace from God that many times, ravished in spirit, she led the souls of the dead either to purgatory or through purgatory to heaven, without any harm to herself."

2. These words are, as we have said, those which the revered bishop Jacques de Vitry related about her. Therefore I, an unworthy friar of the Order of Preachers, have described these things, although in unpolished language, for the edification of readers and especially for the praise of Christ, yet I am perfectly satisfied about the account which has been reported to me. I do not say perfectly satisfied without cause, for I have so many straightforward witnesses to what I have described who were living at that time in the town of St-Trond and who could use their reason, and these things were not done in narrow corners but straightforwardly among the people. Nor has so much time elapsed that oblivion has swallowed up and buried [these occurrences], for I wrote this life not more than eight years after her death. I personally heard other things from people who swore they learned them from her own mouth which no one could have known except [Christina] herself.

3. And whoever reads this might acknowledge that he has believed me by virtue of such witnesses who by no means would deviate from the center of truth even at the risk of losing their heads. We admit – and it is true – that our account surpasses all human understanding inasmuch as these things could by no means have occurred according to the course of nature, although such things are possible to the Creator. Furthermore I would never have presumed to have written this unless the revered bishop Jacques had not previously given testimony to most of these things. For this reason, then, let us fulfil the task by approaching it in this way: first of all we will describe how she was nourished, and then how she was educated, and finally we will describe her deeds, just as we have learned from most truthful and indisputable accounts.

Here begins the life of the holy Christina of the town of St-Trond

4. Christina, the unforgettable virgin of Christ, was born of respectable

parents in the town of St-Trond in Hasbania. After her parents had died, she was left with two older sisters. Desiring to order their life in the manner of religious life, they arranged that the oldest sister would occupy herself in prayer, the middle one to take care of the house and the youngest – that is, Christina – to watch the herds as they went to pasture. Without delay Christ did not fail as Consoler to the lower and more humble office allotted to the girl, but rather he gave her the grace of an inward sweetness and very often visited her with heavenly secrets. Nevertheless she remained unknown to all and the more hidden she was, the more she was known to God alone. This is why Isaiah boasted, when he said "My secret to myself, my secret to myself," for God is a modest lover.

5. It happened that after these events she grew sick in body by virtue of the exercise of inward contemplation and she died. Her lifeless body was laid out in the midst of her friends and her sisters wept copiously over it. The next day when it was borne to the church and while her Requiem Mass was being said, suddenly the body stirred in the coffin and rose up and, like a bird, immediately ascended to the rafters of the church. All those present fled and only her older sister remained behind fearfully and stayed there immoveably until Mass was finished, when she who had been kept in check by the Sacrament of the Church was forced to descend by the priest. Some say that the sensitivity of her spirit was revolted by the smell of human bodies. Finally, returning home with her sisters, she was reinvigorated by food. Her spiritual friends then hastened to her and asked what she had seen and wanted her to explain what had happened. She said to them:

6. "As soon as I died, angels of God – the ministers of light – took my soul and led me into a dark and terrible spot which was filled with the souls of men. The torments which I saw in that place were so many and so cruel that no tongue is adequate to tell of them. There I saw many dead men whom I had previously known in the flesh. Having not a little compassion on those wretched souls, I asked them what place this was. I thought it was hell, but my guides said to me, 'This place is purgatory and it is here that repentant sinners atone for the sins they committed while they were alive.' They then led me to the torments of hell and there also I recognized some people whom I had known by sight while I was alive.

7. After these events, I was carried into Paradise, to the throne of the Divine Majesty. When I saw that the Lord was well pleased with me and wishing me joy, I rejoiced above all measure thinking that I would remain with the Lord forever after. At once the Lord answered my desire and said, 'Certainly, my dearest, you will be with me, but I now offer you two choices, either to remain with me now or to return to the body and suffer there the

sufferings of an immortal soul in a mortal body without damage to it, and by your sufferings to deliver all those souls on whom you had compassion in that place of purgatory, and by the example of your suffering and your way of life to convert living men to me and to turn aside from their sins, and after you have done all these things to return to me having accumulated for yourself a reward of such great profit.' I answered without hesitation that I wished to return under the terms that had been offered to me.

8. With no delay the Lord wished me joy in his response and commanded my soul to be led back to the body. And see how quick the angels were to obey the bidding of the Lord! At the same time that the 'Agnus Dei' ['the Lamb of God,' a liturgical response] was being said for the first time while Mass was being celebrated for me, my soul was standing before the throne of Divine Majesty, but by the time they said the 'Agnus Dei' for the third time, I had been restored to the body by those swift angels. Thus was the manner of my returning and of my departing and I have been given back to life for the improvement of people. Now therefore do not let the things you are going to see in me trouble you because those tasks with which God will charge me are above understanding. Indeed, such things have not been seen among mortals."

9. Then Christina fled the presence of human beings with wondrous horror into deserts, or to trees, or to the tops of castles or churches or any lofty structure [see Symeon Stylites in 12 above]. Thinking her to be possessed by demons, the people finally managed to capture her with great effort and to bind her with iron chains and although she endured much suffering and privation, yet [she suffered] even more from the stench of men. One night, with the help of God, her chains and fetters fell off and she escaped and fled into remote desert forests and there lived in trees after the manner of birds. Even when she needed food (for despite the extreme sensitivity of her body, she could not live without food) and was tortured by a most grievous hunger, by no means did she wish to return home but she desired to remain alone with God in her hiding place in the desert. Therefore, pouring forth a prayer to the Lord, she humbly begged that he gaze on her anguish with the eyes of his mercy. Without delay, when she turned her eyes to herself, she saw that the dry paps of her virginal breasts were dripping sweet milk against the very law of nature. Wondrous thing! Unheard of in all the centuries since the incomparable Mother of God! Using the dripping liquid as food, she was nourished for nine weeks with the milk from her fruitful but virginal breasts. In the meantime, she was being sought by her own people and was found, captured, and bound as before with iron chains – but in vain.

10. After she had been freed by the Lord, she came to the city of Liège.

Thirsting for the most holy flesh of the spotless Paschal Lamb, she begged the priest of St. Christopher's to strengthen her with Holy Communion against the anguish she was suffering from so many things. And when the priest promised he would do so but said that he could not give her Communion right then because he was busy, she was impatient at any delay, and came to a priest at another church and asked for the Body of Christ. He immediately gave in to the prayers of the supplicator and gave her Communion. At once, struck with a certain violent emotion, she fled and left the city. The priest wondered greatly at this fleeing woman and he ran to the other priest at St. Christopher's and they both followed her as far as the rapidly flowing Meuse river. When they reached the river's edge, they rejoiced because they thought they could seize her but, stupefied, they observed the woman in front of them (in bodily form although she looked like a phantasm) enter the deep streams of the water and come out untouched on the other side.

11. Then Christina began to do those things for which she had been sent back by the Lord. She crept into fiery ovens where bread was baking and was tormented by fires – just like any of us mortals – so that her howls were terrible to hear. Nevertheless when she emerged, no mutilation of any sort appeared in her body. When no oven was at hand, she threw herself into roaring fires which she found in people's houses or else she thrust her feet and hands into flames and held them there for so long that they would have been reduced to ashes had it not been a divine miracle. At other times she jumped into cauldrons of boiling water and stood there immersed either up to the breast or the waist depending on the size of the cauldron, and poured scalding water over those parts of her body which were untouched by the water. Although she howled as if she were suffering the pangs of childbirth, when she climbed out again she was quite unharmed.

12. Often in cold weather she would remain for a long time under the waters of the Meuse; indeed frequently she stayed there for six or more days at a time. The priest, however, who was attending to her came and stood on the river bank and adjured her, in the name of Christ, to come out and, thus forced, she would emerge. In the winter she would stand upright on a water-wheel throughout its entire revolution and the waters ran over her head and limbs. At other times she would swim with the current and revolved with the wheel through the waters. Despite this, no hurt appeared on her body.

13. She also stretched her arms and legs on the rack, that instrument of torture on which brigands were usually tormented, and yet when she descended no fracture appeared in her limbs. She would also go to the gallows and suspend herself between the thieves who were hanging there and would so hang for one or two days. As well she would often enter the graves

of dead people and there make lamentation for their sins.

14. On another occasion she rose up in the middle of the night and, provoking the dogs of St-Trond to bark, ran before them like a fleeing beast. The dogs pursued her and chased her through woods so thick with thorns that her whole body was covered in bloody wounds. Nevertheless when she had washed off the blood, there was not a trace of the wounds.

15. Her body was so sensitive and light that she walked on dizzy heights and, like a sparrow, hung suspended from the topmost branches of the loftiest trees.

16. When she wanted to pray, she had to flee to tree-tops or towers or any lofty spot so that, remote from everyone, she might find rest for her spirit. And again when she prayed and the divine grace of contemplation descended upon her, all her limbs were gathered together into a ball as if they were hot wax and all that could be perceived of her was a round mass. After her spiritual inebriation was finished and her active physical senses had restored her limbs to their proper place, like a hedgehog her rolled up body returned to its proper shape and the limbs which had been bent formlessly once again were spread out. Many times she would stand erect on fence palings and in that position would chant all the Psalms for it was very painful indeed for her to touch the ground while she was praying.

17. Her sisters and her friends were greatly embarrassed because of these things and the manner in which they were done, for men thought that she was possessed by demons. They made an agreement with a most wicked man who was very strong and they bribed him to follow and capture her and to bind her with iron chains. Although this worthless man pursued her through the desert, he could not capture her with his hands but he did, finally, catch up with her and broke her leg with a cudgel. She was then brought home and her sisters hired a physician who took care of her broken shinbone. It was for this reason that she was carried to Liège in a cart.

18. The physician knew her strength so he bound her firmly to a pillar in a dungeon where chains hung on all the walls and he locked the doors securely. He then attended to her broken shinbone and bound it with medicated bandages. After the physician had left, she drew off the bandages since she thought it shameful to have any doctor for her wounds but Jesus Christ, and the Almighty did not fail her. One night when the Spirit came upon her, the chains with which she was bound were loosed and, healed from all hurt, she walked around the dungeon and danced and praised and blessed him for whom alone she had chosen to live or die. Her spirit then felt itself to be shut up in a narrow dungeon, and she took a stone from the dungeon floor and in her impassioned spirit she threw it with such force that she

made a hole in the wall. To use an example, it was like an arrow which is more forcefully released the harder it is pulled in the bow. Thus her spirit, which had been restrained more than was just, flew with her body in its weak flesh through the empty air like a bird because "where the Spirit of the Lord is, there is liberty."

19. Nevertheless her sisters and friends never stopped their persecution, for after she had returned to a place where they could seize her, they bound her fast with a heavy wooden yoke and fed her like a dog with a little bread and much water. Christ allowed her to be overcome and to endure tribulation for a time in order that he might show in her the remarkable miracle of his strength. The hardness of the wooden yoke which lay heavily on her neck rubbed her shoulders and caused festering wounds and she was so wasted by these pains that she could not eat her bread. No one there had compassion on her wretchedness, but the Lord marvelously had pity on her and wrought in her that great miracle, unheard of in all previous centuries. Her virginal breasts began to flow with a liquid of the clearest oil and she took that liquid and used it as a flavoring for her bread and ate it as food and smeared it on the wounds of her festering limbs as an ointment. And when her sisters and friends saw this, they began to weep and they struggled no more against the miracles of the Divine Will in Christina and they released her from her chains and knelt down begging for mercy for their injuries to her and let her go.

20. Then using her liberty for lawful and pleasurable things, she suffered pains for the sins of men as we mentioned above. Many people from far and near and religious men and women who lived in St-Trond clustered around her every day to see the wonders God had wrought in Christina. Then, terrified that this highest wonder of miracles might exceed human senses and that the carnal minds of men might see in these divine operations an occasion for evil, she fled the presence of men and ascended into lofty places like a bird and lingered long in the waters like a fish. Her sisters and friends then besought the Lord with earnest prayers that he moderate his miracles in Christina in accordance with the usual state of men. God generously did not disdain the prayers of those who were weeping.

21. It happened one day that, violently stirred by the Spirit, she visited a church in the city of Wellen and coming upon a baptismal font, she completely immersed herself in it. It is said that when this event occurred, thereafter her manner of life was more moderate with regard to society and she behaved more calmly and was more able to endure the smell of men and to live among them.

22. She partook of the Sacrament of the Body and Blood of the Lord

with holy devotion on almost every Sunday, and she said that she received strength of body and a greatest joy of spirit from it. Consequently she, who had given up everything of her own for Christ as well as those things which belonged to her by right and which could have been used for food and drink, used to beg from door to door every day for the common alms of men so that she might bear the sins of those people from whose alms she was fed. Indeed she said that she was driven by the Spirit of God to beg the alms of sinful men because they might thereby be called to a horror of their sins and to a penitent life. Furthermore she said that nothing made God weep more with mercy for sinners than when sinners are moved by mercy towards their neighbors, for mercy and pity never can result in anything but good at the last day. And as these things show by example, so we confirm those things we are telling about the behavior of Christina.

23. It happened one day that she was stirred by God to an intolerable thirst and ran to the table of a most wicked man who was feasting splendidly and she asked for something to drink. Moved by an unaccustomed pity he took a little of the wine and let her drink. Contradicting the opinion of everyone who knew this man, Christina said that at his death he would be called to the grace of repentance and contrition.

24. This is why, as we have said, she was driven to beg for alms from publicans, but when she ate anything given to her as alms which had been wrongly acquired, it seemed to her that she was swallowing the bowels of frogs and toads or the intestines of snakes. When she ate such things, she would cry out as if in childbirth "O Christ! What are you doing? Why do you torment me in this way?" She would beat her breast and her body and say "O miserable soul! What do you want? Why do you desire these foul things? Why do you eat this filth?" Thus it was torture for her to eat any unjust plunder. Yet her tortures were no less painful if a guilty man denied her what she had requested. Once it happened that she snatched away with force something that a wicked man had denied her and she said "Although now you do not wish it, yet later you will not grieve that it has been taken away. Then what is not useful to you now will be profitable."

25. When a sleeve was missing from her gown or when her scapular lacked a hood, she would beg for it from anyone she met because she had been inwardly counseled in her spirit that the person should give it to her. If it was given to her, she gave thanks; if not, and if the person were unwilling and refused her, she took it anyway and sewed it on her own garment. She was not ashamed if the sleeves of her gown did not match or were of different colors. She was dressed in a white tunic and a white scapular which frequently was sewn with threads made from the inner bark of the linden tree

or willow twigs or little wooden spikes and which covered her whole body down to her feet. She did not have shoes but walked with bare feet in all kinds of weather. The food she ate was vile and loathsome. She boiled in water bits of food that had been scraped from dishes which were fit only for the garbage. With this she ate bran bread so hard that it had to be first softened with water. She ate these things only after she had first fasted for two or three days at a time.

26. She fled recognition and praise most energetically and said that those to whom Christ had given knowledge of his truth in their lives were the most tormented in hell and purgatory because of honors like these. When she walked around the town weeping, it was as if she were dying, for God daily showed her the salvation or destruction of those who were near death. When one of the townspeople died whom she knew in the spirit was damned for his sins, she wept and twisted herself and bent herself backwards and bent and rebent her arms and fingers as if they were pliable and not made of bones. All those who saw her found her sorrow so intolerable that hard men could not endure it without the greatest contrition and compassion. When she met people who wanted to be saved, she leaped and jumped so high that it was a great marvel to see. From behavior like this, the people knew the power of her spirit and could easily mark by her joy or sorrow what would happen to the dying in the town.

27. She assisted the dying most willingly and gladly and exhorted them to a confession of their sins, to the fruit of penance, to a hope of everlasting joy, and to a fear of the destroying fire. She showed solicitude and wonderful compassion not only to dying Christians but also to Jews because there was a very large group of them in the town. She said that Christ the Lord was full of mercy to those who wished to be converted to him. He would, however, take full vengeance for the sins of men as was required. Although he was saddened whenever he was forced to do so, he also looked for opportunities by which he might grant salvation to sufferers. When she spoke in this way of Christ the Lord, she was filled with wonderful grace of speech.

28. She also said that there was a place near hell which was ordained by God for the purgation of those who were stained by great sins but who had nevertheless repented at the end. This place, she said, was so fearsome because of its torments that there was no difference between these torments and the pains of hell except that there those who were suffering these pains breathed the hope of mercy. Demons, she said, were present to those who were suffering, who tormented them, but they knew that the more cruelly they were tortured, the shorter their torments would be.

29. She expounded many things with the spirit of prophecy and fore-

warned many to salvation and privately reprimanded many of their secret sins and recalled them to penance. On the occasion of the calamitous meeting at Steppes in October 1213 between the duke of Brabant and his enemies when so many hundreds of men were killed, on that very day this blessed woman cried out as if in childbirth, "Alas! Alas! I see the air full of swords and blood! Hurry, sisters, hurry! Pray to the Lord! Shed tears lest from his wrath he curb his mercy!" And she said to a nun at the monastery of St. Catherine's in St-Trond, "Run, sister, quickly run to prayer! Beg the Lord for your father because he is in great danger!"

30. When another nun at the same monastery was thinking of leaving, Christina said about her, "O empty vessel, you will be the cause of very great scandal to the monastery." Indeed, just as Christina had said, it soon happened that she apostasized from the Order and caused great scandal to the monastery through her unrestrained behavior. When the nun repented of her actions, the monastery found it difficult to take her back and reinstate her, but Christina reproached them and said, "Although you consider her downfall to be a minor thing, yet Christ did not pay so little for her soul but, rather, poured out his blood for her and considered her worthy to die for." Christina did not cease repeating these words until the repentant nun was reinstated.

31. When a nobleman wanted to go on pilgrimage to the Lord's tomb, his wife begged and swore an oath to Christina that she bring him back safe and sound by her prayer. Christina took her oath seriously and offered many prayers, labors and vows to the Lord for the knight that he bring him back safely, but she said angrily to his wife, "Behold, I have brought your husband back safely because of the insistency of your oath, but know now that you will not long rejoice in his presence." The truth of these words soon became clear for a few days later the nobleman died and left his wife and children in grief and desolation.

32. On another occasion she foretold long before the event that Jerusalem in the Holy Land would be taken by the ungodly Saracens. On the day that Jerusalem was captured, along with the Lord's tomb and the cross of Christ, she was in the castle of Loen and knew the event in the spirit. She exulted with great passion over this event and those who were present asked her why she exulted so much. "Rightly," she said, "I exult because today Christ the Lord rejoices with the angels and he exults because so many men have been given the occasion by which they might be saved."

33. When those present asked what this occasion might be, she said, "Know that today the Holy Land has been handed over into the hands of the ungodly and through this event a great occasion for salvation has been

given. Today Christ has produced something worthy from what had been an insult to himself, for the land has been delivered into shame although it had been consecrated by his Passion. Although it shall perish with the world at the end of time, yet by its recovery souls shall endure forever and shall be redeemed by his blood and they shall be turned to the path of justice from the path of injustice, and men shall shed their blood in this affair of the Holy Land and they, in turn, shall repay the death of Christ with great devotion." All who were there greatly marveled and some of them noted the time. Afterwards some of them who had made a pilgrimage in the intervening time discovered that on that very day the fame of the event had reached across the sea.

34. About 1170 she also prophesied a very great famine a long time before it occurred, and Christina prophesied many other wondrous things which have now been fulfilled and which we believe will be fulfilled in the future.

35. She later became very familiar with the nuns of St. Catherine's who lived outside the town of St-Trond. Sometimes while she was sitting with them, she would speak of Christ and suddenly and unexpectedly she would be ravished in the spirit and her body would roll and whirl around like a hoop. She whirled around with such extreme violence that the individual limbs of her body could not be distinguished. When she had whirled around for a long time in this manner, it seemed as if she became weakened by the violence of the rolling and all her limbs grew quiet. Then a wondrous harmony sounded between her throat and her breast which no mortal man could understand, nor could it be imitated by any artificial instrument. Her song had not only the pliancy and tones of music but also the words – if thus I might call them – sounded together incomprehensibly. The voice or spiritual breath, however, did not come out of her mouth or nose, but a harmony of the angelic voice resounded only from between the breast and the throat.

36. While all this was happening, all her limbs were quiet and her eyes were closed as if she were sleeping. Then after a little time, restored to her former self, she rose up like one who was drunk – indeed she *was* drunk [spiritually] – and she cried aloud, "Bring the nuns to me that together we might praise Jesus for the great liberality of his miracles." Shortly thereafter the nuns of the convent came running from all sides and greatly rejoiced in Christina's solace and she began to sing the 'Te Deum laudamus' ['We praise thee, O God'] and all the convent joined in and she finished her song. Afterwards when she was fully restored to herself, she knew what had happened from the tales of the others, and she fled for shame and embarrassment, and if anyone forcibly detained her she languished with a great sorrow and thought herself stupid or foolish.

37. At other times when she had been restored from the state we have just described, she would say in great bitterness of heart, "O wretched and miserable world that does not recognize your Maker! Why do you not consider the forbearance of his patience? If you saw his goodness, you could not be turned away from him, even if the world opposed you. Nay, rather you would love him. But you, O wretched world, are turned aside. You have closed your eyes and do not wish to understand." When she said these things, she cried out with great lamentations as if in childbirth and twisted her limbs and rolled around on the ground and, redoubling her cries, asked why the world did not recognize its Creator.

38. After these events, she left her own home and kin and went to a castle on the border of Germany called Looz where she stayed for nine years with a recluse called Jutta who led a very religious life. There the Lord wrought wonders through her. It was from this recluse that I received many of the revelations which I have written concerning Christina. Indeed this was the reason that I came to her from the far parts of Gaul.

39. While she was in that place Christina went to the vigils of Matins every night after everyone had left the church and the doors were locked. Then, walking on the church pavement, she would utter such sweet songs that they seemed to be the songs of angels and not of human origin. The song was so marvelous to hear that it surpassed the music of all instruments and the voices of all mortals. Nevertheless this song was less sweet and much unequal to the sweet song of the harmony which sounded incomparably from between her throat and breast and which surpassed human understanding. This song, I say, was in Latin and wondrously adorned with harmonious oratorical devices.

40. Although she had been completely illiterate from birth, yet she understood all Latin and fully knew the meaning of Holy Scripture. When she was asked very obscure questions by certain spiritual friends, she would explain them very openly, but she did this most unwillingly and rarely, for she said that to expound Holy Scriptures belonged to the clergy and not to the ministry of such as her. Arising from her very great love of Christ, she greatly and in a wonderful fashion venerated the clergy and especially priests even though on her part she had suffered many injuries from them. She would admonish sinning priests or clerics in great secrecy and with a wonderful reverence and as sweetly as if they were her own father lest they blaspheme the good name of Christ through their public excesses.

41. When Louis, count of Looz and a most noble man, learned of her famous sanctity through hearsay, he began to love her in his heart and to follow sincerely her counsels and advice. Wherever he saw her, he would rise

and run to her and call her his mother and when he did anything against justice or against the Church of Christ or against its ministers, she would weep for him like a mother weeping for her son. She would go to him in his palace and, trusting that she had the protection of a mother, would reprimand him and would obtain from him whatever was owing for the satisfaction of justice.

42. Once when Count Louis was reclining in the churchyard surrounded by many soldiers, she arrived unexpectedly and came close to the head of the count. She raised her eyes and her hands and began to say with a marvelous grace of speech, "O Lord, how beautiful you are!" When the soldiers heard this, they said to the count, "Do you not hear, lord count, how this holy woman praises you?" The count, however, said, "I know who it is that she is praising. I am not he. She praises her heavenly Lord who is the creator of all beauty and the most beautiful of all." She then said, "You have spoken truly. Why therefore do you not love him?"

43. One summer's noon the count was staying in his palace at Looz (which is now destroyed) with the Duke of Limburg and another count and they were talking together. Christine ran unwaveringly to them and cried out to Count Louis, "O most wretched one! Who are you talking to? Behold, he is no friend who is acting like a friend to you and is stretching forth the hand of a traitor!" Fearing the voice of the woman, the traitor immediately fell silent for a time and dissimulated the truth by his words, but the result proved the truth of the. prophecy.

44. When Count Louis was near death he called Christina to him and most persistently begged her to stay with him until the hour of death. She very obligingly granted this and he commanded all the counts who were with him to leave the bedchamber and kept Christina alone with him in the chamber. Without delay the count pulled himself up with all the strength he could summon and lay fully prostrate before the feet of Christina and, with great lamentation, recited to her all his sins from his eleventh year right up to that very day. He did this not for absolution which she had no power to give but rather that she might be moved by this atonement to pray for him. After this he called all his counts into the bedchamber and, following the advice of Christina, he disposed of his goods and then he died. She saw his soul being carried to purgatory and there tormented with the most bitter punishments.

45. The goodly woman was not a little compassionate towards him and obtained permission from the Lord that she might suffer with him the exacted punishment in purgatory. When therefore he appeared to her after his death and asked for help, Christina said to him, "Well then, go hence and fulfil the punishments due your sins according to the Divine Judgment. As

for me, I will accept in my own body a half part of your purgatorial torments which must be exacted." Having taken on these burdens, for a long time afterwards you might have seen Christina in the middle of the night being tormented with burning smoke and at other times with freezing cold. Indeed she suffered torments in turn according to what the soul of the count was suffering. She also watered with her tears the places where the count had been accustomed to sin and she grieved in the places where futile joy had made him happy.

46. In the last year of her life solitude and the desert places were frequently her home. She returned, although most rarely, when she was driven in the spirit, either for the salvation of men or for the partaking of food. No mortal man could, at that time, restrain her when she wanted to go into the desert. When she returned no one dared greet her, no one dared ask her anything. Once she returned at Vespers and passed above the ground right through the middle of a house like a spirit and people could scarcely tell whether a spirit or a material body had passed by, since she barely seemed to touch the ground. Indeed in the last year of her life, the spirit so controlled almost all the parts of her corporeal body that scarcely could either human minds or eyes look at the shadow her body cast without horror or a trembling of the spirit. She then returned to the town of St-Trond and more frequently dwelt in the monastery of St. Catherine's.

47. A venerable man whom I remember, Thomas, now abbot of St-Trond [1239-1248] but then a priest in St-Trond, told me a very meritorious thing about Christina. One dawn he was returning home from Matins with a companion and he saw her going into the church, moving purposefully. They followed her surreptitiously and observed her most secretly from behind a pillar of the church to see what she would do or how she would pray. Without delay she threw herself before the altar as if she were a sack filled with dry bones. Then wailing bitterly she began to beat her breast and her body most often and said, "O miserable and wretched body! How long will you torment me, miserable as I am? What are you doing with me? What is it to you that you keep my wretched soul in you for so long? Why do you delay me from seeing the face of Christ? When will you abandon me so that my soul can return freely to its Creator? Woe to you most miserable one! And woe to me who am united to you!"

48. When she had said these things in this manner, she would beat her body but then, taking the part of the body she would say, as if to the spirit, "O miserable soul! Why are you tormenting me in this way? What is keeping you in me and what is it that you love in me? Why do you not allow me to return to the earth from which I was taken and why do you not let me be at

rest until I am restored to you on the last day of Judgment?" When she had said this, she would sigh and gasp and weep. Immediately afterwards she would rest a little in silence and, burning most purely in God with a holy thought, she would dissolve into a most sweet smile. Then taking her feet with both hands, she would kiss the soles of her feet with greatest affection and would say, "O most beloved body! Why have I beaten you? Why have I reviled you? Did you not obey me in every good deed I undertook to do with God's help? You have endured the torments and hardships most generously and most patiently which the spirit placed on you."

49. Then doubling her kisses, she said, "Now, o best and sweetest body, endure patiently. Now is an end of your hardship, now you will rest in the dust and will sleep for a little and then, at last, when the trumpet blows, you will rise again purified of all corruptibility and you will be joined in eternal happiness with the soul you have had as a companion in the present sadness." Thus gentling her body with words and kisses for an hour, she then uttered that wonderful cry which we have already described and was inwardly filled with such joy that one would have believed that her exterior body would burst. Truly God works wonders in his saints and in situations like this; if I may say, his wonders pass all admiration.

50. At the end of her life, she ate little and very rarely. No longer did she wish to sit and talk with her sisters and the nuns as she used to do but, eating only a little and sleeping only a little before midnight, she went into the desert. In those days, no one ever saw a smile on her lips but she was like one who has been made mad from excessive sorrow. She would wander around praying, weeping and mourning and, for this reason, some people believed that the Lord had shown her even more of the condition and malice of the world. The one thing for which she mourned most frequently with wondrous outcries was that almost all of humankind was being corrupted by an explosion of licentiousness. It was because of this that the most swift anger and vengeance of God was threatening all of Christendom.

51. When the time approached that she should be held fast in the sickness of death, she was overtaken by such an unbroken grace of contemplation that she found it very difficult to direct the attention of her mind anywhere else. At the very end, untroubled by anything, she gently asked Beatrice, a nun at St. Catherine's, that a bed be prepared secretly for her in one of the rooms because her final sickness was close at hand. [Beatrice] quickly did what she was asked and Christina lay down and was overcome by an increasingly serious illness. After three days of this sickness, she asked for the Communion of the Body of the Lord and for the holy oils. When this was done, the Beatrice of whom I have spoken fell down on her knees and openly begged that she

make known certain things before she died. When Christina did not answer, Beatrice thought that her attention was on other things and, postponing her question, left the room to do something else and left her alone for a time.

52. Some people say that, while she was alive, Christina often prayed to the Lord not to honor her in death by any miracles, but to allow her to die the common death of men. In this the Lord also heard her, for before the aforementioned Beatrice could return, Christina called on Christ and gave up her spirit. As soon as Beatrice returned with another nun she found the lifeless body stretched out on the ground after the manner of corpses and truly, I believe, in the care of the angels. Beatrice was fearsomely impatient at this and fell upon the body of the dead woman and began to wail violently. She often interrupted her shouts by asking the dead woman why she had gone to the Lord without her permission [and] without the leave of the sisters. Nevertheless in her vehement spirit, she still had trust and, putting her face to the mouth of the dead woman, she said, "O Christina! You were ever obedient to me in life! I now therefore beseech you and admonish you earnestly through the Lord Jesus Christ, whom you loved with ardent desire while you lived, that you obey me now; since you are powerful and, through him with whom you are now joined, you can do what you want, return to life and tell me what I begged you to reveal to me with great desire while you were alive."

53. Wonderful event! As soon as Beatrice had cried out into the ears of the dead woman, Christina returned to her body and, heaving a great sigh, opened her haggard eyes like one roused from a profound sleep. Turning her grief-stricken face to the one who had called her back, she said, "O Beatrice! Why have you disturbed me? Why have you called me back? Just now I was being led to the face of Christ! But now, my sister, quickly ask me what you want and then, I beg you, allow me to return to the Lord for whom I have longed eagerly." Then Beatrice asked [Christina] her question and received a reply from her. In the meantime the sisters of the monastery gathered together from all sides and Christina blessed them with word and with the sign of the Cross and in this way she who had experienced death three times and died three times passed to the immortal age of ages.

54. She lived for forty-two years after she had first risen from the dead and died around the year 1224. She was buried in the monastery of St. Catherine's just outside the town of St-Trond and there she rested for seven years until they transferred the monastery to a more fitting place which was close at hand. Then all the citizens, together with the clerics and the nuns at the convent, gathered together at the grave of the holy and revered Christina. When they opened the lid and laid it on the side, a grace of such sweetness

seized everyone both collectively and individually that they all cried out together with one mind and one voice, "Christina! You were marvelous in life and now after death you are no less glorious!" No one doubted the grace of healing which had been bestowed on those who had come to her tomb with due faith. We cannot, however, pursue these matters.

55. Therefore see, reader, how greatly we who see Christina suffering so many torments and so much hardship (not, indeed, for herself but for her neighbors) are under an obligation and yet we fear to do penance for ourselves and for our excesses! Certainly a day will come – it will come and there will be no delay! – when we would gladly do much more than this if a place of penance were given to those who would ask for it and thereby make up for lost time. Woe to those who want to buy the oil of mercy after the time of trading has passed! With empty lamps they will beat on the door and will not be able to enter. Rather, he [God] will say, "Amen, I say to you I know you not. Watch ye therefore, because you know not the day nor the hour."

56. Therefore it is brought to an end with an argument necessary for those who are sleeping who, forgetting the day and the hour, do not want to keep vigil with a lamp filled with the oil of good works and with the worthy fruits of penance. Watch therefore because you know not the day or the hour when your Lord will come. What else did Christina cry out during her entire life except that we do penance and be people who are ready at every hour? By the example of her life and with many words, with tears, lamentations and boundless cries she taught more and shouted louder than anyone we have known either before or since through writings or by report about the praise and glory of Christ who, with the Father and the Holy Spirit is God living and reigning forever and ever. Amen.

38. WOMEN'S SPIRITUALITY II: UMILTÀ OF FAENZA

As in the north of Europe, the thirteenth and fourteenth centuries saw an increase in the depth and variety of spirituality among Italian women. While the founding of new religious orders such as the Franciscans and Dominicans opened up a wider choice of careers in the Church for men, women, with less access to education, increasingly restricted admission to convents, and continued exclusion from the church hierarchy found their choices as few as ever. St. Francis's friend and companion, Clare, had wanted to establish an order for women similar to the Rule for men, but ultimately her followers found themselves observing poverty in a strictly cloistered setting as the 'Poor Clares.' Nevertheless, Italian women did develop individual forms of spirituality during this period, especially as mystics, a religious vocation in which the role of women was acknowledged. These women had certain characteristics in common: mostly from the urban middle and upper classes, they rebelled against their parents (especially over issues of marriage) at an early age; their refusal to behave conventionally often ended in escape to a convent from which their angry relatives tried to retrieve them, some-times by force; they preferred a solitary life of prayer and communion with God, con-fined to a room or a cell, and they engaged in harsh and sometimes bizarre ascetic practices. Umiltà of Faenza (1226-1310) is not an extreme example of this type but, like that of her contemporaries Margaret of Cortona and Angela of Foligno, her life suggests an uneasy tension between withdrawal from society and involvement in its institutions (such as marriage), and, in the second phase, between reclusiveness and the demands of conventual living. Her biography was commissioned by her companion and friend, Margaret of Faenza, and addressed to the nuns of the Vallombrosan Order.

Source: trans. Elizabeth Petroff, *Consolation of the Blessed* (New York: Alta Gaia Society, 1979), pp. 121-137; repr. with permission. BHL 4045.

Prologue

1. Dearest sisters, you constrain me to bring within the compass of a single volume, with excessive verbiage removed, the life of St. Umiltà, your mother and mine, an account which has been written in various volumes by various different authors in a variety of ways; and also to set down what I learned from her own true account, since, as you assert, you believe that from her telling I know many things which truly demonstrate her sanctity. Even though the defects of my life, the poverty of my intellect, conflicts over tem-poral matters, and the senseless outcries of her detractors would restrain me from complying with your wishes, nevertheless affection for your holiness has compelled me – a feeling by which, as you know, we have been intimately

bound together from the first youthful period of your arrival here. Accept this eagerly, then, and imitate so holy a mother. Accept into your prayers what the earnest love of him who is your servant in all things has gathered together and now transmits clearly, under precise chapter headings. And should anything seem harsh in following her example, I beg you to consider the brevity of life, the vileness of the body, the inevitability of death, the delights of our heavenly homeland, and the bitter things experienced by Christ; then the way will be led with ease, and all things surely will distill sweetness.

Her early adolescence, marriage, religious life; her transferral to the Vallombrosan Order

2. Rosanese, called Umiltà after her baptism in holy religion, was born in the province of Romandiola, in the town of Faenza, of very noble stock, for her father was Elimonte and her mother Richilda. From her childhood she was intent on divine obedience, occupying her time in constant prayer and generous alms-giving. She commended herself to God unceasingly, submitting her entire self first to Christ, then to his mother who, from then on, she established as her model in all her deeds, and by so establishing her, gained her as a special patroness in all her striving. And so that entrance to the hall of such a great king and such a great queen might lie open in easy efforts, Rosanese instituted as her agent blessed John the Evangelist, not fearing, with him to lead the way, to obtain whatever she would want from him who gave Mary sweetly as a mother and in consequence, from her who accepted John as a foster son, when she was weeping most bitterly at the foot of the Cross. Rosanese, fair with an appearance which she scorned, elegant in conversation, most gracious in her manners, as everyone reported, was dressed very richly one day, as befitting the only daughter of very wealthy parents, for this was the custom of that land. Suddenly she returned to her real self, withdrew into her chamber, and gave herself to prayer. She was silent about what she felt, but having put aside every vanity, she transformed her whole self unutterably. Her parents were very grieved when they thought about this; and because of her attitude concerning the use of ornamentation, her attraction to whatever was lowly, and her association with girls her own age, they lost all hope that they had [for themselves] from her advancement in the secular world and merely tried to insure that she did not secretly enter a convent.

3. As much as she could, meanwhile, she began to give money to the poor, secretly and in public, so that her chambermaids were exhausted by reporting this to her parents. They hid their knowledge of this activity, and

commanded her obedience in all things according to a vow. She expressed her desire to enter a convent to some abbesses of women's houses; each of them agreed, but none of them could see how she might escape from her parents' watch over her, if this was not according to divine providence.

When the emperor Frederick had taken Faenza after a lengthy siege, and had entered the city, his cousin on his father's side heard of her reputation for beauty and was stricken with blind love. He sent many messengers, but none was able to see her. When he discerned that he was accomplishing nothing this way, the young man finally sought her as his bride from her parents. When asked her opinion about this match, the girl's answer was that she wanted Christ as her husband, and no one else. When the youth saw clearly that he had taken on himself an impossible task, he ceased to trouble her further, and publicly reported that no girl like her existed. Although Rosanese perceived all these events quite clearly, she nevertheless remained as much on her guard as before, as long as the said youth was present in Faenza.

4. A short time later, Umiltà's father Elimonte was taken from this evil world with a good ending. Rosanese was married to Ugolotto, a nobleman of the city of Faenza. For nine years she lived with him very happily, never ceasing to have conversations with him about changing his manner of living. He considered this laughable, saying to himself that he would never do any such thing. She gave herself to prayer for days on end, over a long period of time, seeking from God what her husband denied. And while she was persisting quite rightly, in this, her dearest husband fell headlong into a serious illness. Physicians were called in, and they all agreed in the judgment that it would be best for him to live chastely. For if he did not abstain from sex, he would collapse with an incurable and foul weakness, and in a short time he would die a very cruel death. He began to say that from henceforth he would live chastely, and to ask his relatives, and his wife's relatives, to convince his wife to do this too, so that he would not die. When Rosanese had observed all this attentively, she gave devout praises to the Lord who had heard her prayers and she lived with Ugolotto faithfully, as with a brother, as long as he lived. Before he relinquished her as his wife, her husband begat many sons and daughters upon her.

5. This prudent lady, considering that now she might be able to fulfil her desire, unceasingly began to offer him comfort under the guise of protecting his bodily health, hoping to inspire him to enter a religious order for the sake of preserving his vitality. Displaying much sorrow and cruel weeping, he assented to this. He permitted her, after she had given away everything she possessed to the sisters, to enter the convent among the sisters of the monastery of St. Perpetua near Faenza, who were living a holy life under a

rule. In humility he joined the group of external brothers attached to the same convent. Then Rosanese changed her name, and it was announced that from then on she was to be called Umiltà. When she did this, Rosanese had just completed her twenty-fourth year. From that day on, her former husband never saw her with bodily eyes. At once she began to be transformed into another woman, to do the most vile tasks in the monastery with her hands, and to be so knowledgeable in matters of religion that no one doubted that she had come, not from the secular world, but from the desert. To all those who saw her, she was now an example of keeping silence, of prayer, of solitude, of ready and helpful obedience towards the sick and the well equally, and of abstinence and all other difficult works.

6. One particular day, when she was still illiterate, some sisters called on her and bade her read at the second meal, as is the custom among nuns. I think they commanded her to do this for their own relaxation. She bowed her head and took up the book so that she might obey. Having picked it up, she carried it to the appropriate place, opened it and began at this verse: "Despise not the works of God, since they are all true and just." What is more, she spoke such lofty words, keeping her eyes always raised to heaven, that she excited the entire convent, who came running to see this spectacle, marveling in wonderment. And when the sign was given for her to conclude her reading, by saying "you, however," as was appropriate, taught by the Holy Spirit, she concluded in the best possible way. Inside that volume no one was ever able to find the passages that she had read, neither before nor after. From that time on, the convent took care to teach her letters – which she did learn – by getting a woman teacher for her.

7. One time, when she as was afflicted with a tumor in her kidneys, having been assigned a nurse by the abbess (who thought that Umiltà didn't want a doctor), and fearing that the stink of her wound would be disturbing to the convent, she gave herself to prayer. At once, as soon as she arose from prayer, she was cured. When the sister who had been assigned to her as a nurse, intending to treat her in the usual way, discovered that she was cured and that there was no sign of there having been any wound, she asked Umiltà what the explanation for this was, for she was greatly amazed. Having faithfully learned the story from her, with great devotion and with all the facts in order she told it to the other sisters.

8. Sister Umiltà began to leave aside other things and to spend her time in prayer. With all her strength she desired to find some deserted place where she might devote herself wholly to prayer, yet she despaired of finding any way by human aid to escape her strict custody. When this desire had persisted in her for a long time, she one day gave herself to contemplation of the

divine. She did not say what she heard, except that a voice had said that she would leave the monastery the coming Saturday and had made it clear for the entire convent that whatever she should demand earnestly she would have without fail. Considering the height of the walls and of the gate, and the external brothers guarding the door, the convent decided that what she had heard spoken was fantasy; assuming the thing was impossible, they ignored the words. But when that particular night arrived, a voice spoke. "Sister Umiltà," it said, "Arise and follow me." As she was about to obey, she went first to the bed of a certain sister who had been very poor, and hastily snatched up her worn out old tunic, leaving her the better one which she had been wearing. Holding her Psalter in her hand, protecting herself with the sign of the cross, she was placed instantly on the top of the wall. Now while she was there and thinking anxiously about how to get down, the being picked her up invisibly as before, and she left the book behind her on the wall. Since the gates were locked, while she was standing there the invisible being opened them with the brother's key. It brought her smoothly outside, and put her down unharmed beyond the entire convent. She came to a certain river situated near this place, which she walked across, passing over it as if with dry feet. Suddenly she came to herself; she saw where she was, as if awakening from sleep. After giving thanks to God, for his guardianship over her, she hurried with swift steps to the convent of sisters of the Order of St. Clare.

9. When Sister Umiltà had come to this convent, she excited wonderment in all the sisters. Many sisters, and the abbess among them, were dubious, on account of her beauty, about her having avoided danger. However, the abbess showed nothing of her doubts, and with her convent received her very kindly, and quickly enrolled her among themselves. The sisters, hearing of her effort, and being instructed by great edification, were astonished at her exit from such strict custody. They sent for a certain knight named Nicolo, a close relative of hers, for the abbess was unwilling for her to travel alone, and they placed her under his protection, meanwhile pouring forth devout tears at her departure. The knight Nicolo, after he had listened to Umiltà's case sweetly, took her to his home, and placed her in a certain pretty chamber, keeping the key in his own possession, and generously supplying it with whatever she needed. All the time she was there she slept on the bare floor, observing the strictest silence, and occupying herself in constant prayer. She ate no food beyond bread and water.

10. There was a certain religious man attached to the church of St. Apollinaris in the city of Faenza who was supposed to have his foot amputated on the advice of certain experienced men, because he had a terrible disease. He

had heard of Umiltà's reputation and had himself brought there, humbly commending himself to her. Moved by pity, she touched his foot with the sign of the cross. Cured instantly, the overjoyed monk returned home on his own feet, announcing the deed to everyone as he went. Considering this event, the above-mentioned Lord Nicolo managed to remove all obstacles [to Umiltà's practicing a solitary life] and to procure by his petitions the permission, granted I think by the curate, for a cell to be built for her next to his church. They built her cell next to the church of St. Apollinaris in Faenza; it was quite small, with a little window which looked into the church so that she might see and receive the sacraments of Holy Mother Church. It had another window facing outside, where she might receive alms and freely give satisfaction to those who had come to see her, for she had requested that the cell be built in this way. The day was fixed upon for her enclosure; the entire city flocked there; they all cried out, "Let's see the saint!" The abbot of Crispino, to whom the place was subject, proceeded to the church; he gave her the habit of holy religion when he had received her obedience. He undertook to provide her and her maid with necessities. So that in poverty she might follow the example of the poverty of Christ, she refused everything, after giving him thanks. After she was blessed with the sign of the cross she asked for two things: an oratory and a board for sleeping on. She possessed nothing else as long as she lived there, nor would she permit anything to be brought into her cell for any reason.

11. Twelve years she lived in that cell; bread and water alone, with cooked bitter herbs on solemn feast days, this was her habitual diet. She reached the point of such abstinence that three ounces of bread a day were enough to support her thin body. Nor did she ever, during the entire time that she was in the cell, arrange for two meals a day, or for any food other than that mentioned, in any circumstance. On her bare body she always wore a shirt of horse hair, or pig skin with the bristles turned toward her flesh, wearing this in every situation, event, and time, with only a worn and worthless cowl over it, without any warm leather or woven clothing placed beneath it. Sometimes in place of the hairshirt she used a very rough woolen vest, when for some reason that was appropriate. When she was tired of being on her knees, she positioned herself on the aforementioned board. When she was overcome by sleep, she would place her head against the wall, and would fall asleep reciting Psalms or meditating on some divine matter.

12. One day a weasel with a bell on its neck entered her cell. She received it affectionately, as if it were divinely given her as a companion. While she was occupied in prayer, it sat at her feet. It never tasted any of the meat given it carefully while it was there in the cell. Nor did it ever seem to eat any

other food, except what it saw the holy mother Umiltà, to whom it had been divinely given as a companion, make proper use of in the cell. A long time passed in this way, when it perceived that there were ladies who lived in cells next to the cell of its lady. It climbed up to the window, looked at its lady as if in derision, deposited there its bell as if saying farewell, and never appeared again.

Umiltà's husband, who was unable to bear her absence, in charity having parted with all those things which he had given to the monastery with her, earnestly requested to be her companion. Having obtained this permission, he bound himself by the yoke of holy obedience first to the abbot of his monastery, then to her, his former wife, as the abbess; this took place in the aforementioned monastery of St. Apollinaris. He always spoke of Umiltà as Lady, and although he never saw her, as mentioned earlier, in no circumstances whatsoever did he neglect her orders. He lived for three years after he entered the monastic life, and with a holy end finished sweetly this wretched life.

She constructs monasteries near Faenza and Florence and rules there as abbess, famous for miracles even after her death.

13. Bishops, abbots, and other religious clerics began to ask her to construct a monastery in the city; among them was the reverend lord rector, abbot of the Greater Vallombroson Order. Trusting solidly in him, she left her cell and constructed a convent near Faenza, in the place which is called Malta, dedicating it in honor of the Mother of God and placing it under the Benedictine Rule. Being bound by obedience to the aforesaid father and rule, she and her place were perpetually subject to the authority of this same father and of all his successors. The fame of her sanctity began to run here and there; very many magnates put their daughters and wives under her direction, and she taught than to observe the aforesaid rule to the very letter. Nothing of her behavior was changed from when she had been living in her cell. On a certain day, when she had received a particular sister and when she had considered carefully the charge that this woman had fulfilled in a less than good fashion the office of prelate which she held in that monastery, Umiltà found her basely delinquent. What is worse, the woman had often been corrected by Umiltà privately, and had not taken any pains to pay heed to this correction. Being conscious of all this, Mother Umiltà called her before her publicly in chapter, and since she brazenly continued to resist the council of the older nuns, Umiltà committed her to imprisonment. The woman absolutely refused to eat any food. When she had remained in this

state for quite a few days, the abbess made her way to the prison, with crossed arms bowing the knee to her, sweetly imploring her to pay attention to her own salvation. Then the woman prostrated herself at Abbess Umiltà's feet and confessed her crime and willingly did penance, and thenceforth, by living in sanctity, made clear to all that she had been properly corrected.

14. One particular day Umiltà, as was her custom, was visiting one of her sisters who was seriously ill. The sister revealed to Umiltà a sin of hers which she had never confessed to anyone out of shame, mentioning this sin in secrecy between the two of them. Sweetly she encouraged the sister to confess, for she ought to realize with certainty that the coming Friday, at the sixth hour, she would leave this world, and that she would then have to account to God for this sin along with her other sins. The astonished woman came to her senses and publicly, in front of the whole assembled convent, spoke the truth and confessed to a priest with many tears. Then at the appointed hour of the day she entered the heavenly realms. Another time Umiltà went to meet her chaplain, who was coming one morning to celebrate Mass, but she pretended she did not know this, and asked him where he was going. As he was telling her where he was going, she said to him secretly and very devoutly, "First confess, my son, such and such sin which you have committed; then you need not fear to approach the altar in safety." He was confounded, and with many embarrassed tears first told her everything, in order, which he thought only God knew, and then diligently confessed, and never afterward committed such sins.

15. When a certain small fish had been given to her, she told the cellarer that she should make it ready to eat, and that in the morning she should serve it to everyone in the convent. The cellarer, assessing the thing carefully, considering that it would scarcely provide a poor meal for two persons, prepared it diligently in a pepper sauce, and put it on the table in front of the abbess alone. Umiltà looked at it, and in front of the whole convent, picked up the dish with anger, and threw it, with the fish, on the floor. Miraculous event! It was not less honorably placed on the table than it was thrown on the floor, for it stuck together whole as if it were nailed together and made of wood and the entire convent saw it lying on the floor. Then the servant picked it up from the floor, and just as the abbess had earlier commanded, gave some of it to each of the sisters.

When Umiltà the holy mother abbess was in Faenza, one day a certain sister began to bleed so heavily from her nose into a basin that, having despaired of all the remedies for health proposed by the physicians, she was hastening toward her final end, as was obvious to all. When the pious nurse Umiltà heard this, as was her custom she sweetly invoked the supreme physician, made the sign of the cross over her, and at once the sister was completely cured, with all her strength restored.

When heavy snows (customary in her country) threatened to make all the houses collapse and people were unable to provide for themselves, all the extern and conventual brothers came to her and humbly besought her to provide for them and for their people in such tribulation. Having comforted them, she gave herself to prayer, and suddenly the tempestuous weather was put to flight, and a very warm sun came out, so that the snow was melted and the whole storm quieted.

16. When she was making her way to Rome on foot for some difficult business, and had completely given up in exhaustion on the tougher part of the journey, someone appeared to her with a very gentle horse, and put her on it, and talking pleasantly with her, brought her all the way up to the hospice. Having lifted her off the horse, he said farewell; even to that moment he concealed his identity and no one among her companions, neither among the ladies nor among the brothers, saw how he left. When her companions ate at this hospice, she found herself unable to chew such hard bread. Bidding everyone to eat, she got up, and alone in the street while they were eating she gave herself to prayer as was her custom, whenever at any time she would dismount in any place. She fell on her knees and busied herself in prayer without delay, until it was appropriate to attend to other business. At once someone appeared to her, and gave her the whitest bread to eat; and kindly bade her refresh herself with it, and went away. When she had obeyed him, the brothers and sisters who had eaten gathered around her. They were very much amazed when they heard about this business, and praising God they finished the journey begun earlier. When in the aforesaid journey she stopped at the cell of two women recluses, they began to call out to her as soon as they saw her "This is the body who appeared to us in sleep, and taught us how we ought to proceed on the path to God." For this reason they insisted that she stay and rest with them, and just as they had seen in their vision, they devoutly received instruction from her for the greater part of the night.

One night, when she was attending Matins in her monastery, she suddenly made a sign that wine should be brought to her, and gently asked for water. This having been brought, she sent it to a certain seriously ill sister in the infirmary, who was so troubled by thirst that she could not sleep. The sick woman, having given thanks to God and his holy Mother, consumed the drink, and then slept peacefully.

17. Although blessed John the Evangelist had appeared to her many times, and commanded her to build his convent, one night he appeared to her, and

commanded that she should build it, not in Venice as she had planned, but in Florence, promising her that he would bear the spiritual responsibility for that which she had already done in Faenza and that which she should do in the future in Florence; he also prophesied that during her journey on the roads she would pass through trials without reproach. Then strengthening herself with the sign of the cross, she secretly called several sisters to her. She revealed to them what had just happened, and taking nothing with her from the monastery, she entrusted the convent to the prioress; barefoot, accompanied by those whom she had named to go with her, she hastened through the hazards of war unharmed, with all her group, with the Evangelist leading the way. When for a long time she had been disposed to have some relics of blessed John the Evangelist, and yet thought that there was no chance that she might ever have them, she came to Florence as she was traveling in the direction of Pieve del To, where she was received by the rector of Pieve and greeted by all the clerics with rejoicing. The rector told her that if she wished to see the relics of the Evangelist, he would gladly show them to her. Eagerly she accepted his promise, and gazed on them with great reverence. The said rector was so moved by this that he freely made her a present of a casket which he acquired, with the manna of John the Evangelist and his relics in it. With inestimable joy she brought these things to Florence and after an appropriate length of time, built in the Evangelist's honor a church of marvelous beauty.

And so in Florence she was joyously received by prelates and lower clergy, religious and lay people. Having been conducted to her lodgings, outside the city in the plain of St. Ambrose, she was provided for with honor. When her sanctity was observed, she was held in such veneration that there she was proclaimed inestimably as a saint. After she had been staying in Florence almost two years, the piece of land where there is now a monastery was bought from Florence. There she quickly went with those whom she had brought with her from Faenza along with other noble ladies from the city of Florence; she enclosed herself and instructed them (so it was said) to wage war for God singlemindedly under the rule which she had assumed.

18. Her usual activity at this time was gathering stones in the bed of the Mugnone River, located next to her site, for use in building the convent; one particular day she had just loaded the stones on an ass, and was bringing him back to her house, when she met two women, who were both gesturing and grievously weeping over the son of a certain Florentine. Moved by pity, Umiltà gently inquired of them the cause of such intense mourning. They then said to her that with the excuse of a long-lasting illness, and at the bidding of his parents, they themselves had been bringing the youth to them

and then he had died on the journey. They did not use many words but they prostrated themselves at her feet, and with great sobs entreated her to bring back to life the said youth. Then the mother of kindness took him in her arms, carrying him over to the altar of blessed John the Evangelist which at that time was standing in a little house near the road, and placed him above the predella. In sight of the onlookers she devoutly gave herself to fervent prayer. After a long time she got up, exhausted, and taking the boy gave him safe and sound to the women. Umiltà commanded them to tell no one in his family about this as long as she was alive, and to come with her immediately to collect stones.

A certain nobleman named Bernard, knight of Urban, of the city of Florence in the neighborhood of St. Felicity, visited Umiltà one day. Although a layman, he commended himself to her prayers with much devotion. She kindly took him in and urged him to consider the state of his soul, for she knew that on the coming Thursday he was to die, and would have to account to God for all his actions. Although he was most sane and clear-headed, he grew afraid hearing this, and when he returned to his own home he died, on the prophesied day, just as she had predicted.

19. The holy mother, who had once been very beautiful in appearance, very wise in the way of God and of the world, day by day, more and more avid for the path of penitence, sweet-flowing of speech when recalling sinners, pouring forth the wine and oil most wisely in corrections, that she might free sinners, adorned with the possessions of all good customs, most perfected in charity, fell into a lingering illness, if I am not mistaken, at the age of eighty or more, on St. Lucy's Day, December thirteenth. Because of the fervor for doing penance that she always displayed, even when she could not speak, during her illness she kindled in those around her an unbelievable desire to serve the Most High. The twenty-second day of May, 1310, the sixth day of the week at about the sixth hour, with her holy companions standing around her singing Psalms and at the same time weeping bitterly, she entered the heavenly realms. On Sunday, in the church she had built in honor of blessed John the Evangelist, next to his altar on the left side, she was buried with marvelous devotion, being granted the highest honor by secular and religious prelates and other clerks, before a great multitude of the people.

20. Meanwhile the stone placed over her grave began visibly to emit oil. One of the sisters, noticing this, and being fearful that it might be only an illusion, prudently would wipe off the oil from the stone quite frequently and carefully. When she saw by doing this that the occurrence was divine, as it was, she told everyone who came there what was happening. When a wiping of the stone was done, the experience of all was very apparent; on this

account particular care was given to the translation of her body by the Florentines. By the devotion of the faithful, a holy altar was built on the right side of the altar in the same church, in which, on the sixth day of June, 1311, her body, still whole and intact, was taken from that first burial place where it had been buried in the bare ground. Those present at this ceremony included the venerable fathers and lords Antonio, bishop of Florence, Roger the abbot of Vallombrosa, Azzone the abbot of Florence, Gratia Septimus abbot, and many other prelates and lesser clergy and secular people, and various other clerics, and a remarkable multitude of Florentines. The people were allowed to view her body until a solemn mass had been celebrated. This being finished, her body was marvelously adorned and she was buried, as we said, in the place prepared for her with great honor, as was fitting.

21. The reverend lord Albertus, abbot of Razzolo, troubled by a severe weakness in his foot, commended himself to her with the greatest devotion, humbly begging her that she might return his health to him. Scarcely had he completed his prayer when he was freed from sickness completely; since this was a witness to her translation, he announced his cure publicly.

A certain woman, who had been blind for almost fifteen years, visiting the shrine of the saint, sought eagerly for her sight. A certain sister gave her a small water pitcher, which had been placed on the saint's table before her for a long time. Devoutly holding this on her eyes, she was at once totally cured, and was able to return to her home. Umiltà appeared to a certain gravely ill sister of the same monastery, named D., one morning when she was between sleeping and waking. She commanded her to get up from her bed and go to church to hear the second mass, just as she herself was doing; then she withdrew, as quickly as she had come. Instantly obedient, the sister rose from her bed and hastened, healthy and joyful, to hear Mass, offering many thanks to God and his Holy Mother.

A certain young woman, a sister in that same place named Francisca, began to cry out as she was struggling with the extremity of death before the eyes of the entire convent: "Wait for me! Wait for me!" When those standing near her asked her what she saw, she indicated by her nod that it was the holy mother abbess. Having made this clear, she at once went forth to her who had called her.

22. Holy sisters, if I have been more negligent in obeying your requests than you would have wished, I beg you to grant forgiveness to him who has wronged you, although no one can arrive quickly enough for a person who is waiting. Although I have confidently held back from many topics, nevertheless on each individual topic I have touched lightly. I know that your prudence is not hidden, and you see that I have not the gifts to be able to pur-

sue such a heavy task. By your prayers I pray that I will be able to see again her of whom I have written, however feebly, in the presence of Christ in our true native land. She now rejoices perfectly in him for whom she wept copiously, as if over present griefs, during her long life in religion when she saw him dead upon the cross, for our sins most cruelly pierced by nails and then by a lance.

23. And I beg that he who reads this should not be loath to reread it with an eye to correction, where he recognizes that what was written is faulty in some respects, for in things concerning such a great lady, it is more pleasing to see nothing, except what is to be emended by surpassing charity.

Supplement of miracles accomplished during her life and after her death

24. One day, there was but a single loaf of bread to be found in the aforesaid monastery; the hour for eating had already arrived, when the venerable abbess spoke to the cellarer and asked "Why are the sisters not eating?"

And the cellarer replied,"There isn't enough bread here; for except for one very small loaf, we have found no bread in the house."

The abbess, trusting in the omnipotence of her Creator, who established and created all things together from nothing, who is totally in all things, as soon as she heard this commanded the table to be laid in the usual way, and the single loaf to be brought forth at once. The abbess, taking it in her hands and raising her eyes to heaven, said "May the Lord, who fed five thousand men with five barley loaves, cause you to multiply." And having made the sign of the cross over the loaf, she broke it, saying to the cellarer that she should place a fragment of the loaf in front of each sister who sat down to dine, and that the Lord would multiply it in their mouths. The cellarer, hearing and firmly believing this, brought a fragment of the loaf to each person. In truth the sisters, who were thirteen in number, ate until they were very full, with the greatest joy, and there were more pieces of bread remaining left over than had been placed before the sisters earlier.

25. One time a kind of swelling puffed up on the abbess's lips so that she was unable to eat, and the nuns said to her, "Lady, you ought to send for a doctor so you can be freed of this swelling."

The abbess replied that she did not want to do this, and said, "I want the medicine that comes from him who took away my cancer before." And truly, on the following day she was cured. And another time, when the Bolognese army had come to the city of Faenza, the abbess predicted to some nuns that the Bolognese would arrive the following day, enter the monastery, and carry off sheep and cows and anything else they liked. And so she instructed them to hide everything well, so that things couldn't be lost. On the day which the abbess had foretold, the Bolognese came to the monastery, carrying off everything in the monastery except for the clothes that the nuns wore all the time. Out of reverence for the venerable abbess they left the nuns completely unharmed, and returned to their camp

26. Another time it happened that the abbess foresaw by divine revelation a famine to come in the next year. She called the cellarer, asking her what kinds of produce she had, from grain to spelt. The abbess commanded the cellarer that she not make bold to feed the livestock from the said produce but to save all of it from that time on until the following year. And when the cellarer announced this to the other sisters, they all said to one another, "Could our lady really believe that we will, from the great abundance which we have now, come down to such scarcity? Far be this from us!" But when the time drew near in which there were the greatest shortages and hunger, the monastery had so much of the corn and other grain, which the abbess had caused to be conserved, that they felt nothing of the famine, but gave generously in almsgiving during that time. Seeing this, the nuns greatly praised the Lord, whom they perceived dwelt truly with their abbess.

27. A certain lady, leaving the world behind, entered the aforesaid monastery, with all her goods. When after some time she confessed to a priest, the abbess called her aside, asking whether she had made a good confession "Certainly, Lady" she said. But the abbess said "It doesn't seem so to me, for I see that your expression is disturbed." The lady then replied, "I have a particular sin that I have never dared confess to anyone." The abbess then said to her "You cannot be saved unless you confess this sin of yours that you have furtively kept hidden." The lady, however, considering the enormity of her crime, said that she didn't dare confess it to anyone. So the abbess then inquired "Will you confess it to a priest if I tell him with my own mouth?" "How can you know that which I have never confessed to anyone?" the lady asked her, knowing that her crime was hidden from all and visible to no one. The abbess merely replied, "I know it well; I know it well." Then the lady gave consent, saying that she would do whatever the abbess wished. Calling forth the priest, the abbess told him her sister's sin, which she had never confessed to anyone. When the priest announced this to the sister, she was greatly astonished, and confessed her sin to him herself on account of her very great fear. The priest gave her absolution, however, praising God for the sanctity of the venerable abbess.

28. During the hot period, in the month of August, the abbess suffered a continual fever and kept asking only for ice; they told her that it was not then the time of year for ice. Yet the abbess said that they should go to the

well. And the following morning, when they had come to the well, they found in the bucket water frozen in the shape of a half moon. Taking out the ice, they brought it to the abbess, all of them being at the same time amazed.

29. When the abbess saw, through God, that anyone was sinning mortally, it was her custom that she would immediately look at the sinner, with her countenance troubled, seeming only half-alive, with no color in her face. Once, when she was weeping bitterly over Christ's Passion (which she bore always in her heart) she began to wipe her eyes in her usual way with a scrap of cloth she carried with her because of her frequent crying. Looking at this scrap she saw that her tears had been totally transformed into blood. On account of great humility she hid the cloth as soon as she saw this, lest anyone else see it.

30. Another time, when the abbess was staying in the cloister of the aforesaid monastery, having with her a nun who was writing down in short form what she was dictating to her – that is, the book about angels, about the soul, and of many very good sayings, which is in that monastery – when the abbess was having that book written, there were two nuns walking through the cloister, both facing the abbess, who saw on the abbess' shoulder a dove of the purest white, with golden feet and gold beak, which it held in her ear, while she was having the aforesaid book written. At length the nuns reported to the abbess what they had seen with their own eyes. And she told them "It is as you have said; nevertheless, never presume to tell anyone what you have seen."

One particular day when she was having the book written in this cloister, there was heavy rain falling everywhere else in the entire convent, yet not a drop fell on her back or shoulders, and this was obvious to everyone in the cloister.

31. Once a certain woman came to her, bearing with her a granddaughter of hers who was suffering from the disease of scrofula. When the woman reached the abbess, she threw herself at her feet, humbly beseeching her to cure her granddaughter of this sickness. The abbess, pious and humble, although she did not know what the girl's illness was, touched her throat by making the sign of the cross, and blessed her. Presently the woman looked again and saw that her granddaughter was cured, giving thanks to God and to St. John the Evangelist.

32. On the third day after Umiltà's death, a certain monk priest, who was feeling severe pain in his arm and had been unable to celebrate Mass for almost six months, came to the tomb of the abbess; both commending himself to her and giving himself to prayer, he felt himself cured at once, giving thanks to God and to blessed Umiltà. And on the same day there was present

a woman with him, who had been sick for the past five years; almost every day she had been unable to speak, to eat, or even to open her mouth, while she had it, nor did she benefit from any medicine. She came to the most pure body of the blessed Umiltà, and touching her body, began to pray. Returning to her home, she felt herself improved, and after a few days she found herself totally cured, giving thanks to God and to blessed Umiltà. On the same day there came to the tomb where Umiltà's most holy body was already buried a certain woman, who was very devoted to blessed Umiltà and who had suffered a long time from a secret disease. After the woman had grieved and wept much over the grave, praying with her tears, she felt a great consolation, and she began to voice this prayer, as it was revealed to her "O most holy Umiltà, you were filled with patience and charity, by the love of Christ and the grace of his mother; I beg of you that you will always pray for me to the heavenly King, that by your holy merits he marvelously spare me in my crimes." A good forty times she announced this prayer, before she rose from the tomb, because of the joy which she felt. Rising from her prayer, she soon sensed that she was cured, and returned thanks to God and to blessed Umiltà.

33. There was a certain woman who was suffering from a very serious illness. One night when she was sleeping in extreme pain she heard a voice saying to her "Commend yourself to St. Umiltà, for you may know it is by her merits that you can obtain health." And when she had awakened, she devoutly and reverently commended herself to the saint, and soon she felt herself cured. Another woman was suffering the extremities of death, and was saying to her family "Why have you sent for the doctors? Don't you see that my death day is imminent?" Hearing this, her father at once came to blessed Umiltà, and with great affection commended his daughter to her. When he was returning home, he found that a sister of Umiltà's monastery was visiting the sick woman, bringing with her the holy abbess's veil. Binding her head with the veil, the sick woman soon got well, and after a few days was totally cured.

34. There was a woman who, when she came to the monastery, had sought devoutly for something that had belonged to the abbess; she took a small piece of the cloth that the abbess had worn on her back, and returned to Volterra. For in that place there was living a certain person whose hand had been accidentally pierced by glass, and who, because of his severe pain, was unable to find any quiet and peace at all. When the woman touched the hand of the suffering sick man with the said cloth, he was cured in that very spot, giving thanks to God and blessed Umiltà.

Another woman had a son, whose bladder was ruptured and inflamed; when his parents saw that their only son was so dangerously ill, they were deeply grieved. The man, angry in spirit, said anxiously to his own wife "You have taken care of our son very badly!" Soon the mother commended him to blessed Umiltà, and upon rising the next morning, she saw her son very fully cured.

Another woman, suffering such pain in her arm that she was unable to use it except with unbearable agony, sought and found the grave of the venerable abbess. Humbly and devoutly she commended herself to her; and as soon as she had commended herself, she felt herself cured, giving thanks to God and to blessed Umiltà. Then there was a certain nun of the same monastery, who had been filled with pain in her entire body for five years, and had been unable to walk except with extreme torment; she commended herself to the abbess, seeing that no medicine was helping her. When she rose from her prayers, she sensed herself so healed that no pain remained in her, and she praised God and blessed Umiltà.

35. And I, Benedict of Master Martinus, Judge and Notary of Florence by imperial authority and now notary of R.P.D. Franciscus D.G. bishop of Florence, saw and read the original book, containing the said chronicle and what is written below it. And I have listened to it, with the present examples transcribed by the below-inscribed Phillip the notary, and subscribed by the below-inscribed Marsoppius the notary, in the presence of the above-inscribed Lord Matthew, vicar of the lord bishop of Florence; I have listened diligently with these three notaries, and since they are in agreement, having been commanded by the lord vicar, giving to this copy his authorization and decree and that of the court of the lord bishop, and I have here subscribed myself as witness in the customary way, in the church of our Holy Savior in Florence, being present as witnesses Ser Jacopo of Ser Miniato, Ser Pietro of Paganucci, notaries of the episcopal court, in the day, year, indiction, and pontificate as is written at the beginning. . . .

39. THE CONVERSION OF ST. FRANCIS OF ASSISI AND THE FOUNDING OF HIS ORDER

While many important saints were commemorated in one major 'life,' so great was the impact of St. Francis's personality on the church and on popular spirituality that no fewer than three 'lives' were authorized to be written within forty years of his death, which occurred when he was about forty-five, on October 4, 1226. In addition to these and some writings by Francis himself, there is extant in a complex manuscript tradition a large body of material by Francis's companions; a collection compiled early in the fourteenth century and entitled 'The Little Flowers of St. Francis' is the best known. The writer of the first 'life,' Thomas of Celano, had entered the Order in about 1215 and although he was not one of Francis's close companions, he may have known him personally. He was an elegant Latin stylist, given to using the kind of rhetorical ornament and hyperbole that modern readers find less appealing than his contemporaries did, and he was well acquainted with the standard form of hagiography exemplified by Sulpicius's 'Martin of Tours' and Gregory the Great's 'Dialogues' (see 14 and 15 above). Probably because of his scholarly reputation, he was commissioned by Pope Gregory IX to write the first 'life' at the time of Francis's canonization in 1228, two years after his death. Fifteen years later the Order requested from Thomas a second 'life' which would include further material collected by Francis's companions, presumably not available when the first account was written. The following narrative of Francis's conversion and the founding of the Friars Minor is from Thomas of Celano's first 'life.'

Source: trans. Placid Hermann, *St. Francis of Assisi: First and Second Life of St. Francis by Thomas of Celano* (Chicago: Franciscan Herald Press, 1963), pp. 5-38, abridged; repr. with permission. BHL 3096.

How Francis lived in the world before his conversion.

1, 1. In the city of Assisi, which lies at the edge of the Spoleto valley, there was a man by the name of Francis, who from his earliest years was brought up by his parents proud of spirit, in accordance with the vanity of the world; and imitating their wretched life and habits for a long time, he became even more vain and proud. For this very evil custom has grown up everywhere among those who are considered Christians in name, and this pernicious teaching has become so established and prescribed, as though by public law, that people seek to educate their children from the cradle on very negligently and dissolutely. For, indeed, when they first begin to speak or stammer, children, just hardly born, are taught by signs and words to do certain wicked and detestable things; and when they come to be weaned, they are forced not only to speak but also to do certain things full of lust and wantonness. Impelled by a fear that is natural to their age, none of them dares to conduct himself in an upright manner, for if he were to do so he would be subjected to severe punishments. Therefore, a secular poet [Seneca] says well: "Because we have grown up amid the practices of our parents, we therefore pursue all evil things from our childhood on." This testimony is true, for so much the more injurious to their children are the desires of the parents, the more successfully they work out. But when the children have progressed a little in age, they always sink into worse deeds, following their own impulses. For from a corrupt root a corrupt tree will grow, and what has once become wickedly depraved can hardly ever be brought into harmony with the norms of uprightness. But when they begin to enter the portals of adolescence, how do you think they will turn out? Then, indeed, tossed about amid every kind of debauchery, they give themselves over completely to shameful practices, in as much as they are permitted to do as they please. For once they have become the slaves of sin by a voluntary servitude, they give over all their members to be instruments of wickedness; and showing forth in themselves nothing of the Christian religion either in their lives or in their conduct, they take refuge under the mere name of Christianity. These miserable people very often pretend that they have done even worse things than they have actually done, lest they seem more despicable the more innocent they are.

2. These are the wretched circumstances among which the man whom we venerate today as a saint, for he is truly a saint, lived in his youth; and almost up to the twenty-fifth year of his age, he squandered and wasted his time miserably. Indeed, he outdid all his contemporaries in vanities and he came to be a promoter of evil and was more abundantly zealous for all kinds of foolishness. He was the admiration of all and strove to outdo the rest in the pomp of vainglory, in jokes, in strange doings, in idle and useless talk, in songs, in soft and flowing garments, for he was very rich, not however avaricious but prodigal, not a hoarder of money but a squanderer of his possessions, not a cautious business man but a very unreliable steward. On the other hand, he was a very kindly person, easy and affable, even making himself foolish because of it; for because of these qualities many ran after him, doers of evil and promoters of crime. And thus overwhelmed by a host of evil companions, proud and high-minded, he walked about the streets of Babylon until the Lord looked down from heaven and for his own name's sake removed his wrath far-off and for his praise bridled Francis lest he should perish. The hand of the Lord therefore came upon him and a change was wrought by the right hand of the Most High, that through him an

assurance might be granted to sinners that they had been restored to grace and that he might be come an example to all of conversion to God.

How God touched the heart of Francis by sickness and by a vision.

3. For, indeed, while this man was still in the glow of youthful passion, and the age of wantonness was urging him on immoderately to fulfil the demands of youth; and while, not knowing how to restrain himself, he was stirred by the venom of the serpent of old, suddenly the divine vengeance, or, perhaps better, the divine unction, came upon him and sought first to recall his erring senses by visiting upon him mental distress and bodily suffering, according to the saying of the prophet: Behold I will hedge up thy way with thorns and I will stop it up with a wall. Thus, worn down by a long illness, as man's stubbornness deserves when it can hardly be corrected except by punishments, he began to think of things other than he was used to thinking upon. When he had recovered somewhat and had begun to walk about the house with the support of a cane to speed the recovery of his health, he went outside one day and began to look about at the surrounding landscape with great interest. But the beauty of the fields, the pleasantness of the vineyards, and whatever else was beautiful to look upon, could stir in him no delight. He wondered therefore at the sudden change that had come over him, and those who took delight in such things he considered very foolish.

4. From that day on, therefore, he began to despise himself and to hold in some contempt the things he had admired and loved before. But not fully or truly, for he was not yet freed from the cords of vanity nor had he shaken off from his neck the yoke of evil servitude. It is indeed very hard to give up things one is accustomed to, and things that once enter into the mind are not easily eradicated; the mind, even though it has been kept away from them for a long time, returns to the things it once learned; and by constant repetition vice generally becomes second nature. So Francis still tried to flee the hand of God, and, forgetting for a while his paternal correction, he thought, amid the smiles of prosperity, of the things of the world; and, ignorant of the counsel of God, he still looked forward to accomplishing great deeds of worldly glory and vanity. For a certain nobleman of the city of Assisi was preparing himself in no mean way with military arms, and, puffed up by a gust of vainglory, vowed that he would go to Apulia to increase his wealth and fame. Upon hearing this, Francis, who was flighty and not a little rash, arranged to go with him; he was inferior to him in nobility of birth, but superior in generosity, poorer in the matter of wealth, but more lavish in giving things away.

5. On a certain night, therefore, after he had given himself with all deliberation to the accomplishment of these things, and while, burning with desire, he longed greatly to set about the journey, he who had struck him with the rod of justice visited him in the sweetness of grace by means of a nocturnal vision; and because Francis was eager for glory, he enticed him and raised his spirits with a vision of the heights of glory. For it seemed to Francis that his whole home was filled with the trappings of war, namely, saddles, shields, lances, and other things; rejoicing greatly, he wondered silently within himself what this should mean. For he was not accustomed to see such things in his home, but rather piles of cloth to be sold. When, accordingly, he was not a little astonished at this sudden turn of events, the answer was given him that all these arms would belong to him and to his soldiers. When he awoke, he arose in the morning with a glad heart, and considering the vision an omen of great success, he felt sure that his journey to Apulia would come out well. He did not know what to say and he did not as yet recognize the task given him from heaven. Nevertheless, he might have understood that his interpretation of the vision was not correct, for while the vision bore some resemblance to things pertaining to war, his heart was not filled with his usual happiness over such things. He had to use some force on himself to carry out his designs and to complete the proposed journey. It is indeed quite fitting that mention be made of arms in the beginning and it is quite opportune that arms should be offered to the soldier about to engage one strongly armed, that like another David he might free Israel from the long-standing reproach of its enemies in the name of the Lord God of hosts.

How, changed in mind but not in body, Francis spoke of the treasure he had found and of his spouse in allegory.

6. Changed, therefore, but in mind, not in body, he refused to go to Apulia and he strove to bend his own will to the will of God. Accordingly, he withdrew for a while from the bustle and the business of the world and tried to establish Jesus Christ dwelling within himself. Like a prudent business man, he hid the treasure he had found from the eyes of the deluded, and, having sold all his possessions, he tried to buy it secretly. Now since there was a certain man in the city of Assisi whom he loved more than any other because he was of the same age as the other, and since the great familiarity of their mutual affection led him to share his secrets with him, he often took him to remote places, places well-suited for counsel, telling him that he had found a certain precious and great treasure. This one rejoiced and, concerned about what he heard, he willingly accompanied Francis whenever he was asked.

There was a certain grotto near the city where they frequently went and talked about this treasure. The man of God, who was already holy by reason of his holy purpose, would enter the grotto, while his companion would wait for him outside; and filled with a new and singular spirit, he would pray to his Father in secret. He wanted no one to know what he did within, and taking the occasion of the good to wisely conceal the better, he took counsel with God alone concerning his holy proposal. He prayed devoutly that the eternal and true God would direct his way and teach him to do his will. He bore the greatest sufferings in mind and was not able to rest until he should have completed in deed what he had conceived in his heart; various thoughts succeeded one another and their importunity disturbed him greatly. He was afire within himself with a divine fire and he was not able to hide outwardly the ardor of his mind; he repented that he had sinned so grievously and had offended the eyes of God's majesty, and neither the past evils nor those present gave him any delight. Still he had not as yet won full confidence that he would be able to guard himself against them in the future. Consequently, when he came out again to his companion, he was so exhausted with the strain, that one person seemed to have entered, and another to have come out.

7. One day, however, when he had begged for the mercy of God most earnestly, it was shown to him by God what he was to do. Accordingly, he was so filled with joy that he could not contain himself, and, though he did not want to, he uttered some things to the ears of men. But, though he could not keep silent because of the greatness of the joy that filled him, he nevertheless spoke cautiously and in an obscure manner. For, while he spoke to his special friend of a hidden treasure, as was said, he tried to speak to others only figuratively; he said that he did not want to go to Apulia, but he promised that he would do noble and great things in his native place. People thought he wished to take to himself a wife, and they asked him, saying: "Francis, do you wish to get married?" But he answered them, saying: "I shall take a more noble and more beautiful spouse than you have ever seen; she will surpass all others in beauty and will excel all others in wisdom." Indeed, the immaculate spouse of God is the true religion which he embraced; and the hidden treasure is the kingdom of heaven, which he sought with such great desire; for it was extremely necessary that the Gospel calling be fulfilled in him who was to be the minister of the Gospel in faith and in truth.

Francis sold all his goods and despised the money given him.

8. Behold, when the blessed servant of the Most High was thus disposed and strengthened by the Holy Spirit, now that the opportune time had come, he

followed the blessed impulse of his soul, by which he would come to the highest things, trampling worldly things under foot. He could not delay any longer, because a deadly disease had grown up every where to such an extent and had so taken hold of all the limbs of many that, were the physician to delay even a little, it would snatch away life, shutting off the life-giving spirit. He rose up, therefore, fortified himself with the sign of the Cross, got his horse ready and mounted it, and taking with him some fine cloth to sell, he hastened to the city called Foligno [about ten miles or sixteen km from Assisi]. There, as usual, he sold everything he had with him, and, successful as a merchant, he left behind even the horse he was riding, after he had received payment for it; and, free of all luggage, he started back, wondering with a religious mind what he should do with the money. Soon, turned toward God's work in a wondrous manner, and accordingly feeling that it would be a great burden to him to carry that money even for an hour, he hastened to get rid of it, considering the advantage he might get from it as so much sand. When, therefore, he neared the city of Assisi, he discovered a certain church along the way that had been built of old in honor of St. Damian but which was now threatening to collapse because it was so old.

9. When this new soldier of Christ came up to this church, moved with pity over such great need, he entered it with fear and reverence. And when he found there a certain poor priest, he kissed his sacred hands with great faith, and offered him the money he had with him, telling him in order what he proposed to do. The priest was astonished and, wondering over a conversion so incredibly sudden, he refused to believe what he heard. And because he thought he was being deceived, he refused to keep the money offered him. For he had seen him just the day before, so to say, living in a riotous way among his relatives and acquaintances and showing greater foolishness than the rest. But Francis persisted obstinately and tried to gain credence for what he said, asking earnestly and begging the priest to suffer him to remain with him for the sake of the Lord. In the end the priest acquiesced to his remaining there, but out of fear of the young man's parents, he did not accept the money; whereupon this true contemner of money threw it upon a window sill, for he cared no more for it than for the dust. He wanted to possess that wisdom that is better than gold and to acquire that prudence that is more precious than silver.

How his father persecuted Francis and put him in chains.

10. So while the servant of the most high God was staying in the aforesaid place, his father [Pietro Bernardone, a rich cloth merchant] went about everywhere, like a persistent spy, wanting to learn what had happened to his

son. And when he learned that he was living in such a way at that place, being touched inwardly with sorrow of heart, he was troubled exceedingly at the sudden turn of events, and calling together his friends and neighbors, he hurried to the place where the servant of God was staying. But he, the new athlete of Christ, when he heard of the threats of those who were pursuing him and when he got knowledge of their coming, wanting to give place to wrath, hid himself in a certain secret pit which he himself had prepared for just such an emergency. That pit was in that house and was known probably to one person alone; in it he hid so continuously for one month that he hardly dared leave it to provide for his human needs. Food, when it was given to him, he ate in the secrecy of the pit, and every service was rendered to him by stealth. Praying, he prayed always with a torrent of tears that the Lord would deliver him from the hands of those who were persecuting his soul, and that he would fulfil his pious wishes in his loving kindness; in fasting and in weeping he begged for the clemency of the Savior, and, distrusting his own efforts, he cast his whole care upon the Lord. And though he was in a pit and in darkness, he was nevertheless filled with a certain exquisite joy of which till then he had had no experience; and catching fire there from, he left the pit and exposed himself openly to the curses of his persecutors.

11. He arose, therefore, immediately, active, eager, and lively; and, bearing the shield of faith to fight for the Lord, armed with a great confidence, he took the way toward the city; aglow with a divine fire, he began to accuse himself severely of laziness and cowardice. When those who knew him saw this, they compared what he was now with what he had been; and they began to revile him miserably. Shouting out that he was mad and demented, they threw the mud of the streets and stones at him. They saw that he was changed from his former ways and greatly worn down by mortification of the flesh, and they therefore set down everything he did to exhaustion and madness. But since a patient man is better than a proud man, the servant of God showed himself deaf to all these things and, neither broken nor changed by any of these injuries, he gave thanks to God for all of them. In vain does the wicked man persecute one striving after virtue, for the more he is buffeted, the more strongly will he triumph. As someone says, indignity strengthens a generous spirit.

12. Now when the noise and the shouting of this kind concerning Francis had been going on for a long time through the streets and quarters of the city, and the sound of it all was echoing here and there, among the many to whose ears the report of these things came was finally his father. When he heard the name of his son mentioned, and understood that the commotion among the citizens turned about his son, he immediately arose, not indeed to

free him but rather to destroy him; and, with no regard for moderation, he rushed upon him like a wolf upon a sheep, and looking upon him with a fierce and savage countenance, he laid hands upon him and dragged him shamelessly and disgracefully to his home. Thus, without mercy, he shut him up in a dark place for several days, and thinking to bend his spirit to his own will, he first used words and then blows and chains. But Francis became only the more ready and more strong to carry out his purpose; but he did not abandon his patience either because he was insulted by words or worn out by chains. For he who is commanded to rejoice in tribulation cannot swerve from the right intention and position of his mind or be led away from Christ's flock, not even by scourgings and chains; neither does he waver in a flood of many waters whose refuge from oppression is the Son of God, who, lest our troubles seem hard to us, showed always that those he bore were greater.

How Francis's mother freed him and how he stripped himself before the bishop of Assisi.

13. It happened, however, when Francis's father had left home for a while on business and the man of God remained bound in the basement of the house, his mother, who was alone with him and who did not approve of what her husband had done, spoke kindly to her son. But when she saw that he could not be persuaded away from his purpose, she was moved by motherly compassion for him, and loosening his chains, she let him go free. He, however, giving thanks to Almighty God, returned quickly to the place where he had been before. But now, after he had been proved by temptations, he allowed himself greater liberty, and he took on a more cheerful aspect because of the many struggles he had gone through. From the wrongs done him he acquired a more confident spirit, and he went about everywhere freely with higher spirits than before. Meanwhile his father returned, and not finding Francis, he turned to upbraid his wife, heaping sins upon sins. Then, raging and blustering, he ran to that place hoping that if he could not recall him from his ways, he might at least drive him from the province. But, because it is true that in the fear of the Lord is confidence, when this child of grace heard his carnally minded [i.e. worldly] father coming to him, confident and joyful he went to meet him, exclaiming in a clear voice that he cared nothing for his chains and blows. Moreover, he stated that he would gladly undergo evils for the name of Christ.

14. But when his father saw that he could not bring him back from the way he had undertaken, he was roused by all means to get his money back. The man of God had desired to offer it and expend it to feed the poor and

to repair the buildings of that place. But he who had no love for money could not be misled by any aspect of good in it; and he who was not held back by any affection for it was in no way disturbed by its loss. Therefore, when the money was found, which he who hated the things of this world so greatly and desired the riches of heaven so much had thrown aside in the dust of the windowsill, the fury of his raging father was extinguished a little, and the thirst of his avarice was somewhat allayed by the warmth of discovery. He then brought his son before the bishop of the city, so that, renouncing all his possessions into his hands, he might give up everything he had. Francis not only did not refuse to do this, but he hastened with great joy to do what was demanded of him.

15. When he was brought before the bishop, he would suffer no delay or hesitation in anything; indeed, he did not wait for any words nor did he speak any, but immediately putting off his clothes and casting them aside, he gave them back to his father. Moreover, not even retaining his trousers, he stripped himself completely naked before all. The bishop, however, sensing his disposition and admiring greatly his fervor and constancy, arose and drew him within his arms and covered him with the mantle he was wearing. He understood clearly that the counsel was of God, and he understood that the actions of the man of God that he had personally witnessed contained a mystery. He immediately, therefore, became his helper and cherishing him and encouraging him, he embraced him in the bowels of charity. Behold, now he wrestles naked with his naked adversary, and having put off everything that is of this world, he thinks only about the things of the Lord. He seeks now so to despise his own life, putting off all solicitude for it, that he might find peace in his harassed ways, and that meanwhile only the wall of flesh should separate him from the vision of God.

How Francis was seized by robbers and cast into the snow, and how he served the lepers.

16. He who once wore fine garments now went about clad only in scanty garments. As he went through a certain woods singing praises to the Lord in the French language, robbers suddenly rushed out upon him. When they asked him in a ferocious tone who he was, the man of God replied confidently in a loud voice: "I am the herald of the great King. What is that to you?" But they struck him and cast him into a ditch filled with deep snow, saying: "Lie there, foolish herald of God!" But he rolled himself about and shook off the snow; and when they had gone away, he jumped out of the ditch, and, glad with great joy, he began to call out the praises of God in a

loud voice throughout the grove. At length, coming to a certain cloister of monks, he spent several days there as a scullion, wearing a ragged shirt and being satisfied to be filled only with broth. But, when all pity was withdrawn from him and he could not get even an old garment, he left the place, not moved by anger, but forced by necessity; and he went to the city of Gubbio, where he obtained a small tunic from a certain man who once had been his friend. Then, after some time had elapsed, when the fame of the man of God was beginning to grow and his name was spread abroad among the people, the prior of the aforementioned monastery recalled and realized how the man of God had been treated and he came to him and begged pardon for himself and for his monks out of reverence for the Savior.

17. Then the holy lover of complete humility went to the lepers and lived with them, serving them most diligently for God's sake; and washing all foulness from them, he wiped away also the corruption of the ulcers, just as he said in his Testament: "When I was in sins, it seemed extremely bitter to me to look at lepers, and the Lord himself led me among them and I practiced mercy with them." So greatly loathsome was the sight of lepers to him at one time, he used to say, that, in the days of his vanity, he would look at their houses only from a distance of two miles and he would hold his nostrils with his hands. But now, when by the grace and the power of the Most High he was beginning to think of holy and useful things, while he was still clad in secular garments, he met a leper one day and, made stronger than himself, he kissed him. From then on he began to despise himself more and more, until, by the mercy of the Redeemer, he came to perfect victory over himself. Of other poor, too, while he yet remained in the world and still followed the world, he was the helper, stretching forth a hand of mercy to those who had nothing, and showing compassion to the afflicted. For when one day, contrary to his custom, for he was a most courteous person, he upbraided a certain poor man who had asked an alms of him, he was immediately sorry; and he began to say to himself that it was a great reproach and a shame to withhold what was asked from one who had asked in the name of so great a King. He therefore resolved in his heart never in the future to refuse any one, if at all possible, who asked for the love of God. This he most diligently did and carried out, until he sacrificed himself entirely and in every way; and thus he became first a practicer before he became a teacher of the evangelical counsel: "To him who asks of thee," he said, "give; and from him who would borrow of thee do not turn away."

How Francis built the church of St. Damian; and of the life of the Ladies who dwelt in that place.

18. The first work that blessed Francis undertook after he had gained his freedom from the hand of his carnally minded father was to build a house of God. He did not try to build one anew, but he repaired an old one, restored an ancient one. He did not tear out the foundation, but he built upon it, ever reserving to Christ his prerogative, though he was not aware of it, for other foundation no one can lay but that which has been laid which is Christ Jesus. When he had returned to the place where, as has been said, the church of St. Damian had been built in ancient times, he repaired it zealously within a short time with the help of the grace of the Most High. This is the blessed and holy place, where the glorious religion and most excellent order of Poor Ladies and holy virgins had its blessed origin about six years after the conversion of St. Francis and through that same blessed man. Of it, the Lady Clare, a native of the city of Assisi, the most precious and the firmest stone of the whole structure, was the foundation. For when, after the beginning of the Order of Brothers, the said lady [who had run away from home to join Francis at the age of about eighteen] was converted to God through the counsel of the holy man, she lived unto the advantage of many and as an example to a countless multitude. She was of noble parentage, but she was more noble by grace; she was a virgin in body, most chaste in mind; a youth in age, but mature in spirit; steadfast in purpose and most ardent in her desire for divine love; endowed with wisdom and excelling in humility; Clare by name, brighter in life, and brightest in character.

19. Over her arose a noble structure of most precious pearls [her followers, including her sister Agnes] whose praise is not from men but from God, since neither is our limited understanding sufficient to imagine it, nor our scanty vocabulary to utter it. For above everything else there flourishes among them that excelling virtue of mutual and continual charity, which so binds their wills into one that, though forty or fifty of them dwell together in one place, agreement in likes and dislikes molds one spirit in them out of many. Secondly, in each one there glows the gem of humility, which so preserves the gifts and good things bestowed from heaven, that they merit other virtues too. Thirdly, the lily of virginity and chastity so sprinkles them with a wondrous odor that, forgetful of earthly thoughts, they desire to meditate only on heavenly things; and so great a love for their eternal Spouse arises in their hearts from the fragrance of that lily that the integrity of that holy affection excludes from them every habit of their former life. Fourthly, they have all become so conspicuous by the title of the highest poverty that their

food and clothing hardly at all or never come together to satisfy extreme necessity. . . .

How Francis having changed his habit rebuilt the church of St. Mary of the Portiuncula and how upon hearing the Gospel he left all things and how he designed and made the habit the brothers wear.

21. Meanwhile the holy man of God, having put on a new kind of habit and having repaired the aforesaid church, went to another place near the city of Assisi, where he began to rebuild a certain dilapidated and well-nigh destroyed church, and he did not leave off from his good purpose until he had brought it to completion. Then he went to another place, which is called the Portiuncula [about a mile south-west of Assisi, deep in the woods] where there stood a church of the Blessed Virgin Mother of God that had been built in ancient times, but was now deserted and cared for by no one. When the holy man of God saw how it was thus in ruins, he was moved to pity, because he burned with devotion toward the mother of all good; and he began to live there in great zeal. It was the third year of his conversion when he began to repair this church. At this time he wore a kind of hermit's dress, with a leather girdle about his waist; he carried a staff in his hands and wore shoes on his feet.

22. But when on a certain day the Gospel was read in that church, how the Lord sent his disciples out to preach, the holy man of God, assisting there, understood somewhat the words of the Gospel; after Mass he humbly asked the priest to explain the Gospel to him more fully. When he had set forth for him in order all these things, the holy Francis, hearing that the disciples of Christ should not possess gold or silver or money; nor carry along the way scrip, or wallet, or bread, or a staff; that they should not have shoes, or two tunics; but that they should preach the kingdom of God and penance, immediately cried out exultingly: "This is what I wish, this is what I seek, this is what I long to do with all my heart." Then the holy father, overflowing with joy, hastened to fulfil that salutary word he had heard, and he did not suffer any delay to intervene before beginning devoutly to perform what he had heard. He immediately put off his shoes from his feet, put aside the staff from his hands, was content with one tunic, and exchanged his leather girdle for a small cord. He designed for himself a tunic that bore a likeness to the Cross, that by means of it he might beat off all temptations of the devil; he designed a very rough tunic so that by it he might crucify the flesh with all its vices and sins; he designed a very poor and mean tunic, one that would not excite the covetousness of the world. The other things that he had heard,

however, he longed with the greatest diligence and the greatest reverence to perform. For he was not a deaf hearer of the Gospel, but committing all that he had heard to praiseworthy memory, he tried diligently to carry it out to the letter.

Of his preaching of the Gospel and his announcing peace and of the conversion of the first six brothers.

23. From then on he began to preach penance to all with great fervor of spirit and joy of mind, edifying his hearers with his simple words and his greatness of heart. His word was like a burning fire, penetrating the inmost reaches of the heart, and it filled the minds of all the hearers with admiration. He seemed completely different from what he had been, and, looking up to the heavens, he disdained to look upon the earth. This indeed is wonderful, that he first began to preach where as a child he had first learned to read and where for a time he was buried amid great honor, so that the happy beginning might be commended by a still happier ending. Where he had learned he also taught, and where he began he also ended. In all his preaching, before he proposed the word of God to those gathered about, he first prayed for peace for them, saying: "The Lord give you peace." He always most devoutly announced peace to men and women, to all he met and overtook. For this reason many who had hated peace and had hated also salvation embraced peace, through the cooperation of the Lord, with all their heart and were made children of peace and seekers after eternal salvation.

24. Among these, a certain man from Assisi, of pious and simple spirit, was the first to devoutly follow the man of God. After him, Brother Bernard, embracing the delegation of peace, ran eagerly after the holy man of God to purchase the kingdom of heaven. He had often given the blessed father hospitality, and, having had experience of his life and conduct and having been refreshed by the fragrance of his holiness, he conceived a fear and brought forth the spirit of salvation. He noticed that Francis would pray all night, sleeping but rarely, praising God and the glorious Virgin Mother of God, and he wondered and said: "In all truth, this man is from God." He hastened therefore to sell all his goods and gave the money to the poor, though not to his parents; and laying hold of the title to the way of perfection, he carried out the counsel of the holy Gospel: 'If thou wilt be perfect, go, sell what thou hast, and give to the poor, and thou shalt have treasure in heaven; and come, follow me.' When he had done this, he was associated with St. Francis by his life and by his habit, and he was always with him until, after the number of the brothers had increased, he was sent to other regions by obedience

[Fig. 41] The allegorical marriage of St. Francis to Lady Poverty, from a fresco by Giotto in the Lower Church of Assisi (Baring-Gould, *Lives of the Saints*, 11).

to his kind father. His conversion to God was a model to others in the manner of selling one's possessions and giving them to the poor. St. Francis rejoiced with very great joy over the coming and conversion of so great a man, in that the Lord was seen to have a care for him by giving him a needed companion and a faithful friend.

25. But immediately another man of the city of Assisi followed him; he deserves to be greatly praised for his conduct, and what he began in a holy way, he completed after a short time in a more holy way. After a not very long time, Brother Giles followed him; he was a simple and upright man and one fearing God. He lived a long time, leading a holy life, justly and piously, and giving us examples of perfect obedience, manual labor, solitary life, and holy contemplation. After another one had been added to these, Brother Philip brought the number to seven. The Lord touched his lips with a purifying coal, that he might speak pleasing things of him and utter sweet things. Understanding and interpreting the sacred Scriptures, though he had not studied, he became an imitator of those whom the leaders of the Jews alleged to be ignorant and unlearned.

Of the spirit of prophecy of St. Francis and of his admonitions.

27. . . . And then . . . he said with joy to his brothers: "Be strengthened dear brothers, and rejoice in the Lord, and do not be sad because you seem so few; and do not let either my simplicity or your own dismay you, for, as it has been shown me in truth by the Lord, God will make us grow into a very great multitude and will make us increase to the ends of the world. For your profit I am compelled to tell you what I have seen, though I would much rather remain silent, were it not that charity urges me to tell you. I saw a great multitude of men coming to us and wanting to live with us in the habit of our way of life and under the rule of our blessed religion. And behold, the sound of them is in my ears as they go and come according to the command of holy obedience. I have seen, as it were, the roads filled with their great numbers coming together in these parts from almost every nation. Frenchmen are coming, Spaniards are hastening, Germans and Englishmen are running, and a very great multitude of others speaking various tongues are hurrying." When the brothers had heard this, they were filled with a salutary joy, both because of the grace the Lord God gave to his holy one and because they were ardently thirsting for the advantages to be gained by their neighbors, whom they wished to grow daily in numbers and to be saved thereby. . . .

How Francis first wrote a rule when he had eleven brothers, and how the lord pope confirmed it; and how he had a vision of a a great tree.

32. When blessed Francis saw that the Lord God was daily adding to their number, he wrote for himself and his brothers, present and to come, simply and with few words, a form of life and rule, using for the most part the words of the holy Gospel, for the perfection of which alone he yearned. But he did insert a few other things that were necessary to provide for a holy way of life. He then came to Rome with all the aforementioned brothers, desiring very much that what he had written should be confirmed by the Lord Pope Innocent. At that time the venerable bishop of Assisi was at Rome, Guido by name, who honored Francis and all his brothers in all things and venerated them with special affection. When he saw St. Francis and his brothers, he was grievously annoyed at their coming, not knowing the reason for it; for he feared that they might wish to leave their native region where the Lord had already begun to work very great things through his servants. He rejoiced greatly to have such great men in his diocese, on whose life and conduct he was relying greatly. But when he had heard the

reason for their coming and understood their purpose, he rejoiced greatly in the Lord, promising to give them his advice and help in these things. St. Francis also approached the lord bishop of Sabina, John of St. Paul by name, who of all the other princes and great ones at the Roman curia was seen to despise earthly things and love heavenly things. He received Francis kindly and charitably, and praised highly his will and purpose.

33. Indeed, because he was a prudent and discreet man, he began to ask Francis about many things and urged him to turn to the life of a monk or hermit. But St. Francis refused his counsel, as humbly as he could, not despising what was counselled, but in his pious leaning toward another life, he was inspired by a higher desire. The lord bishop wondered at his fervor, and, fearing that he might decline from so great a purpose, he showed him ways that would be easier to follow. In the end, overcome by Francis's constancy, he acquiesced to his petition and strove from then on to further his aims before the lord pope. It was Pope Innocent III who was at that time at the head of the Church, a famous man, greatly learned, renowned in discourse, burning with zeal for justice in the things that the cause of the Christian faith demanded. When he had come to know the wishes of these men of God, he first examined the matter, then gave assent to their request and carried out all that had to be done; exhorting them concerning many things and admonishing them, he blessed St. Francis and his brothers and said to them: "Go with the Lord, brothers, and as the Lord will deign to inspire you, preach penance to all. Then, when the almighty Lord shall give you increase in number and in grace, return to me with joy, and I will add many more things to these and entrust greater things to you with greater confidence."

In all truth the Lord was with St. Francis wherever he went, cheering him with revelations and encouraging him by his gifts. For one night after he had given himself to sleep, it seemed to him that he was walking along a certain road, at the side of which stood a tree of great height. The tree was beautiful and strong, thick and exceedingly high. It happened as he drew near to it, and was standing beneath it, admiring its beauty and its height, that suddenly the holy man himself grew to so great a height that he touched the top of the tree, and taking hold of it with his hand, he bent it to the ground. And so indeed it happened, for the lord Innocent, the highest and loftiest tree in the world, graciously stooped to Francis' petition and desire. . . .

Concerning the fame of the blessed Francis and the conversion of many to God; how the order was called the Order of Friars Minor and how blessed Francis formed those entering religion.

36. Francis, therefore, the most valiant knight of Christ, went about the towns and villages announcing the kingdom of God, preaching peace, teaching salvation and penance unto the remission of sins, not in the persuasive words of human wisdom, but with the learning and power of the Spirit. He acted boldly in all things, because of the apostolic authority granted to him, using no words of flattery or seductive blandishments. He did not know how to make light of the faults of others, but he knew well how to cut them out; neither did he encourage the life of sinners, but he struck hard at them with sharp reproof, for he had first convinced himself by practising himself what he wished to persuade others to do by his words; and fearing not the censurer, he spoke the truth boldly, so that even the most learned men, men enjoying renown and dignity, wondered at his words and were struck with wholesome fear by his presence. Men ran, and women too ran, clerics hurried, and religious hastened that they might see and hear the holy man of God who seemed to all to be a man of another world. Every age and every sex hurried to see the wonderful things that the Lord was newly working in the world through his servant. It seemed at that time, whether because of the presence of St. Francis or through his reputation, that a new light had been sent from heaven upon this earth, shattering the widespread darkness that had so filled almost the whole region that hardly anyone knew where to go. For so profound was the forgetfulness of God and the sleep of neglect of his commandments oppressing almost everyone that they could hardly be aroused even a little from their old and deeply rooted sins. . . .

38. But our first concern here is with the order of which he was the founder and preserver both by charity and by profession. What shall we say? He himself first planted the Order of Friars Minor and accordingly gave it this name. For he wrote in the rule, "and let them be lesser brothers," and when these words were spoken, indeed in that same hour, he said: "I wish that this fraternity should be called the Order of Friars Minor." And indeed they were lesser brothers, who, being subject to all, always sought a place that was lowly and sought to perform a duty that seemed in some way to be burdensome to them so that they might merit to be founded solidly in true humility and that through their fruitful disposition a spiritual structure of all virtues might arise in them. Truly, upon the foundation of constancy a noble structure of charity arose, in which the living stones, gathered from all parts of the world, were erected into a dwelling place of the Holy Spirit. O with

what ardor of charity the new disciples of Christ burned! How great was the love that flourished in the members of this pious society! For whenever they came together anywhere, or met one another along the way, as the custom is, there a shoot of spiritual love sprang up, sprinkling over all love the seed of true affection. What more shall I say? Chaste embraces, gentle feelings, a holy kiss, pleasing conversation, modest laughter, joyous looks, a single eye, a submissive spirit, a peacable tongue, a mild answer, oneness of purpose, ready obedience, unwearied hand, all these were found in them.

39. And indeed, since they despised all earthly things and did not love themselves with a selfish love, pouring out their whole affection on all the brothers, they strove to give themselves as the price of helping one another in their needs. They came together with great desire; they remained together with joy; but separation from one another was sad on both sides, a bitter divorce, a cruel estrangement. But these most obedient knights dared put nothing before holy obedience; before the command of obedience was even uttered, they prepared themselves to fulfil the order; knowing not how to misinterpret the commands, they put aside every objection and hastened to fulfil what was commanded. Followers of most holy poverty, because they had nothing, loved nothing, they feared in no way to lose anything. They were content with one tunic, patched at times within and without; in it was seen no refinement, but rather abjectness and cheapness, so that they might seem to be completely crucified to the world. Girt with a cord, they wore poor trousers, and they had the pious intention of remaining like this, and they wished to have nothing more. They were, therefore, everywhere secure, kept in no suspense by fear; distracted by no care, they awaited the next day without solicitude, nor were they in anxiety about the night's lodging, though in their journeyings they were often placed in great danger. For, when they frequently lacked the necessary lodging amid the coldest weather, an oven sheltered them, or at least they lay hid for the night humbly in grottos or caves. During the day, those who knew how labored with their hands, staying in the houses of lepers, or in other decent places, serving all humbly and devotedly. They did not wish to exercise any position from which scandal might arise, but always doing what is holy and just, honest and useful, they led all with whom they came into contact to follow their example of humility and patience.

40. HUMANISTIC HAGIOGRAPHY: THE WRITINGS OF ST. FRANCIS'S COMPANIONS

Even Thomas of Celano's stylized biography allows the reader a more personal knowledge of the saint than do most hagiographers, whose intention was not to convey the idiosyncratic aspects of the saints' characters but to show how they exemplified the idealized lives of certain saintly types. But the mass of anecdotal material collected and written down by Francis's closest companions and arranged unchronologically after his death as 'fioretti' or 'little flowers' of wisdom increases our sense that we know this man personally as we know few other medieval saints. The difference in style and content is a matter both of the influence of Francis himself and one of doctrine: the Franciscans emphasized the importance of a personal relationship with God. Francis humanized his own religious practices and encouraged others to do the same. In a famous incident which took place one Christmas, near the town of Greccio, he had the scene of the nativity reproduced in the church in which he was to celebrate Mass, bringing in a manger, hay, an ox and an ass to drive home to people the human nature of Christ. Thomas of Celano tells us that "the people came and were filled with new joy over the new mystery." Typically, Francis ordered that the hay should afterwards be given to the animals to eat. The writings of Francis's companions convey simply and directly, often through the saint's own words, his devotion to poverty, humility, and obedience, his encompassing sympathy for the created world, and the personal nature of his piety. The following selections are taken from the 'Legend of Perugia,' thought to be a transcription of the early writings of Francis's friends, Leo, Rufino, and Angelo.

Source: trans. Rosalind B. Brooke, *Scripta Leonis, Rufini et Angeli, Sociorum S. Francisci* (Oxford: Clarendon Press, 1970), pp. 95–283; abridged and repr. with permission. BHL 3114.

How the early friars obeyed the Gospel to the letter.

4. In those days, when St. Francis was with the friars that he then had, such was his purity that from the hour in which the Lord revealed to him that he and his friars ought to live according to the model of the holy Gospel, he wanted to do this to the letter and tried to observe it throughout his life. He ordered the friar who did the cooking for the brothers, when he wanted to give them vegetables to eat, not to put them in hot water in the evening ready for the following day, as is usually done, so that they might obey that saying of the holy Gospel: 'Take no thought for the morrow.' So that friar put them to soak after the brothers had said Matins. For the same reason for a long time many of the friars in the houses where they were living, and especially in the towns, observed this injunction – being unwilling to acquire or accept alms beyond what was sufficient for them for one day.

St. Francis ate grapes with a sick friar.

5. At one time, while St. Francis was still at that house, a friar who was staying there, a holy man who had been a long time under religious vows, was very weak and ill. Seeing this, St. Francis was moved with compassion towards him. But because the friars then, both sick and well, with joking and with patience, treated poverty as abundance, and did not use medicines in their illness but rather preferred to take what was contrary to their bodily needs, St. Francis said to himself: 'If that brother were to eat ripe grapes first thing in the morning I believe they would do him good.' So one day he got up secretly very early in the morning and called him and took him into the vineyard which is next to the church, and chose a vine on which were good grapes ready to eat. Sitting with the friar by the vine, he began to eat grapes so that he should not be embarrassed at eating alone. As they ate the grapes, the friar praised God, and for the rest of his life remembered this compassionate act the holy father had done for his sake, and often with great devotion and shedding of tears he recalled it among the friars.

St. Francis tried to destroy a stone house.

11. At one time, near the date when the chapter [the meeting of the Order] was due to be held – for in those days it was held every year at St. Mary of the Portiuncula – the people of Assisi held a general meeting. They had observed that through God's grace the friars had increased and were daily increasing, and that especially when they all gathered there for the chapter they would have nothing except a poor little cottage thatched with straw, its walls made of withies and mud, as the friars had made it when they first went to live there. In a few days they made there in haste and with great devotion a big house of stone, with limed walls, without the consent of St. Francis, while he was away. When St. Francis returned from one of the provinces and came to the chapter and saw the house that had been built there, he was astonished. Thinking that, by reason of this house, the friars in the houses where they lived and were to lodge might build large houses or cause them to be built, and most of all because he wished that this place should always be the model and example for all the houses of the friars, he arose one day before the chapter ended and climbed up on to the roof of the house and ordered the friars to come up. He began, together with the friars, to throw to the ground the wooden tiles with which it was roofed, wishing to destroy the house. Some knights of Assisi and others who were there representing the city commune to guard the house (because of the crowds and secular folk who were outside the house in great numbers), having gathered from all sides

to watch the friars' chapter, seeing that St. Francis and the other friars wanted to destroy that house at once came up to them and said to St. Francis: 'Brother, this house belongs to the commune of Assisi, and we are here on behalf of the commune. We tell you that you are not to destroy our house.' St. Francis said to them: 'If the house is yours I have no wish to touch it.' He at once got down off it and the other friars who had ascended with him. On account of this the citizens of Assisi for a long time decreed each year that whoever was their *podestà* should be responsible for having it roofed and repaired when necessary.

St. Francis's efforts to keep churches clean.

18. At one time, when St. Francis was staying at the church of St. Mary of the Portiuncula and the brothers were still few, sometimes he went through the villages and churches in the neighborhood of the city of Assisi announcing and preaching to men that they should do penance, [and] he carried a broom to sweep the churches. For St. Francis was very grieved when he entered any church and found it was not clean, and therefore he always, after he had preached to the people and the sermon was ended, gathered together all the priests who were there into some remote spot so that laymen should not hear, and preached to them of the salvation of souls and especially that they should be careful and diligent in keeping clean their churches, altars, and everything connected with the celebration of the divine mysteries.

St. Francis ate from the same dish as a leper.

22. One day, when St. Francis returned to the church of St. Mary of the Portiuncula, he found James there, a simple brother who had come that day with a leper with ulcerous sores. The holy father had strongly recommended this leper and all other lepers who were badly afflicted to him. For in those days the brothers used to stay in leper hospitals and this brother James was, as it were, the doctor of those who were most afflicted, and willingly touched, dressed, and healed their wounds. St. Francis said to Brother James as though criticizing him: 'You ought not to bring Christian brothers here, as it is not seemly either for you or for them.' St. Francis called lepers 'Christian brothers.' The holy father said this because, although it pleased him that James should help and serve them, he did not want him to take those who were badly afflicted outside the hospital, particularly as this Brother James was very simple and often went to the church of St. Mary with some leper; and people were in the habit of shrinking from lepers who were badly afflicted. As soon

[Fig. 42] St. Francis preaching to the birds: on finding a flock of many birds of different kinds, he spoke to them of the gratitude they owed to God, and the birds listened attentively until he gave the sign of the Cross and they flew away (Giotto, reproduced in Baring-Gould, *Lives of the Saints*, 11).

as he had said it St. Francis blamed himself and confessed his fault to Brother Peter Catanii, who was then minister-general [of the Order], because he believed that by rebuking Brother James he had shamed the leper. So he admitted his fault, to make satisfaction to God and to the leper; and St. Francis said to Brother Peter: 'I am going to tell you the penance that I wish to do for it so that you can confirm it for me, and not contradict me at all.' Brother Peter said to him: 'Do as you please, brother.' For Brother Peter was so respectful and afraid of St. Francis and so obedient to him that he did not presume to change his orders even though on that occasion and on many others he was distressed inwardly and outwardly. St. Francis said: 'May this be my penance, that I eat from the same dish with the Christian brother.' This was done, and when St. Francis sat at the table with the leper and the other friars, a dish was put between the two. The leper had sores and ulcers all over him and in particular his fingers, with which he ate, were contorted and bleeding, so that always, when he put them in the dish, blood flowed into it. Seeing this, Brother Peter and the other friars were much upset, but they did not dare to say anything for fear of the holy father. He who wrote this saw it and bore witness.

St. Francis would not help put out a fire.

50. Another time, when he was keeping Lent on Monte La Verna, his companion one day, when it was time for the meal, was lighting the fire in the cell where they ate; when it was lit he came to St. Francis in the cell where he prayed and slept, as it was his custom to read to him the portion of the Gospel which was recited at Mass that day. When St. Francis could not hear Mass, he always wanted to hear the Gospel for the day before he ate. When he came to eat in the cell where the fire had been lit, the flames of the fire had reached the gable of the cell and were burning it. His companion began to put it out as best he could but he could not manage alone. St. Francis did not want to help him, but picked up a skin, with which he covered himself at night, and went out into the wood. The brothers of the place, although they lived far away from the cell, as the cell was a long way from the friary, when they sensed that the cell was on fire, came and put the fire out. St. Francis afterwards returned to eat. After the meal he said to his companion: 'I do not want to have this skin over me any more, since through my avarice I did not want brother fire to eat it.'

St. Francis's love for all creatures.

51. When he washed his hands he chose a place where the washing-water would not afterwards be trampled underfoot. When he was obliged to walk over rocks he walked with fear and reverence for the love of him who was called a rock, and when he recited that verse of the Psalm where it says: 'Thou hast raised me on the Rock,' he used to say with great devotion: 'Thou hast raised me beneath the feet of the Rock.' He told the brother who got wood for the fire not to cut down the whole tree but to cut it in such a way that some part remained and part was cut. He also made this an order to a brother who was in the friary where he was staying.

He told the brother who tended the garden not to plant all the space in the garden entirely with vegetables but to leave some part of the soil where he might grow flowering plants which in their season might produce their brothers the flowers. He used to say that the friar who was the gardener ought to make a beautiful little bed in some part of the garden, putting and planting there all the sweet-smelling herbs and all the plants which produce lovely flowers, so that in their season they might invite all who saw them to praise God, since all creatures say and proclaim: 'God made me for you, O man.' We who were with him used to see him always in such joy, both inwardly and outwardly, over all creatures in general, gladly touching them and seeing them, that his spirit seemed to be not on earth but in heaven. The truth of this is evident, since on account of the great comfort which he had and had had in God's creatures, a little before his death he composed some Praises of the Lord for his creatures to incite the hearts of their hearers to the praise of God, and so that God might be praised by all through his creatures.

St. Francis wanted to be free to give away his clothes.

54. Another time a poor man in poor garments came to a hermitage of the friars and asked the friars for some old rag for the love of God. St. Francis told one of the friars to look through the house to see if he could find some cloth or rag to give him. Going all round the house the friar said he could not find any. So that the poor man should not go away empty-handed, St. Francis went privately, in order that his guardian should not forbid him, took a knife and, sitting down in a hiding-place, began to cut off a piece of his tunic, which was sewn on the inside of the tunic, wanting to give it secretly to the poor man. But as his guardian at once sensed what he wanted to do, he went to him and forbade him to give it, chiefly because it was then very cold and he was ill and really cold. St. Francis said to him: 'If you wish me not to give it to him it is absolutely necessary that someone else procures a piece to give to the poor brother.' So the friars gave him some cloth from their garments at St. Francis's prompting. If the friars lent him a cloak when he went through the world preaching, whether on foot or on an ass – after he began to be ill he could not go on foot and so it was necessary for him sometimes to ride on an ass, as he was not prepared to ride on a horse unless in genuine and very great necessity, and this only a short time before his death when he began to grow much worse – or when he was staying in a friary, he did not want to accept it unless under this condition that, if he met any poor man or any came to him whom the spirit told him was in evident need, he could give it to him.

St. Francis's reply to the novice.

73. On another occasion St. Francis was sitting by the fire warming himself when the novice [who had approached him previously on the same subject]

came yet again to speak to him about [having a] Psalter. St. Francis said to him: 'After you have a Psalter you will want and hanker for a breviary; after you have a breviary you will sit in an armchair like a great prelate, saying to your brother: "Bring me the breviary."' Thus saying, with great fervor of spirit he took some ashes in his hand and put them on his head, drawing the hand round his head as you do when you wash it, saying to himself as he did so: 'I a breviary! I a breviary!' He continued to reiterate this saying many times, 'I a breviary,' drawing his hand over his head. The friar was dumbfounded and ashamed. Afterwards St. Francis said to him: 'Brother, I have been similarly tempted to have books, but in order that I might know the Lord's will in this matter, I took the book where the holy Gospels are written and prayed God that when I first opened the book, he would deign to show me his will in this. After I had prayed, on first opening the book this Gospel saying struck me: "To you it is given to understand the mysteries of the kingdom of God, but to others in parables."' And he said: 'There are so many who ascend willingly to knowledge that he is blessed who makes himself sterile for the love of God.'

The novice asked again. This time St. Francis found the answer, and always used it in future.

74. Many months later, when St. Francis was at the church of St. Mary of the Portiuncula, by the cell past the house on the road, the brother spoke to him again about the Psalter. St. Francis said to him: 'Go, and do as your minister says to you.' Hearing this, the brother started to go back by the way he had come. St. Francis, staying where he was, began to think over what he had said to the brother, and at once called after him: 'Wait, brother, wait.' He came up to him and said: 'Come back with me, brother, and show me the place where I said to you as to the Psalter that you might do as your minister told you.' When they came to the spot where he had spoken these words to him, St. Francis bowed down before the brother and said on bended knee: 'I was wrong, brother, I was wrong, since whoever wishes to be a friar minor ought not to have anything except a tunic, as the rule allows him, and a cord and breeches, and those who are forced to by necessity or illness may have shoes.' From then on he gave this answer to as many friars as came to him for advice in such matters. Wherefore he used to say: 'A man has only as much learning as he can work with, and a religious is as good an orator as he is a worker;' as much as to say: 'A good tree is known only by its fruit.'

St. Francis tamed a cicada.

84. One summer, when St. Francis was at the same house, staying in the fur-
thest cell next to the hedge of the garden behind the house, where after his
death Brother Rainerius the gardener used to live, it so happened that one
day when he went down from that cell there was a cicada on the branch of
the fig tree which was near the cell, and he was able to touch her. Stretching
out his hand he said to her: 'Come to me, my sister cicada.' Immediately she
jumped on to the fingers of his hand and with the finger of his other hand
he began to stroke the cicada, saying: 'Sing, my sister cicada.' Immediately she
obeyed him and began to sing and St. Francis was much comforted and
praised God. For a good hour he held her thus in his hand. Afterwards he put
her back on the branch of the fig tree, from which he had taken her. Then
for eight days running, when he left the cell, he found her in the same place,
and every day he took her in his hand and as soon as he said to her that she
should sing, and stroked her, she sang. After eight days he said to his companions: 'We will give sister cicada leave to depart wherever she wishes, for she
has comforted us enough and the flesh might draw vainglory from this.'
When he had given his leave she immediately went away and appeared there
no more. His companions marveled that she obeyed him thus and was so
tame with him. St. Francis had so much joy in creatures through his love of
the Creator that God, for his consolation both inward and outward, made
tame to him creatures normally wild.

The night before St. Francis died many larks flew low over the house. St. Francis's love for birds and animals, and his concern for them, especially at Christmas time.

110. On the Saturday evening after Vespers the night before St. Francis died,
many birds called larks flew low over the roof of the house where St. Francis
lay and circled, singing, making the form of a wheel. We who were with St.
Francis and have written these things about him bear witness that many times
we have heard him say: 'If I speak with the emperor I will implore him for
the love of God and the intervention of my prayer to make a constitution
and decree that no man should trap sister larks or do them any harm whatever; likewise that all *podestàs* [mayors] of cities and lords of towns and villages
should be bound each year on Christmas Day to compel men to scatter corn
and other grain on the roads outside cities and towns for the birds to have
something to eat, especially sister larks, and other birds, on the day of such a
festival. Out of reverence for the Son of God whom the blessed Virgin his
mother laid that night in a manger between ox and ass, every man ought also

that night to give a good meal to our brothers the oxen and asses. Similarly on Christmas Day all the poor ought to be sated by the rich.' For St. Francis had a greater regard for Christmas than for any other festival of the Lord, since although the Lord may work our salvation in his other festivals, yet, because he was born for us, as St. Francis used to say, it was his concern to save us. Therefore he wished that on that day every Christian should exult in the Lord for love of him who gave himself for us. Every man should with gladness be bountiful not only to the poor but also to animals and birds. St. Francis said of the lark: 'Sister lark has a hood like a religious and is a humble bird, who goes cheerfully along the road to find herself some corn and even if she finds it among the dung of beasts she takes it out and eats it. As she flies she praises God, like a good religious despising earthly things, for her life is always in the heavens. Moreover her clothing is made like the earth, her feathers that is, giving an example to religious that they ought not to have colored and fancy clothing but as if dead, looking like soil.' Because he saw these things in his sisters the larks St. Francis loved them dearly and saw them gladly.

41. THE OFFICIAL *LIFE OF ST. FRANCIS*: THE STIGMATA

Some thirteen years after the completion of Thomas of Celano's second 'life,' the General Chapter of the Franciscan Order commissioned a new version from their minister-general, St. Bonaventure. His 'life,' based on material from the earlier ones which he reorganized under thematic headings, with some controversial passages excised (such as Francis's prophecies, and instances of his more extreme behavior), was accepted as the only official one. As a mark of its status, a shorter version of it was adopted for reading in the liturgy, and the Chapter took the unusual step of suppressing all earlier accounts and related material. The reasons for the suppression lie in the controversies that had developed both within the Order, concerning Francis's true intentions for his followers, and outside it, between the monastic orders, jealous of their ancient prerogatives, and the friars (Dominican as well as Franciscan), eager to assert their new privileges. The major argument within the Franciscan Order was between the Spirituals, those who adhered to the literal interpretation of poverty, and the Conventuals, who stood for a more moderate community life adapted to the needs of study and preaching. St. Bonaventure's 'life' of the founder was both an attempt to make peace among the factions and an assertion of what he felt to be the true spirit of the Order. The famous story of the stigmata, the culmination of Francis's mystical experiences, is included in all three accounts of his life. By the time St. Bonaventure wrote, it was more essential than ever to give a convincing version of this event, since its veracity was being called into question by the Order's critics; his is the account that follows.

Source: trans. Benen Fahy, "Major and Minor Life of St. Francis with excerpts from other works by St. Bonaventure," in *St. Francis of Assisi: Writings and Early Biographies; English Omnibus of the Sources for the Life of St. Francis,* ed. Marion A. Habig (4th ed. rev.; Quincy, Ill.: Franciscan Press, 1991), pp. 729-735; repr. with permission. BHL 3107.

Chapter 13

1. St. Francis never failed to keep himself occupied doing good; like the angels Jacob saw on the ladder, he was always busy, either raising his heart to God in prayer, or descending to his neighbor. He had learned how to distribute the time in which he could gain merit wisely, devoting part of it to his neighbor by doing good, and part to the restful ecstasy of contemplation. According to the demands of time or circumstances he would devote himself wholly to the salvation of his neighbor, but when he was finished, he would escape from the distracting crowds and go into solitude in search of peace. There he was free to attend exclusively to God and he would cleanse any stain he had contracted while living in the midst of the world. Two years

before his death, after a period of intense activity, he was led by Divine Providence to a high mountain called La Verna, where he could be alone. There he began a forty-day fast in honor of St. Michael the Archangel, as was his custom, and he soon experienced an extraordinary in-pouring of divine contemplation. He was all on fire with heavenly desires and he realized that the gifts of divine grace were being poured out over him in greater abundance than ever. He was borne aloft not as one who would search curiously into the divine majesty and be crushed by its glory, but as a faithful and wise servant anxious only to discover God's will, which he wanted to obey with all his heart and soul.

2. By divine inspiration he learned that if he opened the Gospels, Christ would reveal to him what was God's will for him and what God wished to see realized in him. And so Francis prayed fervently and took the Gospel book from the altar, telling his companion, a devout and holy friar, to open it in the name of the Blessed Trinity. He opened the Gospel three times, and each time it opened at the passion, and so Francis understood that he must become like Christ in the distress and the agony of his passion before he left the world, just as he had been like him in all that he did during his life. His body had already been weakened by the austerity of his past life and the fact that he had carried our Lord's Cross without interruption, but he was not afraid and he felt more eager than ever to endure any martyrdom. The unquenchable fire of love for Jesus in his goodness had become a blazing light of flame, so that his charity could not succumb even before the floodwaters of affliction.

3. The fervor of his seraphic longing raised Francis up to God and, in an ecstasy of compassion, made him like Christ who allowed himself to be crucified in the excess of his love. Then one morning about the feast of the Exaltation of the Holy Cross, while he was praying on the mountainside, Francis saw a Seraphim with six fiery wings coming down from the highest point in the heavens. The vision descended swiftly and came to rest in the air near him. Then he saw the image of a man crucified in the midst of the wings, with his hands and feet stretched out and nailed to a cross. Two of the wings were raised above his head and two were stretched out in flight, while the remaining two shielded his body. Francis was dumbfounded at the sight and his heart was flooded with a mixture of joy and sorrow. He was overjoyed at the way Christ regarded him so graciously under the appearance of a Seraphim, but the fact that he was nailed to a cross pierced his soul with a sword of compassionate sorrow.

He was lost in wonder at the sight of this mysterious vision; he knew that the agony of Christ's passion was not in keeping with the state of a seraphic

[Fig. 43] Representations of St. Francis receiving the stigmata; the earliest is by Giotto (Jameson, *Legends of the Monastic Orders,* p. 262).

spirit which is immortal. Eventually he realized by divine inspiration that God had shown him this vision in his providence, in order to let him see that, as Christ's lover, he would resemble Christ crucified perfectly not by physical martyrdom, but by the fervor of his spirit. As the vision disappeared, it left his heart ablaze with eagerness and impressed upon his body a miraculous likeness. There and then the marks of nails began to appear in his hands and feet, just as he had seen them in his vision of the Man nailed to the Cross. His hands and feet appeared pierced through the center with nails, the heads of which were in the palms of his hands and on the instep of each foot, while the points stuck out on the opposite side. The heads were black and round, but the points were long and bent back, as if they had been struck with a hammer; they rose above the surrounding flesh and stood out from it. His right side seemed as if it had been pierced with a lance and was marked with a livid scar which often bled, so that his habit and trousers were stained.

4. When he realized that he could not conceal the stigmata which had been imprinted so plainly on his body from his intimate companions, he was thrown into an agony of doubt; he was afraid to make God's secret publicly known, and he did not know whether he should say what he had seen, or keep it quiet. He called some of the friars and asked them in general terms what he should do. One of them, who was called Illuminatus, was enlightened by God and he realized that some miracle had taken place because the saint was still completely dazed. He said to him, "Brother, remember that when God reveals his secrets to you, it is not for yourself alone; they are intended for others too. If you hide something which was intended to do good to many others, then you have every reason to fear that you will be condemned for burying the talent given to you." Francis often said, "It is for me to keep my secret to myself," but when he heard these words, he described the vision he had just seen apprehensively, adding that the person who had appeared to him had told him a number of secrets which he would never reveal to anyone as long as he lived.

We can only conclude from this that the message given him by the Seraphim who appeared to him on the Cross was so secret that it could not be communicated to any human being.

5. True love of Christ had now transformed his lover into his image, and when the forty days which he had intended spending in solitude were over and the feast of St. Michael had come, St. Francis came down from the mountain. With him he bore a representation of Christ crucified which was not the work of an artist in wood or stone, but had been reproduced in the members of his body by the hand of the living God. "Kings have their coun-

sel that must be kept secret" and so Francis who realized that he shared a royal secret did his best to conceal the sacred stigmata. However, it is for God to reveal his wonders for his own glory; he had impressed the stigmata on St. Francis in secret, but he publicly worked a number of miracles by them, so that their miraculous, though hidden, power might become clearly known.

6. In the province of Rieti a fatal disease had attacked cattle and sheep and carried great numbers of them off so quickly that nothing could be done for them. Then a devout man was told in a vision at night to go immediately to the friars' hermitage where St. Francis was staying and get the water with which he had washed his hands and feet and sprinkle it over the livestock. He got up in the morning and went to the hermitage and got the water secretly from the saint's companions. Then he sprinkled the sick cattle and sheep. The animals were lying on the ground exhausted, but the moment that a mere drop of the water touched them, they immediately recovered their normal strength and stood up and hurried off to pasture, as if there had never been anything wrong with them. The miraculous power of water which had touched the stigmata banished the disease and saved the livestock from the fatal sickness.

7. Before St. Francis went to stay on La Verna it often happened that clouds would form over the mountain and violent hailstorms would devastate the crops. After his vision, however, the hail stopped, much to the amazement of the local people. The unusually clear skies proclaimed the extraordinary nature of his vision and the power of the stigmata which he received there.

One wintertime, because he was weak and the road was bad, the saint was riding an ass belonging to a poor man. It was snowing and the approach of darkness made it impossible for them to reach shelter, so that they had to spend the night under the lee of an overhanging cliff. Francis heard his benefactor grumbling to himself and turning this way and that; he was wearing only a few clothes and he could not fall asleep in the biting cold. He himself was ablaze with the fervor of divine love and he stretched out his hand and touched him. At the touch of his hand, which was warm with the heat of the coal used to purify the lips of the prophet Isaias, the cold disappeared and the man felt as warm as if he had been hit with a blast of hot air from an oven. He immediately felt better in body and soul and he slept more soundly in the rocks and the blizzard until morning than he had ever slept in his own bed, as he used to say afterwards.

It is certain, therefore, that the stigmata were impressed upon St. Francis by God's power, because it is God who purifies, illuminates, and inflames by the intervention of the Seraphim. These sacred wounds purified animals of disease and granted clear skies, as well as physical warmth. This was proved more clearly than ever after Francis's death by the miracles which we shall describe in their own place.

8. Francis was very careful to try and hide the treasure he had found in the field, but he could not prevent everybody from seeing the stigmata in his hands and feet, although he always kept his hands covered and wore shoes. A number of the friars saw them during his lifetime, and to put the matter beyond all doubt they testified to this under oath, although they were good religious and deserved to be believed. Some of the cardinals who were close friends of the saint also saw them and celebrated their praise in various hymns and antiphons which they composed in his honor, thus bearing witness to the truth in their words and writings. In a sermon which he preached in public and at which I was present with a number of other friars, his holiness Pope Alexander asserted that he had seen the stigmata with his own eyes during the saint's lifetime. More than fifty friars with St. Clare and her nuns and innumerable lay people saw them after his death. Many of them kissed the stigmata and felt them with their own hands, to prove the truth, as we shall describe later.

However, Francis succeeded in covering the wound in his side so carefully that no one could get more than a glimpse of it during his lifetime. A friar who used to wait on him carefully gently prevailed upon him to take off his habit and have it shaken out, and as he watched closely he saw the wound. He put three of his fingers on it immediately so that he was able to feel as well as see how big it was. The friar who was Francis's vicar at that time managed to see the wound by a similar subterfuge. Another of his companions, a man of extraordinary simplicity, put his hand in under his capuche to massage his chest because he was not feeling well, and accidentally touched the wound, causing the saint great pain. As a result, Francis always wore trousers which reached up to his armpits, in order to cover the scar on his side. The friars who washed his trousers or shook out his habit found them stained with blood. This clear proof left them with no doubt of the existence of the wound which they afterwards contemplated and venerated with others on his death.

9. O valiant knight of Christ! You are armed with the weapons of your invulnerable Leader. They will mark you out and enable you to overcome all your enemies. It is for you to bear aloft the standard of the High King, at the sight of which the rank and file of God's army take heart. And you bear, nonetheless, the seal of the supreme High Priest Christ, so that your words and example must be regarded by everyone as genuine and sound beyond all cavil. You bear the scars of the Lord Jesus in your body, so that no one should

dare oppose you. On the contrary, all Christ's disciples are bound to hold you in devout affection. God's witness in your favor is beyond all doubt; the sacred stigmata were witnessed not just by two or three, which would have been enough, but by a whole multitude, which is more than enough, and they leave those who are unbelieving without excuse. The faithful, on the other hand, are confirmed in their faith and raised up by confident hope and inflamed with the fire of divine love.

42. THE *CANTICLE OF BROTHER SUN*

The Franciscan tradition of worshiping with music inspired a strong flow of religious verse in the vernacular in the thirteenth and fourteenth centuries. For Francis, song formed an integral part of the worship of God, and several anecdotes relate his love of music: how he often broke into spontaneous song in French (his mother's language) as he traveled the countryside, or pretended to accompany himself with a stick for a violin bow as he sang. The following account from the 'Legend of Perugia' describes how he began to write his most famous prayer-poem, in the Umbrian dialect of Italian, the year before his death, while he was losing his sight and was cared for by the nuns at San Damiano. He added the final verses just before he died.

Source: trans. Rosalind B. Brooke, *Scripta Leonis, Rufini et Angeli, Sociorum S. Francisci* (Oxford: Clarendon Press, 1970), pp. 163-7; "Canticle of Brother Sun" trans. Lawrence S. Cunningham, *Saint Francis of Assisi* (Boston: Twayne Publishers, 1976), pp.58-59; both repr. with permission. BHL 3114.

From 'The Writings of Leo, Rufinus and Angelo'

St. Francis lay there [at San Damiano] for fifty days and could no longer see in daytime the light of day, nor at night the light of the fire, but always remained in the house and in the little cell in darkness. Moreover, he had great pain in his eyes day and night so that at night he could scarcely rest or sleep, which was very bad for him and greatly aggravated the sickness of his eyes and his other infirmities. Also, if at any time he wished to rest or sleep, there were many mice in the house and in the little cell where he lay, which was a lean-to made of rushes attached to one side of the house. The mice ran backwards and forwards over and around him, and so did not let him go to sleep. They even hindered him considerably at the time of prayer. Not only at night but even by day they so tormented him that even when he ate they got up on to the table, so that his companions and he himself considered it must be a temptation of the devil, as indeed it was. One night St. Francis was thinking about how many tribulations he had and began to feel sorry for himself, saying inwardly: 'Lord, come to my help and look on my infirmities so that I may be able to bear them patiently.' Immediately it was said to him in spirit: 'Tell me, brother: if anyone were to give you for your infirmities and tribulations such a great and precious treasure that, if the whole earth were pure gold, all stones were precious stones, and all water were balsam, yet you would consider all this as nothing, and these substances as earth, stones and water in comparison with the great and precious treasure given to you, surely you would rejoice greatly?' St. Francis replied: 'That would be a great treasure, Lord, and worth the seeking, truly precious and greatly to be loved and desired.' He said to him: 'Therefore, brother, rejoice, and rather be glad in your infirmities and tribulations, since henceforth you are as secure as if you were already in my kingdom.' Rising up in the morning he said to his companions: 'If the emperor were to give a whole kingdom to his servant, surely he ought to rejoice much? But if the whole empire, surely he would rejoice much more?' He said to them, 'Therefore I ought to rejoice greatly from now on in my infirmities and tribulations and to find comfort in the Lord, to give thanks always to God the Father and to his only Son, our Lord Jesus Christ, and to the Holy Spirit for the great grace and blessing given to me, because while still living in the flesh he has deigned in his mercy to make me his unworthy servant certain of the kingdom. Therefore I want for his praise and my consolation, and the edification of our neighbors, to make a new song of praise of the Lord for his creatures, which we use daily and without which we could not live. In them the human race greatly offends the Creator and daily we are ungrateful for such grace, because we do not praise our Creator and Giver of all good things as we ought.' Sitting down, he began to meditate and afterwards began: 'Most high, omnipotent good Lord.' He made a song on the creatures and taught his companions to recite it. For his spirit was then in such sweetness and comfort that he wanted Brother Pacifico, who in the world had been known as the king of verses and who had been a really courtly doctor of singers, to be sent for and given some good and holy friars that they might go through the world preaching and praising God. He said he wanted it that first one of them who knew how to preach should preach to the people and after the sermon they were to sing the praises of God as minstrels of the Lord. After the praises he wanted the preacher to say to the people: 'We are the Lord's minstrels and as our reward we want you to live in true penitence.' He said: 'For who are servants of the Lord unless in some measure they are his minstrels who ought to move the hearts of men and rouse them to spiritual joy?' He said this especially of the Friars Minor, who were given to the people for their salvation. He set over the praises of God which he made, that is, 'Most High, omnipotent, good Lord,' the title 'Canticle of Brother Sun,' which is more beautiful than all other creatures and can come nearest to God. Thus he said: 'In the morning when the sun rises, every man ought to praise God who created it, because through it the eyes are lighted by day. In the evening when it grows night, every man ought to praise God for his other creature, Brother Fire, because by it our eyes are lighted at night.' He said, 'We are all as it were blind, and the Lord through these two creatures lights our eyes. Because of this, for these and all his other creatures which we make use of daily we ought always especially to praise their glorious Creator.' This he did and continued to do gladly in sickness and in health, and gladly urged others to praise the Lord. Even more, as his infirmities increased he began to recite the praises of the Lord himself, and afterwards he got his companions to sing, that in thinking of God's praise, he might forget the anguish of his suffering and illness. Thus he did until the day of his death.

The Canticle of Brother Sun

Most High, omnipotent, good Lord
To you alone belong praise and glory,
Honor and blessing.
No man is worthy to breathe thy name.
Be praised, my Lord, for all your creatures.
In the first place for the blessed Brother Sun,
Who gives us the day and enlightens us through you.
He is beautiful and radiant with great splendor,
Giving witness of thee, Most Omnipotent One.
Be praised, my Lord, for Sister Moon and the stars
Formed by you so bright, precious and beautiful.
Be praised, my Lord, for Brother Wind
And the airy skies, so cloudy and serene;
For every weather, be praised, for it is life-giving.
Be praised, my Lord, for Sister Water,
So necessary, yet so humble and precious, and chaste.
Be praised, my Lord, for Brother Fire,
Who lights up the night.
He is beautiful and carefree, robust and fierce.
Be praised, my Lord, for our sister, Mother Earth,
Who nourishes and watches us
While bringing forth abundance of fruits with colored flowers and herbs.
Be praised, my Lord, for those who pardon through your love
And bear weakness and trial,
Blessed are those who endure in peace,
For they will be crowned by you, Most High.
Be praised, my Lord, for our sister, Bodily Death,
Whom no living man can escape.
Woe to those who die in sin.
Blessed are those who discover thy holy will.
The second death will do them no harm.

Praise and bless my Lord.
Render thanks.
Serve him with great humility.
                    Amen.

43. THE CANONIZATION OF ST. FRANCIS

In the early period of Christianity, saints achieved their status through the develop-
ment of popular movements with the support of the local priest: spontaneous gatherings
occurred at the tombs of the "very special" Christian dead, and, in church, accounts of
their lives were read out (hence the term 'legend') on the anniversaries of their deaths,
known as their feast-days. After the age of martyrs had passed, however, it became
more difficult to decide who deserved to be venerated. Sometimes the honor might be
given to undeserving or even non-existent persons, and cults were initiated for financial
reasons. In the light of attempts by some to safeguard against these abuses, and by oth-
ers to gain even more honor for their saint, it became customary to appeal to the bishop
for decisions and to involve synods or councils. By the eleventh century it had become
increasingly common to appeal to the pope in issues of canonization, and at the begin-
ning of the thirteenth, the papacy established its exclusive right to make saints. What
had begun in part as an attempt to promote some saints by appealing to higher
authority thus ended by placing canonization strictly in the hands of the pope. As the
Middle Ages drew to a close the making of a saint could be a long drawn-out process
requiring intensive lobbying at the Vatican and considerable expense for supporters; a
fifteenth-century promoter of the English St. Osmund compared it to outright warfare.
Many of those popularly regarded as saints, like Godric, remained uncanonized for
lack of organized support and funds. The canonization of St. Francis was exceptional:
such was his popularity (and he had known the pope, Gregory IX, personally) that by
the end of his life, canonization was a foregone conclusion. It took place with unusual
speed barely two years after his death, and instead of the customary 'legend' required as
part of the evidence, Thomas of Celano's 'life' was commissioned at about the same
time that the status of saint was conferred. Thomas was thus able to include a typically
fulsome account of the canonization ceremony, which he apparently witnessed, at the
end of his first 'life.'

Source: trans. Placid Hermann, *St. Francis of Assisi: First and Second Life of St. Francis by Thomas of Celano* (Chicago: Franciscan Herald Press, 1963), pp. 109-117; repr. with permission. BHL 3105.

Book 3 of Thomas of Celano's 'First Life.'

The canonization of our blessed father Francis.

1, 119. Therefore the most glorious father Francis, adding an even more
happy end to a happy beginning, most happily commended his spirit to
heaven in the twentieth year of his conversion, and there, crowned with
glory and honor and having attained a place in the midst of the stones of

fire, he stands at the throne of God and devotes himself to furthering effectually the concerns of those he left behind upon earth. What indeed can be denied to him in the imprint of whose stigmata appears the form of him who, being equal to the Father, has taken his seat at the right hand of the majesty on high, the brightness of his glory and the image of his substance, and has effected man's purgation from sin? What else should there be but that he be heard who has been made comformable unto the death of Christ Jesus in the fellowship of his sufferings which the sacred wounds in his hands and feet and side show forth?

Actually, he is already giving joy to the whole world that has been gladdened by a new joy, and he is offering to all the advantages of true salvation. He is brightening the world with the very bright light of his miracles and illuminating the whole world with the brilliance of a new star. Once the world was saddened when it was deprived of his presence, and it saw itself overwhelmed in a pit of darkness, as it were, at his setting. But now, lighted up as the noonday with more refulgent beams by the rising of this new light, it feels that it has lost this universal darkness. All its complaining, blessed be God, has now ceased, since every day and everywhere it is filled most abundantly through him with new rejoicing over the abundance of his virtues. From the east and from the west, from the south and from the north those come who have been helped through his intercession; thus these things are proved by the testimony of truth. Indeed, while he lived in the flesh, that extraordinary lover of heavenly things accepted nothing of ownership in the world so that he might possess more fully and more joyfully the universal good. It therefore came about that he received in its entirety what he had declined in part, and he exchanged eternity for time. Everywhere he is helping everyone; everywhere he is at the behest of everyone; and, truly a lover of unity, he knows no loss because of such division.

120. While he was still living among sinners, Francis went about through the whole world preaching; reigning now with the angels in heaven, he flies more swiftly than thought as the messenger of the most high King and bestows generous gifts upon all. Therefore all the world honors him, venerates, glorifies, and praises him. In truth, all share in the common good. Who can tell what great miracles and who can tell what kind of miracles God deigns to work everywhere through him? What great miracles is not Francis working in France alone, where the king [Louis IX, later canonized] and queen and all the great ones run to kiss and venerate the pillow Francis used in his sickness? Where also the wise and most learned men of the world, of whom Paris [the university of Paris, where Pope Gregory IX had studied] is accustomed to produce a greater abundance than the rest of the world,

humbly and most devoutly venerate, admire, and honor Francis, an unlettered man and the friend of true simplicity and complete sincerity. Truly Francis had a free and noble heart. Those who have experienced his magnanimity know how free, how liberal he was in all things; how confident and fearless he was in all things; with what great virtue, with what great fervor he trampled under foot all worldly things. What indeed shall I say of the other parts of the world, where, by means of his clothing, diseases depart, illnesses leave, and crowds of both sexes are delivered from their troubles by merely invoking his name.

121. At his tomb, too, new miracles are constantly occurring, and, the number of petitions greatly increasing, great benefits for body and for soul are sought at that same place. Sight is given to the blind, hearing is restored to the deaf, the ability to walk is given to the lame, the mute speak, he who has the gout leaps, the leper is healed, he who suffers from a swelling has it reduced, and those who suffer diverse and various infirmities obtain health, so that his dead body heals living bodies just as his living body had raised up dead souls.

The Roman pontiff, the highest of all bishops, the leader of the Christians, the lord of the world, the pastor of the Church, the anointed of the Lord, the vicar of Christ, heard and understood all this. He rejoiced and was happy, he danced with joy and was glad, when he saw the Church of God renewed in his own day by new mysteries but ancient wonders, and that in his own son, whom he bore in his holy womb, cherished in his bosom, nursed with his words, and nourished with the food of salvation. The rest of the guardians of the Church too heard it, the shepherds of the flock, the defenders of the faith, the friends of the bridegroom, those who are at his side, the hinges of the world, the venerable cardinals. They congratulated the Church, they rejoiced with the pope, they glorified the Savior, who with the highest and ineffable wisdom, the highest and incomprehensible grace, the highest and immeasurable goodness chooses the foolish and base things of this world that he might thus draw the strong things to himself. The whole world heard and applauded, and the entire realm that was subject to the Catholic faith superabounded in joy and overflowed with holy consolation.

122. But there was a sudden change in things and new dangers arose meanwhile in the world. Suddenly the joy of peace was disturbed and the torch of envy was lighted and the Church was torn by domestic and civil war. The Romans, a rebellious and ferocious race of men, raged against their neighbors, as was their custom, and, being rash, they stretched forth their hands against the holy places. The distinguished pope Gregory tried to curb their growing wickedness, to repress their savagery, to temper their violence;

[Fig. 44] The story is told by Bonaventure that when traveling to Siena, St. Francis had a mystical encounter with three poorly-dressed maidens whom he called Poverty, Chastity, and Obedience, the chief virtues of his Order. This sketch (school of Giotto) shows the meeting, and the three maidens returning to heaven afterwards (Jameson, *Legends of the Monastic Orders,* p. 256).

and, like a tower of great strength, he protected the Church of Christ. Many dangers assailed her, destruction became more frequent, and in the rest of the world the necks of sinners were raised against God. What then? Measuring the future by his very great experience and weighing the present circumstances, he abandoned the city to the rebels, so that he might free the world from rebellions and defend it. He came therefore to the city of Rieti, where he was received with honor, as was befitting. From there he went to Spoleto where he was honored with great respect by all. He remained there a few days, and, after the affairs of the Church had been provided for, he kindly visited, in the company of the venerable cardinals, the Poor Ladies of Christ, who were dead and buried to the world [St. Clare and her followers]. The holy life of these Poor Ladies, their highest poverty, and their glorious way of life moved him and the others to tears, stirred them to contempt of the world, and kindled in them a desire for the life of retirement. O loveable humility, nurse of all graces! The prince of the world, the successor of the prince of the apostles, visits these poor women, comes to them lowly and humble in their seclusion; and, though this humility is worthy of just approbation, it was nevertheless an unusual example and one that had not been seen for many ages past.

123. Then he hastened on, hastened to Assisi, where a glorious treasure awaited him, that through it the universal suffering and imminent tribulation might be extinguished. At his approach, the whole region rejoiced, the city was filled with exultation, the great throng of people celebrated their happiness, and the already bright day was further illuminated by brighter lights. Every one went out to meet him and solemn watches were kept by all. The pious fraternity of Poor Brothers went out to meet him, and they all sang sweet songs to Christ the Lord. The vicar of Christ arrived at the place and going first to the grave of St. Francis, he greeted it reverently and eagerly. He sighed deeply, struck his breast, shed tears, and bowed his venerable head with great devotion. While he was there a solemn discussion was held concerning the canonization of the holy man, and the noble assembly of cardinals met often concerning this business. From all sides many came together who had been freed from their illnesses through the holy man of God, and from every side a very great number of miracles gave forth their luster: these were approved, verified, heard, accepted. Meanwhile, the urgency of the affairs of his office pressed upon the pope, a new emergency threatened, and the holy father went to Perugia that by a superabounding and singular grace he might return again to Assisi in the interests of this very great business. Then they met again at Perugia, and a sacred assembly of cardinals was held concerning this matter in the room of the lord pope. They were all

in agreement and they spoke unanimously; they read the miracles and regarded them with great reverence, and they commended the life and conduct of the blessed father with the highest praises.

124. "The most holy life of this most holy man," they said, "needs no attestation of miracles; what we have seen with our eyes, what our hands have hand led, we have proved with the light of truth." They were all transported with joy, they rejoiced, they wept, and indeed in those tears there was a great blessing. They immediately appointed the happy day [of the proclamation of Francis's canonization] on which they would fill the whole world with saving happiness. The solemn day came, a day to be held in reverence by every age, a day that shed its sublime rapture not only upon the earth but even upon the heavenly mansions. Bishops came together, abbots arrived, prelates of the Church were present from even the most remote parts of the world; a king too was present [John of Brienne, king of Jerusalem, whose rights were usurped by the emperor Frederick II], and a noble multitude of counts and princes. They then escorted the lord of all the world and entered the city of Assisi with him amid great pomp. He reached the place prepared for so solemn an event and the whole multitude of glorious cardinals, bishops, and abbots gathered around the blessed pope. A most distinguished gathering of priests and clerics was there; a happy and sacred company of religious men was there; the more bashful habit of the sacred veil was there too; a great crowd of all the people was there and an almost innumerable multitude of both sexes. They hurried there from all sides, and every age came to the concourse of people with the greatest eagerness. The small and great were there, the servant and they who were free of a master.

125. The supreme pontiff was there, the spouse of the Church of Christ, surrounded by a variety of his great children and with a crown of glory on his head, an ornament of honor. He stood there adorned with the pontifical robes and clad in holy vestments ornamented with jewels set in gold and graven by the work of a lapidary. The anointed of the Lord stood there, resplendent in magnificence and glory in gilded clothing; and covered with engraven jewels sparkling with the radiance of spring, he caught the attention of all. Cardinals and bishops stood around him; decked with splendid necklaces and clad in garments as white as snow they showed forth the image of super-celestial beauties and displayed the joy of the glorified. All the people stood in expectation of the voice of mirth, the voice of gladness, a new voice, a voice full of all sweetness, a voice of praise, a voice of constant blessing. First Pope Gregory preached to all the people, and with a sweetly flowing and sonorous voice he spoke the praises of God. He also praised the holy father Francis in a noble eulogy, and recalling and speaking of the purity of

his life, he was bathed in tears. His sermon had this text: "He shone in his days as the morning star in the midst of a cloud and as the moon at the full. And as the sun when it shineth, so did he shine in the temple of God." When the faithful saying and worthy of all acceptation was completed, one of the lord pope's subdeacons, Octavian by name, read the miracles of the saint before all in a very loud voice, and the lord Raynerius, a cardinal deacon, a man of penetrating intellect and renowned for his piety and life, spoke about them with holy words and with an abundance of tears. The Shepherd of the Church [Pope Gregory] was carried away with joy, and sighing from the very depths of his being and sobbing, he shed torrents of tears. So too the other prelates of the Church poured out floods of tears, and their sacred vestments were moistened with their abundance. All the people too wept, and with the suspense of their longing expectation, they became wearied.

126. Then the happy pope spoke with a loud voice, and extending his hands to heaven, he said "To the praise and glory of Almighty God, the Father, Son, and Holy Spirit, and of the glorious Virgin Mary and of the blessed apostles Peter and Paul, and to the honor of the glorious Roman Church, at the advice of our brothers and of the other prelates, we decree that the most blessed father Francis, whom the Lord has glorified in heaven and whom we venerate on earth, shall be enrolled in the catalogue of saints and that his feast shall be celebrated on the day of his death." At this decree, the venerable cardinals began to sing in a loud voice along with the pope the 'Te Deum Laudamus.' Then there was raised a clamor among the many people praising God; the earth resounded with their mighty voices, the air was filled with their rejoicings, and the ground was moistened with their tears. New songs were sung, and the servants of God gave expression to their joy in melody of spirit. Sweet sounding organs were heard there and spiritual hymns were sung with well modulated voices. There a very sweet odor was breathed, and a more joyous melody that stirred the emotions resounded there. The day was bright and colored with more splendid rays than usual. There were green olive branches there and fresh branches of other trees. Brightly glittering festive attire adorned all the people, and the blessing of peace filled the minds of those who had come there with joy. Then the happy Pope Gregory descended from his lofty throne, and going by way of the lower steps, he entered the sanctuary to offer the vows and voluntary oblations; he kissed with his happy lips the tomb that contained the body that was sacred and consecrated to God. He offered and multiplied his prayers and celebrated the sacred mysteries [Mass]. A ring of his brethren stood about him, praising, adoring, and blessing Almighty God who had done great things in all the earth. All the people increased the praises of God and

they paid due thanksgiving to St. Francis in honor of the most holy Trinity. Amen. These things took place in the city of Assisi in the second year of the pontificate of the lord pope Gregory on the seventeenth day of the calends of the month of August [16 July 1228].

CHAPTER EIGHT

HAGIOGRAPHIC ROMANCES

Many improbable stories of saints, some of whom were later rejected by the Roman Calendar, circulated widely in medieval Europe and were among the most popular hagiographies. The history of such writings goes back to the apocryphal stories of the apostles and the famous 'Acts of Paul and Thecla,' about St. Paul and a devoted female disciple, that circulated in the first century. Later hagiographical romances in the vernacular are characterized by a practical didacticism, by lively narrative relying heavily on direct discourse and plenty of action, by the absence of historical context (these stories are often situated in an indeterminate time, vaguely that of the Roman persecutions, and in exotic locations), and by the use of plots and motifs also found in mythology and folk tales. Given a lack of historicity in hagiography generally, it is no wonder that the line between what passed as truth and fiction was often blurred. Hippolyte Delehaye describes numerous instances of mistaken identity, anachronism, exaggeration, and the transference of incidents and motifs from myth to hagiography, and the events that gave rise to the story of St. Ursula show how errors could become established truths. At the same time, these stories are mines of information about the preoccupations of medieval writers and their audiences. Chastity, for instance, was a major theme, and the 'life' of the virgin martyr who threw off her feminine weakness and became a soldier for Christ was a staple among these stories. The popularity of this type of hagiography was a major cause of attacks on the cult of the saints in the Renaissance and led indirectly to the great work of the Bollandists, beginning in the seventeenth century, when a small group of Jesuit scholars under the leadership of Heribert Rosweyde and John Bolland developed scientific methods of historical research aimed at separating hagiographical fact from fiction.

44. ST. URSULA AND THE ELEVEN THOUSAND VIRGINS

The earliest extant 'life' of St. Ursula and her army of virgin martyrs was written by a Flemish monk named Herric. He claimed to have received it from a German emissary, Count Hoolf, who had heard it while on a mission to England from the lips of St. Dunstan himself when he was archbishop of Canterbury. This account, fraught with chronological inconsistencies, has been assigned a date between 969 and 976, but from the eighth century on there is evidence of a growing cult of St. Ursula at Cologne. Its basis was a fourth-century stone inscription (now in St. Ursula's church) commemorating a group of unnamed virgin martyrs and the rebuilding of a church in their honor at the place where they died. The details of the legend gradually took shape in calendars, martyrologies, a tenth-century sermon, and the 'Passio' cited above: the name of the princess-leader changed from Pinnosa to Ursula, the virgins accompanying her achieved a specific number, and the circumstances and flight from Britain were added. But by the twelfth century a tide of skepticism was growing and the version of the legend reprinted here (written c.1100) may be read in the context of other events designed to refute the disbelievers, particularly a series of discoveries of quantities of relics belonging to the saint and her followers and found with the guidance of angelic visions. These were to culminate in the revelations of the mystics Elizabeth of Schönau and Hermann Joseph, which however did not succeed in silencing the critics. But despite the skeptics, the cult of St. Ursula and her virgins continued to flourish throughout Europe.

Source: trans. Pamela Sheingorn and Marcelle Thiébaux, *The Passion of St. Ursula*, Peregrina Translation Series 16 (Toronto: Peregrina Publishing Co., 1990), pp. 13-37; repr. with permission. BHL 8428.

The Birth of St. Ursula and Her Marriage Proposal

1, 1. It was during the reign of our Lord Jesus Christ, after his passion, resurrection, and ascension, when people from all the ends of the earth had turned to God, and not even the far corners of the ocean could hide from the fervor of his faith, when the people were assembled together, people and kings, to serve the Lord.

At that time there lived in the lands of Britain a certain King Deonotus, known to God by his life as much as by his name. Since he was devout in all the observances of the Catholic faith, he learned how to govern men so as not to forget the kind of subservience he himself owed to his Creator. He also learned to exact tribute from his subjects in such a way that he always remembered that he owed his very existence to his celestial King. This King

[Fig. 45] A reliquary of St. Ursula depicting scenes from her legend on the side panels, by Hans Memling [c.1430-94], in St. John's Hospital, Bruges. The left-hand panel shows the virgins arriving at Cologne on their way to Rome, in the middle they reach Basel, and on the right they are received by the pope in Rome (Baring-Gould, *Lives of the Saints,* 12).

Deonotus, therefore, bearing the yoke of Christ beneath which he blamelessly soldiered, also blamelessly and most justly ruled over others. In continued fulfilment of the promise of future generations, in the blessing of Abraham's seed, he took a wife who was his equal both in lineage and in the manner of her goodness.

But the wrath of God's justice begins here on earth against vessels of wrath that deserve to be shattered with a double blow and this same wrath wreaks irreparable destruction at the last Judgment. Similarly, God's mercy grants to those who love him a foretaste of the wealth of his goodness, generally even in this life. By this means they learn to await patiently the indescribable glory that the eye has not seen, nor the ear heard, nor has it entered into the human heart.

2. And so while both her parents awaited with highest hope a male child who would be the successor to their earthly kingdom, God's provident mercy – which knows how to grant even more than is prayed for – gave

them a female child. This daughter was endowed with a more than manly spirit, so that she might go before them to the inheritance of the heavenly kingdom, to which they would follow. In this way she could prepare for them many good things which would endure without end. Because she was destined one day to strangle the savage bear (that is, the Devil), following David's example, she received from her parents in baptism the prophetic name of Ursula. This was done through the dispensation of God, for he names those whom he predestines.

Ursula was educated with regal pomp as befitted royal offspring. While she was advancing normally in her physical growth, Ursula began to progress beyond the tender years of her age in the maturity of her character. Even at that point the world had grown repugnant to her, because she was imbued with the teachings of the evangelists. She would meditate on the law of the Lord day and night. And because she sighed in her heart and soul for spiritual marriage with her Bridegroom, all her adornment and glory were not without but within. And now she was able to turn away promptly from all earthly things. These things came about because the highest Artificer wished to polish his pearl for some great ornament of the Church. And it was as if even then he had openly proclaimed to her, "Hearken, O daughter, and incline your ear, because the King desires your beauty."

3. In addition to possessing these and other gifts of spiritual grace, this holy virgin was unrivaled in appearance and wondrous beauty. She was glorious to the eyes of all. But this girl, thinking only on the things of the Lord, loved these qualities less in herself because she knew that they were not very pleasing to the eyes of her own Bridegroom. Since the news had spread far and wide that this very noble girl had such innate virtue, word reached the ears of a certain foreign king. He, being powerful and strong, boasted of his military strength, and ruled widely with barbaric ferocity. He had a son of great natural ability, whom he loved deeply with fatherly affection because he was the successor to the kingdom. Because of his son, this king wanted very much to command respect for his royal grandeur. He began, therefore, to consider that his kingdom would be extended and his name and the glory of his prosperity would be increased if it should befall his son to marry so renowned a girl.

The son was no less determined, inasmuch as he was already entering the years of early manhood. With his father's approval and the further assent of the leaders of the people, he dispatched legates to the girl's father. He sent along many precious gifts. And he made promise of more things – rich cities, tracts of lands, bodies of water, in short, all of his father's realm, and whatever of the world's delights he was able to offer, or had been able to offer. Again and again he calculated the reckoning of the dowry. He also leveled threats as if he would employ a good deal of force, in keeping with the greatness of his name, so that at all events he might exact what he wanted through fear if he did not gain it through flattery and gifts.

4. The legates received their orders from the king and set forth on their journey. When they had traveled a great distance, they approached the girl's father. Once they were granted an ample opportunity to speak, they very assiduously went over the details of the matter that their lord had commanded. After heaping on flattery, like scorpions they unleashed what they believed to be very effective: threats and hostile intimidations. Then the old man, who was prudent and wholly filled with charitable feelings, began to vacillate inwardly. For he thought it most shameful to tear his reluctant daughter, who clung ever more closely to her heavenly Bridegroom, from the embrace of the eternal King and to subject her to the defilement of foreign lust. On the one hand, he might have been willing to spill his own blood on behalf of the Catholic religion and zeal for justice, since for him to live was Christ and to die was gain. On the other hand, the care of the kingdom was entrusted to him, and he despaired of being able to resist with his own armies so savage an assault from that barbarian king. Already he seemed to see taking place right before his very eyes the slaughter of men of every age, the plundering of cities, the rape of married women and girls, the torching of churches, the desecration of shrines, and whatever miseries might at any time befall a defeated people, especially with pagans conquering Christians.

5. Caught up in this dilemma concerning his daughter, the pious king hastened from the presence of the enemy and turned to divine mercy – which was then the only refuge that lay before him – as if to a tower of strength. Wholly bathed in tears, he begged heaven's aid with tireless prayers. In the midst of these events the maiden of God noticed her father's troubled countenance. For although he dissembled, he was unable to hide the fact that she herself was the cause of his distress. Ursula, less anxious for herself, felt sorrow for the anxiety of her father. She swiftly had recourse to her own weapons, just as holy Judith and Esther did for the liberation of their country. She prayed and fasted throughout the night. She was determined to obtain very quickly what she asked for when she addressed the listening ears of her Bridegroom, with whom she was already truly united in spirit. And while from day to night, or rather from days to nights, she continued in vigils and fasting, her limbs collapsing because of her body's weakness, her heart kept vigil with God. She fell asleep for awhile, and through a vision granted by divine revelation she was found worthy to be shown the whole plan of her

life, the number of her co-warriors, and the glorious palm of martyrdom. The outcome of things later bore this out.

6. Therefore, after the first light of the rising dawn, Ursula set about to relieve her father's sorrow. For, indeed, on that day he had to respond to the legates of the powerful king. Light-hearted she came to him, and smiling softly, she said, "My father, do not grieve any further over this matter, but cast your thoughts upon the Lord, who will not give a just man over to endless agitation. And do not ascribe what I say to my girlish years. Understand that last night a voice came to me – despite my unworthiness as the Lord's handmaiden – in a dream of divine consolation. The voice ordered me not to deny the hope of a wedding to the young man who is trying to win my hand in marriage. Nonetheless I shall die unmarried with the seal of my virginity intact.

This must be a legal provision of the wedding and the document of the marriage contract: that you, father, and the young man who entices me to his love shall seek out ten maidens in their earliest youth and most carefully selected as to beauty and lineage. Then you shall assign to me, and to each one of them, a thousand maidens of excellent repute. And you shall prepare eleven ships with triple rows of oarsmen to match our number. Let a three-year period of grace be granted to us for the dedication of our virginity. Once these conditions have been met, whatever is pleasing to God will come to pass. There is no one who can alter the immutable plan of divine love that has been provided for me."

7. The father was gladdened by his daughter's words. He had the legates summoned to the court, approved their requests and, as a legal provision of the marriage, he proposed the condition that the girl had demanded. And he cautiously stipulated, as the most important requirement contract, that the young man, after being reborn to salvation through baptism, must be instructed in the Lord through the Catholic faith for three years.

When they had heard these things the legates traveled home on the road by which they had come, as if their prayers had been answered. Swiftly they returned to their lord without interrupting their journey, since they expected to receive honor, glory and reward for a mission well done. After the mandated conditions had been explained in detail to the very happy father, the son's joy exceeded all measure because of the greatness of his love. As soon as the rejoicing of their leaders became known, as was appropriate a general celebration was held in the whole kingdom. Since he most eagerly accepted the legal provisions of the marriage document, the young man began very ardently to demand of his father that he be initiated at once in Christian teachings. He longed to fulfil the girl's wish through the consecration of baptism.

Now a new levy was declared for a novel kind of army. Everywhere throughout the two realms well-born and beautiful maidens were sought. They were conducted to the palace, where they received feminine ornaments to increase their royal splendor. No less sumptuously did the building of the ships take place, for both kings were equally zealous. Some men felled trees in the forests; others carried them to the shore; some fashioned the hulls; others the thwarts; some fitted the decks together with fine joints; some made this, some that ornament out of gold, silver and bronze. And since each one busied himself, eagerly striving according to his own skill and task, the work proceeded briskly everywhere.

The Nautical Exercises and Journeys to Cologne and Rome of St. Ursula and her Companions.

2, 8. Through the friendship and effort of the two kings, the fleet was wonderfully constructed according to standards of regal splendor, and the group of very carefully chosen girls was completed to fulfil the number assigned by God. Among the seemingly countless girls of the noblest families, Pinnosa, daughter of a certain Duke Maximus, stood out from the others as much because of her innate virtue as because of her lineage. After St. Ursula she was second-in-command of the virgin army. Her father cherished her as a noble comrade with a special bond of filial affection.

After everything had been magnificently completed, the maiden troops assembled before the princess St. Ursula on the appointed day. Girded up as if for naval exercises, they awaited the orders of their commander. Surrounded by her virgin army, which she had wanted for such a long time, the blessed girl Ursula, with a joyful mien and spirit, first gave to God the thanks she owed him. Then she revealed to them, as if to the most loyal comrades in arms, the secret of her plan. With pious exhortations she instructed and strengthened them in the fear of God or rather the love of God, because "perfect charity banishes fear." Moreover the virgin troops, while listening very eagerly, heeded with rapt attention the most beneficial admonitions of their princess. Lifting their hearts to heaven, they raised their hands as if they had already been sworn to Christ by a military oath of allegiance, and solemnly pledged their devotion to every duty of divine religion. With mutual zeal they urged one another on in this undertaking, inasmuch as they had by then one heart and one soul. And since they had already received from above a foretaste of heavenly sweetness, the world and its glory grew vile in their minds.

9. As the sea was nearby, once the signal was given they swiftly flocked to their ships. They deployed the rigging and set out to the open sea. They

practised every kind of exercise: first they steered the ships towards one another, then they scattered. At times they simulated flight, at other times combat. Nothing that occurred to them did they leave untried. As a group of young women they took part in training each and every day. Sometimes they turned back around midday, sometimes at about three in the afternoon and sometimes after spending the whole day in games, they turned back towards evening.

The pious king was often present at this spectacle, along with his very venerable senators and all the leading figures of the realm. And even the common people – as always, greedy for new things – put aside their serious business and applauded the young women's maneuvres. But, emboldened by persistent daily exercise, the girls rowed farther and farther from the shore. It even happened that certain ships, widely dispersed by gusts of wind, scarcely returned before night. Since the young women were withdrawing the pleasure of the spectacle from the people, the prolonged daily wait and the fact that they were jaded with the games caused the spectators to grow weary. As they departed one by one to their own tasks, the crowd gradually drifted away.

10. In this way the young women celebrated their three year prelude to martyrdom with great joy. Now the wedding gifts were being prepared for the appointed day of the marriage, and the young man was spurring his thoughts towards his love of the maiden. Blessed Ursula, though not doubting the promise of the divine vision, nevertheless grew anxious because of her own human frailty. She therefore admonished her virginal companions, whom she had already instructed in the Lord as much by her example as by her words, that at such a critical point in the matter they should beat more insistently upon the door of divine mercy. For, she told them, she feared that they might lose the armour of chastity beneath whose protection they had soldiered blamelessly for their heavenly King. After she had spoken these words, which were like a goad to incite those already running, the maidens devoted to God poured forth tears from the depths of their hearts. Since each one hoped to dedicate her own chastity to God together with that of the princess, they began to invoke the aid of heaven with the most burning anguish of spirit.

11. But the loving God, who is always near for all those calling upon him in true need, did not delay his answer to such pious pleas. He brought forth a wind out of his treasure-house and in the span of one day and one night he carried the wind-driven fleet on a favorable course with the entire number of ships and young women unharmed into the port called Tiel. They gained the shore as they had desired. Then Ursula, the female captain of so great a

[Fig. 46] St. Ursula depicted as the patron saint of young girls, sheltering her virgins beneath her cloak and holding the arrow which caused her death (Hans Memling, reproduced in Jameson, *Sacred and Legendary Art*, 2, 511).

venture, led them in song. She was just like Miriam the prophetess after the escape from Pharaoh's army through the Red Sea. They sang an epithalamium of praise honoring their heavenly Bridegroom. Since it was an army of young women, their marriage song resounded not with clamorous noise but with the symphony of attuned hearts. This song of praise reached the ears of the Lord with the scent of sweetness. After they had spent the night in that place, the young women bought some utensils the next day, for Tiel had a market fair. Then they returned to their ships and, weighing anchor, they rowed upstream and finally arrived at Cologne, that well-known city of Germania, where their bodies now rest in peace.

12. Once they had landed they ate their evening meal and, since they were weary from their day's labor, sleep crept over them. Then the most holy virgin Ursula, who already was pleasing to God because she had embraced angelic chastity, saw in her sleep a man with the radiance and authority of an angel. Standing beside her, he first asked Ursula whether she were keeping vigil through the night. The young woman was terrified at his sudden appearance, in the way a girl might be. So he checked her fear gently, saying, "Daughter, know that you will arrive in Rome, just as you have greatly desired, under the protection of the heavenly God, with this very sweet band of comrades, your sisters. After you have fulfilled your vows, you shall return again to this place in peace with the whole number of your companions. Here, I say to you, eternal rest has been predestined for you by God forever and ever. Here you will sleep in peace. And because you have fought a good fight, you have finished your course, you have kept the faith; as to the rest, a crown of justice awaits you. And in order to receive fully this crown from the just Judge, you shall yield your necks to your persecutors in testimony of your faith. After you have laid down the corruptible burden of your bodies in this place, you will attain to the heavenly bridal chamber with the glory of martyrdom." After he had said these things, the man disappeared.

13. The holy virgin Ursula doubted nothing about an oracle of such great authority. As soon as day returned to the earth, she called together her band of young women and poured into their ears all that she had seen and heard. When they had heard these things, there was general exultation because they had been accounted worthy to suffer violence for the name of Jesus. After they had offered up their praises to God, they decided with singleminded determination to complete their journey more swiftly, for they plainly desired to be set free from their bodies and to be with Christ. So as not to cause any delay in realizing the destiny God had chosen for them, they sailed with a favorable wind, disembarked at Basel, left their ships there, and journeyed on foot to Rome.

In Rome they spent several days visiting everywhere the various shrines dedicated to the saints. Keeping vigil, they commended their souls to God in prayer and, with tears, they composed their inner selves, as if they were already about to proceed quite eagerly to the banqueting hall of the eternal King. Finally, when they had fulfilled their vows, they returned to Basel on the same route by which they had come. Boarding their ships, they sailed down the Rhine with their hulls riding the current. Armed in spirit, strengthening themselves as much against spiritual iniquities as against all the oppressions of persecution, at last they landed at Cologne.

The Martyrdom of the Eleven Thousand Holy Virgins.

3, 14. At that time the barbarian tribe of the Huns had come to Cologne, their presence compelled by the sins of humankind. They had already laid waste with slaughter and fire the lands of the Gauls, as well as of Germany and Italy, so that cities were destroyed, churches were burned, and scarcely the slightest traces of divine religion were left. Although at this very moment the same barbarians, with their inborn ferocity, had even surrounded the city of Cologne in a tight siege, the news had not yet reached the young women arriving there. Because they were already acquainted with the civility of the inhabitants, it was without any kind of suspicion that the young women stepped out onto the land. And see! When the barbarians had learned of the virgins by sending out the swiftest running scouts according to their custom, they suddenly burst upon the young women with a great outcry. Just like wolves descending upon a sheepfold, they slew that infinite multitude with inhuman cruelty.

15. Slaughtering all the young women in their path with bestial frenzy, the henchmen of death made their way to St. Ursula. Moved by her marvelous beauty, they restrained both their hands and their purpose. Then the prince who commanded their heinous crimes, in a fever of lust as if struck by a thunderbolt, put aside his harshness a little and began to condescend to flattery and words of love. "Truly, your beauty," he said, "gives strong outward evidence that you are a girl born of a noble and great parentage." And he swore to her, saying, "If you had come forward earlier to intercede with me, you would not have suffered the loss of a single one of the women in your company. But be consoled and rejoice in your fate, beloved. Do not mourn the death of your young women, for I find you worthy of deserving me — the victor over all Europe, the man before whom even the Roman Empire quakes with fear — as a husband."

But the virgin, thinking on the things of the Lord, scornfully pushed aside this kind of a spouse with the most unrestrained indignation of voice and manner, as if he were the Prince of Darkness. His barbaric mind welled with rage and he bellowed like a wild beast. Not tolerating her refusal, he pronounced the sentence of death upon the blessed virgin, who already longed to be set free from her body and to be with Christ. And so St. Ursula, the queen of the most radiant army, pierced through by the shot of an arrow, sank upon the noble heap of her followers like a heavenly pearl.

She was purified by the royal purple of her own blood as if she had been baptized again. With all her victorious troops she ascended, crowned with laurels, to the celestial palace. For she had faithfully fulfilled in her flesh the suffering still to be undergone by Christ. And so Ursula, that wondrous flower vase of the Lord, was now completed to perfection. Not only did the vase gleam whitely with the lilies of virginity, but it was also adorned with just as many roses of martyrdom. By this means, she reddened more seemingly before the eyes of the lofty Examiner.

16. Now, let some people mislead others and be misled themselves, those who are stupefied by worldly vainglory, who extol the triumphs of their kings with infinite praises as if to the skies. They write this and that about the glory of war: vanquished kings who walk before the chariot, innumerable herds of captives being driven on like cattle, and, furthermore, victorious soldiers shining with weapons and armor of many colors, each one flaunting his military emblems, and the leaders themselves sitting high in golden four-horsed chariots, glittering with golden cloaks. Let them add other things if they wish: a festive day for the city, the joy of proud senators, the shouts of the crowd, and the dancing of the people. But if these things were wisely compared with the triumph of Ursula and her comrades they would have to be called misery rather than glory. For those who are adorned in their royal purple and gold have descended to shadows and eternal torments; whereas these holy virgins, clothed in the vestments of immortality, enjoy the vision of the Lord and the company of angels.

See! According to the voice of the Lord, the fertile earth patiently brought forth a yield which was at once sixty times and a hundred times that of the seed which had been sown. And these virgins at the appointed time went away, they went away weeping as they sowed their seeds, but now coming back, they came back singing, bearing their sheaves. Yes, they even went so far as to lay down the chaff of their bodies before they carried the threshed and well-sifted wheat into God's granary.

Oh, what dancing there was in heaven on this day, and what a gathering of the citizenry of the skies! And besides, what a rejoicing of the apostles! How harmonious the glory of the martyrs and holy virgins exulting in the increase of their order! How pious the thanks of the patriarchs, prophets, and confessors at the time when the souls of the holy virgins earned the right to be made sharers in rejoicing in the presence of our Lord Jesus Christ, who lives and reigns, world without end. Amen.

And so that the people of the blessed city of Cologne – made more blessed by this incomparable treasure – might know how much honor and reverence they forever owed to the virgins' most sacred ashes, they realized when they gained their liberation how precious was the death of the virgins in the sight of the Lord. The people learned how magnificently the blessed virgins were living in the council of the saints, they whose bodies – some lying unclothed – had been so potent. For after the bestial savagery of the Huns had completed their slaughter, God brewed a cup of wrath, confusion, and insanity for these would-be torturers. They were given over to a false perception – they believed they saw as many battle lines of armed soldiers pursuing them as the bodies of the virgins they had slain. And that fierce barbarian horde, accustomed to victory, did not know how to flee, nor did they dare to make a stand.

When the enemies of peace had fled therefore, and peace had been unexpectedly restored to the besieged citizenry, these citizens of Cologne were freed from their long struggle. They burst through the city gates. And see! Everywhere they found the unburied corpses of the virgins on the bare ground. Nor did this discovery deceive them for long. On the contrary, they recognized the clothing, features, and ships of the holy young women who had already passed this way before. They readily understood that the virgins devoted to God had fallen in the agony of martyrdom for the seal of chastity they had determined to preserve. These citizens of Cologne further understood that through the merits of their protectors they had escaped not only death but also barbaric tortures which are harsher than every kind of death. With a single mind, reverencing them not as if they were human but as if they were God in human bodies, they spared neither private nor public expense. They busied themselves, each one, undertaking the task not only with the duty of humanity, but with the zeal of most humble veneration. Some gathered up the scattered and lacerated limbs of the martyrs, some covered them with clothing, some dug the earth, others placed the bodies in sarcophagi. Within a short time, just as may be seen there today, the most holy relics of the virgins rested in peace to the eternal glory of Cologne.

18. From this time divine religion was already growing in Cologne. A custom arose among the people that eventually became a solemn obligation, namely that within the precinct of the virgins' burial place, no one up to this day may bury a body of any dead person.

After a certain length of time had passed, a religious man by the name of Clematius who had been frequently exhorted by God and summoned as if by an embassy of the holy virgins, arrived from eastern lands; in fulfilment of his vow he completed the building of a church, from its foundations, over the most holy ashes in honor of the holy virgins. Therefore, Cologne, praise the Lord, for he has strengthened the bolts of your gates and he has brought peace to your realm and, according to his promised pledge, he has blessed your children within you.

19. There was, however, in the same most sacred military comradeship of virgins a certain girl named Cordula. While the other young women met their deaths in the Passion of Christ, she alone went into hiding that same night in the hull of a solitary ship. The next day she bold-heartedly offered herself to the death she had fled, following the virgin hosts, gaining equal glory in martyrdom. But no one should be shocked at this, as if that blessed virgin had in any way dishonored her crown because of her paltry fear. Neither Peter in his denial nor Thomas in his doubting was driven from the honor of apostleship. For Peter, who through God's will would become a great benefit to the Church, had confidence in himself as a man and asserted that he would die together with his Master. But he became greatly alarmed for his own safety when he heard the insinuation of the maidservant who was the doorkeeper. Yet afterwards he persevered all the way to his own crucifixion, nor did he tremble even before the ruler of the city of Rome.

Perhaps that blessed virgin too, presuming on the purity of her earlier life and on the constancy of her faith, had some confidence in her ability to endure martyrdom. For that reason she had to be humbled so that she might learn to take pride not in herself but in the Lord and, thus humbled, might pass over more gloriously to her heavenly bridal chamber. In the same way faithful David, although he said to the Lord, "I have sworn and am determined to keep the judgments of your justice," soon made a substitution, as if he had relapsed, saying: "I have been afflicted in every way."

Nor should infirm limbs despair of health, if ever in a crisis of suffering they may gradually grow feeble because of human frailty. For the very Mediator between God and men, when taking on the role of those who are weak, said, "My soul is sorrowful to the point of death. Father, if it may be, let this chalice pass from me." So you see, he who had the power of laying down his own life and taking it up again yet desired that the chalice of his Passion might pass from him. There was never any time when the Son might not be harkened to by the Father, but the head was speaking for the feeble limbs, whose role he then had taken upon himself.

Perhaps that heavenly Gardener wished to prune the fruit-bearing branch so that it might bear more fruit. It is the same thing with some statuette that is very finely wrought by the sculptor's skill. The artist contemplates it and files it smooth so that what pleases the eyes of other people may not in any way displease his own eyes. But who has known the mind of the Lord? For this reason it serves no useful purpose to probe God's hidden judgments. As long as faith is sound, there is no danger in not understanding. Clearly it is agreed and always will be agreed that Cordula, the athlete of God, was delayed in order to be tested, not condemned.

20. Consequently, after a long succession of years had gone by, Cordula, the saint of whom we have spoken, appeared in a vision then to a certain recluse called Helmdrude, who was of unparalleled life and particular merit. Addressing Helmdrude as if she were her comrade-in-arms, Cordula asked whether she recognized her. But Helmdrude, although a holy woman and already close to God in spirit, was nonetheless still mortal. And as a mortal creature unable to endure an immortal presence, she shuddered at this personage of divine elegance and authority. For this was a virgin of God, marvelously attired beyond all human skill and she wore on her head a crown interwoven with lilies and roses.

Then Helmdrude, God's handmaid, recovering from her sudden fear, replied that she was unworthy of the recognition of such a great majesty. "For I am still under the dominion of the laws of carnal sin," she said. "But you have already been received into the rank of heaven-dwellers and are a stranger to all fleshly corruption." Then Cordula said, "Know that I was one of the sacred number of the virgins of Cologne. After they triumphed I lived one night longer, but the next day I was eager for death and offered myself of my own accord to those butchers. In that way I died in Christ. I did not desert my sisters, nor did I lose my share in their crown of martyrdom. But although all Cologne now observes with due worship the day of their most glorious death, not even a brief testimony of any kind has yet been made to my name. That is why I come now and impose this task upon you. You must on my behalf inform the nuns who devoutly keep vigil at the burial place of our bodies that when they celebrate the triumphal glory of my sisters, they should also pay me some kind of veneration the very next day. For it affords your sisters little profit that among all those who sleep in that place there should be no reverence for my name alone."

And when Helmdrude inquired what her name was, she was commanded by the virgin to gaze upon her forehead, so that Helmdrude might know for herself, without any doubt, the name she would find inscribed there. Helmdrude complied. She saw and read the separate syllables and discovered what was distinctly written there: Cordula.

21. Helmdrude, God's handmaid, thereupon reported the heavenly dream to the nuns, and it was believed. From then on the custom was established that while the feast of the holy virgins took place the day before, the following day would be devoted to the praises of St. Cordula. But Helmdrude's vision should not be considered by anyone to have a lesser authority, nor should it seem that she had been deluded in a mocking dream. This should be recalled to memory: Peter also while asleep saw in a vessel God's invitation to the Gentiles. And Paul did not doubt that he heard a man from Macedonia calling him into Illyria. And our patriachs, Abraham of course, Isaac, and Jacob, Joseph as well, Gideon and Daniel, saw many great secrets of the heavenly mysteries. The Magi too were instructed while sleeping about the change in their return route. And Joseph, the very foster-father of the Lord, was warned in a dream by an angel to flee into Egypt, and when the persecutors of Christ had died, he was advised to withdraw to Nazareth for fear of Archaelaus, and to dwell there.

(But why are these declarations necessary, when the handmaid of God, to whom this revelation was shown, was so renowned in her life, and of such saintly conduct that she herself had to be considered as the most certain testimony of the truth? For there is a place in Saxony called Heerse, where to this day resides a glorious community of nuns. There that holy woman was born and nurtured. There, with the course of her most holy life complete, her body now rests in peace, although she spent some of her last years in the same holiness on the mountain where the city of Iburg is located. To her way of life and sanctity, there are as many witnesses as there are nuns at Heerse today, or as there were in those days. And it is clear that these witnesses are most truthful since God has now confirmed the words of human beings. For to this day it is frequently reported that at her tomb sight is restored to the blind, the power of walking to the lame, the infirm are restored to the enjoyment of life, and the possessed are cleansed of impure spirits. For these reasons Helmdrude's testimony was reliable and it is impious to doubt that God deigned to unfold a revelation to the saint about the saint, to the bride about the bride, and to the beloved concerning his beloved.)

22. Therefore let the heavenly Jerusalem boast, and let the court of heaven boast, increased by so many worthy citizens, where there is neither slave nor free, male nor female. Let Britain boast, for even while begetting in the manner of Adam, she nevertheless teemed with her native yield of virgins. Let Germany boast, for she gathered in so many, the choicest flowers of the Ocean. Let Rome boast, for she returned the number of virgins that she had received. Let Cologne boast, for she has kept within herself such a treasure. Let your blessed community of nuns boast, entrusting your perpetual

salvation to the patronage and intercession of so many holy virgins served so devotedly. Blessed be the glory of the Lord in that heavenly place!

And you nuns, moreover, protectresses of so many celestial gems, busy yourselves especially in faithful obedience, so that even if you do not achieve a yield of a hundredfold or even sixtyfold, you may at least, in following their footsteps, gather the ears of grain of divine mercy. Let us all together very humbly entreat their most holy patronage and intercession. We do not dare to aspire nor are we able to attain a share in their glory, nevertheless, in my father's house there are many mansions. So through the merits of their just protection may we obtain citizenship in the heavenly Jerusalem, at least at the last Judgment, in the presence of Jesus Christ our Lord, who lives and reigns with the Father and the Holy Spirit, world without end. Amen. Hosanna signifies saving, that is, lead to salvation.

Here ends the Passion of the Eleven Thousand Holy Virgins.

45. FOUR 'LIVES' FROM *THE GOLDEN LEGEND*

The immensely popular and important collection of saints' lives known as the 'Leg-enda Aurea' ('The Golden Legend') was compiled about 1260 by Jacobus de Voragine, a native of Varazze in Italy and a Dominican who became archbishop of Genoa in 1292. It is a compilation of many hagiographical writings in Latin, probably intended as a source book for clerics in search of material for sermons and readings for saints' days. The saints are those of the official church calendar and their 'lives' are organized according to the order of their feast days within the liturgical year, with additional material included for other major celebrations: Advent, the Annunciation, the Passion and Resurrection, the Ascension, and so forth. Jacobus's interests are doctrinal, and the legends as he retells them use narrative primarily to illustrate doctrine. His work became the major source of vernacular saints' accounts in the later Middle Ages and was one of the first works printed, in 1483, by William Caxton. Not all of the 'lives' in the 'The Golden Legend' are hagiographic romances. Many are legitimate retellings, representing the four traditional categories of saint: apostles, martyrs, confessors, and vir-gins. Nevertheless, the emphasis on the miraculous and the extraordinary made it diffi-cult for Roman Catholics to defend the collection at the time of the Reformation, and rendered it an easy object of attack by both Protestant and Catholic reformers. The excerpts reprinted here are examples of a large body of imaginative saints' 'lives' that circulated widely in the late Middle Ages. Two of the accounts ('Alexis' and 'Eustace') emphasize those aspects of domestic tragedy which particularly touched the sensibilities of ordinary Christians during this period, while Mary Magdalene was also well-known as a type of reformed sinner, giver of hope to other sinful Christians, and the embodiment of the contemplative life. 'James the Dismembered' is an extreme example of the violence that characterizes many of Jacobus's accounts, and of his incorporation of doctrine in a narrative apparently designed − at least in part − as an aid to memory.

Source: trans. William Granger Ryan, *Jacobus de Voragine: The Golden Legend. Readings on the Saints* (Princeton, N.J.: Princeton University Press, 1993), 1, 371-383 and 2, 266-271; repr. with permission.

Alexis (BHL 291)

The name Alexis is composed of *a,* which means much or very, and *lexis,* which means word. Alexis, therefore was very powerful in the word of God.

Alexis was the son of Euphemianus, a member of the highest Roman nobility who was in the first rank at the emperor's court. Three thousand slaves wearing golden girdles and silk clothing waited on him. As a high officer in the city Euphemianus was temperate in the exercise of his authority. Moreover, every day he had three tables set up in his house for the poor and for orphans, widows, and strangers in need. He himself served at these tables and did not until late in the evening take food in the fear of the Lord with other religious men. His wife, Aglaë, shared both his religious fervor and his attitude toward others. They were childless until in answer to their prayers the Lord granted them a son, after whose birth they agreed to live in chastity.

Their son was instructed in the liberal disciplines and made rapid strides in all the philosophic arts. When he was still a youth, a girl of the imperial household was chosen for him and the wedding was celebrated. On their wedding night, as he and his bride met in the silence and secret of their chamber, the saintly youth began to instruct his spouse in the fear of God and urged her to remain in the pure state of virginity. Then he gave her his gold ring and the cincture he wore around his waist, and said: "Take this and keep it as long as God pleases, and may the Lord be always between us!" Then he took some of his wealth and went to the coast, where he secretly boarded a ship and sailed to Laodicea, going from there to Edessa, a city in Syria, where an image of our Lord Jesus Christ on a fine cloth, an image no human hand had made, was preserved. Once in Edessa he distributed everything he had brought with him to the poor, put on ragged clothes, and began to sit with the other mendicants in the porch of the church of Mary the Mother of God. Of the alms he received he kept the bare minimum he needed to live on and gave the rest to the other poor people.

All this time his father, sorrowful and mourning over his son's departure, sent his slaves into every corner of the world to look for him. Some of them came to Edessa and were recognized by the son, but did not recognize him and gave alms to him as they did to the other beggars. He accepted the alms and gave thanks to God, saying: "I thank you, O Lord, that you have allowed me to receive an alms from my own slaves." The servants went home and reported to the father that they had not found his son anywhere. His mother, from the day of his departure, spread a sack on the floor of her bedchamber and lay awake at night, murmuring dolefully: "Here shall I stay always in sorrow until I recover my son." The young bride, too, said to her mother-in-law: "Until I hear from my sweet spouse, I shall stay with you, like a lonely turtledove."

When Alexis had spent seventeen years in God's service in the porch of the aforesaid church, the image of the Blessed Virgin that was in the church spoke to the watchman, saying: "Bring in the man of God, because he is worthy of the kingdom of heaven. The Spirit of God rests upon him, and his prayer rises like incense in the sight of God." But the watchman did not know who this man was, so the image spoke again: "The man who sits outside at the door, that's the one." The watchman hurried out and led Alexis into the church. When other people noticed this, they began to pay him reverence, so he left the place in order to escape human glory, went back to Laodicea, and took ship to go to Tarsus in Cilicia.

By God's dispensation the ship was driven by the wind into the port of Rome. When he became aware of this, Alexis said to himself: "I will go and stay unknown in my father's house and so will not be a burden to anyone else." Therefore he waited in the street as his father was on his way back from the palace surrounded by a number of suppliants, and called after him: "Servant of God, give orders that I, a pilgrim, be taken into your house, and that the crumbs from your table be given to me as food. And may the Lord deign to be merciful to you, too, who also are a pilgrim." When Euphemianus heard this, he thought lovingly of his son, gave orders that the stranger be welcomed, and designated a cubbyhole for him in the house. He also provided that the visitor should have food from the master's table, and appointed one slave to look after him. Alexis persevered in prayer and disciplined his body with fasting and vigils. The house servants made fun of him, spilled dirty water on his head, and plied him with insults, but he bore all this with unshaken patience.

For seventeen years Alexis lived unrecognized in his father's house. Then, knowing by the Spirit that the end of his days was near, he asked for paper and ink and wrote out a full account of his life. On a Sunday, after the celebration of Mass, a voice rang out in the church: "Come to me all you who labor and are burdened, and I will refresh you." All present were frightened and fell to their knees while the voice came again, saying: "Seek out the man of God, that he may pray for Rome!" They looked around but found no one, and a third time the voice sounded: "Look in the house of Euphemianus!" Euphemianus was questioned but said he did not know what this was all about. Then the emperors Arcadius and Honorius, in company with Pope Innocent, came to the house. The slave who took care of Alexis came to his master and said: "Could our stranger be the man you are looking for? He is a man of good life and great patience."

Euphemianus ran to the stranger's cubbyhole and found him dead, his face shining like the face of an angel. He tried to take the paper from the dead man's hand but could not. He went out therefore and came back with the emperors and the pope. They went in to the dead man and the emperor said: "Sinners though we are, we two rule the state, and with us is the pontiff who has pastoral care of the whole world. Therefore give us the paper you are holding, and let us see what is written on it." The pope then went up and took the script, which was relinquished readily, and had it read before

Euphemianus and a great crowd of people. The father, hearing what was read, was overwhelmed with grief; his strength deserted him and he fell down in a faint. When after a while he came to himself, he tore his garments and began to pull out his gray hair and beard, threw himself on his son's body, and cried out: "Woe is me, my son! Why have you saddened me this way? Why have you stricken me all these years with grief and lamentation? Woe, woe is me, I see you now, the staff of my old age, lying on a litter and not speaking to me! Alas, alas, what consolation will I ever find?"

The mother, hearing all this, came like a lioness breaking out of a net. Tearing her robes, her hair in wild disarray, she raised her eyes to heaven, then rushed to where her son lay; but such a crowd had gathered that she could not reach the holy body. She cried out: "Make way for me, you men, let me see my son, let me see my soul's consolation, the one who suckled at my breast!" And when she finally got to the body, she lay upon it and lamented: "Alas, my son, light of my eyes, why did you do this? Why have you treated us so cruelly? You saw your father and miserable me shedding tears, and did not make yourself known to us! Your servants hurt you and made sport of you, and you allowed it!" Again and again she prostrated herself upon the body, now spreading her arms over it, now feeling the angelic face with her hands and kissing it. "Weep with me, all of you here present," she cried, "because for seventeen years I had him here in my house and did not recognize him! Because he was my only son! Because even the slaves heaped contempt on him and dealt him blows! Woe is me! Who will give my eyes a fountain of tears, so that night and day I may pour out the sorrow that is in my soul?" The bereaved spouse also ran up weeping and saying: "Ah, woe, woe! Today I am left alone, have become a widow, have no one to gaze upon or lift my eyes to. Now my mirror is broken and my hope gone. Now begins the grieving that has no end!" And the people standing around heard all this and wept loud and long.

Now the pope and the emperors placed the body on a princely litter and went before it into the heart of the city. Announcement was made to the populace that the man of God whom the whole city had been seeking had been found. The people all ran to be near the saint. Any among them who were sick and touched the holy body were cured instantly, the blind received their sight, the possessed were delivered of the demons. Seeing these wonders, the emperors and the pope undertook to carry the bier themselves, in order that they too might be sanctified by the holy corpse. The crowds were so dense that the emperors gave orders to scatter gold and silver coins in the streets and squares, hoping that the common people would be drawn away by their love of money and would let the funeral procession get through to the church. The people, however, checked their greed and in ever greater numbers rushed to touch the saint's most sacred body; but the cortege finally succeeded in getting to the church of St. Benedict Martyr. There they worked continuously for seven days, praising God as they raised a monument adorned with gold, gems, and precious stones, and reverently laid the holy body to rest in it. From this monument emanated a fragrance so powerful that everybody thought the tomb was filled with perfumes.

Alexis died the seventeenth day of July about the year 398.

Mary Magdalene (BHL 5501)

The name Mary, or Maria, is interpreted as *amarum mare,* bitter sea, or as illuminator or illuminated. These three meanings are accepted as standing for three shares or parts, of which Mary made the best choices, namely, the part of penance, the part of inward contemplation, and the part of heavenly glory. This threefold share is what the Lord meant when he said: "Mary has chosen the best part, which shall not be taken away from her." The first part will not be taken away because of its end or purpose, which is the attainment of holiness.

The second part will not be taken because of its continuity: contemplation during the earthly journey will continue in heavenly contemplation. And the third part will remain because it is eternal. Therefore, since Mary chose the best part, namely, penance, she is called bitter sea because in her penances she endured much bitterness. We see this from the fact that she shed enough tears to bathe the Lord's feet with them. Since she chose the best part of inward contemplation, she is called enlightener, because in contemplation she drew draughts of light so deep that in turn she poured out light in abundance: in contemplation she received the light with which she afterwards enlightened others. As she chose the best part of heavenly glory, she is called illuminated, because she now is enlightened by the light of perfect knowledge in her mind and will be illumined by the light of glory in her body.

Mary is called Magdalene, which is understood to mean "remaining guilty," or it means armed, or unconquered, or magnificent. These meanings point to the sort of woman she was before, at the time of, and after her conversion. Before her conversion she remained in guilt, burdened with the debt of eternal punishment. In her conversion she was armed and rendered unconquerable by the armor of penance: she armed herself the best possible way – with all the weapons of penance – because for every pleasure she had enjoyed she found a way of immolating herself. After her conversion she was

[Fig. 47] The woman washing the feet of Christ in Luke 7:37-39 was, in the Middle Ages, identified as Mary Magdalene and was also often conflated with the woman from whom Christ cast out devils, the woman taken in adultery, and with Mary the sister of Martha and Lazarus. Gregory the Great supported this identification which is now rejected by the Roman Calendar (Baring-Gould, *Lives of the Saints,* 8).

magnificent in the superabundance of grace, because where trespass abounded, grace was super abundant.

Mary's cognomen "Magdalene" comes from Magdalum, the name of one of her ancestral properties. She was wellborn, descended of royal stock. Her father's name was Syrus, her mother was called Eucharia. With her brother Lazarus and her sister Martha she owned Magdalum, a walled town two miles from Genezareth, along with Bethany, not far from Jerusalem, and a considerable part of Jerusalem itself. They had, however, divided their holdings among themselves in such a way that Magdalum belonged to Mary (whence the name Magdalene), Lazarus kept the property in Jerusalem, and Bethany was Martha's. Magdalene gave herself totally to the pleasures of the flesh and Lazarus was devoted to the military, while prudent Martha kept close watch over her brother's and sister's estates and took care of the needs of her armed men, her servants, and the poor. After Christ's ascension, however, they all sold their possessions and laid the proceeds at the feet of the apostles.

Magdalene, then, was very rich, and sensuous pleasure keeps company with great wealth. Renowned as she was for her beauty and her riches, she was no less known for the way she gave her body to pleasure – so much so that her proper name was forgotten and she was commonly called "the sinner." Meanwhile, Christ was preaching here and there, and she, guided by the divine will, hastened to the house of Simon the leper, where, she had learned, he was at table. Being a sinner she did not dare mingle with the righteous, but stayed back and washed the Lord's feet with her tears, dried them with her hair, and anointed them with precious ointment. Because of the extreme heat of the sun the people of that region bathed and anointed themselves regularly.

Now Simon the Pharisee thought to himself that if this man were a prophet, he would never allow a sinful woman to touch him; but the Lord rebuked him for his proud righteousness and told the woman that all her sins were forgiven. This is the Magdalene upon whom Jesus conferred such great graces and to whom he showed so many marks of love. He cast seven devils out of her, set her totally afire with love of him, counted her among his closest familiars, was her guest, had her do the housekeeping on his travels, and kindly took her side at all times. He defended her when the Pharisee said she was unclean, when her sister implied that she was lazy, when Judas called her wasteful. Seeing her weep he could not contain his tears. For love of her he raised her brother, four days dead, to life, for love of her he freed her sister Martha from the issue of blood she had suffered for seven years, and in view of her merits he gave Martilla, her sister's handmaid, the privilege of calling out those memorable words: "Blessed is the womb that bore you!" Indeed, according to Ambrose, Martha was the woman with the issue of blood, and the woman who called out was Martha's servant. "She [Mary] it was, I say, who washed the Lord's feet with her tears, dried them with her hair and anointed them with ointment, who in the time of grace did solemn penance, who chose the best part, who sat at the Lord's feet and listened to his word, who anointed his head, who stood beside the Cross at his passion, who prepared the sweet spices with which to anoint his body, who, when the disciples left the tomb, did not go away, to whom the risen Christ first appeared, making her an apostle to the apostles."

Some fourteen years after the Lord's passion and ascension into heaven, when the Jews had long since killed Stephen and expelled the other disciples from the confines of Judea, the disciples went off into the lands of the various nations and there sowed the word of the Lord. With the apostles at the time was one of Christ's seventy-two disciples, blessed Maximin, to whose care blessed Peter had entrusted Mary Magdalene. In the dispersion

Maximin, Mary Magdalene, her brother Lazarus, her sister Martha, Martha's maid Martilla, blessed Cedonius, who was born blind and had been cured by the Lord, and many other Christians, were herded by the unbelievers into a ship without pilot or rudder and sent out to sea so that they might all be drowned, but by God's will they eventually landed at Marseilles. There they found no one willing to give them shelter, so they took refuge under the portico of a shrine belonging to the people of that area. When blessed Mary Magdalene saw the people gathering at the shrine to offer sacrifice to the idols, she came forward, her manner calm and her face serene, and with well-chosen words called them away from the cult of idols and preached Christ fervidly to them. All who heard her were in admiration at her beauty, her eloquence, and the sweetness of her message . . . and no wonder, that the mouth which had pressed such pious and beautiful kisses on the Savior's feet should breathe forth the perfume of the word of God more profusely than others could.

Then the governor of that province came with his wife to offer sacrifice and pray the gods for offspring. Magdalene preached Christ to him and dissuaded him from sacrificing. Some days later she appeared in a vision to the wife, saying: "Why, when you are so rich, do you allow the saints of God to die of hunger and cold?" She added the threat that if the lady did not persuade her husband to relieve the saints' needs, she might incur the wrath of God; but the woman was afraid to tell her spouse about the vision. The following night she saw the same vision and heard the same words, but again hesitated to tell her husband. The third time, in the silence of the dead of night, Mary Magdalene appeared to each of them, shaking with anger, her face afire as if the whole house were burning, and said: "So you sleep, tyrant, limb of your father Satan, with your viper of a wife who refused to tell you what I had said? You take your rest, you enemy of the Cross of Christ, your gluttony sated with a bellyful of all sorts of food while you let the saints of God perish from hunger and thirst? You lie here wrapped in silken sheets, after seeing those others homeless and desolate, and passing them by? Wicked man, you will not escape! You will not go unpunished for your long delay in giving them some help!" And, having said her say, she disappeared.

The lady awoke gasping and trembling, and spoke to her husband, who was in like distress: "My lord, have you had the dream that I just had?" "I saw it," he answered, "and I can't stop wondering and shaking with fear! What are we to do?" His wife said: "It will be better for us to give in to her than to face the wrath of her God whom she preaches." They therefore provided shelter for the Christians and supplied their needs. Then one day when Mary Magdalene was preaching, the aforesaid governor asked her: "Do you think

[Fig. 48] St. Mary Magdalene shown wearing a scarlet cloak; the long hair descending beneath it and the pot of ointment beside her symbolize her penitential ministrations to Christ, and the cave in which she stands recalls the medieval legend of her withdrawal from the world (from a painting by Timoteo della Vite, Jameson, *Sacred and Legendary Art,* 1, 359).

you can defend the faith you preach?" "I am ready indeed to defend it," she replied, "because my faith is strengthened by the daily miracles and preaching of my teacher Peter, who presides in Rome!" The governor and his wife then said to her: "See here, we are prepared to do whatever you tell us to if you can obtain a son for us from the God whom you preach." "In this he will not fail you," said Magdalene. Then the blessed Mary prayed the Lord to deign to grant them a son. The Lord heard her prayers and the woman conceived.

Now the husband began to want to go to Peter and find out whether what Magdalene preached about Christ was the truth. "What's this?" snapped his wife. "Are you thinking of going without me? Not a bit of it! You leave, I leave. You come back, I come back. You stay here, I stay here!" The man replied: "My dear, it can't be that way! You're pregnant and the perils of the sea are infinite. It's too risky. You will stay home and take care of what we have here!" But she insisted, doing as women do. She threw herself at his feet, weeping the while, and in the end won him over. Mary therefore put the sign of the cross on their shoulders as a protection against the ancient Enemy's interference on their journey. They stocked a ship with all the necessaries, leaving the rest of their possessions in the care of Mary Magdalene, and set sail.

A day and a night had not passed, however, when the wind rose and the sea became tumultuous. All aboard, and especially the expectant mother, were shaken and fearful as the waves battered the ship. Abruptly she went into labor, and, exhausted by her pangs and the buffeting of the storm, she expired as she brought forth her son. The newborn groped about seeking the comfort of his mother's breasts, and cried and whimpered piteously. Ah, what a pity! The infant is born, he lives, and has become his mother's killer! He may as well die, since there is no one to give him nourishment to keep him alive! What will the Pilgrim do, seeing his wife dead and the child whining plaintively as he seeks the maternal breast? His lamentations knew no bounds, and he said to himself: "Alas, what will you do? You yearned for a son, and you have lost the mother and the son too!"

The seamen meanwhile were shouting: "Throw that corpse overboard before we all perish! As long as it is with us, this storm will not let up!" They seized the body and were about to cast it into the sea, but the Pilgrim intervened. "Hold on a little!" he cried. "Even if you don't want to spare me or the mother, at least pity the poor weeping little one! Wait just a bit! Maybe the woman has only fainted with pain and may begin to breathe again!"

Now suddenly they saw a hilly coast not far off the bow, and the Pilgrim thought it would be better to put the dead body and the infant ashore there than to throw them as food to the sea monsters. His pleas and his bribes barely persuaded the crew to drop anchor there. Then he found the ground so hard that he could not dig a grave, so he spread his cloak in a fold of the hill, laid his wife's body on it, and placed the child with its head between the mother's breasts. Then he wept and said: "O Mary Magdalene, you brought ruin upon me when you landed at Marseilles! Unhappy me, that on your advice I set out on this journey! Did you not pray to God that my wife might conceive? Conceive she did, and suffered death giving birth, and the child she conceived was born only to die because there is no one to nurse him. Behold, this is what your prayer obtained for me. I commended my all to you and do commend me to your God. If it be in your power, be mindful of the mother's soul, and by your prayer take pity on the child and spare its life." Then he enfolded the body and the child in his cloak and went back aboard the ship.

When the Pilgrim arrived in Rome, Peter came to meet him and, seeing the sign of the cross on his shoulder, asked him who he was and where he came from. He told Peter all that had happened to him, and Peter responded: "Peace be with you! You have done well to trust the good advice you received. Do not take it amiss that your wife sleeps and the infant rests with her. It is in the Lord's power to give gifts to whom he will, to take away what was given, to restore what was taken away, and to turn your grief into joy."

Peter then took him to Jerusalem and showed him all the places where Christ had preached and performed miracles, as well as the place where he had suffered and the other from which he had ascended into heaven. Peter then gave him thorough instruction in the faith, and after two years had gone by, he boarded ship, being eager to get back to his homeland. By God's will, in the course of the voyage they came close to the hilly coast where he had left the body of his wife and his son, and with pleas and money he induced the crew to put him ashore. The little boy, whom Mary Magdalene had preserved unharmed, used to come down to the beach and play with the stones and pebbles, as children love to do. As the Pilgrim's skiff drew near to the land, he saw the child playing on the beach. He was dumbstruck at seeing his son alive and leapt ashore from the skiff. The child, who had never seen a man, was terrified at the sight and ran to his mother's bosom, taking cover under the familiar cloak. The Pilgrim, anxious to see what was happening, followed, and found the handsome child feeding at his mother's breast. He lifted the boy and said: "O Mary Magdalene, how happy I would be, how well everything would have turned out for me, if my wife were alive and able to return home with me! Indeed I know, I know and believe beyond a doubt, that having given us this child and kept him alive for two years on this rock, you could now, by your prayers, restore his mother to life and health."

As these words were spoken, the woman breathed and, as if waking from sleep, said: "Great is your merit, O blessed Mary Magdalene, and you are glorious! As I struggled to give birth, you did me a midwife's service and waited upon my every need like a faithful handmaid." Hearing this, the Pilgrim said: "My dear wife, are you alive?" "Indeed I am," she answered, "and am just coming from the pilgrimage from which you yourself are returning. And as blessed Peter conducted you to Jerusalem and showed you all the places where Christ suffered, died, and was buried, and many other places, I, with blessed Mary Magdalene as my guide and companion, was with you and committed all you saw to memory." Whereupon she recited all the places where Christ had suffered, and fully explained the miracles and all she had seen, not missing a single thing.

Now the Pilgrim, having got back his wife and child, joyfully took ship and in a short time made port at Marseilles. Going into the city they found blessed Mary Magdalene with her disciples, preaching. Weeping with joy, they threw themselves at her feet and related all that had happened to them, then received holy baptism from blessed Maximin. Afterwards they destroyed the temples of all the idols in the city of Marseilles and built churches to Christ. They also elected blessed Lazarus as bishop of the city. Later by the will of God they went to the city of Aix, and, by many miracles, led the people there to accept the Christian faith. Blessed Maximin was ordained bishop of Aix.

At this time blessed Mary Magdalene, wishing to devote herself to heavenly contemplation, retired to an empty wilderness, and lived unknown for thirty years in a place made ready by the hands of angels. There were no streams of water there, nor the comfort of grass or trees: thus it was made clear that our Redeemer had determined to fill her not with earthly viands but only with the good things of heaven. Every day at the seven canonical hours she was carried aloft by angels and with her bodily ears heard the glorious chants of the celestial hosts. So it was that day by day she was gratified with these supernal delights and, being conveyed back to her own place by the same angels, needed no material nourishment.

There was a priest who wanted to live a solitary life and built himself a cell a few miles from the Magdalene's habitat. One day the Lord opened this priest's eyes, and with his own eyes he saw how the angels descended to the already mentioned place where blessed Mary Magdalene dwelt, and how they lifted her into the upper air and an hour later brought her back to her place with divine praises. Wanting to learn the truth about this wondrous vision and commending himself prayerfully to his Creator, he hurried with daring and devotion toward the aforesaid place; but when he was a stone's throw from the spot, his knees began to wobble, and he was so frightened that he could hardly breathe. When he started to go away, his legs and feet responded, but every time he turned around and tried to reach the desired spot, his body went limp and his mind went blank, and he could not move forward.

So the man of God realized that there was a heavenly secret here to which human experience alone could have no access. He therefore invoked his Savior's name and called out: "I adjure you by the Lord, that if you are a human being or any rational creature living in that cave, you answer me and tell me the truth about yourself!" When he had repeated this three times, blessed Mary Magdalene answered him: "Come closer, and you can learn the truth about whatever your soul desires." Trembling, he had gone halfway across the intervening space when she said to him: "Do you remember what the Gospel says about Mary the notorious sinner, who washed the Savior's feet with her tears and dried them with her hair, and earned forgiveness for all her misdeeds?" "I do remember," the priest replied, "and more than thirty years have gone by since then. Holy Church also believes and confesses what you have said about her." "I am that woman," she said. "For the space of thirty years I have lived here unknown to everyone; and as you were allowed to see yesterday, every day I am borne aloft seven times by angelic hands, and have been found worthy to hear with the ears of my body the joyful jubilation of the heavenly hosts. Now, because it has been revealed to me by the Lord that I am soon to depart from this world, please go to blessed Maximin and take care to inform him that next year, on the day of the Lord's resurrection, at the time when he regularly rises for matins, he is to go alone to his church, and there he will find me present and waited upon by angels." To the priest the voice sounded like the voice of an angel, but he saw no one.

The good man hurried to blessed Maximin and carried out his errand. St. Maximin, overjoyed, gave great thanks to the Savior, and on the appointed day, at the appointed hour, went alone into the church and saw blessed Mary Magdalene amidst the choir of angels who had brought her there. She was raised up a distance of two cubits above the floor, standing among the angels and lifting her hands in prayer to God. When blessed Maximin hesitated about approaching her, she turned to him and said: "Come closer, father, and do not back away from your daughter." When he drew near to her, as we read in blessed Maximin's own books, the lady's countenance was so radiant, due to her continuous and daily vision of the angels, that one would more easily look straight into the sun than gaze upon her face.

All the clergy, including the priest already mentioned, were now called together, and blessed Mary Magdalene, shedding tears of joy, received the Lord's Body and Blood from the bishop. Then she lay down full length before the steps of the altar, and her most holy soul migrated to the Lord. After she expired, so powerful an odor of sweetness pervaded the church that for seven days all those who entered there noticed it. Blessed Maximin embalmed her holy body with aromatic lotions and gave it honorable burial, giving orders that after his death he was to be buried close to her.

Hegesippus [a second-century Greek Christian writer] (or, as some books have it, Josephus [a first-century Jewish historian]) agrees in the main with the story just told. He says in one of his treatises that after Christ's ascension Mary Magdalene, weary of the world and moved by her ardent love of the Lord, never wanted to see anyone. After she came to Aix, she went off into the desert, lived there unknown for thirty years, and every day at the seven canonical hours was carried up to heaven by an angel. He added, however, that the priest who went to her found her closed up in a cell. At her request he reached out a garment to her, and when she had put it on, she went with him to the church, received communion there, and, raising her hands in prayer beside the altar, died in peace.

In Charlemagne's time, namely, in the year of the Lord 769, Gerard, duke of Burgundy, being unable to have a son of his wife, openhandedly gave away his wealth to the poor and built many churches and monasteries. When he had built the monastery at Vézelay [site of the great twelfth-century Benedictine abbey and church named after Mary Magdalene, a major center for her cult] he and the abbot sent a monk, with a suitable company, to the city of Aix in order to bring back the relics of St. Mary Magdalene, if possible. When the monk arrived at the aforesaid city, however, he found that it had been razed to the ground by the pagans. Yet by chance he discovered a marble sarcophagus with an inscription which indicated that the body of blessed Mary Magdalene was contained inside, and her whole story was beautifully carved on the outside. The monk therefore broke into the sarcophagus by night, gathered the relics, and carried them to his inn. That same night blessed Mary appeared to him and told him not to be afraid but to go on with the work he had begun. On their way back to Vézelay the company, when they were half a league from their monastery, could not move the relics another step until the abbot and his monks came in solemn procession to receive them.

A certain knight, whose practice it was to visit the relics of St. Mary Magdalene every year, was killed in battle. As he lay dead on his bier, his parents, mourning him, made pious complaint to the Magdalene because she had

[Fig. 49] The translation of Mary Magdalene's body to her church at Vézelay, the center of her cult and an important place of pilgrimage, depicted in a fifteenth-century ms, the *Chroniques de Hainault* (Lacroix, *Military and Religious Life in the Middle Ages,* p. 387).

allowed her devotee to die without making confession and doing penance. Then suddenly, to the amazement of all present, the dead man rose up and called for a priest. He made his confession devoutly and received viaticum [the eucharist], then returned to rest in peace.

A ship crowded with men and women was sinking, and one woman, who was pregnant and saw herself in danger of drowning, called upon Magdalene as loudly as she could, and vowed that if by Mary's merits she escaped death and bore a son, she would give him up to the saint's monastery. At once a woman of venerable visage and bearing appeared to her, held her up by the chin, and, while the rest drowned, brought her unharmed to land. The woman in due time gave birth to a son and faithfully fulfilled her vow.

There are some who say that Mary Magdalene was espoused to John the Evangelist, who was about to take her as his wife when Christ called him away from his nuptials, whereupon she, indignant at having been deprived of her spouse, gave herself up to every sort of voluptuousness. But, since it would not do to have John's vocation the occasion of Mary's damnation, the Lord mercifully brought her around to conversion and penance; and, because she had had to forgo the heights of carnal enjoyment, he filled her more than others with the most intense spiritual delight, which consists in the love of God. And there are those who allege that Christ honored John with special evidences of his affection because he had taken him away from the aforesaid pleasure. These tales are to be considered false and frivolous. Brother Albert [St. Albert the Great, 1206-1280] in his introduction to the Gospel of John, says firmly that the lady from whose nuptials the same John was called away persevered in virginity, was seen later in the company of the Blessed Virgin Mary, mother of Christ, and came at last to a holy end.

A man who had lost his eyesight was on his way to the monastery at Vézelay to visit Mary Magdalene's body when his guide told him that he, the guide, could already see the church in the distance. The blind man exclaimed in a loud voice: "O holy Mary Magdalene, if only I could sometime be worthy to see your church!" At once his eyes were opened.

There was a man who wrote a list of his sins on a sheet of paper and put it under the rug on the Magdalene's altar, asking her to pray that he might be pardoned. Later he recovered the paper and found that his sins had been wiped out.

A man who lay in chains for having committed the crime of extortion called upon Mary Magdalene to come to his aid, and one night a beautiful woman appeared to him, broke his fetters, and ordered him to be off. Seeing himself unshackled, he got away as fast as possible.

A clerk from Flanders, Stephen by name, had fallen into such a welter of sinfulness that, having committed every sort of evil, he could do no works of salvation nor even bear to hear of them. Yet he had deep devotion to blessed Mary Magdalene, observed her vigils by fasting, and celebrated her feast day. Once when he was on a visit to her tomb and was half asleep and half awake, Mary Magdalene appeared to him as a lovely, sad-eyed woman supported by two angels, one on either side, and she said to him: "Stephen, I ask you, why do you repay me with deeds unworthy of my deserts? Why are you not moved with compunction by what my own lips insistently say? From the time when you began to be devoted to me I have always prayed the Lord urgently for you. Get up, then! Repent! I will never leave you until you are reconciled with God!" The clerk soon felt so great an inpouring of grace in himself that he renounced the world, entered the religious life, and lived a very holy life thereafter. At his death Mary Magdalene was seen standing with angels beside the bier, and she carried his soul, like a pure-white dove, with songs of praise into heaven.

Eustace, also known as Placidus (BHL 2762)

Eustace was first called Placidus. He was the commanding general of
Emperor Trajan's armies. Though a worshiper of idols, he was assiduous in
doing works of mercy, and his wife was his partner both in worship and in
good works. They had two sons, and their father saw to it that the boys were
trained in a manner befitting their high station.

Placidus's constant care for those in need merited him the light of grace
that led him to the way of truth. One day while he was hunting, he came
upon a herd of deer, among which one stag stood out by his size and beauty,
and this deer broke away from the others and bounded into a deeper part of
the forest. Leaving his soldiers to follow the rest of the herd, Placidus gave his
full effort to pursuing the stag and did his best to catch it. The deer kept well
ahead of him, however, and finally stopped at the top of a high peak.
Placidus, coming near, pondered how he might capture the animal. As he
studied it, he saw between its antlers what looked like the holy cross, shining
more brightly than the sun. Upon the cross was the image of Jesus Christ.
Christ then spoke to Placidus through the stag's mouth, as once he had spoken through the mouth of Balaam's ass [in *Num.* 22-24, Balaam was rebuked
by his ass for being about to curse the Israelites]. The Lord said: "O Placidus,
why are you pursuing me? For your sake I have appeared to you in this animal. I am Christ whom you worship without knowing it. Your alms have
risen before me, and for this purpose I have come, that through this deer
which you hunted, I myself might hunt you!" There are others, however,
who say that these words were pronounced by the image which appeared
between the stag's antlers.

Having heard what was said, Placidus was stricken with fear and fell from
his horse. After an hour, however, he came to himself, rose from the ground,
and said: "Let me understand what you were saying, and I will believe you."
The Lord said: "I am Christ. I created heaven and earth. I made light to rise
and be separate from darkness. I set seasons and days and years. I formed man
from the slime of the earth. For the salvation of the human race I took flesh
and appeared on earth. I was crucified and buried, and on the third day I
rose from the dead." Placidus, having heard these words, again fell to the
ground and said: "Lord, I believe that you ARE, that you have made all
things, that you convert the erring." The Lord said to him: "If you believe, go
to the bishop of the city and have him baptize you." "Lord," said Placidus,
"do you want me to make all this known to my wife and my sons, so that
they also may believe in you?" "Yes," said the Lord. "Tell them, and let them
be cleansed with you. Then you yourself come here tomorrow morning, and

ΟΛΣ. ΕΥΣΤΑCΙΟΣ.

[Fig. 50] St. Eustace shown in Roman soldier's dress with the stag holding the form of a crucifix in its antlers, by Domenichino (1581-1641). The story of Eustace's conversion through his encounter with the miraculous stag found its way into the legend of St. Hubert whose iconography is similar (Jameson, *Sacred and Legendary Art,* 2, 794).

I will appear to you again and tell you more fully what the future holds for you."

Placidus went home, found his wife in bed, and began to tell her what he had to tell, but she burst out, saying: "My master, I too saw him this past night, and he said to me: 'Tomorrow you and your husband and your sons will come to me!' So now I too know that he is Jesus the Christ!" And right then, in the middle of the night, they went to the bishop of Rome. He baptized them with great joy, giving Placidus the name Eustace and his wife the name Theospis, and called his sons Agapetus and Theospitus.

Morning came, and Eustace, as he had done before, set out for the hunt. Coming near to the place he knew, he dismissed his soldiers on the pretext that their task was to pick up the tracks of some game. Then, standing in the same place, he saw the same vision as before and, prostrating himself on the ground, said: "I implore you, Lord, show your servant what you promised to show him!" The Lord: "Blessed are you, Eustace, for accepting the bath of my grace, because now you have overcome the devil! Now you have trampled on the one who had deceived you! Now your faith will be seen! The devil, because you have left him, will fight furiously against you. You will have to bear many hardships in order to receive the crown of victory. You will have to suffer much, in order to be brought low from the lofty vanity of the world and be exalted again in the riches of the spirit. Do not lose courage, nor look back upon your former eminence, because, through your trials, you are to become another Job. But when you have been humbled, I will come to you and restore you to your erstwhile glory. Tell me, therefore! Do you wish to endure trials now or at your life's end?"

Eustace gave his answer: "Lord, if so it is to be, order the trials to befall us now, but grant us the patience to bear them!" The Lord: "Be of good heart! My grace will guard your souls." Then the Lord ascended to heaven, and Eustace went home and told all to his wife.

Within a few days a lethal plague gripped the men and women who served in his house and killed them all, and not long afterwards his horses and herds perished. Then some lawless men, seeing him despoiled and desolate, broke into his house at night, laid hands on everything they found, and robbed him of his gold and silver and all his goods. Eustace gave thanks to God and, having nothing left, fled by night with his wife and sons: dreading the shame of destitution, they decided to go to Egypt. The king and all the senators were shocked at the loss of their commander-in-chief, especially since they could find no equal to replace him.

The fugitives made their way to the sea, boarded a ship, and sailed away. Eustace's wife was a beautiful woman, and the ship's captain lusted after her.

When it was time to pay their passage and they had nothing to pay it with, the captain commanded that the woman be held on board. He intended to make her his own, but Eustace absolutely refused to agree. When he persisted in his refusal, the master gave his crew the idea of throwing Eustace overboard so that they could have his wife; and Eustace, unable to resist further, sadly left her to them and went ashore with his sons. Weeping, he said to the boys: "Woe to me, woe to you, that your mother is given over to a man who is not of our race!"

They came to a river in flood, and the father did not dare attempt to cross with the two boys at the same time, so he left one and carried the other across. But the river was over its banks, so Eustace put ashore the boy he was carrying and started back to rescue the other. As he reached the middle of the stream, a wolf ran out, snatched the boy his father had just put ashore, and disappeared into the forest. Eustace, despairing of this child, turned again to go to the other one, but a lion came and carried the boy away. Unable to go after either son, since he was out in the middle of the river, the father began to mourn and tear his hair, and might have abandoned himself to the waters had not divine providence restrained him.

Meanwhile some shepherds saw the lion carrying the boy off alive and went after him with their dogs. By God's will the beast dropped the child unhurt and got away. On the other side of the river huntsmen raised the hue and cry in pursuit of the wolf, and freed the boy, unharmed, from the animal's jaws. As it happened, the huntsmen and the shepherds were of the same village, and they kept the boys with them and took care of them.

Eustace, however, did not know that this had happened, and went his way weeping and saying: "Alas, alas! Once I flourished like a tree, but now I an almost leafless! Woe is me! Once I was surrounded by a multitude of soldiers, but now I am left alone, and even the company of my sons is denied me! I remember, Lord, that you told me it was my lot to be tried as Job was tried, but it seems to me that even more ills have come to me than to him. Even if he was stripped of his possessions, he could at least have dung to sit on, but I have not even that! He had his friends to share his misery, but I have only the fierce beasts that stole my sons. Job's wife was left to him, I am bereft of mine. Give pause, O Lord, to my tribulations, and set a guard over my mouth, lest my heart incline to evil words, and I be cast out of they sight!" He went on and came to a certain village, where he stayed and, for a pittance, watched over the fields of those men for fifteen years, while in the next village his sons were growing up and did not even know that they were brothers. The Lord also kept Eustace's wife in his care. The ship's captain, that foreigner, never took her to wife but died leaving her untouched.

In those years the emperor and the Roman people were constantly harassed by enemies. The emperor remembered Placidus, who had fought so valiantly against those same foes, and was saddened to think of the sudden change that had overtaken his general. So he sent many soldiers to different parts of the world, promising wealth and honors to those who would find Placidus. Two men who had served under the former commander came to the village where he was living. Eustace saw them coming across the field, recognized them by their gait, and was disturbed by the memory of his own former high status. He said to the Lord: "Lord, I see these men who were with me, whom I had not hoped ever to see again! Please grant that I may again see my wife! I cannot ask for my sons, because they were eaten by wild beasts." And a voice came to him, saying: "Have confidence, Eustace, because you will soon have back your high honors, and your sons and your wife will be returned to you!"

He went to meet the two soldiers, who did not recognize him at all. They greeted him and asked if he knew a stranger whose name was Placidus and who had a wife and two sons. He professed not to know them. He invited the soldiers, however, to be his guests and waited on them. Then, recalling his former rank, he could not contain his tears, but went outside and washed his face before returning to serve them. Meanwhile the two men looked at each other questioningly, and one said: "Doesn't that man look a lot like the one we're looking for?" "He certainly does," the other said. "We'll watch closely, and if he has a scar on his head like the one our general had, he's the one!" They looked and saw the scar, and knew that Eustace was the man they were looking for, so they jumped up and embraced him and asked about his wife and children. He told them that his sons were dead and his wife in captivity. Then the neighbors hurried in as though to enjoy a bit of theater, and the soldiers boasted about their general's prowess and the glory that had been his. They also informed him of the emperor's order and clothed him in fine garments.

A fifteen-days' journey brought them back to Rome, and the emperor, learning that Eustace was approaching, hurried to meet him and embraced him warmly. He told them all that had happened to him, and they took him immediately to military headquarters and ordered him to take charge. He surveyed his forces and found that they were far fewer in number than he needed in order to face so many foes, so he ordered recruits to be called up from every city and village. Thus it happened that the place where the two sons had grown up was called upon to furnish two recruits. The local people considered the two young men to be the most fitted for military service, and sent them up. Eustace was very pleased to see these two physically robust and morally upright candidates, and assigned them to places in his immediate circle. Off they went to war and won a great victory, and Eustace granted the troops three days of rest in a place where, though he did not know this, his wife kept a modest inn. By God's will the two youths were quartered in this inn, but they were not aware that their hostess was also their mother.

Around midday the two were lounging outside and chatting about their early years, while the mother, seated at a little distance, listened intently. The older son said to the younger: "I can't remember anything about my childhood, except that my father was the commander of the armies, and my mother was a very beautiful woman. They had two sons, me and a younger one – he was very handsome too – and our parents took us one night and we boarded a ship going I don't know where. When we got off the ship, our mother stayed on board, I don't know why. Our father was crying as he carried the two of us and came to a river, which he crossed carrying my younger brother, leaving me behind on the riverbank. When he was on his way back to get me, a wolf came and ran off with my brother, and, before my father could reach me, a lion came out of the forest, seized me, and dragged me into the woods. Sheepherders snatched me from the lion's mouth and brought me up on their own land, as you know. I never could find out what became of my father and the boy." Hearing all this, the younger brother began to weep, and said: "By God, from what I hear, I am your brother, because the men who brought me up said the same thing – that they had snatched me from a wolf!" So they fell into each other's arms, and kissed, and wept.

The mother, having heard the story as the older son told it, spent hours wondering whether these could be her sons. The next day she went to the commander and questioned him, saying: "I beg of you, my lord, to order me returned to my native land, because I am a Roman and therefore a foreigner here." As she spoke to the commander, she noticed certain distinguishing marks and recognized her husband. Unable to control herself, she threw herself at his feet and said: "I pray you, my lord, tell me about your early life, because I think you are Placidus, commander of the armies, and are also called Eustace, whom the Savior converted when you were still Placidus. You underwent one trial after another. Your wife – and I am she – was taken from you at sea but was preserved from degradation. I had two sons, whose names were Agapetus and Theospitus." While she spoke, Eustace studied her carefully and saw that she was indeed his wife. Tears of joy and mutual embraces followed, and he glorified God who comforts the afflicted.

Then his wife said to him: "My master, where are our sons?" He said: "They were carried off by wild beasts." And he told her how he had lost them. "Thank God!" she exclaimed. "I think that as God has given us the gift of finding each other, he will also give us the joy of recognizing our sons!" Eustace: "I told you they were carried off by wild beasts!" She: "Yesterday I was sitting in the garden and listening to two young soldiers telling each other about their childhood, and I think they are our own sons! Ask them! They'll tell you!" Eustace sent for them and, upon hearing an account of their young years, knew that they were indeed his sons. He and their mother embraced them, floods of tears were shed, and kisses exchanged time after time. The whole army cheered and rejoiced, both because these people had been reunited and because the barbarians had been conquered.

When Eustace returned to Rome, Emperor Trajan had died and Hadrian, a still more guilty tyrant, had succeeded him. Hadrian staged a magnificent welcome for the commander and laid on a sumptuous banquet, celebrating his victory and the finding of his wife and sons. The next day the emperor led a procession to the temple of the idols, to offer sacrifice in thanksgiving for the victory. The emperor noticed that Eustace did not offer sacrifice either for the victory or for the recovery of his family, and exhorted him to do so. Eustace answered: "I worship Christ as God and I sacrifice to God alone!" This made Hadrian angry. He had Eustace, together with his wife and their sons, placed in the arena, and had a ferocious lion loosed upon them. The lion came running to them, lowered his head as though adoring them as saints, and meekly withdrew. Then the emperor had a brazen bull heated and ordered the four saints enclosed in it alive. Praying and commending themselves to the Lord, they entered the bull and so rendered their souls to the Lord.

Three days later their bodies were taken out of the bull in the emperor's presence. The bodies were intact, nor had the heat of the fire touched the hair or any other part of them. Christians took the sacred remains, buried them in a most honorable place, and built an oratory there. The martyrs suffered on 1 November, or, according to others, on 20 September, in the reign of Hadrian, which began about AD 120.

James the Dismembered (BHL 4101)

St. James, called the Dismembered because of the way he was martyred, was noble by birth and yet more noble by his faith. He was a native of the city of Elape in the land of the Persians, born of most Christian parents and wedded to a most Christian wife. To the king of the Persians he was well known, and stood first among his peers. It happened, however, that he was misled by the prince and his close friendship with him, and was induced to worship the idols. When his mother and his wife found this out, they wrote him a letter, saying: "By doing the will of a mortal man, you have deserted him with whom there is life; to please one who will be a mass of rottenness, you have deserted the eternal fragrance; you have traded truth for a lie; by acceding to a mortal's wish you have abandoned the judge of the living and the dead. Know therefore that from now on we are strangers to you and will no longer live in the same house with you."

When James read this letter, he wept bitterly and said: "If my mother and my wife have become strangers to me, how much more must I have estranged God?" He therefore inflicted harsh penances on himself in expiation of his fault. Then a messenger went to the prince and told him that James was a Christian, and the prince sent for him. "Tell me," he said to James, "are you a Nazarene?" "Yes," James answered, "I am a Nazarene." The prince: "Then you are a sorcerer!" James: "Far be it from me to be a sorcerer!" The prince threatened him with many kinds of torture, but James said: "Your threats do not bother me, because just as the wind blows over a stone, your anger goes quickly in one ear and out the other!" The prince: "Don't be a fool, or you may die a dreadful death!" James: "That is not death but should rather be called sleep, since in a short time resurrection is granted." The prince: "Don't let the Nazarenes deceive you by telling you that death is a sleep, because even great emperors fear it!" James: "We do not fear death, because we hope to pass from death to life!"

Upon the advice of his friends, the prince now sentenced James to death member by member, in order to strike fear into others. When some people wept out of compassion for him, he said: "Don't weep for me, but mourn for yourselves, because I go on to life, while eternal torment is your due!"

Now the torturers cut off the thumb of his right hand, and James cried out and said: "O Nazarene, my liberator, accept this branch of the tree of your mercy, for the husbandman trims the dry branches from the vine in order to let it grow stronger and be crowned with more fruit!" The headsman said: "If you wish to give in, I shall spare you and bring ointments for your wound." James: "Haven't you ever examined the trunk of a tree? The dry tendrils are cut away, and in due season, when the earth warms, each nub left by the pruning puts forth a new shoot. If therefore the vine is thought to need pruning in order to grow and bear fruit as the seasons revolve, how much greater the need of a man of faith who is grafted into Christ the true vine!"

The torturer cut off the forefinger, and James said: "Accept, O Lord, the two branches that your right hand planted." The third finger was cut off; and James said: "I am now set free from the threefold temptation, and I will bless the Father, the Son, and the Holy Spirit. With the three youths rescued from the fiery furnace I will confess you, O Lord, and amidst the choir of the martyrs I will sing Psalms to your name, O Christ!" The fourth finger was severed, and James said: "Protector of the sons of Israel, you were foretold in the fourth blessing [Jacob's blessing on Judah in *Gen.* 49, 8-12]. Accept from your servant the confession of the fourth finger as blessed in Judah." The fifth was cut off, and he said: "My joy is complete."

Then the executioners said to him: "Now is the time to spare your soul, lest you perish. And don't be sad because you've lost one hand. Many men have only one hand, yet abound in wealth and honors!" Blessed James responded: "When shepherds shear their sheep, do they take off the fleece from the right side and leave the left side unsheared? And if the sheep, a dumb animal, wants to lose all its fleece, how much the more should I, a rational man, not think it beneath me to die for God?" Therefore those impious men proceeded to amputate the little finger of his left hand, and James said: "You, Lord, were great, but you chose to become little and least for us, and therefore I give back to you the body and the soul that you created and redeemed by your blood." The seventh finger was taken, and James said: "Seven times a day I have given praise to the Lord." The eighth was removed and he said: "On the eighth day Jesus was circumcised, and the Hebrew male child is circumcised on the eighth day in order to pass over to the ceremonies of the Law: so let the mind of your servant pass over from these uncircumcised men with their unclean foreskins, and let me come and look upon your face!" The ninth finger was cut off and he said: "At the ninth hour Christ yielded up his spirit on the Cross, and so I, Lord, confess you in the pain of the ninth finger and give you thanks!" The tenth was taken, and he said: "Ten is the number of the commandments, and J is the initial letter of the name Jesus Christ."

Then some of the bystanders said: "O you who were so dear to us in the past, just profess their god before the consul so that you can go on living; and even though your hands are cut off, there are expert physicians who will be able to ease your pain!" To them James said: "Far be it from me to be guilty of so unspeakable a deception! No one who puts his hand to the plow and looks back is fit for the kingdom of God!" The angry torturers came and cut off the great toe of his right foot, and James said: "Christ's foot was pierced and blood poured out!" They took the second toe and he said: "Great above all days is this day to me, for today I shall be turned and go to almighty God." They cut off the third toe and threw it in front of him, and James smiled and said: "Go, third toe, to your fellow toes, and as the grain of wheat bears much fruit, so you at the last day will rest with your companions." The fourth went, and he said: "Why are you sad, my soul, and why do you disquiet me? I hope in God for I will still give praise to him, the salvation of my countenance and my God." The fifth was taken, and he said: "Now I shall begin to say to the Lord that he has made me a worthy companion to his servants."

Then they went to the left foot and took off the little toe, and James said: "Little toe, be comforted, because the big and the little will all rise again, and not a hair of the head will perish. How much less will you, the littlest, be separated from your fellows!" The second was taken, and James said: "Destroy the old house, a more splendid one is being prepared." After the third, he said: "The anvil is made more solid by the blows of the hammer." The fourth toe was amputated, and he said: "Comfort me, God of truth, for I trust in you and in the shade of your wings I will hope until iniquity passes away." The fifth went, and he said: "Look upon me, O Lord, I offer sacrifice twenty times!"

Next, the executioners cut off James's right foot, and he said: "Now I shall offer a gift to the King of heaven, for love of whom I endure these pains." They cut off the left foot and he said: "It is you who work wonders, Lord! Hear me and save me!" They cut off his right hand, and he said: "May your mercies help me, O Lord!" After the left hand, he said: "You are the God who works wonders." Off with his right arm, and he said: "Praise the Lord, my soul, in my life I will praise the Lord, I will sing to my God as long as I shall be!" Now his left arm, and he said: "The sorrows of death surrounded me, and in the name of the Lord I will be avenged." Next it was the right leg, which they cut off at the thigh. Blessed James, stricken with unspeakable pain, cried out, saying: "Lord Jesus Christ, help me, because the groans of death have surrounded me!" And he said to the torturers: "The Lord will clothe me with new flesh, upon which the wounds you inflict will not be able to leave a stain." They were exhausted, having toiled from the first to the ninth hour of the day at dismembering blessed James, but now they returned to their task, taking off the calf of the left leg up to the thigh. Blessed James cried out: "O Lord and Ruler, hear me half alive, Lord of the living and the dead! Fingers, Lord, I have none to hold out to you, nor hands to extend to you; my feet are cut off and my knees demolished, so that I cannot kneel to you, and I am like a house that is about to fall because the columns that support it have been taken away. Heed me, Lord Jesus Christ, and lead my soul out of prison!"

When James had said this, one of the executioners cut off his head. Then Christians came secretly, seized his body, and buried it with honors. He suffered on the twenty-seventh day of November.

[Fig. 51] Dogheaded men carved on each side of a cross at Conchan, on the Isle of Man, one of a number of monuments of Celtic and Scandinavian origin dating from the fifth to the early thirteenth centuries (P.M.C. Kermode, *Manx Crosses* [London, 1907], p. 135)

46. 'LIVES' OF ST. CHRISTOPHER:
THE IRISH *LIBAR BREAC*

The earliest reference to St. Christopher is in a fourth-century Gnostic document called 'The Acts of St. Bartholomew,' which describes him as a convert to Christianity and one of the Cynocephali, a mythical race of dogheaded, cannibalistic monsters. This version remained well-known in the east and achieved great popularity in Russia. Some time before the eighth century it found its way to Ireland, possibly through Greek-speaking monks, and also became known in the west of England, as indicated by the stone carvings found on the Isle of Man and by images depicted in a Cornish wall painting. The Cynocephali are elsewhere mentioned in Isidore of Seville's 'Etymologies,' and are the subject of a letter written by Ratramnus of Corbie, a ninth-century Benedictine monk, to his friend the priest Rimbert. The latter had asked his opinion on whether the Cynocephali were merely animals or were descended from Adam, and therefore in possession of minds and souls capable of salvation. Ratramnus concluded that they were indeed human – a matter of some reassurance to Rimbert, perhaps, since he was traveling to Scandinavia as a missionary and must have wondered whether he would encounter similar creatures there. Ratramnus refers to St. Christopher in his letter as an example of the human nature of the dogheaded, but later versions of the legend played down or omitted the monstrous origins of the saint, and invented the story of Christopher carrying the Christ-child over a raging river, the tale most often connected with him in the west in the later Middle Ages. Modern commentaries suggest that the myth of a dogheaded race originated in travelers' accounts of dogheaded baboons, or possibly from misunderstood deformities such as those caused by hypertrichosis (abnormal hair growth) or neurofibromatosis (facial tumors). Christopher's status was reduced to a local cult by the Vatican in 1969, but in this century of widespread air and road travel he continues to enjoy popularity even among non-Christians.

The 'Libar Breac' is a fifteenth-century collection of Irish saints' lives compiled from earlier sources.

Source: trans. from Gaelic by J. Fraser, "The Passion of St. Christopher," *Révue Celtique* 34 (1913): pp. 309-325.

There was a persecution of the Christians in [the] time of the emperor Decius [249-51], and the holy man Christopher was taken and tortured like the others. Christopher was exceedingly wise, and had observed that the Lord assisted those of the heathen who believed just as much as he assisted the Christians. Now this Christopher was one of the dogheads, a race that had the heads of dogs and ate human flesh. He meditated much on God, but at that time he could speak only the language of the dogheads. When he saw how much the Christians suffered he was indignant and left the city. He began to adore God and prayed. "Almighty God," he said, "give me the gift of speech, open my mouth, and make plain thy might that those who persecute thy people may be converted."

An angel of God came to him and said: "God has heard your prayer." The angel raised Christopher from the ground, and struck and blew upon his mouth, and the grace of eloquence was given him as he had desired. Thereupon Christopher arose and went into the city, and immediately began to stop the offering of sacrifice. "I am a Christian," he said, "and I will not sacrifice to the gods." There came a certain Baceus to him and struck him. "You may do so," said Christopher, "for I will not strike you in return, but I forgive you, for forgiveness is the new Law." Baceus went to the king, and said: "Hail O King, I have news for you. I have seen a man with a dog's head on him, and long hair, and eyes glittering like the morning star in his head, and his teeth were like the tusks of a wild boar. I struck him for he was cursing the gods; but he did not strike me, and said it was for the sake of God that he refrained. I am telling you this in order to know what is to be done with him, for it seems that it is by the God of the Christians that he has been sent, to help the Christians." "Bring him to me," said the king. The bystanders said that a large number of men must be sent for him. "Let two hundred soldiers go for him," said the king, "and bring him hither in chains; and if he resist you, bring his head with you that I may see it."

The soldiers then went to seek him. As for Christopher he went into the temple, and drew his hair round his head in two plaits. He rested his head on his knee, and, after planting his staff in the ground, began to pray. "Almighty Lord," he said, "perform a miracle through me that thy name may be praised; and let this staff send forth shoots." The staff immediately put forth twigs, and leaves and flowers appeared.

A certain woman came gathering roses past the place where he was praying. She looked into the temple, and saw him seated and moaning. She went away then and told another woman that she had seen a magician lamenting loudly. While they were talking in this way, the soldiers came up to them seeking him. The soldiers heard the conversation of the women, and asked them where they had seen the man they were talking about. The women gave them a description of Christopher and told them where he was. The soldiers had not the courage to go to him. At that time a company came from Asia to see Christopher. Christopher was praying with his hands stretched out, and when the soldiers came up to him they said: "Why do you moan in that way?" "I moan," he said, "for all men that do not recognize the Lord God, that is the true God who made heaven and earth." The soldiers said to him: "It is for you we have been sent, to take you with us in chains, in order that you may worship the gods." "I will go with you without chains, if you like," he said, "for God will save me from the power of your father, the devil." "Stay, if you wish," said the soldiers, "or, if you like, rise and go in any direction you please, and we will say that we have not found you." "Allow me to go to pray for a short time that the might of God may be made plain to you." "We cannot," they said, "for our provisions have come to an end." "Give me any you have left," said Christopher, "that I may divide it between you, so that you may see the miracle God will work in it." They gave him thereupon the little they had. Christopher took the remainder, and said: "Almighty God, who didst satisfy the five thousand with five loaves, bless this little portion that the soldiers may be satisfied with it, and that thy grace may be made clear, and that all that will see the miracle may believe." The food immediately increased and grew, so that they all ate as much as they wished. When they had seen that miracle, they believed that he had been sent by Christ. So Christopher and the soldiers came afterwards to Antioch, and were baptized by the bishop, Babilus.

Thereupon they went to the emperor Decius in the city. Christopher told the soldiers to take him to the palace in chains in order that they might not be blamed for not manacling him, for that had been the king's command. And so he was brought to the king. When the king saw Christopher he was filled with astonishment, and was seized with such terror that he fell from his throne. "If it is for fear of God that you fell," said Christopher, "it is well for you, for God will ask of you every one of them that you have harmed without cause." "Whence have you come?" said Decius, "and what is your name?" "I am a Christian," said Christopher, "and Reprobus was my name before I believed, but Christopher has been my name since my baptism. My face tells that I am of the race of Dogheads." "Sacrifice to the gods, Reprobus," said Decius, "and I will give you wealth and priesthood." "It will be distinction in your eyes to destroy me," said Christopher "and your gods will come to nothing, for they are not gods but devils." The king gave orders that he should be taken and his hair knotted together. This was done, and the king said: "Sacrifice to the gods and you shall live." "I will not," said Christopher, "for they are devils." The king gave orders that his whole body should be torn with iron hooks, and that was done. "This temporal pain has no terror for me," said Christopher, "but you ought to fear the eternal pain that you shall suffer." The king, in anger, gave orders that two lighted lamps should be applied to his sides. But the people said that it was not right to inflict such torture on a man of his learning, but that he should be coaxed with gentle words. The king then ordered his chains to be struck off, and it was done.

"Sacrifice to the gods," said the king "and you will be my charioteer." "I will be your servant," said Christopher, "and your charioteer, and do you believe in Christ, and you will have a kingdom in heaven." "That is not satisfactory," said the king, "that you should be trying to make me forsake the gods, and that I should be asking you to sacrifice to them." "I have a good suggestion for you," said one of his retinue to the king: "Let him be put into a separate room with two pretty and well dressed women along with him. As soon as love for the women takes possession of him, he will sacrifice to the gods."

The king thought the plan was a good one, and he sent for two pretty women, and they were put into a separate room with Christopher. Thereupon Christopher prayed for long with his face to the ground. When his prayer was finished, he raised his face. As soon as the women saw him, they were filled with fear and terror, and retreated from him. "We shall die," they said, "if we see more." "Why have you come here?" said Christopher. The women did not answer for fear. He repeated the question, and still they did not answer. "Believe in my God, unhappy women," he said. One of the women said to her companion: "We are in great danger here; if we do not believe in his God, he will kill us, and if we do, the king will kill us." However one of the women, Aicilina, said: "It is better for us to believe in his God that we may have eternal life. Holy Christopher pray for us that God may forgive our sins." "Only believe in the everliving God," he said, "and I will pray on your behalf."

During this conversation a city guard came to them and said: "Come out, you are wanted." When they came before the king, he asked them if they had seduced Christopher. Aicilina replied: "We have believed in his God, for in him alone is safety." The king asked again if they had seduced him and turned him to their gods. "We believe only in the one God who is in heaven," said Aicilina. "As for your gods, they are only stones, and can only hurt those who worship them."

At that the king was enraged, and gave orders that she should be taken and her hair twisted together, and that two stones should be fastened to her hands to break them. This was done, and Aicilina looked at Christopher and said: "Holy Christopher, pray for me." Christopher did so; and then she died. The king ordered her body to be kept without burial.

Then the other woman was brought before the king. The latter said: "Sacrifice to the gods, and I will give you great honor, and I shall have a gold statue made to you." "Only tell me," said Caillica, "where I am to offer sacrifice." The king ordered her to be taken to the temple of the gods to sacrifice, and a herald went before her to announce that Caillica was sacrificing to the gods. The wicked people were glad of that for they imagined that she would indeed sacrifice. So she went into the temple, and on seeing the priest of the temple and the others present, she said: "See how it will be to the great god that I will sacrifice." She then went to the place where the statues of the gods were, and stood before that of Jupiter. "Jupiter," she said, "tell thy servant what to do." The god made no reply. "The gods must be angry with me," she said, "since they do not answer, or perhaps they are asleep." She then said: "If ye have any power answer, and if not, why do ye do hurt to men? God of body and of soul, come to my aid." She drew to her the statue of Jupiter, and it crumpled like wax. She also broke the other statues in the same place, saying: "If ye have any power, why do ye not save yourselves?" Then she was seized and taken to the king's palace. "If we had not seized her," said the soldiers, "she would not have left a single statue undamaged."

"You promised me, wicked woman," said the king "that you would sacrifice to the gods but what you did was to damage them!" "Your gods are wretched creatures," said she, "if a woman can hurt them. He is the true God that no one can harm, and he is my God, and it is in him that I believe." The king ordered two iron nails to be driven through her from her soles to her neck, and a stone to be put on her neck to break it. She looked at Christopher and said: "Holy Christopher, pray for me." He did so, and she died. The king ordered her body to be kept without burial till the body of Christopher joined it.

The king said to Christopher: "Bad is your name Reprobus, and hideous is your appearance, and we prefer that you should die than that the city should be spoilt through your sorcery. Sacrifice to the gods, and you shall not be tortured." "Chief of idolatry and head of unbelief," said Christopher, "I will not sacrifice to your detestable gods who are deaf and dumb; yet I should like to conduct you to the path of life that you might understand the glory of God."

At that moment the two hundred soldiers who had taken Christopher arrived, and laid down their uniforms and armor before the king, and kissed Christopher's feet. The king said: "Christopher is an enemy to me, for he has taken my soldiers from me and destroyed the gods." The soldiers answered: "We are Christians since the day when we were sent for the servant of God. He blessed our bread for us on the way and gave us the grace of God." "I will give you wealth," said the king "if you do not leave me." "What belongs to you," said the soldiers, "that is, your uniforms and arms, you may keep, but as for us, we will follow Christopher." The king immediately ordered them all to be put to death, and their bodies burned. That was done.

Christopher was brought before the king who said to him: "You have deprived me of my soldiers, bold madman." "My only fault is praising God," said Christopher. "You shall be burned presently," said the king. Christopher was then bound and placed on a bed of brass, a large heap of firewood was put upon him, and thirty flagons of oil poured over it; and then a great fire was lit.

When the fire had gone down, Christopher sat up on the bed and said to the bystanders: "I have seen the Master of the City, a tall man and his face beautiful like a ray of sunlight. His garments were as white as snow, there was a crown of pearls on his head, and his glory was unspeakable. There was with him a number of soldiers, and splendid was their appearance. I saw also another chief as black as jet accompanied by black soldiers, and every hair of his head was as thick as an iron chain. A battle was fought between them, and the black king and his company were defeated by the glorious king. He was put in chains and his whole house was burnt and destroyed."

Now when the people saw that Christopher was alive, that not even his hair was burnt, and that he did not smell of fire, they all believed in God, and leaping into the fire drew Christopher out of it. They then said with one voice to the king: "You have been destroyed and vanquished with all your servants." When the king heard the shout of the people, he was filled with great fear and went into his palace.

Next morning the king gave orders that all should sacrifice to the gods on pain of death. St. Christopher and all the Christians then appeared and began to praise God; and his attendants said to the king that the people had turned against him, and that unless he made a brave fight he should himself perish. He rose from his throne and armed himself, and his soldiers also took their arms, and began to slay the Christians. Christopher kept encouraging the Christians, telling them that the kingdom of Heaven awaited them. And on that Sunday ten thousand three hundred and three of the Christians were put to death. The king had Christopher seized and bound in iron chains, and, with a stone attached to him, cast into a dry well in order that his bones might not be preserved. But when the holy man was put into the well, his chains turned to dust and ashes, and angels carried him away to the king's palace. The king was told, and said to him: "Strong is your magic, Reprobus," but Christopher made no answer. The king said again: "Sacrifice to the gods and you shall not be harmed." "Almighty God," said Christopher, "receive my spirit that it may rest in thy glory," and he fell on his knees. The king gave orders that whosoever should not worship the gods should be put to death. Christopher was thereupon taken to the place of execution. Many Christians accompanied him, and asked the executioner to allow him to pray; and Christopher said: "Lord, give to Decius a devil to compel him to gnaw his own flesh and so die. Grant to my prayer that the Christians who are now oppressed may be succored, and give this grace to my body that all who shall have any of my relics may have miracles wrought clearly for them, that they may expel devils, that all diseases may avoid them, that they be prosperous, and that their sins may be forgiven." The angel replied: "Your wish shall be granted you, and it shall be granted you in addition, that if any one be in need he shall be freed from it through your intercession." Christopher then said to the executioner: "Do as you have been ordered," crossed himself, stretched out his neck, and then he was beheaded. However a certain Peter gave a price for the body of Christopher, and took it with him to his city. There was a stream which damaged the city, and the body was buried facing the onset of the stream, and after that the stream did no more harm to the city.

47. 'LIVES' OF ST. CHRISTOPHER: THE SOUTH ENGLISH LEGENDARY

One of the major collections deriving from 'The Golden Legend' is 'The South English Legendary,' preserved in whole or in part in numerous manuscripts, the earliest dating from about 1300. Written in rhyme, 'The South English Legendary,' like its major source, gives the saints' 'lives' in the order in which their feast days fall in the year, and includes material for other festivals. It also adds a number of English saints not found in 'The Golden Legend.' Written probably by a friar or friars, it is lively and colloquial, and aims to hold the attention of lay-people while it teaches them. The following excerpt, translated from the Middle English verse, includes the prologue to the collection followed by the passion of St. Christopher. The latter emphasizes a different tradition of the saint from the Irish 'Libar Breac.' Here he is primarily celebrated for being a giant man of strength, a practical man and an illiterate who is nevertheless filled with God's grace.

Source: trans. from Middle English by M.A. Stouck, *The South English Legendary*, ed. Charlotte D'Evelyn and Anna J. Mill, EETS 235 (rpt. 1967; London, New York, Toronto: Oxford University Press, 1956), I, 1-3 and 340-348.

Prologue

Now flourishes the new fruit that has just begun to grow
That mankind must bring as his true inheritance.
This new fruit of which I speak is our Christian faith
That once was sown on earth, and now brings forth fruit.
So hard and wicked was the land on which it had to grow
That scarcely could anything be grown there.
God himself was the gardener who first sowed the seed –
That was Jesus, God's son, who humbled himself therefore.
Though he himself sowed that seed, so obstinate was man
That it could not take root until it was watered with rain.
With a sweet dew of rain he watered this hard stock,
With his sweet heart's blood he gave his life for it.
Most worthy was the sweet blood that it was watered with.
At last, mingled with his heart's blood, water flowed there.
Then the new seed began to take hold somewhat better.
And yet, after this, many shed their blood for it:
First the martyr St. Stephen and the apostles that had died,
Who gave their blood and their lives to nourish that sweet seed,

And then these other martyrs, who were our Lord's knights,
Who shed their blood for the Christian faith so that it would not perish.
Fierce was the battle that our sweet Lord undertook
And his disciples afterwards, in many places, to support
the Christian faith.
When a king wants to undertake a battle to maintain his rights,
He first arranges his army and prepares them to fight;
In front he sets up his crossbows and his archers too,
His trumpeters to herald him, and his banner.
And then when the king is ready he will go among the vanguard,
To encourage all his men so that none shall flee.
Then in the rearguard bold knights must go
To support their lord's cause and conclude the fight,
And if they behave like cowards, the whole battle is lost.
In this way our sweet Lord was born on earth,
To begin Christianity, and he first planted the stock;
His trumpeters and crossbowmen he sent first before:
That is, the prophets and his patriarchs who went in advance of him
To tell men that he would come, and to amend their ways.
Their enemies were contemptuous and laughed them to scorn,
And tormented them fiercely and slew them all.
Then our sweet Lord himself came down from heaven for this battle,
And took on man's flesh and blood in which he wanted to fight.
He would not begin this battle nor raise his banner
Before he had strength of body and was fully grown:
He was twenty-nine years old before he armed himself for it,
And started to do battle for Christendom.
When he was fully grown he first had himself armed:
He received our baptism in the river Jordan.
His cousin St. John the Baptist armed him there.
At once like a bold king he had his banner raised:
St. John was his standard-bearer and carried his banner before him,
And fought hard like a bold knight until he lost his life.
When the standard-bearer was slain the king was not afraid;
Into the battle he went at once until he was put to death.
And yet, for all his painful death, he would have lost his rights
If his knights in the rearguard had not known how to fight all the more
    bravely.
They followed the example of their Lord – they would not flinch –
Neither the apostles nor the martyrs, until they were put to death.

[Fig. 52] St. Christopher, copy of an early woodcut now in the John Rylands Library, Manchester. On the left of the saint are figures symbolizing the active life (a laborer toiling uphill with a sack of grain) and, on the right, the contemplative life (a hermit holding a lantern). The Latin inscription says 'On whatever day you look upon the image of Christopher, on that day you will surely not suffer an evil death' (Jameson, *Sacred and Legendary Art*, 2, 447).

Well ought we to love Christendom that has been bought at such a price,
With the heart's blood of our Lord, pierced by the spear.
People love to hear stories of the battles of kings
And of knights who were bold; most of it is lies.
Whoever is eager to hear stories of such things
May learn of fierce battles here – no lies are these! –
Of apostles and martyrs who were bold knights,
Steadfast in battle, and did not flee for fear;
Who while they lived endured wicked men tearing their limbs.
I shall tell about them in order, as their feast days occur in the year.
I shall begin at New Year's Day for that is the first feast,
And go from one to the next in order, as long as the year lasts.

Chapter 53: St. Christopher (25 July).
(British Museum MS. Cotton Julius D. IX f. 118a)

St. Christopher was a Saracen in the land of Canaan –
In his time there was no man anywhere so strong.
He was twenty-four feet tall, and very thickset and broad.
If such a man weren't strong I'd be surprised.
All the people of the country where he was would flee from him,
So it seemed to him that no one should oppose him.
He said he would not stay with any man unless he were
The highest lord over all men, and with no-one else.
He traveled in search of such a man until he was told
Of the highest man who was on earth and wielded the most power.
St. Christopher searched for him far and wide; at last he found him.
The king asked him who he was, and also who he was looking for.
[Christopher] told him who he was and that he wanted to serve
The highest man anywhere, who would submit to no-one,
If he could find such a man. The king replied
That he esteemed no man, nor did he submit to or fear anyone.
Both were pleased with one another. Christopher served him for a long time.
Now the king loved the sound of the fiddle and singing
So that one day a certain minstrel played lively [tunes] for him
And in his song at last he named the Devil.
When the king heard that, at once he crossed himself.
St. Christopher took good heed of this; he wouldn't move a foot
Until he knew the reason. The king didn't want to say.
Christopher said, "Unless you explain, I'll stay no longer."

Then the king saw no alternative. "Dear Christopher," he said,
"It was because he named the Devil, for I fear him greatly."
"And so" said Christopher "he is a higher master than you."
"I can't very well contradict that now" said the king.
"Good-bye then!" said the other, "I will never again stay with you;
I shall seek out the Devil and serve him if I can find him."
The king and all his people were sorry that he would not stay.
He journeyed forth to seek the devil, and yet he didn't go far
(For that wicked scoundrel is always at hand for those who have gone over to
    him).
When Christopher reached a town he saw many people coming
With great splendor, well mounted, very haughty and proud.
Christopher met them boldly – he was afraid of nothing;
The leader who was very proud came and met him at once.
"Fine sir" he said, "What sort of man are you and where do you think you're
    going?"
He said "I am in search of employment, and I will serve no man
Except my lord whom I seek: the high Devil of hell."
"Fair brother" said the first, "I am he; you are most welcome to me.
I will bestow on you the best employment that you want to choose."
Christopher saw his great following, and that he had great power.
He was pleased with such a lord and master.
The master called all his men away except for their two selves,
So as to teach his craft privately as they went along.
As they traveled, discussing this wicked employment,
A cross stood on the road; the Devil grew afraid.
He withdrew far off into thorns and briers
(May [he] never come in a better place, for that is good enough for [him]!)
And they all withdrew there, for each felt the need to lament,
And when the cross was passed, they turned again to the open road.
Christopher asked [the Devil] the reason; he was reluctant to say.
"Indeed," said [Christopher], "unless you tell me, I'll never again serve you."
"Christopher," said the Devil, "I will gladly tell you,
As long as you serve me afterwards the better for it, with all your strength.
By means of a cross such as the one you see, the high God that was here
Overcame and brought to grief me and all my companions."
"Then he is higher than you," said Christopher, "and wields more power."
"I can't deny it," said the other, "it grieves me sorely."
"Then a curse on longer employment with you!" said Christopher,
"If I may, by any means, know anything about that high man."

[Fig. 53] St. Christopher as a giant, from a picture by Paolo Farinati (1524-1606) (Jameson, *Sacred and Legendary Art,* 2, 446).

Forth he went to seek our Lord; far and wide he went.
At last he found a hermit; he approached him at once,
And told him everything, and how he was looking for a certain man.
The hermit said, "Blessed be he who brought you to this knowledge,
For he is your Lord, dear son, he created you man,
And with his own flesh and blood on the Cross he bought you.
You must suffer somewhat for him and fast each Friday."
"I've never fasted" said the other, "and I can't do it now."
"You must go to church" said the hermit "and say your prayers too."
"I don't know what that is," said Christopher, "and I certainly can't do it."
"Well," said the hermit, "you're strong, and here nearby is a river
Which no one can cross unless he rides higher up.
For forgiveness of your sins, you must make your dwelling here,
And when anyone has need of you, you must carry him over."
He agreed to that at once, for forgiveness of his sins.
The hermit gave him baptism, and sent him off.
Christopher made a small dwelling beside the water.
In his hand he carried a long rod as his staff.
When anyone wanted to cross the water, he lifted him upon his back,
And took his staff and carried him over, stepping firmly and quickly.
Because he was so strong and so tall, there was no one too heavy
For him to carry boldly into the deep waters.
One night a voice came from the other side of the water, crying out:
"Christopher, hail, hail!" and asking to be carried across.
Christopher arose at once and took his staff in hand
And went out, and found no one when he reached the land.
He had scarcely got home when it cried out again there;
He went forth and could find no one, any more than he did before.
Still it cried out the third time after he had reached land.
With his staff he went out again, and found a little child standing there.
That child asked him, for charity, to carry him across.
"Well, come out here" said Christopher, "I didn't know where you were."
He lifted the child lightly up and tossed him in his arms.
As he carried this child it continued to grow heavier,
And the water increased too. Christopher was very afraid
Of drowning; the child was so heavy that at last he could scarcely stand.
He had never been so nearly overcome; at each step he groaned and gasped,
And he dared not throw the child down in case he might drown.
When he reached land – and it seemed to him a very long time-
He set that child down upon the ground, and stood there to cool off.

"Who are you?" he said, "So light, and yet grown so heavy –
So heavy that I was often on the point of drowning.
If all the world had rested upon me, it seems to me that it wouldn't have been
    so heavy."
Said the child, "No wonder, Christopher, if I was heavier
Than all the world, for truly I am more than all the world,
And I made all the world out of nothing, and all that is.
And so that you may see the truth of what I have said, fix your staff in the
    ground
And it will live and bear fruit and grow in a short time."
After that he didn't know what became of this child. Christopher took his
    staff
And fixed it in the ground, and the next day, it happened [as he had said].
Then he was more certain than he had been before, and loved our Lord the
    more.
He went forth to follow him and preached God's commandment.
He heard where Christians were brought into torment.
He went there to comfort them, so that they would not waver.
"Be strong," he said "and steadfast, and do as I teach you."
The judge leapt up at once, and struck him below the ear.
"Are you" said he "one of them? You shall suffer hard for it."
"Sit still" said Christopher, "I tell you, strike no more;
For if I weren't a Christian man, I'd avenge myself right now.
You believe in these idols made of wood and stone
Which can no more do miracles than so much wood.
You shall see something of my Lord's power from my staff."
He stuck his staff in the ground and at once
It lived and grew and bore fruit right in front of them all.
He said, "You should believe in a God, who can accomplish [deeds of] such
    power."
Because he was so huge, they did not dare to speak a bold word to him,
Because of the fair miracle of his staff, and because of his preaching too.
In that place he converted to God more than seven thousand men.
St. Christopher traveled towards a kind of wilderness
To lead his life in God's service, as our Lord sent him grace.
The justice described in the king's presence the kind of man he had seen
Converting that folk; he had not dared come near him because of his
    strength.
Then the king ordered two hundred knights to search until they found him,
And to take him and bring him at once, bound fast.

These two hundred knights set out well armed immediately;
In a short time they came to Christopher; they all looked at him;
They dared not come close to him but fled for home,
And when they got there they said they could not find him.
"What! You cowards!" said the king, "Have you not found him?
If he's alive I shall have him bound securely."
He sent another two hundred knights to seek him far and wide
Never to return until they brought him with them.
They set out well armed, and when they saw Christopher,
They stopped and dared go no closer, nor scarcely [did they dare] to set eyes
    on him,
For he was so terrifying and so huge that they hardly dared behold him.
With a little leap he could have made them run at once.
This good man made fun of them, and asked them what they wanted.
The knights said "We daren't do with you what we're supposed to do,
Because the king ordered us 'bring him and tie his hands securely.'
If you want, we'll tell him that we couldn't find you."
"No, for God's sake" said Christopher "then you would get blamed for it.
I will go with you gladly to see what he wants done."
Against their will he made them all bind him fast like a thief,
And lead him forth and tie his hands very tightly behind his back.
On the way Christopher taught them God's commandment,
So that before they came home to the king, each one had been baptized.
And nevertheless, they led him forth in bonds to the king.
"Lo, sir," they said, "Here is God's knight; now we have found him."
This king sat high upon his throne, but at once, as soon as he saw him,
He fell to the ground in terror so that he nearly broke his neck.
The knights came to [his help] at once and when his wits returned to him,
He said, "Christopher, change your mind and abandon your baptism."
"Good man," said the other, "You might as well be quiet about it:
You have bound my body fast; do what you want with me."
"Certainly sire" said the knights who had brought him there,
"We have accepted baptism; we will not abandon it."
Then the king in great wrath had Christopher put into prison,
And bound the knights fast, and cut off their heads too.
When the knights were beheaded, the king took thought,
And brought two of the most beautiful women to St. Christopher –
One was called Nite, the other Aquilline – to change his mind.
When these two women saw Christopher as he stood in prison,
It seemed to them that his face was brighter than the sun or the moon.

"Have mercy, Christopher!" they cried loudly. "Baptize us now!"
Christopher taught them their creed and baptized them there.
The king ordered them to be brought forth the next day to see how things
    were going,
And he believed they had brought the good man into lechery.
The women gave him an easy answer, as if they cared nothing for him.
"What's this?" said the king, "have you been converted?
Honor your gods, I advise you, if you hope for my favor."
"Our gods deserve to be honored in a fair place," said these women;
"Therefore sweep the streets so that all the people may see,
And we will honor them indeed as it is right, and lawful."
The king had everything done as they said, quickly and very gladly.
When the idols were finally brought into the street
Both these women took their girdles and tied them securely to [the idols],
And dragged them the length of the street and hacked them to dust there.
They said "Go and fetch doctors to heal them!"
The king was nearly mad with rage, so he had one woman hung
And heavy rocks tied to her feet, so that her death throes would be painful.
When this woman was hung up her limbs burst from within,
Neck and sinews and the rest too; she received the joy of heaven.
He had the other woman put into a fierce fire, but no flames came near her.
When he saw that, he had her head struck off.
Thus both these holy women went into the joy of heaven,
Through the grace that our sweet Lord sent them, by means of Christopher.
The king had Christopher brought and asked him at once
Whether he would serve the idols or go to his death.
Christopher forsook their idols and their service too.
The king at once ordered him to be placed on a gridiron
And roasted with fire and pitch, but when he was laid on it
The gridiron melted away like wax. The fire at once was quenched,
And he rose up unharmed. Then the king was enraged,
And had him bound to a pillar, with knights posted around him.
They shot him lethally with sharp fierce arrows –
More than two hundred knights shot at him with longbow and crossbow,
But no arrow touched him, for all stayed in the air
Hanging around him, as though waiting.
When the king saw this, he approached furiously;
An arrow that hung over Christopher quickly made its way to him,
And struck out both his eyes, and [pierced] far into his head.
Then the king stopped in agony as if he'd lost his wits.

"Foolish wretch," said Christopher, "What has become of your power now
Against the One that you have begun [to fight]? You're a very feeble fighter.
I pity your misery, and I shall reveal [something] to you:
For it is my Lord's will that tomorrow you shall martyr me.
Smear your eyes with my blood and good sight will quickly return to you."
At this the blind king had hope, [for he] understood this well.
The next day he had [Christopher's] head struck off, and smeared himself
    with the blood,
And had good clear eyesight; at once he changed his belief.
He gave this holy man a fair burial, and believed at once in God,
And received baptism along with all his men,
And went into the joy of heaven. And so that was much better for them
Than to go to the torments of hell, and to serve their idols.
Thus at the last St. Christopher went to the most high God.
Now God bring us to that same joy to which he brought Christopher's soul.

48. AN OLD FRENCH *LIFE OF*
ST. MARGARET OF ANTIOCH

Despite, or rather because of, the fanciful episode of her encounter with the Devil in the form of a dragon and her subsequent victory over him, Margaret was one of the most popular virgin martyrs venerated during the Middle Ages. Eight versions of her life, based on two earlier Latin texts, exist in Old French from the thirteenth century; she is included in 'The Golden Legend,' and many versions exist in Anglo-Norman and Middle English that indicate her special popularity in England. The Old French version reprinted here is preserved in over a hundred manuscripts, mostly from the four- teenth and fifteenth centuries, and makes use of dramatic devices similar to those employed in 'The South English Legendary.' It is also an example of the extremely popular 'virgin martyr' story, of which Christina, Dorothy, Agnes and Barbara are also typical.

Source: trans. from Old French verse by Brigitte Cazelles, *The Lady as Saint: A Collection of French Hagiographic Romances of the Thirteenth Century* (Philadelphia: University of Pennsylvania, 1991), pp. 218-228; repr. with permission.

After the holy Passion
Of Jesus Christ, when – on Ascension day –
He ascended into Heaven,
The world was filled with many good people,
Who led a devout life.
Through the preaching
Of the apostles and the martyrs,
The Holy Spirit worked so well
That many people were believers,
Among the old and the young, including children,
Matrons, and maidens.
The good news spread in such a way
That a young maiden
By the name of Margaret
Heard of Jesus Christ,
Of the tortures he suffered,
Of eternal life
(Which she knew to be neither a lie nor a fable),
And of the eternal Kingdom of God.
She abandoned the Saracen [pagan] law,
Was baptized and purified,
And started loving God
With all her heart.

[Fig. 54] Three early renaissance images of St. Margaret of Antioch (Jameson, *Sacred and Legendary Art,* 2, 518 and 520).

But she hid her faith
From her father and friends.
She devoted herself to God so totally
That neither honors nor riches
Could ever convince her to seek another friend [male suitor]
Never
Will she look for the company of man
Or seek marriage,
And she will turn down any such request.
Theodosius, her father, was
A Saracen, and so was
Her mother.
Her father hated her deeply.
But her mother loved her
On account of her beauty,
Fair body, fair face,
Knowledge, courtesy, and wisdom.
Her parents did not live long
But died within two years.
She found herself an orphan.
She lived with a wet nurse
Who had raised her since childhood.

It was she who had initiated Margaret
Into the teachings of Christianity.
The wet nurse knew Margaret's devotion,
Her mode of life, and her thoughts.
Margaret, who was without pride or sin,
Called her her lady and master.
Everyday, Margaret would tend the sheep of her wet nurse
And lead them to the fields,
As she had no concern for the vain world.
Her clothing was poor,
But her body was beautiful and comely,
Her eyes bright, and her face shining.
Filled
With God's grace,
She cared for no other love
Than the love of God.
This was the only payment that she cared to receive,
While God was her only investment.
It happened one day,
As she was tending her wet nurse's sheep,
That Olymbrius passed by,
He who was the lord of the land.
He stared at her,
Not looking at her clothes,
But at her fair and graceful body,
Which was beautiful and enticing.
He continued on his way,
But did not forget her.
Shortly afterwards, he sent a messenger to her,
For he wanted to know her name
And whether she would accept to love him.
The messenger arrived
And approached the maiden.
"Maiden," he said, "may God be with you!"
She answered him without anger,
Or anguish,
Simply saying: "May God bless you too!"
Then he delivered this message:
"Maiden," he said, "my lord,
Who happened to pass by some time ago,

Sends me to you, for he would like you
To give me your name,
And to tell me whether you would accept to love him.
He wishes to know who you are, what is your lineage,
Who are your parents,
And by what law and faith you abide."
"Lord," she says, "in my childhood,
I was baptized as a Christian.
I have given my love to God,
In such a way that no offer
Could ever prompt me to have another friend."
"Fair lady," he says, "know
That you could find yourself the recipient of many riches.
Be the friend of my lord,
And you will live in great honors.
Great honor and great power
Will be yours through him.
Do as my lord begs you to do.
Reconsider your decision,
And come along with me
On this horse."
"Friend, give up your arguments.
You will never convince me.
I am the servant of Jesus Christ."
Discomfited by her response, the messenger
Leaves at once without farewell.
He goes back on his horse and departs.
He then describes to his lord
The merit and virtue
He has found in the maiden:
"She did not care a whit,
For what I told and promised her.
For she has put in a better place
Her heart, which she will not give to you.
You will never be her lord or spouse,
Not one single day for the rest of her life.
She has no desire for your love."
Olymbrius becomes angry,
His rage changes his appearance.
His nostrils flare, he gnashes his teeth,

And his face loses color.
He greatly resents
The fact that the girl has rejected him.
He is determined to make her pay for it.
The following day, he calls for her,
Asking that she be brought before him,
So that he can take his revenge.

[Margaret proclaims herself a Christian, telling Olymbrius that she is the servant and friend of her Spouse Jesus Christ. She is at once disrobed, hanged, and whipped.]

Blood springs like a fountain,
Running down her body.
Neither Olymbrius, nor his soldiers,
Nor any of the onlookers
Could stand to look at her,
Because of the running blood
And the sufferings she endures.
Olymbrius, the evil traitor,
Cries out to her: "Sister Margaret,
Trust me and follow my orders!
You will then be able to regain health.
Trust me, you will do wisely,
For I will take you in marriage."
And all those who stand around her
Cry to her: "Sister, listen to our lord!
Trust him, you will do wisely,
For our lord is offering you
A very rich marriage indeed.
Do not waste your beautiful youth,
Out of childishness or madness.
Save your body, save your life!"
The maiden hears and listens
To the noise and the shouts of the people.
And she reacts
To what they tell her:
"Ha," she says, "how evil are your counsels!
You see me suffering,
And you think that God has forsaken me?

But no. He is still protecting me.
Your thoughts are mad indeed,
You who advise me
To abandon for your lord
The friendship of my Creator.
If my body endures these tortures,
My soul will ascend even more happily
To Paradise, in the company of the saints.
This martyrdom is but a bath
Which purifies my body and soul.
Through it, my soul is protected
From the ordeal of eternal death.
It will indeed allow me to avoid sin.
Go away, men and women!
Your words and your arguments
Are worth no more than an apple,
For Jesus Christ is with me."

[Olymbrius now orders that she be thrown into a dark cell.]

She is brought to the entrance of the jail,
All bloody and naked.
But before entering,
She crosses herself.
As they push her inside,
She changes color and becomes pale,
Because of the darkness of the cell.
He would have a harsh and mean heart,
He who could throw her in there
And refrain from weeping.
As soon as she is inside,
She bows at once,
And kneels on the ground.
With sweet words, she calls on God
To rescue her.
She sighs and weeps,
Saying: "Help me, sweet and fair God!
This place is so dreadful
That I do not know where I am.
And I trust no one,

Sweet God, except you.
I have been greatly shamed, degraded,
And tortured.
May you give me promptly your counsel.
And may you grant me, through your grace,
To see face to face
The one that causes my torments.
I must protect myself from him.
Indeed, I do not know
How I could have wronged him."
Having finished her prayers,
She looks in the direction
Of one of the corners of her fearsome cell.
Presently, she sees a huge dragon appearing.
He is dark and extremely hideous,
With black hair,
A huge head,
And long and wide ears.
His eyes are big and large,
Glowing like fire.
Flames come out of his nostrils,
And with them, an evil smell.
His round and irregular teeth are ugly.
The inside of his mouth is darker than iron.
His beard and hair
Look like pure gold.
His breath is so foul
That the whole cell reeks.
Seeing him approaching her,
Margaret does not know what to do.
She does not dare make a move.
There is no escape from the dragon.
Fear makes her tremble.
With his tongue,
The dragon lifts her up by the feet.
She falls down on the ground,
And he swallows her up in one gulp.
But the sign of the cross that she had made
Has imprinted her, in such a way
That the serpent is pierced in the middle.

When the maiden sees the opening,
She emerges from the dragon,
Healthy and unharmed,
And more confident in God's love
Than ever before.
Soon after, a dark man,
Who did not look like a Christian
But was blacker than an Egyptian,
Appears and approaches her.
She whose trust is in God
Asks him boldly:
"And who are you? I order you,
In God's name, to answer me."
"And so I will, if you intercede for me
Before your God, who harmed me greatly
When he caused my brother to be split open,
In the name of your love and prayers.
You have indeed made him pay dearly
For the sufferings you have endured.
The pain has become his."
"Who is your brother?" "Ruffin.
Most painful was his death,
Which I now deeply grieve.
This is what prompted me to come here,
To torment you, to harm you,
And to avenge my brother's death."
"What is your name?"
"They call me Beelzebub,
And rightly so.
I am the king and lord of all the devils.
I never cared for goodness,
Loving only the worst of sins.
I have swallowed in my belly
The riches, the goods,
And the possessions of many people.
I have friends and soldiers
That I send in order to deceive
Those who, I can see,
Act out of lust
And have no care for virtue.
I watch over them so closely

That I promptly induce them to sin.
And when I hold them in my nets,
Great are my joy and my satisfaction.
Such is indeed my reaction, when I can catch one of my prey.
It was I who inspired the wrongs you endured,
I who caused your capture, and your tortures.
And you can expect far more,
Unless you agree to obey
The one who holds you in his power."
When the maiden hears his words
And discovers that he is the one who caused her ordeal,
She rushes at him,
Pulls him down by the hair,
And holds him tight.
She puts her foot on his chest,
And beats him a great deal.
Under the strain of her pressure,
He cries out, begging for mercy:
"Ha! lady, lift up your foot
And let me regain my breath!
For I can hardly breathe."
"Ha!" she says, "mad and evil man,
Despicable and foul creature,
Beast full of iniquity,
Threat to my virginity,
Be careful not to harm me,
If you ever want to get up!"
"I promise you, in all honesty,
That I will never do to you
Any cruel, mean,
Harmful, or foul deed,
If you let me escape.
Take your foot away, for it hurts me."
She lets him go, and he disappears.

[Margaret resumes her prayers, thanking God for having protected her. There is a sudden earthquake. Then a dove appears, carrying a rich crown.]

All the witnesses who were near the cell
And who saw God's glorious deeds,
Began to wonder.

There numbered more than four thousand,
Men, women, and children.
They all converted and praised God.
And Margaret asked God to bless them.
When Olymbrius heard
About the conversion of these people,
He became enraged.
So great was his cruelty,
That he ordered that they be taken
Outside the walls of the city,
And that they be beheaded
In a field called Lymet.
He could not wait one more day.
When this evil deed was accomplished,
He then ordered that Margaret be taken
Out of her cell at once.
"Go," he tells his soldier,
"And cut her head off!
There is no better way for me to take my revenge.
Her resistance will thus come to an end."
The soldier who holds the sword
Goes where his lord has sent him.
He conveys his lord's edict word for word,
Asking her to kneel
And to offer him her neck,
So that he can cut her head off more easily.
For he does not want to miss his target.
She kneels at once,
Lowers her head, and offers him her neck.
But as he is lifting the sword,
He looks to his right,
And sees that God, accompanied
By his angels, is standing at Margaret's side.
The soldier becomes frightened.
As if bewitched,
He can no longer move his feet,
Nor lift his arm.
He is dismayed and confused.
"Maiden," he says, "get up at once!
I will never strike you,

Rest assured."
She tells him: "Friend, why?
For you will never join me
If you do not kill me now."
"I will not do it, for Jesus Christ
Is beside me, who forbids me
To do such a thing."
"Friend, if you have seen God,
Do what you must do, thus allowing me
To join my Creator and to adore him in Heaven.
For I have no care to remain in this world any longer."
And the soldier agrees.
She starts praying devoutly:
"I ask for your mercy, Good Lord, and present you with this request:
May all those who will write
My life, or have it written,
Receive your forgiveness, whatever their sins,
Sins which are never hidden to you.
I, Margaret, also pray to you,
God, that you give me power
To protect any pregnant woman,
If she crosses herself
With a book containing the story of my life,
Or opens it,
Or places it on her body,
So that she be granted a safe delivery.
And may you also grant me the following:
May any woman who commemorates me,
In a church founded in my name,
Be granted – when she finishes
Her prayers,
And after listening to the story of my martyrdom –
That the fruit of her womb not die,
At the time of conception,
Or during pregnancy.
And when her time comes,
May her infant be in good health,
And free from any physical or mental deformity.
I ask you also to grant me this request:
May he be never wrongly judged nor deprived of his rights

– In a court of justice or in a suit –
He who will have, on that day,
Remembered my life.
And may he who gives
– To any church where there are proofs
That my life is true –
Candles of oil or wax,
Be protected from all perils.
I also ask you, good God,
That you protect the places
– Where my life will be written –
From the power of evil spirits,
And from fires caused either by lightning or by storm.
May the evil spirit never visit these places,
And may they be inhabited by the Holy Spirit,
In goodness, peace, and charity.
And may joy, honor, and good luck
Be bestowed on any man or woman
Who lives at a place
Where my life is written."

[Descending from Heaven, a dove tells Margaret that her requests will be granted. Margaret is then beheaded, and the angels carry her soul to Paradise.]

Theotimus, the man who saw to it
That Margaret's martyrdom be recorded,
Along with the prayers she said while in prison,
Had these writings sent to every church.
Thanks to him, it became known to everyone
That Margaret had departed from this earth.
This news inspired
Many ill people to go to the place where she was martyred,
In order to be cured of their afflictions.
There was no one,
Upon touching her tomb,
Who did not find himself healed at once.
Whether bitten by a snake or suffering from fever,
They were all cured forever.
And I can tell you more:

There, songs of angels were often heard,
As well as the moaning
Of unbelievers, who came to Margaret's tomb,
Lamenting
The miracles made by God,
On account of his friend who lay there.
Margaret died at this place.
May God, who sees everything,
Grant his glory
To those who remember her.
She is now in a good place
Where she knows only bliss.
Let us pray to God that everyone
Be granted to go directly to Paradise.
Let us say amen, that God may grant our request.

CHAPTER NINE

EPILOGUE

The cult of the saints became a major issue in the controversies that raged between Roman Catholics and Protestant reformers from the fourteenth century onwards. While critics of the abuses associated with pilgrimage and relics had long existed within the Church, the reformers went further since they denied the role of the saints as intercessors and made the claim that Christ was the only true mediator. They were willing to acknowledge only that the saints set the best example of holy living for other Christians. At the Council of Trent in 1563 the Roman Church reaffirmed the principle of the intercession of the saints, and directed that the faithful should be instructed to pray to them. This remains an essential difference between Roman Catholic and Protestant Churches today. Where hagiography was concerned, 'The Golden Legend' was a focus of attack by both Catholics and Protestants, but orthodox 'lives' and collections of 'lives' continued to appear during the fifteenth and sixteenth centuries, including Mombritius's 'Sanctuarium' (Milan, before 1480) and the 'De probatis sanctorum historiis' of Lawrence Surius (Cologne, 1570-75), which combined hagiography with a polemic against the Protestants. On the Protestant side John Foxe produced his 'Book of Martyrs' in English (1563) with a dedication to Elizabeth I. It was intended as a polemic against the Catholics and included a calendar of Protestant martyrs. Alban Butler's 'Lives of the Fathers, Martyrs, and Other Principal Saints' (1756-59), a collection of some 1600 'lives' of saints, was a further response from the Catholic side. Today the work of establishing texts and determining their historical value continues in the hands of the Bollandists, of Vatican researchers into the claims of candidates for canonization, and of numerous other scholars worldwide.

[Fig. 55] A portrait of Wycliffe made in 1581 by Jean de Laon, Geneva (Lacroix, *Military and Religious Life in the Middle Ages*, p. 409).

49. A REFORMER'S VIEW OF THE CULT OF THE SAINTS

One of the earliest salvos in the attack by reformers on the cult of the saints was fired by the Englishman John Wycliffe (c.1330-1384). Educated at Oxford, where he received his Doctor of Divinity and was for a time Master of Balliol, he went on to receive an income as the sometime-absentee rector of parishes in the university's gift. His interests took a political direction in 1374 when he was appointed by Edward III to take part in discussions with papal representatives on such matters of perennial dis- agreement as the taxes owed to Rome and the authority to make church appointments. A prolific writer and preacher, Wycliffe argued for the pre-eminence of the Law of God over the authority of the established Church, and for a direct relationship between Christians and the Divinity. He promoted the translation of the Bible into English, and preached against the mediating roles of both saints and priests. Under the powerful protection of John of Gaunt, Wycliffe escaped arrest when brought before the ecclesias- tical authorities in 1377. However, following the Peasants' Revolt in 1381, in which some of the leaders professed similar ideas, his writings were condemned by the arch- bishop of Canterbury and banned at Oxford. Even many who had earlier supported him could not accept his argument against transsubstantiation (the doctrine that during the sacrament of the Mass, the eucharistic substance of bread and wine is changed into the body and blood of Christ). Wycliffe's suspicion of outward signs and materialistic rituals fed his attacks on the cult of the saints, as the following excerpts show. They are taken from his treatise 'De Ecclesia,' completed in 1378. His followers, persecuted in the fifteenth and sixteenth centuries, were among the earliest of a new breed of Protestant martyrs.

Source: trans. M.A. Stouck from Johann Loserth, ed. *Johannis Wyclif: Tractatus de Ecclesia* (rpt. 1966; London: Trübner & Co., 1886), pp. 44-46 and 465-466.

On the Church 2: Canonization and Miracles

. . . Although there may be strong evidence from the testimony of the Roman church that an individual whom it canonizes is a member of the church triumphant, and even stronger evidence if God performs miracles on behalf of the saint, nevertheless on this question both sorts of evidence can be illusory. For as canon law itself indicates, the church both deceives and is deceived (as is clear from book 5 of the Decretals [of Gregory IX], in the title "On the sentence of excommunication" beginning "A nobis"). [For the church] excommunicates many, at one time or another, who are guiltless and fully acceptable in God's sight; and conversely it often absolves and inscribes in the catalogue of saints [the martyrology] those whom God would rightly condemn. God forbid that any Christian should think that salvation requires every faithful person to believe explicitly, concerning this or that person can-onized by the church, that he is a saint, since then we would have a creed that was far too long [to recite]. Nor should we believe explicitly that any particular individual is not a saint, but rather we should avoid consideration of such things, stick to what is more probable, [and] believe with reservations, or doubt with pious caution. As far as other saints [are concerned] – that is to say the apostles, the martyrs and the saints of the early church – we believe without misgiving and acknowledge that they are saints; but when it comes to more recent saints who are canonized because of lineage, petition or gifts, we ought not to put such great trust in them. It is not my intention to cut off any who have been canonized or to argue that they are not part of the church triumphant; but if I believe that they are, it is with a certain reverent doubt, since I also know that it is possible they are not. Since this is the case, I believe implicitly what I cannot know for certain, and I do not wish to prove beyond a doubt that whoever is on Christ's side is a saint, although I believe unhesitatingly that many of them are. Nor do recent miracles neces-sarily give true faith to everyone, since the devil may be given the power to punish the sin of an adulterous generation that seeks for signs and renounces the requisite faith in things unseen; thus by these unchristian portents many are led astray (these portents are discussed in Book Six, chapter six). More-over, it is the custom nowadays for any natural wonder performed by God to be called a miracle, and thus many are tempted to draw the wrong conclu-sions since any created thing seems to be a miracle of God. But in formal terms a miracle is understood as God's own wonderful operation in a crea-ture, and thus it is not the saints who perform miracles, although sometimes they are the occasion of them, as when God performs a miracle because of the insistence of their prayers or [because of] their merits. And then those saints are said to have performed the miracle as a subordinate agent or in a lesser capacity, as the case may be. And the ability to discern the miracle is hidden from all except for those to whom God wishes to reveal it. And I wish that all these ceremonies and signs were not increased in our church, since the deeds of the saints and all other rites are only praiseworthy to the extent that they lift the spirit to the love of our Lord Jesus Christ. Moreover it seems to many that the faith, brought into confusion by prayer to the saints, would unite Christians in belief in Christ more closely – and so more intensely, securely and better – if such a crowd of saints were not introduced daily. For we cannot understand clearly whether an individual saint is blessed or damned, or whether he is destined to be among the reprobate or the elect. Thus our understanding is confused through doubt and ignorance about particular cases, along with a clear knowledge of what is common to all. So also, multiple canonizations beyond the limits of the Old Testament and of our own early church are partly useful and partly harmful; but it is likely that for many they are more harmful, since a great number of observances that destroy the liberty of the church are the cause of many errors. And every such saint would pray for us more effectively if his cult were abandoned and we loved our Jesus more. For there are many saints unknown to us, but more blessed than those who have been canonized, who help us more by praying than those saints whose feasts we honor with special devotion, since the saints' love and prayers, in accordance with the worthiness of the supplicant, are most beneficial to those who prefer to love God [rather than the saints themselves].

On the Church, 19: The Cult of Relics

. . . Such culpable blindness and the excessive and covetous cult surrounding relics cause many people to be falsely drawn into the penalty of sin. And so in many countries greed often causes churches to buy parts of a human-being so that he may be canonized as a confessor or martyr and is then more honored by pilgrimages, by sumptuous offerings and by the ornamentation of his tomb with gold and precious stones than the body of the Mother of God herself, or [the bodies] of the apostles Peter and Paul or of other famous saints. And the proof of these things lies in the fact that they can be done truly and meritoriously, and that the priests to whom this is unknown give their approval so that it may be so. I reject no act of this kind and I approve of none, or of very few, because those making pilgrimages, worshiping relics and accumulating wealth could be much more usefully occupied if these things were abolished. Indeed from things done in the law of Christ and in scripture [the Gospels] it seems to follow that all those engaged in these things could be better employed, and therefore they sin gravely if they fail to be so. I pass over the sins which pertain to the other side in this matter, and how the same was done by the Pharisaic fathers of the Old Testament, not from the new law effectively founded for us, but as highly dubious, and injurious both on the part of the relic-worshipers and on the part of the relic-owners. For just as in the old law the signs of an adulterous generation grew stronger as the Jews turned aside from the worship of invisible things, so under the new law, as love of heavenly things grows sluggish, it is appropriate that human traditions and the rites of earthly ceremonies prevail, since religion and the desire for heavenly things have been set aside. . .

For it is right that the Devil in the guise of holiness should seduce men into hypocrisy by the illusion of material signs, because the sins of the people require this, and the Devil sees that the people are more apt to be seduced in this way.

50. A HERETIC'S CONFESSION

The extent to which the Lollards, as Wycliffe's followers were called, knew his writings at first hand is unclear, but the success of his ideas in attracting adherents can be measured by the fact that in 1428, forty-four years after his death, he was considered such a serious threat that his remains were exhumed, burnt, and scattered as a sign that he was to be known as a heretic. Fierce persecution of the Lollards continued well into the sixteenth century. Many of them were prepared to go further than Wycliffe had done in condemning the saints and their cult. The following excerpt is taken from the records of a series of trials held at Norwich between 1428 and 1431. Norwich had become a center of Lollardy, with some of the leaders fleeing there from persecution in Kent. Though the trial records do not name Wycliffe, the accused confessed to similar beliefs: they were opposed to the sacraments, to the church's possession of temporal goods, to tithing, swearing oaths (which medieval law required in some circumstances), and to all aspects of the cult of the saints, even though Wycliffe himself had praised those saints he believed to be genuine. The punishment for the Norwich heretics after recanting was generally flogging, carried out during solemn parish processions on Sundays or in the public square on market day. Some, however, endured death by burning, including William White and Hugh Pye, leaders of the group named in Hawisia's confession. Hawisia's husband Thomas was a well-to-do shoemaker, and several members of his household came under suspicion; as a group however the Norwich Lollards were not wealthy, and included glovers, tailors, carpenters, a butcher, and a miller.

Source: modernized from Middle English by M.A. Stouck, from the edition by Norman P. Tanner, *Heresy Trials in the Diocese of Norwich, 1428-31,* Camden Fourth Series, Vol. 20 (London: The Royal Historical Society, 1977), pp. 140–143.

In the name of God, before you, worshipful father in Christ, William, by the grace of God bishop of Norwich, I, Hawisia Moone, the wife of Thomas Moone of Loddon of your diocese, your subject, knowing, recognizing and understanding that before this time I have been very close in secret with many heretics, knowing them to be heretics, and I have taken them in and given them lodging in our house, and I have hidden them, comforted, supported and maintained them and favored them with all my might — and the names of the heretics are these: Sir William White, Sir William Caleys, Sir Hugh Pye, Sir Thomas Pert, priests, John Waddon, John Fowlyn, John Gray, William Everden, William Bate of Seething, Bartholomew Cornmonger, Thomas Borell and Baty, his wife, William Wardon, John Pert, Edmond Archer of Loddon, Richard Belward, Nicholas Belward, Bartholomew Monk, William Wright and many others — who have often kept, held and maintained schools of heresy in private chambers and secret places of ours, in which schools I have heard, conceived, learned and reported the errors and heresies which are written and contained in these indentures [formal agreements], that is to say: First, that the sacrament of Baptism performed by water in the form customary in the church is nonsense and of no account, for all Christ's people are sufficiently baptized in the blood of Christ, and so Christ's people need no other baptism.

Also that the sacrament of Confirmation performed by a bishop is of no avail, nor [is it] necessary to have it, since when a child has acquired discretion and is able, and wishes, to understand the word of God, [that child] is sufficiently confirmed by the Holy Ghost and needs no other confirmation.

Also that confession should be made only to God, and not to any other priest, for no priest has the power to remit sin nor to absolve a man of any sin.

Also that no-one is bound to do penance prescribed by any priest for [them] to do for their sins which they have confessed to the priest, for it is sufficient penance for all kinds of sin if every person refrains from lying, back-biting and wicked deeds, and no-one is bound to do any other penance.

Also that no priest has the power to make Christ's true body at Mass in the form of bread, but that after the sacramental words spoken at the Mass by the priest, only material bread remains.

Also that the pope of Rome is Father Antichrist, and false in all his deeds, and has no power before God, any more than any other ignorant man, unless he [the pope] is more holy in his way of life, and the pope has no power to create bishops, priests or any other orders, and he whom the people call the pope of Rome is no pope but a false extortioner and a deceiver of the people.

Also that only he who is most holy and most perfect in his life on earth is the true pope, and these mass-singers who are called priests are not priests, but they are lecherous and covetous men and false deceivers of the people, and with their clever teaching and preaching, singing and reading, they rob the people pitifully of their goods with which they sustain their pride, their lechery, their sloth and all other vices, and they keep on making new laws and new ordinances to curse and kill cruelly all other people who criticize their wicked manner of life. . . .

Also that no-one is bound to fast in Lent, Ember Days, Fridays nor on the vigils of saints, but on all such days and times it is lawful for all Christ's people to eat flesh and all kinds of food without differentiating, as they please and as often as they are hungry, just as much as on any other day when no fast is ordered.

Also that no pilgrimage ought to be performed or made, for all pilgrimages serve for nothing but only to give goods to priests who are too wealthy and to deck out barmaids and make innkeepers proud.

Also that no honor or reverence ought to be done to any images of the crucifix, of Our Lady or of any other saints, for all such images are only idols and made by craft of man's hand, but honor and reverence should be done to the image of God, who alone is man.

Also that all prayer ought to be made only to God, and to no other saints, for it is doubtful if there are such saints in heaven as these mass-singers endorse and command [us] to honor and pray to, here on earth.

Because of these and many other errors and heresies I have been called before you, worshipful father, who have the care of my soul. And may you be fully informed that my aforesaid affirmation, belief and way of thinking are open errors and heresies and contrary to the doctrine of the Church of Rome, wherefore I [am] willing [to] follow and pursue the doctrine of holy Church and to depart from all manner of error and heresy, and turn with good will and heart to the unity of the Church. . . .

In witness of these things I write here below with my own hand a cross.

51.ERASMUS: *A PILGRIMAGE FOR RELIGION'S SAKE*

Born in Rotterdam c.1466, Erasmus has been called the greatest humanist of the northern Renaissance. He was ordained a priest in 1493, but the restricted life of a formal religious was uncongenial to him, and he eventually obtained papal sanction for a career of independent study, teaching, and writing. He traveled widely and became friends with many English and Italian humanists. An enemy of dogmatism in all its forms, he corresponded with Luther but wrote against the reformers. His 'Colloquies' had a mixed reception. Intended for use in schools to teach Latin, they were widely popular but were also censured, notably by the theological faculty of the Sorbonne which charged that the descriptions of religious life were impious or even heretical. 'A Pilgrimage for Religion's Sake' was first printed in 1526, and grew out of visits made by Erasmus to the shrines of Our Lady of Walsingham and St. Thomas à Becket at Canterbury. A decade later, when Henry VIII destroyed the shrines and confiscated their treasures, this colloquy was reprinted anonymously as a useful piece of propaganda, but the abuses described by Erasmus had been the subject of a long tradition of earlier complaint within the church. 'Menedemus' means 'stay-at-home,' and 'Ogygius' may imply 'simple-minded' or 'stupid.'

Source: trans. Craig R. Thompson, *Ten Colloquies of Erasmus* (New York: The Liberal Arts Press, Inc., 1957), pp. 56-91; repr. with permission.

Menedemus, Ogygius

Menedemus. What marvel is this? Don't I see my neighbor Ogygius, whom nobody's laid eyes on for six whole months? I heard he was dead. It's his very self, unless I'm losing my mind completely. I'll go up to him and say hello. – Greetings, Ogygius!

Ogygius. Same to you, Menedemus.

Menedemus. Where in the world do you turn up from, safe and sound? A sad rumor spread here that you'd sailed in Stygian waters [died].

Ogygius. No, thank heaven; I've seldom enjoyed better health.

Menedemus. I hope you'll always be able to refute silly rumors of that sort! But what's this fancy outfit? You're ringed with scallop shells [symbol of St. James of Compostella, see 25 above], choked with tin and leaden images on every side, decked out with straw necklaces, and you have snake eggs [rosary beads] on your arms.

Ogygius. I've been on a visit to St. James of Compostella and, on my way back, to the famous Virgin-by-the-Sea, [at Walsingham, Norfolk] in England; or rather I revisited her, since I had gone there three years earlier.

Menedemus. Out of curiosity, I dare say.

Ogygius. Oh, no: out of devotion.

Menedemus. Greek letters, I suppose, taught you that devotion.

Ogygius. My wife's mother had bound herself by a vow that if her daughter gave birth to a boy and he lived, I would promptly pay my respects to St. James and thank him in person.

Menedemus. Did you greet the saint only in your own name and your mother-in-law's?

Ogygius. Oh, no, in the whole family's.

Menedemus. Well, I imagine your family would have been no less safe even if you had left James ungreeted. But do please tell me: what answer did he make when you thanked him?

Ogygius. None, but he seemed to smile as I offered my gift, nodded his head slightly, and at the same time held out these scallop shells.

Menedemus. Why does he give these rather than some thing else?

Ogygius. Because he has plenty of them; the sea nearby supplies them.

Menedemus. O generous saint, who both delivers those in labor and gives presents to callers! But what new kind of vowing is this, that some lazy person lays the work on others? If you bound yourself by a vow that, should *your* affairs prosper, *I* would fast twice a week, do you think I'd do what you had vowed?

Ogygius. No, I don't, even if you'd sworn in your own name. For you enjoy mocking the saints. But she's my mother-in-law, custom had to be kept. You're acquainted with women's whims, and besides I had an interest in it, too.

Menedemus. If you hadn't kept her vow, what risk would there have been?

Ogygius. The saint couldn't have sued me at law, I admit, but he could have been deaf thereafter to my prayers, or secretly have brought some disaster upon my family. You know the ways of the mighty.

Menedemus. Tell me, how is the excellent James?

Ogygius. Much colder than usual.

Menedemus. Why? Old age?

Ogygius. Joker! You know saints don't grow old. But this newfangled notion that pervades the whole world results in his being greeted more seldom than usual. And if people do come, they merely greet him; they make no offering at all, or only a very slight one, declaring it would be better to contribute that money to the poor.

Menedemus. An impious notion!

Ogygius. And thus so great an apostle, accustomed to shine from head to foot in gold and jewels, now stands a wooden figure with hardly a tallow candle to his name.

Menedemus. If what I hear is true, there's danger that other saints may come to the same pass.

Ogygius. More than that: a letter is going round which the Virgin Mary herself wrote on this very theme.

Menedemus. Which Mary?

Ogygius. The one called Mary a Lapide.

Menedemus. At Basel, unless I'm mistaken [a reference to a famous statue of the Virgin at Mariastein near Basel].

Ogygius. Yes.

Menedemus. Then it's a stony saint you tell me of. But to whom did she write?

Ogygius. She herself gives the name in the letter.

Menedemus. Who delivered the letter?

Ogygius. Undoubtedly an angel, who placed it on the pulpit from which the recipient preaches. And to prevent suspicion of fraud, you shall see the very autograph.

Menedemus. So you recognize the hand of the angel who is the Virgin's secretary?

Ogygius. Why, of course.

Menedemus. By what mark?

Ogygius. I've read Bede's epitaph [in the abbey church at Durham], which was engraved by an angel. The shape of the letters agrees entirely. Also I've read the manuscript message to St. Giles [a scroll placed by an angel on the altar in response to the prayers of St. Giles, mentioned in *The Golden Legend*]. They agree. Aren't these facts proof enough?

Menedemus. Is one allowed to see it?

Ogygius. Yes, if you'll promise to keep your mouth shut about it.

Menedemus. Oh, to tell me is to tell a stone.

Ogygius. But some stones [touchstones, which detect whether gold is true or not] are notorious for giving secrets away.

Menedemus. Then tell it to a deaf man, if you don't trust a stone.

Ogygius. On that condition I'll read it. Lend me your ears.

Menedemus. I've lent them.

Ogygius. "Mary, Mother of Jesus, to Glaucoplutus ["owl-rich," a play on the first name of the Swiss reformer, Ulrich Zwingli]: greetings. Know that I am deeply grateful to you, a follower of Luther, for busily persuading people that the invocation of saints is useless. For up to this time I was all but exhausted by the shameless entreaties of mortals. They demanded everything from me alone, as if my Son were always a baby (because he is carved and painted as such at my bosom), still needing his mother's consent and not daring to deny a person's prayer; fearful, that is, that if he did deny the petitioner something, I for my part would refuse him the breast when he was thirsty. And sometimes they ask of a Virgin what a modest youth would hardly dare ask of a bawd – things I'm ashamed to put into words. Sometimes a merchant, off for Spain to make a fortune, commits to me the chastity of his mistress. And a nun who has thrown off her veil and is preparing to run away entrusts me with her reputation for virtue – which she herself intends to sell. A profane soldier, hired to butcher people, cries upon me, 'Blessed Virgin, give me rich booty.' A gambler cries, 'Help me, blessed saint; I'll share my winnings with you!' And if they lose at dice, they abuse me outrageously and curse me, because I wouldn't favor their wickedness. A woman who abandons herself to a life of shame cries, 'Give me a fat income!' If I refuse anything, they protest at once, 'Then you're no mother of mercy.'

"Some people's prayers are not so irreverent as absurd. An unmarried girl cries, 'Mary, give me a rich and handsome bridegroom.' A married one, 'Give me fine children.' A pregnant woman, 'Give me an easy delivery.' An old woman, 'Give me a long life without a cough or a thirst.' A doddering old man, 'Let me grow young again.' A philosopher, 'Give me power to contrive insoluble problems.' A priest, 'Give me a rich benefice.' A bishop, 'Preserve my church.' A sailor, 'Give me prosperous sailings.' A governor, 'Show me thy Son before I die.' A courtier, 'Grant that at point of death I may confess sincerely.' A countryman, 'Give me a heavy rain.' A country woman, 'Save the flock and herd from harm.' If I deny anything, straightway I'm cruel. If I refer to my Son, I hear, 'He wills whatever you will.' So am I alone, a woman and a virgin, to assist those who are sailing, fighting, trading, dicing, marrying, bearing children; to assist governors, kings, and farmers?

"What I've described is very little in comparison with what I endure. But nowadays I'm troubled much less by these matters. For this reason I would give you my heartiest thanks, did not this advantage bring a greater disadvantage along with it. I have more peace, but less honor and wealth. Formerly, I was hailed as 'Queen of Heaven, mistress of the world'; now I hear scarcely an 'Ave Maria' even from a few. Formerly I was clothed in gold and jewels; I had many changes of dress; I had golden and jeweled offerings made to me. Now I have hardly half a cloak to wear, and that one is mouse-eaten. My annual income is scarcely enough to keep the wretched sacristan who lights the little lamp or tallow candle. And yet all these hardships I could have borne, if you weren't said to be plotting even greater ones. You're trying, they say, to remove from the churches whatever belongs to the saints. Now just consider what you're doing. Other saints have means of avenging injuries. If Peter is ejected from a church, he can in turn shut the gate of heaven against you. Paul has a sword; Bartholomew is armed with a knife. Under his monk's

[Fig. 56] The ruined gatehouse of Walsingham Priory, from a nineteenth-century drawing. The most important site of Marian pilgrimage in England, Walsingham claimed to possess a replica of the Virgin's house in Nazareth and a vial of her milk. Destroyed during the Reformation, it was restored as a place of pilgrimage in the twentieth century (Nichols, *Pilgrimages,* p. 88).

robe William [St. William of Gellone, who fought against the Saracens under Charlemagne] is completely armed, nor does he lack a heavy lance. And what could you do against George, with his horse and his coat of mail, his spear and his terrible sword? Anthony's not defenseless, either: he has his sacred fire. Others likewise have weapons or mischiefs they direct against anybody they please. But me, however defenseless, you shall not eject unless at the same time you eject my Son whom I hold in my arms. From him I will not be parted. Either you expel him along with me, or you leave us both here, unless you prefer to have a church without Christ. I wanted you to know this. Think carefully what to answer, for my mind's absolutely made up. From our stony house, on the Calends of August, in the year of my Son's passion 1524. I, the Virgin a Lapide, have signed this with my own hand."

Menedemus. A dreadful, threatening letter, indeed! I imagine Glaucoplutus will take warning.

Ogygius. If he's wise.

Menedemus. Why didn't the excellent James write to him on this same subject?

Ogygius. I don't know, except that he's rather far away, and all letters are intercepted nowadays.

Menedemus. But what fortune brought you back to England?

Ogygius. An unexpectedly favourable breeze carried me there, and I had virtually promised the saint-by-the-sea [Our Lady of Walsingham] that I would pay her another visit in two years.

Menedemus. What were you going to ask of her?

Ogygius. Nothing new, just the usual things: family safe and sound, a larger fortune, a long and happy life in this world, and eternal bliss in the next.

Menedemus. Couldn't the Virgin Mother here at home see to those matters? At Antwerp she has a church much grander than the one by the sea.

Ogygius. I can't deny that, but different things are bestowed in different places, either because she prefers this or (since she is obliging) because she accommodates herself in this respect to our feelings.

Menedemus. I've often heard about James, but I beg you to describe for me the domain of the Virgin-by-the-Sea.

Ogygius. Well, I'll do the best I can in brief. She has the greatest fame throughout England, nor would you readily find anyone in that island who hoped for prosperity unless he greeted her annually with a small gift, according to his means.

Menedemus. Where does she live?

Ogygius. By the northwest coast of England, only about three miles from the sea. The village has scarcely any means of support apart from the tourist trade. There's a college of canons, to whom, however, the Latins add the title of regulars: an order midway between monks and the canons called seculars [Austin canons, of whose order Erasmus himself was a member].

Menedemus. You're telling me of amphibians, such as the beaver.

Ogygius. Yes, and the crocodile. But details aside, I'll try to satisfy you in a few words. In unfavorable matters they're canons; in favourable ones, monks.

Menedemus. So far you're telling me a riddle.

Ogygius. But I'll add a precise illustration. If the Roman pontiff assailed all monks with a thunderbolt, then they'd be canons, not monks. Yet if he permitted all monks to take wives then they'd be monks.

Menedemus. Strange favors! I wish they'd take mine too.

Ogygius. But to get to the point. This college depends most entirely on the Virgin's generosity for its support. The larger gifts are kept, to be sure, but any small change, anything of trifling value, goes towards the support of the community and their head, whom they call the prior.

Menedemus. Do they live holy lives?

Ogygius. They're not unpraised. They're richer in piety than income. The church is fine and splendid, but the Virgin doesn't dwell there; in honor of her Son she yields that to him. She has her own church, that she may be to the right of her Son.

Menedemus. The right? Which direction does the Son face, then?

Ogygius. I'm glad you remind me. When he faces west he has his mother on his right; when he turns to the east she's on his left. However, she doesn't dwell here, either, for the building is not yet finished, and the place is quite airy – windows and doors open, and Ocean, father of the winds, nearby.

Menedemus. Too bad. So where does she live?

Ogygius. In that church, which as I said is unfinished, is a small chapel built on a wooden platform. Visitors are admitted through a narrow door on each side. There's very little light: only what comes from tapers, which have a most pleasing scent.

Menedemus. All this is appropriate to religion.

Ogygius. Yes, and if you peered inside, Menedemus, you would say it was the abode of the saints, so dazzling is it with jewels, gold, and silver.

Menedemus. You make me impatient to go there.

Ogygius. You wouldn't regret the trip.

Menedemus. Is there no holy oil there?

Ogygius. Silly! That oil exudes only from the tombs of saints, such as Andrew and Catherine. Mary isn't buried.

Menedemus. My mistake, I admit. But finish your story.

Ogygius. As the cult spreads more widely, different things are displayed in different places.

Menedemus. In order, perhaps, that the giving may be more generous; as it is said, "Loot quickly comes when sought by many hands."

Ogygius. And custodians are always present.

Menedemus. Some of the canons?

Ogygius. No, they're not used, lest on a favourable opportunity for religious devotion they might stray from devoutness, and while honoring the Virgin pay too little regard to their own virginity. Only in the interior chapel, which I said is the inner sanctum of the Holy Virgin, a canon stands by the altar.

Menedemus. What for?

Ogygius. To receive and keep the offering.

Menedemus. Do people contribute whether they want to or not?

Ogygius. Not at all, but a sort of reverent shame impels some to give when a person's standing by. They wouldn't give if no one were present to watch them. Or sometimes they give more generously than they would otherwise.

Menedemus. That's human nature. I'm no stranger to it.

Ogygius. Nay, there are some so devoted to the Most Holy Virgin that while they pretend to lay an offering on the altar, they steal, with astonishing nimbleness, what somebody else had placed there.

Menedemus. Suppose there's no witness: would the Virgin strike them dead on the spot?

Ogygius. Why would the Virgin do that, any more than does the heavenly Father himself, whom men aren't afraid to rob of treasures, even digging through the church wall for the purpose?

Menedemus. I can't tell which to be the more astonished at, their impious audacity or God's mildness.

Ogygius. Then, on the north side — not of the church (don't mistake me) but of the wall enclosing the whole area adjacent to the church — is a certain gateway. It has a tiny door, the kind noblemen's gates have, so that whoever wants to enter must first expose his shins to danger and then stoop besides.

Menedemus. Certainly it wouldn't be safe to go at an enemy through such a door.

Ogygius. Right. The custodian told me that once a knight on horseback escaped through this door from the hands of an enemy who was on the point of overtaking him in his flight. In despair he commended himself then and there to the Holy Virgin, who was close by. For he had determined to take refuge at her altar if the door was open. And mark this wonder: suddenly the knight was entirely within the churchyard and the other man outside, furious.

Menedemus. And was this wondrous tale of his believed?

Ogygius. Of course.

Menedemus. A philosophical chap like you wouldn't accept it so easily.

Ogygius. He showed me on the door a copper plate, fastened by nails, containing a likeness of the knight who was saved, dressed in the English fashion of that period as we see it in old pictures – and if pictures don't lie, barbers had a hard time in those days, and so did weavers and dyers.

Menedemus. How so?

Ogygius. Because the knight was bearded like a goat, and his clothing didn't have a single pleat, and was so tight it made the body itself thinner. There was another plate, too, showing the size and shape of the shrine.

Menedemus. You no longer had any reason to doubt!

Ogygius. Beneath the little door was an iron grating, admitting you only on foot. It was not seemly that a horse should afterwards trample the spot the horseman had consecrated to the Virgin.

Menedemus. And quite rightly.

Ogygius. To the east is a small chapel, filled with marvels. I betake myself to it. Another custodian receives us. After we've prayed briefly, we're immediately shown the joint of a human finger (the largest of three). I kiss it and then ask whose relics these are. "St. Peter's," he says. "Not the Apostle Peter's?" "Yes." Then, looking at the great size of the joint, which might have been a giant's, I said, "Peter must have been an extremely big man." At this one of my companions burst into a loud laugh, which annoyed me no end, for if he had been quiet the attendant would have kept none of the relics from our inspection. However, we appeased him with some coins.

In front of the little building was a structure that during the wintertime (he said), when everything was covered by snow, had been brought there suddenly from far away [a reference to the Holy House, supposedly a copy of Mary's house in Nazareth, the original, according to medieval legend, having been miraculously transported to Loretto in Italy]. Under this were two wells, filled to the top. They say the stream of water is sacred to the Holy Virgin. It's a wonderfully cold fluid, good for headache and stomach troubles.

Menedemus. If cold water cures headache and stomach troubles, oil will put out fire next.

Ogygius. You're hearing about a miracle, my good friend – besides, what would be miraculous about cold water quenching thirst?

Menedemus. Clearly this is only one part of the story.

Ogygius. That stream of water, they declared, suddenly shot up from the ground at the command of the Most Holy Virgin. Inspecting everything carefully, I inquired how many years it was since the little house had been brought there. "Some ages," he replied. "In any event," I said, "the walls don't look very old." He didn't dissent. "Even these wooden posts don't look old." He didn't deny they had been placed there recently, and the fact was self-evident. "Then," I said, "the roof and thatch of the house seem rather recent." He agreed. "Not even these crossbeams, nor the very rafters supporting the roof, appear to have been put here many years ago." He nodded. "But since no part of the building has survived, how is it known for certain," I asked, "that this is the cottage brought here from so far away?"

Menedemus. How did the attendant get out of that tangle, if you please?

Ogygius. Why, he hurriedly showed us an old, worn-out bearskin fastened to posts, and almost laughed at us for our dullness in being slow to see such a clear proof. So, being persuaded, and excusing our stupidity, we turned to the heavenly milk of the Blessed Virgin.

Menedemus. O Mother most like her Son! He left us so much of his blood on earth; she left so much of her milk that it's scarcely credible a woman with only one child could have so much, even if the child had drunk none of it.

Ogygius. The same thing is said about the Lord's Cross, which is exhibited publicly and privately in so many places that if the fragments were joined together they'd seem a full load for a freighter. And yet the Lord carried his whole cross.

Menedemus. Doesn't it seem amazing to you, too?

Ogygius. It could be called unusual, perhaps, but "amazing" – no, since the Lord, who multiplies these things as he wills, is omnipotent.

Menedemus. You explain it reverently, but for my part I'm afraid many such affairs are contrived for profit.

Ogygius. I don't think God will stand for anybody mocking him in that way.

Menedemus. On the contrary, although Mother and Son and Father and Spirit are robbed by the sacrilegious, some times they don't even bestir themselves slightly enough to frighten off the criminals by a nod or a noise. So great is the mildness of divinity.

Ogygius. That's true. But hear the rest. This milk is kept on the high altar, in the midst of which is Christ; on the right, for the sake of honor, is his mother. For the milk represents his Mother.

Menedemus. So it's in plain sight.

Ogygius. Enclosed in crystal, that is.

Menedemus. Therefore liquid.

Ogygius. What do you mean, liquid, when it flowed fifteen hundred years ago? It's hard: you'd say powdered chalk, tempered with white of egg.

Menedemus. Why don't they display it exposed?

Ogygius. To save the virginal milk from being defiled by the kisses of men.

Menedemus. Well said, for in my opinion there are those who would bring neither clean nor chaste mouths to it.

Ogygius. When the custodian saw us, he rushed up to it, donned a linen vestment, threw a sacred stole round his neck, prostrated himself devoutly, and adored. Soon afterward he held out the sacred milk for us to kiss. We prostrated our selves devoutly on the lowest step of the altar and, after first saluting Christ, uttered to the Virgin a short prayer I had prepared for this occasion: "Virgin Mother, who hast had the honor of suckling at thy maidenly breast the Lord of heaven and earth, thy Son Jesus, we pray that, cleansed by his blood, we may gain that blessed infancy of dovelike simplicity which, innocent of all malice, deceit, and guile, longs without ceasing for the milk of gospel doctrine until it attains to the perfect man, to the measure of the fullness of Christ, whose blessed company thou enjoyest forever, with the Father and Holy Spirit. Amen."

Menedemus. Certainly a devout intercession. What effect did it have?

Ogygius. Mother and Son both seemed to nod approval, unless my eyes deceived me. For the sacred milk appeared to leap up, and the Eucharistic elements gleamed somewhat more brightly. Meanwhile the custodian approached us, quite silent, but holding out a board [or box] like those used in Germany by toll collectors on bridges.

Menedemus. Yes, I've often cursed those greedy boards when traveling through Germany.

Ogygius. We gave him some coins, which he offered to the Virgin. Next, through an interpreter who understands the language well (a smooth-tongued young man named Robert Aldridge [a Cambridge scholar who worked with Erasmus], I believe), I tried as civilly as I could to find out what proof he had that this was the Virgin's milk. I wanted to know this clearly for the pious purpose of stopping the mouths of certain unbelievers who are accustomed to laugh at all these matters. At first the custodian frowned and said nothing. I told the interpreter to press him, but even more politely. He did so with the utmost grace, such that if with words of that sort he had entreated the Mother herself, recently out of childbed, she would not have taken offence. But the custodian, as if possessed, gazed at us in astonishment and as though horrified by such a blasphemous speech, said, "What need is there to inquire into that when you have an authentic record?" And it looked very much as if he would throw us out for heretics, had we not calmed the fellow's wrath with money.

Menedemus. What did you do then?

Ogygius. What do you suppose we did? As though beaten with a club, or struck by a thunderbolt, we took ourselves out of there, humbly begging pardon (as one should in sacred matters) for such outrageous presumption. Then on to the little chapel, the shrine of the Holy Virgin. At our approach a custodian turns up, a Minorite, and gazes at us, as though studying us; after we go a little farther a second one turns up, likewise staring at us; then a third.

Menedemus. Perhaps they wanted to draw you.

Ogygius. But I suspected something very different.

Menedemus. What was that?

Ogygius. That a sacrilegious person had filched something from the Holy Virgin's ornaments, and that their suspicion was directed against me. So when I entered the chapel I greeted the Virgin Mother with a short prayer, like this: "O thou alone of all womankind Mother and Virgin, Mother most blessed, purest of maidens, we who are unclean come unto thee who art pure. We bless thee, we worship thee as best we can with our poor gifts. May thy Son grant us that, by emulating thy most blessed life, we too, through the grace the Holy Spirit, may be made worthy to conceive the Lord Jesus spiritually in our inmost hearts, and never lose him once conceived. Amen." Kissing the altar at the same time, I laid some coins upon it and went away.

Menedemus. What did the Virgin do at this? Didn't she indicate by the slightest nod that your short prayer was heard?

Ogygius. As I told you, there was a dim religious light, and she stood in the shadows, to the right of the altar. Finally, the first custodian's harangue had so squelched me that I didn't dare lift my eyes.

Menedemus. So this expedition didn't end very happily.

Ogygius. On the contrary, quite happily.

Menedemus. You've brought me back to life, for "my heart had fallen to my knees," as your Homer says.

Ogygius. After lunch we went back to the church.

Menedemus. You dared to, when you were suspected of sacrilege?

Ogygius. That may be, but I was not suspect in my own eyes. A good conscience knows no fear. I wanted to see the "record" to which the guide had referred us. After searching for it a long time, we found it, but the board was hung so high nobody could possibly read it. I'm no Lynceus [a proverbially keen-sighted Argonaut] so far as eyes are concerned, nor am I totally blind, either. So as Aldridge read, I followed along, not trusting him completely in so vital a matter.

Menedemus. Were all your doubts cleared up?

Ogygius. I was ashamed of having doubted, so clearly was the whole thing set forth before my eyes – the name, the place, the story, told in order. In a word, nothing was omitted. There was said to be a certain William of Paris, a holy man, inasmuch as from time to time he was remarkably devoted to searching the world over for saints' relics. After traveling through many lands, visiting monasteries and churches every where, he came at length to Constantinople, where his brother was bishop. When William was preparing to return, his brother confided to him that a certain nun had the milk of the Virgin Mother, and that he would be extremely blessed ever afterwards if by prayer, purchase, or artifice he could get hold of a portion of it. For all other relics he had collected to date were as nothing compared with this sacred milk. From that moment William could not rest until by his begging he won a little of the milk. With this treasure he thought him self richer than Croesus.

Menedemus. Why not? And beyond expectation, too.

Ogygius. He hurried straight home, but death struck on the journey.

Menedemus. How slight, brief, and limited is human happiness!

Ogygius. Aware of the danger, he summons a fellow pilgrim, a most reliable Frenchman. Swearing him to secrecy, he entrusts the milk to him on condition that if he reaches home safely he is to place this treasure on the altar of the Holy Virgin who dwells in the great church in Paris, overlooking the Seine that flows by on each side – the river itself seems to give way in honor of the Virgin's sanctity. To make a long story short, William is buried; the other hurries on; and death takes him, too. In despair of his life, he gives the milk to an English companion, but binds him by many oaths to do what he himself had intended to do. He dies; the other takes the milk and places it on the altar in the presence of the canons there (formerly called regulars, as they are yet at St. Genevieve's). From them he begged a little of the milk. This he carried to England and finally brought to St. Mary-by-the-Sea, summoned to this place by divine inspiration.

Menedemus. Surely this story is very consistent.

Ogygius. More than that: lest any uncertainty remain, there were inscribed, above, the names of suffragan bishops who grant indulgences as extensive as their supply affords to those who come to see the milk and don't neglect to leave a small offering.

Menedemus. How much can they grant?

Ogygius. Forty days.

Menedemus. Are there days even in the underworld?

Ogygius. There's time, certainly.

Menedemus. When the whole supply's been granted, is there none left to give out?

Ogygius. On the contrary: what they grant is inexhaustible. And obviously this is different from what happens to the jar of the Danaides, since that, although continuously filled, is always empty; but as for this, if you always drain it, you still have no less in the jar.

Menedemus. If forty days apiece are granted to a hundred thousand men, each man has so much?

Ogygius. Yes.

Menedemus. And if those who received forty days before lunch were to ask for the same number again at dinnertime, it would be at hand to bestow?

Ogygius. Oh, yes, even if they asked for it ten times an hour.

Menedemus. Wish I had such a money box at home! I'd ask merely for three drachmas if only they renewed themselves.

Ogygius. If the answer to your prayer is to be so large as that, you're hoping to turn into gold completely. But to resume the story. This "proof" was added, with pious simplicity: that although the Virgin's milk shown in a great many other places was of course to be reverenced, nevertheless this was to be venerated more than that elsewhere, because that was scraped from rocks whereas this flowed from the Virgin's own breasts.

Menedemus. How was this known?

Ogygius. Oh, the nun of Constantinople, who gave the milk, said so.

Menedemus. And perhaps St. Bernard [of Clairvaux] informed her?

Ogygius. That's what I think.

Menedemus. The one who in old age was privileged to taste milk from that same breast which the child Jesus sucked. Hence I'm surprised he's called "the mellifluous" instead of "the lactifluous." But how can that be called the Virgin's milk which did not flow from her breasts?

Ogygius. It did flow, but falling on the rock where she happened to be sitting when giving suck, it hardened and then, by God's will, so increased.

Menedemus. Right. Continue.

Ogygius. After this, while we're strolling about, looking at sights of interest before departing, the custodians turn up again, glance at us, point with the finger, run up, go away, rush back, nod; they seemed to be on the point of accosting us if they could find courage enough.

Menedemus. Weren't you at all scared then?

Ogygius. Oh, no, I looked them straight in the eye, smiling and gazing at them as if inviting them to address me. At last one comes near and asks my name. I give it. He asks if I was the man who two years earlier had put up a votive tablet in Hebrew [Erasmus had earlier composed a Greek poem to the Virgin of Walsingham]. I admit it.

Menedemus. Do you write Hebrew?

Ogygius. Of course not, but anything they don't understand they call Hebrew. Soon the protos-hysteros of the college comes – having been sent for, I imagine.

Menedemus. What title is that? Don't they have an abbot?

Ogygius. No.

Menedemus. Why?

Ogygius. Because they don't know Hebrew [Ogygius takes the Syriac word "abbot" to be from Hebrew].

Menedemus. Nor a bishop?

Ogygius. No.

Menedemus. Why?

Ogygius. Because the Virgin is still too hard up to buy an expensive staff and miter.

Menedemus. Don't they have at least a provost?

Ogygius. Not even that.

Menedemus. Why not?

Ogygius. Because "provost" is a title designating office, not sanctity. And that's why colleges of canons reject the name of "abbot." That of "prior" they accept willingly.

Menedemus. But "protos-hysteros" I never heard of before.

Ogygius. Really, you're very ignorant of grammar.

Menedemus. I do know "hysteron proteron" in figures of speech [the figure of speech in which the word or phrase which should properly come last is put first]

Ogygius. Exactly. The man next to the prior is posterior-prior.

Menedemus. You mean a *sub*prior.

Ogygius. This man greeted me decently enough. He tells me how hard many persons toil to read those lines, and how often they wipe their spectacles in vain. Whenever some aged D.D. or J.D. came along he was marched off to the tablet. One would say the letters were Arabic; another, that they were fictitious characters. Finally one was found who could read the title. It was written in Roman words and letters, but in capitals. The Greek lines were written in Greek capitals, which at first glance look like Latin capitals. Upon request, I gave the meaning of the verses in Latin, translating word for word. I refused the small tip proffered for this bit of work, declaring there was nothing, however difficult, that I would not be very eager to do for the sake of the Most Holy Virgin, even if she bade me carry a letter from there to Jerusalem.

Menedemus. Why would she need you as postman when she has so many angels to wait on her hand and foot?

Ogygius. He offered from his bag a piece of wood, cut from a beam on which the Virgin Mother was seen to stand. A marvelous fragrance proved at once that the object was an extremely sacred one. After kissing so remarkable a gift three or four times with the utmost devotion, while prone and bare-headed, I put it in my purse.

Menedemus. May one see it?

Ogygius. I'll let you see it. But if you aren't fasting, or if you had intercourse with your wife last night, I shouldn't advise you to look at it.

Menedemus. No danger. Show it to me.

Ogygius. Here you are.

Menedemus. Oh, how lucky you are to have this present!

Ogygius. In case you don't know, I wouldn't exchange this tiny fragment for all the gold in Tagus [a river in Spain and Portugal]. I'll set it in gold, but so that it shines through crystal.

Then Hystero-protus, when he saw that I was so reverently delighted with this little gift, and decided I was not undeserving of having greater matters entrusted to me as well, asked whether I had ever seen the secrets of the Virgin. This word startled me somewhat, but I didn't dare ask which secrets of the Virgin he meant, since in subjects so sacred even a slip of the tongue can be dangerous. I say I haven't seen them, but that I want to very much. I'm led on now as though divinely inspired. One or two wax tapers are lighted, and a small image displayed, unimpressive in size, material, and workmanship, but of surpassing power.

Menedemus. Size has little to do with producing miracles. I've seen the Christopher at Paris [a statue formerly in the Church of Notre Dame], not merely of wagon or colossus size but fully as big as a mountain – yet he was distinguished for no miracles that I ever heard of.

Ogygius. At the Virgin's feet is a jewel, as yet unnamed by Latins or Greeks. The French have named it from "toad," because it shows the figure of a toad in a way no art could achieve. What's more wonderful, the stone is very small; the image of the toad does not stick out but shines through in the jewel itself, as if inlaid.

Menedemus. Perhaps they imagine the toad's likeness, as we imagine an eagle in a stalk of fern. And similarly, what don't children see in clouds: dragons breathing fire, mountains burning, armed men clashing.

Ogygius. For your information, no toad shows itself more obviously alive than that one did.

Menedemus. So far I've put up with your stories. From now on, look for someone else to convince with your toad yarn.

Ogygius. No wonder you feel like that, Menedemus. Nobody could have persuaded me either, even if the whole Faculty of Theology had maintained it, unless I had seen it, inspected it, and made certain of it with these eyes-these very eyes, I tell you. But you do strike me as rather lacking in curiosity about natural history.

Menedemus. Why? Because I don't believe asses fly?

Ogygius. Don't you see how Nature the artist enjoys expressing herself in the colors and forms of everything, but especially in jewels? Then, how marvelous the powers she put into those jewels: well-nigh incredible, did not firsthand experience give us assurance of them. Tell me, would you have believed steel is pulled by a magnet without being touched, and repelled by it again without contact, unless you had seen it with your own eyes?

Menedemus. No, never, even if ten Aristotles had sworn it to me.

Ogygius. Then don't cry "Incredible!" as soon as you hear about something not yet known by experience. In *ceraunia* we see the figure of a thunderbolt; in *pyropus,* living fire; in *chalazias,* the appearance and hardness of hail, even if you throw it into the midst of the fire; in the emerald, deep, clear sea water. *Carcinias* resembles a sea crab; adderstone, a viper; *scarites,* the fish called scarus; *hieracites,* a falcon. *Geranites* has a neck like the crane's; *aegophthalmus,* a goat's eye (one kind shows a pig's eye, another three human eyes together); *lycophthalmus* paints the eye of a wolf in four colors: golden red, blood red, and in the middle black bordered by white. If you open *cyamea nigra,* you'll find a bean in the center. *Dryites* looks like a tree trunk and burns like wood. *Cissites* and *narcissites* depict ivy; *astrapias* throws out flashes of lightning from its white or lapis-lazuli center; *phlegontes* shows inside the color of flame, which does not die out; in the coal carbuncle you see certain sparks darting; *crocias* has the color of a crocus; *rhodites,* of a rose; *chalcites,* of brass. Eagle stone represents an eagle, with a whitish tail; *taos* has the image of a peacock; swallowstone, that of an adder. *Myrmcecites* contains the figure of a creeping ant; *cantharias* shows a complete beetle; *scorpites* illustrates a scorpion remarkably. But why pursue these examples, which are countless, since nature has no part – in the elements, in living things, or in plants – that it does not illustrate, as if in sport, in precious stones. Do you wonder that a toad is imaged in this jewel?

Menedemus. I wonder that Nature has so much leisure to play thus at imitating everything.

Ogygius. She wanted to arouse the curiosity of mankind, and so to shake us out of our idleness. And yet – as though we had no way of escaping boredom! – we go crazy over jesters, dice, and jugglers' tricks.

Menedemus. Very true.

Ogygius. Some sober people say that if stones of this kind are put in vinegar, the "toads" will move their legs and swim.

Menedemus. Why is the toad dedicated to the Virgin?

Ogygius. Because she overcame, stamped out, extinguished all impurity, infection, pride, avarice, and whatever earthly passions there are.

Menedemus. Woe to us who bear so great a toad in our breasts!

Ogygius. We shall be pure if we worship the Virgin zealously.

Menedemus. How does she like to be worshiped?

Ogygius. You will adore her most acceptably if you imitate her.

Menedemus. Precisely – but that's very hard to do.

Ogygius. Yes, but most glorious.

Menedemus. Go on; continue what you began.

Ogygius. Next he shows us gold and silver statues. "This one," says he, "is all gold; the other one, silver gilded." He adds the weight and worth of each, and the name of the donor. When, marveling at every one, I was congratulating the Virgin on such fortunate wealth, the guide said: "Since I notice you're a devout sightseer, I don't think it right to keep anything from you: you shall see the Virgin's very greatest secrets." At the same time he takes down from the altar itself a world of wonderful things. If I tried to enumerate them all, the day would not be long enough. Thus the pilgrimage ended very happily for me. I had my fill of sights, and I brought away with me this priceless gift, a pledge from the Virgin herself.

Menedemus. Didn't you test the power of your piece of wood?

Ogygius. I did. Before three days passed, I found at a certain inn a man who had gone mad; they were ready to chain him. I slipped this wood under his pillow secretly. He fell into a long, deep sleep. In the morning he woke up as sound as ever.

Menedemus. Maybe it wasn't insanity but delirium tremens from drink. Sleep usually helps that malady.

Ogygius. Joke as you please, Menedemus, but about something else. To make fun of the saints is neither reverent nor prudent. Why, the man himself said that a woman of marvelous beauty had appeared to him in a dream and held out a cup to him.

Menedemus. Hellebore, I dare say.

Ogygius. I don't know about that, but I do know the man's in his right mind.

Menedemus. Did you overlook Thomas, archbishop of Canterbury?

Ogygius. By no means. No pilgrimage is more devout.

Menedemus. I long to hear about it, if that's not too much trouble.

Ogygius. Oh, no, I want you to hear. There's a section of England called Kent, facing France and Flanders. Its chief city is Canterbury. In it are two monasteries, almost adjacent, both of them Benedictine houses. That named for St. Augustine is evidently the older; the one now called after St. Thomas appears to have been the archbishop's seat, where he used to live with a few chosen monks; just as today, too, bishops have residences adjoining the churches but apart from the houses of other canons. (In old time both bish-

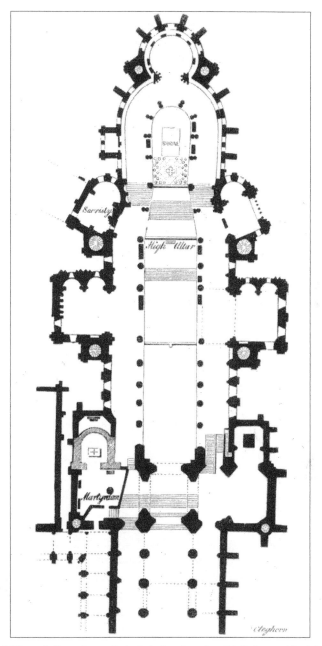

[Fig. 57] Plan of Canterbury Cathedral showing the chief places visited by pilgrims and described by Ogygius in Erasmus's *Colloquy:* the *Martyrium,* site of Becket's murder, at lower left, the sacristy (upper left) and, behind the high altar, the shrine containing Becket's relics (Nichols, *Pilgrimages,* p. 114).

ops and canons were usually monks; evidence abounds to prove that.) The church sacred to St. Thomas rises to the sky so majestically that it inspires devotion even in those who see it from afar. Thus by its splendor it now dims the glory of the neighboring one and, so to speak, overshadows the spot that was anciently the most sacred. It has two huge towers, as though greeting visitors a long way off and making the region ring far and wide with the wonderful sound of its bronze bells. At the south entrance of the church are stone statues of three armed men, who with sacrilegious hands murdered the blessed saint. Their surnames are added: Tusci, Fusci, Berri [William de Tracy, Reginald Fitzurse, and Richard le Breton].

Menedemus. Why is so much honor paid to impious men?

Ogygius. Obviously they have the same honor as Judas, Pilate, and Caiaphas, that band of wicked soldiers whom you see carefully carved on gilded altars. The surnames are added lest anybody in the future speak well of them.

Attention is called to them in order that hereafter no courtier lift a hand against bishops or church property. For those three conspirators went mad after committing their crime, and would not have recovered had they not begged help of the most holy Thomas.

Menedemus. O the everlasting mercy of martyrs!

Ogygius. When you enter, the spacious grandeur of the building is disclosed. This part is open to the public.

Menedemus. Is there nothing to see there?

Ogygius. Nothing but the mass of the structure, and some books – among them the Gospel of Nicodemus – fastened to pillars, and a tomb, I don't know whose.

Menedemus. Then what?

Ogygius. Iron screens prevent you from going any farther, but they permit a view of the space between the end of the building and the choir, as it is called. This is ascended by many steps, under which a certain vault gives access to the north side. A wooden altar sacred to the Holy Virgin is shown there; a very small one, not worth seeing except as a monument of antiquity, a rebuke to the luxury of our times. There the holy man is said to have spoken his last farewell to the Virgin when death was at hand. On the altar is the point of the sword with which the crown of the good bishop's head was cut off, and his brain evidently smashed to make death come more quickly. Out of love for the martyr we reverently kissed the sacred rust of this sword. Leaving this place, we went into the crypt. It has its own custodians. First is shown the martyr's skull, pierced through. The top of the cranium is bared for kissing, the rest covered with silver. Along with this is displayed a leaden plate with *Thomas of Acre* carved on it [a reference to the medieval legend that the saint's mother was a Saracen]. The hair shirt, girdle, and drawers by which the bishop used to subdue his flesh hang in the gloom there – horrible even to look at, and a reproach to our softness and delicacy.

Menedemus. Perhaps to the monks themselves, too.

Ogygius. I can neither affirm nor deny that, nor is it any of my business.

Menedemus. Very true.

Ogygius. From here we return to the choir. On the north side mysteries are laid open. It is wonderful how many bones were brought forth – skulls, jaws, teeth, hands, fingers, whole arms, all of which we adored and kissed. This would have gone on forever if my fellow pilgrim, a disagreeable chap, had not cut short the enthusiasm of the guide.

Menedemus. Who was this?

Ogygius. An Englishman named Gratian Pullus [John Colet, Dean of St. Paul's and Erasmus's friend, since 'pullus' is Latin for 'colt'], a learned and pious man but less respectful toward this side of religion than I liked.

Menedemus. Some Wycliffite, I suppose.

Ogygius. I don't think so, though he had read his books. Where he got hold of them isn't clear.

Menedemus. Did he offend the guide?

Ogygius. An arm was brought forth, with the bloodstained flesh still on it. He shrank from kissing this, looking rather disgusted. The custodian soon put his things away. Next we viewed the altar table and ornaments; then the objects that were kept under the altar – all of them splendid; you'd say Midas and Croesus were beggars if you saw the quantity of gold and silver.

Menedemus. No kisses here?

Ogygius. No, but a different sort of desire came to my mind.

Menedemus. What was it?

Ogygius. I longed to have such relics at home.

Menedemus. A sacrilegious wish!

Ogygius. Admitted, and I begged the saint's forgiveness before I left the church. After this we were conducted to the sacristy. Good Lord, what an array of silk vestments there, what an abundance of gold candelabra! There, too, we saw St. Thomas's staff. It looked like a cane plated with silver. It was not at all heavy, had no ornamentation, and was no more than waist-high.

Menedemus. No cross?

Ogygius. None that I saw. We were shown a pallium, silk to be sure, but coarse, without gold or jewels, and there was a facecloth, soiled by sweat from his neck and preserving obvious spots of blood. These memorials of the plain living of olden times we gladly kissed.

Menedemus. They're not shown to everyone?

Ogygius. Certainly not, my good friend.

Menedemus. How did you manage to make such an impression of devoutness that no secrets were kept from you?

Ogygius. I had some acquaintance with the Reverend Father William Warham, the Archbishop [1504-1532]. He gave me a note of recommendation.

Mcnedemus. I hear from many persons that he is a man of remarkable kindness.

Ogygius. More than that: you would call him kindness itself if you knew him. His learning, integrity, and holiness of life are so great that you would find him lacking in no quality befitting a perfect prelate. Next we were led up above, for behind the high altar you ascend as though into a new church. There, in a small chapel [the Chapel of the Holy Trinity containing the shrine], is shown the entire face [the mitred bust of St. Thomas, known as the Corona] of the saint, gilded, and ornamented with many jewels. Here a certain unlooked-for accident almost upset all our good luck.

Menedemus. I'm waiting to hear what misfortune you mean.

Ogygius. My friend Gratian made a *faux pas* here. After a short prayer, he asked the keeper, "I say, good father, is it true, as I've heard, that in his lifetime Thomas was most generous to the poor?" "Very true," the man replied, and began to rehearse the saint's many acts of kindness to them. Then Gratian: "I don't suppose his disposition changed in this matter, unless perhaps for the better." The custodian agreed. Gratian again: "Since, then, the saint was so liberal towards the needy, although he was still poor himself and lacked money to provide for the necessities of life, don't you think he'd gladly consent, now that he's so rich and needs nothing, if some poor wretched woman with hungry children at home, or daughters in danger of losing their virtue because they have no money for dowries, or a husband sick in bed and penniless if, after begging the saint's forgiveness, she carried off a bit of all this wealth [later plundered and destroyed by Henry VIII] to rescue her family, as though taking from one who wanted her to have it, either as a gift or a loan?" When the keeper in charge of the gilded head made no reply to this, Gratian, who's impulsive, said, "For my part, I'm convinced the saint would even rejoice that in death, too, he could relieve the wants of the poor by his riches." At this the custodian frowned and pursed his lips, looking at us with Gorgon eyes, and I don't doubt he would have driven us from the church with insults and reproaches had he not been aware that we were recommended by the archbishop. I managed to placate the fellow by smooth talk, affirming that Gratian hadn't spoken seriously, but liked to joke; and at the same time I gave him some coins.

Menedemus. I quite approve of your sense of duty. But seriously, I wonder sometimes what possible excuse there could be for those who spend so much money on building, decorating, and enriching churches that there's simply no limit to it. Granted that the sacred vestments and vessels of the church must have a dignity appropriate to their liturgical use; and I want the building to have grandeur. But what's the use of so many baptistries, candelabra, gold statues? What's the good of the vastly expensive organs, as they call them? (We're not content with a single pair, either.) What's the good of that costly musical neighing when meanwhile our brothers and sisters, Christ's living temples, waste away from hunger and thirst?

Ogygius. Every decent, sensible man favors moderation in these matters, of course. But since the fault springs from excessive devotion, it merits applause, especially when one thinks of the opposite vice in those who rob churches of their wealth. These gifts are generally given by kings and potentates, and would be worse spent on gambling and war. And removal of anything from there is, in the first place, regarded as sacrilege; next, those who are regular contributors stop their giving; above all, men are incited to robbery. Hence churchmen are custodians of these things rather than owners of them. In short, I'd rather see a church abounding in sacred furnishings than bare and dirty, as some are, and more like stables than churches.

Menedemus. Yet we read that in former times bishops were praised for selling the sacred vessels and using the money to relieve the poor.

Ogygius. They're praised today, too, but only praised. In my judgment, to imitate them is neither allowable nor agreeable.

Menedemus. I'm holding up your story. Let's have the conclusion.

Ogygius. Hear it, then; I'll be brief. While this was going on, the chief official came forward.

Menedemus. Who? The abbot of the place?

Ogygius. He has a miter and abbatical revenue; he lacks only the name of abbot and is called prior [Thomas Goldston was prior from 1514 to 1517], because the archbishop serves instead of an abbot. For in ancient times whoever was archbishop of this diocese was also a monk.

Menedemus. Well, I wouldn't mind being called camel if I had an abbot's income.

Ogygius. He seemed to me a good, sensible man; something of a Scotist theologian, too [one learned in the philosophy of Duns Scotus]. He opened for us the chest in which the rest of the holy man's body is said to lie.

Menedemus. You saw the bones?

Ogygius. No, that's not allowed, nor would it be possible without the use of ladders. But within the wooden chest is a golden chest; when this is drawn up by ropes, it reveals in estimable treasure.

Menedemus. What do I hear?

Ogygius. The cheapest part was gold. Everything shone and dazzled with rare and surpassingly large jewels, some bigger than a goose egg. Some monks stood about reverently. When the cover was removed, we all adored. The prior pointed out each jewel by touching it with a white rod, adding its French name, its worth, and the name of the donor. The principal ones were gifts from kings.

Menedemus. He must have had a remarkable memory.

Ogygius. Your guess is correct, although practice helps too, for he often does this. From here he leads the way back to the crypt. There the Virgin Mother has a residence, but a somewhat dark one, enclosed by a double row of iron rails.

Menedemus. What's she afraid of?

Ogygius. Only robbers, I suppose, for I've never seen anything more loaded with riches.

Menedemus. You tell me of dark riches.

Ogygius. When the lanterns were brought closer, we saw a more than regal sight.

Menedemus. More wealth than that of St. Mary-by-the-Sea?

Ogygius. It looks like much more. She alone knows her secret wealth. It isn't shown to any but people of the highest importance or to special friends. At last we were led back to the sacristy. There a chest with a black leather cover was brought out, placed on the table, and opened. Immediately everyone worshiped on bended knee.

Menedemus. What was inside?

Ogygius. Some linen rags, many of them still showing traces of snivel. With these, they say, the holy man wiped the sweat from his face or neck, the dirt from his nose, or whatever other kinds of filth human bodies have. At this point my friend Gratian again displayed imperfect manners. To him, since he was English, and a well-known person of considerable standing, the prior kindly offered one of the rags as a gift, thinking he was giving him a present that would please him very much. But Gratian was hardly grateful for it. He touched the piece with his fingers, not without a sign of disgust, and put it back scornfully, puckering his lips as though whistling. (This is what he ordinarily did if he came across anything he thought despicable.) Shame and alarm together embarrassed me dreadfully. But the prior, no stupid man, pretended not to notice this incident, and after offering us a glass of wine dismissed us kindly, for we were returning to London.

Menedemus. Why did you have to do that when you were already fairly close to your own shore?

Ogygius. Yes, I was, but I willingly avoided that shore as much as possible.

It's more notorious for frauds and robberies than any Malean rocks [on the coast of southeastern Peloponnesus] are for shipwrecks. I'll tell you what I saw on my last crossing. Many of us were ferried in a row boat from the Calais shore to a larger vessel. Among the passengers was a poor, ragged French youth. He was charged half a drachma; so large a sum do they wring from each passenger for the very short ride. He pleaded poverty. To amuse themselves they search him, and when they pull off his shoes they find ten or twelve drachmas between the soles. These they take, laughing in his face and jeering at the damned Frenchman.

Menedemus. What did the young fellow do?

Ogygius. Mourned his loss. What else could he do?

Menedemus. They had no right to do such things, had they?

Ogygius. Exactly the same right they have to rob passengers' luggage and to snatch purses whenever they get a chance.

Menedemus. It's extraordinary that they should dare to commit such a serious crime in the presence of so many witnesses.

Ogygius. They're so used to doing it that they think it's quite all right. Many persons watched from the larger boat. In the rowboat were some English merchants, who protested in vain. Those fellows boasted about catching the damned Frenchman as if it were a practical joke.

Menedemus. I'd gladly crucify those pirates as a practical joke!

Ogygius. But both shores are full of such men. "Guess what masters might do when knaves dare do such deeds." [a quotation from Virgil, *Eclogues* 3.16] So from now on I prefer roundabout routes to that short cut. In these respects, just as "the descent to hell is easy" [Virgil, *Aeneid* 6. 126-129] but the return very hard, so entry by this shore is not altogether easy, exit very hard. Some Antwerp sailors were hanging about London; I decided to take my chances with them.

Menedemus. Does that place have such conscientious sailors?

Ogygius. As an ape is always an ape, I confess, so a sailor's always a sailor. But if you compare them with professional thieves, they're angels.

Menedemus. I'll remember that if ever I, too, get the urge to visit that island. But go back to the road I took you away from.

Ogygius. On the way to London, shortly after you leave Canterbury, you find a very deep and narrow road; moreover, it has such steep banks on each side that you can't get out of it. There's no other road you can take, either. On the left side of this road is a little almshouse [at Harbledown, about two miles from Canterbury] for some old beggars. As soon as they see a rider coming one of them runs up, sprinkles him with holy water, and presently holds out the upper part of a shoe fastened to a brass rim. In it is a glass that looks like a jewel. People kiss it and make a small contribution.

Menedemus. On that sort of road I'd rather meet a house of old beggars than a gang of able-bodied thieves.

Ogygius. Gratian was riding on my left, closer to the alms house. He was sprinkled with water, but he managed to put up with that. When the shoe was thrust at him, he asked the man what he meant by this. He said it was St. Thomas's shoe. Gratian turned to me and said heatedly, "What, do these brutes want us to kiss all good men's shoes? Why not, in the same fashion, hold out spittle and other excrements to be kissed?" I felt sorry for the old man and cheered him up with a tip, poor fellow.

Menedemus. In my opinion, Gratian's anger was not entirely unreasonable. If soles of shoes were kept as evidence of a temperate life, I wouldn't object, but I consider it shame less to push soles, shoes, and girdles at one to be kissed. If one kissed them of his own accord, from some overwhelming feeling of piety, I'd think it pardonable.

Ogygius. I won't pretend it wouldn't be better to leave those things undone, but from what can't be amended at a stroke I'm accustomed to take whatever good there is. Meantime, I was pleasing myself with the reflection that a good man is like a sheep, a bad one like a beast of prey. When an adder's dead, it can't sting, true, but its stench and blood are injurious. A sheep, while alive, nourishes by its milk, provides clothing by its wool, enriches by its offspring; dead, it furnishes useful hide; and all of it can be eaten. So rapacious men, addicted to this world, are troublesome to everybody while alive; when dead, they're a nuisance to the living by reason of the tolling of bells, grandiose funerals, and some times by the consecration of their successors – because that means new exactions. Good men, truly, are in every respect useful to everyone: as this saint, during his lifetime, encouraged people to holiness by his example, teaching, and exhortations, comforted the forsaken, and raised up the needy. In death his usefulness is almost greater. He built this very wealthy church; he won more power for the clergy through out England. Lastly, this piece of shoe supports a whole house of poor men.

Menedemus. A noble thought indeed, but since you're of that mind I'm surprised you've never visited St. Patrick's cave, of which marvelous tales are told [a famous site of pilgrimage in Ulster, Ireland, known as St. Patrick's Purgatory, where according to legend some pilgrims witnessed the tortures of hell]. To me they're not entirely plausible.

Ogygius. On the contrary, no story about it can be so marvelous that it is not surpassed by the fact itself.

Menedemus. And have you been in it, then?

Ogygius. I sailed in Stygian waters, to be sure; I went down into the jaws of Avernus; I saw what goes on in hell.

Menedemus. You'll do me a favor if you'll be kind enough to tell me about it.

Ogygius. Let this serve as prologue to our conversation; and it's long enough, in my opinion. I'm on my way home to order dinner; I haven't lunched yet.

Menedemus. Why haven't you? Not because of religious observance?

Ogygius. Oh, no, because of a grudge.

Menedemus. A grudge against your belly?

Ogygius. No, against greedy tavern keepers who, though they won't serve a decent meal, don't hesitate to charge their guests outrageous prices. I get even with them in this way: if I expect a good dinner with an acquaintance, or at an inn-keeper's who is a little less niggardly, my stomach won't stand much lunch; but if luck has provided the sort of lunch I like, I get a stomach-ache at dinnertime.

Menedemus. Aren't you ashamed to seem so stingy and mean?

Ogygius. Menedemus, those who take shame into account in such matters, believe me, are bad bookkeepers. I've learned to keep my shame for other purposes.

Menedemus. I long to hear the rest of the tale, so expect me as a guest for dinner. You'll tell it more comfortably there.

Ogygius. Well, thanks very much for inviting yourself, since so many who are pressed to come decline. But my thanks will be doubled if you'll dine at home today, for my time will be taken up with greeting my family. Besides, I have a plan more convenient for us both. Have lunch at your home tomorrow for me and my wife. Then I'll talk until dinner – until you admit you're satisfied; and if you like, we won't desert you even at dinner. What are you scratching your head for? You get dinner ready; we'll be sure to come.

Menedemus. I'd prefer stories I wouldn't have to pay for. All right: I'll furnish a bit of lunch, only it will be tasteless unless you season it with good stories.

Ogygius. But look here! Don't you itch to go on these pilgrimages?

Menedemus. Maybe I'll itch after you've finished talking. As matters stand now, I have enough to do by going on my Roman stations [processions to certain churches in Rome on certain days].

Ogygius. Roman? You, who've never seen Rome?

Menedemus. I'll tell you. Here's how I wander about at home. I go into the living room and see that my daughter's chastity is safe. Coming out of there into my shop, I watch what my servants, male and female, are doing. Then to the kitchen, to see if any instruction is needed. From here to one place and another, observing what my children and my wife are doing, careful that everything be in order. These are my Roman stations.

Ogygius. But St. James will look after these affairs for you.

Menedemus. Sacred Scripture directs me to take care of them myself. I've never read any commandment to hand them over to saints.

INDEX OF TOPICS

Topics are listed by document number and, in some cases, by books or sections and chapters within that document. Thus, 39.2.1 is a reference to document number 39, Book 2, section 1; 19.25 is a reference to document 19, section 25. If a topic appears several times in a document, no section or chapter number is given.

Afterlife 3, 7, 10.14, 15.34-35, 20.13, 23.19, 25.8, 36.7, 36.48, 37.6-7, 37.44

Angels 3.11-13, 14.7, 36, 37.6-8, 41.3, 45, 51

Animals 1, 2, 3, 8, 10, 11.26-27, 15.8, 18.11, 18.14, 18.28, 19.25-27, 20.9, 26, 27, 36, 37.14, 38.12, 40.51, 40.84, 40.110, 41.6-7, 42, 45

Antichrist 14.24

Asceticism 8.2-3, 9, 10, 11, 12, 14.26, 15.1, 16, 18.32, 21.31, 36, 37, 38.11, 45

Burial 1.11, 1,18, 2.5.1, 6.6, 7.12, 8.4, 10.16, 11.25, 11.27, 14.6, 14.b, 15.34, 15.37, 17, 18.30, 22, 25.8, 35, 36.62, 38.19-20, 45

Cannibalism 2.5.1

Canonization 43, 49

Charity 8.1.1, 14.3, 16, 18.19, 21.24, 21.29-30, 36.13, 38.3, 39.1.8, 40.54

Childhood 3, 13, 16, 18.1, 21.11, 21.29, 21.35, 23.9, 39.1.1, 39.1.2, 44.2, 45, 48

Church

    Alexandria 8.3

    Asia Minor 2

    Ephesus 7

    Gaul 2, 14, 16, 18, 19, 28, 29, 30, 31, 32

    Germany, 18.2, 32

    North Africa 3, 4, 5, 6

    Rome 32

    Smyrna 1

    Spain 25.9

    Switzerland 18

Conversion 8.1, 14.2, 14.5, 39.1.3, 39.1.36, 45, 46, 47

Devils 8, 14, 15, 16.30, 18.7, 18.12, 36, 47, 48

Dreams and Visions 3, 12.3, 14, 15.22, 16.38, 18.26, 32, 35, 36, 39, 41.3, 44, 45

Easter and Lent 11, 16.6, 21.18-19, 21.28, 23.15, 23.16, 36.47

Education and Literacy 8.1.1, 11.20, 15.2.1, 15.2.3, 19.9, 37.40, 38.6, 38.30, 39.1, 40.73, 40.74

Excommunication 25.7, 27

Exorcism 8.3.13-14, 9.9-13, 14, 16.33, 18.7, 18.15-18, 23

Farming 8.3.13, 18.6, 36, 40

Female Sanctity 2, 3, 4.4, 5, 11, 13, 15.33, 15.34, 16, 21, 37, 38, 44, 45, 48

Food 8.1.2, 8.3.11, 9, 10.10, 11, 12, 21.31, 25, 35, 36, 37.9, 38.15, 40.4-5, 40.22, 50

Franciscan Order 39, 40, 41, 42, 43

Hagiography 14.1, 15.Prol., 18.Prol., 19, 21.1-2, 36.57-8, 37.1-3, 38.1

Heresy 7.6, 8.4, 14.6, 15.31, 31, 50

Humiliation (of saints) 29

Hunting 18.10, 26

Iconoclasm 31, 50

Incest 2.5.1

Indulgences 26, 51

Jews 1, 12.27, 20.14, 23.13, 27, 33.3.6, 37.27

Levitation 11.10, 37.5, 37.9, 37.15-16, 38.8, 45

Lust 8.1.2, 11.14, 11.19, 15.2, 15.8, 36, 45, 48

Marriage 16, 21.13, 21.22, 26, 38.4-5, 44.5-7, 45

Martyrdom 1, 2, 3, 4, 5, 6, 8.3.11, 20, 22, 23, 44, 45, 46, 47, 48

Miracles

    General 15, 21.32, 23, 41, 49, 51

    Healing 8.3.14, 11, 12.11, 12.16, 14, 15, 16, 18.31, 18.34, 19.19, 19.22, 23, 25, 28, 32, 34, 36, 38.10, 38.20, 38.24-34, 41.6, 43, 45, 46, 47, 48

    Concerning natural phenomena: 8.3.14, 12.18, 14.13-14, 15, 16.11, 16.12, 18.27, 19.19, 20, 21.33, 23.3, 27, 28, 32.1.10, 34, 35, 36, 37, 38.28, 41, 46, 47

    Raising the dead: 14.7-8, 15.32, 16.37, 36, 37.53, 45

    Punitive: 14, 15, 25.11, 28.33, 28.83, 34

Monasticism (see also Asceticism) 8.3, 8.4, 9, 10, 11, 12, 13, 14, 15, 16, 17, 18, 19, 26, 35, 37.30, 38.13, 44.21-22

Music 36, 37.35, 37.39, 42, 43.126

Odor of Sanctity 1.15, 2, 3.13, 4.2, 28.62, 32.2.4, 36.63, 45

Pagan Cults 14, 18.6, 18.8, 22, 45, 46, 47

Persecution 1, 2, 3, 4, 5, 6, 7, 8.3.11, 10.2-3, 20, 22, 37, 39.1.11-15, 45, 46, 47

Pilgrimage 21.27, 22, 23, 24, 25, 26, 27, 31, 35, 36.4-5, 36.9, 44, 45, 49, 50, 51

Poison 15.3, 15.7, 15.27

Poverty 8.1-2, 8.5, 10.17, 21.24, 38.10, 39, 40, 45

Prophecy 3, 8.3.14, 8.4.18, 12.19, 13.19, 14.21, 15, 36, 37.29, 38.26, 39.1.27

Relics 1.18, 2.5.1, 6.5, 10.16, 15.38, 16.38, 18.6, 18.11, 20.11, 23, 26, 27, 28, 29, 30, 31, 32, 33, 34, 35, 36.63, 38.17, 45, 49, 51

Repentance 11, 13.13

Sacraments 11.22, 21.19, 37.10, 37.22, 49, 50

Saints

    Aegidius (Giles) 25.8, 36.4, 51

    Aethelthryth 20.14

Alexis 45

Antony 8, 9, 10, 19.9, 51

Augustine of Hippo, 5, 22, 23, 26

Bartholomew, 51

Benedict, 15, 19.5, 20.1

Bernard of Clairvaux, 51

Blandina 2

Botolph 35

Caesarius of Arles 25.8

Christina of St-Trond 37

Christopher 46, 47, 51

Clare 39.1.18-19, 41.8, 43.122

Columbanus 18

Cuthbert 20.14, 21.Prol., 36.8

Cyprian 6

Desiderius 18.11

Dunstan 20.1, 21.5

Edmund 20, 35

Edward the Confessor 20.21, 21.5

Eustace 45

Faith 25.8

Felicitas 3, 5

Francis of Assisi 39, 40, 41, 42, 43,

Gall 18

Genesius 25.8

George 51

Georgius 28.100

Germanus 16.16

Gervasius 23.8.1, 28.46

Giles (see Aegidius)

Godric of Finchale 36

Gregory the Great 15, 19.1, 20.12, 21.20

Gregory of Tours 7, 28, 29, 30

Helena 21.17, 24.6-7, 28.5

Hilary of Poitiers 14.5-7, 16.14, 16.17, 28.5

James the Dismembered 45

James the Great 25, 51

Jerome 10

John the Baptist 25.8, 36, 47

John the Evangelist 24.2, 38.17-19, 45

Justina 15.33

Justus 33

Lawrence 20.12

Maiol 19

Mallosus 28.62

Marcellinus and Peter 32

Margaret of Antioch 48

Margaret of Scotland 21

Marina 13

Martha and Mary 16.17, 21.8

Martin of Tours, 14, 16.14, 16.17, 16.37, 16.38, 19.6, 19.12, 25.8

Martyrs of Lyons and Vienne 2

Mary (Mother of God) 11, 18.11-24, 34, 36, 37.9, 45, 51

Mary of Egypt 11

Mary Magdalene 16.17, 25.8, 36.31, 45

Mary of Oignies 37.1

Maurice 18.11

Maurus 15

Maximin 45

Médard 16.12

Mitrias 29

Nicholas 24.3, 36.47

Paul 24.2, 25.8, 51

Paul of Thebes 10

Peter 36.56, 44.19, 45, 51

Perpetua 3, 5

Placidus 15

Polycarp 1

Protasius 23.8.1, 28.46

Radegund 16, 17, 28.5

Sanctus 2

Sebastian 20.7, 32.1.1

Sergius 30

Seven Sleepers 7

Sexburgh 20.14

Scholastica 15.33

Stephen 2.5.2, 18.22, 23, 28.33

Symeon Stylites 12

Thomas à Becket 26, 36.49-50, 36.53, 36.63, 51

Tiburtius 32

Trophimus 25.8

Twenty Martyrs 23.3

Umiltà of Faenza 38

Ursula 44

William of Gellone 51

Saracens 8.3.13, 10.6, 10.12, 12.16, 13.17, 19.24–25, 24.5, 25.7, 27, 37.32, 48

Sermons and Preaching 4, 5, 8.2, 18.25, 18.29, 26, 27, 39.1.23, 39.1.36, 40, 43.125, 45

Shipwrecks 16.31, 24.1, 24.4, 25.7, 27, 28.82, 45

Shrines 20.11, 22, 25.9, 26, 27, 28, 32.1.15, 35, 36.4, 38.32, 43, 51

Stigmata 41, 43.119

Torture 1, 2, 3, 4, 7, 8.3, 10.3, 37, 45, 46, 47, 48

Translation (of saints' bodies) 32, 35, 38.20, 45

Trials 1, 2, 3, 6

Uncorrupted bodies 10.17, 20.10–12, 20.14

Virginity 37, 39.1.19, 44, 45, 48

ACKNOWLEDGEMENT OF SOURCES IN COPYRIGHT

Chapter One

The Martyrdom of St. Polycarp, Bishop of Smyrna, is taken from: trans. E.C.E. Owen, *Some Authentic Acts of the Early Martyrs* (Oxford: Clarendon Press, 1927), pp. 32-41. Reprinted with permission.

The Passion of SS. Perpetua and Felicitas is taken from: trans. H. R. Musurillo, *Acts of the Christian Martyrs* (Oxford: Clarendon Press, 1972), pp. 106-131. Reprinted with permission.

Tertullian's Address to the Martyrs is taken from: trans. Rudolph Arbesmann, *Tertullian: Disciplinary, Moral and Ascetical Works,* in *The Fathers of the Church* (New York: Fathers of the Church, Inc., 1959), 40, pp. 17-29. Reprinted with permission.

Augustine Preaches on the Feast of SS. Perpetua and Felicitas is taken from: trans. W. H. Shewring, *The Passion of SS. Perpetua and Felicity MM together with the Sermons of S. Augustine upon these Saints* (London: Sheed and Ward, 1931), pp. 45-59, abridged. Reprinted with permission.

The Trials and Execution of Cyprian is taken from: trans. E.C.E. Owen, *Some Authentic Acts of the Early Martyrs* (Oxford: Clarendon Press, 1927), pp. 95-99. Reprinted with permission.

The Age of Martyrs in Legend: The Seven Sleepers of Ephesus is taken from: trans. William C. McDermott, *Monks, Bishops and Pagans: Christian Culture in Gaul and Italy, 500-700* ed. Edward Peters (reissued 1975; Philadelphia: University of Pennsylvania Press, 1949), pp. 199-206. Reprinted with permission.

Chapter Two

Christianity in the Desert: St. Antony the Great is taken from: trans. J.B. McLaughlin, *St. Antony the Hermit, by St. Athanasius* (London: Burns Oates and Washbourne, 1924), pp. 1-122 abridged. Reprinted with permission.

The First Hermit: St. Paul of Thebes is taken from: trans. Marie Liguori Ewald, *Fathers of the Church: Early Christian Biographies,* ed. Roy J. Deferrari (rpt. 1964; Washington, D.C.: The Catholic University of America Press, 1952), pp. 225-38. Reprinted with permission.

A Harlot in the Desert: Mary of Egypt is taken from: trans. Benedicta Ward, *Harlots of the Desert: A Study of Repentance in Early Monastic Sources* (Kalamazoo, Michigan: Cistercian Publications, 1987), pp. 35-56. Reprinted with permission.

A Famous Pillar Saint: Symeon Stylites is taken from: trans. R. M. Price, *A History of the Monks of Syria by Theodoret of Cyrrhus* (Kalamazoo, Michigan: Cistercian Publications, 1985), pp. 160-171. Reprinted with permission.

Chapter Three

The Life and Miracles of St. Benedict is taken from: trans. Odo John Zimmerman, *St. Gregory the Great: Dialogues* (New York: Fathers of the Church, Inc., 1959), pp. 3-6 and 55-110. Reprinted with permission.

Venantius Fortunatus's Life of St. Radegund is taken from: Jo Ann McNamara ed., *Sainted Women of the Dark Ages,* Chapter 4, "Radegund, Queen of the Franks and Abbess of Poitiers" (translation of *Monumenta Germaniae Historica: Auctores Antiquiores* 1: 271-275; and *Scriptores rerum merovingicarum* 2: 358-405). Copyright 1992, Duke University Press. Reprinted with permission.

Radegund Writes to the Bishops is taken from: trans. O. M. Dalton, *The History of the Franks, by Gregory of Tours* (Oxford: Clarendon Press, 1927), 2, pp. 418-21. Reprinted with permission.

An Irish Missionary: St. Gall, by Walahfrid Strabo is taken from: trans. Maud Joynt, *The Life of St. Gall* (London: Society for Promoting Christian Knowledge; New York and Toronto: Macmillan, 1927), pp. 58-111 abridged. Reprinted with permission.

A Mirror for Monks: The Life of St. Maiol, Abbot of Cluny, by Odilo, Fifth Abbot of Cluny is taken from: trans. P. E. Dutton, from *Sancti Odilonis abbatis Cluniacensis V De vita beati Maioli abbatis libellus,* ed. M. Marrier and A. Duchène in *Bibliotheca Cluniacensis* (Brussels and Paris, 1614), cols. 279-290, and repr. In J. P. Migne, *Patrologia Latina,* 142, cols. 943-962; printed with permission.

Chapter Five

St. Augustine on the Rites at the Martyrs' Tombs is taken from: trans. Gerald G. Walsh and Grace Monahan, *Saint Augustine: The City of God Books 8-16* (New York: Fathers of the Church, Inc., 1952), 8, 27, pp. 74-76. Reprinted with permission.

Pilgrimage and Miracles in North Africa is taken from: trans. Gerald G. Walsh and Daniel J. Honan, *Saint Augustine: The City of God Books 17-22* (New York: Fathers of the Church, Inc., 1954), 22, 8, 9, pp. 440-451. Reprinted with permission.

The Pilgrim's Guide to St. James of Compostella is taken from: trans. James Hogarth, *The Pilgrim's Guide: A 12th-Century Guide for the Pilgrim to St. James of Compostella* (London: Confraternity of St. James, 1992), pp. 3-88 abridged. Reprinted with permission.

Pilgrimage as Metaphor: The Canterbury Tales is taken from: trans. David Wright, *The Canterbury Tales* (London: Fontana Press, 1964), pp. 5-21 abridged. Reprinted with permission.

Chapter Six

Gregory of Tours: the Power of Relics is taken from: trans. Raymond Van Dam, *Gregory of Tours: Glory of the Martyrs* Translated Texts for Historians, Latin Series 3 (Liverpool: Liverpool University Press, 1988), pp. 22-4; 26-7; 52-3; 69; 86-7; 106-9; 123-4. Reprinted with permission.

The Humiliation of St. Mitrias is taken from: trans. Raymond Van Dam, *Glory of the Confessors* Translated Texts for Historians, Latin Series 4 (Liverpool: Liverpool University Press, 1988), pp. 73-75. Reprinted with permission.

The Affair of St. Sergius's Fingerbone is taken from: trans. O. M. Dalton, *Gregory of Tours: History of the Franks* (Oxford: Clarendon Press, 1927), 2, 7, 31 pp. 308-309. Reprinted with permission.

Criticism of the Cult of Relics: Claudius of Turin is taken from: trans. A. Cabaniss. Reproduced from: *Early Medieval Theology* edited by George E. McCracken (Library of Christian Classics Series 9) pp. 241-248. Used by permission of Westminster John Knox Press.

Theft of Relics: the Translation of SS. Marcellinus and Peter is taken from: trans. B. Wendell, *The History of the Translation of the Blessed Martyrs of Christ Marcellinus and Peter: the English Version* (Cambridge: Harvard University Press, 1926); revised by P. E. Dutton, pp. 239-264. Reprinted with permission.

False Relics and Imposters is taken from: trans. John France, *Rodolphus Glaber: The Five Books of the Histories* (Oxford: Clarendon Press, 1989), pp. 181-185. Reprinted with permission.

Fundraising with Relics: the Monks of Laon is taken from: trans. Paul J. Archambault, *A Monk's Confession: The Memoirs of Guibert of Nogent* (University Park, Pennsylvania: Pennsylvania State University Press, 1996), pp. 174-181. Reprinted with permission.

Chapter Seven

Women's Spirituality I: Christina the Astonishing is taken from: trans. Margot H. King, *The Life of Christina of St-Trond by Thomas of Cantimpré* (Saskatoon: Peregrina Publishing Co., 1986), pp. 1-33. Reprinted with permission.

Women's Spirituality II: Umiltà of Faenza is taken from: trans. Elizabeth Petroff, *Consolation of the Blessed* (New York: Alta Gaia Society, 1979), pp. 121-137. Reprinted with permission.

The Conversion of St. Francis of Assisi and the Founding of his Order is taken from: trans. Placid Hermann, *St. Francis of Assisi: First and Second Life of St. Francis by Thomas of Celano* (Chicago: Franciscan Herald Press, 1963), pp. 5-38 abridged. Reprinted with permission.

Humanistic Hagiography: the Writings of St. Francis's Companions is taken from: trans. Rosalind B. Brooke, *Scripta Leonis, Rufini et Angeli, Sociorum S. Francisci* (Oxford: Clarendon Press, 1970) pp. 95-283 abridged. Reprinted with permission.

The Official Life of St. Francis: the Stigmata is taken from: trans. Benen Fahy, *Major and Minor Life of St. Francis with excerpts from other works by St. Bonaventure* in *St. Francis of Assisi: Writings and Early Biographies; English Omnibus of the Sources for the Life of St. Francis,* ed. Marion A. Habig (4th ed. rev.; Quincy, Ill.: Franciscan Press, 1991), pp. 729-735. Reprinted with permission.

The Canticle of Brother Sun is taken from: (1) trans. Rosalind B. Brooke, *Scripta Leonis, Rufini et Angeli Sociorum S. Francisci* (Oxford: Clarendon Press, 1970), pp. 163-7 and (2) trans. Lawrence S. Cunningham, *Saint Francis of Assisi* (Boston: Twayne Publishers, 1976), pp. 58-59. Reprinted with permission.

1.[tab]The Canonization of St. Francis is taken from: trans. Placid Hermann, *St. Francis of Assisi: First and Second Life of St. Francis by Thomas of Celano* (Chicago: Franciscan Herald Press, 1963), pp. 109-117. Reprinted with permission.

Chapter Eight

St. Ursula and the Eleven Thousand Virgins is taken from: trans. Pamela Sheingorn and Marcelle Thiébaux, *The Passion of St. Ursula.* Peregrina Translation Series 16 (Toronto: Peregrina Publishing Co., 1990), pp. 13-37. Reprinted with permission.

Four Lives from The Golden Legend (Alexis, Mary Magdalene, Eustace, James the Dismembered) is taken from: trans. William Granger Ryan, *Jacobus de Voragine: The Golden Legend. Readings on the Saints* (Princeton, N.J.: Princeton University Press, 1993), 1, pp. 371-383 and 2, pp. 266-271. Reprinted with permission.

An Old French Life of St. Margaret of Antioch is taken from: trans. Brigitte Cazelles, *The Lady as Saint: A Collection of French Hagiographic Romances of the Thirteenth Century* (Philadelphia: University of Pennsylvania, 1991), pp. 218-228. Reprinted with permission.

Chapter Nine

Erasmus: A Pilgrimage for Religion's Sake is taken from: trans. Craig R. Thomson, *Ten Colloquies of Erasmus* (New York: The Liberal Arts Press, Inc., 1957), pp. 56-91. Reprinted with permission.

READINGS IN MEDIEVAL CIVILIZATIONS AND CULTURES
Series Editor: Paul Edward Dutton

"Readings in Medieval Civilizations and Cultures is in my opinion the most useful series being published today."
— William C. Jordan, Princeton University

I—Carolingian Civilization: A Reader, second edition
edited by Paul Edward Dutton

II—Medieval Popular Religion, 1000–1500: A Reader, second edition
edited by John Shinners

III—Charlemagne's Courtier: The Complete Einhard
translated & edited by Paul Edward Dutton

IV—Medieval Saints: A Reader
edited by Mary-Ann Stouck

V—From Roman to Merovingian Gaul: A Reader
translated & edited by Alexander Callander Murray

VI—Medieval England, 1000–1500: A Reader
edited by Emilie Amt

VII—Love, Marriage, and Family in the Middle Ages: A Reader
edited by Jacqueline Murray

VIII—The Crusades: A Reader, second edition
edited by S.J. Allen & Emilie Amt

IX—The Annals of Flodoard of Reims, 919–966
translated & edited by Bernard S. Bachrach & Steven Fanning

X—Gregory of Tours: The Merovingians
translated & edited by Alexander Callander Murray

XI—Medieval Towns: A Reader
edited by Maryanne Kowaleski

XII—A Short Reader of Medieval Saints
edited by Mary-Ann Stouck

XIII—Vengeance in Medieval Europe: A Reader
edited by Daniel Lord Smail & Kelly Lyn Gibson

XIV—The Viking Age: A Reader, second edition
edited by Angus A. Somerville & R. Andrew McDonald

XV—Medieval Medicine: A Reader
edited by Faith Wallis

XVI—Medieval Pilgrimages: A Reader
edited by Brett Edward Whalen

XVII—Prologues to Ancient and Medieval History: A Reader
edited by Justin Lake